The four books of *The Nature of Order* constitute the ninth, tenth, eleventh and twelfth in a series of books which describe an entirely new attitude to architecture and building. The books are intended to provide a complete working alternative to our present ideas about architecture, building, and planning — an alternative which will, we hope, gradually replace current ideas and practices.

Future volume now in preparation

THE PROCESS OF CREATING LIFE

Great Hall color mockup in progress, Eishin campus, Japan, 1984

THE
NATURE
OF
ORDER

*An Essay on the Art of Building and
the Nature of the Universe*

BOOK ONE
THE PHENOMENON OF LIFE

BOOK TWO
THE PROCESS OF CREATING LIFE

BOOK THREE
A VISION OF A LIVING WORLD

BOOK FOUR
THE LUMINOUS GROUND

THE CENTER FOR ENVIRONMENTAL STRUCTURE
BERKELEY CALIFORNIA

in association with

PATTERNLANGUAGE.COM

Published by The Center for Environmental Structure
2701 Shasta Road, Berkeley, California 94708
CES is a trademark of the Center for Environmental Structure.

ISBN 0-9726529-2-2 (Book 2)
ISBN 0-9726529-0-6   (Set)
LIBRARY OF CONGRESS CATALOGING-IN-PUBLICATION DATA
Alexander, Christopher. The Nature of Order: An Essay on the Art of Building and the Nature of the Universe /
Christopher Alexander,   p.   cm.   (Center for Environmental Structure Series; v. 9–12).
Contents: v.1. The Phenomenon of Life — v.2. The Process of Creating Life
v.3. A Vision of a Living World — v.4. The Luminous Ground
1. Architecture—Philosophy.   2. Science—Philosophy.   3. Cosmology
4. Geometry in Architecture.   5. Architecture—Case studies.   6. Community
7. Process philosophy.   8. Color (Philosophy).
I. Center for Environmental Structure.   II. Title.
III. Title: The Process of Creating Life.
IV. Series: Center for Environmental Structure series ; v. 10.
NA2500 .A444   2002
720'.1—dc21   2002154265
ISBN 0-9726529-2-2 (cloth: alk. paper: v.2)

Typography by Katalin Bende and Richard Wilson
Manufactured in China by Everbest Printing Co., Ltd.

BOOK ONE
THE PHENOMENON OF LIFE

PROLOGUE TO BOOKS 1-4

BOOK TWO
THE PROCESS OF CREATING LIFE

BOOK THREE
A VISION OF A LIVING WORLD

BOOK FOUR

THE LUMINOUS GROUND

I dedicate these four books to my family:

to my beloved mother, who died many years ago;

to my dear father, who has always helped me and inspired me;

to my darlings Lily and Sophie;

and to my dear wife Pamela who gave them to me,

and who shares them with me.

These books are a summary of what i have understood about

the world in the sixty-third year of my life.

THE
PROCESS
OF
CREATING
LIFE

* *

THE CONCEPT OF LIVING STRUCTURE

In order to provide a background for Book 2, it is necessary to summarize what I have, I believe, accomplished in Book 1, THE PHENOMENON OF LIFE.

The basic idea is this: *Throughout the world, in the organic as in the inorganic, it is possible to make a distinction between living structure and non-living structure*. In nature, most structures which appear (whether organic or inorganic) are living structures to a fairly high degree. This is a class of structures which does not pertain exclusively to organisms or organic life. It is a more general class of structures, existing within the very much vaster class of all possible three-dimensional structures.

As I use it, the term "living" applied to structure is always a matter of degree. Strictly speaking, every structure has some degree of life. The main accomplishment of Book 1 is in making this distinction precise, in providing empirical methods for observing and measuring degree of life as it occurs in different structures. Perhaps most important, I gave in Book 1 a partly mathematical account of living structure, so that we may see the content of living structure, its functional and geometric order, as an established and objective feature of reality.

In nature, almost *everything* has living structure: waves, sand, rocks, forests, thunderstorms, birds, snakes, and moss. That is why, I think, scientists have not previously drawn attention to the existence of the class of living structures, nor to the distinction between living and non-living structure. It has not, in physics, or geology, or biology, or chemistry, so far been a necessary distinction.

In primitive society builders also needed no distinction, because within the processes available to them, nearly everything made by people had living structure, just as systems in nature do. By and large, traditional builders, even as recently as a hundred years ago, also still made buildings, fields, and artifacts which had living structure.

But in the past century, we have, for the first time, become able to conceive, design, make, manufacture, and produce non-living structure: kinds of things, arrangements of matter, buildings, roads, artifacts which do not belong to the class of living structures and which, for the first time, focus our attention on the distinction.

Thus the objects, buildings, and landscapes created by human beings in the past century have, very often, been outside the class of living structures. More exactly, they are often systems with significantly low levels of living structure, much lower than occurs in nature. That is something new in human history.

For reasons which will become clear in the next chapters, I believe that many of these new artifacts and buildings — including, for instance, the apparently harmless developer-inspired motels of our era or our mass housing projects — are structures which can be *thought*, invented, created artificially, but they cannot be generated by a nature-like *process* at all. Thus they are, structurally speaking, monsters. They are not merely unappealing and strange. They belong, objectively, to a class of non-living structures, or less living structures, and have thus, for the first time, introduced a type of structure on earth which nature itself could not, in principle, create.

Living structure: Lemon groves, Lake Garda

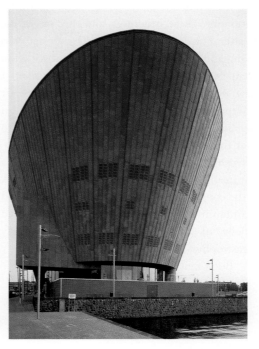

Non-living structure: Technology center, Amsterdam

Living structure: Shelter for the homeless, San Jose

Non-living structure: Nussbaum museum, Osnabrück

It is this event which has stimulated my investigation into these structures, and encouraged me to attempt a definition of the difference between living and non-living structure. The distinction compels attention because — if the arguments I have put forward in Book 1 are legitimate — it is important that we, as a people on Earth, learn to create our towns, buildings and landscapes so that they too — like nature — are living structures, and so that our artificial world is then a nature-like system. As I have suggested in Book 1, the consequences of living our daily lives and maintaining human society in a world composed chiefly of non-living structure, are nearly catastrophic.

But I am jumping ahead of myself, since what I have just said already depends on the conclusions of this book. My present starting point is simply this: there is such a thing as living structure, and there is an objective distinction between systems which have relatively *more* living structure and systems which have relatively *less* living structure.

The distinction has been brought to the fore by the history of 20th-century design and construction, which forced our attention — for the first time — on the fact that not all structures made by human beings are living ones.

The question is, How is living structure to be made by human beings? What kind of human-inspired processes can create living structure?

REAL LIFE CREATED BY A PROCESS IN THE CARIBBEAN

In the photograph opposite, we see a situation which would, normally, be classified as poverty. The houses are rudimentary, the road is roughly paved, two of the men are barefoot. Yet for all its poverty, which is certainly real, we can detect the residue of living process in this scene. The men are happy, evidently. They are talking and smiling and dreaming with quiet enjoyment. The road goes just where it is needed. It interferes little with the land, and leaves it harmonious. The houses, made of wood and corrugated iron, are placed in convenient spots, the right distance apart, making a lively spot between. The vegetation of the mountain is largely untouched. In this scene — both in its human happiness and in its architecture — we see a case of wonderful life. We see the impact of hundreds of acts, done by different people, making a living street where, rich or poor, people are truly comfortable. The ordinary old porch, steps, windows, and doors — how pleasant the way they sit with the street. One man sits happily, half on his side, comfortable, looking at his friend, and leaning on the ground. The trees, the columns, the deck chair, the tree branches have all happened step by step, with the hardly conscious adaptation of each fence-post, path, seedling, each season of painting. Buildings and plants, even the people with them, have unfolded together, making something comfortable, ordinary, and profound.

It should be repeated again and again, and understood, that the capacity of a society to create living structure in its architecture is a dynamic capacity which depends on the nature and character of the processes used to create form, and to create the precise sequence and character of the unfoldings that occur during the daily creation of building form and landscape form and street form.

For this purpose I shall, in the chapters of this book, move from the technical language of structure-preserving process to the broader and more intuitive language of living process. I shall define a living process as any process that is capable of generating living structure. But, as we shall see in the book, the concept — and its implementation — require a wider and more everyday understanding of what is involved, an understanding which fits with the daily acceptance of day-to-day process and generic process — in

*Ease of living, Guadeloupe, French West Indies. Modesty of means matters much less
when the environment has grown in support of ordinary things. Here there
is charm, comfort, joyfulness in the buildings as a part of life.*

short, one that can be compatible with everyday individual and social process and with the institutionalized process of professions like architecture, and of the other social activities which play a major role in shaping the environment.

Above all, the living processes which I shall describe, are — as it turns out — enormously complex. The idea that all living processes are structure-preserving turns out to be merely the tip of a very large iceberg of hidden complexity. The subject of living process is a topic of great richness, which is likely to keep us occupied for centuries as we try to master its variety of meanings and its attributes and potentialities.

A SOURCE OF LIFE

All this will have direct meaning in the world around us. If carried out, it will change our conception of our own life, and of our world. Above all it will change the character of our results. What may appear superficially as an informal, relaxing, rambling roughness of the Caribbean photograph is actually a far deeper order than the norm. It is what we experience as *life*. That is where real stories are made; where human beings experience a measure of the freedom, and difficulty, and incongruity of being human. It is not hard to be at ease in such places. They invite us to be what we are, and they allow us to be what we are.

It must be recognized that — morphologically speaking — to generate such complexity is a different task from generating the lifeless hulks portrayed in chapter 4, which have been the aspirations of too many clients and developers and architects in the modern age. This real life is an *entirely* different matter. The means needed to create this real life, to create living structure in the true meaning of the word — that has an order of difficulty we architects have almost never contemplated yet. Indeed, the small example of the street in Guadeloupe gives only a tiny glimpse of the true nature of complexity.

PREFACE

ON PROCESS

The Belousov-Zhabotinski process
See chapter 1

1 / A DYNAMIC VIEW OF ORDER

In Book 1, I tried to rearrange our definition of architectural order in such a way that it forms a basis for a new view of living structure in buildings and landscapes, escaping from the mechanistic dilemma.[1]

Book 1 invited us to see the world around us — buildings, plants, a painting, our own faces and hands — as field-like structures with centers arranged in a systematic fashion and interacting within the whole. When a structure is living we will feel the echo of our own aliveness in response to it.[2] Book 2 takes the necessary next step of investigating the process of how living structure creates itself over time. A child becomes an adult without ever losing uniqueness or completeness. An acorn transforms smoothly into an oak, although the start and endpoint are radically different. A good building or city will unfold according to the living processes that generate living structure. What I describe throughout Book 2 is a comparably new view of architectural process, with a focus on architectural processes that are capable of generating living structure. It is my hope that a world of architecture, more suitable for human life, will emerge from this new view of living process and of what process *is*.

Book 2 invites us to reconsider the role and importance of process and how it is living or not. It is about the fact that order cannot be understood sufficiently well in purely static terms because there is something *essentially* dynamic about order. Living structure can be attained in practice, and will become fully comprehensible and reachable, only from a dynamic understanding. Indeed *the nature of order is interwoven in its fundamental character with the nature of the processes which create the order.*

When we look at order dynamically, the concept of living structure *itself* undergoes some change. Book 1 focused on the idea of *living* structure, and the viewpoint was geometric, static. In Book 2, I start with a second concept, based on the idea of an *unfolded* structure. The point of view — even for the structure itself — is dynamic.

The two conceptions of structure turn out to be complementary. In the end we shall see that living structure and unfolded structure are equivalent. All living structure is unfolded and all unfolded structure is living. And I believe the concept of an *unfolded* structure is as important, and should play as essential a role in architecture, as the concept of *living* structure. Thus we shall end up with two equivalent views — one static, one dynamic — of the same idea.

2 / THE NECESSARY ROLE OF PROCESS

The task of architecture may be simply stated. We seek to make a living architecture: that means an architecture in which every part, every building, every street, every garden, is alive. It has tens of thousands of living centers in it. It has rooms, gardens, windows, each with their own life. It has stairs, passages, entrances, terraces, columns, column capitals, arches. In a living environment, each of these individual places is a living center in its own right. The window is a glorious living center with light, comfort, view, and so on. The window sill is a living center, with shape, seat, a place for a vase of flowers. Even the smallest part of the most insignificant room, a forgotten corner, has the quality of a living center. Even the smallest part of the physical structure, a brick, the mortar between two bricks, the joint of one piece of wood with another, also has this living character.[3]

What process can accomplish the subtle and beautiful adaptation of the parts that will create a living architecture? In a certain sense, the answer is simple. We have to make — or generate — the ten thousand living centers in the building, one by one. That is the core fact. And the ten thousand centers, to be living centers, must be beautifully adapted to one another within the whole: each must fit the others, each must contribute to the others, and the ten thousand centers then — if they are truly living — must form a coherent and harmonious whole.

It is generally assumed that doing all this well is the proper work of an architect. This is what an architect is supposed to do. It is what an architect is trained to do. And — in theory — it is what an architect knows how to do. There is a general belief that *how* it is done by the architect and others is part of the mystery of the art; one does not ask too many questions about it. Questions about *how* it is best done — by what process — are rarely raised. Yet in this book I shall argue that careful thought about the adaptation problem shows that it *can* only be done successfully, when following a certain very *par-*

ticular kind of process. This does not mean that there is one ideal process which must be used. There are many thousands of different processes which can succeed. But to succeed, these processes must meet definite conditions — defined in the chapters which follow. Processes which meet these conditions, even though there may be thousands of them, are limited. They are rare and precious, compared with the millions upon millions of processes which are used daily for conceiving, designing, and building by architects and builders all over the world.

Many of the processes used today, sadly, are nearly *bound* to fail. We see the results of this failure all around us. The lifeless buildings and environments which have become common in modern society are not merely dead, non-living, structures. They are what they are precisely because of the social *processes* by which they have been conceived, designed, built, and paid for. No matter how skillful the architects, no matter how gifted, no matter how profound their powers of design — if the process used is wrong, the design cannot save the project.

Thus we shall see that processes (both of design and of construction) are more important, and larger in their effect on the quality of buildings, than the ability or training of the architect. *Processes* play a more fundamental role in determining the life or death of the building than does the "*design.*"[4]

3 / ORDER AS BECOMING

In many sciences, it has become commonplace to consider process as an inescapable part of order. In physics, for example, forces themselves are now seen as processes, and the structure we observe in the world of atoms and electrons is known to come about as a result of the continuous play of subatomic processes defined by quantum mechanics.[5] In biology, the structure of an organism is understood to be inseparable from the process which creates and maintains it: an animal, at any instant, is the ongoing result of certain genetically controlled processes which create the organism to begin with, and which continue to create that organism throughout its life. A cloud is a transitory by-product of the condensation of water in the atmosphere. The waves of the ocean are the flowing product of the process of interaction between wind and water.

The sand ripples in the Sahara are the product of the process by which the wind takes sand, picks it up, and drops it. The mountain is the temporary product of the folding and heaving of the earth. The flower is the temporary product of the unfolding of the bud and seed pod under the driving influence of DNA. In each case, the whole system of order we observe is only an instantaneous cross section, in time, of a continuous and ongoing process of flux and change.

These insights originated 2,500 years ago with Heraclitus and his assertion that we can never step into the same river twice. But arriving at this understanding in modern science has been a difficult affair. D'Arcy Wentworth Thompson, describing the origins of biological form in 1917 as a necessary result of biological growth, had to struggle intellectually, showing again and again by example that biological form could only be understood as a product of the growth process.[6]

Much more recently, the physicist Ilya Prigogine took decades, and many books and papers, to show that physics must be understood as a directional process — and that the way classical physics viewed phenomena without the orientation of time was fundamentally at odds with

reality and was incapable, therefore, of describing some of the most important physical phenomena. As Prigogine wrote in 1980: "*in classical physics change is nothing but a denial of becoming and time is only a parameter, unaffected by the transformation that it describes.*"[7]

Now, at the turn into the 21st century, the "process" insight has finally arrived in most scientific disciplines. Gradually, a modern view has come into focus where we understand that it is the transformations from moment to moment which govern order in a system.

However, despite the great progress made in many sciences and humanities, the concept of process has not yet become a normal part of the way we think about architecture. The words Prigogine used in 1980, criticizing mainstream 20th-century physics, could still be applied equally to contemporary mainstream architecture. *Our current view of architecture rests on too little awareness of becoming as the most essential feature of the building process.* Architects are much too concerned with the design of the world (its static structure), and not yet concerned enough with the design of the generative processes that create the world (its dynamic structure).

4 / PROCESS, THE KEY TO MAKING LIFE IN THINGS

I think of my friend Bill McClung making his meadows in the hills of Berkeley.[9] The near-wasteland of brush and eucalyptus, an overgrown and damaged landscape on the fringes of Berkeley becomes under his hand, something beautiful, alive.

Day after day, he goes up, gathers wood. He cuts poison oak and brush and thorn. He mows grassland, takes out bushes which have overgrown, takes out a tree which prevents another tree from having the light, from having its magnificence. He makes a pathway where I can walk, where he can walk.

Gradually, by cutting and removing, with a careful eye, he forms meadow: patches of grassland where the light falls, bounded by trees, looking toward a landscape, looking out toward the bay.

From something nearly destroyed, beautiful patches of land are formed. He clears the land of that scrub which makes the land too vulnerable to fire. He opens it, concentrates its beauty. Under the hand of this embellishment, each part becomes better; its uniqueness is preserved; its character intensified.

When he is done, each meadow has a different character. Each is ordinary, but a jewel,

Meadow in the Berkeley hills, mown and taken care of by Bill McClung, 1996

an individual jewel. The fabric of the jewel-like living meadows all together, if he succeeds, will cover the ridge of the Berkeley hills.

When I ask him what makes him keep doing it, he answers, "The knowledge that I am making life: that something living is being enhanced. That keeps us inspired. It makes it worthwhile. It is a tremendous thing."

But then I ask him, pushing, "Isn't it really more the actual pleasure of each day? You go, and go again, because each day, each hour, is satisfying. It is simple work. You enjoy the sunshine, the open air, the physical sweat of carrying, and cutting. The smell of the grass as it opens up, the dog running in the grass, the comments of the neighbors." And there is also the feeling of community, as people living near this bit of park begin to recognize Bill as a fixture, hope that he will keep on coming back; they appreciate what he does. His act makes him part of a community. And most of all, it is just pleasant, worth living for. The hours and minutes spent are rewarding in themselves.

I ask him if this pleasure in the process he is following is not worth almost more than the knowledge that he is making something come to life? He acknowledges my comment and admits, "Yes, this daily ordinary thing is almost more important than the other."

But it is the two together: the daily pleasure, breathing in the smell of the newly cut grass, with the deeper knowledge that goes with it that in this process he is making a living structure, up there on the ridge of the Berkeley hills.

On the other hand, processes which work against the existing life of a place, which fragment it, ignore it, cut across it, do damage. Even when they only *ignore* the wholeness or defy it with the best intentions, damage is done, disorder begins to occur. And as we watch the progress of the world, its growth, its change, we find that various acts — coming either from outside or from inside the thing itself — may be helpful or unhelpful to this wholeness which exists. This happens because the wholeness of any given thing may be helped or hindered by the character of the parts which it contains.

Once we recognize the possibility that some centers will be helpful to the life of an existing wholeness, while others will be antagonistic to

A 15th-century Hispano-Moresque tile, made by the cuerda seca *technique, the use of rope to form the lines*

it, we then begin to recognize the possibility of a highly complex kind of self-consistency in any given wholeness. The various centers within a wholeness may be in harmony with one another in different degrees, or at odds with one another in different degrees. And this is where the degree of life, or degree of value, in any given thing comes from.

Thus we see that each given wholeness has a certain history: the wholeness becomes more valuable if the history allows this wholeness to unfold in a way that is considerate, respectful, of the existing structure, and less valuable if the steps which are taken in the emergence of the wholeness are antagonistic to the existing structure.

What is fascinating, then, is the hint of a conception of value which emerges dynamically from respect for existing structure. We do not need any arbitrary or external criterion of value. The value exists within the unfolding of the wholeness itself. When the wholeness unfolds unnaturally, value is destroyed. When the wholeness unfolds naturally, value is created.

That is the origin of living structure.

Look at this Hispano-Moresque tile of the 15th century. When we first look at it, we see a beautiful design, harmonious, orderly, well-conceived, beautiful space and color. In contemporary terms, all this would appear to be part of the design of the tile, since it is the geometry of the finished tile, it seems to us, that causes this. We think of its beauty as a result of design.

But when I handled this tile, looked at its surface, held its weight, looked at the glaze, and started to ask myself how I would make a tile like this, the thing took on quite a different character. I saw that the particular lines of the design are formed by raised ridges in the clay. The separate colors of the different glazes are kept separate by these ridges, so that the liquid glaze, at the temperature of the kiln, cannot "run." As I thought more about how to do it — if I were actually making such a tile — I began to see that the sharp, almost hard design, the brilliant separation of glazes which makes the colors beautiful, and even the design itself, the character of straightness, curvature, and the formal quality of the line, are all by-products of a

San-ju-san Gen Do, temple of the thirty-three bays, Kyoto, 13th century. Here, too, the beauty of this building, the wonderful harmony of its construction, arise as value that appears in the process of craft, from a gently unfolding wholeness. The unfolding of the woodwork is so complex, and yet so pure, that it reaches great spiritual depths.

particular kind of process which must be used to make such a tile.

I believe the design was made by laying thick rope into the soft clay. It is the *rope* which allowed the maker form such complex shapes, with perfect parallel lines, and perfect half-round troughs. In my studio my assistant went further to understand how it had been done, and made a clay impression of the tile's surface in reverse. This reverse — a raised embossed impression taken in modeling clay — was even more impressive, and more beautiful than the tile itself. I realized that this — the negative impression — must have been the actual thing which the maker made, and that the tile was then cast from it in clay.

The further I went to understand the actual process which had been used to make the tile, the more I realized that it was this *process*, more than anything, which governs the beauty of the design. Perhaps nine-tenths of its character, its beauty, comes simply from the process that the maker followed. The design, what we nowadays

Interior, San-ju-san Gen Do, Kyoto. The interior is empty, except for one thousand golden Buddhas, carved, carefully placed, and revered.

think of as the design, followed. It was almost a residue from the all-important process. The design is indeed beautiful, yes. But it can only be made as beautiful as it is within the technique, or process, used to make it. And once one uses this technique, the design — what appears as the sophisticated beauty of the design — follows almost without thinking, just as a result of following the process.

If you do not use this technique — process — you cannot create a tile of this design. An attempt to follow the same drawing, but with different techniques, will fall flat on its face. And if I change the technique (process), then the design must change, too. This design follows almost without effort from this *technique*. It is the process, not the design, that is doing all the hard work, and which is even paving the way for the design.

Thus the making, the physical processes of shaping, carving, drying, glazing, and firing the tile, are the ways in which this tile gets its form, its life, even its design. The "design" of this beautiful work is not more than a tenth of what gives it its life. Nine-tenths come from the process. We see the same phenomenon in a far more complex work from 13th-century Kyoto. In San-ju-san Gen Do, the temple of the thirty-three bays, we see the imprint of years, the imprint of care in the pieces of wood that have been lovingly matched to their position so well that seven hundred years later they still impress the heart. It is the mark of the plane on the wood which makes the wood, hundreds of years later, touch our hearts. It is the process used by the temple priests to lay out the foundations and cornerstones which places the building so beautifully in the land. It is the care of the goldsmith — the carving process and the carving tools, the process of making the mold — which gives each of the one thousand buddhas its unique personality, yet allows it to be ultimately the same and so, capable of teaching us, through one thousand manifestations, that we feel the true nature of all things.

This gradual rubbing together of phenomena to get the right result, the slow process of getting things right, is almost unknown to us today.

5 / OUR MECHANIZED PROCESS

During the 20th century, we became used to something very different.

Consider the "normal" building process we have become used to in recent decades. A client specifies a program in which building areas are mechanically set out as requirements. In the case of a large building, this program is then made more precise (and often more rigid) by a professional programmer who sets it forth arithmetically in a table of square footages. An architect designs the building at a drawing table and is held to the program, rigidly, not to the evolving whole. The drawings are then checked by an engineer who is separate from the process and responsible for making the building stand up. A soils engineer very possibly works out the foundation, separately again. The final engineering drawings are then checked by a building inspector and by a zoning officer — again a separate process. In many cases, the zoning officer who checks them has not been to the site. Even if the officer has done a site visit, he or she has little or no authority to create any coherent relation between the building and the site, in relation to the site's special conditions. Once the drawings are approved, they are sent out to bid, by a contractor who has not been part of the design process, looks only at the drawings, but shares none of the vision. The drawings are also checked by a bank. The individual parts of the drawings may be sent out to bid by subcontractors, who are even more remote from the task at hand. Many of the objects, components, which will be used in the construction of the building are factory-made. They have been designed and constructed with no knowledge of the building at all; they are mentally and factually separate from its existence, but are brought into play only by a process of assembly.

During the building process, corrections cannot be made without huge expense to the client. Thus the assembly process is insensitive to almost any new wholeness which appears during construction. The landscape work is done by a separate architect, who specializes in plants. The actual gardening — that is, the preparation of the ground, planting of trees, flowers — is done by yet another person acting under orders, and once again contractually removed from the human feeling, light, and action of the building.

The interior, very often, is done by yet *another* person — an interior decorator. This person, *again* remote from any previous reality, will also assemble pre-constructed components and modules to try and produce a whole. But the elements are, at the end, almost inevitably separate and cold in feeling, harsh in content, without origin in human meaning. They do not reflect the feelings of the building's occupants; nor do they arise naturally from the wholeness of the building shell and from the seeds of a direction which that shell already contains. Even the building's paint is often applied as an afterthought, as if it were an independent act. And the very paint, itself, is once again chosen from among a system of mechanically component-like colors, none of which was conceived in the context of the building, but which exist, precooked, in a catalog.

Present-day town-planning practice — mainly based on zoning — is equally mechanical in character. It is largely independent of the people most directly affected, and is controlled by appointed officials, who often do not even visit the site where a particular building is to be built. The zoning ordinance — a map of an imaginary future, used as a control device — is prepared by others. The process is based, in considerable part, on the needs of the developer-controlled, profit-oriented marketplace, and on the assumption that agreement about deep value is impossible in principle. Achievement of subtle or spiritual character in a town under these conditions — which are a large-scale replica of the conditions surrounding smaller-scale mechanical building process — is once again hardly possible.

You might say of these examples, "But this surely is all process. Isn't that good?" The trouble is that it is *mechanical* process only, something which subverts the inner fire of true living process.

In a mechanistic view of the world, we see all things, even if only for convenience, as machines. A machine is intended to accomplish something. It is, in its essence, goal-oriented. Like machines, then, within a mechanistic view processes are always seen as aimed at certain ends. We think of things by the end-state we want, and then ask ourselves how to get there.

This mistake was widespread in the 20th century. For example, in the extreme 20th-century view of some mechanistic sociology, even kindness might have been seen as a way of achieving certain results: part of a bargain, or a social contract, which had the purpose of *getting* something.[10]

Real kindness is something quite different, something valuable in *itself*. It is a true process, not guided by the grasp for a goal, but guided by the minute-to-minute necessity of caring, dynamically, for the feelings and well-being of another. This is not trivial, but deep; sincerely related to human feeling; and not predictable in its end-result, because the end-result is not a goal. Unlike the goal-oriented picture, which is imposed intellectually on our substance as persons, real kindness is a process true to our essential human instinct and to our knowledge of what it means to be a person. But the machine-age view showed a process like kindness as being oriented toward a *goal*, just as every machine too has its purpose — its goal, what it is intended to produce.

Like the mechanical 20th-century view of kindness, the 20th-century mainstream view of

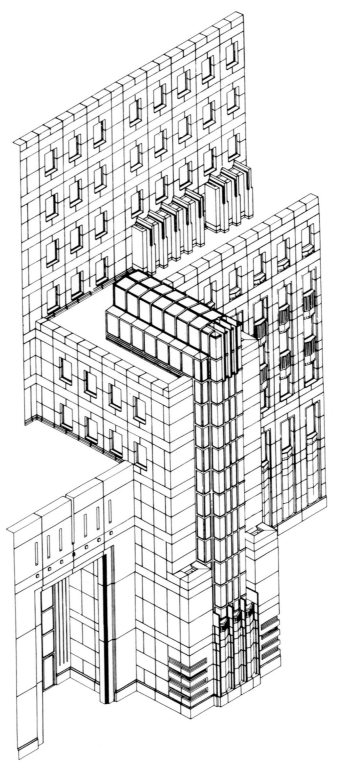

Our mechanized process: a building designed and made by a process which is mechanical

Our mechanized process: a building planned and designed and made by a process which is not only mechanical technically, but which is also mechanical in human terms, bureaucratic and corporate

building was goal-oriented and mechanistic, aimed mainly at end-results, not on the inner good of processes. Building was viewed as a necessary way to achieve a certain end-result. The design drawn by the architect — the master plan drawn by the planner — was the purpose, these were the goals of the art. The process of getting to the goal was thought to be of little importance in itself, except insofar as it attained (or failed to attain) the desired goal.

The mechanistic view of architecture we have learned to accept in our era is crippled by this overly-simple, goal-oriented approach. In the mechanistic view of architecture we think mainly of *design* as the desired end-state of a building, and far too little of the *way* or *process* of making a building as something inherently beautiful in itself. But, most important of all, the background underpinning of this goal-oriented view — a static world almost without process — just is not a truthful picture. As a conception of the world, it roundly fails to describe things as they are. It exerts a crippling effect on our view of architecture and planning because it fails to be true to ordinary, everyday fact. For in fact, everything is constantly changing, growing, evolving. The human body is changing. Trees bear leaves, and the

leaves fall. The road cracks. People's lives change from week to week. The building moves with wind and rain and movement of the earth. Buildings and streets and gardens are modified constantly while they are inhabited, sometimes improved, sometimes destroyed. Towns are created as a cooperative flow caused by hundreds, even millions, of people over time.

Why is this process-view essential? Because the ideals of "design," the corporate boardroom drawing of the imaginary future, the developer's slick watercolor perspective of the future end-state, control our conception of what must be done — yet they bear no relation to the actual nature, or problems, or possibilities, of a living environment. And they are socially backward, since they necessarily diminish people's involvement in the continuous creation of their world.

In all this, *process* is still not present as something essential, only as something mechanical.[11] In our profession of architecture there is no conception, yet, of process *itself* as a budding, as a flowering, as an unpredictable, unquenchable unfolding through which the future grows from the present in a way that is dominated by the goodness of the moment.

6 / POSSIBILITY OF A NEW VIEW OF ARCHITECTURAL PROCESS

I shall argue that every good process in architecture, and in city planning also, treats the world as a whole and allows every action, every process, to appear as an unfolding of that whole. When living structure is created, what is to be built is made consistent with the whole, it comes from the whole, it nourishes and protects the whole.

We may get some inkling of this kind of thing by considering what it means to *design* a building, and to compare it with what it means to *make* a building. Naively, I make a building if I actually do it myself, do it with my own hands.

This sounds like fun. But of course that is impossible for all but the very smallest buildings. More deeply, what it means for me to *make* a building is that I am totally responsible for it. I am actually responsible for its structure, its materials, its functioning, its safety, its cost, its beauty, everything. This is in marked contrast with the present idea of architecture, where as an architect I am definitely *not* responsible for everything. I am only responsible for my particular part in the process, for my set of drawings, which will then function, within the system, in a strictly limited fashion that is shut off from the whole. I have limited responsibility. Like a bureaucrat, I play my role, but "don't ask me to be responsible for anything — I am just doing my job."

When I *make* something, on the other hand, I am deeply involved with it and responsible for it. And not only I. Whether I am head of some project, or a person making some small part of it, the feeling of total responsibility is on my shoulders. In a good process, each person working on the building is — and feels — responsible for everything. For design, schedule, structure, flowers, feeling — everything.

I remember a few years ago meeting an old man who told me he had put the last I-beam on the Empire State Building. He had also placed the highest steelwork on the towers of the Golden Gate Bridge. As he told me about the riveters and welders he used to work with, he described a kind of special ethic they carried with them: while doing their work, five hundred or a thousand feet above the ground, they were conscious, among themselves, that whatever they did — every rivet, every weld — was their responsibility and theirs alone. It was up to them to make a thing that was to last forever. It was in their hands, and there were no excuses.

This was vastly removed from the "I-am-just-doing-my-job" attitude which exists in the fragmented and mechanical process most often followed today, where the demarcation of responsibility is socially and legally drawn to make sure each person does *not* feel responsible for the whole.

I do not suggest that making should be re-introduced for reasons of nostalgia. But I shall prove that a process which is not based on making in a holistic sense, *cannot create a living structure*. And I shall demonstrate hypermodern processes, many using the most advanced techniques of the present and of the future, in which a new form of *making* dominates our attitude.

In every sphere of nature, and in every sphere of human effort, there are trillions upon trillions of possible processes. Of these trillions, only a few are *living* processes — that is, actually capable of generating living structure. That does not mean that living processes are rare. There are, of course, still billions of them among the trillions. All the processes which generate nature — including what we understand as physics, chemistry, biology, geomorphology, hydrodynamics — they are *all* living processes, because they do virtually all generate living structure, at least most of the time. However, there is an even larger number of *possible* processes which fail to create living structure.

Since human beings are the first creatures on Earth who have managed to create non-living structure, the need to focus on non-living processes is new. Indeed, we have only even *seen* non-living structure and non-living process for the first time in relatively recent decades.

Traditional society almost never saw these non-living processes. Although traditional society was filled with human-created processes — human-inspired and human-invented — it was dominated by living process. Human beings in traditional societies, by and large, used living processes.

Non-living process is a recent arrival on the planet Earth. It is only in the modern era, and chiefly in the last 50-100 years, that human beings have given widespread use to processes of all kinds which are non-living, which therefore generate quantities of non-living structure.

However, since the distinction between living process and non-living process has now become visible, and since, for the time being, we have no precise conception or definition of living process, it has become urgent that we try to get one.

In this book I make an effort, perhaps for the first time, to make this distinction and to lay a basis for a theory — and for a form of daily practice — which allows for a world in which living process, hence living structure, dominates the world and its creation.

NOTES

1. Wholeness, defined structurally, is the interlocking, nested, overlapping system of centers that exists in every part of space. For definitions, see Book 1, chapter 3, and Book 1, appendix 2.

2. For a precise definition and analysis of living structure in buildings, see Book 1, throughout, and especially chapters 1, 2, 4, 5, 8 and 11.

3. Also explained and argued in detail throughout Book 1.

4. One of the few texts, and perhaps the first, to make a dramatically clear statement about the vital role of process in building was Halim Abdelhalim's THE BUILDING CEREMONY (doctoral thesis, University of California, Berkeley, 1981). Another striking exception is the book by Stewart Brand, HOW BUILDINGS LEARN: WHAT HAPPENS AFTER THEY ARE BUILT (New York: Viking, 1994), which clearly identifies the dynamic history of the building as one of its most salient features.

5. Richard Feynman, THEORY OF FUNDAMENTAL PROCESSES (New York: W. A. Benjamin, 1961).

6. D'Arcy Wentworth Thompson, ON GROWTH AND FORM (Cambridge: Cambridge University Press, 1917; reprinted volumes 1 and 2, 1959). Also Brian Goodwin, HOW THE LEOPARD CHANGED ITS SPOTS (New York: Simon and Schuster, Touchstone, 1994).

7. Ilya Prigogine, FROM BEING TO BECOMING (San Francisco: W. H. Freeman, 1980), p. 3.

8. I am aware of one provocative counter-example, in the following passage by a philosopher, Bruno Pinchard: "It is on the subject of architecture that Aristotle achieves great precision in the presentation of his dynamics, when he analyzes the reality of the buildable as such and distinguishes it from the finished construction. Now the architecture is not only in the house that is built, but in the act of building itself. The mover in architecture is not only the mental image of the project in the architect's mind. Particularly for the great theorists of Vitruvian humanist architecture, who tried hard not to reduce the origins of architecture to the primitive hut, it is the architect's job to direct work on the site and so to transform the plan according to the necessities of the climate of the materials at his disposal. This amounts to drawing a distinction between the idea of the house and its form, its programming and the carrying out of the opus. In other words, the architect's final cause is not simple (the architect is not just a space technician), and it may be said that there is no classical architecture that does not carry in its realization the trace of the processes of its construction." From Bruno Pinchard, Appendix to René Thom's SEMIOPHYSICS, A SKETCH (Boston: Addison Wesley, 1990), pp. 237–38.

9. Bill McClung, my friend and editor, is a fire commissioner in the city of Berkeley and spends much of his life now making meadows in the Berkeley hills, converting fire-hazardous brush to something more alive and beautiful.

10. See, for example, Evans Pritchard and other early 20th-century functionalist discussions of social contracts.

11. See the preface to Book 1. Our understanding of process, like our understanding of order, has been severely compromised by the value-neutral Cartesian picture, and in a similar fashion. In the case of static order at least, everyone knows that things have value; the mistake has been in the fact that we have been encouraged to think that the value of an object is subjective. Process presents a deeper problem since, in our time (with some exceptions), we are not used to evaluating it at all, even in subjective terms. We have yet to learn that, objectively, there is life-creating process and life-destroying process.

PART ONE

STRUCTURE-PRESERVING
TRANSFORMATIONS

I start with an overview of a scientific question. Throughout the natural world, one sees myriad examples of systems which "come into being." Indeed, as we think about it, in natural systems there is nothing else BUT this "coming into being." Everything is coming into being, continuously.

Yet we have relatively little theory that allows us to grasp this process of coming into being. Although there have been many discussions in the last two decades about chaos, catastrophes, bifurcation, and emergence, about the generation of complexity from interaction of simple rules, about the processes that have become known as chaos theory, and the way that new structures emerge by differentiation and bifurcation, still, even now, there is not enough coherent scientific theory that tells us how these processes really work geometrically.

In the first four chapters I focus on the idea that a living process always has enormous respect for the state (and morphology and form) of what exists, and always finds a next step forward which preserves the structure of what exists, and develops and extends its latent structure as it creates change, or evolution, or development. This is the process which is "creative."

In chapters 1 and 2, I address these issues for cases in the natural world, and provide the outline of a tentative approach that helps us understand the unfolding of geometry in biology and physics. This theory provides the underpinning for what follows. In chapters 3 and 4, I turn my attention to the BUILT world, to towns and buildings and to the way the emergence of living structure in towns and buildings may be understood within the context of theory.

The searchlight on nature will show us that many of the processes we have come to accept as normal in architecture and city planning and development are, from a process point of view, deeply flawed. They are, as matters stand today, incapable in principle of generating living structure. For this reason the near absence of living structure in our built contemporary world cannot be a surprise to us. It follows, inevitably, from the flaws of the processes we have come to accept as a normal part of our society, and it will change only when the processes we use in our society, are changed.

CHAPTER ONE

THE PRINCIPLE OF UNFOLDING WHOLENESS IN NATURE

1 / INTRODUCTION

How does nature create living structure?

Living structure, as I have defined it, is not merely the structure we find in living creatures — organisms and other ecological and biological systems. It is, in a more general sense, the character of all that we perceive as "nature." The living structure is the general morphological character which natural phenomena have in common.

In Book 1, I have tried to describe and characterize this living structure in very general terms. In the sense introduced in Book 1, the living centers which appear in any given physical system have varying degrees of life. They have life because they are composed of other living centers that support and sustain and intensify each other. I remind the reader that in this way of thinking, living structure refers not to the biological systems in the world, but is a general character, appearing through all systems, organic and inorganic, of the natural world.

The way that centers manage to support and intensify each other in such living structure is chiefly governed by the repeated occurrence of fifteen geometric properties defined in Book 1.[1] They are identified as: 1. LEVELS OF SCALE, 2. STRONG CENTERS, 3. BOUNDARIES, 4. ALTERNATING REPETITION, 5. POSITIVE SPACE, 6. GOOD SHAPE, 7. LOCAL SYMMETRIES, 8. DEEP INTERLOCK AND AMBIGUITY, 9. CONTRAST, 10. GRADIENTS, 11. ROUGHNESS, 12. ECHOES, 13. THE VOID, 14. SIMPLICITY AND INNER CALM, 15. NOT-SEPARATENESS.

What I call the living structure of nature — that which we see in the natural world around us — is also largely governed by these fifteen properties and their interaction and superposition. Chapter 6 of Book 1 contains many examples that show the field of centers and its associated fifteen properties in rocks, animals, plants, clouds, rivers, landscapes, crystals. Again and again, throughout the worlds studied in physics, chemistry, biology, geology, fluid dynamics, ecology, crystallography, cytology, and molecular biology, we find densely packed structures of centers in which thousands of centers support each other.[2] Thus nature creates living structure every day, in sand, in rivers, in clouds, in birds, in running antelopes. It does it, both in the organic and inorganic realms, apparently without effort.

But why does living structure, with its multiplicity of centers and their associated fifteen properties, keep making its appearance in the natural world? *Why*, and *how*, does living structure keep recurring in these widely different domains? What is the mechanics of the process by which living structure is made to appear, so easily, in nature? What is the process by which this kind of structure repeatedly, and persistently, occurs?

Oddly enough, the persistent appearance of living structure in nature is not easy to explain. That is why, in this book about architecture, I start by trying to understand nature in a new way. Once we have that understanding, we may have a basis for thinking about architectural process and for identifying processes which are capable of creating a living world in the realm of architecture. In a good building, as in nature, there is also living structure. Each living center contains thousands of living centers; and the centers support each other in an intricate pattern. But as we see from the many 20th-century buildings which lack this structure, there is — at least in modern society — some kind of immense practical difficulty in creating such a living structure in the real world of buildings. Indeed, the very large number of recently built buildings which lack living structure suggests that for some reason it is especially hard for us in our present period of history.

Yet nature manages the task rather easily. That is why I say, "To learn how to create living structure in buildings, we had better start by looking at nature."

2 / NOTE FOR THE SCIENTIFIC READER

In what follows, I shall argue that the emergence of new structure in nature, is brought about, always, by a sequence of transformations which act on the whole, and in which each step emerges as a discernible and continuous result from the immediately preceding whole.

This thought, obvious if taken naively, but profound and difficult if taken literally as a piece of science, relies entirely on the possibility that we can form a coherent and well-defined idea of what is meant by "the whole," and of what is meant by a structure which grows from the whole, and preserves the wholeness while it is moving forward. Such a thought is well-nigh impossible today, because in spite of the uses provided by David Bohm of the word "wholeness," there is in science today no concise or well-defined idea of wholeness as a structure. Yet without a well-defined idea of the whole, the thought I have expressed here cannot be completed or used. The nub of the point which governs the thinking of this book, is that we *are* able to approach clear thinking about this issue, and have enough of a well-defined formulation of what wholeness "is" to see the outline of a new theory built on this foundation.

Although I cannot claim to have fully solved the problem, I believe that in Book 1, I have given a sufficient description and definition of "the wholeness" so that it may be understood as a well-defined structure which occurs in all configurations.

Briefly, recapitulating passages of Book 1, the wholeness is what we think of as the "gestalt," the broad gestural sweep of a figure, or of a configuration. In the Belousov reaction (images shown on page 27 below), it is the "curly-Y" figure — the lily-shaped figure — which has two halves sweeping away from each other, and containing between them a V-shaped center. That is what exists in picture 2, and what exists, already, in an earlier form, in picture 1. The 2nd stage has emerged from this wholeness, and has preserved it, even as it introduces other structure. In the stages 2 and 3, we see another gestalt, which emerged from the first — a pair of round whorls or spirals — partly present in the picture 2, and fully developed in picture 3. As we go from picture to picture, or from stage to stage of the reaction, we see a continuous series of such configurations, in which the deep gestalt of each stage forms, grows, swells, develops, and gives rise to a new configuration.

It is this process, which I mean by "emergence of the wholeness" and by "emergence of the configuration from the wholeness."

What I have said, in Book 1, is that this wholeness is in principle amenable to mathematical treatment and description. A wholeness consists of a recursively nested system of centers, all more or less living ones (according to the definitions of Book 1). It displays the fifteen properties, and in a sense one might say that the fifteen properties are the primitive configurations from which all wholeness is built. In more detail still, considering the arguments and examples of Book 1, appendix 3, the wholeness may always be viewed as a nested system of local symmetries, and it is the *configuration* of the system of nested local symmetries which gives us the character of any particular wholeness, in any particular configuration.

I claim that even in continuous phenomena (such as curves, curved surfaces, organic forms in three dimensions such as leaves or organs, or in configurations of subtle gestalt such as gradients and smoothly meandering curves) *it is always the wholeness, as defined here*, in terms of the strong centers which appear, and in terms of local symmetries, which provide the handle of this wholeness.

What I call the wholeness is, to a very rough degree, a mathematical representation of the overall gestalt which we perceive, or which we are aware, which gives the character to the configuration, and which forms, what an artist might call, his most intuitive apperception of the whole.

Now, in simple outline, what I claim in this chapter, and in many succeeding chapters, is that natural process — and all living processes — come about as a result of sequence of transformations which emerge from, and act upon, this wholeness — bearing in mind that the wholeness is a well-defined thing, not an artistic

thing — and that it is indeed from this wholeness, not previously identified in science with precision, that all growth and morphology emerge.

And yet I must apologize. Although I have given a nearly adequate definition of what this means, I have not given precise enough treatment, yet, to provide a strict mathematical treatment. What follows then, should be understood as proto-mathematics, where a structural idea, mathematical in principle, is available, and may guide our thought — but the hard work of formulating a mathematics with which one can calculate, has only just begun.

With this shortcoming in mind, please regard the following discussion, and presentation of examples, with some forgiveness. I have come as close to being accurate as, at present, I know how.

3 / THE NEED FOR A GENERAL EXPLANATION OF THE WAY THAT LIVING STRUCTURE IS CREATED

When we look at nature, we can nearly always find an explanation for any *one* of the fifteen properties as it appears in any *one* particular instance. Take BOUNDARIES, for example. Conventional plasma physics can be used to explain the appearance of the plasma boundary layer that forms around the sun. Hydrodynamics can be used to explain the silting up of the mouth of a river like the Rio Negro, where it flows into the Amazon, to form a pattern of streams bounded by great swaths of silted mud deposited by stream flow. Biological studies suggest why a cell is constructed to have a thick boundary layer, larger in volume than the nucleus of the cell. It is needed as the zone where chemical exchanges happen.

But it is quite another matter to give a general explanation which tells us why massive and substantial boundaries *will, in general, tend to occur again and again, throughout nature, within three-*

dimensional systems. This question involves a level of morphological thinking which has no familiar language in contemporary mathematics.

I have argued in Book 1 that the fifteen properties are necessarily associated with living centers and are the ways in which centers appear in the world, come to life, and cooperate to form other living centers. But that, in itself, does not explain why they keep appearing. We need a more systematic, general explanation. It is extremely hard to formulate a general rule for any one of the fifteen properties which gives us a convincing explanation as to why that property appears again and again and again throughout nature.

This issue is far from trivial. Although recent developments in complexity theory have shown how linked systems of variables, under the right conditions, will cooperate to form emergent order, that in itself does not yet tell us why the particular kind of order formation I have

*Boundaries created by hydrodynamic process of silting at the edges of stream flow:
formation where the Rio Negro runs into the Amazon*

*Boundary formed by magneto-nuclear and plasma
processes: the corona of the sun*

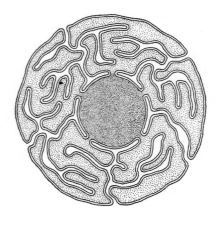

*Boundary formed by cytological process
in a mammalian cell*

identified as living structure, keeps on recurring, time after time.[3]

Yet there does, in an enormous number of empirical cases, appear to be a process which produces centers — and above all "living centers" — packed with density of other centers and hence with life. Why do *these living centers* appear? Why does living structure appear in the world? What is it — in the detailed history of natural systems, with its mechanical causation — that can, step by step, keep on making the fifteen properties appear *in general*, and that therefore, in general, causes the repeated creation of living structure in the inorganic and organic world?[4]

4 / CREATION OF STRUCTURE AS IT OCCURS IN NATURE

In what follows, I invite the reader to look at examples, while considering the existence of a fundamental principle which I call the principle of *unfolding wholeness*. This principle states that, *in the evolution of an otherwise undisturbed system, the wholeness W is progressively enhanced and intensified*. This wholeness, as defined in chapter 3 of Book 1, is the system of strong centers which occurs in space.[5]

According to this principle, the transformations which occur in the system take whatever wholeness exists at any given instant and continue it and intensify it while, broadly, maintaining its global structure, so that at the next instant that wholeness is more pronounced; as time goes forward, the wholeness gets progressively intensified, step by step by step. It is this process — I maintain — which is responsible for the creation of living structure. When the wholeness is intensified again and again, precisely that structure we recognize as living (with its fifteen properties) will begin to appear. In this view, then, the appearance of living structure in the world is caused by the repeated application of the principle of unfolding wholeness to every system.

I believe the principle of unfolding wholeness is consistent with most present-day physics and biology. It is also consistent with recent thinking in non-linear dynamics, catastrophe theory, and bifurcation theory.[6] It is, however, a principle which is not automatically given by anything currently identified in these disciplines. As such, it is a new principle, necessary, I believe, in order to explain the appearance of living structure in the world.

If we examine the wide variety of cases from nature which I present in the next few pages, we shall see that they *all* show a particular kind of structure-preserving, smooth unfolding. That is true, even when systems pass through bifurcations and catastrophes. In each case, there is a path of development that is notable for being smoothly structure-preserving in a way that keeps the global structure intact. In the terms I have defined in Book 1, it is *wholeness* which exhibits smooth unfolding.[7] That is, the structure I have defined as the wholeness, as it changes from state to state over time, follows a path where the centers which constitute the wholeness (and particularly the large ones) are changing as little as possible. The wholeness is essentially preserved at each step, and the new structure is introduced in such a way that it maintains and extends — but almost never violates — the existing structure. It is globally structure-preserving. That is why the unfolding seems smooth.

In the following pages I illustrate sequences for such processes in the following cases:

Formation of a spiral galaxy.
The formation of a frog embryo.
A breaking wave in the ocean.
Formation of a milk-drop splash.
Formation of vortices on the surface of Jupiter.
Evolution of different beaks in subspecies of Hawaiian finches.
Flight of a pigeon.
The sequence of the Belousov–Zhabotinski reaction.
Evolution of mollusks.
Formation of a plane surface on a growing crystal.
Development of algae.
Stages of development of a common mushroom.
Bacterial growth.

Collapse of a smooth cylinder under buckling.
Growth of quasi-crystals in alloys.
Formation of a planetary moon.
Generation of slime mold.
A glass plate shattering.

Other examples are scattered in the text which follows in this chapter and the next.

Sand waves forming in wind-blown sand.
Growth of a snow crystal.
Evolution of a river bed.
Development of an angiosperm seed.
Evolution of the feathers of archaeopteryx.
The quantum process which creates electron orbits within atoms.

In all these cases, when we look at the sequence of development, we see a sequence which is essentially *smooth* in character.[8] That means, within the sequence, *each state follows, without breaking structure, from the state before.* The structure of the state before (its wholeness) develops, evolves, changes — but is still visible in the next state. Even in those important cases where an entirely new structure is introduced — often the most important moments in the sequence — the new structure is still introduced in such a way as to maintain the essence, the underlying structure, of the previous state. This smoothness of evolution is visible in all the examples, essentially without exception. Even in those cases where there is a catastrophe — the mathematical term for the appearance of some new feature, not visible in the symmetries of the previous state — this catastrophe always begins as a feature *which is essentially consistent with the symmetries of the earlier state*, and which then develops, and continues to develop, as the new source of structure, thus still allowing a smooth and consistent evolution of structure.[9]

FORMATION OF A SPIRAL GALAXY - THE DRAMATIC SPIRALS OF M51

The genesis of the spiral form in a galaxy comes about because a disk of pre-galactic mate-

The spiral galaxy M51

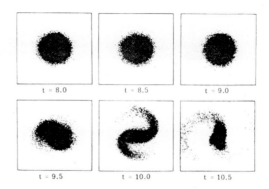

Computer simulation of the process of the emergence of the spiral in a galaxy. At each step, we see a smooth transition from the previous state, preserving most of the structure of the wholeness of the previous state.

rial, spinning as it does, includes some random motion. The random perturbations give rise to an oscillating pattern of gravitational waves of rarefaction and compression. As this wave system develops, it can go only to two or three large-scale forms. Much of the time, it goes to a two-armed spiral. The two-armed spiral is one of the simplest transforms of a slightly perturbed oscillating disk of material in which a gravitational wave appears.[10] The second illustration shows a computer simulation of the process. When you break the infinite symmetry group of the rotating disk, you are left with the simplest symmetry group consistent with rotational motion: a spiral with arms.

A breaking wave

A BREAKING WAVE IN THE OCEAN

Here we have a catastrophe creating radical new structure. When the wave breaks, the smooth, curved top of the unbroken wave slowly becomes a point, and this point then curls over when the wave breaks. Finally, the broken wave turns into many drops which form the splash.

Even here, when the curve turns into a cusp with a sharp point, only one new differentiation is introduced. The system of centers which existed in the volume of the water, on the air-water interface and next to the water in the air, are, for the most part, maintained. One small bit of new structure is added — the cusp — and this tiny bit of structure, gradually introduced and extended, becomes more and more extensive in its impact, and finally makes the wave break, and forms an entirely new system of configurations.

In each case, if we look carefully at Thom's diagram, and at my diagram to the right, we see that the system of centers which constitutes the wholeness in the ongoing wave is extended and maintained and developed, but never violated.[11]

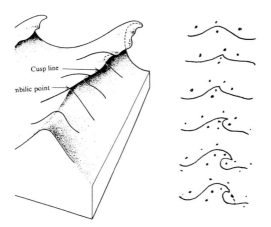

René Thom's diagram of a breaking wave, showing the smooth appearance of the catastrophe

Gradual change of centers as the wave breaks

THE FORMATION OF A FROG EMBRYO

The embryo starts as a ball of cells. The ball splits down the middle. An axis is introduced. The wholeness of each stage is consistent with

Stage number			Stage number			Stage number		
	Age-hours at 18°C			Age-hours at 18°C			Age-hours at 18°C	
1	0	Unfertilized	7	7.5	32-cell	13	50	Neural plate
2	1	Grey crescent	8	16	Mid-cleavage	14	62	Neural folds
3	3.5	Two-cell	9	21	Late cleavage	15	67	Rotation
4	4.5	Four-cell	10	26	Dorsal lip	16	72	Neural tube
5	5.7	Eight-cell	11	34	Mid-castrula	17	84	Tail bud
6	6.5	Sixteen-cell	12	42	Late gastrula			

*Seventeen stages in the development of
a frog's embryo*

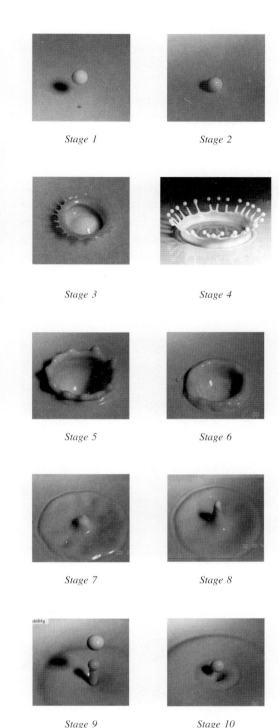

Stage 1   *Stage 2*

Stage 3   *Stage 4*

Stage 5   *Stage 6*

Stage 7   *Stage 8*

Stage 9   *Stage 10*

the wholeness of the previous stage. The centers which exist in the wholeness at each stage — both large centers dominating the big pattern, and small ones locally — are largely left intact by the next transformation. The next transformation introduces new structure, usually in the form of new asymmetrically placed *local* symmetries which induce new layers of structure — hence a new differentiation — but rarely or never disperse the underlying deep structure of the old, even when it changes things.[12]

EVOLUTION OF A SPLASHING DROP

Although this splashing drop sequence shows the appearance of a new structure (which is in mathematical terms catastrophic because new features appear in a non-continuous fashion from old features) what is important is that nevertheless, once again, the actual transitions are still smooth. In the photographs above, the change from one frame to the next is always gentle.[13]

FORMATION OF VORTICES ON THE SURFACE OF JUPITER

In the photograph, we see a complex system of vortices on the surface of Jupiter.

The diagrams show a much simplified but similar system. Below are shown four stages in a computer simulation of dynamical appearance of vortices from a smooth laminar flow in a simple system similar in general type to the vortices on Jupiter. If we look at the transition from stage to stage in the simulation, at each stage we see a comprehensible and relatively modest transition. Although the last stage is markedly different

Similar vortices on the surface of Jupiter

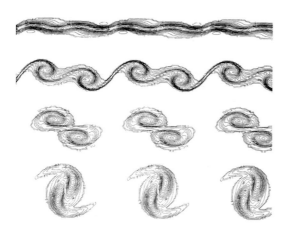

Computer simulations: step-wise evolution of vortices from laminar stream flow

from the first, the transition from each stage to the succeeding one is morphologically smooth. Stage 1 of the system is a double wavy line. Stage 2 maintains the wavy undulation, but introduces whorls and S-shapes which roughly preserve the undulating form. In Stage 3, the complex alternating S-shapes collapse to form separated double whorls, while losing the binding S-shapes. In stage 4, the pairs of whorls collapse further to coalesce in a single S, which nevertheless preserves the doublet form of the previous stage. At each step, the wholeness structure is preserved, though extended, each time changing in overall quality, but largely without losing the global structure present in the previous stage — even while new structure is being created.[14]

EVOLUTION OF DIFFERENT BEAKS IN SUBSPECIES OF HAWAIIAN FINCHES

Here we see an example from the evolution of species: a family of finches in their conjectured evolutionary sequence. In this instance, for the first time, we have a case where it is not the wholeness *itself* which is unfolding in the sequence shown, but rather the genome which gives birth to a sequence of different wholenesses. The wholeness in each finch is generated by the genes in the embryo, interacting with the biological environment as the embryo grows. This genetic structure is also a kind of wholeness, but a *latent* wholeness, contained within each bird in its genetic material. This latent wholeness, capable of generating the wholeness of the bird, itself also evolves and is transformed by transformations much like those that go from one wholeness to another. In evolutionary time, the system smoothly moves from the wholeness created by one genetic sequence to another wholeness, far separated in time. What is evolving smoothly, behind the scenes, is the wholeness latent in the genetic material of these different finches.[15]

In the diagram, we see displayed the evolution of the different subspecies. Starting at the

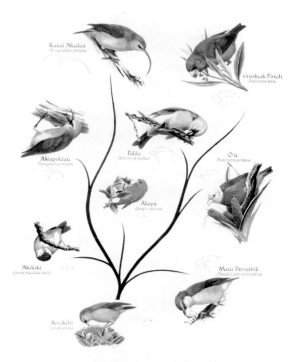

Evolutionary tree of Hawaiian finches

bottom of the picture and moving upward through the evolutionary tree, we see how, in the process of evolution, the transitions from species to species are once again smooth and structure-preserving. Even though the variation of different beaks is great, the transitions from one to the next are always "nice."[16]

FLIGHT OF A PIGEON

Here we see the same smoothness in steps that are only microseconds apart. Each stage —

Sequence of positions in the flight of a pigeon. Here again, the wholeness unfolds smoothly: each wing position evolves smoothly from the structure of the previous state.

and configuration — of the bird's flight follow smoothly from the previous one. In each state, we see the wholeness of the previous state, almost entirely preserved as a structure, with insertion of a minor modification on the whole. Although the motion passes through phases, utterly unlike each other, from step to step there are no abrupt transitions.[17]

THE SEQUENCE OF THE BELOUSOV-ZHABOTINSKI REACTION: CHEMICAL SCROLL WAVES

The Belousov-Zhabotinski reaction: waves in a chemical system

Consider these famous photographs of the chemical waves studied by Ilya Prigogine and others. Although the patterns formed in the dish of chemicals are startling, and although the last stages are entirely unlike the first stages, still, once again, if we examine each stage, we see a simple and natural evolution from pattern to pattern, without apparent discontinuity.

At each step the wholeness — the overall sense of the pattern in its global configuration — is preserved, and the changes occur within the respectful maintenance of global structure of pattern, form, and the underlying system of centers.[18]

EVOLUTION OF MOLLUSKS

Once again, the evolution of organic species: intermediate stages in the evolution of one mollusk subspecies to another. In this instance, the transitions are almost invisible, the path is so smooth.[19]

Stages in the evolution from one species of mollusk to another. See the comment under "Evolution Of Different Beaks In Subspecies Of Hawaiian Finches."

FORMATION OF A PLANE SURFACE ON A GROWING CRYSTAL

A very simple example. Since incoming molecules prefer to go to the stickiest part of a growing crystal — i.e., to the places where there is the greatest binding energy from molecules

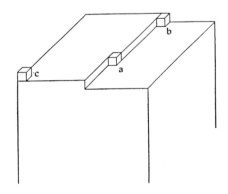

Growth of a plane face of a salt crystal. Of the three possible types of location, the one which has the most binding energy, and hence the most "stickiness" for an incoming molecule (marked "a" above), is the one which, when repeated, creates a plane face.

Growth of a crystal as a whole: stages of capping process in growth of a crystal of ammonium dihydrogen phosphate

already in place — this has the effect that the plane face will attract molecules in such a way as to continue the plane face. Irregular arrangements in which new molecules would sprout randomly, on the plane surface, are extremely unlikely to occur. The effect is that the plane surface perpetuates itself, and the wholeness is preserved. The crystal grows in a way that most of the time preserves the wholeness.[20]

GROWTH OF CRYSTAL AS A WHOLE: STAGES
OF CAPPING PROCESS IN GROWTH OF A CRYSTAL
OF AMMONIUM DIHYDROGEN PHOSPHATE

In the more elaborate case of a crystal such as this pyramidal crystal form, even when a non-pyramidal slice of the material is placed in a solution, the ragged edges grow so fast that they quickly move upward and downward at the proper angle for the crystal (caused by the chemical bonds). In this wholeness, *W*, the *edges* appear as the strongest centers and cause the most rapid growth; they then develop spontaneously in a way that continues and extends the structure.[21]

DEVELOPMENT OF ALGAE:
SUCCESSIVE STAGES OF DEVELOPMENT
OF A COLONY OF GOLDEN ALGAE

If we read from A to H, we see the gradual creation of stalks, until finally we have an entire sprouted structure. What happens at any given stage is always a natural evolution from the previous structure. For instance, when we go from D to E, it looks as if something entirely new has happened. But the wholeness of stage D already has a unique condition at the top end of the stalk. Thus, from the point of view of the wholeness, there is already a latent center there at the top of the stalk. The fact that at stage E this is

embodied by a system of sprouting buds is entirely consistent with the latent wholeness that was there before. The same is true in the transition between F and G.[22]

STAGES OF DEVELOPMENT OF
A COMMON MUSHROOM

AND

BACTERIAL GROWTH: DEVELOPMENT
IN THE MYCOBACTERIUM
CHONDROMYCES CROCATUS

Both these examples — the mushroom on this page and the bacterium on the next — show

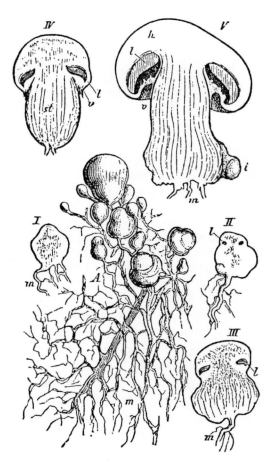

Development of a common mushroom

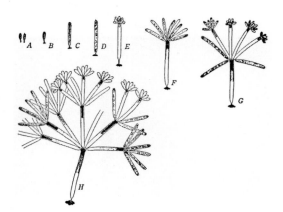

Buds sprouting in Golden algae, step by step, in such a fashion that the structure of the previous stage is always preserved

Growth of a bacterium

Buckling of a hollow cylinder when compressed

an organism budding, sprouting, and becoming many-limbed, always under a slow growth process while preserving structure.[23]

COLLAPSE OF A SMOOTH CYLINDER UNDER BUCKLING: BUCKLING INTO SYMMETRIC PATTERN OF DIMPLES

A thin cylinder, buckled by uniform pressure from above, shows a remarkable symmetric pattern of dimples. This phenomenon is intuitively unexpected. Present thinking suggests that, as buckling occurs, the infinite group of rotations characteristic of the smooth cylinder is reduced and replaced by a finite group of rotations, which is one of its subgroups. So, as it buckles, though it has to give up some structure, most of its structure (defined in this instance by the finite symmetry group) is preserved. See also the discussion in chapter 2, page 63.[24]

FORMATION OF A PLANETARY MOON

This picture shows the theory of moon formation that the French mathematician Jules-Henri Poincaré formulated in the late 19th century. Even though it is now fairly certain that Poincaré's pear-shaped blob theory does not give an accurate picture of the sequence that actually takes place, I still show it because the picture sequence shows the typical character of an unfolding sequence in beautiful and intuitive

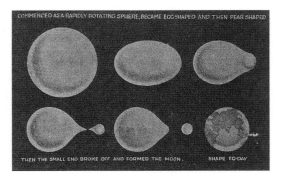

Poincaré's (incorrect) theory for the evolution of a planetary moon. I show it in spite of its inaccuracy because it was one of the earliest attempts to see the unfolding process in action.

terms. In the absence of a more accurate modern picture once again, in this theory, we see a smooth sequence of unfolding, in which each stage seems to presage the following stage. The evolution, though highly dramatic in its overall results, shows an almost imperceptible structure-preserving character, as it moves from stage to stage.[25]

GENERATION OF SLIME MOLD: FOUR STAGES OF AGGREGATION OF DICTYOSTELIUM

It is remarkable that even in the case of cell aggregation, as in the slime mold pictured here, the coalescence of the thousands of particles and their gradual formation into a coherent blob once again shows smoothness at every stage. Even here, we can see the wholeness preserved, as the form unfolds.

What happens mechanically, in this case, is that the chemical agent acrasin is diffused. The concentration gradient of the acrasin, sent out by the individual swimming cells, becomes a basis for orientation, and as a result the thousands of cells then slowly swim toward each other. Remarkably, the cells give the impression of swimming toward a center, even though this center is only manifested, mechanically, as a chemical gradient in the water. In fact, the concentration of acrasin is simply highest at the center of gravity of the individual swimming cells. This center of concentration, once formed, then becomes a real entity in the ensuing configuration because of the chemotaxis it induces. The swimming cells are mechanically influenced by this center of concentration, and the increasing aggregation of cells then intensifies the concentration further, yet further increasing the physical creation of the entity we see as a center in the mold.[26]

A GLASS PLATE SHATTERING

Even here, in a violent event, the process is completely smooth. Shattering glass seems sud-

Step 1: Bullet enters.

Step 2: Effect starts on far side of glass.

Step 3: Effect spreads out through glass in bowl-like shear zone.

Step 4: Effect widens: the shear cone in the glass is severed.

Four stages, only microseconds apart, showing how the explosive shattering of the glass when the bullet hits it, is a well-formed developmental process, in which each configuration leads, and gives way, smoothly to the next.

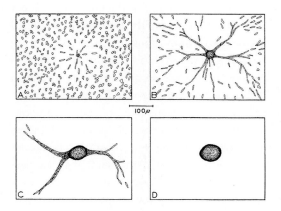

Generation of a slime mold body from individual cells by coordinated aggregation

den because, to us, it happens very quickly — in microseconds — and in our own time scale it appears disturbing, alarming, sudden.

But when we examine the actual sequence of events over time, and consider the stages of the evolution, one microsecond at a time, as seen below, we see a process in which yet again each new stage develops from the previous stage quite smoothly. The big, winged form, which develops as the smash propagates, itself originates with a tiny crack, visible in the second picture. If we look at the structure that exists in the second picture — the bullet, and the plane which it in-

duces tangent to its tip and parallel to the glass plane — create a configuration in which one can almost sense, or see in advance, the big, winged curve which is about to form. The coming curve is first latent in the structure, and then develops smoothly from the structure as the inevitable next geometric phase of unfolding.

The shattering of the glass itself depends on latent dislocations present in the material before the impact, which are enlarged after impact. Even this most violent and most catastrophic event arises smoothly from the wholeness that was there.[27]

5 / APPEARANCE OF THE FIFTEEN PROPERTIES

In all these natural examples, one thing stands out. The process of formation that occurs in nature — whether it happens in microseconds or over millions of years, whether it is large or small, whether it comes from the organic or the inorganic world — is in every case *smoothly structure-preserving*. Each of the sequences in the last pages shows a sequence where successive stages are so alike as to be hardly distinguishable. Yet what is accomplished overall, from the beginning to the end of each sequence, is enormous. New form comes into being. Morphogenesis occurs. New form that is, in almost every case, unpredictable from the initial state appears smoothly via a sequence of tiny continuous changes.

The sequences are not merely smooth. We have, in every case, a sequence in which new structure grows organically, holistically, from the structure which is there already. One whole gives rise to another.

It is this smooth and elegant "becoming" or unfolding of the whole which is the characteristic of nature. The continuity and smoothness of unfolding wholeness may seem obvious. Indeed, in a certain sense, it *is* obvious. Yet, as a creative process, it is sharply at odds with the human

process of creation we have come to expect in contemporary art and architecture.

And throughout these examples, the fifteen properties appear again and again. We see LEVELS OF SCALE appear in mushrooms, in planetary systems, in vortices, in shattered glass. We see STRONG CENTERS almost everywhere, in the formation of galaxies, in the Darwinian evolution of a bird's beak, in the growth of a colony of algae. We have seen BOUNDARIES in the sun's corona, in the boundary of the living cell, in the banks of the Rio Negro River as it pours out into the Amazon. We see ALTERNATING REPETITION in vortices and in the buckling cylinder and in the evolution of the feathered and winged *Archaeopteryx* from dinosaurs (page 41). We see POSITIVE SPACE in the formation of the frog embryo and in the wing positions of the flying pigeon and in the breaking wave. We see GOOD SHAPE appearing in the form of leaves and mushrooms, in the Chladni figures on a vibrating plate (shown in Book 1), in the spirals of the Belousov-Zhabotinski reaction, in the bends of a meandering river (page 36). We see LOCAL SYMMETRIES in crystal growth, in flowers, in the formation of slime mold. We see GRADIENTS emerging in stream flow of a river, in the distribution of twigs and branches on a tree (page 39). We see ECHOES and their associated angles showing up in crystals, metals, geological formations, and sand ripples (page 35). ROUGHNESS appears throughout, as a consequence of the fine adaptation present in all unfolding, since each shape can be minutely adjusted, without needing rigid geometry. CONTRAST appears as the result of differentiation in the formation of a galaxy, as in the dimples of a buckled cylinder. DEEP INTERLOCK AND AMBIGUITY appears in the unfolding of a mushroom,

and in the vortices of turbulent flow. We see SIMPLICITY AND INNER CALM in the surface of a lake as in the line of dewdrops on a spider web (page 64) and in the buckling cylinder. We see THE VOID make its appearance in the gaps between the clouds and in the eye of a hurricane. We see NOT-SEPARATENESS in river-bed ecology, in the vegetation of a forest, and in the imbrication of the human lung. In all these processes, living structure emerges slowly, steadily.

Why this happens still needs to be explained.

6 / THE FIFTEEN PROPERTIES EMERGE DIRECTLY FROM THE UNFOLDING OF THE WHOLE

Let us consider two examples, both from embryology, in rather more detail. I want to show that the unfolding of these embryos (which I characterize as wholeness-preserving) follows a particular path, and that during the path the form evolves in a way that gradually increases the extent to which the fifteen properties are present, and developed.

If you look at the mouse foot first, you see that it starts, essentially, as a blob. This is literally true, of course. It is an undifferentiated cell mass with relatively few features of its morphology, yet visible. In a period of about four days, the forelimb and foot are formed, and as we see it forming, we see that it develops as a whole, and as an articulated whole, which displays the fifteen properties, more and more strongly. CENTERS become visible, both in the limbs, the fingers, and the joints. We see ALTERNATING REPETITION in the space between the fingers; we see BOUNDARIES at the ends of the different bone segments (what will later turn into muscle and ligament); GOOD SHAPE is visible in the shape of the hand as a whole, and the shapes of individual bone segments become swollen and beautiful. LOCAL SYMMETRIES are plainly present in the formation of the whole, in the paired forelimb bones; ECHOES

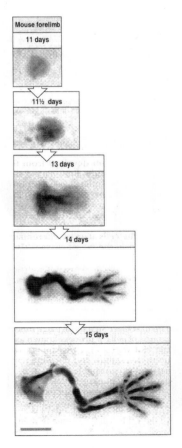

Development of mouse foot

is strongly visible in the similarities of all the different bones, and the fact that the angle-character of all the bones are strongly alike; GRADIENTS are visible in the gradient from small finger to large, and in the distribution of finger joints from base to tip; LEVELS OF SCALE are beautifully present, and within two days, develop in the size of bones, the hierarchy of sizes, and the hierarchy of visible components; even THE VOID, oddly, makes its appearance in the gap between the two forelimb bones.

How should we view all this activity, and how should we interpret it? Biologists have, of course, accumulated a great deal of information about the way that chemical gradients, in the cells, create patterns by position.[28] But what remains missing from their analysis is the way in which this thing moves forward *as a whole*, retains its coherence *as a whole* from start to finish, and how the coordination of the different parts, and the beauty of the whole thing, is maintained.

The same occurs in the formation of the seed of a flowering plant (Shepherd's Purse or *Capsella bursa-pastoris*). The sequence shown gives the development of one seed, after the

flower itself matures. We see the appearance of strongly differentiated lumps (top and bottom), forming defined and distinct CENTERS; we see formation of DEEP INTERLOCK, in the indentation, of LOCAL SYMMETRIES in the appearance of the two cotyledons; the final beautiful and compact GOOD SHAPE of the whole is obvious. ROUGHNESS pervades, and is of the essence in the cell packing, to permit good shape to be formed; POSITIVE SPACE appears in the cell shapes, in the invagination, and in the whole. Once again, literal minded examination of what the individual cells do, as they split and migrate, does not account for the beauty of the unfolding process, nor for the beauty of the result.[29]

Yet the beauty and coherence of the result is the most remarkable feature of the process.

The fifteen properties do emerge from an unfolding, which protects and enhances the whole, and in the differentiations which occur, as the whole develops, it is always the fifteen properties, one or another of them, which guide the differentiations. In effect, it is as if the kinds of differentiation which can occur, are enumerated, and restricted to the possibilities laid down

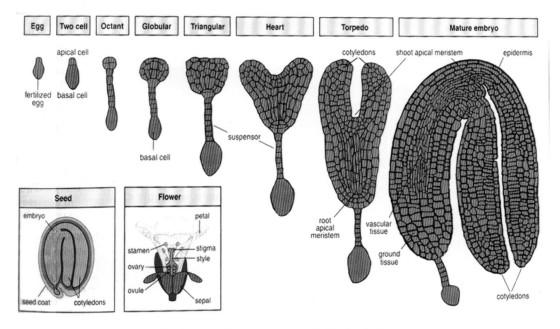

Development of an angiosperm seed: Shepherd's Purse

by the fifteen properties. It is these fifteen properties which do all the work, of making the whole, and of making the whole beautiful. The chemistry and cell migrations are the mechanisms which do the work, but they are simply not the principal thing which is going on.

7 / PREVIOUSLY OFFERED EXPLANATIONS OF EMERGENCE FROM THE WHOLE

Throughout centuries of study of nature, many, many cases of emergence of form from the whole have been observed and studied. Many have been matter-of-fact. Rarely, until now, has it been seen as necessary to propose new mechanisms of emergence. Generally speaking, the emergence of form in the world has been seen and understood as a relatively straightforward mechanical emergence of the product of different causal laws.

The possibility that a new principle, altogether, might need to be invoked, and above all, that the unfolding of the whole might have to be seen, in its own right, as a fundamental principle of nature — these are relatively new ideas. And certainly we shall not wish to propose or invoke an entirely new principle, if this is not absolutely needed — if it is not *required* — by the failure of existing explanations.

Let us therefore examine some existing explanations, as we have them today:

MECHANICAL ORIGINS OF LIVING CENTERS

The simplest kind of explanation is just mechanical and "accidental." For example, here is a classic mechanical explanation for one particular system of centers: the appearance of ALTERNATING REPETITION in the wave-like ripples of wind-blown desert sand. Suppose we have a desert or a dry beach surface with millions of grains of sand about equal in size and weight. Any grain that is slightly irregular sticks up; as the wind blows over the sand, it will pick up any grain that sticks up, and will carry it a certain distance, where it drops it, once again "sticking up." Since the grains are similar in size and weight, the wind tends to carry them all the

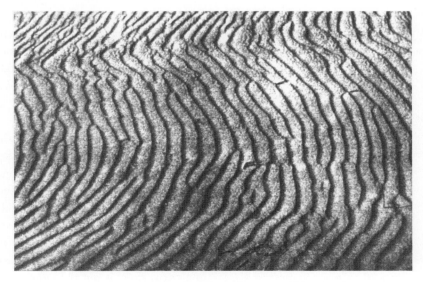

Alternating repetition formed as ridges in wind-blown sand

same distance. Wherever an irregularity occurs, it tends to be repeated by this "wavelength" downwind. Gradually any ridge-like pattern is duplicated, one wavelength downwind, by a second ridge. This second ridge will then be duplicated by a further ridge, another full "wavelength" downwind. After the wind has been blowing for some time, the sand has an overall pattern of wave-like ridges which lie at right angles to the direction of the wind. They are not waves at all; the apparent wavelength is simply the distance that the wind carries an average grain of sand.[30] This purely mechanical explanation shows how, in this particular case, ALTERNATING REPETITION — repeating ridges alternating with valleys — is produced. The explanation for its appearance is entirely mechanical. The local mechanics of the situation create a pattern in the whole.

In similar fashion, we have looked at the case of the growing salt crystal, where LOCAL SYMMETRIES are created in the faces of the crystal. As we have already seen, crystals grow as they do because new atoms attach themselves to the array of atoms in the corners with most binding energy. As a result, plane faces emerge, even though there is no guiding hand making the faces of the crystal plane. The larger whole, and the local symmetries which form the plane surface, arise from the action of the local mechanics.[31]

STRONG CENTERS and GOOD SHAPE appear in loops of a meandering river, because of the

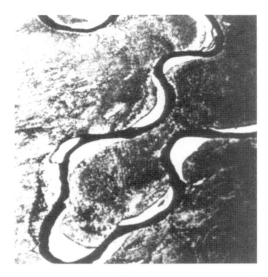

Strong centers and good shape formed by mechanical process: meandering loops are formed by centrifugal processes in the evolution of a river

mechanical action of stream flow. When a minor irregularity occurs — the start of a bend — centrifugal force throws the water in the top layer outward, thus eroding the outer bank of the curve still further and then, balanced by downstream deposition of silt, gradually creating a full concave curve which we see as a loop or a meander in the river.[32]

In these mechanical cases, the whole — the marvelous pattern of the whole — emerges from the interaction of small events and local circumstances. The whole itself appears almost as if by accident. Certainly, in these cases, there does not appear to be a need for any explanation in which the whole itself takes a hand and guides events.

The classical picture of nature was of a system formed and guided entirely by such local mechanical laws.

But these local explanations are far too specific to answer our questions. Although each can explain a particular phenomenon, they are not generalizable, and they give no general insight into the general question: why do ALTERNATING REPETITION, or LOCAL SYMMETRIES, or GOOD SHAPE appear repeatedly *in general?* The process which forms alternating repetition in a cirrus cloud is not the same as the process

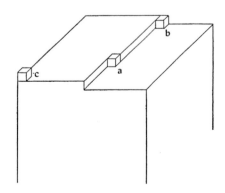

The adherence of the individual molecules continues and enhances the plane face of the crystal.

which causes grains of sand to form ridges in the sand. The process which forms good shape in a Gingko leaf (page 70) is not similar to the process which forms the beautiful full-bellied loops in a meandering river. Nor do these mechanical explanations give much insight into the still more basic question: why, most generally of all, is there an overall tendency in nature for living structure to appear?

THE PRINCIPLE OF LEAST ACTION

The fact that individual mechanical explanations are too limited, and that the wealth of morphogenesis which occurs in the world needs a unifying explanation within which all morphogenesis may be seen as having a common origin, has been the subject of much speculation. Since the efforts of Gottfried Wilhelm Leibniz in the 17th century, there have been many attempts to formulate a more general basis for understanding morphogenesis. Nearly all have sought, in one fashion or another, to explain how the wholeness of the world in the large is responsible for the emergence of form in its holistic aspects. Among the most significant is the principle of least action, first formulated by the French

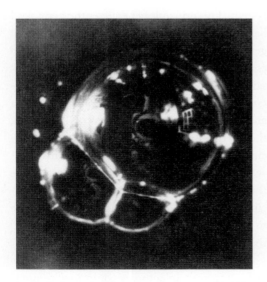

A spherical soap bubble, or complex system of bubbles, takes that shape which has the configuration of least potential energy.

mathematician Maupertuis about 1744, restated in the 19th century as Hamilton's principle, and still in use today as a vital component of quantum field theory.[33] The principle says that the evolution of any dynamic system will always follow the path of least work.

Let us see what THE PRINCIPLE OF LEAST ACTION is trying to do.

Consider a soap bubble. A single bubble floating in air is roughly spherical. What is the process that makes it spherical? We can understand the local surface tension as a system of forces. But it is hard to understand the effect of all these forces on the bubble as a whole, by studying these individual local forces acting locally. It becomes easier when we recognize that, for a given volume of air, the bubble takes that shape which minimizes the surface area. The resulting form happens to be an example of GOOD SHAPE. But why does it happen? When the surface area is minimized, the potential energy is minimized. Might we say that morphogenesis occurs because of a general tendency for systems to move towards a state with minimum potential energy? Many systems do evolve in the direction which minimizes their potential energy. The deeper problem is that we are then faced with the question, Why should the potential energy be minimized?

Or consider two wires of equal resistance that are wired in parallel to a battery. The electric current then distributes itself equally. This is so familiar that it seems obvious. It also happens to be a case of LOCAL SYMMETRY. Yet what physical principle is causing the symmetry? We can explain it by using Ohm's law ($I=V/R$, implying that the two currents must be equal if the two resistances are equal). But *why* is it true? To get a deeper explanation of why the currents in the two wires are equal, we can make a further assumption about systems: we can explain the configuration of the larger structure, the whole, by assuming that the flow of electricity distributes itself in such a way as to minimize the rate of heat production. If translated into electrical terms, this more general principle becomes

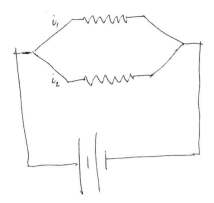

If the wires have equal resistance, the current balances itself equally between the two parallel wires.

equivalent to Ohm's law, and gets the right answer; it predicts that the currents will be equal. But why should *this* formulation get the right answer? Why *should* the rate of heat production be minimized *in general systems*? What is it about nature that makes it act to minimize the rate of heat production?

The same question arises in many forms. If I tell you that soap film in a bubble arranges itself in such a way that the potential energy of the bubble's surface is minimized, this explanation helps because it is a profound principle which helps us predict the bubbles in complex configurations. Since it predicts correctly, we know that it is true. But that does not help us understand the *existence* of the principle. *Why* should the potential energy be minimized?

A river meanders with a certain characteristic kind of bend, a wide curve, and the curves are spaced at about ten times the width of the river. These meanders occur in such a way as to minimize the energy consumption at the bends. So in this case, the principle of minimum-energy consumption is responsible for STRONG CENTERS in the bends of the meander, for GRADIENTS, GOOD SHAPE, and POSITIVE SPACE.[34] The branches of a tree branch, roughly, at that angle which makes the consumption of energy, in the sap-flow, a minimum. In this case, LEVELS OF SCALE are again produced by another version of the minimum-energy principle.[35] But *why* does a

river move in just that way which consumes least energy? *Why* does a tree branch in such a way as to make the work which the sap does a minimum. Why is that? What kind of principle is this?[36]

We can work out the fact that trees branch in such a fashion so that the flow of sap does the least work. The bee's honeycomb is arranged in such a way that the angle of joining is the most efficient. We can show that a normal leaf is shaped in such a way as to produce the shape in which the weight is supported by the least weight of material.[37] The river winds in such a fashion as to have the least expenditure of flow energy and least heat loss from friction. Light travels through a composite medium in such a way as to minimize the time taken by the ray.

Why, and why, and why? Hardly one of these principles has a complete and satisfying *mechanical* explanation. It is always the global effect of some larger principle, calling for least energy, or least work, coupled with the detailed mechanics, which finally provides the explanation.

The principle of least action was formulated essentially to summarize these many principles and others like them. The principle says that the "action," *S*, the rate of expenditure of energy twice integrated over time, is minimized in any system. This principle generalizes the examples I have given, and many others. It is one of the most general principles of this kind ever discovered and essentially underlies all the others. Max Planck said of it, "Present-day physics is completely governed by a system of differential equations . . . this entire rich system of differential equations, though they differ in detail since they refer to mechanical, electrical, magnetic and thermal processes, is now completely contained in a single theorem, the principle of least action."[38] The principle is now viewed by physicists as indispensable to the underpinning of modern quantum field theory.[39]

But like the simpler minimum-energy principles, this principle, too, is not in *itself* comprehensible enough, nor intuitively general or convincing enough, to explain the complex

Elm tree branches with constant branching angle

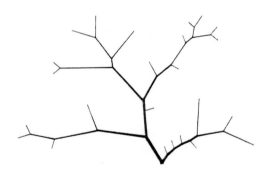

Diagram of constant branching angle

appearance of the fifteen properties in living structures. There are so many *different* explanations for these kinds of phenomena. For example, Peter Stevens was able to provide three equally convincing explanations for the meander pattern of an evolving river. All three give correct numerical predictions for the curvature and frequency of loops. Yet they are quite different from one another. One is based on least-energy consumption: essentially least action. One is based on the action of centrifugal force. One is based on the fact that the highest probability path for a fixed-length random walk between two points will

take the form of a meander.[40] The three are not numerically equivalent.

So the uneasy sense exists that there is more here than meets the eye. Various holistic explanations have been formulated. No single one of these holistic explanations is clearly "the" origin of the other explanations. Under the surface, something still more general must be going on. Some still more fundamental unifying explanation is needed, something which truly underlies all phenomena.

NON-LINEAR DYNAMICS

There is a new class of explanations which some believe may give us such a general kind of explanation. In the case of current flow, the global behavior of current in distributing itself in an electrical system can be simulated by a model in which individual electrons choose the path which is least constricted. The global behavior then comes about from interactions of individual local behaviors. Since the arrival of high-speed computers, it has become possible to simulate the behavior of many complex systems

Acetabularia: the algae studied by Brian Goodwin

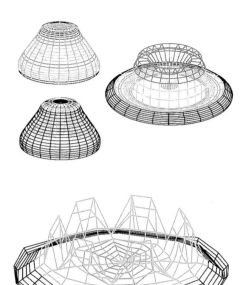

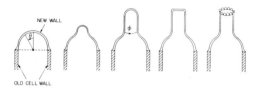

Sequence of changes needed to form the characteristic whorl at the tip of Acetabularia: sectional view

Computer simulations of the order-seeking process which generates the cap, the indented cap, and then the whorl

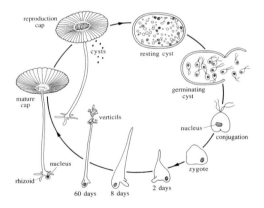

Life cycle of Acetabularia

by making up simple rules which approximate the behavior of component elements, and then simulating the interaction of these rules.

With the help of this approach, we have been able to create (and thus explain) many large-scale configurations similar to those we see in nature. More generally, in recent years the new science of complexity theory, and the study of non-linear systems modeled by computer, have provided an entirely new class of explana-tions for the forms we see in nature. Prigogine, Thom, Mandelbrot, Feigenbaum, Kauffman, Goodwin, and hundreds of others have demon-strated that highly complex, ordered phenomena can arise as a result of relatively simple interac-tions among variables linked by non-linear equations.[41] These non-linear systems, which can usually not be solved by arithmetic tech-niques, have become accessible to study largely through the use of computers which simulate, in effect, the path of the evolving system over time.

Some of these techniques have produced spectacular results. Realistic-seeming sno-wflakes, turbulence in liquid systems, formation of clouds, weather prediction, simulations of the formation of mountain ranges, the breaking of waves, and embryonic morphogenesis have all become accessible to study. In all these cases, the technique involves interaction of a few variables, iterated in the computer in such a way as to produce results similar to the natural systems being studied.

The literature has grown profusely. There are by now thousands upon thousands of pages of such simulations, many of them seeming to provide accurate approximations of the phenomena they simulate.

Have we, then, finally understood how nature works? And, most important for our discussion here, have we understood the origin of the fifteen properties, and the appearance of living structure throughout nature?

Central to the studies in complexity theory, is the discovery that these systems converge to attractors (small regions in the state-space of the system), and that because of the mathematical behavior of the state-space, order will arise in these systems spontaneously, under suitable conditions. This discovery has recently held out the promise that the evolution of biological organisms, and the problems of development and growth in organisms, may be orderly in large part because of the mathematical properties of the state-space for these systems (according to Kauffman, Goodwin, et al.).

However, even with these very powerful techniques, what has so far been explained is still a little thin from a practical point of view. At least for the present, the specific appearance of the fifteen properties, and the emergence of living centers in the world, are hardly more clear now than before. Although certain specific structures appear and can be explained as a result of these dynamical systems (see, for instance, the

results of Brian Goodwin's classic work, shown opposite), just as simpler mechanical schemes can explain simpler cases, the *general* features of the living systems which I have described in Book 1, and above all the features which give them life as I have defined it, so far remain largely unexplained.

So, even with these techniques, the appearance of living structure in the world has so far only just been touched. While these techniques may one day explain a great deal, the one specific thing we need to understand in order to make better buildings — that is, the appearance of the fifteen properties — has barely even been opened as a topic.

STILL OTHER KINDS OF STRUCTURE CREATION, ALSO NOT EASILY EXPLAINABLE

There are still other types of structure creation — also showing the appearance of the fifteen properties — which seem unlikely to be explained either by the least-action principle or by spontaneous order creation from non-linear systems.

Biological evolution is perhaps the most obvious. The selection mechanism postulated by Darwinian theory always had difficulty explaining features of the evolutionary sequence, when these features can only be arrived at along a path which involves steps that are not themselves advantageous. For example, *Archaeopteryx* (the first bird) had feathers and used its feathered wings to fly. This is clearly an evolutionary advantage. But how would a partly developed wing, with little tufts — presumably the precursors of feathers — get any selective advantage? This is harder to understand. Although Stephen Jay Gould and Richard Dawkins have made good arguments for step-wise advantages being enough to move the evolving genotype towards complex functional order, these arguments are not yet entirely convincing.[42]

Similar questions can be asked about the famous bombardier beetle (which injects its prey with poison).[43] What form did the poison-

Artist's reconstruction of Archaeopteryx — a dinosaur-like creature found in Jurassic limestone together with fossilized feathers, and believed to be the first feathered bird

injecting mechanism have when it was half-way developed? How was it advantageous in an incomplete form? Or, if not, how did evolution select toward the half-formed injecting mechanism as it evidently must have done (to get to the fully developed one)? Rational discussion of this issue has been complicated in recent years by the creationist community who believe that organisms were formed by God's design and believe that the bombardier beetle somehow supports their case. In response to the irrational character of the creationist argument, many scientists have been spending their energy trying to insist, "no it is not God's design, Mr. Creationist, it is by a series of step-wise changes, gradually evolving," instead of answering the difficult question about how the very sophisticated machinery was actually arrived at, step by step.[44] Of course (for me anyway) the question is not "Was it by God's design, or was it step-by-step?" No doubt it was step-by-step. But how does step-by-step *actually* accomplish its results when the result requires sophisticated and complex global geometry to work.

Consider this case more carefully. The beetle defends itself by squirting hot poison. The mechanism which does it is pretty darn complicated. When you ask how it evolved, can one honestly say that it came about *merely* as a result of a series of random mutations causing steps, each of which was advantageous, by itself, at the time it happened? Along the way you have various half-formed squirt guns. Does a half-formed squirt gun work at all, or is there a pattern-like tendency which makes transformations toward coherent patterns (based on the fifteen properties) which then tend to produce coherent mechanisms for geometric reasons — *and the selective pressure then finds a use for these beautiful and coherent mechanisms to gain advantages.*

Is it not possible that the emergence of large-scale pattern — global order — comes about *merely* from many small Darwinian step-by-step changes, but modified and improved by some kind of directional twist in the dynamics of the evolving system which makes it go towards global patterns of a certain sort, and that it is this pattern-seeking or pattern-creating tendency which must be taken into account, *together* with selective advantage of small steps, if one really wants a satisfactory explanation of the evolutionary sequences in detail?

According to this view, the evolving system of the genetic material ITSELF *causes evolution to follow certain pathways, not only because of selective pressure from outside, but also by virtue of its own internal dynamical ordering tendencies. The results of evolution are then to be understood mainly formed not by Darwinian selective pressure acting from outside, but by pressures created by the geometry and dynamics of the evolving genetic system itself.* One powerful outline of such a theory has been published by Stuart Kauffman, who believes it may be caused by system effects of the coupling between an evolving genotype and its fitness landscape.[45] Another version of such a view was was put forward about 1960, by Lancelot Whyte, who thought it might be an internal interaction among the molecules of the evolving chromosome.[46]

If true — and such theories seem to hold promise for explaining many problems that have been glossed over by neo-Darwinian evolutionists — it means that there is essentially something in the *geometry* of living systems which contributes order by itself: that the biological material evolves, and advances, on the basis of some tendency to order embedded in the very action of the process, and interacting with the Darwinian selection.

Although there is some growing acceptance of this view, the specific proposals made by Kauffman do not yet explain in detail how this purely geometrical evolution works, nor do they give sufficient detail to allow us to explain anything particular. Explanations have yet to be given. So the tendency for evolution to create geometrically ordered biological structures remains (so far) largely unexplained by detailed theory.

Other examples of morphogenesis also pose puzzling questions. For instance: a growing bone

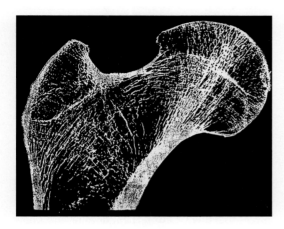

The end of a bone

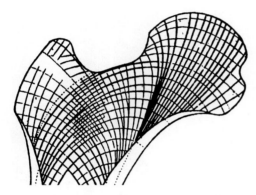

Lines of tension and compression in the bone are perfectly orthogonal: thus making the bone almost perfectly efficient.This is accomplished because the bone always adds material where the strain is greatest.

physics. For example, the shapes of snow crystals, with their endless variety of hexagonal symmetry, are even today not yet fully explained (page 44). Each snow crystal grows as it falls through freezing moist air, and each crystal is unique in its configuration. But the puzzling thing is: why are the six arms of one crystal so nearly alike? Each crystal has overall hexagonal symmetry. The general symmetry and the 60-degree angle it is based on are explained by the angle of the hydrogen and oxygen atoms in a water molecule, and by the accretive process which builds the crystal from these molecules. But why is the detailed structure on any one of the six arms of a given crystal so *exactly* like the structure on

adds material at that point where the stress is greatest — so that the resulting shape of the bone, which emerges from the growth, tends to equalize the stress in every part of the bone.[47] This requires a mechanical process in which the growth tissue simply gets added on at the point where stress or strain energy is greatest. The idea is simple. Even the mechanism may be clear once molecular biologists have isolated the particular mechanism responsible for translating strain energy to growth. But *how* is it happening? The idea of selective advantage acting over generations seems absurdly remote from the simplicity and directness of the growth process itself.

And puzzles of order formation remain even in simple domains of elementary chemistry and

Different naturally occurring snowflakes. Note the second-order symmetries which make each arm similar to the other arms in great detail, with no obvious mechanical explanation of how this happens.

the other five arms? Starting from the center of the snowflake, molecules are added, one at a time, to form the crystal. How is it that what is happening at the end of one arm is duplicated almost exactly by what is happening at the end of five other arms, hundreds of atoms away, even though the pattern is different for each different crystal? Diffusion-aggregation explanations have managed to simulate a rough overall symmetry of this kind when the crystal growth is com-

Diffusion-Aggregation simulation of a snowflake made by H. Eugene Stanley. Though broadly accurate as a loose generalized picture of a snowflake, the deep structure of the local symmetries inside the arms that we observe in nature, and the similarities from arm to arm, are not even remotely as pronounced — indeed are barely visible at all, in the simulation.

pressed, so that the spatial constraints help to form something with these local symmetries.[48] The crystal shapes generated by these diffusion-aggregation models are something *like* naturally occurring snow crystals (see illustration above). But the phenomenon occurs, also, in an open crystal where atoms are further apart, like these illustrated. The nearly identical detail on the six arms is not explained by any present diffusion-aggregation model that I know of. And saying that the same formations arise because of the same conditions of temperature and pressure does not explain the really remarkable symmetries, subsymmetries, and sub-subsymmetries which occur in the patterns forming on the six arms and sub-arms of these crystals.

A still more powerful example of unexplained form creation has been put forward by Roger Penrose. His famous quasi-symmetric til-

ing pattern of stars and pentagons has been found in naturally occurring crystalline alloys discovered by Dan Schechtman and his colleagues; and has now been extended to a wider class of crystals known as quasicrystals.[49] Penrose has stated that the order seen in these quasicrystals requires a non-local ingredient in their assembly. In his words: "In assembling the pattern, it is necessary from time to time, to examine the state of the pattern many atoms away, if one is to be sure of not making a serious error when putting the pieces together."[50] How, then, does nature know how to do it? The molecular assembly must ap-

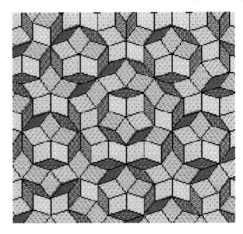

Quasicrystal tiling discovered by Roger Penrose, and occurring naturally in certain metallic crystals

parently be guided by a process which acts on the basis of the larger-scale order. Recently published suggestions about the practical mechanism by which these long-range forms of order are created in the case of the metal alloys, do indeed propose non-local action — via such things as electronic resonances which act in the large, and overlapping clusters of atoms which are capable of being coordinated by larger scale geometry. [51]

In each of these puzzling cases, it appears that some inherently geometric principle of form-creation is at work, encouraging a coherent large-scale order to emerge. We do not yet know what it is. All we know for sure about it is that in each of these examples new geometric form — with an increase of living structure and large-scale order — springs, in steps, from an older form.

8 / A PRINCIPLE OF UNFOLDING WHOLENESS

I propose an analysis that is, in principle, capable of answering these unanswered questions about how living structure emerges.

In the cases we have looked at, we see that again and again, in nature, living structure seems to "emerge." Along with the operation of the local laws, something is going on, rarely explained by local laws alone, which makes living structure, coherent centers, and the fifteen properties appear in the large. Why does this happen?

I suggested in Book 1 that these fifteen properties are the glue from which wholeness is constructed. Asking how they come about in the world is, in another form, therefore the same as asking why wholeness itself comes about in the world. And this is no less than asking how living structure comes about. The wholeness, when it is more intense, is created from the wholeness or life of individual centers. Why do centers arise at all? Why do centers become more intense or more alive? What is it that makes wholeness altogether become more intense, more alive with time?

Mixed in with this question, there is an important minor puzzle. Living structure, and the fifteen properties, clearly do not appear in the world *all* the time. Even though nature manifests these properties frequently, we know that whatever law of nature is making them appear is a law that doesn't always apply. Why do I say that? Because in some cases of human artifacts we have seen very clearly that they do not have the fifteen properties — so whatever law it is that creates these properties in nature, must be breaking down at least in some of those human-inspired cases. We know that buildings sometimes *do* have the properties, and sometimes do *not* have them. Traditional society often seems to have created them, contemporary society seems to have created them less often. So, if there is a law of nature which is creating these fifteen properties, this law is a temperamental law, which only works *sometimes*.

Be clear what this means. The law of gravity is a law of nature. It is not temperamental. It applies everywhere, all the time. It applies in traditional society, and it applies in modern society. But whatever law is making living structure appear is different. Evidently, it sometimes breaks down and fails to operate. That is what makes it so extremely hard to understand how it can be acting *in nature*. When I say I want to understand some general law which is responsible for making the fifteen properties appear in nature, whatever this law is, it must also explain why it is temperamental, why it breaks down sometimes at some scales, and why it breaks down specifically at the macroscopic scale in the building production of modern society.

Even the principle of least action, highly general and holistic in nature though it is, does not explain why the fifteen properties keep on occurring in the world.

What then is the explanation for the appearance of centers and of the fifteen properties in nature? I believe the wholeness which I have introduced in Book 1 sheds a great deal of light on the puzzle, and can give us a consistent way of explaining what is going on.

Look again at the variety of cases I have given as examples. Behind the scenes in *all* of them, there is what *appears to be* a consistent thrust toward order. In the terms which I have explained earlier in this book, there is, in all of them, a process in which the fifteen properties are appearing more and more strongly. Through this process, then, centers are getting created and strengthened.

Is it possible to think about all these cases in a way which is fundamentally the same? I believe it is. Underlying all these cases there is a geometrical principle, reminiscent of the principle of least action, but more general. This principle may be formulated as follows: *the evolution of any natural system is governed by transfor-*

mations of the mathematical wholeness and by a tendency, inherent in these transformations, for the whole to unfold in a particular direction.

In more detail, I postulate that every natural system has a disposition, a tendency caused by the most simple way forward for the system to move in the direction which preserves wholeness. I do not mean that it preserves wholeness in some pious emotional sense, nor that it "wishes" to preserve wholeness. *I simply mean that wholeness, which I have defined as a structure of symmetries and centers (Book 1, chapter 3 and appendix 1), will always have a natural dynamic of such a nature that as many as possible of these symmetries (and especially some of the larger ones) are preserved as the system moves forward in time. As the system evolves, it destroys these symmetries and larger centers* AS LITTLE AS POSSIBLE. It *maintains* as much of the structure of symmetries and centers as possible, and *destroys* as *little* of the structure of symmetries and centers as can be managed while yet moving forward.

This idea is consistent with ideas of symmetry-breaking that have recently made their appearance in modern physics, but it is more comprehensive and, as an idea, more extended.[52] As noted, it is, in character, somewhat like the principle of least action, except that it is purely geometrical in character, not arithmetical and not energy-based. It explains the mechanical cases because its effect on systems is almost the same as the law of least action. It is capable of explaining the cases covered by non-linear dynamics, because it introduces something like a geometric attractor into the dynamical systems. And it also explains the enigmatic point about the negative effect of human intervention and the unfortunate human ability to create *non*-living structure. While nature may well have a dynamical tendency to preserve wholeness, it is possible for human beings to violate this tendency, simply by acting in a way which is disrespectful of the wholeness (either on purpose to gain something, or by mistake simply because they fail to see the wholeness accurately).

Further, the nature of the wholeness, coupled with this principle, explains how new structure — the creative and most interesting aspect of nature's morphogenesis — comes about. As we saw in Book 1, the centers which occur in a given wholeness, especially the larger ones, appear at first in a diaphanous, weak, and latent form. If the dynamical system acts to preserve and extend these centers, which appear first as weak, nearly invisible structures in a cloudy chaos, the intensifying process will then effectively create entirely new structures, merely by strengthening these centers. As they become strong, as latent centers get strengthened, entirely new and hitherto unseen structures emerge.[53] And, in cases of death and decay, order appears there by means of a similar process that sweeps structure away, while yet preserving many essential symmetries.

Thus the principle of unfolding wholeness has great promise as a way of explaining form creation. It introduces little that is new, is consistent with existing physical theory on almost all points, and yet creates an entirely fresh perspective which can explain the emergence of living structure, without our having to resort to a teleological "urge for life."

That is what I propose. I do not know whether the principle of unfolding wholeness is, like the principle of least action, simply a concise way of gathering together and understanding a host of individual physical results caused by known laws and processes — or whether it is a *new* autonomous principle, more fundamental than the others, and acting with them, causally, to produce results. It is probably wisest for the time being to keep an open mind on this question, and assume that it is indeed merely a way of describing known results. But there remains the possibility that if new predictions about physical processes were to follow from this principle, that one may indeed then consider it as a deeper and more significant way of looking at nature. In either case, this principle describes an important aspect of the behavior of all complex systems.

9 / EMERGENCE OF LIVING STRUCTURE

Because a system is conservative — because it tends to preserve and extend the existing symmetries and centers — it also tends to reinforce the *larger* centers which exist, and to make them stronger. This we shall see in more detail in chapters 7–16. We may thus give a stronger formulation of the principle as follows: *at each moment in the emergence of a system, the system tends ("prefers") to go in that direction which intensifies the already existing centers in the wholeness in just such a fashion that the new centers reinforce and intensify the* LARGER *configuration or wholeness which existed before.*

I suggest that all nature appears as the product of the unfolding wholeness. This means that the living structure we see all around us — in the organic world and in the inorganic world — is not merely a result of interaction of densely coupled systems, but that the wholeness which occurs in space *necessarily* unfolds in such a way as to create more and more life because through the impact of these transformations, larger wholes are created, intensified *more often than they are destroyed or weakened.* As a result the centers necessarily become more and more profound; and that nature is, in this sense, reaching forward to some kind of order; even though this order is invisible, unpredictable, and not "created."

What this means is that life and living structure will appear in the world inevitably: not by some magic probabilistic occurrence, but because the nature of things — and, in particular, the mathematical way in which space gives rise to structure which reinforces wholeness — sees to it that living structure comes into being as part of its most normal evolution. This argument implies that all the processes we know — including the relatively simple mechanical processes, the physical processes governed by the law of least action, the coordinated behavior of complex systems which has been identified from recent work in chaos theory and catastrophe the-ory, and the evolution of organisms — are *all* governed by this simple, yet deep regularity, which binds these widely different cases together as a common underlying thread.

I should clarify the extent to which this new principle of unfolding wholeness might genuinely be a *new* principle separate from other known principles, and to what extent it is merely an unusual way of stating what other well-known principles and laws governing the evolution of physical systems already say. Once again, I take the history of the least-action principle as a way of explaining the situation. The principle of least action is a separately formulated mathematical principle that appears to cover the evolution of most physical systems. It is not separate from other known laws; but nor is it already covered by what they contain. For example, the equal distribution of current in two parallel wires may be deduced from Ohm's law, as referred to above; it may also be deduced from the principle of least action: thus in this one instance the principle adds nothing to Ohm's law, and is equivalent to it, in what it predicts. Yet in other cases, such as the form of a hanging chain, the catenary form may be deduced only from some version of the law of least action, or from the law of least potential energy. Here the principle of least action does more work for us. The different explanations overlap, are sometimes equivalent, and sometimes the law of least action gives new insight into the behavior of a system which is not known or deducible from other laws of physics.

I believe the principle of unfolding wholeness could turn out similarly. In some cases what this principle enunciates is something already covered by known laws, as in the case of the crude appearance of crystal forms, or as in the cases of known development of morphology under laws of pattern formation that have been worked out in biology. However, the principle is not *merely* another way of expressing results we have already. In other circumstances, the principle of unfolding wholeness adds something which complements and deepens — may occasionally even replace — our understanding of known laws. That may be because it is deeper, or a more telling formulation, or because it covers cases that are not easily understood without it. Or it goes deeper, and may be said to be something lying deeper below the surface, under all laws of physics, at the same time that it is consistent with the expression and operation of known physical and biological laws.

There may be special insights to be gained for the case of biological systems. I believe it may even turn out that the apparent mysteries of embryological morphogenesis, and even the anomalous and unexplainable appearance of new organic forms that appear in evolution apparently without selective advantage, will be more easily understandable when we consider that the evolution of any system from time t to time $t+1$, is governed by a process which works on the centers visible in the system at time t, strengthens some of these centers in a way which preserves and enhances as much of the structure as possible, and destroys as little as possible. That causes the emergence of new, more definite, forms — and it is the trajectory or pathway of this step-wise evolution, that defines the trajectory of each natural living system.

10 / A FINAL COMMENT ON ARCHITECTURE

Whatever else may be said about physics and biology, and the smoothness of the unfolding wholeness we observe in nature, one enormous observation follows for architects.

The history of architecture, especially in the period from 1600 to the present, and culminating in the thought of the 20th century, has been based on the idea that the architect's vision arises, almost spontaneously, and at all events suddenly, in the breast of the architect — a vision obtained from inspiration, that arrives full-fledged, from "thin air" — and that the quality, depth, and importance of the architect's vision comes from this mysterious moment. Contemporary students tremble as they try to attain this mystery.[54]

Yet if the observations of this chapter are held to be true about the production of living structure, and if, as I have suggested, living structure *always* arises slowly, by successive transformations of what exists, gradually, gradually, and then decisively changes slowly until a new thing is born, then the view of the unfettered architect-creator that has been fostered in the last four hundred years, must be completely wrong.

It is not the way that profound living structure can be created in buildings, it never was, and it never could be. Our idea of what it means to design a building, and to create a profound building form, must be changed for ever by this knowledge.

NOTES

1. Even when, as in inorganic nature, they are not living systems from a biological point of view.

2. In the way I have tried to describe in chapters 4–6.

3. Complexity theory, as it is generally known in broad terms, emanates from the Santa Fe Institute and is embodied in the work of many writers during the last fifteen years. In particular Stuart Kauffman, THE ORIGINS OF ORDER (New York: Oxford University Press, 1993); Brian Goodwin, HOW THE LEOPARD CHANGED ITS SPOTS (New York: Simon and Schuster, Touchstone, 1994); and Murray Gell-Mann, THE JAGUAR AND THE QUARK (New York: Freeman, 1994).

4. It is very important for me to remind the reader that my use of the phrase "living structure" does not refer merely to what is conventionally known as living structure in biological materials, but also to that living structure, defined in Book 1, that is found much more widely throughout what we call "inorganic" nature and also, on occasion, in human artifacts and works of art.

5. Detailed definitions are given in Book 1, appendix 1.

6. See, for example, Murray Gell-Mann, THE JAGUAR AND THE QUARK; and David Abraham, THE SPELL OF THE SENSUOUS (New York: Pantheon, 1995).

7. As I said in Book 1, each wholeness is, in effect, a nested system of LOCAL SYMMETRIES. In any part of space we have a nested system of centers, each one having certain symmetries, and this system of all the local symmetries *is* the wholeness.

8. In using the word "smooth," I am referring not to the smoothness of mathematical functions (which are smooth when continuously differentiable) but, in a more intuitive sense, to the smoothness of the transitions in the global structure. This smoothness is defined precisely in chapter 2.

9. The terminology originated with René Thom, STRUCTURAL STABILITY AND MORPHOGENESIS: AN OUTLINE OF A GENERAL THEORY OF MODELS, trans. from French by D. H. Fowler (Reading, Massachusetts: The Benjamin/Cummings Publishing Company, 1975).

10. Richard G. Kron, ed., EVOLUTION OF THE UNIVERSE OF GALAXIES (Berkeley: University of California Press, 1989); Brian Swimme, Ian Stewart and Martin Golubitsky, FEARFUL SYMMETRY: IS GOD A GEOMETER? (Oxford: Blackwell Publishers, 1992), pp. 137–41, figs. 6.5 and 6.7.

11. René Thom, STRUCTURAL STABILITY AND MORPHOGENESIS, p. 79, fig. 5.18.

12. Stewart and Golubitsky, FEARFUL SYMMETRY, p. 153, fig. 7.3.

13. Ibid., illustration p. vii, plate 13.

14. Ilya Prigogine, FROM BEING TO BECOMING: TIME AND COMPLEXITY IN THE PHYSICAL SCIENCES (San Francisco: Freeman, 1980), pp. 16–17.

15. This situation is very much more complex than the unfolding of the wholeness itself, and I do not know how to describe it accurately. Nevertheless I feel it is vital to include this kind of case, since I am convinced that the principle of unfolding wholeness applies, by extrapolation, to this more complex situation, and that it, too, should ultimately be understood in this way. The same applies to the evolution of the bird's wing, discussed later in this chapter.

16. Roger Lewin, THREAD OF LIFE: THE SMITHSONIAN LOOKS AT EVOLUTION (Washington D. C.: Smithsonian Books, 1982), p. 58.

17. Stewart and Golubitsky, FEARFUL SYMMETRY, p. 219, fig. 8.19.

18. Prigogine, FROM BEING TO BECOMING SCIENCES, p. 200.

19. Roger Lewin, THREAD OF LIFE, p. 54.

20. John Tyler Bonner, MORPHOGENESIS: AN ESSAY ON DEVELOPMENT (New York: Athenaeum, 1963), 33, fig. 4.

21. Ibid., p. 105, plate 1.

22. Ibid., p. 93, fig. 34.

23. Ibid., p. 99, fig. 38.

24. Stewart and Golubitsky, FEARFUL SYMMETRY, p. 13, fig. 1.5.

25. Ibid., p. 132, fig. 6.3.

26. John Tyler Bonner, "Evidence for the Formation of Cell Aggregates by Chemotaxis in the Development of the Slime Mold *Dictyostelium Discoideum*," JOURNAL OF EXPERIMENTAL ZOOLOGY 106 (1947): 1–26.

27. Harold E. Edgerton and James R. Killian, FLASH, (Boston: Hale, Cushman, and Flint, 1939).

28. Lewis Wolpert, PRINCIPLES OF DEVELOPMENT, 208–12

29. Ibid., 305–7

30. Christopher Alexander, "From a set of forces to a form," in Gyorgy Kepes, THE MAN MADE OBJECT (New York: George Braziller, 1966) pp. 96-107. Precise explanation of the wind-carried sand forming wave-like ripples is given in the text.

31. See Humphries' discussion of crystal structure, in L. L. Whyte, ed., ASPECTS OF FORM (London: Lund Humphries, 1968).

32. Luna Leopold and Walter B. Langbein, "River Meanders," SCIENTIFIC AMERICAN 214 (June 1966): 60–70.

33. For an excellent summary of Maupertuis's principle and Hamilton's function, see Stefan Hildebrandt and Anthony Tromba, MATHEMATICS AND OPTIMAL FORM (New York: Scientific American Library, 1986).

34. See the discussion, for example, in Peter S. Stevens, PATTERNS IN NATURE (Boston: Little Brown & Co., 1975), pp. 92–96.

35. Ibid., pp. 116–23.

36. Excellent general discussion of such minimum principles appears in Stefan Hildebrandt and Anthony Tromba, MATHEMATICS AND OPTIMAL FORM (New York: 1984) and in Richard Feynman, Robert Leighton, and Matthew Sands, THE FEYNMAN LECTURES ON PHYSICS, vol 2, (Reading, Massachusetts: Addison-Wesley, 1964), pp. 19-1 to 19-14. In some cases the whole can be understood as a result of purely local considerations. For example, there is a sophisticated approach to minimum-path questions for quantum phenomena such as the shortest path of a light ray, in which one expresses the global behavior purely as a result of local behaviors. This approach is typified by the sum-over-paths method for photons, where large-scale behavior in a light ray appears as a statistical result of the motion of photons taking all possible paths, with appropriately assigned probabilities. See Richard Feynman, QED (QUANTUM ELECTRODYNAMICS), (New York: 1985).

37. See Book 1, chapter 6, note 35.

38. Max Planck, AKADEMIE ANSPRACHEN (Berlin: Akademie Verlag, 1948), pp. 41-48.

39. Murray Gell-Mann, THE QUARK AND THE JAGUAR (New York, W. H. Freeman and Co., 1994), pp. 207-9.

40. Stevens, PATTERNS IN NATURE, pp. 94-96.

41. Armin Bunde and Shlomo Havlin, eds., FRACTALS AND DISORDERED SYSTEMS (Berlin: Springer Verlag, 1991); René Thom, STRUCTURAL STABILITY AND MORPHOGENESIS; Prigogine, FROM BEING TO BECOMING; Gerald Edelman, TOPOBIOLOGY, (New York: Basic Books, 1988); Stuart Kauffman, THE ORIGINS OF ORDER (New York: Oxford University Press, 1993); John Briggs, FRACTALS; THE PATTERNS OF CHAOS (New York: 1992); and hundreds of others.

42. Steven Jay Gould, "Evolution as Fact and Theory," from HEN'S TEETH AND HORSE'S TOES: FURTHER REFLECTIONS ON NATURAL HISTORY (New York: Norton, 1994) 253-62, and Richard Dawkins THE BLIND WATCHMAKER: WHY THE EVIDENCE OF EVOLUTION REVEALS A UNIVERSE WITHOUT DESIGN and THE SELFISH GENE (New York: Oxford University Press, 1996 and 1976).

43. An important article by Mark Isaak, shows how indeed the squirt gun could be achieved in small step-by-step increments (he gives one possible scenario with biological and chemical details of each step). See Mark Isaak, "Bombardier Beetles and the Argument of Design," published on the Internet, http://www.talkorigins.-org/faqs/bombardier.html, dated 1997. But even in this important article the holistic character of the squirt gun and its coherence as a whole, though absolutely necessary to the success of the step-by-step process, is not accounted for.

44. Isaak, ibid.

45. Kauffman, AT HOME IN THE UNIVERSE (New York: Oxford University Press, 1995), 180-89.

46. First put forward by Lancelot Law Whyte, in INTERNAL FACTORS IN EVOLUTION (Oxford: Pergamon, 1960).

47. Tension and compression in bones is discussed in detail by D'Arcy Wentworth Thompson, ON GROWTH AND FORM (Cambridge: Cambridge University Press, 1917; reprinted vols. 1 and 2, 1959), pp. 975-88.

48. H. Eugene Stanley, "Fractals and Multifractals: the Interplay of Physics and Geometry," in Bunde and Havlin, FRACTALS AND DISORDERED SYSTEMS, pp. 1-49, especially pp. 8-9.

49. D. Schechtman, I. Blech, D. Gratias, and J. W. Cahn, "Metallic Phase with Long-Range Orientational Order and No Translational Symmetry," PHYSICS REVIEW LETTERS 53 (1984): 1951.

50. Roger Penrose, THE EMPEROR'S NEW MIND (New York: Oxford University Press, 1990), p. 436 and footnote 7 on p. 449.

51. Recently published suggestions about the practical mechanism by which these long-range forms of order are created in the case of the metal alloys, do indeed propose such things as electronic resonances which act in the large, and overlapping clusters of atoms which are capable of being coordinated by larger scale geometry. See F. Axel and D. Gratias, BEYOND QUASICRYSTALS (Berlin: Springer/Les Editions de Physique, 1995).

52. Stewart and Golubitsky, FEARFUL SYMMETRY, throughout.

53. This process follows the same route of leveling and sharpening that I once described, in great detail, for the emergence of coherent form from infants' scribbles, and the process is nearly the same. See Christopher Alexander, "The Origin of Creative Power in Children," BRITISH JOURNAL OF AESTHETICS (1962) vol 3, no. 2: 207-26.

54. In how many 20th-century architectural competitions, or artistic competitions, for example, was "originality" one of the criteria used by the judges for establishing the winner?

CHAPTER TWO

STRUCTURE-PRESERVING TRANSFORMATIONS

1 / STRUCTURE-PRESERVING TRANSFORMATIONS

In chapter 1, I introduced the idea that every natural process is somehow "smooth." I suggested that in parallel with its other known physical explanations each process is also governed by a new principle of unfolding wholeness. I suggested, in general terms, that all living structure — all those systerms which possess what we may otherwise call "the character of nature" — follow naturally, without effort, from this kind of principle working under the surface as part of other known processes.

What does it mean to say that a process is "smooth?" I define a smooth transformation as a transformation which preserves structure and wholeness: and from now on I shall refer to these types of transformations as structure-preserving transformations. My claim in Book 2 is that the intricate and beautiful structure of living centers comes about naturally, and most of the time without effort, as a result of the repeated application of structure-preserving transformations to the wholeness which exists.[1]

Have a look at the sequence of sketches on this page. At each step, there is an addition or injection — a new center of some kind is introduced. But this new center is not added randomly like a foreign body. It grows out of what was there before. Thus, the dark small circle in D2 occupies a position which is already hinted at in the previously existing circle. There is, if you like, a faint "fuzz" at the center of the empty circle in D1, a halo or latent possibility caused by the structure of D1, which draws attention to its own middle. This faint fuzz begs for intensification or elaboration. If you were doodling, then elaborating the middle of the circle, where this fuzz exists, is one of the most natural things to do.

What I call the faint fuzz at the middle of D1 is not merely an intuition. It exists there for describable mathematical reasons. In the plain circle, a zone in the middle of the circle exists because it is a locus of intensity differentiated

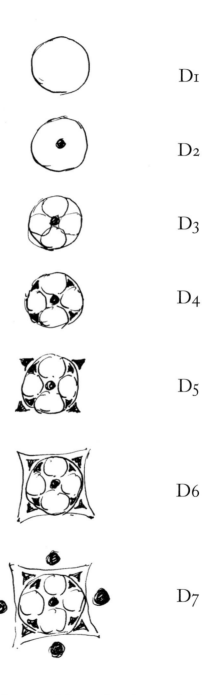

D_1

D_2

D_3

D_4

D_5

D_6

D_7

A sequence of six transformations, starting from an empty circle

by a different system of symmetries, caused by the other symmetries present within the circle. For example, if I draw all the tangent circles on the inside of the circle D1, they all overlap or generate this spot thus giving this spot special saliency. The saliency is a precise phenomenon caused by overlapping symmetries and centers from round about. We intuit it as a fuzz. But it is an actual structure present in the mathematics of the space.

If I now darken this fuzz spot, as in D2, I am intensifying an existing center, albeit one which was at first latent and somewhat weak. By intensifying this center, I create a new balance among the system of centers, and indeed cause a modified system of centers throughout the disk. The wholeness is changed, since the relative strength of centers has changed. The centers have not changed greatly, only slightly. Yet this slight change changes the wholeness of the entire configuration, and by our making the intensification, a new structure more highly differentiated than before has been created. This is what I call a structure-preserving transformation.

I should like to make some observations about the structure-preserving transformation $D_1 \longrightarrow D_2$ that we have just looked at.

(A) First, this structure-preserving transformation is not unique. Other existing and latent centers could have been chosen for intensification. However, there are not an unlimited number of choices. Relatively few acts intensify the structure which exists, while there are thousands of random acts which would *not* intensify the structure.

(B) The new structure has more life than the previously existing empty circle. Not greatly more life, but slightly more, and noticeably more.

If you are not sure about this, please use the criteria of Book 1, chapters 8 and 9. According to those criteria, you will see that D2 has more life than D1.

(C) The D2 is arrived at by taking the whole, the *wholeness* of D1, and intensifying *that*. In other words, it arises from the structure as a whole, not from a fragmented portion of the structure. And it arises from a process that enhances and embellishes that whole.

(D) Even in this very rudimentary transformation, as the new whole, D2, emerges, some of the fifteen properties already begin to appear more strongly. The smaller disk in the middle has CONTRAST, it has GOOD SHAPE, its size is chosen so that the empty ring of space around it forms a BOUNDARY and so on. Thus in parallel with the intensification, the life of the whole is growing both as measured by the appearance of STRONGER CENTERS, and as measured by the appearance of geometric properties which support the increasing life of the new centers.

If I had chosen the black disk to be smaller, the boundary would have been less strong, and the contrast and good shape less marked. So the particular form of intensification was chosen to maximize the effect of preserving and enhancing the structure which exists, so as to give D2 as much new life as possible, without losing or going away from the structure of D1.

(E) Please note that nothing entirely *new* has been injected — the newness has been created by intensification of what exists. Thus the procedure is both conservative (it respects the previously existing structure) and innovative (it creates new structure, not previously visible in the older structure of D1).

Without any difficulty, the reader can see for himself how the transformations $D_2 \longrightarrow D_3$, $D_3 \longrightarrow D_4$, $D_4 \longrightarrow D_5$, $D_5 \longrightarrow D_6$, and $D_6 \longrightarrow D_7$ all work in the same way, and the five points A–E occur in each of these transformations.

D7, the last of the series, is a novel configuration, arrived at from the plain circle by these structure preserving transformations. In a similar way, natural but new configurations emerge continually from their contexts as dynamical systems go forward.

Of the five points just made, it is point (E) which is most important and most striking. We have seen how a mechanical process, following from adherence to structure that exists according to well-defined rules of transformation will *by itself create entirely new and previously unseen structure.*

Thus the creation of morphological novelty, biological invention, artsitic creation, architectural invention . . . may all be understood as products of a relatively simple process. This possibility arises because there is invisible or semi-visible structure present, and active, within the structure that exists — and it is this structure which gives birth to new possibilities and new combinations at every step, even through it is a relatively mechanical procedure.

All that is required is that this mechanical procedure is sensitive to the *whole* and is influenced by and guided by the structure of the whole. That is the secret of morphological emergence in natural phenomena. It is also, I maintain, the secret of all artistic and constructive human-inspired acts of creation.

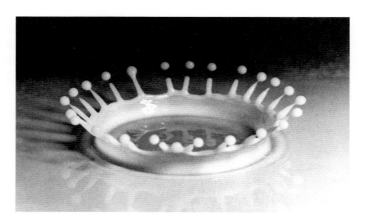

Centers forming during the unfolding of a milk-drop splash. The full sequence of which this is a part has already been shown on page 25. Detailed discussion and explanation of the structure-preserving transformation which creates this particular phase is given on page 66.

Later in the chapter, using the idea of structure-preserving transformations, we shall be able to define the principle of unfolding wholeness in more precise terms that will tell us how the fifteen properties — and all living structure — arise from this principle without any complex teleological explanation. We shall see, for instance, why the splashing milk drop forms a strong living center as it falls, and why and how other phenomena in nature take their form, and become densely packed with living centers, simply as a result of repeated unfolding of the wholeness.

Later, we shall see, too, how at least potentially, the system of architecture and planning and care of the land, can move the built environment forward, also, by structure-preserving transformations that extend and enhance the wholeness that exists, and so keep on drawing the future from the present.

2 / STRUCTURE-PRESERVING TRANSFORMATIONS
FURTHER DISCUSSION

Let's start again. On the right, there is a sketch of a square drawn on a sheet of paper. Below that, I show various ways you might modify the square, add something to it, transform it.

If I ask you to modify it in a way which *preserves* or continues or extends the structure which exists in the square, you will probably draw something like one of the (A) sketches in the first row below.

The original square

A. Transformations of a square which preserve its structure

B. Transformations of a square which destroy its structure

If, on the contrary, I ask you to modify the square in a way which *destroys* or damages or contradicts the structure which exists in the square, you will probably draw something like one of the (B) sketches in the second row.

In both cases, your intuition tells you roughly what to do. Intuitively, we understand the concept of preserving or destroying structure. This means, of course, that in some form we must have an intuitive idea of the structure which *exists*. That concept is not new: the structure which exists is, of course, the wholeness as I defined it in Book 1. It is the field of centers. But

we must also have an intuitive idea of a transformation which preserves or extends a structure, and an intuitive idea of a transformation which destroys or contradicts a structure. This *is* new. Except in chapter 1 of this book, I have not previously (in Book 1) suggested that the wholeness which exists contains a seed or direction that points the way toward those transformations which are kind to it and away from those transformations which are unkind to it. But the demonstration I have just given shows that there is indeed some way in which a transformation of a structure which exists can be kind or not-

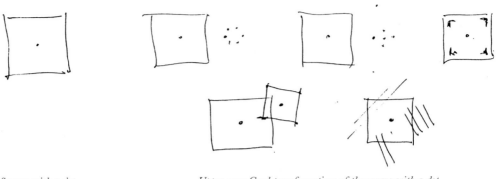

Square with a dot

Upper row: Good transformations of the square with a dot
Lower row: Bad transformations of the square with a dot

kind — structure-preserving or structure-destroying, more consistent or less consistent with the structure that exists.

A preference for movement towards the structure-preserving transformation is almost exactly what we have seen in the examples of chapter 1. Throughout nature, we see a continuous smooth unfolding of the wholeness which preserves structure at every moment, even when it seems to be introducing new structure. That is what happens even when a bullet shatters a piece of glass (page 31). It is what happens when a seed grows into a plant. It is what happens when a waves breaks or a river meanders.

Here are some more examples of structure-preserving transformations. At the top of the page, I take one of the transformed versions of the square: the square with a dot in the middle. I make *further* marks to transform *this* figure further. Again, these marks may be structure-preserving or not. The three in the top row *are*

structure-preserving. The two in the second row are *not* structure-preserving. The transformations in the first row, even though they bring in new structure and open up new directions, preserve and enhance the wholeness of the square with the dot. The transformations in the second row also bring in new structure, but they do it in a way which violates the structure of the square with the dot. Its structure is weakened or destroyed.

The idea of structure-preserving transformations is quite general. If we are faced with any configuration at all — simple or complex — and we are asked to modify it by adding elements or making changes, we can distinguish between types of additions and changes which preserve or enhance the structure and types which weaken or destroy the structure.

It is the structure-preserving transformations which give us the key to the creation of wholeness. Look at the situation (below) where

Two trees; two trees plus hammock; two trees with bench around one of them.
Putting in a hammock leaves the wholeness of the two trees intact: putting a single round bench around one of the trees leaves it somewhat less intact.

*Plan 1: A first possible site plan, rather conventional in charac-
ter, which is NOT structure preserving. Although this plan follows typical design character for a typical building in the 1970s
or 1980s, the placing of the volumes, the badly formed exterior
space, and the lack of structure-preserving done to the two streets
and to the sunshine in the south are all negative.*

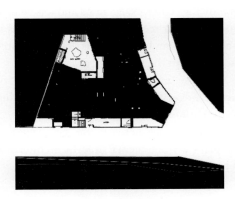

*Plan 2, as built: A site plan which IS structure-preserving.
It shows the unusual configuration caused by
the fork, and two bent streets.*

*The view of our apartment building in Tokyo after
completion. It kept the character of the neighborhood
alive because it was structure-preserving in so many ways.*

two very similar trees are standing close together
(first diagram). If I string a hammock between
them, this is a structure-preserving transformation. The wholeness of the two trees with the
hammock is similar to the wholeness of the two
trees without the hammock (second diagram).
Another structure-preserving transformation
occurs if I put a single bench around one of the
trees (third diagram). However, this transformation is slightly less structure-preserving, since it
introduces an asymmetry that was not there before, and changes the larger wholeness
substantially.

To explain the point with a complex, full-
scale example from architecture, I give the example of an apartment building I built in 1987. It
was built at an acute-angled fork in a busy Tokyo
street. The fork had an unusual angle; both
streets were (and are) narrow. I show two possible plans for the building, considered while it
was in the earliest design process. One of them,
highly conventional from the point of view of architectural planning, circa 1970–80, and done as
an exercise by someone in my office, is made of
several rectangular volumes arranged to fill the
site as nearly as possible. It is not structure-preserving. The other, following the street contours
as they are, forms a volume which was unusual
by the standards of 1987; but it is more structure-
preserving. It enhances the spatial volumes of

the two streets. The second plan is also more structure-preserving for the neighborhood as a whole. It is the plan which we subsequently built. The photograph to the right of the plans shows the apartment building when it was finished.

On this page, I give a second similar example of real built things, but they are much more modest in scale. This shows how the same principle affects even the smallest things in the environment: the following two everyday illustrations from the Berkeley hills show how ordinary this process is. The photographs are of two mail boxes on a street near my house. The first, on the left, is very simple. The person needed a mailbox, put it on a stick, and let the grass grow around it. It is beautifully structure-preserving and sensitive.

In contrast, on the right, is another mailbox, from a house further down the street. It is almost the same kind of mailbox. You see that the owner of this mailbox has built a kind of pyramidal structure under the mailbox, evidently trying to make it "nice." In our language, you might say that this person was trying to make a STRONG CENTER. Should he not get some brownie points, then? No. The center he created has too little to do with the context of the situation where he created it. The reason is that, compared with the first one, this center has less relation to the grass, flowers, and driveway around it. It did not arise as naturally from the wholeness of its location. Thus it is a more isolated, more self-aggrandizing center, exaggerated and less helpful to its context. It seems a bit overblown. And it seems overblown because it is less structure-preserving than the first mailbox.

As these examples suggest, examples of structure-preserving and structure-destroying transformations are visible all around us.

The difference between the two types of cases plays a fundamental role in architecture and in the evolution of all living structure.

Mailbox which is structure-preserving. The landscape, steps, grass, and their wholeness are preserved by the insertion of the mailbox.

Mailbox which is not structure-preserving. The center which is created under the mailbox does not arise naturally from the surrounding wholeness.

3 / THE OBJECTIVITY OF
STRUCTURE-PRESERVING TRANSFORMATIONS

What is more structure-preserving and what is less so is, in principle, an objective matter.[2]

In a series of experiments carried out in my laboratory in the early 1980s, my students and I demonstrated that an observer's awareness of transformations which are structure-preserving is well defined. For a great variety of cases, we found that the judgments of whether a given transformation is or is not structure-preserving are agreed on by many people. I believe that these judgments reflect an objective mathematical reality.

The subtlety of the judgment is shown in the example below, where different transformations of an octagon were rated by a group of eight people. The transformations in the upper row are clearly structure-preserving. Eight out of eight people found them to be so. In the lower row, the transformation on the left was felt to be ambiguous, but somewhat structure-destroying (four people thought so; three did not know). The third transformation was clearly and unani-

mously felt to be structure-destroying (eight people thought so). The second and fourth transformations were seen as mainly structure-preserving with some ambiguity (in the second, four people thought so, four did not know; in the fourth, five people thought so, three did not know).

We found that we could rate the goodness of a structure-preserving transformation, approximately, by the number of people who considered it to be so. However, the issue cannot simply be settled by a vote. As I have explained (Book 1, appendix 3) people see the wholeness in a given situation with varying degrees of accuracy and subtlety. The goodness of a given structure-preserving transformation can be assessed accurately only by a person who sees the wholeness accurately. It is, in the end, not a judgment of opinion, but a judgment about the wholeness which actually exists.

Surprisingly, it turns out that this judgment is objective and well-defined even in those cases

structure-preserving *8*
don't know *0*
structure-destroying *0*

structure-preserving *8*
don't know *0*
structure-destroying *0*

structure-preserving *7*
don't know *1*
structure-destroying *0*

structure-preserving *8*
don't know *0*
structure-destroying *0*

structure-preserving *0*
don't know *3*
structure-destroying *4*

structure-preserving *4*
don't know *4*
structure-destroying *0*

structure-preserving *0*
don't know *0*
structure-destroying *8*

structure-preserving *5*
don't know *3*
structure-destroying *0*

where people find it difficult to be specific in *defining* the structure which exists.

This point became clear in a fascinating result which we obtained experimentally. We asked people to make a diagram or drawing of the structure which they perceived to exist in something. Because the field of centers is complex and hard to draw, the diagrams people made, even of the same structure, were different from person to person. Different people selected different aspects of the field of centers to draw and did not manage to catch all of it. However, in spite of these differences, we found that the agreement about which transformations *are* structure-preserving, and which are *not*, is much higher among people who have first attempted to draw the structure, *even when they disagree about that structure and have drawn it differently*. Evidently, the awareness of structure *itself*, the fact that a person's mind is focused on the *structure*, not on other more superficial aspects of design, makes the judgment of which transformations are structure-preserving and which are not more objective, and increases people's agreement about that judgment.

My last example shows the depth and subtlety which may be involved in making judgments about what is structure-preserving and what is not.

I show a vertical rectangle (below, left) and three possible transformations of this rectangle (below, right). Among these three, it is relatively easy to agree that the one on the left is the least structure-preserving. Essentially the vertical sensation and wholeness of the first rectangle A is lost, is more compromised, by the fragment which lies floating in it, and especially because this fragment has a niche in its upper edge: that makes the form altogether more inconsistent with the vertical gestalt of the outer rectangle, and therefore less structure-preserving.

But what of the other two, those on the right, B and C. Each contains an indented vertical rectangle, and on the whole both seem to complete or extend the original rectangle, with some success. When we try to make a careful assessment, we are drawn into very subtle considerations about wholeness — of what the wholeness of the rectangle is really like, and what the wholeness of these two transformed rectangles are like. If we try to feel the wholeness of the rectangle, we sense a vertical and "rising" quality in its wholeness. The inner rectangle of B, has two turret-like features sticking up, and at first we may feel that the rising quality is supported, and enhanced by this feature. The inner rectangle of C, which seems turned down somehow, at first seems to contradict this rising quality, and would seem therefore to be less structure-preserving or enhancing. However, when we look at it longer, we see that the inner small indent at the bottom edge, is itself actually pointing upward, and in the end, in my experience, it is this which will be felt to be the more structure-preserving of the two. Here we are drawn into the most subtle questions of whole-

A plain vertical rectangle

  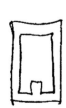

Three transformations of the vertical rectangle, A, B and C. The one on the right is most structure-preserving. Most people feel this to be true, intuitively. Yet the difficulty of defining it, and explaining why, emphasizes the deeply subtle nature of the wholeness.

ness. This is not only revealing of the experimental difficulties which may be faced, but also redoubles our awareness that a purely mathematical treatment of the wholeness, and our ability to define it successfully in abstract terms, is still far away.

4 / REPEATED APPLICATION OF STRUCTURE-PRESERVING TRANSFORMATIONS

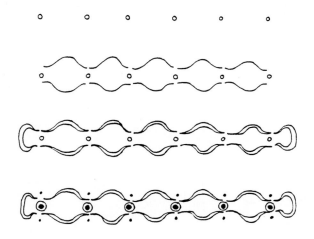

A sequence of patterns which develop from a row of dots

Let us look, now, at the effect of a sequence of repeated structure-preserving transformations on a simple pattern.

In the drawings on pages 61–2, we see what happens when we start with a simple nearly empty structure and keep on transforming it under conditions where each transformation is structure-preserving. The results are nice. Perhaps not spectacular, but, to the extent that structure is preserved, the resulting patterns are pleasing and harmonious.

We also see that centers begin appearing more and more densely in the patterns.

This is inevitable. We start with the wholeness of the empty space. It has a system of weak centers, latent, not strongly visible. Then we embellish this space in some fashion which supports, brings out, the structure that exists: that means that certain centers, already existing latent in the wholeness, are now brought out and revealed more strongly by the structure-preserving transformations.

In my laboratory studies, my students and I made a further important discovery. If we have a sequence of transformations, all of which are structure-preserving, then the result of these transformations is almost always beautiful. Good transformations do not cause any upheaval. So to get a good project, we merely have to make a sequence of structure-preserving transformations. When we do so, a good design evolves smoothly, almost automatically.

However, even a single bad transformation can upset the smooth unfolding. If we make one transformation which destroys structure, in the middle of a sequence of good ones, things become

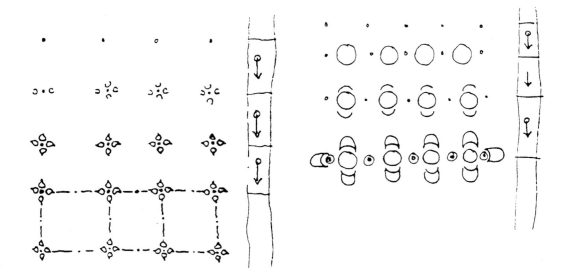

A sequence of structure-preserving transformations

A sequence of structure-preserving transformations

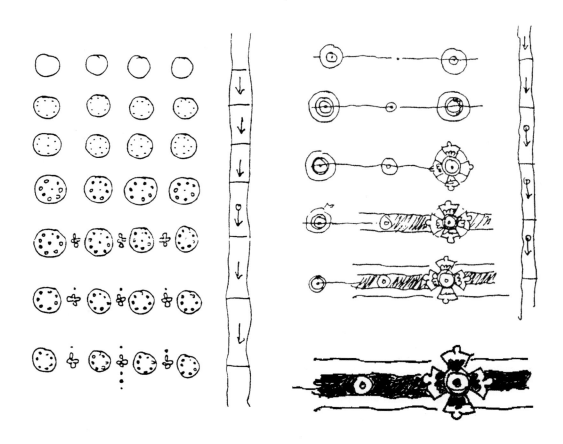

A sequence of structure-preserving transformations

A sequence of structure-preserving transformations

ugly very quickly; the structure which arises then is no longer consistent with the field of centers. We also found that the effect of this one bad transformation is very hard to recover from. It is as if, in dealing with the wholeness, we are dealing with a delicate material which remains in good condition as long as we are nice to it. But the moment we send it off the rails, we have lost touch with its underlying origin in reality, and it is then very hard indeed to bring it back.

We see from even these simple examples that the repeated application of a structure-preserving transformation creates rather densely packed, rich systems of centers.

5 / MINIMUM SYMMETRY BREAKING

Nature, too, creates beautiful structures which are governed by repeated application of structure-preserving transformations. In this connection, I think it is useful to remark that what I call structure-preserving transformations are very closely related to what has become known as "symmetry breaking" in physics.[3]

You may recall the smooth metal cylinder I described in chapter 1, which, when buckling under compression, takes on a uniform pattern of dimples all over its surface. The explanation given for this phenomenon, still not entirely un-derstood, goes like this: before buckling, the uniform cylinder has a very big symmetry group on its surface. Since each point is essentially like every other point, it has the infinite symmetry group of rotations. This means, simply, that every point is like every other.

Now, when the cylinder buckles at a certain critical moment because of the compression, one little point — the weakest — will pop out first. The moment this happens, even only a tiny amount, say one-hundredth of an inch, the symmetry which existed before all around the cylin-

Buckling of a hollow cylinder when compressed

der is broken. It no longer exists. But at this moment, so the argument goes, the system acts in such a way as to keep as many symmetries as possible. Just a few symmetries are knocked out by the occurrence of the small deformation. The metal of the cylinder then rearranges itself in such a way as to keep as many of the previous symmetries as possible, and only removes those which are forced out by the buckling. Thus the buckling takes on a form which has fewer symmetries: it still has a rotational group of symmetries; only now it is a finite group. The claim, which is not really explained, is that the system acts in such a way as to remove as few symmetries as possible, and then rearranges itself with all the remaining symmetries left intact.[4] This claim is really a minimum change argument: *the system acts to preserve as much of its structure as possible.*

Ian Stewart and Martin Golubitsky give another example which is helpful. Consider the dew on a spider's web. As we know, the dew often forms in regularly spaced drops. We assume, I think, that this occurs because of surface tension. But Stewart and Golubitsky state that the surface tension is not enough to explain the drops. If the filament were perfectly uniform, the dew would spread out in a single cylinder coating the thread all along its length, without any drops. The explanation of the drops goes as follows. Again, somewhere, there is an irregularity. The perfect infinite symmetry of the thread coated with dew is thereby broken. The system "tries" (their word) to save as much of the symmetry as possible, while incorporating the irregular spot, and comes up with a system of equally spaced droplets. This still has the translational symme-

Dew drops on a spider's web. Note the extraordinary regularity of drop size and spacing, explained in the text. This poor quality photograph is the most beautiful example of this problem I have found, so I used it rather than substitute a sharper, less beautiful picture.

try as before, but less of it; and the irregularity lies between the drops. Again, the system wants to preserve as much symmetry as possible: when the perfect symmetry of the endless thread is broken, we get the slightly less perfect symmetry, but symmetry nonetheless, of the regularly spaced line of droplets.[5]

These are examples of explicitly structure-preserving transformations from the literature

of physics. In each case, the wholeness is a system of symmetries and centers. When something is done to the wholeness, or some effect is introduced, differentiation is created. The particular differentiation which occurs is that one which is most fully structure-preserving. This means that a step forward is taken which leaves intact as much of the structure of centers and symmetries as possible.

6 / HOW THE FIFTEEN PROPERTIES APPEAR IN NATURE FROM THE UNFOLDING OF WHOLENESS

Let us now return to the fifteen properties which define living structure.[6] In nature, all living structure containing these properties comes into being without effort as a direct result of unfolding wholeness.

Think about the wholeness dynamically. Everything is changing constantly. Every process which occurs on earth continuously changes, transforms, modifies the wholeness which exists. So the wholeness is continuously evolving. At any given moment, in any given region of space, there is a wholeness W_t. At the next moment, this gives way to another wholeness W_{t+1}. The transformation of W_t to W_{t+1} is the way the world unfolds: $W_t \longrightarrow W_{t+1}$. Everything is covered by it.

What happens when the unfolding is *smooth*? The transformation is structure-preserving. At any moment t, there is a certain wholeness, W_t. At the next moment t+1, this leads to a new wholeness, W_{t+1}, which is *consistent* with the previous wholeness W_t; indeed, the next step, W_{t+1}, is one of the relatively few steps (of all possible steps forward) which is *very deeply* consistent with the wholeness W_t.

What this means, in a nutshell, is that during the transition to W_{t+1} the centers in W_t are not violated. They are preserved. Thus, in general, additional centers will be created that reinforce and strengthen the centers that already exist. In the cases where centers are taken out (death,

pruning, simplification), they are removed, still, in such a way as to leave as many as possible of the larger centers intact. Under these circumstances, as layer upon layer of smooth unfolding takes place, what develops is a system of centers which is stronger, crustier, and more imbricated, and in which the centers (at first hundreds, then thousands, or tens of thousands) all reinforce and intensify one another.

The dense character of living structure, arrived at by a layered dynamic process in which wholeness is always being preserved as much as possible, *is exactly the character which has been described in Book 1, chapters 5–6.*

All this hinges on the fact that wholeness (as defined in Book 1, chapter 3) is entirely *made* of centers. Since it is made of centers, a transformation which preserves the structure of the wholeness must then preserve most of these centers.

From this it follows that the new centers which are created at each step will be related, *through repeated new appearances of the fifteen properties,* to the previously existing centers.[7] I have asserted, in Book 1, chapter 5, that the fifteen properties are the fifteen ways in which centers can enliven one another. Hence, if under a structure-preserving transformation, new centers are being added that enliven or deepen the existing centers, this means that the fifteen properties must slowly come into being, step by step, with each new transformation. Otherwise, the new centers will not enliven or deepen the older ones.

I am asserting that (to a first approximation) there are only fifteen ways in which this intensification of centers by other centers can take place. In other words, the presence of the fifteen properties in a naturally evolving structure, will increase as the evolution goes forward, as a direct result of the repeated use of structure-preserving transformations. Here are some examples of how it works.

1. LEVELS OF SCALE. For example, within a given center A or directly near it, we shall find smaller centers, B, one level of scale smaller. That happens because any perturbation or irregularity which develops near A causes the start of a latent center B. As this latent center gets stronger, the strengthening will then cause a nucleation near the first center. The nucleation *must* be at a jump in scale, since if too similar in size it would not preserve the structure.

In the milk-drop splash, the splash first forms a ring — the first center. The perturba-tions around the edge of the ring then aggregate in smaller drops — smaller, obviously, than the main ring, but not tiny. Their diameter is about one-quarter to one-tenth the size of the ring, and they give the milk-drop splash its LEVELS OF SCALE.

The process is quite general. If a large center is developing, and within it, somewhere, a small dot occurs (randomly), then to intensify this small center under structure-preserving trans-formations without disturbing the larger center, the small center must be kept *substantially* smaller than the first; yet if it is *too* small, it does nothing to enhance the larger one. If it has a scale at which it does not disturb and yet actively enhances the first center, the second one will be *just* one order of magnitude smaller than the big one. Repeated application of a process which enhances structure must create the property LEV-ELS OF SCALE.

Although the smaller drops that form around the crown of the splash break the infinite symme-try of the original continuous ring, they will now be arranged in a regular ring and be of roughly equal size. This is the same as saying the smaller drops must preserve the structure of the original

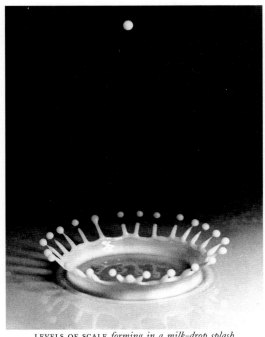

LEVELS OF SCALE *forming in a milk-drop splash*

STRONG CENTERS *forming in a flowering plant*

splash without drops, and must therefore still keep the "ring" structure. They can do this only if they preserve a symmetry around the center of the splash. Thus the perturbations that make the milk splash not only have LEVELS OF SCALE, but also make a strong center.[8]

2. STRONG CENTERS. Under structure-preserving transformations, STRONG CENTERS keep on increasing.

In the growth of a flower, a field effect takes place, caused by chemical gradients in the sap. As one center forms, the position of the flower-head and the point of growth that will become a bud — stem, sepals, petals, and other parts of the flower — then develop and arrange themselves to support the flower that is forming. The medium of the transmission is the sap, containing ribosomes, enzymes, all together then creating a chemical field effect which stimulates growth of smaller centers placed in positions to enhance the original bud, and gradually giving rise to the fully formed flower as a center.

In general, in any system where one center forms, as structure-preserving transformations occur, other smaller centers will then emerge, will be intensified and themselves strengthened in just such a way that by virtue of their position and arrangement they intensify the first center. This causes the field effect around the first center which I have described (under my discussion of strong centers in Book 1, chapter 5). Gradually, it will occur around every center.

3. BOUNDARIES. At any moment in the evolution of a system, each center which exists has a latent boundary zone around it just by virtue of the nature of the center, separating it from adjacent centers and joining it to them. The boundary zone is the zone where the steepest gradient of differentiation falls off around the center, thus distinguishing it as a center. In one form or another it must occur, by definition, around any center. Under structure-preserving transformations, this latent boundary zone will intensify and encourage new centers to form within the

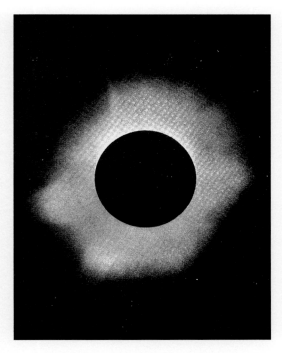

Formation of a BOUNDARY *in the sun's corona*

boundary zone, as it strengthens the existing center, ultimately creating a big boundary which is strong in itself.

This is what happens in the sun's corona, in the piling of silt along the Rio Negro where it goes into the Amazon, or in the formation of the boundary around a human cell. The main center brings with it a boundary zone, and then (in many cases, like the cell) soon this boundary zone is filled with activity, forming additional and smaller centers that ultimately become structures in themselves.

The process is quite general. Gradually, under structure-preserving transformations, centers form boundaries, and the property BOUNDARIES will be found repeatedly throughout space.

4. ALTERNATING REPETITION. Inevitably, in every structure, events (and local structures) repeat. This is typical at all scales. Atoms, waves, leaves, grains of sand, cirrus clouds — all have repetition of some type of center, many times, spread through a portion of space.

ALTERNATING REPETITION: *waves and spaces between the waves*
in wind-blown sand in the sand dunes of the Sahara

Consider the sand waves which typically occur in the wind-blown sand of big sand dunes. The crests come at more or less regular intervals, because the wind carries each sand grain a typical distance (determined by wind speed, and grain size). This causes a simple repetition. But as the wave crests grow, not only the crests, but also the depressions *between* the waves crests form. The structure-preserving transformations in the system then act to intensify both the hill-like shape of the crests, and the bowl-like depressions of the valleys. Both crests and valleys become more and more well-shaped, as a result of the structure-preserving transformations. The so-called empty space — actually space formed and shaped by the crests — then repeats *its* characteristic form, thus creating a second system of centers which repeat. These spaces become coherent, and alternate with the crests themselves, which, as centers, also repeat. The overall effect is ALTERNATING REPETITION.

The effect is general. In *any* repetition there will, obviously, be latent centers (not yet fully existing centers) in some of the spaces between adjacent centers in the repetition. Assume, then, that a structure-preserving transformation occurs. The latent center between some pair of centers will develop and become a center in its own right. If the spaces between the repeating centers are themselves similar (as they will often be), this center-forming process will gradually occur in each one of the centers lying between the first system of centers — thus forming a second system of repeating centers tucked between the first system. After a number of transformations of this kind, there will be ALTERNATING REPETITION throughout the repetition.

5. POSITIVE SPACE. Consider a small zone of empty space somewhere in a system that is currently not inhabited with strong centers. By virtue of its geometry, at least some regions of this empty space will have a weak latent quality as centers. Like the empty space between two adjacent blobs, they will be center-like but undeveloped. Sooner or later, by moving material to make the shape of this "empty" space more coherent, structure-preserving transformations make these latent centers in the space more and more center-like. As they become centers they become more positive in shape. They will gather

themselves together and differentiations will occur around the edge to intensify the shape and make it still more center-like.

Look at the packing of kernels in a bit of wood tissue. While the tissue is growing, the wood cells press against one another, deforming their shapes, much as bubbles in a mass of bubbles keep their coherence under their own internal pressure, balanced against the pressure of nearby bubbles. Just so with the cells in the wood tissue, until each bit of space is made positive.

Under structure-preserving transformations, such a process will occur quite generally in any system. Gradually, each bit of space that has any latency to be center-like gets formed more and more strongly as a center. As the empty space is filled, pushed, pulled, connected, each bit of it becomes a center, and slowly becomes more positive. The property POSITIVE SPACE slowly makes its appearance throughout the space.

6. GOOD SHAPE. Consider an emerging shape within a developing whole. The shape often exists, at some early stage, as a weakly formed "possible" shape, not yet very sharply defined. As

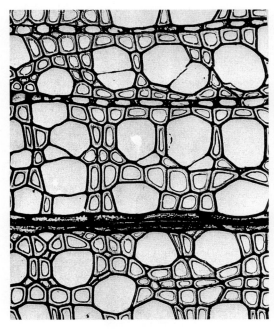

POSITIVE SPACE *in the cell structure of wood tissue*

GOOD SHAPE *as it forms in a breaking wave*

GOOD SHAPE *of a single Ginkgo leaf*

The centers which form in the growing Ginkgo leaf.
It is the formation and strengthening of these centers
which then create a beautiful form, and
GOOD SHAPE *in the leaf.*

structure-preserving transformations are applied, the latent centers which appear both within this shape and next to it, even if only dimly present, will be strengthened and made into a more definite center.

As a wave forms, at first it has a gentle shape, the rising swell of the wave-form. Then, as the wave develops, the shape becomes more and more pronounced, the non-homogeneity at the cusp becomes pronounced, the curl emerges as an independent center and finally, as the wave breaks, its shape becomes extreme and filled with centers.

As a ginkgo leaf forms the simple, relatively homogeneous curve around the compartments gives way to a curve in which each compartment becomes more pronounced, thus slowly creating a profound GOOD SHAPE.

Under structure-preserving transformations of a form, one by one, the vaguely existing centers within the shape are replaced by definite centers; as a result the shape strengthens. Gradually, throughout the space, just that character emerges that I previously defined as GOOD SHAPE: each shape is redefined so that it is made throughout of well-formed centers.

7. LOCAL SYMMETRIES. The centeredness of a given center is almost always strengthened by local symmetry — not always, but *almost* always.

For example, as electron orbitals form around an atom, the orbitals become symmetrical. The Jahn-Teller theorem establishes a connection between the symmetry of molecular configurations and the stability of degenerate electron orbitals. Any orbital which was neither symmetrical nor antisymmetric but was instead unsymmetrical with respect to reflection would, when squared,

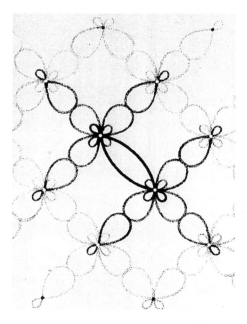

LOCAL SYMMETRIES *in the electron orbits*
around a complex molecule

yield a physically impossible probability distribution. In short, under evolution of the atom's quantum processes, the orbitals that form are locally symmetrical throughout.

More generally, during structure-preserving transformations, symmetrical and near-symmetrical evolution of centers maintains global structure, while "cleaning up" structural debris. Thus, at least some centers get reinforced and strengthened by LOCAL SYMMETRIES that intensify local centers. As structure is preserved, the density of LOCAL SYMMETRIES will typically increase: local symmetries, sometimes distorted to accommodate to other nearby structures, will appear more and more often throughout the space.

8. DEEP INTERLOCK AND AMBIGUITY. Along an edge between two zones, random perturbations will form disturbances which start as latent centers. As these randomly occurring latent centers get intensified, the centers go in one direction or another, into either one zone or the other zone along the edge. In many cases, there are additional functional constraints which make it desirable for these "edge" centers to belong to the larger centers on both sides of the line.

In the meandering river shown in the photograph, the centers formed along the two banks of

the river have the river as a common edge. Gradually, as the history of the river develops, the centers shift. The centers which form on either side — both quiet places, and turbulent places in the stream — dig into and form an imbricated structure where the two parts of the land get spatially interlocked.

Very generally, along an edge which separates major centers, as minor centers along the edge get strengthened, they often swell in dimension, and penetrate more deeply into the zones of the two larger centers on either side of the edge. As a result of this process, centers are established which interpenetrate the larger centers, causing DEEP INTERLOCK. In those cases where the new centers may belong, functionally, to either one side or the other, the formation of the new centers will often also cause spatial AMBIGUITY.

9. CONTRAST. One result of a structure-preserving transformation is to give each center more distinctness, more differentiation from its surroundings. The differentiation can take many forms, but often requires opposition of contrasting polarities, either in density, or material, or charge, or color.

This effect can have surprising forcefulness. It is comparable to the process of leveling and

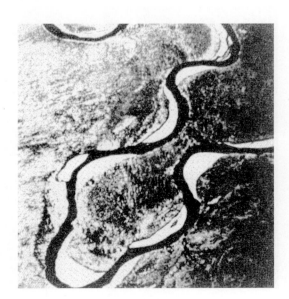

STRONG CENTERS *and* GOOD SHAPE *forming in the bending and winding of a river*

CONTRAST, *as it appears in the camouflage of a zebra's skin*

sharpening that occurs when we make a black and white xerox copy of a finely shaded photograph with gray tones. Differences get increased, so that the forms stand out more sharply.[9]

Increase of differentiation between peaks and valleys in an evolving mountain range is of this type; so are formations of the electric charge caused by differentiation of positive and negative; so are the differentiation of hard bone and soft tissue in a growing embryo. The process is so fundamental that it appears not only in obvious cases of polarity such as charge, but even in inexplicable cases of pure visual patterns like the zebra's coat. Technically, the patterning of the zebra's coat comes from growth diffusion mechanisms, under the control of genes. It has been claimed that this striping helps to camouflage the zebra in a shaded forest (where the zebra is protected from predators when seen against the striped pattern of light and dark falling through branches); also on the plains (where it is claimed that the stripes make the individual animal less distinguishable from the herd). But these evolutionary explanations are dubious and contradictory. What we can say for sure is that somehow the diffusion process autonomously causes a pattern of strongly contrasting pigmentation. Somehow the structure-preserving transformation starts with the weaker contrast of an earlier horse-like species, and intensifies it.

To accomplish CONTRAST, structure-preserving transformations increase the contrast of a pattern by intensifying both its internal differentiation and its differentiation from the surrounding environment.

10. GRADIENTS. When a center appears, the ongoing structure-preserving transformations do what they can to intensify that center. As a consequence, the space around the center will gradually be re-organized to include GRADIENTS of various kinds, which orient themselves toward that center, strengthening it by means of a field effect.

Above, for instance, we see a mountain where many simultaneous gradients exist from the lower slopes to the topmost peak: gradients of slope,

GRADIENTS *in the landscape and atmosphere around Mount Fuji*

temperature, ecology, climate, plant-life, geological differentiation, and density of plant and animal species. All these gradients, from the warm

GRADIENTS *in a spider's web*

lower levels in a mountain range to the higher altitudes, where peak, rock, snow, and air have a different character, help to support the centeredness of the mountain peak, and make the mountain stronger. Some of these gradients come from a very long time ago, geologically (gradients of physical slope, rock type). Others come about as a result of climate gradients consequent on the altitude. Others then follow, as a result of bioclimes and vegetal adaptation.

A spider's web starts at the middle. The spider works her way outward from the middle in a spiral. In each successive ring of thread, the total enclosed area of the web-cells is about equal and the threads get closer together, as the spider has to walk across radials that are further and further apart, and needs something to hang onto. We may also think of this as an area-based effect, because the spider can only straddle a "cell" of roughly fixed area when walking, thus creating a pattern with rough centers related by an inverse square law for the radial dimension as a function of distance from the middle. As a result, centers forming a gradient make their appearance in the space.

More generally, whenever there is a center, for different but vaguely similar reasons, the geometry of space is likely to induce phenomena that fall off with something like an inverse-square law from the middle simply because of the geometry of space, thus creating GRADIENTS. In supporting and strengthening the center, these inverse-square related gradients will develop, thus forming gradient phenomena. As a result we may expect to find a variety of graded phenomena following formation of any center, where field strengths of the GRADIENTS point toward the centers, so reinforcing and strengthening the existence of the center. Slowly gradients will make their appearance throughout the space, around many of the centers.

11. ROUGHNESS. As a system comes to order, the structure-preserving pressure to form centers — especially larger centers — will often refine boundaries, edges, shapes, and connections in unusual and *apparently* inelegant ways that look like

ROUGHNESS *developing in crystal growth*

inaccuracies. However, these apparent inaccuracies are a direct result of careful and highly subtle adaptations, that come about inevitably as a result of the structure-preserving process.

For example, in a system of growing crystals, the crystals take on different shapes and sizes. This is not only because of random fluctuations in the nutrient of the crystal growth but also because, as the large configuration emerges, in order to maintain the wholeness of the system in the large, more material is needed to fill in gaps in one spot while another spot is more crowded. To preserve the wholeness, ROUGHNESS and variations have to appear among the centers that the crystals form. To guarantee that the smaller centers really do work to form larger centers, the smaller ones are often made irregular, are syncopated in shape and arrangement, to fit the smaller centers smoothly into larger ones.

Slowly, in any structure-preserving process, ROUGHNESS always makes its appearance. Even among individual atoms, we see roughness. That is, we find imperfect similarity from one atom to the next within a crystal, even when the atoms are of the same type. Note, though, that ROUGHNESS is only an *apparent* irregularity. Really, it is a necessary feature, the outward sign of deeper order as larger centers are perfected.

12. ECHOES. In any system where there are structure-preserving transformations, it is nearly inevitable that the same process will be repeated, locally, through zones of the system. In addition, some processes will be repeated, but with minor modifications according to context.

In the weatherbeaten face of this old man, the lines and angles make a similar pattern all over his face. Centers are organized with a similar morphology. This comes from the structure-preserving process. The folds in his skin are made by a similar process in different parts of his face; each one, locally, is the same process, applied to a different bit of flesh and skin. What results?

ECHOES *in the lines of an old man's face*

ECHOES appear from point to point throughout his face.

This is quite general. In every structure-preserving process, we shall find a great many cases where similarities of process create similar systems of centers — hence structural similarities, or ECHOES of similar angles and shapes — which bear a family resemblance to one another in the different centers where they appear.

13. THE VOID. Part of the process of structure-preserving requires cleaning out from time to time, just as an orchard must be pruned. When a situation appears where there are too many centers, too crowded together, in a confusion of structure, a structure-preserving process must be applied to the situation, since the conglomeration of centers becomes so confused that it begins to undermine the coherence of the centers. That means the process must act to discern the deep structure, the most important structure beneath the confusion. This important structure must then be preserved and the rest cut away.

As a result, structure-preserving transformations frequently act to create THE VOID. As structure is preserved, the transformations act to preserve distinctness. One of the ways this happens most frequently, is that dense highly differentiated structure gets set off against empty, clean smooth structure, and distinctness is maintained,

We may also express this by saying that crowded complex structure often ends up living at the edge of a much larger homogeneous void, and that the contrast between the intricate structure and the vast emptiness is needed to maintain the structure of the intricacy. In one illustration, we see the formation of voids in the Great Barrier Reef as a natural counterpart to the formation of living structure around the voids.

A similar process occurs at cosmological dimensions. There are huge structures in the cosmos, containing dense filaments of galaxies hundreds of light years in length, and these filaments are formed around vast volumes of relative emptiness. Current models of the formation of struc-

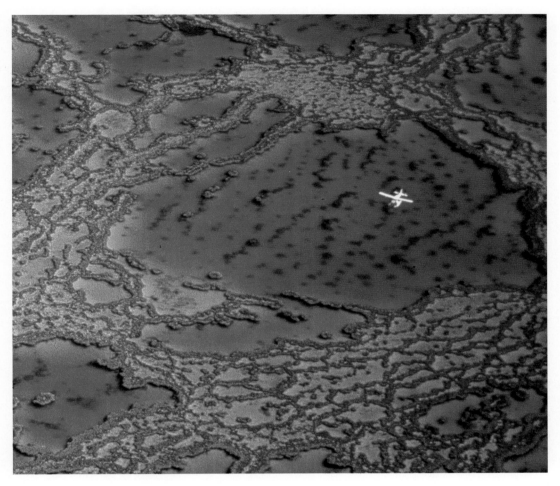

VOIDS *in the formation of the Great Barrier Reef*

ture in the early cosmos do not adequately explain the extent of these "empty" areas. However, the repeated application of structure-preserving transformations explains it as a result of the specialized symmetry operations that are needed to preserve structure in the unfolding whole.[10]

14. SIMPLICITY AND INNER CALM. As the cleaning out of irrelevant structure continues, centers will be further intensified by simplification. Slowly, a state appears in which nothing unnecessary remains present and in which all irrelevant or confusing centers that irritate the structure or reduce the value or importance of other centers are removed. This simplification occurs in nature constantly.

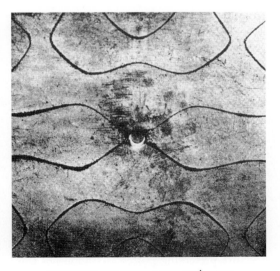

SIMPLICITY AND INNER CALM: *sand pattern left on a vibrating plate*

INNER CALM *in a Tuscan landscape*

For instance, in the shape of the Chladni figures formed in sand on a vibrating plate (page 75), the sand moves toward the still spots in the standing wave. The standing wave, under the impetus of structure-preserving transformations, must take the simplest form. Even when people act as part of nature, such a process continues: in the field in Tuscany shown in the photograph, the cypresses simplify and substantiate the meadow. All is made simple and calm. Irrelevant and confusing structure is removed. Only the essential structure is allowed to remain, in a kind of simplification that is reminiscent of Occam's razor.

The SIMPLICITY of the state comes about naturally as the result of the structure-preserving process.

15. NOT-SEPARATENESS. The more the structure-preserving works, the more it brings out the underlying unity which exists in any system. This unity is preserved, and intensified, by the structure-preserving action. Thus throughout, as the structure develops through its uncompleted forms, the pressure to unify, and unify continues, by creating links, by wrapping each center into a web of other centers, tying everything together.

It is worth understanding just how the structure-preserving process accomplishes this.

In the ecology of the lake edge (photograph, right), we see that the weeds, water, small creatures, bacteria, mud, and reeds in the shallow water create an unbroken tissue of organisms. Each part becomes wedded more firmly to the others. Exaggerated differences are eliminated.

In general, as the finishing touch to the structure-preserving process, small infill centers for fine-tuning are placed to create a pervasive sheet-like unity. Gradually, during this process, each part becomes inseparable from the others, allowing NOT-SEPARATENESS to appear.

NOT-SEPARATENESS *that has developed at the edge of a lake*

8 / FIFTEEN TRANSFORMATIONS

Let us now consider the fifteen properties, not merely as *results* of structure-preserving transformations, but *as the names of particular types of structure-preserving transformations themselves.*

Take, for example, LEVELS OF SCALE. We have seen in the previous section that levels of scale (viewed as a geometric property) will arise in a system naturally, as a result of structure-preserving transformations. We may, alternatively, think of LEVELS OF SCALE as a *transformation itself* which *introduces* levels of scale into a given structure. Thus, for any given structure, this transformation may be thought of as injecting into it, new centers which provide more beautifully articulated intermediate LEVELS OF SCALE. This transformation, whenever applied to a structure S_1, is likely to create a new structure S_2 that is a structure-preserving extension of S_1.

Similarly, LOCAL SYMMETRIES may be viewed as a transformation which injects local symmetry into emerging centers, strengthening weaker centers by injecting local symmetry into them. And BOUNDARIES may be thought of as a transformation applied to a structure S, which strengthens one or more centers in S by providing fat boundaries (themselves consisting of centers), to intensify and better define the coherence of the original centers. All three — LEVELS, SYMMETRIES, BOUNDARIES — are both property *and* transformation.

In general, all the geometric *properties* identified in Book I are also associated with dynamic *transformations* which will inject these geometric properties into the system of centers of any emerging, growing whole.

Let us consider in a little more detail, how the transformations work.

The LEVELS-OF-SCALE transformation introduces intermediate-sized centers to fill out the hierarchy of scales that exist in a given wholeness. In this case, some zone that has been loosely distinguished, is differentiated further into smaller parts. This can happen so that these new parts are similar in size to one another, but one level smaller than the center which is being differentiated. In another application of this transformation, a large center is made more coherent and distinct by the introduction of smaller parts, which then act together with the large center to form a recognizable and distinctive hierarchy.

The STRONG-CENTER transformation is the most fundamental transformation of all (and will be discussed further in chapter 7). Any weak center which exists is made more emphatic by this transformation. It may be more strongly differentiated, more strongly defined, more strongly integrated by virtue of its differences, or more sharply drawn and distinguished. Of course, all the transformations help, in some form, to achieve this fundamental goal. However, the transformation itself, in a primitive form, acts to give weight and definition and distinction and centeredness, to any weak center which has begun to crystallize in any given field.

The BOUNDARY transformation. Here the evolution of a given wholeness may take this form: First a zone of space is slightly different from its surroundings — a cloudy but distinctly differentiate zone with some "character" appears. How then, may this be further differentiated. One thing that can occur, is that the boundary transformation is applied. In this case, the zone (a ring zone, or spherical zone) becomes more distinct, and a thick boundary zone starts forming in a discernible way.

The ALTERNATING-REPETITION transformation generates a repeating pattern of similar entities, within a previously undifferentiated field. The way it works, though, it simultaneously generates a second pattern of repeating centers, interlocking and alternating with the first. This transformation is the most basic way that a large system may be given a structure as a repeating field of many repeating smaller entities.

The POSITIVE-SPACE transformation makes strong positive space by creating new centers in the space between other centers, thus strengthening and shaping spaces between the other centers that are not yet centers themselves. This is one of the most powerful of the fifteen transformations.

The GOOD-SHAPE transformation takes an existing center or system of centers (often formed by earlier application of the ALTERNATING-REPETITION transformation). The transformation intensifies the products of the alternating repetition, by strengthening them, making them more distinctive — and this is done by applying the GOOD-SHAPE transformation and POSITIVE-SPACE transformation in the weakly existing centers in such a way that any loosely formed shape which exists in the space, is made more marked, stronger, by giving more life to the centers within the shape. The effect is to make a more beautiful, more living, shape.

The LOCAL-SYMMETRY transformation strengthens a center (or system of centers) by making the center (or each center in the system) have an internal axis of symmetry. The symmetries induced are only local, and do not extend beyond the limits of the center, and may sometimes even be used only to strengthen or "symmetrize" the kernel of the center. This is often the way in which an emerging center first receives its strength. Shortly after an entity is differentiated and made to stand out from its ground the symmetry transformation then sets it up as a strong center in its own right.

The DEEP-INTERLOCK transformation takes an existing structure, especially in its boundary zones, and weaves the distinct opposing parts at the boundary into a tighter, less separated, union by physically creating connections in which part of one enters into the other, and vice versa. This imbrication of the boundary cements the whole (the structure plus its context); the transformation helps to unify the growing whole. It would be unusual for this transformation to happen at the outset of a differentiating process.

The CONTRAST transformation is a kind of sharpening which occurs. In a system where two types of centers occur the transformation works to increase the distinction between the two kinds; it separates them more sharply from one another, thus creating a field of more strongly contrasting entities. The contrast may be achieved by color, darkness, polarity, or by other physical characterics. The polarity of the two, generates a more well-knit system as a whole in which the two kinds of centers can complement each other better.

The GRADIENT transformation creates transitions of size and character. In response to an uneven, or non-homogeneous field, certain aspects of size, shape, weight, darkness, spacing, are made to vary systematically — thus introducing coherence of a new kind into an almost random-like field of structure. The gradient transformation thus begins to create structure where none was visible before. In other cases, a simple polarity or position, or axis, engenders a gradient, and the inner parts and centers are then given features which vary systematically according to this gradient. In this case the GRADIENT transformation can have a very large, global, field effect within an extended zone. It has a surprising ability to order complex and inchoate structure, without greatly bending or changing circumstance.

The ROUGHNESS transformation. In the course of making positive space, strong centers, local symmetries, or alternating repetition, it is often necessary to introduce or pack in irregular variants of repeating centers, to make things work out. The roughness transformation uses intentional irregularity to find the most regular fit possible for a given configuration, and one which permits things to work out successfully and simply in the large. It is of enormous importance. Wholeness would not be possible without it.

The ECHOES transformation applies procedures, angles, and shapes and shape-character of certain repeating centers to other centers in the field, thus generating a widespread family resemblance among different centers and so strongly unifying the whole.

The VOID transformation is at work getting rid of garbage. Areas which are relatively undifferentiated, and which do not need their differentiation, are cleaned out and made more homogeneous, and defined by a boundary zone which is attached, surrounded, by more differentiated structure. The transformation also preserves an imitation of the greater undifferentiated VOID.

The SIMPLICITY transformation, like the void transformation, also cleans, simplifies. However, it works by removing unwanted centers, differences, and other kinds of complexity, throughout the structure, where the void does it by creating a single homogeneous zone in one place. The simplicity transformation gets rid of unnecessary structure by reducing it.

The NOT-SEPARATENESS transformation may be thought of as a kind of knitting. In applying this transformation to an existing object or system of centers, modifications are made to the centers and their surroundings so that the center gains more of the subtle substance from its surroundings; and at the same time the surroundings gain more of the substance inherent in the center. The effect is that the two are brought closer together, forming a more indissoluble unity. All in all, the purpose of the transformation is to unify, to knit together, to create a texture in which the separateness of any given entity is reduced.

The way the NOT-SEPARATENESS transformation most typically works is somewhat similar to the effect of the color transformation called MUTUAL EMBEDDING (Book 4, chapter 7, page 192). When operating on two major areas, A and B, that are differentiated from one another, the transformation takes pieces of A and copies them inside B, and takes pieces of B and copies them within A. The result is that A and B become more associated, more allied, more united, and less distinct from one another. The not-separateness transformation may occur early or late in the differentiation of a structure. Essentially this transformation binds the entity which is being created and its surroundings more tightly. This may be accomplished by a variety of specific means including ECHOES, DEEP INTERLOCK, BOUNDARIES and so on. However, the overall unification of an entity and its surroundings, is a transformation in which the two distinct entities (a center and its context) are made more connected, more similar, more different, more interlocked, more reminiscent of each other, more complementary, more distinct, less distinct, and more united. The transformation stretches them apart and binds them together, making inside and outside less distinguishable.

Even under circumstances where the general principle of unfolding wholeness governs, what is it that makes these specific transformations occur? I do not know exactly how to answer this question. But loosely, one may compare it to the way that there are geometrical limits on the number of possible arrangements that can occur in space — as, for instance, in the limited number of different ways regular elements can be repeated to form crystals.

The inherent limitations of space have the effect that, for purely mathematical and geometrical reasons, there are only a certain small number of ways that a given wholeness can be extended, while preserving its essential structure. I have discussed this issue a number of times in Book 1, also in chapter 1 of this book. Although I cannot claim to give a rigorous proof that the fifteen transformations are the only ways to extend and conceive a given wholeness, I believe that this is true, and that a more sophisticated mathematical treatment will one day be able to show why it is true.

The fifteen transformations form a coherent system. We have in them, a limited palette of transformations which may be made to act on a given system. These are the fifteen most basic ways in which structure-preserving transformations can be made to occur. Every differentiating process is accomplished, in a structure-preserving way, by successive application of these fifteen transformations. The range of possible sequences and combinations, and the range of results which can be achieved by this type of differentiation, is amazingly rich and varied.

We see now that the fifteen properties are not merely observable end-products of structure-preserving transformations. They provide the base transformations from which, in practice, *all* structure-preserving transformations are made. The world of nature — what we think of as nature, and what we think of as natural (whether it is brought into being by the innocent operations of nature, or made carefully by the thoughts and hands of men and women) is that world which is brought into being by repeated application of these fifteen transformations, applied again and again, to enlarge, and deepen, and evolve, and magnify the beauty of the world which exists.[11]

We shall return to the subject of these transformations throughout this book, and especially in chapter 7 and in chapter 16.

9 / A NEW VIEW OF THE NATURAL WORLD

As wholeness unfolds under the fifteen structure-preserving transformations, these fifteen associated geometric properties necessarily appear more and more often, and more densely, while latent centers are progressively being differentiated and intensified. This is why the living structure appears in nature.

Living structure appears in the wholeness as a direct result of repeated unfolding. If the evolution of the natural world follows a step-by-step

Mountain landscape after millions of transformations

Detail of mountainside after millions of transformations

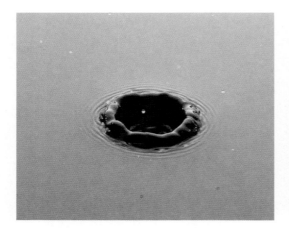 

Water drop splashing under the impact of the fifteen transformations

process in which each step is structure-preserving, it will then follow that the fifteen properties will appear more and more often, and that the life or degree of life in the wholeness will increase steadily.

This is true for an evolving waterdrop, as shown above. It is true for a mountain. Let us consider the existence and development of a mountain over eons. At any given moment, the mountain has a certain wholeness. This wholeness is the huge system of centers with their relative degrees of life. To make the description more complete, we add dynamics: the fact that the wholeness is changing and evolving in a systematic way with time. At any moment we have the wholeness of the mountain as it exists, and in addition, the mountain is subject to glacier movement, mud slides, erosion by wind and water, earthquake activity, plants growing, animals moving. Daily, as a result of these processes, the mountain undergoes change in shape. Let us try to understand these processes in terms of centers. The wholeness of the glacier sliding in the valley, includes the angle of slide, the rocks being crushed by the grinding motion, the flow of water coming out of the melting glacier, the eroded banks of the stream caused by the flow of water, and so on. All these features of the system inhere in systems of centers, and we can ascribe to each center a saliency according to its degree of coherence. The glacier itself exists as a center. So does

the moraine beneath it. So does the stream of water, and so do the eroded riverbanks.

As the mountain moves forward in time, old centers are preserved, new centers are generated, often in a way that intensifies the old centers. The structures of greatest coherence tend to preserve themselves in this action of the mountain. As the centers continue the process of helping one another in their wholeness, the mountain changes, and evolves.

To grasp the underlying nature of this process clearly and systematically, we need just the one assumption: *Throughout the process, centers will always tend to form in such a way as to preserve and enhance previous structure — and this means, in such a way as to help sustain other existing and emerging centers.* Mathematically, this structure-preserving process will then be embodied in the fifteen possible transformations I have described.

As the mountain follows the principle of unfolding wholeness, the fifteen transformations will be applied again and again, and as this happens the fifteen properties will show up again and again, simply because they emerge when an evolving system follows this law.[12] These are the geometric properties which arise in space when centers increase their centeredness by following a path in which they get intensified. If we remove our Cartesian blinders, that is exactly what we do observe.

Most of the time, the mountain — or equally, the star, frog, river, crystal — unfolds in a way which exhibits the fifteen properties more and more as centers get established, and as the centers help intensify each another. We get ALTERNATING REPETITION in the smaller valleys down the major valley. We get LEVELS OF SCALE in the different valleys, peaks, and rocks. We get STRONG CENTERS in the peaks and valleys. We get BOUNDARIES between the glacier and the valley floor. We get LOCAL SYMMETRIES in the peaks. We get POSITIVE SPACE in the valley spaces between the hills. We get ROUGHNESS developing within the local symmetries.

For every natural system which evolves, we see the fifteen properties developing as the trace of the system's evolution, a product of the field of centers' gradual intensification and of the action of the fifteen transformations. So the fifteen properties define not only the different ways a system can be whole, statically, but — as transformations — the various ways in which any system evolves naturally — *provided that it is allowed to become whole naturally, under the gradual rubbing together of its processes.* In any case, nature has these fifteen properties, and has the field of centers in it, because, at least for the most part, it demonstrates an undisturbed unfolding process in which each wholeness gives way to a next wholeness that is consistent with the previous one.

This, I believe, is an essential model which teaches us the real meaning of living structure, and which shows us these phenomena as naturally existing phenomena of beauty which will occur without effort *in any world where the wholeness is allowed to unfold smoothly and truthfully, without disturbing previously existing centers.*[13] Once this is clear, we shall then have a vision of the world in which the world itself — *all of it* — animals, plants, mountains, rivers, buildings, roads, terraces, rooms, and windows — is part of a single system and a single way of understanding.

10 / IN BUILDINGS, TOO, ALL LIVING STRUCTURE GROWS NATURALLY FROM STRUCTURE-PRESERVING TRANSFORMATIONS

In the world of building, specifically, this insight also has much to say. It means, too, that at each step forward the next step in an evolving building or in an evolving design, the system should (to preserve and generate a living character) do as much as possible to maintain the structure of the wholeness where it occurs, intact, and introduces the minimum new structure which is absolutely necessary, nothing more. The wholeness, then, can be preserved, enhanced, extended, and intensified. It is occasionally pruned and trimmed; and only very rarely destroyed altogether.

As we shall see next, this concept will greatly deepen our appreciation of human actions in the art of building.

During the past century we have been used to understanding value as a subjective, culturally influenced phenomenon which depends on private individual judgment. However, within the framework of wholeness, we may begin to conceive of value as an objective phenomenon which arises inevitably from the existence of the wholeness as a structure. Distinctions of value — the distinction between one thing which is more valuable, and another which is less valuable — come directly from the wholeness, and from the degree to which unfolding has been "truthful" — by that I mean, guided by the fifteen transformations I have identified as structure-preserving, and by combinations of these fifteen transformations.[14]

This is a startling and new conception of ethics and aesthetics. It describes good structure as a structure which has unfolded "well," through these transformations, without violating the structure that exists. The structure we know (from Book 1) as living structure, is just that kind of structure which has unfolded smoothly and naturally, arising step by step from what exists, preserving the structure of what exists, and allowing the "new" to grow in the most natural way as a development from the structure of "what is." This startling view provides us with a view of ethics and aesthetics that dignifies our respect for what exists, and treasures that which grows from this respect. It views with disfavor only that which emerges arbitrarily, without respect for what exists, and provides a vision of the world as a horn of shimmering plenty in which the "new" grows unceasingly from the structure that exists around us already. That this horn of plenty is inexhaustible, and that we may conceive an everlasting fountain of novelty without ever having to beat ourselves over the head for the sake of novelty per se — that may perhaps be one of the greatest potential legacies of this new view of the world.

NOTES

1. Living centers are defined in Book 1, chapter 4.

2. Although, like the judgment and perception of wholeness, accurate observation of this fact is highly dependent on the observer's degree of *awareness*.

3. Ian Stewart and Martin Golubitsky, FEARFUL SYMMETRY: IS GOD A GEOMETER? (Oxford: Blackwell, 1992), throughout, especially pp. 51–52.

4. Ibid., p. 13.

5. Ibid., pp. 20–21.

6. First introduced in Book 1, chapters 5, 6, and in chapter 1 of the present book, page 18.

7. Again, this hinges on points developed in Book 1. To see this in more detail, check back to the explanation of the fifteen properties in Book 1, chapter 5, pp. 143–242. These are the ways in which wholeness-enhancing transformations occur.

8. Another instance of the symmetry-breaking argument discussed on page 63.

9. This process of increasing differentiation has been extensively discussed in the literature on cognition as "leveling and sharpening." See, for instance, Christopher Alexander, "The Origin of Creative Power in Children," BRITISH JOURNAL OF AESTHETICS, Vol. 3, No. 2, July 1962, pp. 207–26, reprinted in Hilda Present Lewis, ed., ART FOR THE PREPRIMARY CHILD, Spring 1972, pp. 33–49.

10. Lee Smolin, THE LIFE OF THE COSMOS (New York: Oxford University Press, 1997).

11. A view of this process as a basis for ecology, coupled with the idea of structure-preserving transformations as the fundamental approach to ecological architecture and to man-made ecology is briefly discussed by Sim van der Ryn and Stuart Cowan, ECOLOGICAL DESIGN (Washington, D.C.: Island Press, 1995), p. 72. As Van der Ryn and Cowan describe it, a design works when it articulates new relationships that preserve the relevant ecological structure.

12. As I have suggested in chapter 1, I believe that the theory of structure-preserving transformations, and unfolding of wholeness to form new wholeness, is consistent with, and extends, catastrophe theory and bifurcation theory and helps to show how new living forms arise from complex dynamic systems in a fashion that is consistent with much recent mathematical thinking. However, the detail of a mathematical connection, showing how both theories are part of one, consistent picture, has yet to be determined.

13. See discussion of chapters 5, 6 and 7.

14. We shall see later that the differences of value we are familiar with in different cultures, or among individuals, all arise naturally as the result of different wholenesses which lead to different healing and development. In every case, what is good is simply the superposition of natural unfolding from one wholeness to another, repeated thousands upon thousands of times.

CHAPTER THREE

STRUCTURE-PRESERVING TRANSFORMATIONS IN TRADITIONAL SOCIETY

1 / INTRODUCTION: SMOOTH UNFOLDING AS THE ORIGIN OF LIFE IN BUILDINGS

Any part of the world we build will have life if it is created by structure-preserving transformations, and will not have life if it is not created by structure-preserving transformations.

This apparently simple statement, if true (as I have argued in chapters 1 and 2), has enormous repercussions.[1] The modern world we build, because its construction is driven by our attitudes about money, production, design, building, and planning, breaks from smooth unfolding at almost every stage. As a result, the processes which we presently have make it very difficult to create life in the world. Yet traditional building almost universally contained processes which, like nature itself, depended on structure-preserving smooth unfolding at every stage.

The absence of life we recognize as a familiar problem of the past century does not come about merely because modernistic design was ignorant of the structural principles expressed in Book 1. It comes about, far more profoundly, because the *processes* which create objects, artifacts, buildings, neighborhoods, agriculture, forests, towns, roads, bridges — nearly all fail to have the character of unfolding wholeness.

This means that even if we architects were to understand completely the living structure described in Book 1, and tried to put this structure into our designs, if we were nevertheless trying to get our buildings conceived, designed, and built by the social processes which currently exist — the buildings would still inevitably break life and could not have life. That is because it is, ultimately, the process, not the design, which gives life to a building.

Thus the issue of process is immense. In its impact on the quality of architecture, it is more important than the static structure of the designs.

2 / SMOOTH UNFOLDING IN THE TRADITIONAL WORLD OF BUILDING

Twenty years ago, in THE TIMELESS WAY OF BUILDING, I tried to explain the essential quality which existed in traditional society, and which allowed the buildings of traditional society to support life. From the perspective of this book, we may see the same points more deeply. However, many of the examples in THE TIMELESS WAY OF BUILDING are still valuable, and I suggest that the reader consult that book, if just for the photographs which showed a vanishing world and the existence of life in that world.[2]

Let us consider an example of traditional building: the construction of canoes in traditional Samoa. Traditional Samoan canoe builders sang a song which, line by line, told them what to do, in order to build their canoe. The song begins "First find your tree," and then goes on to describe, line by line, what must be done next — cut down the tree, strip the branches, hollow the trunk, shape the prow — all the way to the carving of the traditional ornaments which will appear on the canoe.

The design is not done on paper. The design emerges from the *process*, which is described, step by step. The organic nature of the finished canoe comes about as a result of the interaction of the simple steps, their nearly rigid sequence, and the impact they have on the emerging canoe, which becomes unique because of the uniqueness of the tree and of the builder who is making it.

Above all, this sequence is structure-preserving. At each step, the operation which is performed is designed to follow the emerging canoe, to induce new structure in it, in a way which preserves and continues what has been begun. Although what happens in any given canoe will always be unique, the process described in the song guarantees that the operation being performed always fits beautifully and naturally into the gestalt of the canoe, as far as it has been created so far. Structure is preserved. Centers multiply and grow. The whole becomes alive.

The tipis of the North American Plains Indians were built by a similar kind of process: The form is defined by, created by, the steps of the process. Long poles are made to lean against each other, their feet forming a rough circle on the ground. Where they cross, the poles are tied together. Skins are stretched over the weave of twigs and poles. A fire hole is shaped at the apex of the cone. Decoration is applied to the skins around the door. Again, this process defines the building. There is no design. The building arises from the process. Each tipi is unique because

Building a tipi among the Blackfeet: The form is defined by, created by, the steps of the process.

the process interacts differently with each reality (different site, saplings, weaving, skins, builder, weather at the time of erecting and so on)— but the tipi grows from a smooth process, and has its life because of the smoothness of the process.

In traditional society, processes of craft are almost always structure-preserving throughout their history. The weaving of a traditional carpet is done under conditions where each next step is based on the previous steps: at each step, the weaver looks at the wholeness, judges it, and makes a next step which extends the wholeness. The same is true of buildings. As I have observed earlier, the mode of perception typical of "primitive" people tends to be holistic. There is no motivation which will tend to make people fracture the wholeness at any stage. This is, in many ways, the type of process which has been called unconsciousness, or primitive. It takes the wholeness, continues it, enhances it, develops it.

On this page and the next, I show the evolution of a wall painting inside a traditional house

in Mali. The pattern is drawn out and painted, step by step. Obviously, it is not made from a blueprint, perfectly anticipated in advance. It is worked out in the situation, then painted and embellished, all stemming from the actual situation which presents itself, unfolding gradually step by step. This wall design is an almost perfect realization of structure-preserving transformations, unfolding gradually and creating a living structure in this room.

The pattern looks and feels almost like part of nature, because of the smooth unfolding and unpredicted character. Its details appear on the wall almost as a surprise, even though the general character is, of course, known in advance.

On the next two pages, I show a simple example of a medieval textile pattern which *itself* is generated following structure-preserving transformations and which is, therefore, wholeness-preserving and has life.[3] This design is *itself* created by a series of steps which preserve the wholeness of the earlier stage and enhance

Scratching in the design

Drawing out the design

The completed wall

it, develop it, and extend it. At the time this pattern was incorporated into a textile in the 15th century, this process was still the norm.

The loom I show below is the humble instrument used to create these structure-preserving transformations, and the great carpet on the facing page, from the Vienna Museum of Applied Arts, shows the magnificence of work which can be created by this simple process of unfolding.

On a larger scale, the same process applies to the making of traditional timber buildings. First the builder chooses the best place for the building. He steps out the foundation. The building is placed with regard to trees and slope and windbreaks. The foundation is built as an extension of the ground. The walls are built as extensions of a nearby mountain or a street. The roof and its overhang are built as an extension of the wall.

On page 92 we see one stage of this process of traditional carpentry: adzing logs and the log work which arises from this process. As with weaving a textile on a loom, each log is cut, shaped, and modified according to its position in the larger whole. The variety of detail work which follows in the carved and shaped logs, is lovely and almost endless. And, of course, we can see that buildings made like this have a natural quality: The fifteen properties come into existence in every log as a result of the adzing process, wholeness upon wholeness has emerged from wholeness. The process is step by step, slow, and not perfectly predictable. Above all, it allows

The process which creates the carpet

Step-by-step growth of a 15th-century textile pattern

The simple steps shown in the diagram, extended and extended: this magnificent carpet, woven in 16th-century Tabriz, shows how the simple and repeated application of the unfolding process can create a breathtaking beauty.

Felling a tree

Adzing logs

the maker to adapt each part, each board, each log, just as much as is needed to make them come out right.

One might say: but the shape of modern timbers, too, is determined by the modern lumber-milling process, just as ancient timbers were shaped by the process of the adze. But there is an enormous difference. The modern process leaves no room for feedback. The process goes on without regard for the character of each log and its position in a building. The traditional adzing process allows each timber to be hewn, shaped, and carved according to its place in the house. And there is constant feedback going on. With almost every stroke of the adze, or the carving tool, the carver looks at what he has done, judges it, checks it against the wholeness to see if it fits — and, as a result, he keeps the structure-preserving process on course. If it goes off course, even a hair, he steers it back again. None of this is possible with the process of a modern cutting mill or with the process of assembly which follows.

Doorway of a Swedish log house showing adzed logs

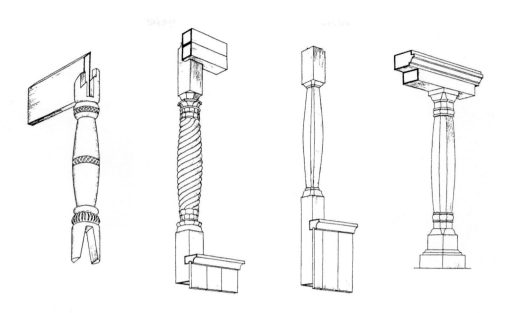

The forms of log adzing, still showing the effect of the adze

Traditional Norwegian doorway: subtlety and refinement of the log work

A Norwegian farm in winter. The buildings sit so close to the ground that they seem to be a part of it; the snow just runs around them.

These features of the traditional process allow the maker to create a lovely harmony within the building. In this case, the unfolding process has immediate practical results. Because the maker can allow each step to follow from the previous step, what he does is simple, well adapted, and profound. We see it and feel it in the constructed details.

In traditional building cultures, the same thing happens with the siting of a farm. Consider the following further example: a beautiful bit of grass and meadowland in Norway or in the Austrian alps. If a house is to be built on land such as that, it is well-made when it leaves the wholeness of the meadow unimpaired, intact. With a traditional Austrian farmhouse, we sense that it has left the wholeness undisturbed and beautiful, and has therefore even increased the beauty of the place. On the other hand, a tract-built house often disturbs the beauty of a mountain, kills its beauty, is wrongly placed on the

slope, and doesn't make sense with the existing stands of trees, contours, streams. We view a house as badly made if it disturbs or fragments the wholeness of the meadow. And this process continues. Once the house is built, the new configuration of the house and meadow has its own wholeness — different from what it was before. Sometime later, we build a fence. Once again,

An Austrian village where the beautiful step-by-step adapation of the houses to the land is very visible

Another Austrian village: again a typical traditional environment, which has grown by unfolding

we view the fence as well made if it leaves the wholeness of the house-meadow intact. We view the fence as badly made if it disturbs the wholeness of the house-meadow. The wholeness keeps on developing, step by step. In many cases, it evolves in a fashion which is comfortable and continuously preserves and extends the wholeness. In other cases, it evolves in a fashion which fragments and destroys the wholeness.

There are so many ways in which this simple process can be violated that it is a small miracle when it occurs unblemished, and, of course, in traditional societies it did not always unfold as perfectly as some of these examples may suggest.

But at its best, the process seeks to establish, step by step, how a building is to be sited, then formed, and then finished, under conditions which once again create a living whole. The essence of the process is that each step creates fine adaptation, creates a beautiful relation between what has gone before and what is being done. The building is created by attention.

In the doorway steps shown below (from Italy), we can almost see the trace of the process by which people lifted one stone at a time to make the stairs to their house, put the stones just where they wanted them, and stopped when the stairs were just right. The unfolding process allows — sustains — minute adaptation in every detail.

Here is a more complex example from Italy: a light-filled passage, made in stone and plaster. Again, the masons worked step by step, unfolding the whole, in such a way that the beautiful light fills the passage. In a modern process, the feedback that allowed such fine adjustment to be made would not have been there. This beauty of soft light could never have been produced in a set of drawings. But also, the love of the whole, the love of life, which is visible in this soft harmony, has been replaced by other attitudes — concentrating on design ideas, on concepts, not on the simple fact of the existing whole. Again, what led to this finely tuned harmony is the love and care which allowed the unfolding process to create this vault, step by step, until it was just right in every detail.

Consider larger buildings: the cathedral at Chartres, the Potala in Tibet, a Chinese palace. In cases like this, the building process sometimes lasted for hundreds of years. But even over such a long period, at each step there was respect for what existed in the land and for what had come before in the construction process. And the next step, most often tiny, then did everything it could to be harmonious and continuous with what had gone before. Sometimes, even a single step took years. For example, the design decisions taken in building the Duomo in Florence, layer by layer, including the unusual decision to place

These steps were worked into place and roughly smoothed, just where the builders wanted them, the size they wanted them, and the height they wanted them.

The size and shape of the archway and the soft light could never have been worked out so beautifully, if not by simply doing it, adjusting it, until it was just right.

round windows in the clerestory, took years — and involved hundreds of discussions, year after year, with the Florentine citizens.[4] When we look at the plan of Florence, the sequence of roads leading from the Ponte Vecchio, past the Duomo, to Brunelleschi's foundling hospital by the university, we can almost see, smell, reconstruct, the unfolding which happened over several hundred years to make this sequence. The process went on, not only spread out in time, but spread out and shared by hundreds of people, each doing his and her part to make the step-by-step adaptation happen, each person naturally a part of the unfolding process. Each step is structure-preserving. For reasons we shall discuss more fully in chapter 18, each builder, each family, does things almost without effort which make sense within the whole, which contribute to the whole, which extend, continue, and deepen, the wholeness which exists.

In the case of a big city — Prague, St. Petersburg, Kyoto, Cairo, Lhasa, Amsterdam — the result was that hundreds of millions of actions, taken one by one over several centuries, together created a living whole, because every step — at any rate, almost every step — was structure-preserving. The tradition told the builders *how* to do this, and told them that they *must* do this.

If we look at the evolution of traditional Amsterdam (page 99), we see how gradually the canals were formed, bridges were built to span (and thus enhance) the canals, edges were formed for the canals, houses were built one by one along the canals — all enhancing the canals — and slowly, over two or three hundred years, a wonderful living harmony was built.

And why did it work? Because, again, all or almost all the actions taken were structure-preserving, structure-enhancing. At every step, minute adaptation was occurring. Everything fit perfectly into the whole.

What is remarkable is that the structure-preserving process which goes on in the large scale — as we see from the evolving plan of Amsterdam, the entire structure of sea, land, canals,

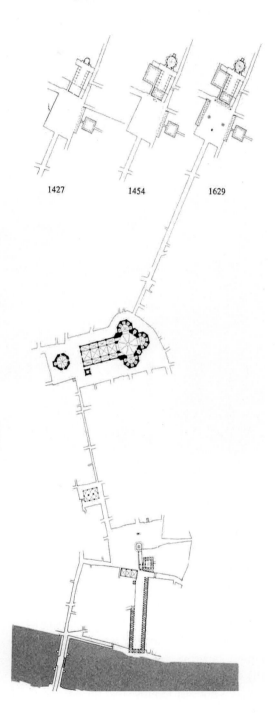

1427   1454   1629

The structure which appeared in Florence during the 13th to 15th centuries. We can see, from the character of this plan, how it has emerged from structure-preserving steps. In detail, we see it at the top, where the sequence of construction near Brunelleschi's foundling hospital is shown.

The cathedral in Florence arises out of the sea of houses, preserving, extending, even making heavenly, the structure that is already there.

and bridges — is accompanied by a parallel process which forms the streets and allows them to unfold. This, in turn, is followed, in parallel, by another process, in which the windows, doors, steps, buildings, flower boxes, and railings are unfolded too — all going forward in parallel — and leads, in the harmony which results, to the almost bursting joy we see in the skaters on the canal.

It is not easy to prove that the process which went on in a traditional town or in a traditional building was structure-preserving, but I believe it was.

It is true, too, that the very largest and most imposing structures were built by the unfolding process. In the houses along the canals of Am-

sterdam, you can see the impact of time. Each board, window, step, was added in enough time for it to be fitted perfectly for use. Thus the whole governed the position and shape of each board as it was added. We can see and feel the underlying sequence of unfolding. Just to look at the resulting structure, we can feel the sequence of what it must have taken to make it.

Imagine a process in which, at each step, some new center is created (or intensified), and that this center is already present weakly in the previously existing wholeness.[5] Under these conditions, what is done next always has a natural and comfortable relation to what existed before: it has a similar structure and never violates the previously existing structure.

98

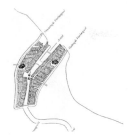

Amsterdam, 1400

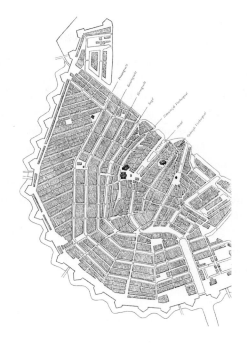

Amsterdam, 1600

Amsterdam, 1800

The city, and the fun of the people, grow out of the loving extension that every step has made.

What we get from such a process is a system of centers which is elaborated by other centers, in which, then, each center is connected upward, downward, and sideways to myriad other centers, in which the centers bolster and intensify one another. *What we get, then, is a particular kind of structure in which all the centers — gradually — take on this encrusted, densely structured character, of being made of other centers.*

And while this is going on — as in nature — the fifteen properties that give life to the emerging centers develop easily.

The Turkish tomb illustrated here, was plainly created by a center-making process, an unfolding, in which centers, large, small, and intermediate, were created steadily, one by one. And look at the structure this process created! Within the plan we see LEVELS OF SCALE; we see ALTERNATING REPETITION; we see BOUNDARIES; we see STRONG CENTERS; we see POSITIVE SPACE; we see THE VOID; we see DEEP INTERLOCK; we see LOCAL SYMMETRIES; we see GOOD SHAPE; we see NOT-SEPARATENESS. Comparing inside and outside, we see ECHOES, and CONTRAST is strongly visible

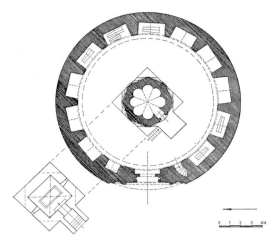

Plan 27. Tercan, Mausoleum of Mama Khātūn

The Mausoleum of Mam Khatun. The powerful geometry comes from the repeated application of the unfolding process.

throughout, in the pervasive contrast between solid and empty space. And in the center, especially, we see GOOD SHAPE and INNER CALM. Only GRADIENTS are not really visible here.

So, in this one tiny building, only a few feet across, fourteen out of the fifteen properties appear,

Kutahya, Imaret of Yakub Bey II. Powerful geometric forms, unfolded from the centers in the wholeness, and unfolded and unfolded until they become profound and powerful

Interior of the Church of the Transfiguration, Kizhi, Karelia, 1714

virtually without effort, as a result of the direct-ness of the unfolding which took place while it was being formed.

The beautiful, harmonious geometry — what to us seems like a miracle of design and thought — arises naturally and easily because the unfolding creates internal conditions in which the natural wholeness of space gives rise, through structure-preserving transformations, to a co-herent and harmonious whole.

This harmony results because of a state of mind in which the makers actually *see* the whole-

ness directly and accurately: that is, they see the system of centers that forms the wholeness. Once one sees these centers and not something else, the centers get intensified, get "dug-in" by the structure-preserving process, and even very pow-erful "design-like" geometric forms arise, as they have done in this tomb. Under other circum-stances, one would assume that such powerful ge-ometric forms have been designed. But the design is of the unfolded kind I have just explained, not a design born from a process of casually looking for forms on paper. The same is true in the other

The process of patching and plastering a Nubian house

stone-vaulted interior sharing the page with the tomb, and in the wooden interior shown on page 101. In both cases, again, it is the unfolding process, derived from the wholeness, which gives the power to the forms and the geometry.

In this process, the traditional town becomes a vibrant living thing. By the repeated application of the structure-preserving transformations, the environment is filled with the fifteen properties. And, in the vital and practical sense I have described in Book 1, this environment is then functionally and practically alive — alive in common-sense terms, alive in emotional terms. It makes people feel alive to be there. Plants and flowers bloom. Cows, dogs, horses, cats, fish, birds, and insects are all there in their well-

being. The air is fresh. The storm blows. The water runs. Shadows glide over the fields. Evening red light colors the bushes. Tiles crack. Plums fall on the ground.

All this — what appears as a romantic image of well-being — arises in that place because the process which has created it, and which creates it every day, is naturally structure-preserving at every step. Like the carpenter's shop in which every tool and every bench is placed just right, in which every tool is ready to hand because after decades of use it has been adapted perfectly, every nail to its position, the environment as a whole is perfectly and harmoniously adapted. It is not an elaborate thing. Just common sense, shaping every tiny part within the whole.

3 / LOVE OF LIFE

In order to make buildings by unfolding — hence by structure-preserving transformations — it is necessary, truly, to pay attention to the wholeness in the world. This "paying attention to the wholeness" is essentially synonymous with love of life.

After all, the wholeness — that wholeness which exists around us at a given place and time — is indeed the *whole*-ness. Paying attention to the wholeness means that a person is paying attention to the whole, to everything: to the life of water, other people, the thirst of a stranger, the stars in the black sky. It means paying attention to the emptiness of the desert, to the passion of an old woman sitting on her doorstep, to one's own passion, to the passions of the people all around, to the running of the water on the ground, to a banana skin on the ground, to

The love of the landscape — hedges, trees, and fields — makes it possible to grow these hedges,
just as they have to be, as an extension of the land.

the laughter of children, to the smells of dinner being cooked. It means loving the glistening white plaster on the wall, the subtle evening light. It means taking in the whole, enjoying it, seeing it all, bathing in it, *loving* it.

Of course, love in this sense does not enter in when nature blindly carries through its structure-preserving transformations. But *for a person*, doing a structure-preserving transformation means paying attention to all this, grasping it fully, taking it all in — loving it — and then extending it. For a person to become part of that wholeness, to extend it, love does — must — enter in.

And I believe one can state truly that in traditional society, the actions, step by step, and small adaptations which make up the structure-preserving transformations are indeed born of this awareness and love of everything around.

When a gardener plants a hedge as an extension of his land, it is in his love for the insects, cows, leaves, wind, rain, and grass that he makes this hedge, to extend the whole.

When Indians build an enormous platform, gazing across the valley at the mountains, it is the love of these mountains which forms their knowledge of the whole and makes it possible to build a porch and columns which truly extend the sweeping whole.

When the people of a Brazilian community in a favela — the poorest of the poor — leave an open space between their houses where children

The love of the distant mountains makes it possible to build this porch, with its tall columns, as an extension of the mountain land

Brazil: a favela in the hills above Rio de Janeiro. Even in this poor favela, it is the love of children and their life which makes it possible to allow this empty place between the miserable houses to survive and thrive and support the children playing. Is there any play as vigorous as this, in our cities today or in our suburbs? There is not, because the making of streets is not supported by the same intense love of the children's life.

can play, it is not just their poverty but love of the children, love of the children's games, appreciation of the child's reality which allow and encourage the preservation of this empty place — not distorted by the technicalities of planning rules or impositions of traffic. Poor as the favela is, this open place comes from structure-preserving transformations of that wholeness which includes the children, and preserves and

extends their love of children. We, in our sophistication, have lost that love — perhaps not in our hearts, but certainly in our technical willingness to allow the love of children to be overlaid with less important "necessities."

This Turkish family (page 106), sitting on their veranda and drying out and sorting their food — it is the love of their own life together, and love of the food, which allow them to build

To this Turkish family, sitting on the veranda, the love of daily life makes it possible to grasp the whole and build all the details which preserve and extend the structure of their daily actions.

and shape this veranda, step by step, as a proper celebration of their family reality.

Even in the biggest buildings of traditional society, it is this love of life — love of the whole — which manifests itself in the smallest actions. It is, then, this love of life which is em-bodied in the conception of a building, in its detail, in its execution — because the wholeness that people paid attention to really was the whole, really was *all* of life, and people were not ashamed or too frightened to respond to *all* of it in their actions as builders.[6]

NOTES

1. If, as I have argued, natural structures get their life only from the smooth unfolding of the wholeness, it must follow that structures we build also will have life if they are created by unfolding wholeness, and will not have life if they do not.

2. Christopher Alexander, THE TIMELESS WAY OF BUILDING (New York: Oxford University Press, 1979).

3. This textile pattern appears in a medieval Italian painting and is recorded by A. H. Christie, TRADITIONAL METHODS OF PATTERN DESIGNING (Oxford: Oxford University Press, 1910) reprinted as PATTERN DESIGN (New York: Dover, 1969). See E. H. Gombrich, THE SENSE OF ORDER: A STUDY IN THE PSYCHOLOGY OF DECORATIVE ART (Oxford: Phaidon, 1979), p. 80.

4. For a related matter, see the diagram of the 400-year growth of the Palazzo Publico, Siena, taking the building construction from the year 1284 to the year 1680, see Alexander, Ishikawa, Silverstein, Angel and Abrams, THE OREGON EXPERIMENT, p. 69.

5. To understand the practical content of the next paragraphs it may be helpful for the reader to look, once again, at the definition of wholeness as given in Book 1, appendices 1 and 2, DEFINITION OF THE WHOLENESS and A DETAILED EXAMPLE OF THE WHOLENESS, *W.*

6. However, it must also be said that it is not only a matter of love, since the wholeness is not so easy to see. For this, see once again Book 1, appendix 3, COGNITIVE DIFFICULTY OF SEEING WHOLENESS.

CHAPTER FOUR

STRUCTURE-DESTROYING TRANSFORMATIONS IN MODERN SOCIETY THE FAILURE OF UNFOLDING

1 / WHY ALL PROCESSES DO NOT CREATE LIFE

Is *every* building process a process of unfolding wholeness? Is the creation of order, or life, in buildings and in towns *inevitable*? Does the life, the deep wholeness formed by the fifteen properties, appear mechanically, and inevitably, as a result of *any* building process?

Evidently not!

Let us recapitulate what happens in a system when it evolves under the rule that the wholeness is preserved and intensified: at each step, some center is developed to become more complex. This means that additional centers may be formed to support it. The centers inherent in the wholeness W_1 at time t_1 are extended, strengthened, and developed to make a new stronger wholeness W_2 at time t_2. We have observed, already, that there are only about fifteen ways in which new centers can strengthen or preserve the centers which exist. Thus the structure-enhancing transformations which occur as W unfolds keep on creating these fifteen properties. This will happen so long as the structure keeps on evolving under the rule that the next state $W_{(n+1)}$ at time $t_{(n+1)}$ is a deeper wholeness than the wholeness W_n which existed at time t_n.

I have argued that in the absence of any interference this unfolding — and the consequent increase of order — will tend to keep on happening in nature. Whether we are in the realm of physical particles, or hydrodynamics, or biology, the wholeness does indeed keep on getting preserved, mainly because there is no way, in the normal operation of the laws of physics, that this structure can be destroyed even when it is being transformed. Even death and destruction, *as they occur in nature*, are still structure-preserving processes. Although they destroy particular configurations, they most often preserve and continue and extend the *whole*.

In traditional societies, the building process often followed the natural process rather closely. Wholeness was preserved and extended by the

actions people followed in then-accepted building process.

But in human society, it is not *guaranteed* that building actions will be wholeness-preserving. This aspect of building is by no means automatic. From the moment that human beings appear on earth, the unfolding of the world is potentially governed by an entirely different principle. Humans guide their actions according to a mental "picture" of the situation, according to schemata, rules, images, and ideas.[1] Because people make things according to such conceptual *pictures* of what we *wish* to do, each moment in the unfolding of a given place, the next step in the unfolding of the world at any given locus, is now governed by those images.

The images, or schemata, which people use to guide their actions may be wholeness-preserving, or they may not be. Governed by images, building processes are therefore capable of being of such a nature that they increase and extend existing wholeness. Governed by schemata, building processes are also quite capable of being of such a nature that they pay no attention to existing wholeness. Sadly, what we architects most often did in the 20th century did not pay attention to existing wholeness.

Thus, although traditional society did often manage to sustain an unfolding process like nature, modern society has almost lost the knack. For a variety of reasons, in modern society the rules of the game — the schemata and images — have become more and more willful, more rule-bound, less and less in touch with the wholeness that exists, and the procedures, too, the everyday processes through which buildings and the world are made, lost the essential features which made them able to create living structure.

In traditional times, people had a world-picture which was in one way or another consistent with the wholeness. But in modern times, this is no longer true. Often the conceptual picture a person has of the reality in a particular place is an invented convention, or an image, sometimes even a willful invention, thought up, and then carried out. But as I have explained in chapter 3, and in appendix 3 of Book 1, such conventions and images and inventions can too easily be at odds, with the wholeness that exists. In many cases it is even difficult for people of our age to *see* the wholeness as it is.[2]

Thus the world has entered a new phase. What is made, what is built now, what develops in the world, is governed by images and rules. It is no longer automatically governed by the existing wholeness. It is now governed by what we decide.

Many of the buildings in this chapter are structure-destroying in their internal geometry, just as surely as this freeway, built through downtown Providence, destroyed the structure and fabric of that community.

2 / INTERIOR STRUCTURE OF BUILDINGS

I would like to emphasize that the problem of structure-destroying transformations applies to the relation which a building has with the world around it: a successful living structure will only come about when the building enhances, and supports the wholeness which exists in the world around it, and thus contributes to a growing fabric of urban space and beautiful protected land. Obviously that has not been happening, in recent years, and it must now be our first concern.

At the same time, the process of design and construction we architects have been following has almost equally drastic negative effects on the *interiors* of the building designs we have created. The process has become so bad, that the internal components of our buildings — rooms, walls, plan, structure, and details — are not structure-preserving even within the fabric of the emerging and created buildings themselves — so that the great majority of modern buildings have the character of being awkward assemblies of unrelated components and parts, and altogether lack the necessary structure to make buildings coherent, living, as designs in themselves.

Ugliness and loss of structure-preserving transformations in two pseudo-traditional buildings, Arundel, England. The buildings on these pages are structure-destroying to themselves, in their internal geometry, just as surely as the freeway built through downtown Providence (page 109) destroyed the structure and fabric of that community. These buildings do not preserve the structure of their surroundings; nor of their own substance.

The structure-destroying aspects of the building process within the building designs we have been making is almost more drastic than the first, larger kind of structure destruction of the world beyond the buildings. It is more invisible, and harder to understand. It is comparatively easy to see that cutting a freeway through a coherent urban area, is a destructive act. It is much harder to understand that the prefabricated balconies on the mass-produced buildings of recent decades, or the willful shapes of much modernist high design, are equally structure-destroying when seen in the context of the building form itself. Yet what we call bad design or harsh, unfeeling architecture, comes about precisely when the design and construction go forward in this clumsy manner.

In the pages of this chapter I shall try to draw attention to these two problems, equally.

The highly repetitive structural scheme makes no adaptation to the location of the structural bays, or to relative closeness to the ground. A structure-preserving process would reflect the structure at each place in the building, as a function of the position and condition of that particular place, thus creating an organic structure.

Here the buildings do not respond to one another, each part fails to grow out of its context, instead we have atomic assemblies, conceived conceptually, in isolation. Although the designer would argue that there is an over-riding design scheme, which relates the buildings to one another, it is superficial. The larger windows, visible in three nearly identical locations, do not grow naturally out of a circumstance that existed in the unfolding process; rather they reflect the designers attempt to compensate for a lack of true living structure, with a designed image that looks like the real thing, but is not. Its falseness is very easily visible.

3 / THE ADVENT OF STRUCTURE-DESTROYING TRANSFORMATIONS TO THE MODERN WORLD

Consider the famous case of Algiers. The structure of the town of Algiers, up until about 1940, was informal and highly organized in the loose way shown in the plan on this page and in the photographs that follow. Then the French government introduced a huge band of high-rise apartment buildings, right through the middle of the most beautiful part of the town. This new construction, supported by Le Corbusier's master plan, was really like a giant slash through the town. It preserved no structure, destroyed hundreds of thousands of living centers. But more than that, the new centers which were created are not related to any aspect of the land, the sea, the town.

The three important centers at the sea front: were the Sea Palace, the Old Mosque, and the Turkish Mosque. Thought of as jewels by the people of Algiers, they formed a natural triangle, and a structure-preserving transformation would have connected them, upheld them, in-

tensified them, and allowed them to become focal points of the changing modern city of Algiers. But instead, they were essentially wiped out, ignored, and the plan which was adopted is the one shown on the next page.

In that plan, the casbah, too, the rambling, complex morphological structure shown on page 114, was slashed, ignored, and overwhelmed by something that preserves and extends none of its structure.

This process, occurring between 1940 and 1980, was almost an archetype of a sequence of structure-destroying transformations. It occurred because the French government, working with then too-brutal images of architecture, could persuade themselves that this was the "right" thing to do, that it was in the interests of architecture and society. In other words, the concepts (in this case, those of our "modern movement" in architecture as of about 1940) seemed to justify the wild slashing of the previous structure.

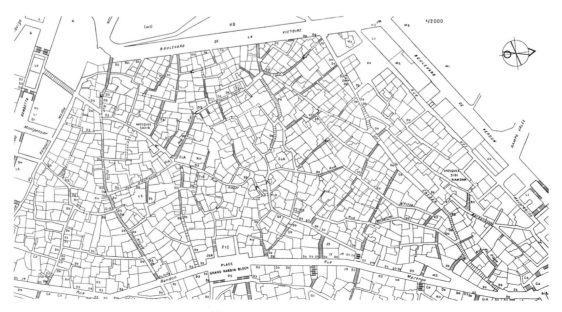

The structure of Algiers as it was

The sea front of old Algiers

What is perhaps more mild and more accurate to say that under the mental spell of these concepts, people in Algiers — administrators, government officials, and so on — became confused about the wholeness which was really there, became indifferent to it, perhaps could no longer even see it. Failing to see it, then of course they did not act according to it. Their ability to make accurate structure-preserving transformations largely disappeared. The capacity to make life was then largely gone.

We may also see the arrival of the same structure-destroying process as it was in Algiers, and in nearly every other place on earth, in a number of other ways.

By the middle of the 20th century, modern planning departments were rigidly organized bureaucracies, in which clerks behind the plan-

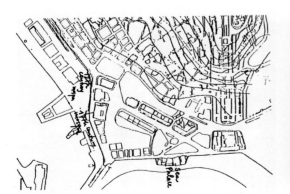 

Map of the three focal points along the old sea front: the Sea Palace, the Old Mosque and the Turkish Mosque. These were the primary centers which should have been extended, but were not (Left). The Sea Palace (Right)

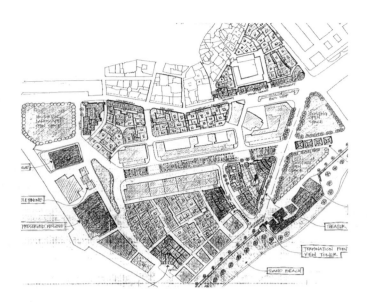

The structure destroyed, as the planners wanted it to be

ning desk had to follow rigid rules in giving or withholding permission for new building projects. These departments were almost always understaffed and were often overworked. A project which, at a single stroke, created several thousand new dwellings, in an apparently simple set of rectangles, was a planner's dream. It reduced work and, indeed, for the poor staff of an over-

worked planning department, made immense practical sense. After dealing with one set of drawings, for three thousand dwellings, their quota for a whole year was done. Imagine the difficulty, by contrast, in applying planning rules to three thousand separate houses, also in a year: to do it, the planners would have had to process (completely) more than eight per day — some-

Old Algiers before 1940: the casbah

Old Algiers before 1940: the Old Mosque

The beginning of the slash: preparation for high construction destroys Algiers.

thing virtually impossible according to the rules and regulations they had to follow. So, understaffed and forced to adhere to a certain set of procedures, the planners were strongly biased toward the gigantic, because it made life possible for them.

There was no conspiracy here. Just a set of procedures which were introduced, with the advent of modern bureaucratic society, with almost total ignorance as to their unintended consequences. Many planning departments, the world over, still suffer from this problem today.

Banks, too, were heavily involved. So were socially inspired efforts to create good housing for working people. Governments sought to create housing by methods which would provide

The slash completed: structure destroyed

bank loans and low-rent apartments. A process of building gradually, with available money (typical in traditional society), was replaced by a process in which buildings were financed with bank loans, thus requiring immediate payback of the interest and capital. This process is the same in a socialist economy, where the government pays back the loan, as it is in a capitalist economy, where private investors pay back the loan but also hope to make further profit. Paying back the loan becomes the underlying process, and the buildings which are created become artifacts charged mainly with the achievement of the loan.

4 / OTHER EXAMPLES OF STRUCTURE-DESTROYING TRANSFORMATIONS

So, from a scientific standpoint, one would have to say that after several thousand years, the traditional building process, which had been capable of creating living structure because it rested on unfolding, and on a process in which people's actions were consistent with nature, was — historically — a temporary state of the world.

With the arrival of the modern age, about 1900, the situation changed decisively. For many reasons, the processes that came into use, and are still in common use today, permit, encourage — in many cases, even force on us — a variety of building processes which are *not* structure-preserving. Some are accidentally structure-destroying, caused by the fluctuating character of modern society. Some are based on rules which have to be followed by functionaries in highly mechanized institutions (banks, planning departments, construction companies, and so on) but which fail to encourage (or most often even to allow) adaptation to subtle circumstances of wholeness. Others are worse, and actively promote ugliness in the search for profit. Of course, greed is not new. But the late 20th-century search for profit took place under an entirely new set of conditions — that is, under conditions which were more likely to be structure-destroying than greed used to be, in Roman times, say, or in the medieval era.

Above all, the decisions about plans and design became based on institutions, procedures, concepts, theories, and ideas that were most often at odds with the wholeness that exists. Transportation has its own theories, and ways of calculating. Development has its pressures. Insurance forces rigid forms of exit and entrance on buildings. Building regulations force narrowly defined acceptable staircases. Methods of production force a type of mechanical imposition of grid-like arrangements on building shape. And, of course, there are a variety of pressures — from banking, industry, and other modern social institutions — which cut across the unfolding process more generally, and do not allow it to be structure-preserving.

Indeed, most of them are not based on awareness of wholeness as a real structure in any respect at all. As I have observed, modern people are, very often, not holistic perceivers. Instead of seeing the wholeness and acting on it, they (especially if they are educated in verbal concepts at modern institutions) now perceive according to invented categories, which often blind them to the wholeness which exists.

The existence of structure-destroying transformations as a norm in society, instead of structure-preserving transformations, is thus in part also linked to a breakdown in the perception of wholeness itself.

Consider the following example from a town in southern California. A certain neighborhood in Pasadena, as it was about 1960, had wide sidewalks, green trees and lawns, nicely plastered

Mass-produced housing, anywhere, and nowhere, 1970

Mass-produced housing, anywhere, and nowhere, 1970

Mass-produced housing, anywhere, and nowhere, 1970

two-story houses. Now imagine a condominium built in this neighborhood, with parking at ground level and the building in the air above the parking. The asphalt of the parking lot covered the ground floor. In the normal mode of perception that existed in the mid-20th century, a person might have viewed such a new condominium with disappointment; even so, that person would have felt obliged to accept it. She would have thought of it as "only her opinion" that the condominium was ugly, and was doing damage to the neighborhood.

However, once people learn to recognize that the wholeness in the neighborhood is an actual structure which really exists, their reaction is more informed, and they may be able to see this kind of event quite differently and, in this instance, as structure-destroying. They become aware of the particular wholeness of this city of Pasadena, with its wide sidewalks, green trees, and plastered two-story houses, *as an objectively existing structure*. The wholeness includes lines of trees along the street: there are centers of space, formed by the

lines of trees and front yards, as long as a city block, parallel to the street. Beyond these large centers of space, there are front lawns and hedges, which cooperate to form other large chunks of space, which in turn cooperate with the biggest ones to form the particular character of Pasadena.

There are quite specific centers which make up this wholeness. A condominium set over a parking lot destroys these centers for a distance of several hundred feet around. The centers induced by the parking lot under the building seep outward, and capture the street. They interrupt the centers formed by the trees. They disturb the rhythmic repetition of deep front gardens. Other acts of construction, differently designed, may protect the wholeness of the neighborhood if they leave the largest and strongest centers intact. For instance, a new building with a front lawn will tend to do so. Another building of the right height, with a beautiful garden in front, harmonious in character with the other buildings and with the sidewalks and trees, also helps to sustain the wholeness.

Pasadena: a street with beautiful trees, and a definite wholeness formed by the trees and sidewalks

This example of the condominium in Pasadena is commonplace enough. We experience the environment ravaged, in similar fashion, by subtle destruction of wholeness thousands of times a year. It is not only the creation of arbitrary, greedy office blocks, hotels, and housing developments which distort and harm the land. The processes are also *internally* structure-destroying, as we see in the next examples.

Look, for instance, at the two bridges illustrated on page 120: one is the Sydney Harbor bridge; the other the Sakura bridge in Japan.

An old Pasadena courtyard that opens naturally off the street, preserving its wholeness and its harmony (Left). Pasadena street, the structure of its wholeness destroyed by a condominium over parking garages. This condominium, with parking underneath and rooms above, destroys the structure of the street, and spoils the neighborhood. The structure-destroying transformation is not merely bad design. It destroys the wholeness that is there. Serious damage is caused to the street, and to the neighborhood.

The Sydney Harbor bridge

One feels strongly that the Sydney Harbor bridge is somehow consistent with its surroundings, and extends and enlarges them. The ship, the harbor, the city buildings, and the water: the bridge looks as if it grew out of them, is part of them. It continues the structure which they create, thus unifies and cements the world.

Japanese bridge over the Sumida river: structure-destroying.

The Sakura bridge, over the Sumida river, Tokyo, on the other hand, is more featureless: it has a peculiarly abstract relation to the water and to the banks on either side. The photograph looks almost like a model, it is so lacking in detail, or in detailed adaptation to specific circumstances around it. The bridge does not extend the world, or cement its unity, or make it more living. Above all, the centers which it creates have no origin in the landscape, or in the banks on either side of the water. It almost seems to have been made on a whim, by someone trying to be inventive. Certainly it does not grow naturally out of the situation. So this second (as it happens, more modern) bridge, built about 1985, is more structure-destroying than the Sydney Harbor bridge, built about 1935.

The differences between these not dissimilar examples are perhaps slight. We begin to learn, in this more subtle example, to see shades of distinction which make it easier to focus on what is more structure-*destroying*, and what is more structure-*preserving*. Becoming aware of such shades of distinction gives a realism and

Here the tract forms a disconnected island in the desert, utterly remote from the beauty of the barren mountains, from the brown desert sand. In color, position, character, morphology, it is separate and structure-destroying.

subtlety of discrimination to our judgments and makes the matter more interesting and more real.

Mass construction of tracts, like the one shown on the previous page, provides a further example of structure-destroying process, when viewed in relation to the natural terrain. In the example shown here, the developer-island in the desert stands in stark contrast to the subtle and beautiful morphology of the desert sand and desert mountains. The particular repetition of the tract, if one looks at it carefully, is entirely different from the repetition and qualities inherent in the mountains or in the desert sand. It cuts across them, does not nourish, or protect, or continue in a beautiful way the structure which nature has begun.

And there is a further sense in which such planned communities, and indeed nearly all developer-built artificial communities, are based on structure-destroying transformations. This comes not from their failure to be consistent with the land where they are built, but merely from the fact that they are planned *at all*, rather than "grown."

To understand this, it is necessary to think about the natural growth of a community. Consider a new piece of land. Say for the sake of argument that someone has made a master plan for this land. But instead of implementing the master plan, let us assume that half a dozen houses are built there where people feel like building them. The people live there. A particular small path to a beach becomes a favorite route. A small bar sets up on a corner. Work begins on an accessible corner of land and some light manufacturing occurs there. Already these humble beginnings cause a series of flows and vectors in the land, which — if allowed — would naturally govern the placing of the next houses. But the position of these "natural" houses and roads will be entirely different from the "planned" arrangement proposed by the master plan. The plan already differs. If we repeat the "natural" process, shops will occur in places quite different from the ones on the plan; roads will have different locations, gardens will

flourish in positions where the land bears fruit (not on the locations of the master plan); others will fade. Slowly a community arises, naturally. Being structure-preserving, each step of development grows from the actuality and living process of the previous stage. The result is an entirely different structure from the one portrayed in the plan.

But what we see in the photograph on page 121, is a master plan carried out and built without regard for such a gradual, adaptive, structure-preserving process — indeed, without the benefit of such a process. It is only the structure-preserving process which lets the plan become complex, well adapted, and alive. The rigidly executed plan is bound to end up dead.

The next example is equally instructive. On the top of the following page is a picture of a Brazilian community, near the Amazon. At the bottom of the page is a picture of a new town, also on the Amazon. Superficially they are similar. Both are on the Amazon, both have a radial form (one circular, one semi-circular). In theory, they could be similar. But the upper example is structure-preserving, and has been made by an unfolding process. The lower is structure-destroying, and was not made by an unfolding process.

What is going on? Why, and in what detailed respects, is the lower one structure-destroying and the upper one structure-preserving?

Consider the upper. The green Amazonian landscape is left where it is, the radial paths leave it and are related to it. The wheel is imperfect; it is united with the slight undulations of the land. The houses at the ends of the spokes are structure-preserving to the wheel. The core is structure-preserving to the community. The geometry itself arises naturally, and keeps itself intact.

Now consider the lower. The radial form is imposed. It has no immediate emotional meaning, and does not arise from an emotional core. It comes from a concept in a planner's mind, not as a structure-preserving gesture toward the river. The river landscape is not left intact, or

Amazon rain forest village: this circle is structure-preserving to the rain forest.

enhanced. The half wheel turns its back on it. The edge of the river, one of the primary centers in the landscape before this town was planned, has not been enhanced. Indeed, the form of the half circle reduces the importance of the river edge as a center. In this specific sense again, it is structure-destroying.

Now, perhaps, you may begin to see how very profound the idea of structure-preserving transformations really is, and how deeply subtle it is as a principle, if we were to seek to adhere to it. The wholeness, though objectively present, is a very subtle structure. Adhering to the wholeness, and extending it, are *very* subtle processes.

Another Brazilian settlement, on the banks of the Rio Branco. Here the same circular forms (now half circles) are not structure-preserving. They are a formalist intrusion into the landscape, without a natural relation to the river or to the town community.

5 / EXAMPLES OF STRUCTURE-DESTROYING TRANSFORMATIONS IN INDIVIDUAL BUILDINGS

The negative character of structure-destroying process which occurs commonly in planned communities has a far less obvious, but far more extensive impact on the world through the interior geometry of individual buildings.

Let us examine this picture of a stucco bank building, recently built in Southern California. What we may see in this building — as in so many individual buildings of modern times — is that it is not true to its own parts, is structure-destroying to its *own* structure, at odds with its *own* structure.

This may take some explaining. I want first to remind you, from chapter 3, that each thing, each building, at any given moment has its own wholeness — that is, the configuration of centers which exist in it, which create its gestalt, its morphology, its organization as a whole. It is perfectly possible, then, for some feature of a building to be at odds with another, for one feature to cut across the existence of some other feature. The building illustrated here has big rounded corners, for example. But these rounded corners are at odds with the existence of the building, and with its wholeness. The building is after all made of two plane walls meeting at right angles on a street corner. And inside the building, indeed inside this very corner, there are rooms. Both inside and outside the wall, then, there is a natural wholeness which is "corner-like."

A corner, formed by the meeting of two planes at right angles, generates a naturally occurring system of centers defined by local symmetries. For example, there is a pronounced axis along the corner itself; there are tangent planes outside the corner which occur, latent in the

Conventional stucco bank building from southern California. Here the geometry is meaningless. Unlike the Turkish tomb on page 125, here the centers, such as they are, have not arisen naturally from the wholeness and its centers: they have merely been superimposed on the lath and plaster by the willful pencil of the architect.

space; there are convex squarish tubes of space on the inside of the corner. All these are latent in the space. Any structure-preserving process will, to a large extent preserve these latent centers. But to make a curve which squashes the corner into a curved plane, destroys nearly all these latent centers and introduces other quite different ones. It is in this precise sense that a round corner on such a building made of plane walls at a corner of a block, violates and destroys structure. To round the corners in the fashion this designer has done is therefore at odds with the most basic nature of the building.

We may see this vividly, and more widely, if we imagine the sequence of steps (decisions) which the designer made while conceiving this building. It is not hard to imagine that the entire sequence will have been structure-destroying, one step after the next.

Let us ask ourselves what must have happened to create this form. Most important, looking at the form, we do not see in it a step-by-step process — a trace of a way in which each part was adapted to the other parts. The entrance, for example, is not well adapted to the street. That is because there was no moment at any time in the process of designing and building it, that the position, size, height, and surface of the entrance were unfolded — that is, shaped from knowledge of its position on the street itself. Instead, this building was (quite clearly) designed on a drawing board. Since unfolding did not occur, the building's entrance does not work.

The same thing may be said about the windows. These windows were not placed by a person who became aware of the light, the view outside, the rooms inside, and then placed them, sized them in just such a way as to enhance the wholeness which was there. Instead, once again, these dark windows high up in the building are conceptual, unrelated to the wholeness which is there. Because they were not unfolded, they do not work.

The same is true of the base of the building. The base of the building — in a sense there is none — did not arise as part of an unfolding process from the land that was there before, which then became extended by the new structure that was to be there. Again, the base is a thought — like thin paper — not a reality which has grown from the actual situation. And once again, because of this, it does not work. It is probably vulnerable to water penetration. It is probably not very strong in earthquake or against cracking. Certainly it is not a place where plants can grow. It is not a place where a person can be comfortable, sitting or leaning or standing against the wall. *The lack of unfolding not only makes the building ugly; it also makes sure that it does not work.*

But there is an even more basic problem. The geometry itself, the form of this bank building, is harsh and ugly, too. This has arisen because the sequences of operations which led first to the conception of the building (its design), and then to its construction, were themselves — all of them, one step at a time — structure-destroying. Indeed, such a building is the end-product of a long history of structure-destroying transformations. That is what we intuitively recoil from.

In the plan of the Turkish tomb which I showed before, and have shown again here, the forms have unfolded naturally from the wholeness. It is this which makes the fifteen properties pervasive in the plan. The empty space has, natu-

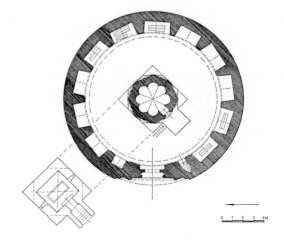

The Turkish tomb again. The powerful, even grave, geometry comes from the repeated application of the structure-preserving process itself to the latent symmetries of empty space; hence the traditional simplicity and depth.

Common land of a huge new French housing project. It has the appearance of community, as a diagram, but in the details, in the people, their bodies, the atmosphere, we see, smell, sense the desolation that exists. This desolation is a direct result of structure-destroying transformations in the design and construction process.

rally latent within it, the repetition of centers, the rhythms of regularity and symmetry, lying undeveloped and nearly invisible. As the structure-preserving process went to work on this homogeneous symmetry-laden round space, the familiar forms of traditional architecture appeared, inevitably.

In the bank building, no such process happened. The forms did not unfold from gradual intensification of the latent centers and symmetries in empty space. They came — I am afraid we must conclude — from artifice, from invented creations in the designer's mind. And it is this lack of congruence with the nature of space which ultimately is the mark of its ugliness, and of its environment-destroying nature.

Consider the further examples of buildings shown here and the next pages. We see things that are similar. The geometry is stark, harsh, not well adapted to itself internally. Again and again, this comes about from a failure of un-

folding, and from a procedure (during the design stage) which must have been structure-destroying.

Look at the Marriott hotel in San Francisco. The geometry is so contrived that it does not even arise, naturally, from itself. In a purely geometric sense, this geometry could not have arisen as a result of a sequence of unfolding operations (even on the drawing board). It has been "created," with intent, to be as interesting as possible. All naturalness of unfolding is gone from its form, and from its detail.

Of course, this geometric awkwardness, what one might even call horribleness, has practical consequences, too. Consider, for example, a contemporary building process which establishes a certain apartment within an apartment building in a certain location. It has a given envelope; a given entrance; a given height. Does the process then continue to make that envelope, height, entrance, as beautiful as possible? Typi-

Marriott Hotel, San Francisco, built about 1990: a form so much at odds with itself that it can allow almost no relationships to occur, internally or externally.

most beautiful light, but merely where it happens to appear on the drawings. Yet the process of designing and then building this apartment, is not one which can correct these mistakes. Indeed, the concept that the internal plan of the apartment may be mistaken is not even legitimate in our contemporary or normal thinking about the architecture of development and building apartment buildings. The apartment building simply has its plan. The building official stamps it. The general contractor builds it. And it appears on the earth, not as a result of a steady series of slow, sensible adaptations, but as an arbitrary accident which appears all at once, with no opportunity for correction or common sense. It is for this reason that the finished apartment is unloved; there is no geranium by the door, no occasion for it, no opportunity for it.

Look at the ground floor of the Japanese building complex at the bottom of this page. It gets its form, again, from the drawings. But again this form did not unfold gradually, smoothly, one step at a time. It simply appeared in the mind of the creator, was transferred to paper, worked out, and then built.

And the same is true of its construction details. The top of a traditional brick wall, whose coping stone appears sensibly and naturally as a result of the process of building the wall, protects the wall from damp and frost. It forms an edge,

cally, it does not. Nor does it make the apartment work as a living space. The entrance passage does not make any profound sense with the location of the entrance. The main room of the apartment is not oriented toward the view, or toward the

Japanese building, postmodern era. Again, a geometry at odds with itself. It looks smooth, peaceful. But that is a facade; the building cannot support life, because the process that created it has not allowed the form, and place, to unfold.

a seat, a top. It arises naturally and gradually. But the wall and floor of this place are quite different. They have inclined planes, strange spaces. These inclines and spaces have not arisen as a natural step in any sensible process. They simply appear as a result of an idea — or perhaps, more accurately, a whim — in the mind of the architect. I feel sorry to have to say this about an architect. But these features have not appeared as steps in a series of structure-preserving transformations. There has been no smoothly flowing emergence of a whole. The building jumps, abruptly, suddenly, into existence, without sense, without merit, without opportunity for criticism, without opportunity for correction.

Many designs which we now consider "modern" have the character that they *could* not, under any circumstances, have arisen as a result of a structure-preserving, step-by-step process. They can be created when conceived on paper. They are conceptual. But in their abstractness, they are barren, not of flesh, and they could not possibly have been created as a result of an authentic process of unfolding.

What this means is not only that these buildings have the familiar ugliness of so much modern design. Most often, they also do not *work*. Being conceptual — not based on step-by-step application of practical reality — they do not fit practical human needs; they do not fit gradually and softly into the harmony of the world which envelops them. They stand, awkward, unrelated to all that is around them. And this is to be expected, simply because they have not been created by an unfolding process.

Inevitably, they do not work.

6 / SOME SYMPATHY FOR THE ARCHITECTS WHO MADE THESE THINGS

I do not, directly, blame all the architects who have made these buildings in so many places on the earth. I believe it is inappropriate to feel anger toward them — though one certainly may feel it from time to time because of the destruction of so much that is beautiful.

Rather, I believe we must acknowledge that the architects (often our own colleagues) who drew these buildings, and then had them built by methods and processes far from their control, deserve our sympathy for being placed in an impossible position. What has caused the new tradition of structure-destroying forms of this era, are mainly the machine-like processes of planning, conceiving, budgeting, developing, construction contracting, construction labor, and so forth. The architects who fully accepted the modern machine have hardly been more than pawns in the game which is much larger than they are.

However, even with sympathy, I do not think one can avoid the realization that many ar-chitects have been sucked into a cooperation with the structure-destroying program of modern society, very much as if we were the advance-men, the ad-men, paid to make a series of unworkable social forms palatable to people by making something inherently bad seem glamorous. After all, it was we architects who invented such slogans as "the house is a machine for living in" and the "spirit of the age" to provide artistic justification for the new machine-linked kind of building process.

And the kind of architecture created in the past century — whether by the modernists from 1930 to 1960, or by the postmodernists from 1970 to the 1990s — did serve the inherently machine-like production process which existed during those years. Engaged in the process, we architects covered up its defects, made it seem palatable, made it seem — even if only marginally — acceptable. Yet that production process which we justified and which many people came to believe in is inherently incapable of creating life.

It is unfortunate that many of us — instead of standing against this production process, and trying to create a workable and life-creating process — instead chose to stand with the money and the jobs, becoming spokesmen and propagandists for the problem.

7 / THE THRALL OF IMAGES

During the 20th century, the negative impact of our profession on human life did not stop quite there. It is true that architects took part in — and enthusiastically embraced — the structure-destroying transformations which became normal in the second half of the 20th century. We even became apologists for these destructive transformations. But our profession — architecture itself — then added a special quality that exacerbated the situation. This came about with the onset of images. Images in the 20th century had a unique power, where image became divorced from reality, and often more important than reality. Among architects, photographs of buildings in magazines became more important than the buildings themselves.[3] Buildings were judged — at least by members of our own profession — more by the way they looked in magazines, than by the satisfaction people felt when using them.[4]

Worst of all, one might say that because of the new role of images in society, many of us began to believe our own propaganda. The images we created in support of the overall unworkable system of structure-destroying transformations began to have an authority of their own, began to form the backbone of an accepted style. These were at first the images of Le Corbusier and Mies van der Rohe; then images of Archigram; more recently the images of such architects as Daniel Libeskind, Ricardo Bofil, Mario Botta, Peter Eisenmann, Michael Graves, and Renzo Piano.[5]

These images were highly destructive. As a result of the fame of such architects younger architects then wanted to be like that, too, and perpetuated this style of work, with all its inher-

ent life-destroying qualities. Yet it all came from images, hardly ever from life.

Through the ideas distributed by these images, gross defects of the production system became embodied (and enshrined) in the architectural establishment, creating images which are inherently impossible to get by unfolding, and (perversely) fixing these as the target of our aims as architects. In the last part of the 20th century this process, supported by schools of architecture, created a generation of young architects who were — by their predilections and by training — virtually unable to understand a life-creating production process.

To understand the perversity of the images which were so widely distributed, it is necessary to look carefully at what an unfolding process does when it is being applied successfully to the design of buildings. The essence of the successful unfolding is that form develops step by step, and that the building as a whole then emerges, coherent, organized. The success of this process depends, always, on sequence.[6] A building design can unfold successfully only when its features "crystallize out" in a proper order. In order to be successful, each step of the unfolding creates new form that preserves the wholeness of the previously unfolded form, yet is rooted in common sense so that simple realities are adhered to. Land, sun, rooms, structure, all take their shape, step by step, in a coherent and well-adapted manner that guarantees living structure to the emerging whole.[7]

The essence, in all cases of unfolding, is common sense. You want to make a house. At each moment, you ask yourself, What is the most important thing I have to do next, which will have the best effect on the life of the house? Then you do it. I am looking at the front door, and I ask myself how I would like to walk from the street to the front door. Then I make the steps in the right place. I look at the windows in the living room, and I ask myself, What is the way I would like to make the windows, so that they give the room most life? When I make the terrace outside the house, I stand there, trying to imagine which kind of enclosure for the terrace will make me most comfortable. Once I understand the answer, then I build it.

It goes on like that. It is not complicated, not pretentious, but simple and obvious. It is just common sense.

But this common sense, and above all the structure-preserving character of unfolding, is deeper than it seems. A student once asked me if one could equally well illustrate the results of unfolding with pictures drawn from the works of Le Corbusier. Could you, in fact, create the designs of Mies van der Rohe, Botta, Le Corbusier by the same process? The answer is that you could *not*.

The essential point is this. Suppose you *do* start with an *idea* of a building — as Mies, Le Corbusier, Botta all typically did. All of them started with a certain idea, a certain *image*. Imagine, then, that at the time of starting a house design in this fashion, as they did, you also start with an image or idea in your mind. Let us say, merely for the sake of concreteness, imagine that you start with the image of a cylindrical house (for example) like the house illustrated on the next page. Now you start an unfolding process, a structure-preserving process, *on the site*, carrying this image in your mind. If you do really and truly follow the wholeness of land, site, and emerging building, and allow the wholeness to unfold — then, gradually, each part of the initial (and arbitrary) image will slowly give way to common sense: that is, to reality, to the wholeness of what is there, rather than to the idea of it you carry in your image. Slowly, then, your image of the position of the cylinder will give way to an

understanding of what the *site* says about position and distribution of volume in relation to slopes, trees, view, access, and privacy. Your image of the building volume will give way to what the *site* tells you about the most appropriate volume, something harmonious with the contour of the land. Your image of the height will gradually give way to what *the site and the emerging volume* say about the height. Gradually, slowly, step by step, every part of the preformed "image" will dissolve, because reality — and common sense — will lead to something different. Finally, even the windows, the window details, the very steps, walls, wall caps, and window sills — will all crumble from whatever form they had in the image, and will give way to something which is determined by the unfolding of the whole. The position, the volume, the height, the position of the door, the height of the floor off the grade, the probable positions of windows, roof shape, and so on, will then have been determined by realistic adaptation, and by emerging common-sense understanding of what is needed and of what is there.

As we conduct this thought-experiment, we are led to a shocking conclusion. It turns out that the images of Le Corbusier, Mies, Botta, and others like them *cannot*, IN PRINCIPLE, *be created by an unfolding process*. Anything that starts with an imposed image, if then taken step by step through an unfolding process, will change — often drastically — as it unfolds. If you truly follow unfolding (and structure-preserving transformations) at every step, features of the design based on an extraneous image will not survive. In other words, many of the buildings we have inherited as icons of the modern movement are arbitrary, and do not — deeply — make sense at all. The wrongness of their form — of so many of the buildings of the 20th century, and including, in many cases, famous buildings of Le Corbusier, Mies van der Rohe, Botta, Graves, and so on — becomes apparent in the fact that they cannot be generated by an unfolding process.

Cylindrical house by Botta. This cannot be produced by an unfolding process. It is controlled by an image, which would dissolve if taken step by step through a sequence of structure-preserving transformations.

The question asking whether an unfolding process might (in theory) be used to generate them, is fascinating, *because the unworkable character of this suggestion goes to the very root of the subject of wholeness and life*, and to the profound defects in modern architecture. When we look carefully at the reason why one could not get the cylindrical house of Botta, for example, by an unfolding (and structure-preserving) process, it all comes down, in the end, to the fact that to keep this arbitrary cylinder as the house form, you would have to follow a path in which you are *not* moving forward step-by-step on the basis of the existing wholeness. Instead, you are leaping to a complete form (probably at odds with the environment) without any possibility of life-giving adaptations: and you have to maintain this arbitrary form, rigidly, in the face of common sense. When you do embrace steps that might otherwise be structure-preserving steps, preserving the

land, entrance path, best daylight in the rooms, and almost every other practical matter or matter based on human feeling, you go in one direction, the direction of life; but to keep the image, instead you have to go all at once, from beginning to end, on the basis of an *idea*.

As I have tried to explain earlier, it is just the appearance of images in human thought which first deflects the natural unfolding process, distorts it, destroys it, and begins to create ugliness. Here we come across the very same issue from a different point of view. A natural process goes step by step from one wholeness to the next, according to the natural unfolding. But the use of images invents structure which can run contrary to what is, imposes it "across" the grain of what is real. This is precisely what causes the destruction.

Looked at from this perspective, the much-hailed "great" works of architecture of the early

20th century were hardly better than questionable nonsense, seriously inadequate if looked at as living structure. The famous works of Mies van der Rohe and Le Corbusier and Louis Kahn came about precisely because of the *intentional* nature of the thought which created them, and the not-unfolded nature of the thought. It is this intentional nature — the presence of arbitrary idea and image — which distorts the process, makes it not-unfolding, makes it contrived.

What I mean is that an unfolding process never runs at cross-purposes with the structure that exists, and is always consistent with the deep structure that exists. An unfolding process, by its nature, produces things that are alive. The image-driven process, by its nature, produces things which are dead.

An unfolding process *could not, in principle*, produce the works of Botta, or Mies, or Le Corbusier. And that is why life cannot be achieved through the philosophy, or process, or images which these architects — the once revered forefathers of modern architecture — and others like them created during the 20th century.

Let us break to reconsider the early years of modern design, the style of the architecture of the last sixty years. The core of the modern design movement — a striving for originality, newness, a breaking with tradition — was fundamentally a structure-destroying force which denied us the real processes of unfolding that create living structure. Thus, of necessity, in the architecture of the late 20th century, in order to make buildings, within the framework of this structure-destroying process, many of us architects, perhaps without realizing it, lived in a world of fake, taught by fake, worked by fake, and transmitted the fake as an essential part of what we did.

This evolution began with Le Corbusier and Mies van der Rohe. It was continued by Frank Lloyd Wright in his last works, the Guggenheim Museum and the high-rise Oklahoma tower, where he abandoned his search for living building, and opened the door to the start of image-architecture. More intense image-production was then taken up by the so-called New York "whites" such as Gwathmey, and followed by fully postmodern works like the Lloyds' building in London, and by Farrell in his enormous image constructions of the late 20th century.

Wright did, I believe, use an unfolding process in his earlier works — especially in the great

The arbitrariness of modern design is quite visible here: this structure has not unfolded from any natural sequence. It has been thought out, consciously and arbitrarily, as an image. Luis Barragan, The Fountain of the Lovers.

Le Corbusier, The Marseille Block

Le Corbusier, La Tourette

Frank Lloyd Wright, Guggenheim Museum, exterior

Frank Lloyd Wright, Guggenheim Museum, interior

prairie houses and Unity temple; and including, too, several large buildings such as the Johnson Wax office building. His later buildings, like the Guggenheim Museum, came about by a more image-driven process. The Guggenheim Museum turns its back on Fifth Avenue, stands in disconnected isolation, a beautiful shape, conceived as an image, not by structure-preserving transformations, violating the fabric of Fifth Avenue that existed there.

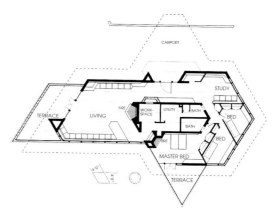

Frank Lloyd Wright, Don M. Stromquist residence, Bountiful, Utah

Le Corbusier's Chandigarh, the Pregnant Oyster in London (near Hammersmith flyover), the works of the later 20th century followed, with few exceptions, the image-driven process. The process of structure-destroying transformations throughout society, outside buildings and inside buildings, reached absurd levels of celebration and acceptance.

8 / MASS-PRODUCED BUILDING AND CITY FORM

Sadly, the image-conscious abstraction of the most outrageous architect-designed buildings of the 20th century soon became an excuse for accepting commercial non-architect buildings that shared the same character not because of willfulness, but only because the process which created them lacked the self-correcting benefits of slow unfolding and adaptation.

The lack of reality which appeared in a broad cross-section of "high" and "artistic" architecture of the mid-20th century provided justification, validation, and therefore an intensification of mass-production and mass-modern planning, where the images driving egocentric building design often arise, for rather different reasons, in the most common building and planning of our late 20th century — thus completing the circle of cause and effect.

Let us look back at the examples of housing projects which I showed earlier in the chapter. They are typical of apartments all over the world, very high density, cheaply built, damaging to the street, damaging to live in, people packed in like sardines, and damn the consequences.

What we have here are projects created by a certain set of processes, procedures, which were taken as normal during the 20th century. A public-housing authority designed low-cost useful buildings; let them to a contractor; and got them built — again, by definition, a process in which unfolding cannot occur. In such a process, most of the kinds of steps which are needed for unfolding are impossible — not (this time) because anyone *wanted* to exclude them for image reasons — but because the practical methods of modern procedure just *did* not include them.

Indeed, people can hardly conceive a modern process which has living features. And the efforts of high-style architects, creating lifeless images and what they considered as élan, were often used to justify the continuation of these development procedures. In these cases we do not have the ego of an architect to blame. Many of these mass buildings which shaped the 20th-century world were almost innocent. Some were made by idealists in the housing department of socialist countries. Others were made by developers trying to make a living, and trying to provide housing for a capitalist context. The two look almost the same.

In both cases, the processes which generated the buildings from start to finish were different from an unfolding process, and therefore created results unlike the coherent, organic, living structures that were needed and are possible.

Of course, there is some relationship between the images of the professional architect, and the greed of the capitalist developer. Indeed, one might say that the very *idea* of city images, or plans, and the very idea of city planning as an activity, is itself inherently at odds with the idea of unfolding, and at odds with the idea of the land giving rise gradually, and of its own accord, to natural extended city form. The modern developments we know too well, associated with huge sums of money, and with vast profits in the hands of developers, necessarily *depend* on images — because it is the images which first draw investors, and then potential buyers, to the land. Thus, the very core of the financial process that fuels urban development is consistent with the ideology of 20th-century developers, and at odds with the organic harmony of towns and land.

9 / CONCLUSION

In a living system what is to be always grows out of what is, supports it, extends its structure smoothly and continuously, elaborates new form — sometimes startling new form — but without ever violating the structure which exists.

When this rule is violated, as it was, far too often, in 20th-century development, chaos emerges. A kind of cancer occurs. Harm is done. All in all modern society succeeded, in the last century, in creating an ethos where buildings, plans, objects . . . are judged only by themselves, and not by the extent to which they enhance and support the world. This means that nature has been damaged, because it is ignored and trampled upon. It means that ancient parts of towns and cities have been trampled, because the modernist view saw no need to respect them, to protect them.

But even more fundamental, it came about because the idea of creativity which became the norm assumed that it is creative to make things that are unrelated (sometimes disoriented and disconnected just in order to be new), and that this is valuable — where in fact it is merely stupid, and represents a misunderstanding, a deep misapprehension of how things are. Creativity comes about when we discover the new within a structure already latent in the present. It is our respect for what is that leads us to the most beautiful discoveries. In art as in architecture, our most intelligent and most wonderful creations come about, when we draw them out as extensions and enhancements of what exists already.

The denial of this point of view, is the chief way in which 20th-century development destroyed the surface of the Earth.

NOTES

1. The idea that human events and social processes are governed by schemata — that is, by images, rules, concepts — has been widely discussed in anthropology, experimental psychology, and cognitive psychology. In psychology, it was pioneered by Frederick Bartlett. In art history, Ernst Gombrich also described this approach to art and building, in ART AND ILLUSION (London: Phaidon, 1960). It is recognized — indeed is nearly axiomatic — as the basis for all anthropology. People have a fairly simple way of acting, based on rules and schemata — and they follow these rules. See discussion of chapter 15, endnote 1. For reasons which are only now becoming clear, the rules a given society follows may be tuned to the proper and successful evolution of a living whole, or they may not be.

2. Book 1, appendix 3: COGNITIVE DIFFICULTY OF SEEING WHOLENESS.

3. During the late 1970s, a number of authors began shining light on the absurdity of modern architecture: Tom Wolfe, FROM THE BAUHAUS TO OUR HOUSE, and Peter Blake, FORM FOLLOWS FIASCO, were two of them.

4. The London journalist Mira Bar Hillel, writing in the LONDON EVENING STANDARD, has published studies in which, remarkably, it was shown that less than 50% of buildings designed by architects in England during the decade 1980–1990, were visited by their architects after completion and occupancy. That reveals, succinctly, our professional lack of concern for practical success in our own buildings.

5. These are all architects once well known in different decades of the 20th century. If I am right about my views, and a more sane approach to building does prevail, many of these names will in all likelihood be forgotten in the future.

6. See chapter 7, THE FUNDAMENTAL PROCESS, and chapter 11, THE SEQUENCE OF UNFOLDING.

7. One example of such a process, useful for illustration, and looked at in detail from beginning to end, is presented in the appendix of this book. Others, at different scales, are presented in Book 3. Yet others, taken from the contemporary unfolding of the modern world, are given on pages 137–74.

INTERLUDE

INSPIRING MODERN CASES WHERE
UNFOLDING DID OCCUR

Passionately, I love the modern era. I loved the 20th century, and I love what I have lived, so far, of the 21st. People sometimes ask me whether I would rather live in another era, and I always answer, unhesitatingly, "No, I like this time best." I would choose no other.

My joy at a life spent in California, riding the freeways, and the intense inellectual and social freedom and excitement, knows few bounds. Even the commercial strip gives me a kind of joy, because it reflects human desire: in a perverted form, yes. But it is still essentially human. Of course the destruction of the earth which we have witnessed is discouraging, without a doubt: and one cannot avoid acknowledging the fact that as a people and as a civilization we have caused much destruction. However, that by itself does not mean that everything is wrong with our era, or that we should turn our backs on it. If we are honest, we can still love what we are, we can find all the good there is to find, and we may find ways to enhance that good, and to find a new kind of living world which is appropriate for our time.

Since I feel so strongly about this, I have, as a counterpoint to the pessimisim of chapter 4, written this next chapter which extols the beauty of our era. I mean it as a source of inspiration, and as a source of hope. And I mean it, too, to be instructive, to show us that perhaps we have been looking in the wrong direction, and at the wrong examples.

Very bluntly stated, we may have forgotten to look for real life as it occurs today, all around us, because we have been too obsessed by the dead sales-images created by corporations, by architects, by planners and developers. We may even have lost sight of the real goodness of life in our everyday experience, because television and magazine images of what is "good" have taken hold of our minds too deeply, and made us forget what is close to us.

The examples which follow are intended to remind us what real life is in its more modern forms, as it exists around us now. I ask you to reflect on the examples I show in the next pages. These examples can teach us a more constructive attitude to what life is, and to what living structure is when it exists around us NOW. *I want to refresh the reader with some inspiring (and sometimes surprising) examples of this special life, which show the marvelous character of living structure that is* POSSIBLE *in our glorious present time.*

This can be an antidote to facile images, and can provide a starting point from which we may examine the reality of living process with a fresh mind.

CHAPTER FIVE

EXAMPLES OF LIVING PROCESS IN THE MODERN ERA

1 / THE WONDROUS CHARACTER OF LIFE
IN MODERN TIMES

Matisse and his birds. The life of this moment was not created by design. It was created by the result of small processes and their results—moving a cage, letting the birds out, drawing the bird, and so on. Such life could never be caused by conscious "design," only by a living process.

During the discussion of chapters 3 and 4, I drew a sharp distinction between the structure-preserving processes common in traditional societies and the rampant structure-destroying transformations common in our own era. This sharp comparison was useful for ease of comprehension.

But of course, not all buildings or all places built in the 20th century were lifeless. I will complete part one, the first group of chapters, by describing, now, the peculiar, special kind of life that is characteristic of our modern era. It is a love of life surviving in the smoke and ugliness and music of our time, drawing on the mass clothes and radios and computers; drawing on the informal shirtsleeve era that has entered our hearts with the American experiment throughout the modern world; drawing on the raucous and soft nature-loving urban motion of our era.

There is a passionate and wondrous feeling to be found in the activities of our age, sometimes in places hidden away, and found, surprisingly, all over the world today, as, in the midst of poverty and pain, people find a new freedom and a new opportunity to be themselves, and to take their own adventures.

The life which seems best, in our world, is that life which comes from efforts that are uncensored, natural and straightforward, from impulses close to our emotions, our sense of joy and freedom, and close to people's everyday, inner emotions and to our unsupported and peculiarly vulnerable human heart.

It is this which I hope you will see in the examples of this chapter, and which you will — I hope — be willing to accept as an illustration of what we should try to find when we approach true life in our time, most closely.

2 / A WIDE RANGE
OF STRUCTURE-PRESERVING PROCESSES
AND LIVING PROCESSES

In all the following examples, an emerging new architecture is visible. All the examples share a certain *character*. They are generally rather unassuming, not too image-conscious, yet profound

The soul of our future architecture: house interior, Sri-Lanka, by Geoffrey Bawa

and moving. They are not especially glamorous or glitzy in their substance. Often, they are ordinary. Occasionally, they tend toward the archaic. Some are unpretentious, rough — one might say, even raw. Yet at the same time many have a beautiful geometric coherence. This coherence is visible in two photographs of work by Geoffrey Bawa. It is visible, too, in the photograph of Matisse drawing his birds while the birds, in their freedom, sit on the cage. This is the kind of ease and life-based coherence which I regard as the seed of our future architecture.

House interior, Sri-Lanka, by Geoffrey Bawa

The photograph on this page and that on page 141 show the interior of Geoffrey Bawa's own house, built slowly over many years, mainly during the 1970s. One feels, in these pictures, something graceful, and beautiful. I would judge from the photograph that especially the light, but also the care in every single thing, and every part, even the finish of the plaster on the stair, mattered to him, and he took care with each tiny part of it, perhaps slowly thinking it and working it, for years.

The process used, I think, was very straightforward:

· *Keep on gradually making the whole slowly.*
· *Work at each thing until you like it.*
· *Concentrate on beauty of the light.*
· *Repeat this, over and over again.*

In most of the following examples, the rough steps of the generating process are shown in italics, line by line, each line preceded by a dot.

LOWER MANHATTAN ISLAND

Large events in cities often preserve structure. The palm trees planted along the sea front at Nice preserve the structure of the edge between the buildings and azure sea. The blinking advertisements at Piccadilly Circus preserve, and support, the hectic character of the traffic which whirls and stops and noises there. In the case of Manhattan, the taller buildings at the crossroads of the streets and avenues preserve and intensify the structure of centers latent in the grid. Which part of the process was structure-preserving, and which was not? The placing of the grid on the land, in the first place, was not structure-preserving. However, being homogeneous, it did less harm to the land than some other more artificial configuration might have done. Once given the grid, the process allowed unfolding to occur. There were no restrictions to the individual buildings — in the early days not even height constraints. Feedback came from the fact that each owner's building reacted to the configuration of the others.

The process in which major streets became avenues (with the up-and-down flow of traffic heavier than crosstown traffic) forms STRONG CENTERS; the process by which buildings are built to the fill the blocks (POSITIVE SPACE); the process by which the largest buildings end up on corners thus forming anchor points for the block, and markers for the crosstown streets — it is these which form the characteristic architecture of the plan of New York: all these, which together create the characteristic profile of the island, are unfolding processes — and to the extent they are at work, the beautiful — though

surprising and manmade — character of Manhattan is an unfolded one.

Can we guess at the process which created this considerable life? The photograph below, taken about 1950, shows a period in the history of the city when the docks were active, and when the area around Wall Street at the south end of Manhattan island was in its highest period of growth.

· *Each new building around the Wall Street area contributed to the cluster of high density centered on the Stock Exchange.*
· *Shared awareness that the Stock-Exchange was being formed was so strong that the highest buildings began to group themselves around the Stock Exchange.*

New York City, 1950. Even the massive city blocks are placed to preserve structure on the grid of Manhattan island. And it is the unfolded structure which results, its character, which makes New York loved and desired.

· *The docks, ripe with the coming and going of transatlantic liners and commercial vessels, grouped themselves around that area, forming a boundary zone around the larger center.*
· *Each wharf that was placed helped to form another center within the boundary zone.*

· *Each individual wharf thus helped to strengthen Wall Street as a center.*
· *Yet smaller centers then formed within the docks themselves — in the shape of cranes, wharves, jetties, and railroad lines — to serve the ships.*

RAILROAD TRACKS IN MINNESOTA

Train tracks, bridge, engineering works and trains, St. Paul, Minnesota. The reality of railroad, cranes, ships, water, and bridges unfolded to make a living landscape in the industrial 20th century.

Railroad lines have to preserve the complex structure of the hills and of the very limited gradients and curves a train can manage. These matters are so practical, and so demanding, that the structure-preserving nature of the engineering follows naturally. The "architecture" of the railroad tracks, which then forms naturally, is formed by the trackbed in its alignment through the land, by the rails on that track bed, the gentle transition curves, the signals and signal boxes. In these elements we find ALTERNATING REPETITION, LOCAL SYMMETRIES, LEVELS OF SCALE. The step-by-step process allows adaptation to occur gradually. The resulting architecture is simple, direct, real.

· *A new track is to run across the yards.*
· *The bridge is placed to leave a wide open area on the lower level*
· *This will allow marshaling of stock cars without obstruction.*
· *The new track alignment leading to the bridge will be worked out to form gentle straights and curves — hence centers — on the upper track, and on its approach lines.*
· *Each track bed is given its own integrity as a center*
· *Laying down the track, smaller centers are made by the railroad ties, the spaces between the ties, and the steel chairs which support the rails.*

PLANTING DAFFODILS IN THE GARDEN

When we garden, we instinctively act to preserve existing wholeness. Many gardens in the world, are made this way continually: Planting a row of flowers against a house where the sun shines; putting a seat at the base of an old tree; raking the leaves; putting stones at the edge of the lawn; planting fruit trees in the sheltered spots where they will ripen. The architecture of the garden unfolds directly from this process.

Because the process is free to be unpredictable, it can go where it wants to, step by step, day by day, afternoon by afternoon, for years. Since the gardener is free, more or less, to exercise his own judgment, and can react to what works and what doesn't work, the things which fail simply die, or get removed. As a result, on a relatively tiny scale, we see hedges, trees (STRONG CEN-TERS), lawns (THE VOID), flower borders (BOUNDARIES), fences and gates (DEEP INTER-LOCK AND AMBIGUITY). Unlike the buildings of our time, which are often more contrived, we often find a great naturalness and simplicity in the architecture of the gardens which emerge from this direct unfolding process. Here is the process I followed, when planting my garden.

· *I first tried to feel the deep structure of the land, its wholeness. I walked the lawn many times, trying to get a feeling for the major centers there — the great willow tree, the wall, the driveway, the laundry line, the flowerbeds against the stable wall, the feel of the lawn as it sweeps towards the meadow.*
· *I looked at the space of the whole garden and lawn together, asking how to plant the daffodils.*

Daffodils at Meadow Lodge, Sussex. I planted these daffodils to enhance the lawns, all around the edges of the lawns, where lawn meets driveways and path. They form the most beautiful boundary, in spring, adding to the life of the lawn. It is something quite wonderful.

· *I asked myself where I could put the daffodils, that would do the most good within the life of this garden.*
· *To embellish the lawn — one of the larger existing centers — I decided to plant the bulbs in the lawn itself.*
· *I tried to make the lawn as strong a center as possible by planting the daffodils to form a ring around the empty lawn.*

· *To make smaller centers too, I grouped the daffodils in clusters, along the lawn's edge. This had the effect that one could still walk easily, without crushing them.*
· *I checked what I had done, to make sure that the step which I proposed really would intensify the feeling of the whole.*
· *When I was finished, and felt it was reliable, we ordered the bulbs, and planted them.*

CUSTOMIZING TRUCKS AND MOTOR BIKES

A hand-painted, hand-customized Harley Davidson from one of the Hells Angels

Oddly enough we find examples of unfolded structure in quite a few machines and in bits of machinery. In the case of certain special machines, we sometimes find them imbued with love and attention by their makers or their owners. The maker modifies the machine by welding, bolting on extras, attaching, cutting, bending, to make the machine unique.

In the case of things where there is a lot of pride — as in the trucks owned by long-distance truck drivers, or the bikes owned by motorbikers, this activity of preserving structure extends to special paintwork, special ornaments, and special interiors, comforts, and ancillary machines. Here, for instance, is a brief summary of what might be a living process for modifying a motor bike:

· *Buy a standard bike.*
· *Customize its mechanical aspects.*
· *Redo the paintwork.*
· *Using intuition, paint a design which follows from, and embellishes, the shapes suggested by the bike's metal components.*
· *Often this will lead to special, and unique, ornament.*

TIMES SQUARE IN THE RAIN

Times Square in the pouring rain, 1959

The rain, here, normalizes everything, and makes human what might otherwise be less so. The cars, the few people walking, the glistening street and sidewalks, and the flood of rain, wipe out the pretentious and artificial. What is left, is more humane.

The appearance of the elements, drowning even heavy construction and big buildings, so that the unfolding of human events is unhindered by any image or conception.

I think it is true to say that what we see in the photograph, the state at this one moment, has unfolded. What we see at this instant is the product of creation, an ordinary place with not much in the way of controls.

· *Individual shop owners and companies build what they wish to.*
· *There are few controls.*
· *Advertisements are blinking.*
· *There is no overriding harmony.*
· *The rain comes.*
· *The cars go where they can.*
· *The people are running.*
· *Paper is swept away by the flood.*

This sounds ordinary enough. Yet in recent new city centers, this straightforward rawness has been replaced by something sanitized, devoid of human content, governed by the image of what sells — not even by the human process itself, as here.

THE GOLDEN GATE BRIDGE

Very large examples abound in engineering works, embankments, dams, and bridges. The Golden Gate Bridge is one example. The name of this bridge is so compelling as a description of the red-orange structure that few people remember that the gap between San Francisco and Marin County was *itself* called the Golden Gate long before the bridge existed. That gap, where the setting sun shines, where the hills come close to each other, and open westward from the Bay to the Pacific Ocean, is a beautiful and magical place. It was so, long before the bridge. The builders of the bridge, however, understood this wonderful place so well, and did indeed preserve its structure so profoundly, that a rare thing happened: the Golden Gate as formed by nature became even more intense, more beautiful, when complemented and completed by the steel, red-painted, bridge. Construction of the bridge itself, both in placement and in detail, was a structure-preserving act, so deeply so, that nowadays we think of the bridge itself as "the" Golden Gate.

Here it is the architecture of the gap which has been formed by unfolding: the presence of a strong center; the local symmetries; the good shape of the curves of the cables; the many levels of scale in the steel members; the gradients in the spacing of bays within the towers. One might say that all this is simply engineering.

I prefer to think that Joseph Strauss, the bridge engineer, sensitive to the harmony of the beautiful gap, filled in this structure in such a way as to complete the gap. He was inspired to make things the right size and shape by the beauty and importance of the task which told him what to do. It was that, perhaps, which made him able to react naturally to the beauty of

The Golden Gate Bridge: how beautifully it preserves the structure of the western entrance to the San Francisco Bay.

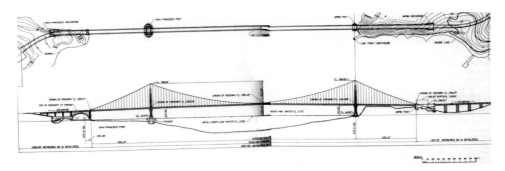

The overall layout of the bridge

Half-way through the early stages of the cable-spinning process, a man waves from one of the bridge towers.

The cables, completed, hang loosely across the towers, before the vertical cables are put in place.

the site. His structure-preserving process on such an immense project may have run along these simple lines:

· *Choose the site and the end points of the bridge.*
· *Get the position of the two towers.*
· *From the vertical loads, get the height of the towers and the curve of the parabola.*
· *From wind and earthquake forces, get the requirements for the towers.*
· *Choose the steel dimensions and cell dimensions to form a gradient in the structure of the towers, with increasing mass and dimension near the ground.*
· *Detail the Vierendeel truss form of the towers and design the gussets at the horizontal-vertical connections.*
· *Size the anchorage of the cables.*

The beauty of the bridge came from a second process, too. Unlike many 20th-century arti-

facts, this bridge got its shape from the process used to construct it. As the cables were hung across the towers, they fall into a catenary; which, then, as it gets loaded with the smaller vertical cables, and finally the deck, was transformed into a parabola.

· *Build the towers.*
· *Spin the cables, while stretching them across the towers.*
· *Anchor the cables by pouring the massive foundation blocks at either end.*
· *Attach the vertical cables to take the deck load.*
· *Build the deck.*
· *Complete the bridge.*

The beautiful shape of the bridge, was thus actually *generated*, dynamically, during the process of construction.

This can be said of relatively few 20th-century building works.

CHAIRS IN THE LUXEMBOURG GARDEN, PARIS

Sometimes, in cities, unfolding wholeness dominates in much smaller and more intimate actions: a road which follows the contours of a hill, a jumble of cafe chairs and tables along the bank of a river. In the photograph here, we see industrially produced chairs, arranged by people, after World War II, looking for sunshine in the Luxembourg gardens in Paris. This photograph shows a life-seeking process, where unfolding has occurred. The process is clearly not part of traditional society. And, looking back on it from today, we may view it as a rarity, still. But nevertheless, the blithe looseness of arrangement and the sunshine shows us that this is possible, even perfectly ordinary, in post-traditional society.

Because the process was unimportant, no one felt they had to control it; it was left perfectly alone, and therefore able to become only what was necessary. This is where the gift of the unfolding lay. The fifteen properties are visible throughout this photograph, showing the extent that the unfolding of geometry and space led to real life in this very ordinary circumstance.

The architecture which developed — an arrangement of chairs, the formality of the boundary, the informality of the chairs, the placing in groups according to the way people wanted to sit, social groups, lovers, and sunshine — made it completely natural.

PING-PONG PLAYERS ON A STREET IN SHANGHAI

This scene from Shanghai shows the structure-preserving and unfolding process vividly, in an ordinary event from modern urban life. The man and boy choose the place to play in an area constrained by bikes, sidewalk, and doors. They push the table into the sun; as they play the area around them clears gradually, as if by itself, but actually as a result of their playing. They have the freedom to adjust the table; feedback comes to them as they experience the convenience or inconvenience of the position of the table, how well it works to play. They change it to make it more convenient. The result, unpredictable? Obviously, it was not planned or worked out in advance — they went where the process led them.

Even in this very simple case we see an architecture: at the core, the mass of the table, simple, central: the two players in relation to this largest whole: the players arms forming the third level, extended; at the ends of their arms, the bats — and all this surrounded by the more loosely arranged boundary of building wall and bikes. This architecture — the whole which forms — is distinctive, unitary. But it has unfolded naturally; it was not drawn. I suspect it went like this:

· *The man and the boy moved fast. They pulled the table out to a place where people could walk around it — probably in a place where they had played before.*
· *They set the table up so each of them had enough room at the ends to stand and make his shots — this is the creation of smaller centers at either end.*
· *They also placed the table so that it made rather a nice larger area outside their apartment: creating a larger center.*
· *Watching the sun, feeling the wind, they put the table where they could to make the over feeling of the situation as good as possible.*
· *Then, while playing, smaller centers were formed by the bats, the balls, and the motion of their wrists.*

*Luxembourg Garden, Paris, 1949. Chairs, tables, shade, sunlight, a railing, the water.
The peaceful leaves drift, preserving the structure of this Paris garden,
and creating an unfolding in the modern world.*

*An old man and a boy playing ping-pong on the sidewalk in Shanghai. How unerringly they place the table: they don't
care who is coming, what they care about is putting the table where they can have a good game. And it is this blissful
unconsciousness which makes the structure-preserving quality of their table, and their game, so accurate.*

FRENCH HIGH-SPEED TRAIN (TRAIN DE GRANDE VITESSE) UNDERGOING SIMULATED TUNNEL TESTS

Wind-tunnel test on the TGV, France

The very high-speed trains developed by the French, were given their shape gradually, not in the field, but in computer simulations. When a train enters a tunnel, pressure waves run the length of a tunnel, and these waves can cause pain to eardrums, and can potentially shatter glass. A simulation can simulate such pressure waves with accuracy, making it possible to modify different shaped noses, after examining the intensity of the pressure waves for different shapes. By testing different nose shapes, and studying the pressures waves in a computer simulation, a highly adapted shape is achieved. This process led to the very long nose of the TGV trains, since the longer nose and specific shape minimize the intensity of the pressure wave.

This process, similar to organic adaptation, allows shape to be generated by a dynamic process in an evolutionary way. Such computer simulations are playing a bigger and bigger role in achieving good fit for buildings and other artifacts.

TICKER-TAPE PARADE, BROADWAY, NEW YORK CITY

When I found this picture, I thought it must be something from the 1930s. Then I discovered it was a parade from 1981, celebrating the return of the Iranian hostages. By the end of the 20th century, the sometimes too-cynical acceptance of the lifeless products of the production-machine had made us insensitive — even something as ordinary and wonderful as this parade looks as if it came from a more distant past.

The photograph shows how the thrust toward life exists even in the biggest high-production, choreographed circumstances.

Ticker-tape parade, Broadway, New York City, 1981

FRANK LLOYD WRIGHT'S BUILDINGS

In writing this chapter, I wanted, from an early stage, to include Wright's Imperial Hotel; something one thinks of as one of the major buildings of the last 100 years. Yet when I compared it, recently, with the examples I have shown, I found the building itself of a lesser natural quality than many of these examples: there had been less unfolding in it. Beautiful as it was — and it was very beautiful, I was lucky enough to be there,

myself, before it was torn down — in life and freshness it did not hold its own with many of the more ordinary examples I am showing in this chapter.

But the essence of Wright's genius lay in the plans he made. His early plans, especially, in their articulate form, were comparable with the beauty of some of the great plans of traditional buildings. They have the unfolded character

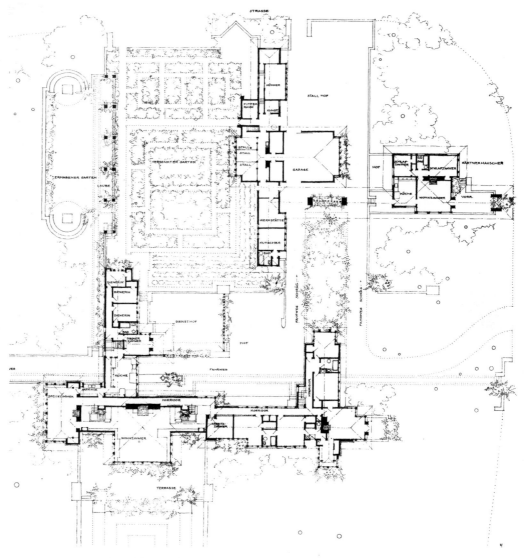

Plan of the Coonley House, Riverside, Illinois, Frank Lloyd Wright, 1908

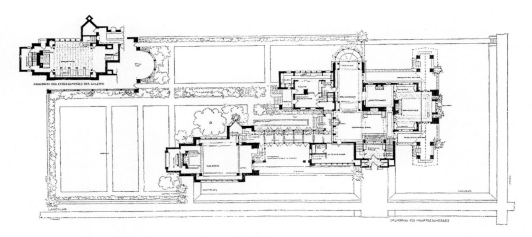

Plan of Wright's Dana house

more strikingly than almost any other aspect of his oeuvre.

Here I show the plans of the Coonley house, built in Illinois in 1908, and of the Dana house. They look so natural, as if the plans were created 1, 2, 3, 4, . . And yet, while they have that wonderful character of one thing being done after another, they also have a strong, profoundly strong physical and geometric order. Somehow he had the trick of making these plans both utterly coherent, and yet natural as if they had just fallen off his pencil.

The key to the very deliberate and coherent structure which Wright's plans had in them, was the following sequence that I believe must have underlain the creation of the plan.

· *Create exterior space, as positive: his gardens, as in the Coonley house, had very coherent rectangular areas as their elements.*
· *Place buildings, loosely, to form these rectangles and strengthen them.*
· *Locate and shape the main rooms.*
· *Create a structural grid, very formal and rhythmic, for the buildings and main rooms.*
· *Make the structural elements well-shaped and rectangular, the pivots of the structural grid.*
· *Place secondary rooms within the shell.*
· *Syncopate the structural grid to accommodate rooms and smaller rooms.*

Wright's Coonley house

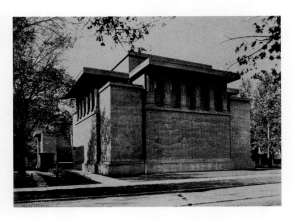

Wright's Unity Temple, 1901. Another kind of building, with the same kind of structural order.

The structural order visible in the plans, is also clearly visible from outside the buildings.

Inside a house in White City Jabavu, Soweto, South Africa, 1987

Apartment house in Manaus, Brazil, 1995

INSIDE A HOUSE, WHITE CITY JABAVU, SOWETO
AND
WALKWAY OF AN APARTMENT HOUSE, MANAUS, BRAZIL

In both the places shown on the left, people are comfortable, normal. At first one may say, well, these people are happy even though in each case they are in what seems like a very rudimentary room, or gallery. But why does that show a living architecture? Are these places made by unfolding?

Yes, it is true that in daytime, without the people enjoying themselves, these places might look not so good, perhaps even miserable. But the point is that, simple or not, poor or not-so-poor, the people are allowed, by the place, to be what they are. These people — judging from their faces in the pictures, anyway — are free in themselves — perhaps because they are not relying on money for joy — and certainly, I think, because there is so little extra in the situation. In Soweto, a table, chairs, bottle, light bulbs, not much more. The generative system in a society, which creates a living world, is something more subtle, more important, than the machine which creates the buildings. What is at stake — what must be kept, and used, and benefited from, in any living world — are the dynamic generative processes which created these situations as a whole, in Soweto and in Brazil.

HOUSE-PROUD OWNER, MEXICALI, MEXICO

This house was designed and built in 1976, for $3,500, by Lilia Duran and her husband, as part of a program of construction I undertook in Mexico. Here are a few excerpts from the step-by-step process followed:

· *Walk about on the site, and select the site with other families.*
· *Place the main room of the house.*
· *Place the front door.*
· *Decide how the porch will create a relation to the common land.*
· *Use special foundation blocks to form the edge of the slab.*
· *Place and pour the slab.*
· *Using specially made cylindrical blocks, build the porch columns.*
· *Build beam forms, place steel, pour the beams.*
· *Place the baskets to form the vaults.*
· *Trowel lightweight concrete on the basket.*
· *Whitewash the columns.*

It was an uncomplicated making process, perhaps only sophisticated in its simplicity (see Book 3, chapters 11 and 12, for details).

Lilia Duran, in the porch of her house:
Houses by Christopher Alexander,
Mexicali, Mexico, 1976

The Upham house, Berkeley, California, 1993

THE UPHAM HOUSE, BERKELEY, CALIFORNIA

This example (by CES) is given in considerable detail in the appendix. Illustrated opposite, for reference, is a moment in the process of unfolding, when window openings in the living room were being settled.

· *As the ground floor slab is placed we begin to consider the room divisions within the context of the whole.*

· *Asking what we can do next that will do most to give this wholeness the most positive increase of life, we identified the exterior wall bays, the division into windows, and the fine-tuning of room-to-room partitions.*

· *Thus the rooms were formed as centers.*

· *As we ask this question, we necessarily direct ourselves to centers, the units of energy within the whole, and ask, at each step, which one center could be created (or extended or intensified or even pruned) that will most increase the life of the whole.*

· *As we work to enhance each bay as a center we do it to try, as far as possible, to increase the life of each room as a new living center.*

· *As we shape the outline of each room, of necessity we also shape the neighboring room as a center, paying attention to the way the partition shapes both at the same time.*

· *We check to see if what we have done has truly increased the life and feeling of the whole. This is possible, as a group process, within the framework of the way we were working (see photograph opposite, top left). If the feeling of the whole has not been deepened by the step we have just taken, we wipe it out. Otherwise we go on.*

· *We then repeat the entire process with the newly modified whole.*

· *We stop altogether when there is no further step we can take that intensifies the feeling of the whole.*

Upham house: settling positions of columns, to form the bays, and window openings of the living room bay window.

Upham house: the finished living room, and bay window, whose design and proportions came from the process shown on the left.

COMMUNITY CENTER IN INDONESIA, MADE BY THE FAMILIES FOR THEMSELVES

This community center in Kali Cho-de, Yogyakarta, Indonesia, was built by the families who live there, 1985.

Here a living process, in the hands of people making a building for themselves, creates a special character, and a special uniqueness in the parts. This is a public building. But even the bays have their own character. It is not the designed, conscious character a designer might try to insert: it is an authentic differentiation, a joy, which arises naturally from living process, and comes about because the adaptations are locally controlled.

THE DANUBE PROMENADE AT ESZTERGOM, HUNGARY

The walk was built around 1950, by the communist government of Hungary and by the government which followed. It was sensitively made, with strong centers both in the walkway and in the balustrade, and though made of simple and massive materials, these centers reinforce the life of the whole. This place looks so much like a product of traditional culture that it is hard to realize it was done fully within processes of the 20th century.

· *The process started with planting trees along the Danube footpath.*

· *The trees were planted in 1920; as they grew, they strengthened the center formed by the river.*
· *The walk along the river edge was strengthened as a center, by making it wider and more comfortable. That happened during the 30s.*
· *Finally, in the 50s, the walk was made into a full promenade by construction of the reinforced concrete wall along the edge. This both protects the pedestrians from the steep river-bank, and also — with the trees on the inner side — makes the path itself even stronger as a center, thus finally very strongly enhancing the river.*

The walk along the Danube Canal, Esztergom, Hungary. The trees were planted around 1920. The walk itself is made of concrete, and was built around 1950. The whole fits together with the river almost perfectly.

The edge of the Amazon River at Belém

THE EDGE OF THE AMAZON RIVER AT BELÉM

Ordinary, typical artifacts of the late 20th century. A table, folding steel chairs, an iron railing, concrete wall, boats, cars in the distance, beer mats. Yet this place has a romantic quality — no wonder these lovers are kissing there. What has generated it? Unconcern, mainly.

· *The easiest chairs, the cheapest, were used.*
· *Painted yellow, for joy.*
· *The easiest table.*
· *The beer mats were provided by the beer company.*

· *The concrete wall base, and the iron railing, were put in by someone. The old cannon, was left from generations before.*
· *There is, in this landscape, the work of hundreds of people, leaving their trace, without concern for images.*

It comes about, this life, because no one has controlled it. The generative process is free, popular, with no rules or regulations — there is no image; no *desire* for control, by anyone.

This car repair shop is very ordinary. In spite of a rugged, nearly grimy quality it is close to the heart in the concrete sense that we feel close to it, not removed from it, as demonstrated by the experiments of Book 1. This, too, comes from the straightforwardness of the process which generated the arrangement.

FAMILY-OWNED GAS STATION, ALBANY, CALIFORNIA

Here once again, something ordinary: the interior of an automobile repair shop. I have printed this picture in Book 1 (chapter 9) because, ramshackle and unappealing as the gas station might appear at first, it is surprising in the extent some kind of inner harmony reaches us when we ask if it reminds us of our own self (see discussion in Book 1). I mention the family owners because I think it is no accident that it is a hard-working family who run this particular gas station, struggling for money, being practical, and having neither time, nor money, nor interest, in the superficial order of a corporate satellite gas station which is more dependent on image and appearance. As a result:

· *First, the hydraulic jack and hoist are carefully positioned.*
· *Spare parts are stacked where there is room for them.*
· *Tools remain lying where they were last used*
· *Cables are run where they have to.*

All these practical steps create an unfolding process which has no predictable outcome. The process is based entirely on feedback from the practical. And, of course, it occurs piece by piece. This shop, with its practical and unimpressive quality, has its own architecture, caused by the making of centers where they had to be made.

A tennis court, at sunset, in the Berkeley Rose garden. How the tennis court, with its asphalt surface and wire mesh enclosure, fits into the land and the trees.

TENNIS COURT AT SUNSET IN THE BERKELEY ROSE GARDEN

How the tennis court, with its asphalt surface and wire mesh enclosure, fits into the land and the trees.

Here the architecture — consisting of an asphalt platform, chain-link netting, uprights, a small platform nestled in the slope — follows from the unimportance of the place, and the care for the bowl of the rose garden and its bowl-shaped terrain, which was to be disturbed as little as possible. That impulse occasioned the way this court was nestled into the curve of the slope, unobtrusively, leaving the whole intact.

What is most interesting to me about this example, is the way that items which are normally not harmonious, create a genuine harmony. Asphalt, the surface of the tennis court, is not typically harmonious. Nine-foot high chain link fence is not typically harmonious. Yet here, these very modern and industrial materials, become unified with nature in the nicest, touching way. The process was as follows:

· *Mark out the rectangle for two tennis courts.*
· *Cut the slope, to leave flat benches, but harm the natural slopes as little as possible.*
· *Grade the soil and put in crushed rock.*
· *Place an asphalt surface on the benched area.*
· *Erect posts by drilling into the ground.*
· *Span wire netting for the surround.*
· *Place doors and tennis net-posts.*

It is no more complicated than that. The easiness of such a process, and lack of conscious design, occurs again and again and again as a key to successful unfolding.

STEEL TOWERS OF HIGH VOLTAGE TRANSMISSION LINES NEAR THE DUMBARTON BRIDGE, SAN FRANCISCO

These towers might easily be dismissed as ugly by an ardent nature lover, but I believe they are structure-preserving.

Here is a picture which may shock you. These high-tension transmission towers of the Pacific Gas and Electric Company (PG&E), stand across the flatlands of the marshes near the Dumbarton Bridge in the San Francisco Bay. These towers might easily be dismissed as ugly by an ardent nature lover. But I believe they are structure-preserving, not structure-destroying. They leave the flat structure of the Bay marsh alone; they are structurally beautiful in themselves; their even spacing is quiet and helps avoid creation of a competing structure; and they make a place for pelicans and sea birds to roost. They are innocent, too, not designed. Engineers simply used steel, bolts, and cables in a simple way without trying to "design" something. In the context of our human population, the flat open wilderness of the Bay marshland is enhanced,

not harmed, by their presence: it is, to me, a synthesis of nature's wild reality and our industrial reality.

By comparison, the hundreds of wind turbines at Altamont Pass, near Oakland, California, loved by ecologists (intellectually) because they harness wind energy, are nevertheless strongly structure-destroying. They do not leave the hills of Altamont alone; they are not innocent in themselves. Thousands of giant propellers, mounted on smaller pylons, crowd together, disturbing sight, slope shapes, hill curves, grass color, and sound. Ecological they may be, but the turbines have made a mess of Altamont Pass.

One has to look at such examples very, very carefully indeed to distinguish what is genuinely structure-preserving from what is actually structure-destroying.

Willis Polk House, San Francisco, built in 1898. This house, built on the very top and steepest part of Russian Hill, is informal and beautiful: it unfolds majestically, but in casual 20th-century fashion, as it tumbles down the hill. Yet the rooms inside are formal and wonderful.

WOODEN ARCHITECTURE OF SAN FRANCISCO

The Polk House. A very early house of the modern era, built when San Francisco was still largely undeveloped. The house stood on the once-grassy slopes of Russian Hill, a place now crowded with high-density towers. A seven-story wooden structure, it fits the slope carefully. Within, the formal rooms have a beautiful heavy timber order, each room differently shaped by its position, and the house then somehow connects them to form a whole. In this case the architecture of the whole which develops — the massive timber members, the heavy, low, squat rooms, the rambling structure on the slope — all arises from a relative natural-ness of a period before building inspectors. The artist's freedom of action and intensity in the formation of the individual rooms allows the architecture to unfold.

Cars, buildings, windows — a suburb of Buenos Aires, 1997

OFFICE AND PARKED CARS, ARGENTINA

I particularly like this picture. The office, with its wall, cars, plants, windows, is so unassuming. For all its randomly parked cars, one feels that it may be relaxed, probably quite fun to be there — and above all, that it is probably comfortable, unoppressive there. It is typical, yet a nice relaxed atmosphere, a living atmosphere. Something to be proud of: a lot of events, and a lot of people have had their hands involved in making this place reach its present state. That is why it is so comfort-able, and so important, in a minor way, as an example. It may seem ordinary, and indeed it is. But it is worthwhile to find such a good example of the most ordinary artifacts of our time — cars, steel windows, posts, air-conditioners — assembled in such a harmonious and living way. It came about, I believe, because the economic conditions, perhaps the temperament of Argentineans, allow a looseness which gives permission for the process to find its proper harmony.

FIELDS OF RAPE, GUIZHOU PROVINCE, CHINA

This photograph from China typifies our modern era. Although the scene is natural, and although the farming involved is relatively straightforward, the cultivation of such a large area, with such masses of rape seed, is industrial in quality, uniquely of our century.

   The structure-preserving character of the living process is strongly visible. The two conical mountains and the plain between — how profoundly intensified by the stark yellow, bursting into bloom at harvest. Is it an artistic process? It is only a harvest. Yet, it is a living process; being living it intensifies the land, and enhances, preserves, intensifies, the structure of the land.

   What the farmers did was simple.
· *Till the ground, working around the large rocks which stand up high.*
· *Plant seed according to their varieties.*
· *Provide for irrigation and access for equipment.*

Fields of rape in Guizhou province, China, 1990

SQUATTER HOUSING IN GUATEMALA

There are millions of houses on earth, built during the 20th century, which exhibit at least *aspects* of unfolding. These are the millions of shelters built by homeless people for themselves, squatters on invaded territories, cases where every box, cardboard, corrugated iron, stick, and concrete block has been gleaned, or harvested, from a dump, or paid for with the tiny surplus left over after a week of work. These houses are hardly beautiful. The circumstances are bare bones, and the people struggle with a poverty many readers of this book will only just be able to imagine.

But, in the midst of this biting struggle, decisions are made by a family, and a ragged cloth, a raw window made from a sheet of plastic, are placed where they are needed — they rise in direct expression of need, desire, function, and circumstance. However crude, these elements are adapted to life. Millions of people, housing themselves in this fashion, have created the beginnings of new cities, which are more organically connected to their own wishes, and to the slopes of the hills, to the position of sun and wind, than the developer's clean boxes.

Squatter housing, Guatemala

Vegetable plots: This picture shows a remarkable living order, generated naturally by the process of people working on the land, Yunnan, China, 1994

Terraced landscape, Guizhou province, China, 1992

VEGETABLE PLOTS, YUNNAN, CHINA

This picture (page 168) shows a remarkable living order, generated naturally by the process of people working on the land.

It is peculiar, and of our time. A friend of mine commented that it has nothing to do with the 20th century. Yet this is an illusion. Could this picture have been taken in the 19th century or in the 18th century? It could not. The clothes are already from our century: the ease of the people is of our time, too. They are serious *and* they enjoy themselves; it is a special mixture that is only of our time. And that is why it is inspiring to me. It is just this character which looks like something from another time, and yet is, in fact, peculiarly appropriate and generated in our time, that so makes me love to live in this century, and why I would not want to live in any other.

And, here, too, the liveliness is generated by special living processes, which are more colorful, more of our era; there is a helpfulness in their tools, a comfort in their clothes. This is not the world of Breughel or of Hiroshige. It is the world of the Rolling Stones and of the computer age, which happens to have found expression in a group of fields tended by modern farmers.

TERRACED LANDSCAPE, GUIZHOU PROVINCE, CHINA

Here (page 169) the imprint of process on the land, and the resulting construction of living order, is easy to see:

· *To contain the irrigation water on the slopes, terraces with an outer bund wall are built.*
· *The walls follow the contours, necessarily, to make the labor most efficient.*
· *Each little plot is under separate control.*
· *Soil and mud are harbored and preserved, within each enclosure.*
· *Crops are planted and irrigated and looked after.*
· *Steps are built from terrace to terrace, to allow the farmers to move around as easily as possible.*

AFRICAN JAZZ

Another example of human joy, and the way that this joy is encouraged and supported by a highly organized environment. What did it take to create the environment which could support this music, adequately?

· *Get on the platform.*
· *Put the microphone where you want it.*
· *Start the drums.*
· *Start the music.*
· *What else matters?*

Here we see one of the most basic human environments: music, a platform and a microphone. It is almost as basic as it can be. Photographed here are Thoko Shukuma and the Lo Six. "Shukuma" means "get you moving," and for two years she and the Lo Six toured South Africa. A great singer, what she needed was the platform and the microphone, the flat boards, her friends in the Lo Six. That was a living world.

Once again, what seems simple, is highly complex, perfect for what it does, and yet it would be viewed with scorn by a designer, who could not charge money for it, nor create an image that would suit his business. Yet the environment is truly organic, just right for what it supports, and highly organized, in a deeper way than we are used to recognizing.

3 / LIVING PROCESSES

The freedom, joy of spirit, and benign adaptation which has occurred in most of the examples, comes from the way a simple (and therefore unhampered) process (sequence of steps) is able to interact with environmental conditions. Thus what I have referred to as the "rough, rambling" quality of so much that is good in the environment, comes from the light-hearted, yet profound adaptation which such a simple stepwise process encourages, and which a more formal or controlled design process cannot achieve.

African Jazz, South Africa, 1956

The examples in this chapter all exemplify what I define as living process. Most of the examples have structure-preserving aspects. Within their limits, each one creates a highly adapted, living world. And in each case, the process itself was also benign. In most of these cases, it was itself good as a process, good, not harmful, for the people who engaged in it, whole-making for them, not fragmenting.

I hope that you, like me, simply *like* these examples, feel inspired by them, and can sense, in some intuitive fashion, why I would view the processes which created them as living processes. It is important to notice that these cases — and this is common to all of them — have a certain roughness, an almost uncharacteristic form-quality which makes them more humane than the more consciously created "image" architectural designs of the 20th century that we know from magazines and advertising. And the examples also have a new kind of coherence. An emerging character, a new kind of architecture, is visible in them.

This character — visible, I hope, throughout the photographs of this chapter — is carefully chosen. I have chosen examples with this character, because it is precisely in this character that their life resides. The places shown are living structures *because* they have this character.

It might be said that my examples, because they have this special quality — including coherence, roughness, and humanity — are not modern enough, not as modern as other examples that one might choose to illustrate the creations of the 20th century. But my point is just the opposite. I believe the rough humanity visible in these pictures, is no less modern, than the titanium struts, glass, plastic sheets, and shimmering homogenous facades we presently *think of* as modern. It seems to me, indeed, that the kindlier, and more engaging morphology which appears in the world when living processes are at work, is what is needed, socially and biologi-

cally, for our survival — and that in the future, this, not the other, will ultimately be seen as a truer product of our modern age. The slick glittering sheets will seem, in retrospect, from some future age, a strange historical aberration caused by ad-men of the 20th century, not by a profound respect for our biology.

My cases show a wide-ranging sample of living processes in the modern world where unfolding, to a greater or lesser degree, *was* taking place. In each case, in one way or another, familiar modern processes have been channelled to allow form to emerge — sometimes beautiful and coherent form — flexible, life-enhancing, allowing adaptation. The goodness of the results is visible both in the evident life of these examples, and in the profound and interesting fact that the unfolding generates an "architecture."

We may find inspiration in these modern processes since they not only give us a more positive outlook on our sometimes less-than-positive world, but they also give us practical guides for imagining the kinds of process which can realistically create living structure in our world. Many are unexpected. Some of them are more gross, more powerful, than one might expect. Others are surprisingly delicate, in their own robust way. But, overall, it is the robustness and excitement of these examples which marks the good of our era, and its potential for life. I have given, for most examples, a short sketch of the kind of process which created the thing in question. I have not attempted accuracy with these roughly sketched processes. It has mainly been my intent to show that the morphology of the example comes, in large part, from relatively simple steps. And I have tried, as strongly as possible, to show that the good essence of these examples comes more from the *process* than from an imagined *design*. In a few cases there is conscious design, as well. But in all these cases, it is the *process* which dominates, and the process which gives the thing its *life*.

4 / THE UNDERLYING PROCESSES WHOSE TRACES
WE HAVE SEEN

I started, in this chapter, trying to make a collection of objects and places that I feel have life, a real life in the 20th-century context; places that were vibrant, truly of our time, and flowing with love, or excitement, or energy.

As I assembled these pictures, I tried to find, in each case, what kind of process seemed to have created them, and in what respects it might be characterized as an unfolding process. These I have written down.

In every case, the process is straightforward, simple, and above all it is free: it allows the real-ity of the situation, the human needs, human joys, to find expression.

Gradually, as I assembled more and more descriptions of this kind, something dawned on me: these step-by-step processes are very simple, very straightforward. What they all have in common is that they are virtually unhampered by concepts or by too much thought about the intricacy of design. The tortured manipulations of 20th-century architectural practice do not show up in these examples. These processes are all simpler and more direct, their makers more

Look again, at the edge of the River Amazon at Belém: a railing, tables, chairs, the lovers are perfectly at home.

forgetful, or unworried, about the consequences. An unworried, unhesitating sequence of actions, creates unfolding, and creates life — because it is direct, motivated by practical concerns, and because each step takes care of something not taken care of in the moment before.

Look again at the case of the riverfront at Belém.

· *Pave the river's edge.*
· *Put a railing there.*
· *Find a couple of tables.*
· *Put some chairs.*

What looks like an informal, rambling process is in reality a more highly organized process than any currently practiced by architects or planners. It is a process which allows (and encourages) each thing that must be located to find its shape and position, thus achieving a refined organic structure which merely *seems* informal. The depth of the organic structure and its refinement is visible in the eyes of the lovers and in the fact that they chose this place, instead of another, as the spot where this moment in their lives could develop.

How different all this is from the anal-retentive up-tight worry about design, in which factors A, and B, and C, and D, and E, and F . . . all have to be manipulated together, before the designer and the planner and the client and the bureaucrats can be satisfied. We have seen some thing in the examples of this chapter which is far more robust. Each process does something — just one thing — which is important, practical, and creates good feeling. Then it does another. Then it does another. There is no manipulation and distortion of the structure, trying to predict where it is going, trying to make sure everything is OK. There is a sublime confidence, and practicality, and simplicity.

If we do one thing at a time, and if what we do is wholesome and sound, then whatever comes next will work. We do not have to tie it down ahead of time for fear of some imaginary potential catastrophe of "design." Instead, we just go step by step, doing what is required as well as we are able, with confidence that the next thing, too, will work out somehow when its time comes, but that it need not be worked out now.

The places of the 20th century which I have shown have life because they are all done with confidence, optimistically, with love of life, without the planner's excruciating attention to "problems" which is so often used (unintentionally, perhaps) as a hammer to destroy life and to destroy living structure. That is what is truly remarkable, and so hopeful about most of these examples. In these examples, through glimpses of the passing 20th century, we may see our modern era in its glory, and we may learn a vital lesson about what to do.

PART TWO

LIVING PROCESSES

With structure-preserving transformations established as the foundation of all living process, we may now go on to a more elaborate and detailed account.

In the present way of thinking about architecture, one is supposed to design a building completely, occasionally even plan a whole neighborhood, and then use the description (the design, with its plans and drawings) as a specification from which to build. But the essential idea of Book 2 is that it is precisely in this way that architecture has gone wrong, and that it is because of this that living structure rarely appears in contemporary buildings. Instead of using plans, designs, and so on, I shall argue that we MUST *instead use generative processes. Generative processes tell us what to* DO, *what* ACTIONS *to take, step by step, to make buildings and building designs unfold beautifully, rather than detailed drawings which tell us what the* END-*result is supposed to be.*

This idea, obvious to biologists, is not yet obvious to architects nor to most people in our society overwhelmed by 20th-century ideas of architecture. It is therefore helpful to read the following eloquent and simple passage explaining the difference between descriptive process and generative process. The passage comes from Professor Lewis Wolpert's PRINCIPLES OF DEVELOPMENT *(New York: Oxford University Press, 1997), page 21.*

THE EMBRYO CONTAINS A GENERATIVE RATHER THAN A DESCRIPTIVE PROGRAM

All the information for embryonic development is contained within a fertilized egg. So how is this information interpreted to give rise to an embryo? One possibility is that the structure of the organism is somehow encoded as a descriptive program in the genome. Does the DNA contain a full description of the organism to which it will give rise? The answer is no. The genome contains instead a program of instructions for making the organism — a generative program — in which the cytoplasmic constituents of eggs and cells are essential players along with the genes like the DNA coding for the sequence of amino acids in a protein.

A descriptive program, like a blueprint or a plan, describes an object in some detail, whereas a generative program describes how to make an object. For the same object the programs are very different. Consider origami, the art of paper folding. By folding a piece of paper in various directions, it is quite easy to make a paper hat or a bird from a single sheet. To describe in any detail the final form of the paper with the complex relationships between its parts is really very difficult, and not of much help in explaining how to achieve it. Much more useful and easier to formulate are instructions on how to fold the paper. The reason for this is that simple instructions about folding have complex spatial consequences. In development, gene action similarly sets in motion a sequence of events that can bring about profound changes in the embryo. One can thus think of the genetic information in the fertilized egg as equivalent to the folding instructions in origami: both contain a generative program for making a particular structure.

Lewis Wolpert

Essentially the same thing can be said about the way — the ONLY *way, I believe — that it is possible to generate buildings or communities that have life. Living structure in buildings can only be* GENERATED. *It cannot be created by brute force from designs. It can only come from a generative program — hence from a generative process existing in the production process of society — so that the building — its conception, plan, design, detailed layout, structural design, and material detail are all unfolded, step by step in* TIME.

The generative processes I am speaking about start from the structure-preserving processes I have described in chapters 1–5. But they will be described in the next chapters, as part of a detailed society-wide system, in such a way that we may contemplate a complete system of living processes that could be responsible for the construction of the built world all over the Earth.

It is as if — we might say — we are to create a complete genetic system for the production of living structure in our built world.

I believe such a system of living processes can be described precisely, can be made practical, and can be implemented. If it can be done, implementing such a system on a world-wide scale could represent one of the greatest transformations of the Earth in modern history.

So we come to the core of Book 2. In the next chapters I try to specify not only what I mean by living process in technical detail, but also what characteristics are operationally necessary to any process which is a "living" process — in other words, what is necessary to ANY *and* EVERY *process which is capable of generating living structure.*

The practical crux of unfolding, the essence of every living process (what is sometimes described as "emergence" by physicists and biologists) is that it is above all a GEOMETRIC *process. That is surprising, and not widely understood. The unfolding is geometrical in its* ESSENCE. *Although there are many side features to living process, it is fundamentally the unfolding of coherent* GEOMETRIC *form, even when it appears loose and "organic."*

Further, the geometrical form of a living world and its unfolding are guided above all, by processes and transnformations which create the fifteen properties. These properties have been described at length in Book 1, and I have indicated in chapter 2 of this book why these fifteen properties will necessarily come into being as a result of any life-creating process.

That is the core of what follows in the next twelve chapters.

CHAPTER SIX

GENERATED STRUCTURE

WITH SPECIAL ATTENTION TO THE DIFFERENCE
BETWEEN GENERATED AND FABRICATED
STRUCTURE AND THE HUGE ECONOMIC COST
TO OUR SOCIETY OF THE FABRICATED
STRUCTURES WHICH ARE CREATED BY
CONTEMPORARY ARCHITECTURE

1 / COMPLEXITY

In this chapter, I shall begin to express, operationally and concretely, what real complexity is when we encounter it in a part of the built environment that has life.

Ostensibly, we are surrounded by complexity. The modern city is immensely complex. Buildings are complex. Ecosystems, and the biosphere are still more complex. Computers and computer networks, and software, are all enormously complex. It would be natural to expect, therefore, that we must have a theory of complexity, that we have an effective and sensible way of thinking about the best way to *create* complexity. Faced with the need, growing every day, to create successful complex structures all around us, one would expect that we have at least asked ourselves *how*, in general, a complex structure may become well-formed. We should long ago have asked ourselves this most basic question: *Is the way that we view design, planning, and construction — in all the spheres mentioned, ecosystems, buildings, communities, objects, computers and computer software — the right way to produce sufficient complexity, and does what we are doing have a chance of success?*

And the answer is, that there is a fundamental law about the creation of complexity, which is visible and obvious to everyone — yet this law is, to all intents and purposes, ignored in 99% of the daily fabrication processes of society. The law states simply this: ALL *the well-ordered complex systems we know in the world, all those anyway that we view as highly successful, are* GENERATED *structures, not fabricated structures.*

The human brain, that most complex neural network, like other neural networks, is generated, not assembled or fabricated. The forests of the Amazon are generated, not fabricated. The tiger, beautiful creature, is generated, not fabricated. The sunset over the western ocean with its stormy clouds, that too is generated not fabricated. When we make a fire that really burns, we generate its structure, by placing a few logs, strategically, to create currents of air, radiation between glowing embers, so that the structure of the fire then creates itself. When we cook a souffle, we generate the souffle by initiating transformations among eggs, butter, sugar, and so on: we do not try to build it, like an inept bunch of chopped vegetables, that someone likes to call a salad. Music, possibly most among all things, is generated, even when stimulated by a score: and it may be generated by a more elusive combination of chords and rhythms that "get something going." All this, is true of buildings, too, and of our communities.

2 / THE GEOMETRY OF COMPLEXITY

In broad terms, a generated structure is something that has a certain deep complexity and is created in some way that appears to be almost biological, and reaches deeper levels of subtle structure than we commonly associate with "design," or with designed objects. In a generated structure one feels intuitively, above all that the structure is more complex and more subtle than anything that could be designed or fabricated.

To get a detailed grip on the nature of this generated complexity, we need a perspective which focuses, above all, on the *geometry* of what has been generated. Further, it is a particular aspect of the geometry we are concerned with. We may identify a particular visible physical character of the environment — its "generatedness" — as the sign that it has been made by a living process.

Generated structure: Jaisalmir, Rajasthan, India. Here the wishes of the family, their comfort, and the adaptation of use to structure have been simply carried out, without fuss, all quite direct. Contrast this picture with the photograph on page 184.

For all these reasons, I devote this chapter, almost entirely, to the generated structure of *the geometry* which follows from living process.

When a process creates living structure, we at once see the impact of the process in the geometry as that something that seems like "generated structure." We see it in the photograph on this page. And we see it in the plan illustrated below, on page 182. The geometry is always, when living, what we may recognize as "*Generated*." This is the adjective which best captures what we are looking for, and that will become the talisman of our success in trying to implement a living process. Does the process create generated structure, or doesn't it? This is a most useful practical question, in trying to decide whether a particular process is a living one.

The need to make all parts of the environ ment as generated structures, once established, will help guide us to see the various attributes of living process, in detail. Our search for adequate definitions of living process can then be guided and stimulated by this focus on the geometry of the results.

Once we have the geometry of complexity fixed in our minds as a target, we may then understand better the purpose of the chapters which follow, and will understand that each of the features of living process covered in subsequent chapters, is specifically intended to make the generation of living structure — in its real and necessary complexity — achievable, possible, and likely to succeed. Throughout the discussion, I shall use the concept of a generated structure, and use this term in opposition to the concept of a fabricated structure.

3 / ANALYSIS OF A FEW GENERATED STRUCTURES BY MEANS OF EXAMPLES

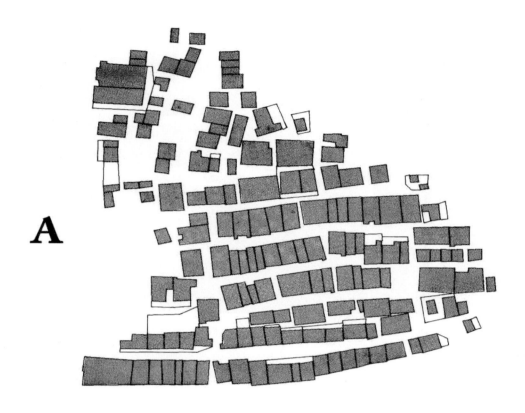

SHILNATH CAMP

0   10   20   50 M

A: A generated structure: Shilnath, Indore, India.

On pages 181–85 there are seven plans of settlements in India. Three of them (A, B, C) are generated structures. Four of them (D, E, F, G) are fabricated structures.[1]

What is it about A, B and C that is different? I should like to suggest, first of all, that most of us share an immediate perception that A–C are more *interesting* than D–G: more complex, more difficult to describe, richer, and somehow more important.

We may feel this in many ways. One person may feel that A–C are more interesting simply as works of art, more interesting to look at, would hold the attention better artistically, if (as plans) they were hung on a wall. D–G are boring, too simple, one stops looking at them after a few moments.

At a slightly more sophisticated level, looking carefully at the plans as plans *of human settlements*, we can see immediately, that A–C are bet-

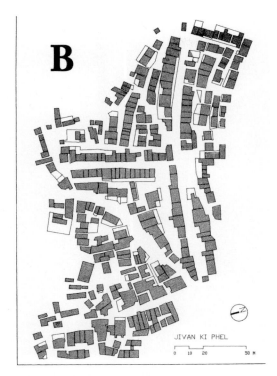

B: A generated structure: Jivan Ki Phel, Indore, India.

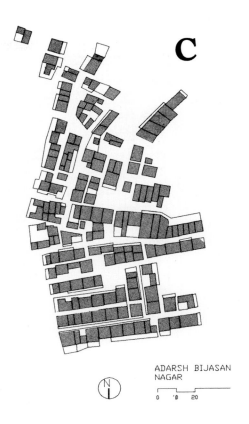

C: A generated structure: Adarsh Bijasan Nagar,
Indore, India.

ter places to live than D–G. The houses are more differentiated; spaces are more satisfying; the experience of being there is richer, each house is unique in shape and position; there are more, and denser, patterns of significant relationships between houses and spaces. With D–G the experience of the actual place will be more sterile, it is less rewarding to be there. Altogether as human, social, and emotional environments, they are less satisfying than A–C.

At least intuitively it is clear, then, that there is something more interesting, more important about A–C than about D–G. The difference hints at something interesting. But what does it mean, what is responsible for the difference we see, and what is the meaning of the difference we see? What is it that makes them profound, what distinguishes them?

My purpose in bringing this out is to ask what the difference is between the two *classes* of objects. What is it about the two classes, *precisely*, that makes the generated structures more interesting and more important?

The concept of "generated" is not quite as straightforward as it seems if one merely looks at the geometry of the plan. For example, architects have thought for two or three decades now, that, in various ways they can simulate the beauty and living character of generated structures and achieve results of greater variety and beauty by doing so. The plan F was made by Rajinder Puri, visibly in an attempt to reproduce the variety of space, the variety of house sizes, and the overall more dynamic character of the generated examples. Yet it still lacks the essential quality of generated structures, and must be firmly placed in the fabricated camp. Its arrangement is created by design, and seems better only in appearance. The essence of its fabricated character is untouched.

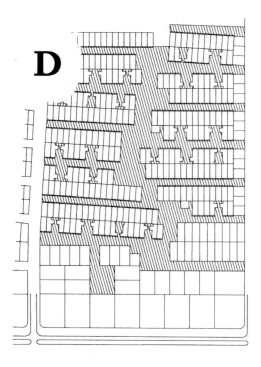

D: A fabricated structure: designed by B. V. Doshi, Vastu Shilpa, and built in Indore around 1989.

The houses built as part of plan D. Although there was a sincere effort to involve families in decisions, it is plain that this is not a generated structure, and the family input has not deeply led to emergence of living structure. Contrast this with the photograph on page 181.

The Plan D was made by my old friend Balkrishna Doshi. In this case the whole idea of the plan is to create a living character by allowing families to make their own house for themselves, plainly a positive ideal, and one which has laid important steps as a precedent. But here, too, the plan itself, its ins and outs, are mechanical — I do not want to say contrived, since they are plainly made with good intent, and with the purpose of making a better living environment. This project was built as drawn, in 1989, and did achieve an important measure of success, as living structure, because of the individually designed house layouts allowed within the rigid structure of the plan. Yet the most important variables which should have been under control of the families, are fixed. The families' contributions are hardly more than minor cosmetic variations within a rigid shell. So this plan, too, lacks the *essence* of living structure, and is not a generated structure. It, too, must be placed in the fabricated camp.

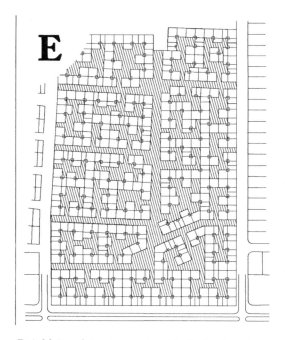

E: A fabricated structure: designed by Carlos Barquin, a theoretical study for Indore, India.

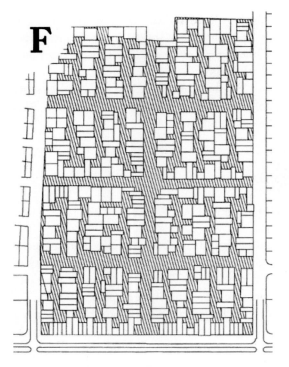

F: Planned settlement by Rajinder Puri, making an effort to create the appearance of a generated structure, but within the framework of a fabricated structure.

G: A fabricated structure: government-designed public housing, Indore, India. The project has had some modest changes over time, which are visible in the in-and-out character of individual dwellings. However, as a whole, the community remains a fabricated structure.

At first sight Plan G looks more generated, and less fabricated than D, or E, or F. And indeed it has more of the character of a generated structure, within the framework of a fabricated one. It is an actual place, made by architects and inspired by a government program of public housing. However, it seems generated only because the houses are all slightly different, house fronts wobble, and the street has minor jigs in it. The variation is a little more real, a little more genuine, than that in plan F, for example. But, although there is an aspect of this plan G that is truly generated, again what is allowed to vary is only a very small proportion of what matters. The core of the plan, most of what one experiences in the actual place, is a lack of living structure at intermediate levels of scale, shows that in its essential quality this plan is still independent of human reality in the houses and in the social groupings: The plan is still a fabricated one.

4 / STRUCTURES THAT HAVE UNFOLDED IN TIME

In the generated structures A–C we have a strong sense that they unfolded over time. We have a feeling, an intuitive certainty that the plans could only have been generated over time.

On the other hand, in D–F it is very clear that the design was created at one moment in time as an *arrangement*. Of course, in a certain sense, D, E and F, too, were created in time. Although the time scale may have been shorter, they still happened in time. The design did not appear all at once in one nanosecond. It may even have taken months at the drawing board to create them. Yet in D–F this length of time is not significant. We know that A–C happened in time in some *meaningful* way, and in a way which mattered, and which gave them their deep essential structure. In D–F, the role of time is insignificant, trivial. Time did not affect the structure, or contribute to its design.

We shall, in the next half-dozen pages, try to understand just what exactly this is, this "meaningful" way.

5 / HOW TO COUNT MISTAKES

When we examine an object, we may see that each element in the object (part, line, edge, position, color, size) represents a decision. In very rough terms, we may say that each line represents a different decision. We may also say that each line has created space on either side of it and near it, and therefore typically represents some four or five decisions about space (through size, convexity, adjacency, organization).

In addition, we must be conscious that larger elements, too (streets, house groups, courtyards, party walls, paths, blocks) — not only the smallest elements — must be included among the elements considered, and decisions about size, shape, and position of these larger elements, too, must be counted, since these also may be either flawed (with mistakes) or well-adapted. In the Shilnath plan (A) there are 150 house lots. Each house lot, as shown on this plan, has possibly four or five lines associated with it, making a total of say, 700 elements or decisions at the lowest level of scale. In addition, we may guess that there are potentially half as many again larger-level elements at a wide variety of different scales. Thus there are about 1000 elements in all, in the Shilnath plan.

Each element has the possibility of being wrong. By that I mean that the element as placed, sized, and oriented, may be *well-adapted* to its neighbors, to the space around it, to the conditions which exist, and to the conditions arising from the structure of the surrounding elements — or it may be *badly adapted* to the neighbors, conditions, space, trees, arising from surrounding elements.

We are going to count the number of possible mistakes, and try to estimate how mnay of these mistakes have been avoided, and how many have been committed, in different types of plan. It is here, that we shall see the vast superiority of generated plans. They avoid mistakes. A fabricated plan cannot avoid mistakes, and in all fabricated plans, the overwhelming majority of possible mistakes, are actually committed.

6 / THE SIGNIFICANCE OF GENERATED STRUCTURE

The significance of generated structure lies in the concept of mistakes. Fabricated plans *always* have many mistakes — not just a few mistakes but tens of thousands, even millions of mistakes. It is the mistake-ridden character of the plans which marks them as fabricated — and that comes from the way they are actually generated, or made, in time. Generated plans have *few* mistakes.

In order to describe what it is that actually happens in time in the case of a generated structure, I shall draw attention to the vital point. Let us consider D, one of the fabricated designs, and compare it with the more organic design of C. We can see that at any given place in C, many small things work. The house has a nice street outside: The house across is in a good relation to it; the space opens out to a place where children can play. The house has a front which is recognizable. Each place has its own uniqueness.

A dramatic way of expressing this idea is to say that by comparison in the fabricated scheme E (which has about 400 houses), each element has the potential for a number of mistakes. Let us make a wild guess and say that the drawing E contains 400 houses, hence about 1600 elements (lines). I shall say (and argue) that in a mechanical scheme like E, each line has roughly five mistakes associated with it. By that I mean that the line was drawn on a drawing board, without any opportunity for the line to be modified, or adjusted, according to realistic perception of actual difficulties and opportunities on the place itself. I claim that in a professional planning/design/development process, this failure of adaptation is inevitable, and that at the time of its creation no process was put in place to remove these mistakes.

By contrast, in C (Shilnath), I argue that each line represents a decision that was put down, one at a time, over a history extended in time, and that each decision was made by people associated with the place, the house, the immediate conditions. As a result of this relatively slower unfolding process, and as a result of the decentralization of the decision-process in different people's hands and in the hands of people intimately associated with the needs of the situation, I shall say, further, that at the time the line is put down, each of the five possible mistakes (that existed in E) is here corrected, by adaptation, and that as a result of the process which allows each line to be considered carefully, and adjusted, these five possible mistakes are eliminated.

The upshot of this comparison suggests that the plan E must inevitably have some 8,000 mistakes in it. There was, in the procedure used to generate this plan, no way to avoid it. Any process which statically determines these elements (lines, edges, and positions) merely by drawing-board planning, cannot avoid having some 8,000 mistakes.

C, on the other hand, has very few mistakes in it — or perhaps, by the same kind of count, at most a few hundred. Thus, the effect of allowing C to grow in time, and to grow gradually, to unfold gradually, is that most of the possible mistakes in it are eliminated, while a designed and planned object such as D will have on the order of 10^4 mistakes in the site plan alone.

That is the enormous difference between a generated thing, and a designed and fabricated thing. In a fabricated/designed thing, it is virtually certain that it will have a huge number of mistakes, reducing the value of the environment, and reducing its ability to support people's daily lives in an efficient and adequate fashion.

7 / A THOUSAND TRILLION POSSIBLE MISTAKES IN A HUMAN EMBRYO

If an embryo were shaped by fabrication, and not generated, the number of mistakes would be unbelievably large.

The human embryo is created by 50 doublings of the cells. Starting with a single cell (the fertilized egg), after 50 doublings, the embryo has 2^{50} cells. During this doubling process that occurs 50 times, each cell has the opportunity to adapt itself, and to remove possible mistakes by position, adaptation, pushing and pulling. The total number of opportunities for correction, then, in the growing embryo, is $(1+2+2^2+2^3+....2^{50}) = 2^{51}$. Reversing the argument, we may express this by saying that the assembly of embryo cells, if not given the chance for adaptation and if instead made by design or fabrication, would typically have 2^{51} mistakes — a truly enormous number, roughly 10^{15}, or a thousand trillion possible mistakes.

That is what would happen if an embryo were designed and built, not generated. If an embryo were built from a blueprint of a design, not generated by an adaptive process, there would inevitably be one thousand trillion mistakes. Because of its history as a generated structure, there are virtually none.

8 / ONE MILLION POSSIBLE MISTAKES IN A COMMUNITY

The number of potential mistakes avoided in the settlement of houses in Shilnath is certainly far less than those avoided in the human embryo. But the principle is the same. In any site plan for a few hundred houses, like the examples D and E and F, there will inevitably be on the order of ten thousand mistakes.

I have estimated, above, that the possible mistakes in a plan for 150 houses, will be about 1000. That is for the site plan alone, only for the *boundaries* of the buildings. In addition, in the type of planned architecture typical of public housing, or development tracts, we have the further possibility of similar huge numbers of errors in each individual house. As we see in the calculation on pages 192, each house, itself, then contains the possi-

bility of some additional 5,000 mistakes per house. If there are 150 houses in a small community, we then have the possibility of approximately (1,000 (for the siteplan) plus 150 times 5,000 (for the houses)) or some one million total possible mistakes in the project as a whole — an egregiously large number. Unfortunately this is not fanciful, but a fact about the way we design and build our houses today.

If we have responsibility for such a plan, or for building such a community, we can only avoid the huge number of inevitable mistakes, by finding some way to make the thing a generated structure, not a fabricated one. This requires deep — very, very deep — changes in procedure.

9 / THE COMPLEXITY THAT WAS GENERATED IN SHILNATH

The primary way in which complexity of structure reveals itself, is in the internal density of significant relationships which exist. When adaptation occurs successfully, and each line or element created is created in such a way as to avoid its possible mistakes, it does this by creating meaningful relationships in every direction.

Let us once again look at Shilnath, and examine the particular part of it which is shown below in the detailed plan (page 189)

blown up to a large scale. Please look at the one small house which is freestanding in the middle of the space shown on the left. This house performs several functions at the same time. First, it is placed in such a way as to close the space to the right. Thus, it makes that space somewhat more private, creates a natural boundary to it, yet leaves it half open to movement and view. We should be aware that this subtle "closing while yet leaving open"

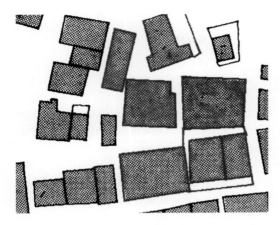

A detail of the settlement at Shilnath. Here we see the profound complexity of overlapping relationships that is typical in every generated structure.

is a human practical matter that concerns the feelings of the people living there, their daily experience, and is something that was plainly done by them to satisfy the way they conduct themselves socially, and emotionally, in their normal daily lives.

Looking again at the small house, with reference now to the long axis it creates, we also see that it is placed to have a relationship with the long house that is above it (on the drawing) and with which it is nearly coaxial. This creates a sense of cooperation and connectedness between these two long houses, and it makes the face of one house face directly to the other. The specific deliberateness with which this is done tells us that once again, it has practical human reasons. Further, the connectedness between the two houses is embodied in the beautifully shaped squarish open space between the two. Again, we see that the makers of these two houses placed their buildings to shape a comfortable space of a certain dimension, which is comfortable for play, conversation, and other things.

We know, too, that the small house, being surrounded by the street, has the capacity to function as a fulcrum at a time of festival, since it allow processions, or dancing, to move around and around the house, without stopping, a common way that people move during marriage festivals and other more informal celebrations. Fur-

thermore, our small house also has an important relationship with the narrow path below it (in the drawing). Also it forms a square space just below it, at the opening to that path. And then, finally, the house also forms an important part of the space on the left (in the drawing), where it helps to shape the end of that space by narrowing it down and forming and endpoint. In this regard the front of our freestanding house also has a significant relation with the fronts of three or four houses to its left (above the forementioned space), by forming a wall, or a facade, or edge of the space, when taken together with these houses.

Our small house thus enters into at least seven meaningful relationships, overlapping and connected. Each of these relationships is embodied as a center, and these seven centers are strong and living ones. Further, the relationships are motivated by practical daily-life concerns, which come from people's most ordinary strivings and needs and wishes. They are not esoteric artistic efforts to create nice space, as a western artist might attempt: Rather they are very mundane, sensible, and practical expressions of real thoughts, feelings, emotions, actions, games, commerce, and neighborly behavior. They are above all down to earth.

Every one of the 150 houses in the Shilnath community enters, in a similar fashion, into multiple overlapping relationships with other houses and other spaces. The subtlety of these relationships, and the connective tissue which they form, is a large part of the life in any living structure. Each of these relationships takes the form of a living center. Since the one example I have been discussing alone creates some seven vitally important living centers, as a result of the extreme carefulness of placing and position, size, and shape, we may surmise that the community as a whole probably contains some 7 x 150 or about a thousand overlapping living centers. This is the true complexity typical of any living structure, and as in this instance, such complexity can only be created when the structure is a generated one.

10 / IN INDIVIDUAL BUILDINGS, TOO, WE MAY ASK WHAT IS THE NATURE OF A "MISTAKE?"

The complexity which I have described in Shilnath and the other generated settlements can be seen, almost without change, in individual buildings, and in objects, too.

In each case, we have a structure in which the edges, spaces, positions, colors, either have — or do not have — the levels of subtle adaptation that I have described.

They have thousands of potential mistakes; and, when fabricated, most of these mistakes do actually occur *in fact*. If generated, there is a chance that these mistakes do not occur, and the object, or building, is harmonious in its existence in the world, and in relation to the things around it.

Whether the mistakes are successfully avoided, depends on the adequacy and subtlety,

of the generating process. In particular, it is essential — absolutely essential — that the adaptation, and the avoiding of mistakes, occurs at several levels of scale, as I described earlier. If this does work, then the adaptation is capable of real, subtle fine tuning. If the adaptation occurs only at one level — what I might call, well-meaning tinkering — this will not work out very well.

Let us consider the kinds of things which are, in my definition, "mistakes."

A window sill may be just right to put thing on — or it may be too small. A window may look at a favorite tree, or it may be placed to look at a wall. The bath maybe built so that one hardly has place to put the soap; or it may be built with a comfortable shelf where soap and shampoo can be without falling off. The light in a room may

Few mistakes: Generated structure of the front part of a house which HAS been generated

Many mistakes: Fabricated structure of the front part of a house in a housing tract which has NOT been generated

be placed to create a comfortable atmosphere at night, small pools of light in just the right places, or it may be merely a light fixture wherever the builder put it. The garage can be a box, barely big enough, or it can have a shelf, or bench, with tools, with a small but adequate window above the work surface. A stair post is either just in the place where your hand comes down as you walk down the stair or not. A paving which warms your feet or your body, because it is colored or terracotta to be absorbent and therefore gets warmed by the sun, works. It is well-adapted to need because of specific small, features that it has.

Each of these things, once again, depends on adjustment, attention to position, dimension, comfort, and adequacy. If missing, they are mistakes of adaptation — adaptations that were not achieved.

Look at the steps of the blue porch, on the left-hand page. It is full of subtle adaptations: the seat up on the right, the railing on the left, the 'wrong' top riser, the boards on the deck, the arched opening framing the trees beyond, and the special choice of paint color giving the trees their special luster. Each one of these is coupled with a careful adaptation that makes life more worthwhile, more practical, without disturbing the harmonious character of the place. But in the porch in the right-hand picture, from a Fort Lauderdale housing tract, the adaptations are missing. Instead of sizes chosen to work right, dimensions are based on cheap cuts made on a 4 x 8 foot sheet of plywood. Windows are standard and cannot be fitted to frame a view or to be just the right size for the feeling of a room or of a view. The height of the ugly slot in the front is done without careful regard for a person entering a house, or, of course, for the concern and special nature of any one particular human being who is to love or cherish this place. The lack of adaptation in the one building, and the fullness and subtlety of adaptation in the other, are clear.

In the next section, we shall see just how many of these adaptations, and how many mistakes, are typical in an ordinary house. The

number is surprising. And in the foregoing argument, it is vital to understand that the beautiful blue porch is not good because it is archaic. Some people might respond to the example by saying, "Well, this beautiful porch is all very well, but it is nostalgic, just something from the past." The point, of course, is not that the porch is ancient or archaic, but simply that it is *better*. It has the deeper adaptation, to its use, to its surroundings, and to its internal orgamization — and is *therefore better*.

Above all the blue porch avoids the two-thousand mistakes which are potentially present in such a porch, and for this very concrete reason is a better, more deeply adapted structure. The battle cry of modern architects, throughout much of the 20th century, which branded such things as nostalgic, irrelevant, not modern, and so forth, was really little more than a wild attempt to justify the huge mistakes modern buildings (and developers and architects) were making daily, by claiming that things which did not make these mistakes were "bad" and "nostalgic."

In fact, of course, the number of mistakes or its contrary — depth of adaptation — has nothing to do with style. In the 20th century, for instance, one of the classes of artifacts which frequently had very good adaptation, were the motorbikes made and adapted by bikers for themselves. Here there was nothing nostalgic at all — merely a community of people with good access to machine tools, welding torches, and a strong desire to make their bikes good for themselves. Long-haul truckers had a similar (not quite so intense) love affair with the cabs of their long-haul rigs, which they also frequently tuned to their own needs, and where once again people managed frequently to reach a relatively mistake-free environment. No nostalgia there!

Nearly all the beautiful and living structures described in Book 1 are, on close examination, generated structures which have precisely this many-level adaptation and overcoming of possible mistakes deep in their fabric, because they were made by processes which *generated* — not fabricated — the structure.

11 / THE FIVE-THOUSAND POSSIBLE MISTAKES IN A TYPICAL HOUSE

H many possible mistakes are there in a typical house?

In order to estimate the number of potential mistakes which can occur in a typical house, it is helpful to consider the fact that a typical house nowadays has about 2000 man-hours of labor in it. During an hour, decisions of dimension and position are being made by a carpenter several times an hour; thus, we have a likely guess that the house contains some 5,000 decision points — each one, again, capable of being done right, or being a mistake, or being done right.

It is fair to say that if any one of these decisions is made blindly, according to design information in a construction blueprint, it is virtually certain that this decision will be a mistake since there is — in general — no way that luck could manage to make the decision come out right. The mistake will be avoided, and the "right" thing done, only if the decision has attention, thought, and mental effort.

Consider the number of physical pieces of material in a typical house: steps, sills, walls, baseboards, floorboards, tiles, shelves, doors, windows . . . A reasonable guess is that there are likely to be a few hundred really important pieces of material of this kind. With each piece there are decisions about position, length, breadth, height, relation to the next thing, extension, connection — again half a dozen or a dozen. All in all, by this method, too, we arrive at a likely number of about 5,000 decisions that can potentially be wrongly placed, and will, inevitably be wrongly placed if they are not given special attention while the house is being made.

It must be said emphatically that this by no means requires an increase in construction cost. The valuable *decision time* need not be done by a highly paid worker — it can be done by family members themselves, provided what they decide can then be built without extra effort or material cost, and the only thing the construction worker or craftsman must do then is to cut, nail, and place material correctly, according to the wishes of the client. This does of course require new forms of contract which provide new relation-

Generated structure: here the wishes of the family, their comfort, and the adaptation of use to structure have been simply carried out, without fuss, all quite direct. Contrast this with the photograph on page 184. Note: this picture is not about "Isn't poverty wonderful." It is about the fact that even with very simple means, people can make themselves comfortable when permitted to do so.

A room (my own library) in which a very large number of adaptive decisions (about 1000) were made, in a relatively short time, and at very low cost. Nevertheless it is a truly generated structure, because every decision, no matter how small, was made in such a way that the resulting relationships became meaningful.

ships between client, craft and labor, and new forms of cost control which can achieve these things in a practical legal framework. The topic is taken up more fully in Book 3.

An example of such a process, where low-cost decisions having a direct bearing on the comfort and harmony of a room, were made in a short space of time (about one week) is presented elsewhere (pages 387–90). An example of its results are shown in the photograph above.

It is also necessary to recognize that the generated character of elements, in a house or anywhere, goes down to the smallest details. Consider, for example, the Japanese tea bowl and the wine glass, shown on the next page.

The concept of mistakes does not only apply to what is functional in the obvious way. A mistake, is ultimately a geometrical problem, which bears on what we call function, and the concept of practical function is only the tip of the iceberg. This matter is fully discussed in Book 1, chapter

11. So, in a small object which appears in the house, within its structure, even within an inch or two, there are also mistakes possible, or harmonies achievable. Let us examine the wine glass and the tea bowl. We may imagine, in each case, that as the object unfolded, centers were latent, and these centers, at the next step were embellished or not, opportunities created by latent centers pressed forward, or left dangling.

In the wine glass we see a number of mistakes. The top of the glass edge of the bowl — not very comfortable for the lips — could have been made rounder; as a boundary, then, it would have had a certain fatness or juiciness, which has not been pursued. The stem of the glass, where it meets the base, is flaccid, and this junction, as a center could have been more beautifully shaped.

But in the Japanese tea bowl, we see such centers have been taken to the fullest, and each latent center, at the time of its making and con-

A famous Japanese tea bowl which, in spite of its appearance of having been "designed," is actually a generated structure—hence its beauty.

A "fabricated" object—a glass made in the Royal Dutch Glassworks, well-designed (perhaps), but utterly dead as an object—because it has no generated structure.

ceiving, pressed home to become a structure of beauty. Of course, when we talk about such intense attention to small details, this is not something that could be carried out in every part of the house, in every domestic utensil, every stair rail. But here, too, thousands upon thousands of mistakes can be made — and *are* made daily in such common objects as the wine glass. They add to the sum-total lack of harmony in the evolving whole. But when taken seriously, even if it is only here and there, in one object such as the tea bowl, or in one special window, the house will gain enormously.

The bowl, in regard to its shape, its glazes, its decoration, the form of the emblem drawn on its surface — all of them are *generated*. At every level the bowl is a generated structure, through and through. By comparison, the wine glass shown above next to the tea bowl, and made by Royal Dutch Glassworks, is stiff and lifeless. It is *not* a generated structure. This is reflected in the fact that the wine glass has not been thought through for comfort. For example the stem is thin, one feels that it is necessary to pick the glass up by the stem — yet this is awkward. The bowl of the glass is not comfortably shaped for the hand. The Japanese tea bowl, on the other hand, is very comfortable to hold. It is made for two hands. the cup is raised from the table, so that

one's fingers fit underneath easily. And the slight, yet extraordinarily subtle curve of the bowl is designed to be comfortable and comforting as the hands go round it.

Let us ask why the tea bowl is so much more "generated" than the crystal wine glass? Why is the glass stiff and lifeless — harsh — while the cup is unified and harmonious — orderly, yet soft? We do see, of course, that the tea bowl is replete with the fifteen properties, as explained already in Book 1, chapter 5. But why does this geometrical quality, as it appears in the tea bowl, come necessarily from the history of this object unfolding in time?

Let me ask this more clearly. In the tea bowl, we see many centers, strong centers, levels of scale, massive boundaries, good shape, deep interlock, and so on. All the fifteen properties are there. And they are largely missing from the wine glass. But what does this have to do with time? What was it that made this structure of centers achievable in the tea bowl?

The answer is complex, and lies at the core of the transformations I shall discuss in chapter 7, but in a nutshell the answer is this: If you want to get a system of centers to appear in that cup or glass, you must introduce them in a certain order, the placing of each depending on infinitesimal subtleties in the structure and geometry, as they have appeared up to that moment. This is what the loose term "unfolding" means. And further, you can only get this structure by allowing the profound and multiple structure of centers to appear in a certain order, so that you get each bit of

the structure by unfolding it — *from* the previous state. Thus the importance of time, is not merely that you have a chance of tinkering and adapting. It also allows you to get each next layer of structure from the previously established layers of structure. Complex, generated structure *cannot be arrived at in any other way.* One structure is established. The next structure is then made to appear within that structure, and *from* that structure. Each stage develops from the previous stage, each one creating the conditions from which the next can be created, and from which it flows. It is in this process that the fifteen properties, and their enormous density, can be achieved. *That is the secret of the whole thing.*

12 / THE SOCIAL AND MONETARY COST OF THE ONE MILLION MISTAKES IN A FABRICATED COMMUNITY

In order to arrive at an estimate of economic damage, we need to find a decisive way of evaluating the importance of generated structures, by making a cost analysis of the mistakes.

The very large number of mistakes which follow inevitably from constructing buildings as non-generated structures is very large indeed. These mistakes are embarrassing, uncomfortable, often ugly. They reduce life in our communities, and fail to support people's lives effectively.

However, the poor environment and the countless inevitable mistakes of adaptation might elicit no more than a few tut tuts from planners or architects or public officials. But the truly dramatic consequence, the devastating impact of these mistakes on our society is not made sufficiently visible by referring merely to these social and psychological discomforts.

What has to be said, is that the whole system of these mistakes, and the way we keep on introducing them into the built world, *is also very costly.* It is exorbitant in cost, and imposes massive economic burdens on society.

Indeed, when we calculate the negative economic effect of fabricated structure, we shall see massive impact in concrete money and fiscal terms, so massive that the sheer number of mistakes must be capable of communicating with the politicians and business leaders of our era.

COST ANALYSIS FOR A SINGLE HOUSE

The mistakes I have referred to are indeed very very costly. I estimate that an ordinary American house contains a density of about 1 decision per cubic foot. That means that a house of 2500 square feet is likely to contain about 20,000 possible mistakes, when the house is *not* generated.

For the library shown on page 193, decisions were made at the rate of about 10 per hour, for twelve days, thus about 1000 decisions in all, in a room 10 feet by 14 feet by 8 feet 6 inches high — about 1200 cubic feet. This yields a potential-mistake density of nearly one potential mistake per cubic foot. The bookshelves are ranged in size, corners are made with special cuts, colors and trim are carefully chosen, each cabinet door, chamfer, and division between shelves, and spacing of dividers, was chosen to increase the function and usefulness of the room. The details of the library are described more fully on pages 387–90.

Although any one of the mistakes by itself is not strongly noticeable, still, the presence of mistakes add up rapidly, and their *absence* controls the monetary value of a building. If the windows are nicely proportioned, the house becomes more expensive. If the window sills are good, the windows, and the rooms are worth a little more. If the windows look towards beautiful views (a function of the window placement, not only of the potential for view that is inherent in the land), the house is worth a lot more money, often as much as $20–30,000 more. If there is a beautifully placed, and cared-for tree, growing by the front door, the house may be worth $10–20,000 more than it would be worth if that tree were not there.

Some mistakes are more costly than others. If the baseboard where the wall meets the floor, is cheap or badly made or badly proportioned, the room is likely to be worth, on the average, $100 dollars less, and the house, altogether, is probably worth $500 less. Here the mistake-cost is about $1 per running foot of baseboard, similar to the figure of $1 per cubic foot for the room. If the view is badly chosen, or the tree by the front door is badly handled, the cost is much higher, on occasion it might even be as high as $5,000 per cubic foot for a few cubic feet.

It is difficult to get a reliable average cost figure for mistakes, but, just as a start, we may contemplate the mistake-costs as lying in the realm of $5–10 per cubic foot, thus potentially as high as $200,000 for a single American house of average size. And, indeed, this is a reasonable number, even though it seems outlandish. The cost of a house which has no mistakes in it, a normal house, in which every detail is perfectly adapted — commonplace at some 'antique' periods of history, but a rarity today — can easily run to the order of $750,000. The difference in value between a house worth $150,000 (which con-

tains 10,000 mistakes) and the same sized house, containing no mistakes (which would be worth, say, $600,000 since it is a rarity today because houses nowadays are so rarely *generated*), might easily be in the range of $450,000 (if such a house were ever to be available at all among the available stock of newly built houses).

In passing, it must also be mentioned that good adaptation is not the prerogative of the rich. In fact it has relatively little to do with the cost level of the house or the income level of the household. In the Indian houses from the communities I have cited earlier in the chapter, total cost of a house may be no more than $3,000 ($US, 1999). And the houses are smaller, say 600 square feet, thus containing only about 5,000 potential mistakes. Yet a small house with the amenity, comfort, charm, and physical rightness which occurs after 5,000 successful adaptations in a proper unfolding, is likely, even in India, to be sought after because it has become so rare, and might well be worth $30,000. Regardless of absolute level of cost, the difference in value between a house which has 5,000 mistakes of adaptation, and one which has none, is like to be on the order of a tenfold difference, no matter what the absolute value of the house may be.

COST ANALYSIS FOR A COMMUNITY OF HOUSES

In the low-cost Indian example, if we use the assumption that house value doubles from $3000 to $6000 when the houses are mistake-free, the loss of value for a community of 150 "fabricated" houses would be $450,000. Using a more accurate guess of $2 per mistake and 5000 mistakes per house, the mistake-cost in a community of 150 fabricated houses would be $1,500,000: a fortune for low-cost housing.

If a community of middle-class American houses has 150 houses in it, the total loss of value in the developer-designed scheme with 20,000 mistakes per house, would be 3 million mistakes, or, at $10 per mistake, on the order of a staggering $30 million of lost value for the community.

13 / DIFFERENTIATION

Needless to say, the highly complex million-fold adaptation of elements cannot occur in random order, or by mere trial and error, nor can it occur successfully through addition, one element at a time. Merely additive processes (like the assembly of an erector set from fixed components that are arranged and rearranged) never lead to complex adaptation, or to profound complex structure.

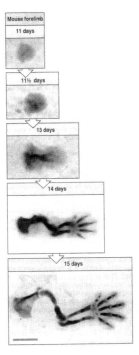

Differentiation in a growing embryo. The unfolding foot of a mouse between the 11th and the 15th day.

The key to complex adaptation in a generated structure lies in the concept of differentiation. This is a process of dividing and differentiating a whole to get the parts, rather than adding parts together to *get* a whole.

In a structure which is differentiated, the structure will not, in general, be made by small piecemeal acts happening in random order. Rather, each step creates the context for the next step in the whole, and allows the process as a whole to lay down, next, what has to be laid down next in order for an orderly unfolding to occur, and to allow a simple and coherent form to arise in which, nevertheless, all the important small details are done just right.

In chapter 7, we shall see an outline of such a differentiating process, and I shall provide a template for a process that I call the fundamental differentiating process, present in all adaptive differentiation. The fundamental process, when present in specific social processes, is capable of generating living structure in buildings and communities. It is, in principle, the key to the effective creation of generated structure in all built form. We shall see how the repeated application of the fundamental process allows large elements to be differentiated to generate smaller elements in such a way that careful, mistake-free adaptation of all elements, at all levels of scale, in the built world can, in principle, be virtually guaranteed.

14 / CREATING HIGHLY COMPLEX OBJECTS

In general, we may say that a complex object will only be successful if it is generated. This is obvious in the case of organisms (animals and plants), which are always generated. But it is less obvious, and so far hardly recognized at all for the complex objects we create such as houses, buildings, rooms, cities, and neighborhoods.

Let us consider the case of software. A typical computer program contains tens of thousands of lines of code; others in daily use contain a million lines, even as many as ten million lines of code.

In recent years some attention has been given to their theory of design, and some improvements have been made in contemporary ways of thinking about their design. Computer scientists have told me proudly that they consider computer programs the most complex objects designed by human beings.

Yet, to date, there is little recognition of the following commonsense point: If indeed the programs are so complex, then it is likely that they, too, will be potentially subject to hundreds of thousands, perhaps millions of egregious mistakes of adaptation. Here I am not only talking about "bugs" — failures which stop a program from running altogether. I am talking about mistakes of adaptation, ways in which the program fails to do what it is supposed to do, fails to meet the needs of the people who use it, or is more awkward, more annoying, less useful, than it is supposed to be. If the analysis given in this chapter is correct, then it is fair to say that truly successful programs can only be *generated*; and that the way forward in the next decades, towards programs with highly adapted human performance, will be through programs which are generated through unfolding, in some fashion comparable to what I have described for buildings.

This chapter was first composed as a lecture to the computer science department at Stanford University. After the lecture, I had a chance to hear comments from many of the computer scientists in the audience. Much of the commentary I heard went something along these lines: "This is really interesting... perhaps you should call it 'evolutionary adaptation' instead of 'generated structures' " and "We computer scientists ourselves often practice various form of evolutionary adaptation in software design. Good software grows, by steps with feedback and evolution, to something better . . ." And so on.

The essence of all these comments was what I call gradualism. It says "Yes of course, in the case of a complex structure, we cannot hope to get it right first time around, so we build it, run

it, test it, fix it, change it . . . and keep on doing this so that it gets better." What has become known as *Extreme programming* is a way of doing this for software development, with a very short cycle of evolution and adaptation, repeated many times.[2]

Of course I am in favor of small steps, of adaptation through trial and error, and of what we may call evolutionary adaptation (see chapter 8). But this is not the central point at all. After listening to all these computer scientists' comments, and taking them to heart, I realized that I had failed, in my lecture, to emphasize the real essence of all generated structures. *The real essence lies in the structure-preserving transformations which move the structure forward through time, and which are primarily responsible for the success of the generating process.* The needed transformations are not merely trial-and-error steps, or some neat way of continually checking and making things better. In chapter 2, I have referred to the fifteen transformations which act, in all structure-preserving transformations, to move a whole structure forward in a deliberate and explainable way. *It is because of these fifteen transformations and their effect,* that a whole may be said to "unfold." It is because of these transformations that a whole becomes coherent, and beautiful. And it is because of this unfolding, and the way the unfolding processes work, that the structure is able to become "mistake-free."

To assume that the point of generated structures is merely slow, step-by-step evolutionary adaptation, is to make the same mistake that early adherents of Darwinism made in biology — to assume that small steps *alone*, modification coupled with selective pressure, would be sufficient to get a genotype to a new state, hence to create entirely new organisms... and so on. This does not work, and is now widely recognized not to work, because it lays too little emphasis on the (hitherto) unknown transformations which actually do the hard work of moving the evolving organism through stages that lead to its coherence and its geometric beauty in the emerging genotype (see chapter 1, pages 42–48)

15 / THE GREEK MARBLE HORSE

Highest example of generated complexity: Greek carving of a horse, 6th century B.C. *Look at the eyes, the head, the forehead ornament, the strap around the nose — each part has been transformed, by transformations originating in the whole, to have* POSITIVE SPACE *and* GOOD SHAPE *which thus intensify the whole.*

What I mean by a generated structure is just such a thing. It is a mistake-free structure which is beautiful and coherent, and which has become beautiful and coherent because of the impact of successive applications of the fifteen transformations which create, bring out, and generate its beauty and its elegance of structure.

The beauty of the generated object, and the connection of this beauty to the mistake-free nature of the generated object, though alluded to in discussion of the Shilnath plan (page 182), is not obvious. Yet this connection, surprising though

it is, is very much the essence of all that follows in the next eleven chapters. It may be made vividly clear, by discussion of an ancient Greek carving of a horse.

Look at the marble horse shown here. Let us consider carefully, what the artist did to make this marble horse, and how the fifteen transformations helped him, and how the mistake-free nature of the carving, and its great geometric beauty, are really aspects of one and the same thing. The artist had, one assumes, seen many horses. His carving is a distillation of what he knew. And how was his structural knowledge distilled in this carving? Let us look at a small part of the horse — for instance the place on the nose, where the straps go across the nose. If we look at the sculpture, we see how each piece — the nose, the space of the nose, its curve, the lay of the strap, the shape of the strap, its particular bulge, the space between the two parts of the strap — these are all positive. They are positive, too, in a real living horse. But a typical "realistic" painting of a horse is different. There, typically, these portions are not living centers with positive good shape, but are much more loosely shaped; all in all there is typically a kind of fuzz of unshaped inarticulate space, lying on the nose, between the eyes, the straps themselves are less beautifully formed. All these fuzzy bits are *mistakes*. To get rid of these mistakes, the individual shapes of space and objects must be made more solid, more clear — and the elements which are fuzzy, vague, must just be cleaned out altogether to leave the rest coherent.

Look at a more complex example. The eye of a horse is a mysterious structure, not easy to capture. It bulges, is visible from the front, yet somehow sits in the side of the head, under the occipital ridge. If you try to make these features literally, the bulging eyeball and the crest bone, you may very easily fail to see the whole in its deepest way. Trivial realist artists often make this kind of mistake. But the ancient Greek sculptor who made this marble horse looked at the wholeness of the eye in a real horse, and saw the way that the eye in the real horse causes a field effect. To create a representation of the *wholeness* — not merely of the details — the artist applied some of the structure-preserving transformations.

He used the ALTERNATING-REPETITION, BOUNDARIES, and STRONG-CENTER transformations, to create a large-scale field effect extending all over the side and front of the horse's head, just as it does in life. To do this, he had to invent something which looks to a modern eye, abstract and unlike a real horse. The lines visible around the eye of the sculpture do not appear in a real horse. Yet in fact the marble horse is more deeply horse-like, has more of the real feeling and presence of a horse than most of our contemporary "realistic" representations, because it is the *wholeness* and its true field of centers which finally appears in the stone, not merely an accurate transcription of details. And the same thing occurs throughout this sculpture. Again and again, we see living centers in the carving: the nostrils, the nose leather, the plate between the ears and on the forehead, The fifteen transformations create beautifully organized positive space in these centers, in a nearly ornamental fashion, throughout the fabric of the head.

This is all highly relevant to our understanding of generated structure, in the following way: What the artist did is roughly what nature does, when structure-preserving transformations preserve and extend the wholeness of a given system. More important, in *any* human-made generated structure, the fifteen transformations must be brought in, in an equivalent fashion, to create the link between the larger whole, and the detailed forms within it.

It is this transformative process which allows a generated structure to become alive and mistake-free — this which allows a living process to generate truly living forms.

16 / CONCLUSION OF THE DISCUSSION ON GENERATED COMPLEXITY
AND
PREFACE TO CHAPTERS 7-17

So, now, pulling together examples and discussions, can we understand what it means to "generate" a structure?

The argument put forward is that the high level of complexity we need in urban tissue, working and dwelling spaces, computer programs, etc., can only be attained when an existing, albeit latent, structure unfolds through differentiation to the needed level of complexity. Each differentiation, i.e. decision, is made in sequence and in context. It is reworked right then and there until it is mistake-free, i.e. , it takes into account all the connecting relationships. This must be done in sequence and in context because the necessary information for a successful decision is not available prior to that step in the unfolding.

This differentiating process is a successive application of the fifteen structure-preserving transformations that both adapt each part to the whole, locally, and, at the same time, preserve and bring forth the deep geometric structure of the larger surrounding whole. It is important to grasp that each differentiation *adds relationships and brings more interdependence among the centers.* Of course, as a result of the many adaptations, and the growing centers and properties, the structure slowly becomes thick with relationships. It is getting denser and denser all the time. And it is vital, for success, that the process is *able* to keep on cramming in more and more relationships, so that the mistake-avoiding adaptations can continue to be generated.

This "cramming" of complexity brings with it a need to constantly clean out any non-functionalities and leave only the most simple possible geometry in place. It is simple structure that allows for maximum relationships (you need only think of the sphere whose simplicity allows

for so many properties at once).[3] The transformations called SIMPLICITY, INNER-CALM, and THE-VOID have as a direct function the task of keeping a structure clean of useless debris and open to the possibility of further useful differentiations.

In short, then, to make room for more and more relationships, there is a cleaning process going on in parallel with the differentiating process. The process keeps cleaning itself out. Any garbage that accumulates has to be flushed out. The process is simplifying itself, getting rid of debris, and leaving itself, at each moment, with the cleanest and most spare structure possible. Only then, can the system be certain that there will always be room for more relationships, and only then will it truly be possible to keep injecting further transformations and maintain a coherent structure. It is this simplifying process, together with the fifteen transformations, which makes the beauty and majestic structure we think of as deep primitive art, or nature generating nature, at its best. Please look at the horse in this way.

A generated structure seeks to maintain and enhance its own internal geometric coherence, to avoid mistakes, and to be open to evolution and differentiation. We can admire Mother Nature generating the deeply beautiful simplicity and complexity of the daffodil is just this way. In fact, there is no other way. Alas, since we are not Mother Nature, when we generate our towns, computer programs, or attempt great art, we have to sweat it out with intense attention to what we are doing.

So now we have a rounded view of what a generated structure is. The structure seeks, above all, to avoid mistakes. To do it, it promotes an activity of structure-preserving transformations, to maintain coherence. In addition, to make the structure capable of containing the vast density of significant relationships which eventually builds up, the process is also cleaning the structure and simplifying itself continually, at the very same time that complexity is building up.[4] To do this, the leveling and sharpening that is typical of a process trying to preserve relationships, and get rid of non-relationship stuff, so that a spruce, spare structure is being built, and we keep moving towards the fine, profound simplicity which is typical of the greatest art, and

typical in nature. This is the only way a profound, well adapted structure can be built.

In the next eleven chapters, 7–17, I shall lay out some of the more important aspects of all living process, which allow a process to embody these concepts and tools, and which provide the core of a theory which shows us how living structure may be generated. The emphasis, throughout, is on the creation and generation of beautiful wholes, made to play their proper part in the great whole.

NOTES

1. The examples of plans on pages 182–85 are taken from a housing study by Witold Rybczynski et al. HOW THE OTHER HALF BUILDS (Toronto: McGill University, Housing Publications, volume No. 9, December 1984.

2. See Kent Beck and Ward Cunningham, http://www.armaties.com/extreme.htm.

3. David Hilbert and Stephan Cohn-Vossen, GEOMETRY & THE IMAGINATION (New York: Chelsea, 1952), "The Eleven Properties of the Sphere," p. 215.

4. Precursors to this kind of thinking can be found in Christopher Alexander, "The Origin of Creative Power in Children," BRITISH JOURNAL OF AESTHETICS, Vol. 3, No. 2, July, 1962, pp. 207-226, where the boiling down of spatial relationships in order to create more coherent forms, is discussed as a feature of children's cognitive development. A PATTERN LANGUAGE also discusses the spatial richness and simplicity that emerges when numerous patterns overlap.

CHAPTER SEVEN

THE FUNDAMENTAL
DIFFERENTIATING PROCESS

1 / DEFINITION

We are ready to examine the general nature of all living process, and to give a definition of living process in the world of building. Let us define as follows: *A living process is any adaptive process which generates living structure, step by step, through structure-preserving transformations.*

As I said in the last chapter, there is a great deal more to generated structures than mere trial-and-error tinkering. When living structure is generated in a building, somehow useful elements of global order slowly make their appearance at many levels of scale, and further, this seems to happen through what I have earlier called structure-preserving transformations. The process by which this occurs has complex aspects. Some are dealt with in chapters 8 to 17. But it will be difficult to understand these aspects without a broad general overview of what is going on.

In general terms, we may put it like this. When living structure is generated, it is not merely done by trial-and-error, rather the process has the feature that a coherent whole emerges, step by step. At each step, the process preserves the wholeness of what was there before. Yet at each moment in the evolution of the structure, from the additional, invisible structure which lies dormant (in the crevices of the structure), the transformations also have the ability to create something entirely new. Thus the process performs the seeming miracle that it respects what is there before, yet also manages to take the structure in a new direction, towards something which was *not* there before. And it does this not by arbitrary insertion of arbitrary new structure, but by pulling on latent aspects of the structure which are there already. Latent, they are there. But they are not yet visible or manifest.

The living process contains the procedure which makes this apparent miracle occur.

2 / THE HIERARCHY OF INDIVIDUAL AND ACCRETIVE PROCESSES

Before proceeding to elaborate this definition, we must recognize an important subtlety: Whether in a major metropolis, in a city, in a village, or in the countryside, generated living structures are made by the interaction of two kinds of process going on side by side:

(1) There are individual processes of design or construction, each one a locally complete, self-contained type of creative process in which a single center — one building, one shop, one room, one garden — of some scope is thought of, conceived, designed, and built, from start to finish. A local process of creation creates one complete center, large or small, from conception to completion. It is done in a controlled and continuous sequence, which happens in one (approximately) continuous time sequence. It does have a completion date.

(2) There is an accretive process which forms the larger structure, piece by piece. Centers — streets, buildings, shops, bridges, gardens — are added, or modified, and accumulated in such a way as to make larger centers — streets, neighborhoods, and so on. Accretive processes of creation are spread out in time and place, and are initiated independently by many different people. The acts of accretion gradually contribute to create a much larger whole, but this overall process generally has no finite beginning or end, and no completion date.

Guatemalan farmer forming and preparing his terraces; both an individual process, and an accretive process.

We may liken this overall scheme of things to the process by which a forest grows. There we also have accretion and local acts. On the one hand, there is a general large-scale process, largely random in sequence, in which many variegated individual acts of growth take place within the extensive (and sometimes tangled) existing structure of the forest. Second, there are thousands of instances of a more local process which are more controlled, each of which happens at a given site where there is a very well-ordered sequence which takes place as a single organism grows under the influence of its DNA, starting from a seed, and ending with a finished organism. In both the forest and the city, the process of accretion is made up of thousands of processes of local, individual growth, and in both cases it is capable of generating a successful, living result. Any definition of living process, must take both kinds of process into account.

All generative processes exist in these two forms. Here (above) is a photograph of of agricultural terraces formed by farmers in the mountains of Guatemala. We see a man working one of the terraces, and we see that his work, and the work of others, has terraced, or repaired the terracing of a whole hillside. Here we have both individual processes and an accretive process. The individual process — what this farmer is doing just now, with his pick — shapes the land, breaks the earth, loosens it, and shapes the slope to drain, be smooth, free of weeds, and ready for planting. And, in his mind, as he does it, there is also present the larger, accretive process in which his (and other people's) individual actions are fitted together to construct an emerging whole. The great pattern of terraces that was formed on the hillside was not formed by one man, but formed by the cooperative and intelligent adaptation of the individual processes to help form the whole.

An individual process that is part of an accretive process. You may ask why I show a medieval example rather than a 21st-century example. The reason is that in this example we see the masons carefully fitting their creative act into the whole around them. That work, in turn, makes larger wholes, as we see in the city of Acca (pages 206–7). Unfortunately, the same can only rarely be said of contemporary acts of building, which often exist in isolation, like cogs of a machine, making the modern city more an aggregation of these cogs, and less a multi-nucleated living whole.

However, the reader may have noticed an anomaly in the logic of the last paragraph. If one looks critically at the distinction between the two basic kinds of acts, accretive and local, one sees an unavoidable fuzziness. In a forest we can see, for example, that there is also a third kind of process in which a single organism, after its initial creation, is also *itself* continually being replenished and repaired. That repair and maintenance process is, once again, an accretive process in which certain new cells (or stems, or leaves, or roots, or twigs) are created within the larger existing whole in order to keep it alive. But this creative-accretive process is now happening within some *part* of an existing organism, not in the forest at large. It is a local version of the accretive process, happening internally within an individual organism.

The example reveals an important truth: every biological event that occurs in the forest is *both* an individual process of creation (at one level) and *also* part of a globally accretive process (with respect to some larger growing whole).

The generative processes which create a physical city have this feature, too. Every process is a process of creation at one level, and part of a larger process of accretion at another level. Something is built locally (room, building, doorway), and that something also helps to play a small part in the establishment and in the (much slower) creation and maintenance of a larger whole (neighborhood, garden, street).

This is the nature of all living process in the built environment. At every scale, every act of formation is both local and global, both creative/complete and accretive/incomplete.

Even a large building, though often built in what we view as a "single" process of design and construction, is itself made from a process-hierarchy of (let us say) 50,000 processes, each one both global and local. Each of the 50,000 processes is globally accretive (in adding to and helping some larger whole in the building) and locally creative (a complete package in its own right, for instance, designing and completing a room, or a wall-panel, or a step of a staircase).

In any living process at all, there is a hierarchy of these two kinds of processes going on. Even in the physically small example shown near the end of chapter 8 — the evolution of a painting by Matisse — the formation of the woman's individual locks of hair is both *part* of such a process, and is *itself* such a process. It creates individual centers, but these are parts of larger centers being formed in the woman's face.[1] And that work on that one painting, if we wish, may be seen as part of a much larger process through which the city of Paris is being formed from hundreds of thousands of processes. Bridges are formed; and within the bridge, girders are formed. Neighborhoods are formed, and within the neighborhood, buildings are formed. To form buildings, rooms and roofs are formed; rooms are furnished, and to furnish the rooms individual chairs and tables are made; these, once again, are formed by processes which make the centers — legs, top, casters, ornament — well or badly.

This hierarchy of center-formation, in one form or another, creates everything in the world. The only important question we must ask, if we are focusing on *living* process and on the capacity of a process to generate *living* structure, is whether these processes add up, whether there arises some coherent living order? That depends, in large part, on the extent to which the smaller processes contribute well to the formation of the larger wholes, whether each individual center is conceived, shaped, and built well according to its contribution to the invention and creation of the larger wholes in which it plays a part.

3 / THE SECRET

Here we come to the core of the secret. The fifteen structure-preserving transformations have the capacity to conserve and to create. They create, generate coherence in the large — and it is *new* coherence that they generate. Yet they are conservative and pull the future from the present.

Further, these fifteen transformations, though simple, guarantee the appearance of orderly, large and larger wholes with beautiful internal geometry. Instead of making aggregates of random structures, they propagate beauty with enormous force, both locally, and in the large.

This is the secret of all living process!

Acca, Yemen: created both by individual process, and accretive process.

4 / DIFFERENTIATION

To understand the way a living process helps us achieve living structure by differentiating space, let us consider, in detail, how space does actually get differentiated, and how a person may use the differentiating process to move steadily, again and again, from latent, half-formed structure to fully developed, coherent structure.

We may understand this human-based differentiation through the same example: the example of a CENTER being made more coherent, stronger, by the creation of a BOUNDARY. Suppose that at a certain stage in the development of a

Differentiation of a center and its surroundings by the creation of a boundary

structure, there is a latent center somewhere. By that I mean that it is a center whose presence can be felt, but it is not yet very strong or coherent. We have the possibility then, of enhancing that center by making a BOUNDARY zone around it. We know (from Book 1, chapter 5) that the strength of the center will be increased if this boundary is large. We may therefore strengthen the boundary, and in doing so, the weak center that existed before will become stronger.

Now, once again, we know (from Book 1, chapter 5) that this boundary will be strengthened, if any latent centers within the boundary are themselves strengthened, and strengthened further if two systems of strong centers are created, which then form an ALTERNATING REPETITION.

We see in these cases how latent centers may be transformed by differentiation (through the use of the fifteen transformations) in such a way

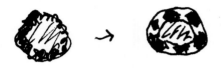

Further differentiation of the boundary, by alternating repetition and positive space

that the system of centers as a whole becomes intensified or more alive. In similar fashion, others of the fifteen properties may be relevant. For example, the use of POSITIVE SPACE and ALTERNATING REPETITION, may take a particular zone or volume of space which forms a weak center, and may strengthen that center. Or comparably, the strengthening effect of a boundary, may be

Differentiation of a system of weak centers by the use of the positive-space and alternating-repetition transformations. The white space between the black lines, and the shape of the black lines themselves, have been modified by the transformations, so that the overall larger diamond visible in the configuration becomes stronger.

intensified by the use of GRADIENTS, which will increase its effect; or a second smaller boundary which forms a gradient, will also introduce LEVELS OF SCALE, once again, to strengthen the effect, and the growing impact on the originally weak, and only latent center.

Two things should be noticed about these transformations.

First, they are purely mathematical, that is, formal. They have their origin only in the nature of space itself, and do not arise as a result of "function." They are used, in all real cases (buildings, biological systems, physical systems) in the service of function — but they are not functional in *origin*. They are pure transformations of space itself, through which the space becomes differentiated, and through which the life of the space is increased.

Second, as a result of the application of these transformations, the life of the whole is increased.

I do not mean to imply that these transformations can be applied blindly, in the hope of getting life to occur. They must always be *appro-priate*. They must act in the service of function; they must be undertaken, always, with an eye to local adaptation, and so on. These matters are taken up in later chapters.

But the essential point is this. We do have a system of transformations which are, in principle, capable of nudging a system steadily towards living structure, and these transformations are precisely those transformations which govern the life of the centers themselves — and hence the whole-ness (which *is* the system of centers), too.

5 / EMERGENCE OF BEAUTIFUL GEOMETRY

To drive the point home, I will give a real example, not only diagrammatic, where we see a beautiful thing emerging, by differentiation, from a sequence of transformations, and where it is clear that it is the transformations that have done the work.

Consider the sequence of transformations, shown on the next page. The diagrams describe the early stages in the evolution of the house plan for the Sanders house, a house we are currently preparing to build in Sonoma County, California. Consider what happens at each step:

Step 1 : Location of the House. A single center is formed. Out of the context, land, view, and nearby buildings, the STRONG-CENTERS transformation sets a position for a house on the edge of the platform in the land, overlooking vineyards below.

Step 2 : Formation of the Courtyard. This single center is transformed, now, under the POSITIVE-SPACE, DEEP-INTERLOCK and NOT-SEPARATE-NESS transformations. A deep center is formed, a courtyard which looks toward the view, is completed by the house, while the house takes three wings, to make the courtyard. These three transformations establish a connection with the land, reach out into the land, and enlarge it.

Step 3 : Differentiation of the House Wings. The previously undifferentiated U-shape is now transformed further. Once again, the primary force of the transformations come from practical considerations — patterns — but the geometric impact arises from the fifteen transformations. In the middle, the ALTERNATING-REPETITION transformation creates a wide porch of square-shaped bays and columns. Each of the three wings is differentiated further: the main room, and largest single center is formed by the LOCAL-SYMMETRY transformation and by the LEVELS-OF-SCALE transformation. And the right hand wing is formed by the BOUNDARY and GRADIENTS transformation. Finally, the entrance, to the left, is formed by the GOOD-SHAPE, DEEP-INTERLOCK, and ECHOES transformations. Throughout, we see the effect of the ROUGHNESS transformation, making rectangles which are as near perfectly rectangular as possible, while yet accommodating to the positive space and to the land, and the angles which they impose.

Step 4 : Differentiation of the House Interior and Expansion of the Garden. The central building is now further differentiated by transformations which create the core of the house: the organization of its living area and kitchen. This arises from intensive discussion about function and

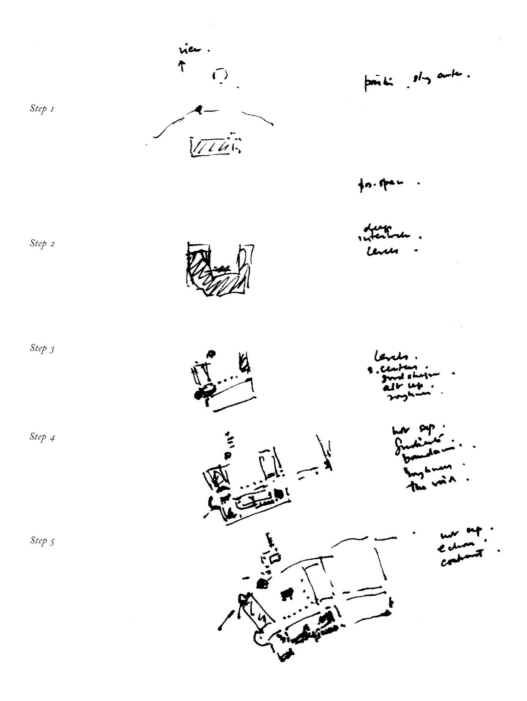

Step 1

Step 2

Step 3

Step 4

Step 5

Step-wise differentiation of the Sanders house

comfort with the family, expressed in the form of patterns: but the geometry is then produced by the action of the fifteen transformations once again. The organization comes from functional considerations — patterns — but the geometri-

cal impact arises from the fifteen transformations.

Step 5 : Further Differentiation of Outlying Areas. The NOT-SEPARATENESS transformation now

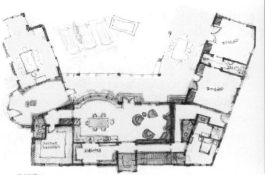 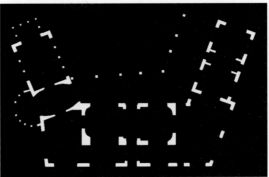

Step 6: The plan of the Sanders house, as it emerges from the previous differentiations through the action of the BOUNDARY *transformation, supplemented by the action of* LEVELS-OF-SCALE, STRONG-CENTERS, LOCAL-SYMMETRIES *and* ROUGHNESS *transformations. Step 7: The right hand drawing shows the structural plan which emerged from this plan shortly afterwards.*

appears several times, to create outlying centers which differentiate the garden, but which above all create an indivisible relationships between the house and the surrounding land.

Step 6 : Detailed Differentiation of the Living Room. The BOUNDARY transformation is very active at the next stage, helping to form coherent space. It shapes the big bow window, the layer of rooms behind the kitchen, the passage and stair behind the fireplace part of the living room, and the overall definition of space and structure which begins firmly to shape the room. Similar effects are visible in the emergence of other rooms visible in the drawing. This action is supplemented by the action of LEVELS OF SCALE, STRONG CENTERS, LOCAL SYMMETRIES in the formation of the alcove window near the bottom of the stair. Throughout the ROUGHNESS transformation acts to make these very strong firmly

shaped centers possible, while respecting the minor irregularities of plan. A plainly visible case appears, for example, in the small lobby to the kitchen inside the main entrance of the house. It has irregular shape to accommodate to external boundary considerations, while nevertheless preserving positive space, local symmetry, and strong centers in the interior of each part of its own space.

Step 7 : Emerging Structure. Next, this plan is transformed in such a way as to form a series of coherent structural bays. This is accomplished mainly by the LOCAL SYMMETRIES and LEVELS OF SCALE operators, through which we form individual coherent POSITIVE SPACE from structural elements like walls and columns. As we see, comparing the left and right drawings, this induces a fairly massive transformation in the whole.

6 / SUMMARY SO FAR

We see how the coherent geometry which makes the thing a unity, and which gives it beauty appears, step by step, as a result of differentiations caused and modified by the fifteen

transformations. Throughout the process, these transformations essentially created the design.

Ideally, then, when things are going well, each center gradually gets shaped appropriately by successive differentiations, and is governed by the larger whole, which it embellishes and helps to shape, and from which it springs. When that happens, everything is going well, and living structure will emerge. This may happen either in the context of an individual building project unfolding, or it may happen in the context of accretion where the construction of an individual building helps to differentiate, and make coherent, the urban space around it.

In cases where the process is less successful, the individual actions that arise within a larger whole are not shaped according to the nature of the larger whole, do not help it or enhance its life. Rather, they are locally unruly fragments (like cancer cells) which do too little locally to sustain and improve the whole.

For reasons given in chapter 4. most 20th-century urban developments were of this latter kind. When I said, there, that contemporary design and planning and development are too often structure-destroying rather than structure-preserving, what I meant was that the fifteen

differentiating transformations were largely missing from day-to-day processes.

On this page we see such an example from Tucson, Arizona, where the process of differentiation seems to have broken down altogether, and has been replaced by a very loose form of aggregation in which the larger wholes are almost never taken care of or healed. In the late 20th century we became used to this. However (though it it has been uncommon for a few decades), the demand that each act of construction in a city should always *help* the larger wholes, and should play a helpful role, is not an overwhelmingly subtle demand. In a generated structure this happens most of the time. An architecture succeeds — and we shall succeed in building living worlds in our cities — when there is a generative process which will allow each part to be shaped correctly, according to its local position, *and in a way that guarantees it has a positive impact on the larger whole.*

This bland-seeming statement has far more teeth than we might at first imagine. If the city of

Tucson, Arizona: Here the accretive process works fails, at almost every step, to generate living structure because the entities formed, though they are formed step by step, are not whole-creating. The result is merely a pile of stuff, unrelated, incoherent, and — for the large part — without much profound life.

Tucson had a living process guiding development, the next acts that took place in the part of Tucson illustrated above would, without effort, include some constructive ways to repair what is there, improve the positive space, make it all more usable, not only for trucks, but for people, too.

If a city can do that one thing all the time, or nearly all the time, everything will gradually work out fairly well; and if we can work out rules of the game so that people all over the world — builders, bankers, lay people — can go forward, doing whatever they do in the world, repairing their surroundings, always accomplishing this one task, then the Earth's environment will steadily be healed. Cities and buildings can become coherent and harmonious, merely as a result of following this rule. From a social point of view, then, what matters are the generative processes, the specific rules of the game which people follow when creating centers. When architects design buildings, are we designing in such a way that the parts we cre-

ate, large or small, contribute to the larger wholes and to the life of the larger whole? When a carpenter places a piece of wood, does the way he does it contribute to the life of the larger whole? When a city-planning official processes a permit, or modifies a permit, does the way he performs this act contribute to the life of the neighborhood?

The rules of the game — the way architects, builders, planners, painters, gardeners, and ordinary citizens play their roles and undertake their actions — that is what controls the form of the world. And the rules of the game needed are precisely those generative processes introduced in chapter 6. The question is, "Are the present rules of the game likely to help people generate a living structure in the larger whole?" It is this question that confronts us. Our aim, to generate a living world, need only to be to tame and redefine the rules of the game, to make them work so that all of us together, as we go about our business, can create a living whole.

7 / THE FUNDAMENTAL PROCESS:

Let us now try to set forth a general model of differentiation. Drawing on the broad picture of local processes and accretive processes — we may see that every process of planning, or design, or construction, or repair — *if it is part of a living process* — will always have a certain general form. This will provide us with the tool we need for a general and powerful way of looking at architecture — indeed at the construction of the built world as a whole.

The idea that there might be a single class of processes at the core of all living processes in society — hence at the core of all building, engineering, and all construction of our world — may shock the modern mind. In the conventional 20th-century way of thinking about architecture we faced a great number of disparate kinds of activity; we had to pay attention to function, flow of people, engineering, building

materials, color, traffic, climate, money, the wishes of the client. In normal professional work, all of these were assumed to be different *in kind*, and required different procedures. Somehow, as architects or engineers, we were supposed to combine these many disparate procedures to produce a successful whole.

I am proposing, instead, that in the course of all planning, building, conceiving, designing, landscaping, or making, at every stage we understand every process to be composed of repeated applications of the fundamental differentiating steps I have described. I believe all living processes are, in effect, combinations or combinations of combinations of this kind of differentiating step. A given living process may have a dozen steps, hence a dozen applications of the fundamental process, or it may have 500 steps, hence 500 applications — and the given building project may still be in the process of being imagined on a computer or a drawing board, or may be under construction, or may have been developing for many years — but the situation is always essentially the same, and the essential nature of each step, each application, is always similar. The core of the differentiating steps lies in the way that centers emerge and evolve and interact.

At each stage in its evolution the process — when a living one — always starts from the wholeness as it currently exists at that moment. The work is complete in some respects, in some respects incomplete. At the next moment, we take a new step — introducing one new bit of structure (always composed of new, living, centers) into the whole. The new structure we introduce may be large, medium, or tiny; it may be physical or abstract; it may occur on the land itself or in a person's mind, or in the collective understanding of a group of people. But the point is that at every stage of every life-creating process, the new bit of structure which is injected to transform and further differentiate the previously existing wholeness, will always extend, enhance, intensify the structure of the previous wholeness by creating further, and stronger, living centers. I therefore regard the group of fifteen transformations which do this work as providing what we may regard as elements of a universal building block — or universal "next step" — for each step forward in all living processes. The structure-enhancing step, which again and again intensifies one center and creates "hooks" to other new centers, might even be called *the* fundamental process.

THE FUNDAMENTAL DIFFERENTIATING PROCESS

1. At any given moment in a process, we have a certain partially evolved state of a structure. This state is described by the wholeness: the system of centers, and their relative nesting and degrees of life.

2. We pay attention as profoundly as possible to this WHOLENESS *— its global, large-scale order, both actual and latent.*

3. We try to identify the sense in which this structure is weakest as a whole, weakest in its coherence as a whole, most deeply lacking in feeling.

4. We look for the latent centers in the whole. These are not those centers which are robust and exist strongly already; rather, they are centers which are dimly present in a weak form, but which seem to us to contribute to or cause the current absence of life in the whole.

5. We then choose one of these latent centers to work on. It may be a large center, or middle-sized, or small.

6. We use one or more of the fifteen structure-preserving transformations, singly or in combination, to differentiate and strengthen the structure in its wholeness.

7. As a result of the differentiation which occurs, new centers are born. The extent of the fifteen properties which accompany creation of new centers will also take place.

8. In particular we shall have increased the strength of certain larger centers; we shall also have increased the strength of parallel centers; and we shall also have increased the strength of smaller centers. As a whole, the structure will now, as a result of this differentiation, be stronger and have more coherence and definition as a living structure.

9. We test to make sure that this is actually so, and that the presumed increase of life has actually taken place.

10. We also test that what we have done is the simplest differentiation possible, to accomplish this goal in respect of the center that is under development.

11. When complete, we go back to the beginning of the cycle, and apply the same process again.

This process, though presented as atomic, is multiple. What appears like a basic unit of process, is itself actually a complex system of processes. At any given moment one center holds our focus. As we make it stronger, we have to strengthen (or create) half a dozen other centers and we try to do this simultaneously. That is a necessary part of making the one center we are working on. If our focus shifts, and we start paying focused attention to one of these other centers that is being worked on, we are then effectively ending one cycle of the fundamental process, and starting a new cycle, now focused on a different center.

In principle (not always in fact) every life-creating process repeats the fundamental process hundreds of times, iteratively, applying it again and again to the product of the previous application of the process. The process stops repeating when no further step can be taken that intensifies the life of the whole.

Such a process will always be structure-enhancing — by definition — because it keeps the wholeness intact, and extends it iteratively. Remember that wholeness in a given region of space is defined by the system of centers that exists there. Repeated use of the fundamental process keeps differentiating the space by enhancing some one or another of these centers (large or small) that is already latent (dimly present, but not yet fully emphasized) in the structure. It keeps on strengthening centers in such a way as to extend and preserve and enhance the whole.[2]

8 / THE CLASS OF LIVING PROCESSES

Using the fundamental process as an intellectual building block, we may reach the concept of a living process. I define a living process as any chain of differentiating steps, each of which carries out the center-intensifying process by means of the fifteen transformations, applying them, iteratively, to the whole. Such a process may serve to guide the design of a great building which is to be uniquely conceived, ordinary day-to-day building design, interior design, nature-conservation, engineering, heavy construction, land management, ecological transformation of a wilderness, or social transformation of a neighborhood.

In one form or another, versions of the fundamental process are used repeatedly in all living building processes. Most living processes are of one of three types:

1. A single use of the fundamental process.

2. A string of steps, each one an instance of the fundamental process, the series strung together one after the other, so that the process may be seen as the sequential creation of living centers.

3. A nested hierarchy of steps, each one an instance of the fundamental process, so that these steps are carried out not in a single precise order, but in a general broad order, each one then calling upon further steps, until the whole is finished.

In all these cases, it is repeated use of the fundamental process which forms the core. A living process may occur in a person's mind while conceiving the idea of a great building. A living process may happen in the cooperative work of a group of people making a park or a building together; it may happen in the actual fabrication or creation of a building element; it can happen in the peripheral processes which govern aspects of buildings, plans, and the environment. The evolution of a neighborhood, design of a major building, painting of a small miniature portrait, laying out and planting a park . . . all, if done in a living process, may follow this model. In all these processes, at every step, the same cycle of structure-preserving events is repeated.

A living process always preserves a certain natural order, and happens in a certain natural sequence. Typically (though not always), we may say that the process moves from larger wholes to smaller ones, first allowing the largest ones to unfold from the context, then growing or filling in smaller ones within the context of the larger whole.

At other times, though, a process goes the other way, beginning with a small thing, which then grows larger, and extends, preserving or developing a larger wholeness. That is what happens when one particular plant grows in a forest. The forest does not first establish a larger plan for the forest as a whole. What happens is that each small process acts to contribute to a (not-yet perfectly defined) emerging larger whole, and keeps developing the wholeness in that way.

9 / PRACTICAL MANIFESTATIONS OF LIVING PROCESS

I emphasize that a living process, as I have described it, is an *idealized* scheme. In the real world of architecture, processes which are living ones do not necessarily resemble the scheme I have described. They are often more informal, and more ordinary.

A couple of examples will make the point. Suppose I am telling someone how to improve a corner of their garden. My advice would be something modest and practical: *Do one small good thing; then do another small good thing; then do another good thing.* Simple as this is, focusing on creation of one good thing at a time, is already likely to work; it will make the garden better. After a person has grasped that idea, I may then point out that sometimes, the good things that we do work even better if each small good thing also helps to achieve some slightly larger good thing. You not only plant a small lilac bush, but you plant it next to a sunny spot where you might like to sit on the grass, and in a way that *contributes* to this larger spot. Then a particularly lovely spot may be created in the garden. If we do *this* kind of thing every time we improve the garden, the process will make the garden better in a bigger sense, and in leaps and bounds. This point is, implicitly, a reference to the creation of larger centers — necessarily part of every living process. But I do not need to mention creation of centers explicitly to have a living process. The

idea of creating centers is crucial. The *language* of centers does not have to be used to make it work.

The same point holds for larger and more public problems. We might formulate a public policy which gives advice about the location of freeways in the landscape. For example: *The position of a new freeway should be chosen to leave beautiful and harmonious land untouched. It must therefore thread its way through a landscape, using as far as possible only the most damaged available bits of land, both for the roadway itself and for the landscape on either side of it.* The effect of this policy on our Earth, if it were widely applied, would be extremely positive. But once again, though it is *implicitly* a living process, since it preserves and extends living centers where they exist, it does not explicitly use the language of centers to achieve it. And it does not need to. It encourages construction of new centers (in the surrounding land and in the freeway) in such a fashion as to increase, not reduce, the harmony of the larger structure of the land. That is what matters.

Society, everyday habit, and professional practice are all filled with rules, policies, generic processes, and homely bits of advice about process. So long as the *content* of these processes — not necessarily their verbal form — makes them living processes, they will help to create living structure in the world. We may judge whether a given real process is living or not by paying attention to the process and asking if its various steps resemble, or do not resemble — in their *content* — the fundamental process. It is a living process when, in *content* — not necessarily in outward verbal form — it accomplishes, and approximates, the scheme I have described.

10 / THE NATURALNESS OF LIVING PROCESS

Living process may be understood well if it is understood to be the most *natural* process in a given circumstance. Suppose, for example, that you are going to lay out your own office for yourself. More or less, you know how to do it. So it does not make sense for me to tell you, shaking my finger at you: *You must use a living process.*

The idea of living process, is, in a sense, only a formal way of talking about your natural process. You already have certain natural instincts about where to sit, how to work, how much space in front, to the side, where to keep your books, and so on. In your own house you do these things naturally, as a matter of course. But the layout process used by big-time corporate furniture installers does not include, or even permit, the natural process I have just described. That is why it destroys life, rather than enhancing it. Part of our difficulty in modern society is that accepted formal processes often fail to include natural processes, and that is how they get things screwed up.[3]

Of course, there are many kinds of natural process. In one natural process you just do one thing after another, as you feel like it. It is natural in the sense that there is no imposed rhythm or order. The rhythm and order is whatever comes from within. But a more wisely achieved natural process may include deeper things, that are not obvious to the do-er. That is closer to Zen, which aims at being completely natural, but is also more deeply wise. If, for instance, you

are placing a fence by a natural process, you may be nailing boards together as the spirit moves you. If I tell you that it is better when the space between the fence boards is more positively shaped — and you discover that the fence becomes more beautiful and gets more life when you do this — then you have a wiser process, which is still natural, but now embellished by a little more understanding. Here you have incorporated the POSITIVE-SPACE transformation, and so modify the process to make it more living. So, you learn something from the theory of living process, and incorporate it in your own natural process, making your own process slightly better.

A living process, with its inherent structure-preserving transformations, is always natural, similar to the best kind of natural process. It incorporates our most natural actions, but it goes deeper, and includes additional centers, which our naive natural process may not take into account. Thus, in laying out your office with a living process, you may pay more conscious attention to the work area next to the computer, make it bigger, create more comfort there, so that it becomes a living space in the room.

Whatever you are doing, whatever process you are following, the concept of a living process usually has the capacity to make it a little better, by making deeper, more profoundly and carefully structured living centers, replete with the fifteen properties — just helping you do a little better what you already do naturally.

11 / EXTREME GENERALITY OF THE CONCEPT OF LIVING PROCESS

What I have defined as living process is — I believe — the minimal, and necessary core of *any* process capable of creating life. In organic nature, some version of living process occurs in the formation of organisms, as I have suggested earlier. In the inorganic natural processes which create living structure in ocean waves, mountains, galaxies, some version of this cyclical structure-preserving process always occurs — as I have suggested in chapters 1 and 2.

And, of course, living processes are a necessary part of any successful process of designing and constructing well-adapted buildings and cities. This conclusion follows directly from the nature of wholeness itself, since centers *must* be created, and *must* meet the condition that all centers are helping other centers, if the structure generated is truly to have life.

What is surprising is that all living processes can be subsumed under this single rubric.[4] If you examine the design and construction of the late 20th-century house shown in the appendix of this book, you will see an attempt to make such living process the basis of nearly all steps taken. If you go back to chapter 5, and look at the many successful 20th-century cases of living process in our modern world shown there, you will see that in those cases, too, it is most often the presence of structure-preserving transformations which makes them work. Whether it is in the development of Manhattan, in the planting of the daffodils in a garden in Sussex, in Matisse's drawing of a woman's face, or in the construction work on a community center in Indonesia — in all the examples the steps taken are, *in their essence*, of the same kind.[5] The steps are similar, regardless of scale. The growth of lower Manhattan deals with the initial conception of an entire area of a city that is two miles across; the example of the railroad yard in Minnesota is perhaps 700 yards long; another example deals with the planting of flowers in a garden perhaps 70 feet across; another governing the placing of a table is hardly more than 70 inches across.

12 / A PROCESS OF CREATING MEADOWS

To end with, I now give a short but detailed and explicit example of one living process at work in the creation of landscape in the San Francisco Bay Area.

The following quoted description of the process refers to me, explicitly, since it was invented and described by my friend Bill McClung, while he was editing THE NATURE OF ORDER. I have left his words exactly as he wrote them, because I find the relaxed language, and his way of talking about the fundamental process in the context of meadows, extremely helpful. It gives real insight which adds to the way one may understand the process, and illustrates its both profound yet ordinary nature very well.

McClung has been engaged for several years in an effort to reconfigure the process of cutting fire-hazardous brush, in the fire-prone California hills on the outskirts of Berkeley and Oakland, in such a way as to make the places useful and beautiful: a significant living structure that is attached to these cities. He contemplates the creation of a 500-foot buffer zone, comprising thousands of acres, wherever wild lands come close to urban areas around the San Francisco Bay, and publishes a newsletter aimed at stimu-

A completed meadow in the Berkeley Hills

Studying a landscape in the mist, deciding what minimal actions will do the most to give it life. The person in the yellow windbreaker is looking for the latent centers in the landscape, trying to identify the centers that should be encouraged, enhanced, and strengthened, and trying, at the same time, to decide what to cut away.

The kind of landscape which results: centers, spaces, and trees are made to stand out; the shape of meadows is lovingly crafted; space becomes more positive. All in all, it is a place where you want to be, because it now has more life. Rex Diederich, ex-fire captain of Berkeley, during his work on the formation of a new wilderness in the Berkeley hills, 1996.

*Typical state of the landscape, before the center-making
process begins: eucalyptus brush*

*Half way through cutting and clearing, the centers begin
to emerge, but are not yet well-shaped or positive. After
most of it is cleared, a meadow starts to form.*

*Women cutting thistle in Tilden Park meadow, 1996, starting to do the actual cutting and removing of brush, to make the
centers, boundaries, and positive spaces
come to life in the landscape.*

lating the creation of beautiful meadows throughout the fire-hazardous areas of the buffer zone.

The following passage is reprinted verbatim from McClung's newsletter.[6]

"Meadows [akin to Old English mädwan to mow] may sometimes appear naturally, but I think they usually are constructed places. In fire mitigation work, we make meadows by cutting and reducing vegetation, from weeds to grass to excessive tree and brush growth. The art of the meadow is in how we apply reduction, and what we do with what we have removed.

"*The Fundamental Operation.* We can produce life in space, according to Christopher Alexander, if we make things following a natural, slow-unfolding process, which involves these steps: *(1) Observe and absorb the deep structure of the whole space.* The deep structure of a potential meadow is usually formed by the shape of the land, the major trees and brush clusters, natural edges, vistas, colors, smells, shadows, the way the sky is revealed and hidden, and important animal and plant life of the place. Such things Alexander call strong centers. *(2) Ask what we can do next to most intensify the life of what is before us, by strengthening the strong centers and wholeness already there. (3) Try to do it.* Life-generating work always involves strengthening existing strong centers, large or small, and in such a way as to make structure-preserving transformations. *(4) Evaluate the result and the new whole-*

Result of the application of the fundamental process: a completed meadow. This picture shows a harp concert in one of the meadows completed by Bill McClung.

ness. (5) Repeat the process step by step. (6) Stop when further improvements in the feeling of the whole cannot be made.

"In a one-acre meadow we might reduce and shape as much as five tons of plant and tree material, choosing what to cut and what to leave, reshaping the space, making it more alive if we are successful, while reducing fire danger by reorganizing fuels downward. The fuels near the ground decompose more rapidly and have less oxygen in a fire. The opening of good spaces where there was dense vegetation is how we make the meadow. The defining feature of the land form is better revealed when the grasses and weeds are cut, brush removed. An important vista is opened by removing dead tree debris. Insects and bugs thrive in the low debris piles, providing food for lizards, salamanders, birds and other animals. Well made, it will feel right. The feeling a place presents to us is a measure of its life. If the meadow feels safe and inviting, it probably is."

13 / NECESSARY FEATURES OF ALL LIVING PROCESS

The concept of living process, although it follows from a simple definition given at the start of this chapter, is complex and rich. At a stretch, it seems to me that it might possibly compare in intellectual breadth and depth to the concept of energy as it was introduced in the seventeenth century. When first introduced, energy (kinetic energy) appeared in the mechanics of Descartes and Newton, as $mv^2/2$. Gradually, during the following centuries, the concept evolved continuously, becoming more and more rich, more extended, and applying to an ever wider range of phenomena, until in the 20th century we saw the equation of mass and energy and the nearly universal format of energy underlying in one form or another nearly all the substance of the universe.

Perhaps the concept of living process has comparable potential to evolve its meaning. It is an intuitively accessible idea; it has enormous capacity to develop and expand. At this early stage, whatever is said, can hardly be more than a first approximation of an idea which must still be deepened and broadened in the next decades, as our understanding of it grows. We can, however, at least try to pin down some of the more important features which the concept has — in an early form. No matter how it is expressed, I believe future understanding of living process — if the concept survives in future generations — must have at least the following features:

1. A living process is a step-by-step adaptive process, which goes forward in small increments, with opportunity for feedback and correction at every increment (chapter 8).

2. It is always the whole which governs, in a living process. Even when only latent, whatever greater whole is latent is always the main focus of attention and the driving force which controls the shaping of the parts (chapter 9).

3. The entire living process — from beginning to end — will be governed and guided and moved forward by the formation of living centers in such a way that the centers help each other (chapter 10).

4. The steps of a living process always take place in a certain vitally important sequence, and the coherence of its results will be dependent to a large extent on the accuracy of this sequence which controls unfolding. (chapter 11).

5. Parts which are created during the process of differentiation must become locally unique; otherwise the process is not a living process. This means that all repetition is based on the uniqueness of the locally shaped parts, each adapted, by the process, to its situation within the whole (chapter 12).

6. The formation of centers (along with the sequence of their unfolding) is guided by generic patterns which play the role of genes (chapter 13).

7. Every living process is, throughout its length and breadth, congruent with feeling and governed by feeling (chapter 14).

8. In the case of buildings, the formation of the structure is guided geometrically by the emergence of an aperiodic grid which brings coherent geometric order to built form (chapter 15).

9. The entire living process is oriented by a form language that provides concrete methods of implementing adapted structure through simple combinatory rules (chapter 16).

10. The entire living process is oriented by the simplicity transformation, and is pruned, steadily, so that it moves towards formation of a beautiful simplicity (chapter 17).

In the next chapters I shall discuss these ten features of living process in detail. It is my hope that the reader can gain enough practical understanding from these discussions, to begin applying this kind of thinking to real cases of design and planning and construction. It is my hope, too, that a person can use these ideas to help shape his or her own procedures, and to approach gradually a more and more profound version of living process, that is rooted in these ideas. I am reasonably certain that, for any process to be a living one, these ten essential features, *at least*, must be present.

I would like the reader to consider my discussion of living process in the next ten chapters as applying to every conceivable process in society, and to every architecture-creating process, at any scale, in which the reader is herself/himself involved.

I cannot see a way of entering the 21st century — the century of biology — without some conception of living process. To create living structure in our world, profound sequences originating in the fundamental process, in some form, must be used again and again. The more we understand about creating life — in buildings, towns, pictures, artifacts — the more we will gradually come to realize that life comes about in them when, and because, and only be-cause, we are repeating the fifteen structure-pre-serving transformations again and again and again: And when we do, when we unfold the structure of the world successfully through differentiation, the results will always be the same, in some profound fashion, though infi-nitely various in their detail.

NOTES

1. See chapter 8, page 242–43.

2. If necessary, check back to the definitions of wholeness given in Book 1, chapter 3 and appendix 1.

3. The concept of naturalness has been very strongly emphasized and developed by Karl-Henrik Robert in the Swedish, and now world-wide, movement known as The Natural Step. See "Educating a Nation: The Natural Step," IN CONTEXT, Spring 1991.

4. I maintain that the definition of living process is completely general. During the last twenty years, I have tested versions of this process in hundreds of projects, at many different scales. Many are described in Book 3, A VISION OF A LIVING WORLD. I have taught this process as the core of design and planning and construction, in one form or another, to generations of my students. I have taught it to them in the context of engineering structures, where they have used it to make beautiful and efficient structures. I have taught it to them in the context of lay-ing out neighborhoods, where they have used it to plan streets and houses, and guide the human process of plan-ning. I have taught it to them on construction sites, where they have used it to shape, form, improve, give spirit to the physical process of construction and the details they build. I have taught it to landscape architecture students who have used it to shape and enliven land. I have taught it to ecologists who are now trying to use it to define the larger-scale ecological systems of a geographic region, es-pecially visible in Stuart Cowan's work in the Pacific Northwest. I have taught it, in part, to my friend and edi-tor Bill McClung, who has added it, injected it, into his already beautiful feeling for the process of making fire-safe meadows in the Berkeley hills. I have taught it, of course, to architects, all over the world, now laying out the form, circulation, shape, and character of very large buildings. I have taught it to city-planners laying out streets and neighborhoods in cities like San Francisco and Tel-Aviv, and in rural areas of Papua New Guinea: they include Yodan Rofe, Ken Costigan, David Week, and others. Aspects of what I have suggested here have played a role in the formulation of a new theory of the city by colleagues like Andres Duany, Peter Calthorpe, and Dan Solomon. They founded the Congress of New Ur-banism welding such ideas into existing practice, and now practice them as they seek to establish pedestrian ar-eas in cities.[8] I have taught it to engineers like Gary Black who now practice it in the use of finite-element analysis, in a way based on the fundamental process, in the cre-ation of new engineering structures. And I have taught it to planners who practice it in establishing the rules, gov-ernance, and urban design which contribute to this prac-tice. I have even taught a version of it to my students in my painting classes, where many of them learned to make beautiful pictures.

All of these living processes are, in one fashion or another, made up from repeated application of the fundamental differentiating process. The fundamental process is the *one general* underlying step which is the building block of every process capable of generating life. We may do all of architecture, all construction, all farming, all forestry, and all bridge-building, all road building by following this simple fundamental operation thousands and thousands of times. This is the structure-preserving, differentiating step which is required to get life into the world.

5. For example, in lower Manhattan the process ex-plicitly paid attention to the whole while parts were cre-ated. The picture the financiers and developers had of a close group of buildings, allowed the individual place-ment of the buildings to form the larger center which we now recognize as Wall Street. If they had not had the desire to place the buildings in a close-knit group, the buildings would not have formed this coherent center, and would instead have merely been isolated skyscrapers, as they are in Dallas or Phoenix today.

6. Reprinted from William McClung, "How to Make a Meadow Following Alexander — 1," published in THE BUFFER ZONE, 2, (1998), page 3.

7. Note 7 for text on page 227. Discovery of the mech-anism responsible for the appearance of the 250 cell types, is due to Kaufmann, see Stuart Kaufmann, AT HOME IN THE UNIVERSE (New York: Oxford University Press, 1995, Viking paperback edition, 1997), pp. 106–12.

APPENDIX / ON THE HUMAN EMBRYO
SOME PARALLELS BETWEEN REPETITION OF THE FUNDAMENTAL PROCESS
AND MORPHOGENESIS IN EMBRYOS

We may gain appreciation of the character of living process in architecture by comparing it to the biological unfolding of a fertilized egg in an organism — the morphogenesis of an embryo. Every living process resembles, in general terms, the process which underlies the unfolding of an embryo.

To see the significance of the parallel, I make a few observations about morphogenesis. The process is remarkably simple in broad outline. It starts with a single cell. The first cell divides, and then divides again. All in all, in the case of a human embryo, there are some 50 cell divisions (happening all across the board about once every five days), creating an organism with about 2^{50} (10^{15}) cells; the fully developed human being. And within that organism containing 10^{15} cells, there are only about 250 cell types.[7] We know from this, that the rules of development must be simple. Some standard differentiating transformations (not unlike the transformations I have defined) must occur, be repeated 50 times, and so generate the complex, fully formed newborn human being. The simple transformations work because, being context sensitive, they take different forms in each context within the embryo, and thus produces appropriate and different results in each place where they are used.

The steps themselves are simple too. For instance, at an early stage, the ball of cells is spherical. At that stage, one particular spot gets marked, thus differentiating the sphere and forming an axis within the sphere. Later, that axis becomes the spinal column. The spot, now a mark at one end of the spinal axis, will later become further differentiated to form the head. At another stage, the ball of cells develops three layers that will later become the skeleton, the organs, and the skin.

So the process of differentiation is, in principle, simple. One can imagine that the transformations which occur at each stage must be quite straightforward, too. Yet later in the process it creates hands, feet, eyes, brain — deep complexity. So far (1998) the embryo's transformations have not been completely identified or well understood. Even in this era of supersophisticated computer simulations, the nature of these steps has so far eluded us. Of course it will be done soon. But it is interesting that something so simple, and so fundamental, has not yet been fully mapped or understood. Although the transformations are applied 10^{15} times, in the course of the transformations only about 250 different cell types arise. The ongoing transformations will, of course, generate these different cell types in response to different contexts. Again, it is remarkable that these transformations are so simple, and yet capable of creating such great complexity, architectural coherence, and beauty.

It is interesting too, that the body is replete with repetition. Structures *repeat*. We have perhaps 100 eyelashes, five fingers on each hand, hairs, toenails, muscles, bones — all repeating. Repetition — gigantic repetition — is the underpinning of the whole system, as it is of every structure in nature.

Yet this repetition is of an unusual type. When we think of repetition, we normally think of *repetition by addition*. I take some pennies out of my pocket, and lay them on the table, in a row. Repeating the same element, I get the repetition by addition. But the organism does not get repetition by addition. It gets it, most typically, by differentiation and division. A certain volume is filled with a wave structure, which then divides into five lines, and the wave crests then become fingers. The waves were created by filling a certain zone, dividing it. Most of the repetition in the organism comes from division, not from addition. This is a far more subtle type of thing. The whole determines the parts. Parts are formed according to their position in the whole. Repeating units are formed by division of a structure into roughly equal parts, which then divide and differentiate further to get their form.

Consider, further, the actual transformations which occur in the embryo. At each cell-splitting that occurs, we may imagine a function which sets up the particular differentiations that occur in a particular zone of space. In some form, these transformations will obviously be hierarchical, each one taking place within some bounded part of the emerging body, and producing different results according to the local contexts where they occur. For instance, what happens next in the emerging head area is obviously different from what happens next in the emerging foot area. In this sense, what actually happens during the emergence of the fully developed body is vastly more than just fifty events. There are fifty time intervals in which such transformations occur. But in each time interval, there may be ten, or a hundred, or a thousand essentially different contexts or spatial zones, and the master process applies, then, to one thousand different versions of the transformation to the one thousand different loci, and has different effects according to the different contexts in those different zones. Thus we have not fifty, but many thousands of individually different transformations, happening during the nine months of morphogenesis, each one specific according to the context where it occurs, and each one then bringing into being new differentiations which ultimately create new structure, and create new contexts for further transformations of the same type, in the next round.

In architecture, too, all living processes are built in some form from what I have called "the fundamental process." They create new centers shaped according to the whole where they occur. Like the transformations which occur in the embryo, these creative processes are versions of a general transformation. But, like the master process of the embryo, these architectural transformations can be carried out by people in many different places, in the myriad different contexts of the built world. They may be applied again and again to different emerging structure in any part of the world. When we apply them successfully, we shall get coherent results, much as the general transformations in the embryo get consistent and coherent results in all their spheres of influence.

CHAPTER EIGHT

STEP-BY-STEP ADAPTATION

GRADUAL PROGRESS TOWARD
LIVING STRUCTURE

1 / INTRODUCTION

Possibly the most basic and necessary feature of any living process is the fact that it goes *gradually*. The living structure emerges, slowly, step by step, and as the process goes forward step by step there is continuous feedback which allows the process to guide the system towards greater wholeness, and coherence, and adaptation. This is obvious, of course. To a biologist or ecologist it is self-evident.

Yet in architecture it is far from self-evident. Neither the process of design, nor the process of construction in modern conventional processes work like this. Instead there is a conception of a desired end-state (the design), and the system of architectural and constructional processes is geared up to *producing* this desired end-state, efficiently, and at all costs as it was initially defined—almost entirely without realistic feedback and improvement and adaptation while the processes are going on. Changing architecture to a new form in which feedback *does* occur, will require a massive transformation.

In any case, the core of *all* living process is step-by-step adaptation—the modification and evolution which happen gradually in response to information about the extent to which an emerging structure supports and embellishes the whole. *It is a necessary, unavoidable core.* And in good architecture and good city-building, too, this was historically always present as a necessary core.

Indeed, historically, all building process—both during the design phase, and during construction—worked because they went forward in an overall context that allowed slow, careful, adaptation to occur step by step. In the gigantism and rigidity of the examples of chapter 4, what fails to work is not only that they are structure-destroying. They are structure-destroying, in large part, *because* the procedural context in which these giant 20th-century projects were taking place—even the design process itself during its early stages—simply did not permit step-by-step adaptation to occur, not during design, not during construction, nor indeed after construction or during maintenance.

However, even in our own time, there are examples, living examples, where we see things that *were* made step by step, by gradual step wise adaptation. The wholesome and often beautiful pictures of life in our age shown in the pictures of chapter 5 have this character. They are not the modern norm. They are almost accidental, and extraordinarily different from the image-structures which many architects have sought to impress upon our cities as the modern norm. But they are inspiring, because they show us what happens when this is done right.

2 / BACK TO GENERATED STRUCTURE ONCE AGAIN

The heart of the issue may be grasped by focusing on the geometric character of living structure—in buildings or in anything else. The most fundamental thing about a living process is that the *geometry* of living structure is markedly different *in kind* from the geometry of design done on a drawing board or on the drafting system of a computer.

I make an analogy between a building and a daffodil. Suppose we want to make a perfect, beautiful, living daffodil. Suppose, for the sake of argument, that we could specify it, cell by cell, atom by atom. And suppose we had a tool, micro-tweezers so fine that we could place each atom just where we wanted to. Would it then make sense to make a blueprint of every one of

Daffodils

the billions of atoms in the daffodil, and then use the micro-tweezers to assemble the daffodil according to the blueprint? Would it be dead or living? One's intuition says that it would be dead in form, in substance, even if great care were taken. And, as I have said in chapter 6, it would also be dead in large part because it would have trillions of mistakes in it.

In short, to make a *living* daffodil, we would, of course, simply plant a bulb and let it grow. We know, intuitively, that the growth process is the secret of the daffodil. The living flower comes from the fact that it has unfolded, step by

step. What matters is that it has unfolded right and, each layer following upon layer, has created living tissue that makes sense. That is the daffodil that blows in the breeze, and moves us with its yellow petals and its yellow core.

To make a building — one which lives — is not such a different matter. It, too, must be allowed to unfold. And that means that, like the daffodil, it must take form step by step, in real time, both before construction and during construction. The geometry of living structure *cannot* be created by static design and production. As in the daffodil, it can be created only by the

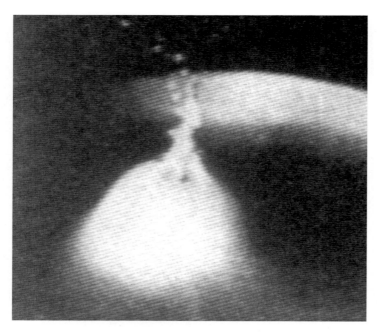

The beautiful, complex shape of a falling water drop

unfolding process itself. This is a fact about the geometry of living structure. We cannot cheat. We cannot fake it. We cannot create unfolded living structure by drawing it *as if* it had unfolded and then building it by different means. It really must unfold, in real time.

Consider a falling water drop. The shape of the drop is a kind of squashed, distorted sphere — not at all the perfect tear drop of popular conceptions. I contend that the shape of this particular kind of squashed drop, as it actually is, *cannot* be drawn or designed by a drawing which tries to get its shape right, but that, instead, it has a complex geometry which can only be arrived at step by step, as in the process which actually happens in the microseconds when the drop is forming in the air. In short, it is a shape arrived at by a beginning shape which is then operated on, transformed, operated on, transformed, many times over, by the laws of physics acting in concert, to differentiate the whole as a system, repeatedly, until in the end the shape reaches the one we know as the flattened falling drop. It is the *history* of this process, and the thousand steps which form this history, that create the shape.

The shape *can* be created by a computer simulation, because such a simulation, at least in principle, may resemble the real process by creating a succession of adaptations that build up the shape gradually. But it cannot be created by a static, non-dynamic act of draftsmanship or design. It is in the nature of the falling water drop that its shape can only be created dynamically.[1] The shape of the water drop has living structure, as defined by the criteria of Book 1. It is also, from what I have just described, a *generated* structure, arrived at by unfolding.

Let us consider an architectural example. I have discussed the Nolli plan before (Book 1, page 173): the plan which records (after the fact) 18th-century Rome, its streets, paths, squares, and public buildings.[2] The spaces have immense vitality and life. The geometry is animated; it varies, each bit is different, yet the whole is harmonious. Where does its great beauty and vitality come from? It comes from the fact that each place in it was created by real people, pushing, rearranging, moving, placing buildings, building walls, until their particular bit of space became comfortable for them. It seems amazing

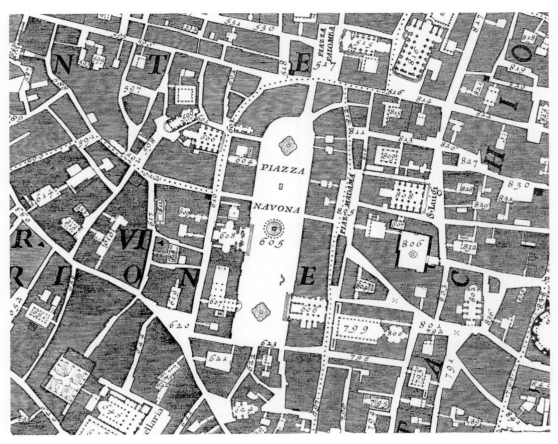

The Nolli plan of Rome: hundreds of positive spaces

that we should be able to sense this in the end-product, the plan, where we can no longer directly see the imprint of their hands, as we can on the stones they laid. But that, I believe, is the fact. We look at the final shape, even in plan form, and recognize it to be the residue of a long, step-by-step, adaptive process.

This is not an intellectually derived conclusion. It is, I believe, a direct perception. We recognize that the shape arrived at in the plan of Rome is an especially complex shape, having a kind of geometric character, which can only be created by this step-by-step adaptive process. What we see, and cherish, in the living architecture of Rome is a geometry which was formed gradually by successive adaptations, happening one by one over time. It is this creation of the shape in time, step by step, which is fundamentally and categorically different from the shapes which are created statically at the drawing board or by design. This, once again, is what I mean by a generated or *unfolded* structure. It has a characteristic, recognizable *architecture*, which cannot be created by any static means such as "design" or "fabrication."[3]

The picture on the next page shows the character of a newly constructed outdoor stair which was made by unfolding. This stair is modest, but has an unmistakable character that has arisen, once again, because the stair was made gradually, not conceived at the drawing board, but conceived and executed, in real time, in the real situation. A further discussion of this stair and the process of its making, is given in chapter 16.

It is my contention that the shapes of a truly living architecture — whether ancient, modern, or still to come in the far-distant future — if living, can only be of this nature. In plan, in section, in

Living structure: an exterior stair between terraces on one of our modest houses. You can see, and sense, that this stair and its balustrade evolved and unfolded. It does not have the geometry of a pre-ordained design, rather something which was adapted and grew according to circumstance and need while it was built. The George House, Pleasant Hill, California, 1998

Insofar as unfolded buildings are lovable, what we love about them is not their age but the rightness which we experience in them. This rightness got into them *as a result of a step-by-step unfolding process.* We can see and feel the rightness. And we see it and feel it because it has a different geometric character from the character which is created by "design."

The 20th-century examples in chapter 5 are lovable — and promising and hopeful — because they, too, have this character. Whether in a single machine, like a modern motorbike, or in a highly complex bit of engineering like the TGV train or the Golden Gate Bridge, or in the houses and apartments along the Amazon, or in the modern Chinese farming landscapes, we see and feel the rightness of the architecture — the global rightness of structure which pervades the whole. The form, coherent from its adaptations, has been unfolded in time, tending to create the fifteen properties throughout its fabric, and to make every part unique and coherent within the whole.

To have a modern version of such a process in our time, we must have a process in society that is capable of generating the form of buildings dynamically, step by step.[4] This *must* be true both of the process of design and of the process of construction. What comes about — if it is to be alive — *must be* a system of shapes which are created dynamically, in time, by gradual adaptation.[5] This is the essence of all life-creating processes. Gradually, step by step, both during the design process and during the building process, the process gets things right.

construction, and in details, they must have that geometrical character which is recognizable as unfolded structure. They must have been created step by step — dynamically — both while they were being thought out and while they were being made. This is an unfolding process.

3 / GETTING THINGS RIGHT

We may start to visualize the necessary process by considering what it means to build a front doorstep correctly. Suppose I want to make a front doorstep outside a house, and I want to make it just right. I have to see what the right

size is. That means how wide, how deep, how high. I am concerned, of course, with trying to make it comfortable. That means comfortable to look at, comfortable to step on, to walk on, perhaps comfortable to sit on or to clean. But how can I tell if it is comfortable in these ways until I have it, or at least until I have it partly?

For example, I can't really tell if the step is just the right height and depth to walk onto comfortably without trying it out. But to try it out I must have something which is solid enough to walk on. And it isn't just the height that is important. There is also walking up *onto* the step, and then walking on, into the house, often another change in height. All this depends on the length of the step, too.

I can get an idea of what feels right by using stones or bricks or blocks to help myself find out what seems to work. I can also do it with lumps of wood, with anything almost that gives me some opportunity to test it out, and check it for its comfort. Then I can build the step. Or I can do the same even *while* I am building the step: for instance, I can lay a course of block or brick, then check it, and then adjust it with an inch of mortar on top if it seems too low, or with an extra half-block of depth if it seems too short. At all events, if I want something harmonious, I cannot separate the process of actually building the step, and of having it materialize concretely, from the process of figuring it out and gradually finding out what to do.

Another project, where these steps were worked into place and roughly cast, just where we wanted them, at the size we wanted them, and at the height we wanted them.

These processes tie in directly with the creation of living centers. As I make the doorstep, I am trying to make each part of it a living center. That means, for instance, I want to find the exact depth and width which make the top a strongly felt center. To do it, since this strong centeredness of the top step is created out of the wholeness of what surrounds it, I must literally "get" the step — its size, shape, height — from the surroundings, and from the wholeness of the surroundings. The existence of the step as a center comes about as a function of the centers in the path, wall, garden, ground, and trees all around. It arises from the wholeness of these existing centers in such a subtle way that I could never hope to get it right merely by studying drawings of the surrounding centers, or from memory, or from any other indirect method. It is only when I am actually standing inside the wholeness of what exists that I can reliably create a step which will be a true living center inside this wholeness.

Thus to create a living center at all — even in this one tiny case — I must try to do it in the actual place, and be thinking while I do it. Such a dynamic process is a necessity which must be going on in order to make living centers *at all*.

The example of a doorstep is very small. It is, in size and scope, no more than one millionth of the size of an average modern building.[6] So, to get a fully adapted world, the same principle has to be extended to cover all scales including even things which are a million times as big. It has to cover even the largest works of construction in our environment. What is needed for all this is an ultra-modern process — by that I mean a process far beyond our present understanding of planning and construction — which can build streets, bridges, concert halls, housing, shops, and factories in a way that creates satisfying adaptation as well as it does in my example of the simple doorstep. That means a process — no matter how complex — which allows each part, each decision, each aspect, to be measured, thought about, tested, made just right, and which then goes on and on and on, repeating thousands of times, creating living centers.[7]

4 / STEP-BY-STEP ADAPTATION

To grasp the real difficulty of an adaptive process in which thousands of adaptations have to occur, imagine a small system with thirty variables. Let us say that the state of each variable is represented by a coin, successfully adapted when it is heads, unsuccessfully adapted when it is tails. My goal is to get all thirty coins lying heads up on the table in front of me. Now, consider two possible approaches to achieving this goal:

(A) THE ALL-OR-NOTHING APPROACH. I toss the coins all at the same time — all thirty coins at once — and then look to see if they have all come down heads. If not, I spin them all again, look at them all again, again check to see if they are all heads. If not, I start again. In this approach, the essential rule is that they must all come down

heads together. Even if twenty-nine come down heads, but one comes down tails, it is not good enough. I have to do it again, until all thirty come down heads at the same time. With this approach, it will obviously take a very long time indeed to get the system to the desirable state (all heads). In fact it will take on the order of 2^{30} trials (about 10^{10}). If I could do one trial per second, this would take 10^{10} seconds or some three hundred years.

(B) THE STEP-BY-STEP APPROACH. In this approach, I spin one coin at a time. When it comes down heads, I leave it lying on the table, and go on to the next coin. Here I am doing the adaptation step by step, one step at a time. With this approach, it will take on the order of about two seconds per coin, or about sixty sec-

Forming centers in the early stages of a house-building process in Mexico. From the very start, the emphasis is on step-by-step adaptation: design and construction are integrated. Christopher Alexander, Julio Martinez, Howard Davis, and others, Mexicali, 1976.

onds altogether — roughly one minute to complete the adaptation.[8]

The step-by-step approach works. The all-or-nothing approach does not work. This is the secret of biological evolution. During the course of evolution, the adaptation of the thousands and millions of variables that must occur to make one successful organism happens step by step, essentially one gene at a time. That is what makes evolution possible. It would be impossible for nature to "design" a system as complex as an organism all at once.[9]

The same *must* happen when a building is designed and built, if it is to be well adapted and to have living structure. A building has too many aspects, too many variables. We cannot get each aspect of the building right unless it is possible to work out one aspect at a time. This

is how we get the system of thirty coins to be all heads, except that in a building it it must be possible to do this for *thousands* of variables, one after the other, both during design and construction.

We may infer, then, that to make things come out right in the built environment, to bring adaptation into society and to regain our capacity to make buildings and streets *just right* — there is a simple condition that must be met. *The process must go gradually, in a way that allows assessments, corrections, and improvements to be made about the degree of life which occurs throughout the structure, at all scales and at all levels. This process must occur continually throughout conception, design, and construction.* And the process must be sufficiently widespread to affect all scales of building and construction.

5 / FEEDBACK

Of course, it is not enough merely to go step by step. As part of the step-by-step adaptation, there must also be a *feedback* process.

In traditional society, while a thing was being made, it was also *continually* being assessed for its degree of life — checked, corrected, improved, checked, corrected. This assessment was driven by some criterion of how much life the thing had — in some form, anyway — and the process was effective in allowing this criterion of life to guide the thing. Naturally, the thing, whatever it was, then gradually became alive.

However, in modern society — especially in those cases I have illustrated in chapter 4 that are plainly negative — neither the design process nor the construction process provide opportunity for gradual step-by-step feedback to influence the whole. Whether or not degree of life is noticed as an attribute while the building is being conceived, drawn, and built, this perception has little opportunity to influence the whole. *Feedback is not allowed to be effective.*

So, to work well, a living process must not merely be step by step. It must be step by step *with* a built-in feedback of such a kind that each step taken can be checked at once for the increase of life which will occur, accepted if it has it, rejected if it does not.

It sounds obvious. But it is not what happens in the processes of architectural design and construction that contemporary architects typically follow. During design, typically, we start with a schematic drawing. This drawing, being complex, usually contains hundreds (if not thousands) of decisions. Yet these decisions, if we separate them from one another, have been made on paper without one of them being tested.[10] Of course, at some stage the drawing is shown to the client, and the client has the right to comment on a completed whole. But by that time, the drawing, in its outline, is all but set, containing hundreds of untested decisions. Often not one of the hundred steps which led to its creation has been tested, nor have we, the architects, had

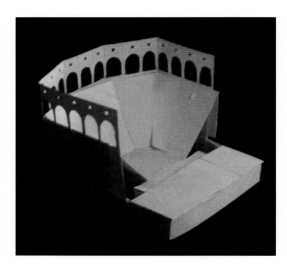

Small paper model of an intimate auditorium for the Mountain View Civic Center: the first step in finding a good form

available to us a contemporary method of designing which can give us real feedback, step by step, as we work it out.

For illustration, consider the design of a large concert hall. How could this be done step by step? The usual way we undertake such a task is to conceive ideas for a possible design, begin to make drawings, develop the idea, work out the periphery of the building, work out the structure, the cost, and so forth. At later stages, acoustic engineers and lighting consultants come in. In this usual process, there is little or no *true* feedback throughout this long sequence of events. There are comments from the client, from others in the office, and so forth. But little *true* feedback about *the actual behavior* of the proposed building. Surprisingly, given the complex nature of the three-dimensional configuration of a large auditorium, there has, during the normally accepted design process, usually been little or no empirical feedback of a realistic sort about whether the concert hall works. Is it comfortable? Is it pleasant? Can one see? Is the feeling of the hall profound? Is the light good? Is the atmosphere what is wanted? These things have been discussed with the client, no doubt. But have they been *tested empirically* to see if the current configuration, as designed, actually has these

functional features that are wanted and believed in by the designer?

In order to make such a design process go step by step with feedback, the following thing would have to happen: *continuously, while making the design,* we would have to model the hall in a three-dimensional form sufficiently close to a person's real experience of the finished hall, so that this model would enable us to make realistic judgments about atmosphere, feeling, acoustics, etc., and would help us to make *improvements in the three-dimensional form* as we go along.

The crux of the difficulty is to find a medium in which we can make sufficiently subtle three-dimensional simulations. The core of architecture lies in the complexity of the three-dimensional configurations which are created, and in the difficulty of inventing them, unfolding them, visualizing them. The real site, in the real world, is a good place for simulations of building position, volume, and so on. But the complex interior configuration of a building — with spaces perhaps hundreds of feet across, perhaps several stories high, and complex in their feeling — how are we to achieve this, so that we can feel what is happening, and keep changing it, until it is really good?

Computer simulations cannot — at present — do these things at the necessary level of subtlety or depth. There are some kinds of computer simulation that provide real feedback about the behavior of a building after it is drawn. One example is the use of finite element analysis for structural design, described in Book 3.[11] There we draw a structural configuration and receive direct feedback from the computer about its structural behavior, allowing us immediately to improve the configuration again and again, until it reaches a stable and harmonious form. This works. The locomotive example on page 152 is similar: the wind tunnel test is not happening in a real wind tunnel, but in a computer simulation of a wind tunnel. The simulation gives immediate feedback about the shape of the locomotive nose, thus allowing the nose to be changed, then retested, until a good shape emerges.

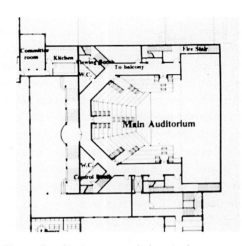

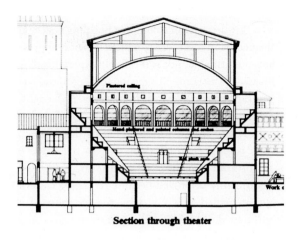

Section through theater

The small auditorium was worked out in the paper model on the left. By playing with the paper model we could find a beautiful and intimate and exciting configuration which was intense and comfortable. Many experiments were made. We cut here, made the sides steeper, made the center smaller, made the arches around the perimeter— on and on—until it settled down to be a shape in which one could imagine feeling genuinely alive.

The plan and section drawn here came after—not before—the paper model on the left was made. After adjusting the model, getting sizes and angles right, putting in the arches, making the steepness of the auditorium slope just right, we could then finalize the design in early hardline drawings. The feedback from the model while making and developing the model is what made it possible to make it beautiful.

Cardboard and paper model used during design of another auditorium, the Eishin Great Hall, in Tokyo. The model allowed me to judge, then modify, the light and space as they would affect people inside.

Years later: a concert in progress in the finished Eishin Hall. Positive results of the early model work are visible, and further elaborations have also become part of the whole.

But the *effect* of a complex building space on the people in it is more complex; it is not, at present, quantifiable, nor is it reliably experienced by means of the three-dimensional images and supergraphics in computer simulations. As a result, no amount of computer simulation tells us what we want to know, which is, "How does it feel, what is its visceral effect on us?" In the absence of this kind of feedback, the building cannot be significantly improved because its *feeling* cannot be intensified. That is why the creation of a building design, by contemporary means, only very rarely succeeds in having a profound effect on us.

There are practical solutions to this problem. One approach that helps is the use of a long series of simple, cheap, quick, paper and cardboard models which can be tested, modified, tested, modified, rapidly, one after the other, so that a good solution has a chance to evolve. Very simple, intentionally rough paper and cardboard models do work. You tear, cut, tape, patch, and paste as you go, making the model better all the time. You can only do this if you have a model so crude that you don't mind cutting into it, and so roughly made that tape, scraps, bits, and pieces do not distract from the effect of the whole.[12] In today's practice, such models are rarely used for design purposes. Models *are* very often used for *presentation*, but that is quite another matter, one that does not contribute to design or feedback.

6 / THE RESULT MUST BE UNPREDICTABLE

To make the feedback meaningful in a step-by-step process, the process must be open-ended, hence partly unpredictable. It must *lack* a fixed, predetermined end-state. This is necessary because adaptation itself means nothing if changes cannot be made in response to the process of adaptation. By definition, such changes cannot be foreseen.

In traditional society, the evolving building was always in some degree allowed to go where it wished to go, or where it needed to go. Traditional society allowed its objects and buildings to be unpredictable in their details, and therefore genuinely allowed them to unfold. But in the more typical, more heavily mechanical production of our modern society — and especially in the structure-destroying cases I have referred to — the end-product is fixed too early and too rigidly. For a variety of reasons — legal, financial, and procedural — under modern conditions the thing is fixed too exactly, too far ahead, and has far too little freedom to unfold. Because of social and legal norms introduced in the second half of the 20th century, the end-product was more and more often required to be exactly like the blueprints — the plan, the master plan, the drawings, or the design — and no longer allowed to deviate from them. It thereby shut off, nearly altogether, the possibility that useful testing or adaptation could occur. But when adaptation and feedback are working, the result *must* be unpredictable. There must be tacit recognition that the end-result is not yet known.

This means not only that the end-result of a building project must be unpredictable during design. That is obvious. But to be effective in creating living structure, it cannot help also being unpredictable during *construction*.

Consider the windows in a house. In order to make rooms wholesome, the windows must create good light in the rooms, and must also create a good connection with near and distant views. But what is a "good" connection? It depends on important minutiae of the real situation. If a house is being framed, and I stand in one of the emerging rooms, I will see exactly where the actual landscape outside makes me inclined to look. But the precise way that the landscape outside speaks to me, at that moment, is very subtle indeed. It may depend on the foliage on the trees, on the brightness of the sky, on the sound which comes from the outside, on the presence or absence of a distant mountain peak. The matter is so subtle that a change of a few percent in the remoteness of that distant mountain peak may altogether change the direction I feel like looking when I stand in that room. If the peak is close enough so that it is salient in some subtle way, it becomes the dominant center in the outside world, and I orient myself more towards it. If it is slightly more distant and subdued, it may become secondary in feeling, and my principal feeling of orientation may then be shaped more by the trees that are a few hundred feet away. Though such a change is slight, it may have a very big effect on the result: In one case, I may feel like facing northwest; in the other case, I may feel more like facing west. Thus the impact of this distant and subtle consideration will fundamentally change my judgment about how to place the windows in the room.

This kind of judgment *can only be made well in the real world*. No detailed architectural drawing, no matter how careful, can reflect this kind of subtlety. The information needed to make the judgment includes the wholeness of the foundations, walls, building mass — which do not even exist at the time the building plans are made. You need the real building, in its emergent state, to make this judgment accurately.[13]

Recent advances in the theory of morphogenesis, especially the so-called butterfly effect, support what I am saying here, in a wide variety of contexts.[14] The essential point of the butterfly effect is something like this: If we examine a complex natural system evolving, each next stage of its evolution depends on its previous stage. Mechanistic 19th-century science created a thought-model in which the next stage would be easily predictable from the previous stage. But it turns out that the world is not like the mechanical thought-model. More sophisticated discoveries have made it clear that in a complex system the next stage is dependent on the current configuration of the whole, which in turn may depend on subtle minutiae in the history of the previous wholes, so "trace-like" that there is no way to predict the path of the emerging system accurately ahead of time.[15]

The key point of this new type of theory — divergent evolutionary paths leading from tiny differences to very large differences of end-result — is exactly the one which I argue must occur in building living structure. Accurate perception (and treatment) of a window during the construction of a building may lead, at first, to minor differences but, within a few steps, to entirely different larger configurations. In this sense, even one small detail can completely change the necessary whole which is most in harmony with the situation, and this difference can only be seen dynamically as the whole unfolds.

What is more, the window which is different then leads to an even larger difference at the next step. One window may require a door inside the house to be placed one way; another may require a plan which moves the internal partition and does away with the door altogether. And then, at a third stage — still only a few weeks away in real construction time — this divergence in the unfolding of the building interior could have results for the organization of people's movement through the building, or for gardens, or for artificial light throughout an entire region of the building. Thus the field of centers which is at the very heart of living structure — *is inherently so subtle that it can only be created dynamically, and is inherently unpredictable in the precise definition of its end-state.*

7 / UNFOLDING OF A PAINTING BY MATISSE

I should like to leave the reader with a graphic image of what step-by-step adaptation means in the context of our modern era. I will do this by showing step-by-step adaptation as it occurred in the evolution of one painting by Matisse. It gives a foretaste of what is coming in the following chapters.

I have a film, in my library, which shows Matisse painting. He is working on a painting, *Woman in a Chair*, a study for what ultimately became *The Cloak* (1946). Eight stills from this film are shown on these two pages.[16]

What is fascinating about the short film, which shows him working for about ten mi-

nutes, is the dance-like quality of his hand and his brush. The hand hovers, quivering, above the canvas. Every now and then, it dips down, and he touches the canvas. Then the hand goes up again, and hovers, oscillating, dancing, above the painting. He seems to be looking for that part of the painting which most urgently needs the next center. Then, after a few more seconds of this quivering motion, he finds it again, the hand goes down, the brush touches the painting, and another center is formed. Then his hand rises again, and the quivering, oscillating motion starts once more, until once more, it dips down to make the mark which forms the next center.

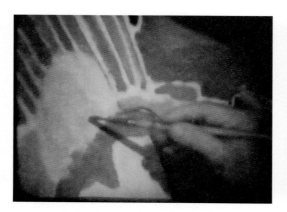

Step 1: Matisse painting Woman in a Chair: an early moment in the process

Step 2 in the process

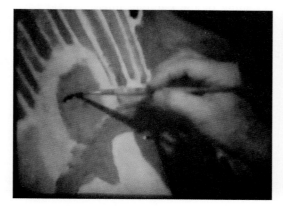

Step 3 in the process

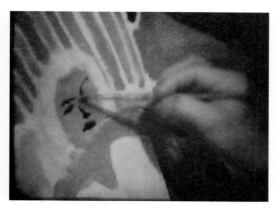

Step 4 in the process

His hand is uncanny in its certainty. He looks, listens, watches, finds, then his hand goes straight down to make the mark. Again and again and again, the process is the same.

The most fascinating and perhaps most important thing about this process is the unfolding of the *architecture* of the painting. In these eight stills, we see how, and how surprisingly, the architecture unfolds.

I wish I could show the incessant hovering, trembling vibration of his hand, as he moves from step to step. Even when he is thinking, his brush quivers. Then it darts down to do a step, all the time quivering, then retreats, quivering again, while he thinks some more.

In step 1, it starts with the POSITIVE-SPACE transformation. As shown on the opposite page, the outline of what is to be a woman's head is only partially present, formed as a void of blank canvas surrounded by the positive space of the stripes already painted in. That is already a surprise. It is not the way a person concentrating too narrowly on the head itself would go about it. Yet it is this which is needed by a living process, and this which commits the painting to a true architecture. Concentration on space, as in the spaces of the Nolli plan of Rome, paves the way for a beautiful and ordered whole.

As Matisse moves to step 2, he forms a BOUNDARY: actually, he darkens the face, forming now a light space where later the hair will be. Again, it is the space which governs, and the dark mass which will be the woman's face looks almost strange at this stage, yet it forms an architecture in the frame of the light boundary, that is the hair-to-be.

Step 5 in the process

Step 6 in the process

Step 7 in the process

Step 8 in the process

In step 3, Matisse tentatively places small dark lines which will swell later to become the eyes: these lines divide the face into two zones, and it is the GOOD-SHAPE transformation that mainly governs the formation of the curved eyebrow.

In step 4, we see the main lines of the face, darkly touched in, forming now an extended architecture. These lines are not so much reminiscent of the woman as they form a coherent architecture in the volume of the face.

In step 5, the nose and eye are more intensely drawn, so that their own internal architecture begins to means something. Suddenly, the hair comes in, a writhing mass of curls, darkly and definitively touched in.

In step 6 more has happened in the boundary — now made of centers which are the woman's curls. This, too, is surprising, since this darkness, darker than the face, reverses the positive and nega-

tive, and places the architecture of these curls within the light boundary that was the space of the hair up until now. We see here how the curls form an architecture with the stripes of the chair behind: The light specks in the hair connect her head to the wall.

In step 7, a line is drawn under the woman's chin, now clearly making her head stand out from her body and her chest, placing also the white line of her breast in relief, making the whole three-dimensional.

In step 8, the side of her face gets additional curls and tresses, lapping over her shoulder and completing the structure of the head.

Throughout, the quivering, focused attention of Matisse's brush — the play of brush and feedback to the brush — nearly dances and forms the architecture, step by step. What is remarkable is the extent to which the visage

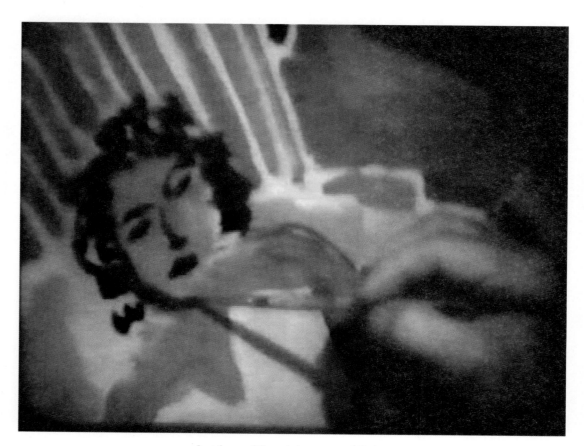

Last frame of the painting, seen at full size

lives, and the extent to which an architecture is formed in the face by means of the fifteen transformations. It is an architecture which ancient builders knew, but which too many of us have now forgotten — because the process used today is not a living process any more.

8 / ARCHITECTURAL IMPLICATIONS

What is the essential difference between Matisse's successful process and the unsuccessful process typical of our professional architecture today? Suppose an architect at a large commercial office like Skidmore, Owings & Merrill is drawing his design, and then makes the claim that what he is doing is just like the Matisse process.[17] Can we answer? Is there an objective distinction between the one process and the other?

The critical difference is the absence of feedback. In Matisse's process, each step is a small step forward from a previously existing reality. The next step is taken as a feedback and as a response to the reality of the actual painting, as it emerges. That is what keeps the thing on track, and what keeps making it better. *Matisse is watching the actual painting; his hand is hovering over it.* He drops down one more spot of color, in response to the real thing. Each move he makes is based on the direct feedback from the real thing, and the real feeling as a whole, which the evolving painting creates. The process therefore has a good chance of making the real painting better all the time.

The architect drawing at his table or on his computer is an entirely different case. The architect is drawing the building. But since it is not the real building which is being formed, *nor any simulation which might come close to creating feelings and sensations like those which the real building will ultimately create in the user's mind, the architect cannot tell, while he is drawing and from what he draws, what would really be going on in the actual building if it were built.* He gets no realistic feedback from the drawing on paper because one cannot judge the real behavior, the nature of the real building, by looking at the lines on paper. Of course, this architect, if challenged on this point, might claim that this is just where his experience lies: that he can tell, from the pencil lines, what the real building would be doing and that it is this ability which makes him an architect. But this is a polite fiction. It is a polite lie on which our 20th-century architecture was based. The truth is that *no one* can tell what the three-dimensional reality of the building is going to be based on a few pencil strokes or a few lines on a computer screen. You cannot tell what the light is like, what the view is like, where the plants will grow, where you feel like walking, where you feel like sitting, what natural intuitive response a group of people will have to a particular room (if it is too high, too low, too wide, too narrow, too strangely shaped, too distant in feeling from the garden or from the room next door), where the sun is going to shine on the floor in winter, whether one can hear sounds from one room to the next, and so on — a thousand things. And it is because of this ignorance about real things that we do not get feedback from the pencil sketch.

That is why what we architects do with our pencil sketches is *not* in the least like what Matisse did when he painted the *Woman in a Chair.* At best the architect is drawing something, and his next step is a reaction to the drawing. Each pencil stroke is thus only a reaction to a previous set of pencil strokes. Since it is not, at any step, based on feedback about reality, there is every chance — one might say there is a certainty — that this process is going to go off the rails. It is the lack of continuous responses to reality which makes the process used by big commercial offices highly vulnerable, and which makes it — inevitably — unsuccessful.

Emoto Apartment Building, Komagome, Tokyo, Christopher Alexander, Hajo Neis, Ingrid King, 1987. This full-size three-story mockup in Tokyo, done in paper to study the effect of the elevation design and materials on the street at actual size, was done to make sure that the street was helped by the building. Mockup by Hajo Neis.

That is the idea we must aspire to in architecture. We must imagine a world where, whether it is a building, or a street, or a room, or a bridge, the conception, design, and the construction — and ultimately the maintenance too — go forward in very small steps with feedback, so that they can be corrected. It is this self-correcting aspect of the building process which has all but vanished in recent times.

To create a living world, successfully, we must again find ways of making all building processes move forward in this experimental, responsive fashion. That one thing alone, as a kind of bedrock for all design and all planning and all building, will change the world. We must reject the statist conception in which the future is planned now, and embrace a new world of architectural design in which the future of each building is not known, remains open to experiment and change, and above all to success.[18]

9 / OVERALL IMPLICATIONS

I hope I have established, in your mind, that creation of complex buildings, towns, streets — both in design and construction — *will succeed in getting life only if it goes forward step by step, with feedback, in a minutely careful process of adaptation which can, continuously, get things right.*

This conclusion, if accepted both within the discipline of design and within the discipline of construction, must lead to a watershed in thinking about the environment. It lays a necessary foundation to all of what this book contains, since it defines what is, in my mind, an ineluctable condition, necessary to all unfolding, hence to all living process aimed at building living structure in the world.

In substance, it implies that our present forms of planning, design, construction, and production are, nearly all, deeply flawed. Since they do not include step-by-step adaptation — and cannot in principle do so, so long as they stay as they are — it implies that these forms of production must be changed.

Awareness of the idea that living process is both necessary — and likely to change our means of production entirely — is perhaps only now beginning to sink in.

NOTES

1. The absolute and primary nature of process and history of a process in determining the geometry of any natural system was emphasized again and again by D'Arcy Wentworth Thompson, ON GROWTH AND FORM (Cambridge: Cambridge University Press, 1917; reprinted 1959). Throughout, and especially 1–21.

2. Book I, page 173–74.

3. What I mean here by "design" is a static process in which shape, or form is created by a single process, collapsed in time, where the features of the design do not emerge, sequentially, in response to one another, but more or less all at once. This process lacks the intervention of feedback which guarantees that the system is coming to order, and creating life, at each step, but instead the whole form comes into being entire, before it is checked. Although many architects might say that they do this when they are drawing, in fact they do not. The real sense of the process is entirely different.

4. The appearance of Stewart Brand's highly important HOW BUILDINGS LEARN: WHAT HAPPENS AFTER THEY'RE BUILT (New York: Penguin, 1995), is a significant step in our growing awareness that a dynamic unfolding process with step-by-step adaptation is necessary for buildings in modern society.

5. The content of this comment may be illuminated for the reader by considering the dozens of detailed examples in the appendix of this book on building a single house, A SMALL-SCALE EXAMPLE OF A LIVING PROCESS: .

6. Say the step is 1 meter by 1 meter by 20 cm. A large modern building might typically be 50 meters by 100 meters by, say, 40 meters high: all in all, 1,000,000 times the volume of the step.

7. In recent years, a new theory of adaptation has made its appearance: the theory of complex adaptive systems pioneered by John Holland. This theory tries to study the general conditions under which adaptation can occur. The theory is extremely general. However, the mathematics have become increasingly more sophisticated, so much so that general and powerful results have been obtained. See, for instance, John Holland, ADAPTATION IN NATURAL AND ARTIFICAL SYSTEMS: AN INTRODUCTORY ANALYSIS WITH APPLICATIONS IN BIOLOGY, CONTROL AND ARTIFICAL INTELLIGENCE (Cambridge, Mass.: MIT Press, 1992).

8. This argument is based on Ross Ashby's example of an adaptation process in which one hundred coupled variables are all set at the same time, versus a process in which one hundred variables are set one by one. See W. Ross Ashby, DESIGN FOR A BRAIN (New York: John Wiley & Sons, 1960) and Christopher Alexander, NOTES ON THE SYNTHESIS OF FORM (Cambridge: Harvard University Press, 1964). As Ross Ashby showed, in his more sophisticated version of the argument, without such a step-by-step process, it is statistically *impossible* to achieve the adaptation in a reasonable time.

9. See Richard Dawkins, THE SELFISH GENE (Oxford: Oxford University Press, 1980), and THE BLIND WATCHMAKER (New York: W. W. Norton & Co., 1996), for a powerful analysis of this problem, and for a definitive explanation.

10. When I say that a typical design drawing represents as many as a hundred decisions, I am talking about the small, item-by-item decisions which happen in an unfolding process. Of course, we could also claim that a typical schematic or development drawing is just one decision. But my whole point is that this one schematic drawing actually contains a plethora of small decisions that can be separated from one another. When you count

them in this fashion, there may indeed be as many as a hundred in a single drawing.

11. Book 3, chapter 7, pages 218–26.

12. One example of this kind, providing more detail about the use of rough cardboard models as the basis for design of a full-scale large auditorium in Tokyo, is described in Book 3, chapter 15.

13. It is interesting to note that this necessarily unpredictable aspect of the design process was well known historically. It was even referred to in testimony in the British parliament (PARLIAMENTARY RECORDS, London, 1812) by a builder who was concerned that estimating buildings by detailed specification, rather than by an undifferentiated overall price per square foot, would affect, negatively, their ability to make the fine-tuning changes which they knew to be essential to a building's success. This information was given to me privately by Professor Howard Davis, and is discussed in his book THE CULTURE OF BUILDING (New York: Oxford University Press, 1999), page 193.

People will, no doubt, *again* ask themselves whether computer simulations might be able to play a role in substituting for the real. I have answered this already in the text, but I should say — again — that I doubt it very much, because I doubt that a computer simulation — at least as we understand that idea today — could catch the subtleties of the wholeness accurately enough to give you the proper insight. One day it may be possible. But even if some future kind of computer simulation could catch the feeling of the building so that one could make effective and realistic judgments about how to increase the feeling, the point is (also) that the needed judgments can *also* only be made on the basis of events which are emerging dynamically, and are hence too complex, too ramified, to be known at the stage we normally consider as the "building-plan" stage today. Whether one uses the real building or some simulation of it, it is necessary to make this judgment as near as possible to a time when all the information is available, and at a time when the impact of the full emerging wholeness can be seen, and felt, and judged.

14. For a popular account of the butterfly effect (the impact of a butterfly flapping its wings in Japan, two weeks later affecting the weather in Brazil) see, for example, James Gleik, CHAOS: MAKING A NEW SCIENCE (New York: Penguin, 1988).

15. Take, for example, the evolution of weather patterns, a subject which stimulated much complex system theory. It turns out that the general direction taken by the weather, at point X in space and time, may depend on the density of clouds at the preceding point in time. But surprisingly, a change in the sixth decimal place (a tiny change) in the earlier state may lead to two entirely different and divergent evolutionary paths. If the density is 0.145672, within two days the system may go towards tornado weather. If the density is 0.145673, within two days the system may go toward high-pressure clear weather. Within a few cycles, apparently minute differences in the whole can have colossal results in the unfolding of the whole. Our understanding of this new point, which originates with chaos theory and complex systems theory, has led to a variety of mathematical models, which try to get the holistic behavior and make predictions based on holistic behavior, not on minutely detailed parameters.

16. The sequence of stills of Matisse painting *Woman in a Chair* is taken from the film MATISSE, made in 1946.

17. Skidmore, Owings & Merrill, one of the biggest mid-20th-century architectural firms, was committed to the high-technology use of prefabricated components in design and to the separation of design from construction.

18. This is a conception which, in the words of Virginia Postrel, will make dynamists of us. Virginia Postrel, THE FUTURE AND ITS ENEMIES: THE GROWING CONFLICT OVER CREATIVITY, ENTERPRISE, AND PROGRESS (New York: The Free Press, 1998). See especially the discussion of dynamist and statist attitudes, throughout the book. Postrel's argument is very similar to the argument of this chapter, and extends my argument in a number of useful ways.

CHAPTER NINE

THE WHOLE

EACH STEP IS ALWAYS HELPING TO ENHANCE
THE WHOLE

1 / INTRODUCTION

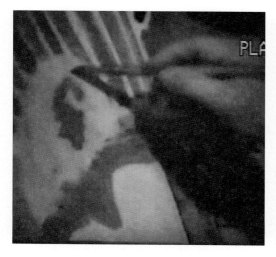

Step 1: The overall form of the face is established as a whole

Step 6: The line making the ringlets of hair does not so much give the particular ringlet shape, as it contributes coherence to the life of the entire configuration

Chapter 8 says that in a living process everything that happens, goes step by step. Now, we may ask, What exactly is it that *happens*, step by step? To this question, there is one answer above all others. Above all, there is the fact that each step *enhances the whole*. When we look at Matisse drawing the woman's head and placing a dark mass in the area of her hair (see above) the action does not so much have concern with a particular ringlet

of hair, but to a far greater extent with the overall balance, coherence, and form *of the whole*. That is what dominates his activity. That is what makes the painting work. That is the mark of a great painter in his activity.

This seems rather obvious. But unfortunately, it is not obvious, and is, in the activity of our age, very far from obvious, in a vast number of accepted human activities — for example, in the process of city planning and zoning.

2 / COMMON SENSE

One would imagine that at least the *goal* of bringing life to larger wholes would be understood and respected. In America of the 1980s I discovered, with something of a shock, that even this is not always so. In 1988, Dan Solomon and I were appointed by the City of Pasadena, California, to write a new zoning ordinance guiding and controlling the design of new apartment

buildings throughout the city. In an early draft of the ordinance, as one of the major processes in a new set of rules to be following by any applicant for a new apartment building project, I included a draft rule which stated: *"Any proposed new apartment building must help the life of the street and of the neighborhood in some tangible way."*

This is the most obvious common sense. Almost any non-profesional person who hears this, would have a reaction something like, "Well, yes, ... of course.... what is new about this? It is the obvious thing to do. A good idea."

But that is not what happened in Pasadena. The chairman of the Planning Commission was outraged by this proposal and asked me, at the very first public hearing where I presented it, what I meant by introducing it. I told him that what I wanted to do was to create a positive impetus, so that from the very outset, each developer would be required to think about helping the street where a building was to be built, to think of making a positive contribution to the street, and would know, in advance, that he was required to do something which would make the street better in a form that could be explained and understood. My rule did not require that it be provably *effective*, nor did I try to specify detailed guidelines as to the meaning of the proposed rule. It was (to make a start on such things) merely a process requiring demonstration that attention had been given to this issue, that a developer had asked himself sincerely what he could do to make any given new building project help the city block where it was to be built.

The chairman of the commission, when he heard my explanation, leaned forward from the dais of the hearing room, and first asked me in heavily ironic but angry tones if I was a Communist, and then requested that I remove this item from the draft without further discussion.

I tell this story partly because it is important, I think, for readers of this book to understand well in advance, to be prepared, perhaps, for a lack of sympathy even on such a deep and obvious matter concerning the living structure of the world. It does not mean that structure-preserving processes are impossible to achieve. It just means that in many circles, it may be necessary to prepare the ground rather carefully, so that people understand the point of what one is trying to do.

But I also tell this story for another more important reason. I wish to draw attention to the individual difficulty that each one of us must face when we try to keep hold of the conception of living process. The president of the Pasadena Planning Commission was antagonistic, certainly. But unfortunately there is some negative voice like this sitting inside most of us, sometimes even inside our own heads, discouraging us from really and truly making every process structure-preserving to the larger whole. This is a kind of mental inhibition (sometimes fueled by ego, sometimes by greed) which continually makes us focus on the local, *and forget, or ignore, the extent to which we must make something living or beautiful happen in the large* — or forget that it is our responsibility, at every turn, to heal and make more whole, the structure of the world.

3 / THE WHOLE

Let us say, then, that extension, enhancement, and deepening of the whole is the crux and target of all living process. Living processes have to do with the creation of wholes. Artistically, the essence of the builder's art, is always to create a whole. When a building succeeds, it is because we perceive it, feel it, to be a magnificent whole, whole through and through, one thing.

It is not common to find this today. We may even say that the ugliness we see all around us, comes largely from the fact that builders — architects, contractors, developers — no longer know, or only rarely achieve, the making of a building which is truly one with its surroundings.

Thus, whatever a living process has to say about architecture, whatever it can teach us, and

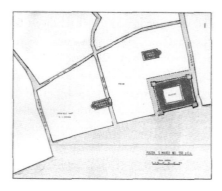

About 560 A.D.

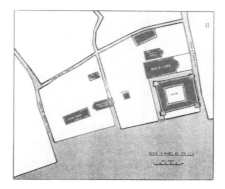

About 900 A.D.

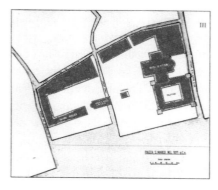

About 1160 A.D.

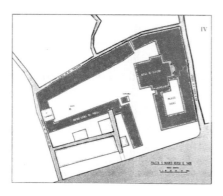

About 1300 A.D.

It is the whole, above all, which evolves; it is the whole which guides. Here is a shortened version of some of the steps in the evolution of Saint Mark's Square, Venice. All in all, these steps took about 900 years to complete. Nevertheless they went one step at a time, and the whole, people's SENSE *of the wholeness, was the underlying force always guiding the next increment.*

whatever it can give us, *above all it must give us this*: the ability to make a living whole.

This is problematic, of course. It is an enigmatic subject. We cannot make something whole, for example, unless we make it united with its surroundings. So, to be whole, it has to be "lost," that is, not separate from its surroundings, part and parcel of them. And the pieces within a living whole, they must also have a special quality. So, the thing which is to be whole, and extends out into the world around it, must also contain wholes *within* it, and these smaller wholes must be part of the larger whole in feeling. So each is to be distinct, to be an entity. Yet it is to be invisible in order to be lost and not separate from the larger whole. Making

a building whole, is an immensely complicated task. But, in any case, making the whole is the essence, the beginning and the end of our work as artists. *And (according to chapter 8) this is to be done while going step by step.*

Let us then start articulating the way that a living process can help us to create a whole. It is possibly helpful to remind ourselves that although this task may tax our creative powers, nature manages it more easily. When a crashing waves breaks, it is a whole. When a mountain rises up from the landscape over the eons, it becomes a whole. All this is achieved, apparently, by structure-preserving transformations. So if we hope to be like nature (and we can hardly aspire to anything stronger) we should,

About 560 A.D.   *Latent centers*   *New building position*   *Hospice first phase c.700*

About 700 A.D.   *Latent centers*   *New building position*   *First basilica built 832*

   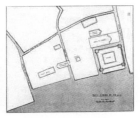

About 832 A.D.   *Latent centers*   *New building position*   *The Campanile built 976*

  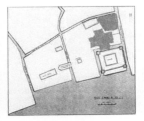 

About 976 A.D.   *Latent centers*   *New building position*   *Cruciform St. Mark's, 1071*

About 1071 A.D.   *Latent centers*   *New building position*   *Piazza extended c. 1100*

Each row represents one four-step cycle in the process: 1 context, 2 latent centers, 3 possible action, 4 new construction.

About 1100 A.D.   *Latent centers*   *New building position*   *Gateway built c. 1250*

About 1250 A.D.   *Latent centers*   *New building position*   *Ospicio Orseolo built 1309*

About 1309 A.D.   *Latent centers*   *New building position*   *Doge's Palace built c. 1400*

About 1400 A.D.   *Latent centers*   *New building position*   *Old Procuria built 1532*

About 1532 A.D.   *Latent centers*   *New building position*   *New Procuria c. 1600*

Each row represents one four–step cycle in the process: 1 context, 2 latent centers, 3 possible action, 4 new construction.

in principle, be able to extract the whole in what we make, derive the whole — the shape and substance of our work — always going step by step, and by concentrating, at every stage, on the emergence of a new, living, breathing, feeling, whole.

4 / TO BE GUIDED BY THE WHOLE, WE MUST PAY ATTENTION TO THE LATENT CENTERS & ENHANCE THEM

Consider the evolution of St Mark's Square, shown on page 252. I would like to say that this process, lasting about 1000 years, achieved what it did because the work was always going forward as a whole, and people were paying attention to the whole. But, you may quite reasonably say, What whole? The whole which became visible at the end of the 1000 years was plainly not visible or even thinkable when the work started around 560 A.D.. So *what* whole, exactly, was guiding the work, pulling the work forward, guiding the next step towards some greater whole?

We may see the answer in the series of diagrams on pages 253–54, showing a very simple iterated process. In each row in the matrix of diagrams, we see a certain configuration at a particular date, then we see the latent centers that were visible at the time of that configuration, then we see a dark mass indicating the decision about where new construction would be undertaken to strengthen and intensify the latent center, and then we see the result of construction — the plan of an actual building built in that position taking the configuration as a whole to a new plateau.

In the next row of diagrams, we see the process repeated, going forward from the new configuration. After ten applications of the iterated process, we see the beautiful, wonderful configuration of St. Mark's square as it arose from the process.

This process has indeed focused on the whole, and been guided by the whole. But the whole, at each moment, is discerned by paying attention to whole configuration as it is *together with the centers latent in that wholeness*. This technique is quite general. In order to understand well what it means "always to enhance the whole," we need to grasp clearly the relation between *preserving* structure and *enhancing* structure. What, precisely, is the relation between a transformation that is structure-*preserving*, and one that is structure-*enhancing*? How can these two apparently different ideas be reconciled?

To explain, I go back to basic theory first presented in chapter 2. The idea is that a structure-preserving process on the one hand transforms and *preserves* structure and on the other hand the idea that this structure-preserving transformation then also *enhances* the whole. The two can be reconciled, because in every wholeness, in every structure, there are *latent* centers. These are centers caused by the overall configuration, dimly present in the structure, yet not yet fully developed. These centers are part of the structure, they are truly there, they are present. But they have not yet been developed, even though they are *capable* of development. In developing these latent centers, one is then both respecting the structure which exists, yet also paving a path to some as-yet unborn new structure. Even though the structure which then emerges is a new one, it has its roots in the old structure.

To do this right, and to pave the way to this conservative and life-giving emergence, one must both preserve the structure which exists, and its wholeness, yet also *enhance* the wholeness — and that means enhancing the *latent centers*, those that are not yet fully recognized.

5 / THE MODERN PROBLEM OF DESIGN

To understand the application of this principle to a more general case, let us take next an example of a process of *design*. Design *itself*, of course, is a process and, as in every other process, the quality of what is designed will flow from the quality of this process. What then, is a design process like when it is governed by a living process in the designer's mind. As any designer will tell you, it is the first steps in a design process which count for most. The first few strokes, which create the form, carry within them the destiny of the rest.

How then, in a living process, do we take the first steps of design so that a beautiful, coherent whole begins to take shape?

In the early stage we must concentrate, of course, on broad structure, on the emergent structure of the *whole*. A difficulty is that we do not have a good notation for the emergence of form during this early process. The notation that architects traditionally use is a language of drawing or computer representation. Using this notation, we try to get the glimpse of an idea, and then put this down as a simple sketch, or as a simple model. But such a sketch always includes too much information, too early, so that the sketch (or computer drawing) is invariably over-specific. Sketches and computer drawings are seductive and may be interesting. But if only 20% of the information in a sketch is based on real decisions that have been taken by a living

process in the designer's mind, and the remaining 80% is arbitrary stuff entered into the drawing only because the notation (sketching) requires it, trouble inevitably follows.

We therefore need a notation, or a way of representing emerging form, which stays closer to what is actually known at each moment. Here I wish to introduce the idea of morphological "ripples." What I mean by a morphological ripple is a partially generated form, in which some global configuration exists in the space under consideration, but it is not yet clearly located, or dimensioned, or even characterized — it is a fieldlike configuration which, though fuzzy, firmly sets some feature of the *whole*, and plays a decisive role in giving character and feeling to the end result.

It is important that the first steps — the morphological ripples — should focus only on the broadest, most global features of the emerging design. Often these "global" features will extend across the full diameter of the area being considered. At each step, another "ripple" introduces one more feature of the whole. To contain these ripples without distortion, I find it best to work, not on paper, not in a drawing on the computer screen, but *in the mind's eye*, preferably while standing in the real place itself — but at the very least in the presence of an extremely realistic model showing the broad features of buildings and terrain in three dimensions.

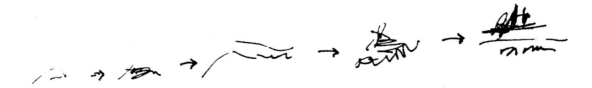

Diagrammatic representation of the evolution of new form through stages which differentiate the form,
and create morphological ripples of increasing complexity.

More important still, as a first stage in the design process, I usually make a word picture of the building. That is, I spell out, IN WORDS, what the building is like, what it is like to arrive to it, what the space in front of it is like, how the building forms the space, what happens as you enter, what happens inside the building, where its main rooms are, what their special beauty is, what it is like to go out, from these rooms, to the outdoors. All in all, a vision of the finished building IN WORDS — as beautiful as I can make it.

It is essential to form this vision of the emerging building *in your mind's eye*, not in sketches on paper. Words and interior visions, when seen with your eyes closed, are more labile, more fluid, transformable and three-dimensional, than sketches or physical designs. They allow the unfolding to go forward more successfully. In the mind's eye, the centers which evolve, one by one within the living process, are not hampered by arbitrary information and decisions that come too early. A word picture in the mind's eye is in a medium in which we can see only what the words describe, and nothing more. A picture on paper or computer representation, on the other hand, says too much, and often therefore contains information and decisions which are arbitrarily added, and which have not — themselves — come from use of structure-preserving process. If I say that a building towers above me, when I approach it, this says something qualitative about its height, but does not yet describe the exact height (in feet), nor does it describe its shape. This feature may well come from a structure-preserving transformation. But if I make even the most rudimentary drawing (on computer screen or paper) the drawing has

an actual height (implied by proportion), and it has many features of shape, width, volume, articulation, which have not in fact been generated by the fundamental process.

Thus the drawing pad and computer screen are poor media for an unfolding process. They are not media where a living process can easily go to work.

By contrast, the best canvas for the evolution of form for a new building is the inner eye, the mind's eye. The vision in the mind's eye contains little that is not actually generated by the living process. When you close your eyes, you see certain things which arise from the word picture. The word-picture, indeed, captures just what you have seen, so far, in your inner eye. And the mind's eye, as it works when your eyes are closed, has the same power as the words. It adds little that is not actually seen, but what it does add is real, and germane, and flexible. The vision floats in your mind, a hovering clear picture, defined only in those aspects you want to define, and undefined in others.

The process of building such a vision in your mind must itself follow the differentiating process, step by step. The vision is built one morphological feature at a time. You start by saying to yourself, and seeing, one thing, the most important thing about the building. That will be captured in its height, its position, is quality, its color. It might be a brooding light that emerges from the building, or it might be the gardens which precede it, and lead to it. It is, in any case, the first global, holistic aspect of the building which you see, when you close your eyes and imagine the building as the context requires that it should be.

6 / AT EACH STEP DECIDE ONLY WHAT YOU KNOW WITH CERTAINTY

As the living process goes forward, repeating the fundamental process again and again, and

applying the fifteen transformations as needed, one feature is built up at a time. When we are sure of the first, we add a second. When we are sure of the first and second, we add a third.

How do you determine these steps which must be taken, and their sequence? (see also chapter 11). What steps do you take, in what order? The most basic instruction I can give you as a guide for a living process, *is that you move with certainty.* That means, you take small steps, one at a time, *deciding only what you know.* You try never to take a step which is a guess or a "why don't we try this?" Large-scale trial-and-error, shots in the dark, simply do not work. Rather, you move by slow, small decisions, deciding one thing, getting sure about it, and then moving on. When — on the one particular small issue at hand — you feel certain enough that you have it right, *then* you move on to the next small decision.

When I say that you should move in small decisions, I do not mean that the decisions should be small in physical scale. Rather, I mean that the *content* of each decision should be limited to a particular subject, to some feature of the design, disconnected from other matters, and floating, to an extent, by itself.

As far as the *scale* of the decisions is concerned — that, on the contrary, should be rather large. At the beginning, especially, you need to work mainly with the largest questions. Many of the issues you need to settle, in the early stages of your work, have to do with the whole, the global quality of the design.

It is always crucial to take a good first step. Each step is, in a sense, a return to the whole and a starting over with a "first step." So, in the same breath, we must recognize that to take a good step, the main problem is to *avoid* taking any of the many possible false steps. A numerical comparison is useful. Suppose, for example, that at a given stage in a process there are a hundred possible next steps available and we must choose among them (the next decision in the design). It will generally be agreed, I think, that more of these possible next steps are likely to be bad than good. Of the 100 possible choices, there may easily be as many as 90 or 95 next steps which will make the thing worse, relatively few, say 5 or 10 next steps which will make it better. What we can be sure of is that there are more bad steps than good ones. How, then, do we find the few good ones? There is no special reason that we should be lucky enough to hit one of the small number of good next steps, by accident, as we consider the possibilities.

If we reason this out, we may then draw the following conclusion. It is more likely that the first possibilities that present themselves to our minds will be bad ones, rather than good ones. We should therefore be extremely skeptical about the first possibilities that present themselves to our minds. We should run through the possibilities very fast, *and reject most of them.* If we do accept one, we should accept it, reluctantly, only when we finally encounter something for which no good reason presents itself to reject it, which appears genuinely wonderful to us, and which demonstrably makes the feeling of the whole become more profound.

This is not the behavior that an architect typically uses. Rather what happens often is that the architect expects that "inspiration will strike." He is — too often — obsessed with his own creativity — jumps at what he has determined — and then loves it to death, unexamined, but goes on with it because he believes that it came from inspiration.

But of course, if one merely jumps at the image that presents itself, and if one carries a self-deluded idea that it *must* be good because it came up in one's own brain — the chances are great that this first or second, or third "inspiration" is something not good, but more likely something bad. Further, the possibility of willful distortion, caused by the architect following an idea or a desire to create a never-before-seen impression, is also capable of obscuring the process, and leading it up a blind alley.

Virtually all the shocking blunders and horrors of modern and postmodern architecture may be understood like this. They turned out bad mainly because they were *unexamined experimentally.* The designer did not take the time to examine the different possible steps in the evolution of the form and, at each step, seek out — with care — *that one of these which has the deepest feeling*: hence which of the possible steps does the most to extend and protect the world in that place.

The vital point is that this is an empirical matter. It can be discovered by experiment (in the real place, or in a model, or in other sufficiently "real" simulations). But it will not be discovered, unless the experiment is *done* — through models and in the designer's mind, while the designer is running through possible steps to take. The one exception occurs when the designer is deeply in touch with the wholeness that is there, and can summon up, very rapidly, a genuine structure-preserving transformation as an intuitive response which springs directly from the wholeness, in the designer's mind. We shall see, in chapter 14, how this can best be achieved by relying on feeling.

One might say that the process I have described is obvious. Certainly it is not very different from what people *say* they do. But there is a vast difference between what people say they do, and what they actually do.

7 / THE PROCESS OF CAPTURING THE WHOLE

To illustrate the process of differentiating a whole, step wise, by application of structure-preserving transformations and feeling, what follows is part of a conversation with Bill McClung. He asked me to illustrate a few steps in a design process trying to gain a vision for the reconstruction and improvement of Claremont Canyon: a wild canyon running east-to-west in the Berkeley Hills, three miles long, and containing some 900 acres of brush and trees. Bill asked me to describe how I would initially go about forming a conception of the design.

I explained that I would start with the whole, and treat it *as* a whole, and use the feeling of the whole which seemed to emerge from what is there today. As the discussion went forward, I showed him how, one by one, different morphological features of the whole came to my mind, and how I was trying to see (and imagine) these features, in such a way that gradually, by superimposing one on top of another, we would get a growing picture of the whole. Always, this work had to do with the whole.

FIRST CHANGE IN THE WHOLE. I started by remembering what it was like to stand at a spot high on the southern canyon wall, looking at the northern slope (roughly the view shown on pages 260–61). I looked out at the canyon. Rugged. Many hues of green. I ask myself what is the biggest difference this canyon might have, *as a whole*, compared with the way it is now. What could we conceive that might be better, as a whole, than it is today? Here I was asking myself for changes in the whole, that would improve our feeling about the whole, that would make us respond to it, as a whole, with deeper feeling.

I was particularly conscious of what it is like to drive up the canyon. There is a single road, rather enclosed, at the bottom; one can hardly see out beyond the road; and one is certainly aware that the canyon itself is almost entirely inaccesssible from the road. Thus, to all intents and purposes it is not there, since most people who see the canyon see it as drivers, from the road, yet cannot actually see it. The single thing that would change it most, as a whole, is the feeling that one could approach the canyon, reach it, enter it, enjoy it.

So the first really big change in the whole that I could imagine, was to imagine it all as being *reachable*; accessible, for people, walking, perhaps driving, on bicycles, for animals; while yet in its wild and natural state. With this in mind, I began to imagine a repeating texture of

Lower part of Claremont Canyon, Berkeley

barely visible paths — sometimes wide comfortable broad paths, not paved, perhaps ten feet wide ... following contours — a network of these broad paths, on both canyon walls, among the vegetation, connected, perhaps criss-crossed by smaller paths going up and down the walls. The texture of these broad paths, a network of paths, and the texture of this network, tiny in relation to the hugeness of the canyon, makes the place accessible. We feel, as we enter, that it is ours because we can reach places. We can get into it. Tame it. Reach it. Enjoy it. From this we have a first thing, an overall geometric texture in the whole.

Bill and I talked about this. He asked me if I felt certain about it. No, my answer was, I am uncertain, perhaps 50% or 60% of this idea might be useful as a clue to the whole.

But it is still a very rough idea, very rough, not thought out in relation to the whole. I need to see more of the canyon, to see if such a thing makes sense. There is no reason to try and decide it now. I don't go on with this. Rather, I just let it sit in our minds.

SECOND CHANGE IN THE WHOLE. Then, thinking out loud. The network of broad paths as a structure, it may not be big enough. Although a vision of such a network has a coherent texture, it is not clear enough as a *whole*, not big enough, in relation to the valley as a whole. What are the features of the canyon as a whole, that could intensify it *as a whole*? Bill suggests open grass lands of a special shape. I believe that this is still too detailed. The landform of the hills and mountains, the land form itself, the beautiful shapes of hills and the rugged, yet soft contours,

Upper part of Claremont Canyon, Berkeley

lost now, but potentially recoverable. I begin to imagine a form of trimming, or pruning, which reveals the slopes and shapes of the hills themselves, differentiating and strengthening the GOOD SHAPE, not willful but emerging from the larger whole. Yes, that is more like it, it may be a form which becomes graspable as a whole, where we might visualize — and then actually see — the canyon as a whole, a whole geometric shape, a whole form, even wrinkled and organic and rugged, still visible as one thing. So now we have some feeling for an overall shape.

THIRD IMPACT ON THE WHOLE. I suggest next, that ideally there would be a center which marks the canyon as a whole. At first Bill takes me too literally. There is a flat land, at Glen Jones's place, he tells me, a few acres flat, right in the middle. It seems like a natural

center. But I know that place. No, I tell him, that is the wrong place, that is just the *middle*. It is not a center which arises from the whole and lifts it up.

He asks me to say more. I tell him that I am still looking, in my mind, for some way of being, which will allow the canyon to impress us as a whole. I talk about the road winding up the canyon. Ideally, if at the head of the canyon, the place where the crossroads is and the saddle into the next canyon, if there, standing at the saddle, there was a castle, almost like a castle at the headwater of the glen. But it is in the wrong place, because the real center of the land is further to the left, where the mountain is steeper and more rugged. That is where this imaginary building should be, at the head of the canyon, to mark the spot.

Sketch showing all six global features forming a new whole

FOURTH STEP IN THE EVOLUTION OF THE WHOLE. This is a very general process I am following. Looking at the whole, I ask myself where, and how, the whole might generate a vector which indicates some center that is the head and heart of the whole. If I could find such a point, then we might try to emphasize that point, place some smaller intense center of great beauty (a building like a jewel) there, so that this casts influence downward, and strengthens the center of the canyon as a whole. Thus we are beginning to imagine a two-center system: one center the larger canyon itself, one the smaller jewel-like building, each of the two strengthening the other.

FIFTH CONTRIBUTION TO THE FORM OF THE WHOLE. I talk briefly with Bill, once again laying emphasis on the fact that the process we are following is concerned with the whole at every moment. Each step we take, everything I try to do, is to visualize a feature of the whole, large enough in its impact to help form the whole, and chosen so that the *whole* creates deep feeling in us. What kind of whole will do that? What formation as a whole will do it? We talk about texture. I describe for him, the way that the overall statistics of material, is one of the most important features of any system or structure, *as a whole*. Applying this

to Claremont Canyon, Bill and I speak of grassland — he suggests perhaps 50% open grass land, 50% trees (Oaks and Eucalyptus). The texture is vital. In some places open land — void — is itself is one kind of texture; in another place dense cover is a texture, or a texture full of holes (spongy) is another. The overall quality of the canyon, in this way, will help us to grasp it, and design it, as a whole.

SIXTH CONTRIBUTION TO THE FORM OF THE WHOLE. Bill then suggests, What about the road at the bottom of the canyon as another main center? My answer is that the road is already a center now, but that it is not a very inspiring one, it does not help to form a vision of the valley as a beautiful and living whole. But what if, Bill says, the road is flanked on either side by a green swath so that instead of just the road alone, it is a smooth green valley, with occasional trees, the stream coming down, a wide green swath forming the base of the whole canyon, perhaps 100 yards wide, following the land, jumping down the cascading terrain? Here we see BOUNDARIES, large boundaries, entering into the formation of LEVELS OF SCALE. That contributes more to the vision of the whole, because it is big enough, morphologically, to have real impact on the whole, and transforms it towards a state which has a deeper feeling.

8 / THE WHOLE THEN EMERGES FROM THESE TRANSFORMATIONS

You see how simple, but inspiring these kinds of steps can be. They are modest; but as we imagine them, a transformed whole takes shape in our mind, and more and more vividly we can imagine what it would be like to be there. It arises smoothly in our mind, unfolding from the whole which exists at present.

Part of the picture is very much given to the fifteen properties: CENTERS, BOUNDARIES, ALTERNATING REPETITION, GRADIENTS, GOOD SHAPE, LOCAL SYMMETRIES, DEEP INTERLOCK, ECHOES ... These properties are the language in which the picture, as it differentiates in your mind, naturally presents itself.

By retaining the picture in verbal form, but by insisting, while we create it, that the content of what we imagine is very physical and global — in other words, that the separate features each make significant contribution to the form and feeling of the whole — we gradually work towards a configuration for the valley in the large which is a design for the whole canyon.

We have decided nothing yet. But as we talk, each of these ideas remains, in verbal form, part of a strongly, powerfully felt visualized whole. Closing my eyes, I see each of the six things Bill and I have discussed. They coalesce freely in my mind, to form a single larger picture — still not complete, of course. They have an inspiring quality. It is not like the rather dead and inaccurate information one gets from a drawing, which would be wrong in so many places, and which — anyway — would not give us the inspiration we need about the design of the whole. It is more vivid in the mind's eye. Yet, if called upon to draw it, or to indicate the structure on a physical model of the canyon, I could do so at once.

What we have achieved is a loose-limbed, connected structure of structures, beginning to have the character needed by any living center.

It begins to have subsidiary centers — at least defined by type. We begin to feel how the whole goes together. We begin to feel what is important, and what less important. We are beginning to have a coherent vision of the whole which will work, and which can be elaborated.

All the work I have done, in trying to get this whole, is to pay attention, one by one, to features of it *as a whole*. I seek, have sought, those features which will most restore its feeling. All of them are rooted in the canyon as it is — so by its essence what I have been doing was always structure-preserving. And the main thrust, the main impetus, is to create a new *whole*, not existing before, just right for this place, yet arising out of what is there now.

Throughout, I am led forward in the discussion by asking what feature will create a deeper feeling in that place. I ask about the feeling. I ask myself what the whole would be like if it had the most profound feeling as a whole I can imagine. I close my eyes. The answer comes autonomously.

And let me say a word more about the fifteen properties, and the way that, quite naturally, they enter in. In the preceding perception and discussion of wholeness we see the fifteen properties, appearing both in the description of the whole, and in the emergence of a growing whole. That is because the fifteen properties are attributes of wholeness, and because all wholeness relies on these fifteen properties as its essential underpinning.

For example, we see the hillside... it has a homogeneous structure of grass and shrubs, which we would like to leave undisturbed. Yet we seek to introduce paths into the whole. To enhance the structure we then imagine a homogeneous network of evenly spaced paths, parallel to contours, small in scale, yet weaving a web or texture whose wholeness — like the slopes and bushes themselves — is rather homogeneous in the large, and thus leaves the wholeness of the hill intact.

Later we get a glimpse of the whole as needing a focus ... so we look for the natural focus — in this case, it happens to be the "head" of the valley, forming a natural center — and then intensify this center by first imagining (and ultimately building) a building there which forms a natural center to the canyon, in the right place, and which, with the canyon as a whole, forms a new more powerful center, consistent with the previous structure but enhancing it.

9 / MICROCOSM OF A PROCESS WHICH IS GUIDED BY THE WHOLE

To leave the reader with a clear, and intuitive small image of what it really means to make each step of a process enhance the whole, I shall close this chapter with an example of a painting. The example is intended to show, for painting, what a living process is like in its wholeness-enhancing nature.

This process started with a ship in the Port of Oakland. I caught a glimpse of a cargo ship for a few seconds as I was driving home on the Bay Bridge one day. What stayed in my mind was the wholeness of the scene; by this I mean the wholeness of the ship, water, bridge, port. This wholeness is visible to some extent in the painting illustrated. It does consist, of course, of the turquoise hull, the red waterline; the two cranes against the sky. But there is a *large* aspect to the wholeness, not so easily described. This is the blackness of the bridge around me, and from which I saw the scene; the light around the white cranes; the distant darkness of the Port of Oakland, rhythmically visible through the cranes and the ship; the overall color sense, the black, the white, the turquoise and flashes of red; the shimmer on the water.

All this was the wholeness of that place, visible for an instant. Concretely, the wholeness was experienced, and remembered, as a kind of light. I remembered the quality of this wholeness, its structure, not by remembering a pattern of centers as described in Book 1, but by remembering the melody of this wholeness as a single struc-

ture. I experienced this melody as a feeling, or as a kind of light. Then, when I went back to my studio, and started the painting, I tried to create an object which re-established this wholeness, which shone with that light, that melody. So, I was trying to copy, not the details of the scene but the *wholeness*, the *life*. Then, in trying to capture this life as a whole, I constructed a variety of details, until these details made *that* feeling and *that* wholeness and *that* life shine out.

In general, the important thing is that the process was not based on details, but on the whole. At the moment I saw the ship, I concentrated on the particular feeling of light which existed at that moment. I tried to retain this structure in my mind. I made a quick mental note of the main colors: dark blue-green water; the ship pale turquoise, red stripe above, red below; cargo containers red and white; the two white cranes, silhouetted against the dark gray billowing fog. That was as much as I had time for. What I felt at that moment and remember even now, was the particular kind of light, the wholeness of the scene — *not its details, but a particular colored light, which occurred as a whole.*

Later, in my studio, I began trying to re-create this wholeness. In doing this, I was not trying to make the scene realistic in the ordinary sense. I was not trying to paint the ship in detail, or the water in detail, or the bridge in detail. If I had been doing this, I would have been trying to build the wholeness from the details. But that

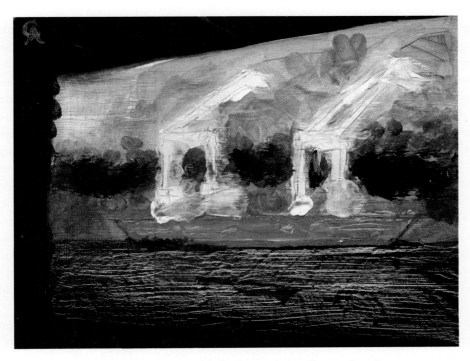

Cargo ship in the Port of Oakland, 9 x 12 inches, oil on wood panel

would not have worked, and that is not what I did. I simply began placing colors on the paper, in the hope that the vivid life-filled light which I had seen would somehow begin to shine forth from the painting. That is what I cared about. So, I was not drawing *from* life, but trying to create a drawing which would *give off* life, making an autonomous construction (at first, in colored pencil on a piece of card, later in oils on a board).

When I began, the picture didn't have the real light of the actual scene at all, nor did it shine with the actual feeling I felt when I saw the scene. I tried a pinkish red, the stripes were too equal. I made the top one thinner. I made the red more red. I put deep ultramarine in the water. It became too sweet. I realized at a certain point that the blackness of the bridge members played a role, and I put them in — not because of realism, but because the black changed the light. I made layers of gray behind the ship — one of them almost black in order to make the others more brilliant. Much later, I decided to put violet streaks in the upper layers of fog. I have no idea if there was anything like that in the actual

situation. But when I put in those flashes of violet, the boat began to shine in the way it really was shining when I saw the scene the day before. I had already tried pink, violeted gray, more white . . . each time I noticed a change of some kind, but not the creation of the light.

It wasn't until I put the flashes of violet in the sky that the boat began to shine. The same with the small touches of light green near the cranes. Again, I don't know if there was anything like that it in the actual situation. The green doesn't represent trees, or grass, or green containers, or anything that I actually saw. What I know is that when I put in these touches of green, the cranes began to have a life, the wholeness began to shine with light, in a fashion something like the actual scene.

In the same way I made the cranes more white, less white, I made the light turquoise more blue, more green, more gray, kept on changing it, until it began to give out light. In the case of the water I remember what it actually was like, a very dark green turquoise. But I didn't try to capture the color I remembered. What I did was to work at the blue, the green, working over layers of green, layers of a grayish blue, touches of ultramarine — finally a coat of thin gray over the whole, until it made the boat shine and made the bridge shine. In the final version, I scratched the dark blue of the water to make whitish lines in it. Objectively, the actual water on that day was not like this. It was dark, and didn't have many highlights. But when I scratched the dark blue of the water, the overall light in the painting became more like the real light. The *whole* was more accurate. The detail was in some mechanical sense *less* accurate — but that had little practical meaning. It was the *wholeness* which mattered.

In this process, the wholeness generates the details. This is what I mean by a new kind of process. The living wholeness guides every step. The details are born, created, brought into existence, only to create that wholeness and its feeling as accurately as possible. It is the life of the whole which matters.

Oddly, though, as a result of this process, the painting seems very realistic. It creates the same feeling as the scene itself created in me at the moment when I saw it. But it became realistic because it was generated from the real life of the *wholeness*, not because of slavish mechanical copying of details.

And, as I did earlier, I will say a word or two about the way the fifteen transformations entered into the process by which the whole emerged. Once again, the focus on wholeness, and the attempt to enhance the whole (this time through color) brings with it, naturally, some of the fifteen properties in the geometric structure which creates the color. The Bay Bridge from which the scene is drawn, is a big BOUNDARY, solid black, intensifying the color of the ship. The scratches forming the sparkle of the waves provide ALTERNATING REPETITION and ROUGHNESS, and intensify the wholeness of the water. The stripe along the ship, is sized and placed to form a hull and a boundary and LEVELS OF SCALE. The cranes and white flecks of paint form ECHOES in the sky.

In each case the appearance of the property in question is present in the wholeness observed originally (the bridge itself) and plays a key role in forming the wholeness in the painting because that, too, is made of structures of centers which enliven one another through the fifteen properties. This structure of the picture may then be intensified and used, in the process of unfolding, to accentuate the wholeness, and to create a vivid version of that whole, *exactly by underlining and increasing the action of the emergent fifteen properties, one at a time.*

10 / IN SUMMARY

In a living process, what is always happening is that every step (large or small, whether it comes late or early) is done in such a way as to increase the beauty — the life — of *the whole*. The process starts with a vision of a possible whole that comes out of the circumstances, that is felt as something which grows out of the form of the world. Every step is made with the idea that the feeling of this very large whole is being made deeper, more intense.

Even if it is only a tiny step, this is still the guiding rule.

CHAPTER TEN

ALWAYS MAKING CENTERS

SO THAT EVERY CENTER IS SHAPED BY THE NEXT STEP
IN THE DIFFERENTIATION

1 / EMERGING CENTERS WHICH HELP THE WHOLE

I shall now describe, in some detail, the process through which differentiation, applied again and again, generates a complete building, center by center, until thousands of centers, at dozens of levels of scale, completely determine the design.

In Book 1, I have given extensive description of the way that a living wholeness is a structure of STRONG CENTERS, centers existing at many scales, mutually reinforcing each other and forming a field. I have shown also that many of these centers which are present when a structure has life are not chiefly obvious distinct *components* but very often nearly invisible pieces of space whose "centeredness" acts within a shape to make it a GOOD SHAPE, acts between elements of space to make POSITIVE SPACE, or acts in such a way as to make almost invisible harmonies, relationships, and comfortable NOT-SEPARATENESS in space as a whole. All this, I have summarized by calling the wholeness a "field" of centers.

When a living whole is to be built step by step, it is clear, therefore, that what must be created, throughout the space, are precisely all these centers from which the wholeness gets its strength. Let us therefore now discuss, concretely, the way that centers are *made*, and the way that they are shaped so as to contribute to the wholeness and the life of the whole.

Of course the question that arises is, How is this to happen? What kinds of center-creating steps can have such an impact that is both piecemeal (step by step) and yet also helping to repair and enhance the whole in its wholeness at each step forward.

The answer comes from the theory of wholeness itself.[1] Centers are not atomic, and are not in any normal sense building blocks.[2] They are nevertheless the units of increase for all development, which allow a whole to unfold without damaging the wholeness. That is because centers are above all, labile, they are *foci* of wholeness, they are not *things*, but regions, qualities, focal points of centeredness which as they change, as they are improved, are ideally suited to enhance and enlarge and extend the whole while making that wholeness benefit, while they are fused into the wholeness, as they go forward.

So, for life to be created, what must be built, extended, added, at every moment, at every next step, is a center: a field of centeredness which is to be injected into the structure of the growing whole. This is not a process of adding a building block of some kind. It is a question of injecting a field-like centrality into the existing wholeness at that point where it can do most good to enhance and sustain the structure of the wholeness as it was before, while also now nudging it forward to a new, more living state.

Given this point of view, what then is happening when something unfolds? New centers are formed, and as they form, the space rearranges itself, not only locally, but in the neighborhood of the newly forming center. POSITIVE SPACE occurs as centers are made more definite, ordinary centers are made STRONG CENTERS. And as POSITIVE SPACE occurs, and stronger centers occur, the structure becomes more definite, more clearly differentiated, more articulate.

The dominant feature of a process that is working correctly is summarized in the statement: *at every step, the process does its utmost to enhance the structure of the whole, and shapes its parts to make this enhancement happen.* The complementary view of the same point is that the parts are formed within the whole and by the whole. Most important is the constant focus on larger wholes, and the awareness in each small act, and in each small piece that is created, the process is contributing to the significant shape and organization of larger wholes within the structure. Every small part is shaped in order to play an effective role in the life of the larger structure.

In a mechanical process, parts are formed independently of the whole, and then added together to form an aggregation. In a living structure, the parts come into being within the whole, they break out from the whole, they are determined and shaped by their presence in the whole, and above all they transform the whole according to the latent structure which exists in it. That is the rule which marks the living, and distinguishes it from the mechanical.

2 / A SNOW BLOCK IN AN IGLOO

Consider the traditional process of making an igloo from snow blocks. The igloo is a roughly round structure, built by cutting big rectangular blocks of snow and placing them to form the wall — first the base of the wall, then the curving part of the wall top, as it curves inward, and finally the roof. The snow block, when it was first cut, was a roughly rectangular block. But as soon as one put it in place, it had to be pushed, trimmed, and squashed to make it conform to the emerging roundness of the igloo both in plan and in section as one formed the vault.

Here is a perfect example of the way awareness of the whole may shape the part. The part starts out autonomous. But because the snow is malleable, moldable, cuttable, and shapeable, it is adapted to the whole as soon as it is put in place: the whole evolves, and the part gets shaped according to its position in the whole. Later, it melts into the whole, and becomes almost indistinguishable any more. And what of the centers which are forming, during this process? The blocks themselves are forming slowly, each one getting a more distinct more highly differentiated shape, according to position, GOOD SHAPE and STRONG CENTERS emerge. The spaces between the blocks, being closed up, become co-herent centers too, and they become more positive as space, and themselves more center-like. NOT-SEPARATENESS appears as they become inseparable.

If we analyze carefully what is going on in such a situation, we see two directions of influence. First, obviously, the part is *influenced* by its position in the whole. The snow block is not modular, but uniquely shaped according to its position and contribution to the shape of the round, domed igloo. Second, the part is made in such a way as to *increase* the life of the emerging whole *in its large aspects*. The igloo, as a shape and as a whole, gets better as the new block is put into it, has more living structure than before: It is improved. With each added block, the wholeness is extended and made stronger. This is very different from construction of a warehouse from modular panels. In the warehouse you see more of the parts as they go up, but the building is not getting better. The igloo gets better, since each new snow block creates opportunities for refinement and improvement as it is introduced. The small centers (snow blocks) are formed to help the life of the larger center (igloo), and in the process are shaped by the emerging whole.

3 / A POWER STATION MADE TO HELP A VALLEY

Let's take a larger example, and imagine that we are responsible for placing a power station in the Austrian Alps, in a particularly beautiful valley, with lovely peaks and forests visible. It would be easy enough to say, "We cannot build a power station there, it would be too damaging." But let us imagine, further, that for some reason it is necessary to put it there. Just saying no, does not solve the problem.

What does it mean, now, to place this new power station so that it protects and preserves the life of the whole?

We must establish, of course, roughly how much land is needed. (I emphasize the word roughly, for reasons that will be clear in a minute.) Let us say that what is needed is about fifteen acres. We will also have an idea of how big the structure is likely to be (again, I say "likely" because we need flexibility in the process of thinking this out).

Imagine now, that we begin to look up and down the valley for places of about fifteen acres, imagining a building of about the height we know is likely. We are looking for a place where this kind of building will do the least damage. That is, we can imagine all the possible places, and ask which, of all those we can find, has the least negative impact on the beauty of the valley.

Of course, then, we shall not put it in a particularly beautiful place, or a prominent place. We look for a place which is tucked away, behind a secondary peak, in a small side valley behind a hill . . . something like that.

But, indeed, we must do more than that. We wish to find the place for the power station which does most good for the whole: that is, for the valley. Now we know that with the power station, inevitably there is a budget, not only for the buildings and equipment, but also for perimeter things such as roads and secondary engineering. We need to look for a place which can *benefit* from the expenditure of the capital which will go with construction of the power station.

So we look for the ugliest, most damaged place in the valley, one that is somewhat unobtrusive. In this damaged place, we look for the place which is going to hold the main buildings. Perhaps the access road can be used to improve some part of a rock slide, a destroyed area.

During this process, new more living centers emerge, places that were damaged, incoher-ent, become more alive, and new STRONG CEN-TERS and BOUNDARIES are formed in them, space is made more positive. And those places where centers are already alive — often the most beau-tiful parts of the natural wild — are left intact, and not disturbed.

When we have finished, we will have man-aged to place the power station in the valley in a way that is almost invisible, and — at the same time — while building it also manage to im-prove secondary land features like retaining walls, engineering of water, slopes, and so on, with the overall effect that something more beautiful can be made of the whole.

To do all this, we not only keep on looking while we are in the place itself. We also keep on taking pictures, then drawing in the volume of the power station so that we can see just where it will be, what it will look like — and whether we are right in thinking that it can make the valley better.

This is all very sensible. I think we must acknowledge, though, that it is different from the way these things are normally done according to most modern planning processes. In the typi-cal planning and development process, the power company chooses a place which is to their advan-tage (cheap, easy access, and so on). The planners then accept or reject the site (with some negotia-tion, and often with political pressure to accept). Then the building is built. Such a process is not a living process, because it has no component which draws attention to the good of the whole landscape where this is to occur.

What I propose is quite different. The smaller center (the fifteen-acre site of the new power station) is placed and formed and shaped in its entirety in such a way to to bring the most good to the larger center (the whole valley). The benefit to the region of Earth where this power station is to be built is obvious. But as things stand, the center-forming process is not repre-sented in the present process by any present polit-ical power, or by any operational step in the present process. Yet, in principle, such a process is clearly possible.

4 / AN OPERATIONAL BASIS:
HOW EACH CENTER, AS IT IS FORMED, MAY BE
CHOSEN TO HELP INCREASE THE LIFE OF THE WHOLE

The snow block helps to form an emerging, imperfectly defined idea of a half-spherical building, which is seen in the builder's mind, and is a target of his actions — imprecise, yet clear enough to steer the cutting and shaping of the individual blocks towards this larger whole. Each block starts as an undifferentiated block, without much existence as a center, then becomes a living center as it is shaped, pushed, trimmed, to take its position in the whole.

The Austrian power station, when correctly placed, is a center guided by a vision of the whole valley, as it might be, a beautiful valley, uncontaminated. This vision steers the work of finding the right place for the power station, and that process in turn then shapes the design of the power station as a living center — makes it detailed, differentiated, realistic, and helpful — because of the contribution that it makes to the living structure of the valley.

The rule I proposed for apartment houses in Pasadena (given on pages 250–51) was designed to help the emergence of the street as a useful, social, beautiful place that could be enjoyed by everyone. The process was (without a blueprint of such a street) to be driven only by the "idea" that each applicant finds some way of helping the larger whole to emerge.

In each of these three cases "the life of the whole" is not too hard to see. It is perhaps only hard to force oneself to make the smaller centers *contribute* to that life. But, one might argue that a person does not have a sufficiently clear vision of the (as yet unknown) whole to be able to make a small act contribute. In the case of the Pasadena street, an unwilling developer might say that he does not yet see how he might contribute, because he does not grasp what the street is supposed to be like. But knowing what to do does not mean knowing what the target is. It means,

having the ability to go towards an unformulated whole, because the life and wholeness of the system is visible, "feelable" as a process, even in the absence of a concrete model of the desired end-state. The key fact, and the essence of all living process, is that experiments *can* be devised to help us to determine what the wholeness needs, where it is going, *what* is most structure-preserving to the present whole, *what* contributes to the life of the whole. As I have demonstrated (pages 253–54) this is an experimental task that can be successfully performed by identifying latent centers, then strengthening them.[3]

By staring at the street, by considering it, by seeing it in one's mind's eye, trying to see the latent centers, then closing one's eyes and imagining what could be there that might best help the street . . . the important thing is that such experiments can be done, they do bring results, and the results have measurable degree of life to an extent that is verifiable and sharable (at least to reasonable degree). My experiments have shown repeatedly that when different people make this effort, they are then slowly able to agree which proposed actions are more structure-preserving or life-bearing, and which actions are less so.[4] Like the mirror-of-the-self tests of Book 1, chapter 8, this is a task which people can do with success, if they have good will — and there will be at least substantial agreement about the results when different people do it together.

Thus it puts the process of unfolding on an operational basis. And, as we shall see next, this process can be applied to every step in the emergence of a building design. Everything that happens in the sequence of events when we design a building, from the first vague ideas to the complete elaboration of the details, can be understood as a progressive unfolding of stronger and stronger centers.

6 / WHY IS IT SO DIFFICULT TO FORM CENTERS BY DIFFERENTIATION? AN ILLUSTRATION FROM POSTMODERN ARCHITECTURE

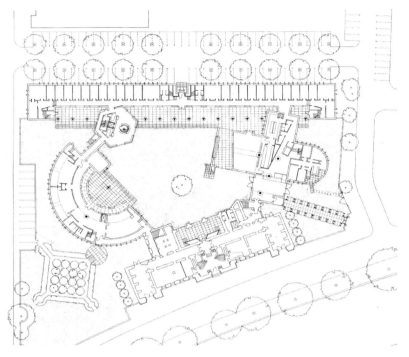

Plan of the Berlin Library, by James Stirling

Nevertheless, the work can be difficult. To illustrate in some detail, *why* this can be difficult, I take a rather well-known building by a prominent 20th-century architect, James Stirling's Science Library in Berlin.

At *first* glance, this building looks as if it has many strong centers in it. When we look at the plan of this building, especially, it seems on the surface, to have several rather good centers. The half circle, the hexagon, the long arcade all stand out in the plan shapes. Are these not the very centers I have been writing about? And does the process of design which went in to this building, therefore not serve excellently, as an example of how to make centers?

But it is harder than that. This architect obviously was trying to make centers. Let us consider them. The columns, for instance, are triangular. That is unusual, and seems, at first, to be clever and interesting. The triangular form is a strongly marked shape. Certainly, one might assume, this column will then be felt as a center. He has succeeded in making these centers strong.

But if we go carefully, we see that this is not really so. The triangular shape of the column, does not create a strong center in the space next to it. Further, because it is hard to do, he did not make any substantial centers either at the bottom of the column, or at the top. That possibly came about because the triangular shape does not easily lend itself to that purpose. The structural connection we do see at the top of the columns, is not a strong center, but a rather awkwardly

The triangular columns of the Stirling library

shaped connection detail. It must have been hard to do anything else. So again, making this center, he failed to make smaller centers which support the large center.

At the bottom Stirling placed the triangular column on a round base. If you look at the connection and ask if it forms a mirror of the self (Is it, profoundly, a picture of your own self?) — you will almost certainly say that it is not.

You see that it is not so easy. One has to be rather careful in shaping things, if one is to succeed in making centers come to life.

Going back to Stirling's plan, let us look at the apparent centers in the plan: the half circle, the hexagon, the Greek cross, and so forth. There are four defects which can be most easily identified in these centers of the plan.

Smaller centers. If we look inside the centers, we find that the thing is subdivided into rooms and spaces which do not form strong centers in themselves. This shows the brittleness of the form. The half circle is an empty shell, which is not made up of smaller centers. By comparison, a true center is itself made of smaller centers which are centers too. The rooms are centers: passages, entrance, odd corners by the stairs — are all centers.

Focus on the triangular columns

Incongruity of the triangular column on a round base

Image-like copies of other centers. If we look at the ground plan, it is noticeable that the centers which exist are very dissimilar — they do not form a family, but seem isolated, distinct. This happens because they are, quite literally, cut and

pasted from history books. One is the stoa. Stirling calls it the stoa. The half circle is like a Greek theater or arena. Stirling calls it the arena. The cross-formed plan is an almost perfect replica of an Armenian or Byzantine church.

This is typical of postmodern architecture — which gains its forms and plans, by making copies of historical plans and images — and literally cutting and pasting them into the plans.

Centers do not emerge from the surrounding wholeness. One asks oneself, How may this be criticized? What is really wrong with it? What goes wrong at a deep level? And what is it that prevents these so-called centers from being real centers, when they are made like this?

Because these forms have been cut or pasted into the plan, they do not have the capacity to emerge naturally from what is there. Thus, they are isolated, in a realistic and literal sense. They do not emerge by transformations of the surrounding structure. Instead, they are cut and transplanted. Thus, they appear context-less, and cut off. They do not extend the surrounding structure. And for this reason they fail to create the seamless structure which is typical in a living field of centers.

From a structural point of view the essential point is this. A real center starts many diameters outside its skin or boundary — the structure beyond contributes to the centeredness. This is an essential attribute of any real center. But these centers, because they are cut and transplanted, do not have this feature. They are very weak centers, because they do not extend outward far enough.

Centers do not help form any larger centers. The centers also do not cooperate to form larger centers. For example, the open space between these buildings could be a center. It is not. This is not because of its irregular shape. A similar courtyard, with a more irregular shape, might be beautiful. Certainly, it is not necessary for the courtyard to be regular rectangle. But the key thing is that the different and separate centers remain separate. They do not cooperate to form any-

Overview of the whole

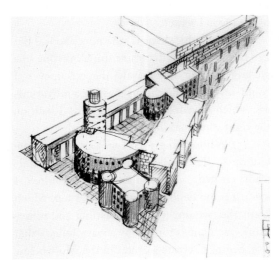

Diagram showing the geometric elements,
heavily shaped, but without actual life

thing. So they remain silly, trivial in feeling — above all because structurally they do not have the proper character.

On first analysis it looks as though the Stirling library is faulty because the *details* are too crude. And they *are* crude. The pure cylinder columns, the triangular wedges of roof and slab — they are unsubtle and academic in their geometry. But the deeper problem, is that successful *larger* wholes do not appear in the building, it has not made larger wholes. The smaller centers — already weak — do not succeed in forming larger centers, or in making the larger centers live.

Are the centers in the building, then, *indeed* good centers? It appears that under the surface, the thing has profound defects structurally. The centers which seem so strong and center-like, are very, *very* weak.

In the way I have described, the level of understanding which existed among postmodern architects was often too simple. One sees, and feels, a limitation in the building, some strange, perhaps unnatural feeling, that exists in the building. If you read the magazines, it would appear (and architects sometimes claim) that they are doing these things on purpose, something done intentionally by the architect in order to be clever.

However, I feel rather, that making the field of centers is quite hard. Although artists and builders of traditional society understood this well, often profoundly, present-day artists and architects often simply underestimate it, do not realize how hard it is, nor how profound it is.

Respect for the unfolding process, may be increased by this example. When it comes to working out a building, achieving something which has living centers in it and in which living structure of the whole occurs is quite a trick.

7 / THE PLAYFUL CORE OF THE MATTER

To illustrate the theoretical point, I should like to review the nature of the center-making process itself. The nub of the fundamental process says that at each step, strong centers are to be created, step by step, in space.

The work of creating geometric centers, in a piece of land, is really a *geometrical*, physical activity. It has to do with making things in space that are really centers. This activity is something so *geometrical*, so *formal*, that it is almost automatic; it is really an artist's song, a free process of creating geometry like singing in the bath, or letting a line of paint follow the paper.

To suggest this idea, and to prepare for the discussion which follows, I start with something that may seem trivial, a doodle, because it has no significant content. And yet, it *is* a process of creating centers. It *is* an embodiment of the fundamental process. And because it is so simple, yet creates new structure without effort, it is intensely interesting. The reader might like to try a similar exercise.

First doodle. This is what happened during the five minutes or so it took to draw it. I started with a soft pencil, and I went into it very, very fast, so all of what happens, happens so fast I am not in control, and the process is almost autonomous.

(1) First, a single little dot, which I started with my soft pencil, and then slashed away at it, starting to enlarge it.

(2) I was using my arm in a way that produced diagonal strokes, so the shape grew very quickly into a sort of horizontal form, which had a bit of a wave in it. This was the first center.

(3) Then, since I was drawing the diagonal strokes so fast, the pencil slipped and went down below. Immediately I began to enlarge this section making it into some sort of shape which was really no more than a bulge towards the bottom — with, at this stage, nothing more than a rough convex outline — this was the beginning of the second center.

(4) Since this shape is still amorphous, I began trying to make the whole thing into one single larger center. Because the shape is uneven, I could only see to do this by making a mirror image which repeated the same as what I had, on the right, thus making a larger center.

(5) While doing this, I was also paying attention to the smaller centers which I had already created, and to maintain their force, I made a more deliberate wave in the top, which keeps the two upper centers distinct and something (each one is formed by a wavy bulge), that also, begins to create a center in the white below it.

(6) And at the same time I am also paying attention to the same thing — the white space — in the lower part of the figure. Once again, in order to maintain the center which I have already created, at the bottom, I make an indentation at the lower edge — if I had

(1)

(2)

(3)

(4)

(5)

(6)

(7)

(8)

(9)

(10)

(11)

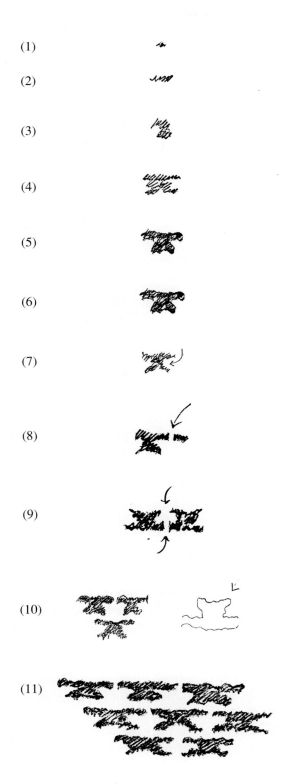

First doodle. The first eleven steps in the process. These steps took altogether perhaps one minute to complete.

smoothed it out, the bottom would be like a trapezium, and would have lost its smaller centers.

By now I have spent perhaps 10 seconds drawing.

(7) I now started to pay attention to the white — as you can see, there is already the beginning of a "shape" in the white indented area between the top of the thing and the bottom of the thing.

(8) Looking at it, I wonder how I can make a center out of that, and while I am thinking already begin another of these T-shaped things to the right, because the presence of the black, a little distance away, already begins to enclose the white, and gives me the promise that I can make the white space into a center. While making this white area into a center I am also paying attention to the upper part of the white, the narrow space between the bars of the two black Ts, which is a yet smaller center in the white.

(9) As I complete the second T, and look at the white centers which now lie between the two, I carefully pay attention to the drawing of the black, to be sure that these emerging white centers have a really nice shape.

(10) I am now struck by a remarkable thing — that the larger white center I have just formed is very similar in shape to the bottom of the black T, but upside down. As I continue in the centering process, I decide to place another T-shaped thing below the two that I have already drawn, in such a position that the wavy bar of the third black T will make a nice white space and make a complete upside down T-like figure in the white.

This is the first time in the whole process, that anything resembling a conscious thought has appeared in my mind. Most of what I described up to now has been almost automatic.

(11) I became lazy for the next minute or so, and just drew a bunch more of the same T shapes, trying to get the centers made in the white, and the centers made in the black, to be strong. I was aware that the waviness of the T-top was important, and that I was doing it differently each time, but just hanging on, trying

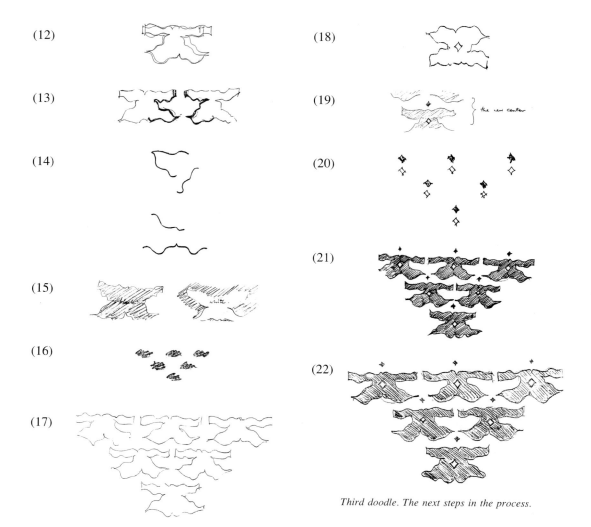

(12)

(13)

(14)

(15)

(16)

(17)

Second doodle. The next steps in the process.

(18)

(19) the new center

(20)

(21)

(22)

Third doodle. The next steps in the process.

to keep the strength of the centers intuitively, without trying to understand it.

By the time I had completed this first black and white drawing, then, about sixty seconds had gone by.

Second doodle. I decided, now, to try and capture the possible unity of the smaller and larger centers working together a bit more strongly by making a line drawing of the whole.

(12) As I drew this second version of the T-forms, I was now consciously trying to create smaller centers which occurred in small places around the boundary of the T-shape, and had to

replace the rough bulges of the rough shaded drawing, with something more definite.

(13) With the consciousness of the need for these smaller centers, I found myself making sharp points at various places. I was once again paying enormous attention to the empty space between the forms, making sure that these spaces had as definite a shape as the T-shaped things themselves, but most of all paying attention to the centers which were forming along the lines themselves as I was drawing them.

(14) These curves themselves are made of centers. For instance, the curve which forms the point on the outside corner, has to be a double S curve, so as to make the space positive, and also make the corner sharply pointed.

(15) Also, the similarity between black figures and white figures has changed. In the second drawing, each takes its own shape.

(16) When I had drawn the first Ts in the top two rows, I felt a strong need for a larger center than any I had drawn so far. I made the whole array symmetrical, with an overall triangle, which contained nicely placed spaces between.

(17) This large center seemed OK, but still not powerful enough to hold one's attention.

Third doodle. To give the individual shapes more force, and to knit the whole fabric together, I now — half idly — put a diamond inside each one — and began to shade the figures grey, leaving the diamond white.

(18) This I did consciously, hoping that I would thus connect the inside of the center of each T (the white diamond), with the outside of the Ts (also white).

(19) The whole thing began, for the first time, to have a feeling of being one overall larger center. I took further steps. I was aware that the space between the top of one T and the bottom of the white space above it, was incoherent — it needed a center there — so I drew a black diamond above each white diamond to hold the forms together, and to create a center there — and to knit together the white and the black.

(20) The *pairs* of diamonds together form a new system of centers.

(21) At the same time, the six black diamonds together form a larger triangle of diamonds, which itself also forms a new center.

(22) The whole process emerges simply, from the desire to knit space together, as strongly as possible, by forming centers at all scales.

During the making of this doodle, I probably applied the fundamental process more than 100 times.

8 / DIFFERENTIATION OF AN IMAGINARY BUILDING STRUCTURE-PRESERVING CREATION OF LIVING CENTERS

Let us apply the fundamental process to a building example. Here I use the same playful technique that I used on the doodle, but now show an example within the more normal process of designing a building — even though it is still playful — so far still just a game.

Step 1. The simplest center, is a symmetrical convex bit of space, with an axis. It is something that looks like this. It feels like a center. It forms a center.

Of course, as simple as it is, it doesn't have much life. It is a center. But it doesn't exactly inspire me to say: Yes, it has life. What do I need to do to it, to give it more life, to make it more a picture of myself?

Step 2. To make the center stronger, it will help to orient and intensify the axis which is latent in it. So I might say, now give it a "head,"

that means give it strength by means of a second center, which helps the first center. This gives the thing LEVELS OF SCALE.[2] Together the second center and the first center, make a third center. The head adds levels of scale. Depending on how the head is made, it may help GOOD SHAPE. Also, if the detail of the head is just right, then the body of the thing — the first center, will have more a quality of being THE VOID.

I can move this head around, and try and try to place it so that the whole configuration is more profound, feels more a picture of my self; has life.

Of course this depends on what it is. If it is a small place outside the front door, it is one thing. If it is a vase, it is another thing. If it is a door, it may be another thing, once again. It might be a window over the door. It might be an ornament in the upper part of the door.

Step 1: A simple thing, bi-axially symmetrical

Step 3: At the same time I can hardly stop myself: I start sketching in minor centers at the tail end, and along the sides, anticipations of further centers to come — and ways of intensifying the original body

Step 2: The simple thing gets a second center which intensifies the first.

Step 4: Now both major centers get a boundary which includes the minor centers from step 3. The boundaries are thick and themselves made of centers, which appear as shadows still. Are they niches, storage, alcoves, statues, places where something might grow.

Step 3. Suppose I have done that, and I want to deepen it further. I might say, well, now it is time to try and make it more centers, by thinking about THE BOUNDARY. What is around the edge, what boundary will form the center most deeply. I start, perhaps just by making something thick and definite around the whole thing — or perhaps around its body. I will probably make this boundary up from smaller centers — so I am not just making a thick thing around it, but somehow trying to make smaller entities, smaller centers around it — so that the first center becomes stronger.

Step 4. If I am skilful, I will do it so that the second center, the head, is also bounded somehow, perhaps with a smaller and more subtle boundary, so that I begin to feel a GRADIENT — GRADED VARIATION — in the passage from body to head, and in the passage from boundary to body, and from boundary to head.

Step 5. As far as we have got with steps 1–4, we still have a separate entity, a building with a nice shape, but relatively little connection to the world around it. Now we apply the NOT-SEPARATENESS transformation and the

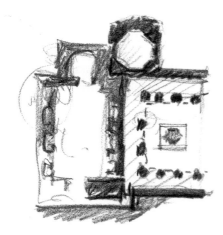

Step 5: Not-separateness. The powerful center is now surrounded and embedded in a field of other centers: it disappears, and gets itslife, most strongly, in the end, because it disappears.

POSITIVE-SPACE transformation, in such a way as to create — almost mysteriously, a connection to the building's surroundings. These transformations create new centers; but they do it in a way which makes the world lock together more. It is not entirely obvious how this works. The new centers that are created are scattered, they connect, they are incomplete, suggesting a breaking down of boundaries — partly it is a feeling in the drawing, only. But all in all, the way these transformations work to generate such connectivity in the world is impressive and important.

From it the body-head-boundary which I have started making, has become seamless, inseparable from its surroundings — not standing out too much, just a slight, and beautiful entity, crowning, or celebrating, modestly, the place where it is in the world.

And of course, to make this center have real life, there also have to be living centers all around it in the world: in the spaces next door to it. This is in effect what POSITIVE SPACE does.

What is it that I have been doing in applying these transformations? I am not trying to be clever. I am not trying to follow any special archetype, ancient or modern. I am just trying to make that thing, which, when its centers have been created, will most honestly make me feel a tremor, make me feel that my life is (even if only slightly) illuminated by the existence of this thing.

And at each step, among the various steps I have described, I had to keep asking myself this: Is it going in such a direction? Does it start to make me feel that life can be worth-while? Does it make me tremble, and feel on the edge of the chasm of life, so that all the uncertainty and fear of everyday life, is wrapped up, made worth something, summarized and justified, by the existence of this thing?

Most often the answer is, No. Ten times the answer comes back, *No*. But sometimes, if I feel even a little tiny bit of yes, I can move the building more towards the yes. And if I keep on looking for that yes direction, gradually it does come into existence.

But I haven't done anything until, *because of the existence of the center emerging in my care*, my life is more worth while than it was before, and my knowledge of the meaning of existence has become more real.

That is a tall order. It is a great demand. Perhaps too great a demand. But that *is* the demand, anyway, that I must make of things, while I am making them. It sounds pretentious, perhaps. But it isn't really. I discuss it in detail in Book 4. Being afraid of such magnificence is only the sad underside of our too mundane late 20th century.

It is important to understand that everything that happened in this example and in the shirt-doodles in the previous section, was structure-enhancing. In *Step 1* the first rectangle comes into being from the blank paper. In *Step 2*, the head gets put on it, to preserve and extend the deep structure of the rectangle as it appears in the sketch. The mid-points get put on in *Step 3*, to preserve and extend that structure. The thick boundary with all its additional centers, gets put on to extend that structure, in *Step 4*. And in *Step 5*, the courtyard, with its arcade, is stitched onto the rectangle and its boundaries, and grows naturally out of them, in order to preserve and extend the structure of *Step 4*.

Of course, in a real example, to make sense in a real context and a real culture, this playful technique which I have just shown, has to be combined with knowledge of realistic generic centers — as discussed in chapter 13. Instead of just making up geometric centers, as I have done in this little example, we also include with them some real generic centers, which have to respond to the geometry of the evolving design and to the wholeness of the culture, by using the patterns of the pattern language we have chosen. The way this works is fully discussed in chapter 13. I do not discuss it in this chapter because I am, first, merely trying to illustrate how all design is a "center building process." Once we have that clear, we can then go on, in chapter 13, to ask where the centers come from, in their inspiration.

In any case, although this example just given is trivial, it contains within it, the fundamental operation, repeated many times. The process of unfolding is always governed by the repeated application of this fundamental operation, thousands and thousand of times, over and over again. Outwardly, this repeated operation seems to take very different character at different moments. At one moment I have to think how the building works. At another, I have to try and decide the overall shape of the building. At another moment, I have to decide on its structural systems. At another time I am concerned about the parking, or the street. At another time I am concerned with the color in a single room. Superficially, it seems difficult to see all these apparently distinct operations, as versions of the same fundamental process. Nevertheless, I wish to re-emphasize that it is indeed this fundamental process which presents itself in a thousand versions.

The design is not necessarily growing on paper, nor necessarily on the actual site. At first it is only growing in my mind. In my mind, I am aware of this field, which is the thing that the building is going to become. At any given moment in the evolution of my thought about the building, I know a certain amount about this field (and, of course, so long as it is unfinished, there is always some part that I do not yet know). So I have in my mind, a kind of partially finished field (wholeness) which has some of its structure sketched in, some of its structure not yet sketched in. At each moment, I am struggling to get more clear about this emerging field.

Since the field is entirely made of centers, the state of my knowledge at any given moment, is always given by some set of centers, which to whatever stage of evolution they have reached, defines and encompasses what I know about the building so far. The simplicity of this idea, lies in the existence of the centers. Since the field exists only in virtue of its centers, it means that everything I know, at any given moment — absolutely everything — is always summarized by some system of centers. At the beginning of any project, I have very little understanding — and may only grasp half a dozen centers — and those only hazily. At the earliest stage it may even be just one, and that abstract, not concrete. Much later in the process, as my understanding deepens, I know and can feel hundreds — and later thousands — of centers in the evolving complex.

This does not mean that the thing is simply becoming more and more encrusted in my mind, becoming more complex in a numerical fashion. Simplicity is of great importance, and sometimes, I may get a great insight by removing material or structure. But even when it is one center which is growing in my mind, the intensity of life of this one center, as it grows, comes from the cooperation of, at first two or three, then dozens, and finally thousands of complex centers. Thus, even if at a certain stage in the unfolding, all that happens is that the shape of a particular arch becomes more refined, the increasing refinement, will be manifested in my mind, in the form of a growing understanding of a beautiful shape — the good shape of the arch — and this will come about because I have learned and seen, and created, a shape that is the product of dozens of smaller centers which cooperate to give beautiful life to the shape of the curve.

So, this slowly growing field, as it takes shape in my mind really is governed and harnessed by the repeated fundamental process. It is this operation through which I increase the subtlety of the centers which form the field.

9 / THE JULIAN STREET INN

To contrast with the weakness of the centers in the example of the Berlin library, I now show an example of a complete building which is somewhat similar in size, function, and character — but in which the centers have more substantial life. This is the Julian Street Inn in San Jose, California, a shelter for homeless people, which my colleagues and I built in 1987–88. It is at the intersection of Julian and Montgomery Streets and provides shelter and beds for about one hundred people.

The theoretical example of pages 279–82, made up for illustrative purposes, contained perhaps half-a-dozen main centers; even if we count all the centers, a few dozen centers at most. Let us now look at the design and formation of a real building, where there are several hundred major centers, and all in all (including all the smallest ones) hundreds of thousands of centers in the building. In the following example, efforts were made to make all these centers living.

The building process started, of course, with a list of generic centers (patterns), which we worked out with some of the homeless people in San Jose. People were living — at that time — under bridges in the bitter cold. In my discussion with them, I found that the most vital thing, from their point of view, was territory, the desire that this building be their territory. I formulated the idea of large gardens for summer; of individual private small rooms like those on a sleeping-car train, as private space for beds; of a comfort-able gathering place where people could wait — sometimes for hours, before the place opened.

When they and I together began to apply these patterns to the site, we quickly took a few steps in establishing major centers, as centers unfolded from the site, and from the cultural patterns.

At the outset, the issue was simple: to find a way of making this building a place where people, frightened, lonely, often dirty, from the life on the street, could find a safe haven, a home for a few days. My aim was to make the building, as far as possible, a place where they could feel safe, and feel normal. I wanted it, also, to be a place where I myself would like to stay, giving each person their own dignity, as much as I would want it myself if I stayed there.

I had several meetings with homeless people in the area, told them that I wanted them to design it with me, and that we should try to make it as friendly as possible. They told me then, from the very beginning: the main issue is "who has the key?" It was clear that establishing private domains, places which people could see as theirs, was the most vital feeling. Beyond that, we were looking for a system of large scenters which could provide a haven for the sanctity of private territory.

The very first thing was to fit the building to the long curve of the road, at the Julian Montgomery intersection, keeping intact the centers which existed in that curve (illustration 1).

Illustration 1: Getting the position of the building in relation to the site

Illustration 2: Conceiving two courtyards, in relation to the curved site boundary, and the existing shed.

The next thing, provision of comfortable and quiet gardens, was difficult on the small site, and I suggested that we build two courtyards, internally to the building, and placed everything around them (illustration 2).

Placing the building mass around these two, on the curvilinear site, was hard. The next thing to emerge were the centers on the building mass, forming uniform segments along the curved boundary, and forming, in effect, a boundary to the courtyards (illustration 3).

Next, the most important interior center of the building, the dining hall, came between the two courtyards, thus, by its placing, and shape, emphasizing and giving life to the two courtyards (illustration 4).

Then, a colonnade running the length of the building, connected the two courtyards, and thus animated them (illustration 5).

Each of these centers, when formed, took the shape that was "left over" within the field of the whole, and made something of it, within that field. The centers created in this way do not have striking individualistic shapes like the centers in the Berlin library, but they have shapes which are softer, arising from the fabric of the space and its wholeness as they present themselves, yet as far as possible reasonably coherent as centers, with the potential to become beautiful if detailed well, while fitting in comfortably to the whole and leaving the structure of the whole intact. That is what makes them living. The main courtyard is off-rectangular, a trapezium. The second courtyard has a fillet in the corner to make the awkward acute angle go away. The entrance lobby, consists of two spaces, each coherent in itself, but necessarily placed at a slight angle to each other, so as to allow each (within the curved building envelope) to maintain a coherent relation with the spaces next to it.

Such "fitting in" is a necessary feature of a successful adaptive process, and it is this, of course, which is responsible for the complex geometry of nature. Thus the pattern of the building as a whole, was formed by a fairly short sequence of steps, each forming some aspect of the

Illustration 3: Getting the shape of the building from the curve of the street, with the dining hall (marked dark) then formed as the major center, which strengthens the rest.

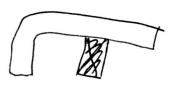

Illustration 4: Emphasizing the main dining hall through shape and position, as a strong center.

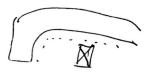

Illustration 5: forming the interior arcade as a strong center

building, and each forming one or more centers; the form of the whole is the result of this very short sequence.

Next came some lesser centers. One was an entrance courtyard where people could wait, shaltered, before the building opened up at night. Once the entrance courtyard had been placed, a sequence of two lobbies had to be placed, one closer to the outside, one close to the interior of the building. Once this sequence had been placed, step after step was taken like this.

At each step the intent was to make the space as good as possible, while not juggling spaces, rather doing each one correctly — and then taking the consequences morphologically and allowing the next one to be formed in relation to the first.

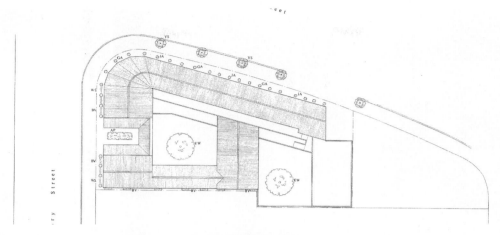

Site plan of the finished building

At the next level of structure, further centers emanate from the bigger ones. A curved wall follows the curve of the road, making a center in the street.

Internally, two gardens, enclosed within the site in donut form, formed major centers. Benches along the outside curve of the building, make the building welcome. The entrance is another courtyard, enclosing space where people can shelter. The main arcade ties the gardens together with the buildings. The dining hall develops at a key spot in the middle, strengthening the two major courtyards.

Each of these centers is supported by still smaller elements — details — as far as possible also made as living centers to make the larger centers stronger, and make them come to life. The column bases and capital. The fountain, and its tiles. The base of the building. The arches of the dining hall. The beautiful curved windows in the dining hall.

Finally, as I shall explain in the following section, the ornaments themselves were conceived and worked through, in such a way that they were also made, as far as I could manage it, from living centers.

In this building, the fundamental process draws everything from the existing wholeness and from the process of preserving structure. This does not only govern plan and overall vol-

ume design; it governs even very small building details.

How is this all different from Stirling's Berlin library. Is it honestly true to say that one has more living centers than the other. Could one not make up a story, similar to the one I have just told, about the design elements in the Stirling library? What is it then, about the Julian Street Inn, and its centers, and the way its centers are made, which gives them a special life, which makes them more authentic, or more deeply adapted, more truly derived from the wholeness which is there?

In my discussion about the Berlin library, I said that there are four main weaknesses: (a) Lack of smaller centers; (b) Centers being image-like copies of other centers; (c) Centers do not emerge from the surrounding wholeness; (d) Centers do not help form any larger centers

In this building, as a result of the repeated use of the fundamental process, I believe it can be seen that the centers *do* meet the four conditions which are lacking in the Berlin Library example:

1. *In most cases, each center does have strong smaller centers.* Look, for example, at the column capital. The capital is a strong center. It has a shaped top which is a strong center. That top has bands which are strong centers; etched relief shaped in

The main courtyard

the ornament and forming strong centers in the zig-zags; tiled inserts which form strong centers; diamonds painted on the tiled inserts, even these are strong centers.

2. Centers do originate in the essence of the building: they are not image-like copies of other centers. The fountain is not copied from any fountain. It arises from the corner position and its strength as a center comes, in part, from this position. The main courtyard feels old; but it is not an image copied from any actual place, it has strength as a center which arises from the nature of the courtyard, the arcade, shade, walking, grass, light.

286

One of the main entrances

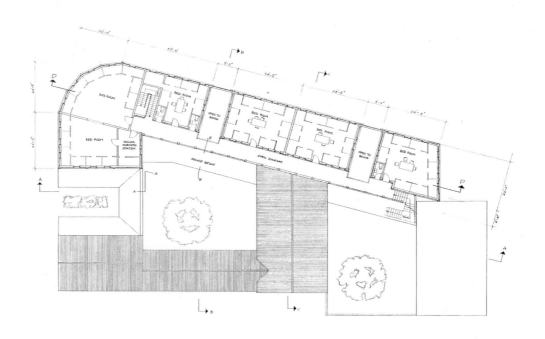

Upstairs plan showing sleeping areas around the courtyards

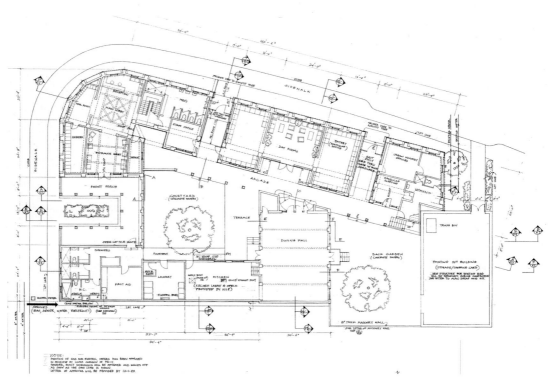

Downstairs plan showing communal rooms, arcade, and courtyards

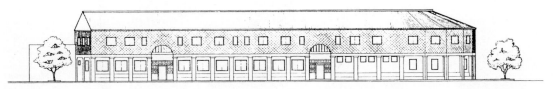

North Elevation

West Elevation

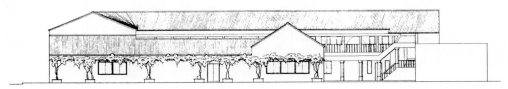

South Elevation

Elevations and sections of the finished building

Stair to the sleeping rooms

Fountain and roses

Benches in the sun, along the Julian Street side of the building. Most of the fifteen properties — ALTERNATING REPETITION, BOUNDARIES, STRONG CENTERS, THE VOID, GRADIENTS, NOT-SEPARATENESS, GOOD SHAPE, LEVELS OF SCALE, LOCAL SYMMETRIES, *and others — are visible, all of them generateed by the living process*

3. *Centers do emerge from the surrounding wholeness.* The ornament of the capital arises from its position on the square column. The tiles on the wall originate from the wall-surface itself. The roses grow near the fountain, from shade, sun, water, grass.

4. *Centers do form larger centers.* The entrance archway is formed and shaped to intensify the wall. The fountain really does intensify the corner of the garden. The arches in the dining hall, are placed and shaped, even in their smallest details, to make the space radiant as a whole.

Thus the presence of living process — a careful adherence to the principle that all centers which are created should as far as possible be made living through the fifteen transformations — does help to make a larger living structure in the building and its surroundings.

Details on the capital of an arcade column
These details form smaller centers (the band, the boundary, the diamond, the zigzag lines) — and within these smaller centers yet smaller centers have been formed. That is how the capital gets its life.

The dining hall

10 / EMERGENCE OF STRONG CENTERS AT FINE SCALE IN THE JULIAN STREET INN

I have not yet spoken much about the way that the space of details, too, needs to be unified and made coherent, in order to give it life, and how this act of unifying detailed material and space will *itself* only succeed to the extent that we make everything a center, and each center a strong field of centers. This can be a very intricate and subtle business.

Here is an example from the tiled wall of the building. I had decided early on, that the exterior second-story wall would be a diagonal checkerboard of concrete and tile. At first, I had as-sumed that I would simply make the checkerboard out of plain terracotta tiles and concrete.

Then, when I noticed that the color of the two together did not shimmer enough, did not melt enough, I felt that some additional color, or ornament was needed to unify it. I tried putting in plain green glazed tiles, in place of the terracotta ones, at random. Nothing good happened. It had a plain and ordinary quality which was not pleasant.

Then I thought it might be desirable to hand glaze the tiles, and put more detail on them

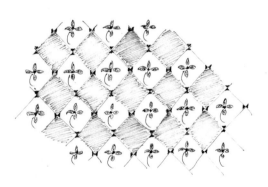

(1) My sketch of a flower pattern of blue blossoms

(2) The blossom pattern we tried in actual tiles

(3) Ornamental tile with a cross shape

(4) Trying a cross shape, with centers at the ends of the cross arms, forming further centers

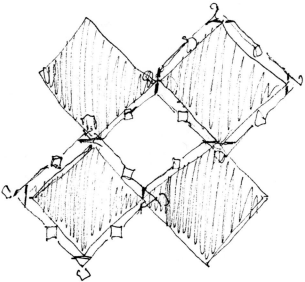

(5) Sketch of a design with blue dots in which there are
about forty centers per tile

(6) Sketch replacing the dots with diamonds, thus paving
the way towards a design with knots and braids

in the underglaze drawing. First I tried flowers (illustrations 1–2). The individual tiles were pretty. And the design seemed nice. But even though there were more centers now they still didn't really unify the space of the wall.

Next I tried a kind of design which paid attention to the whole wall, and tried to make a pattern which would bring the wall together. This is the tile in which I placed little dots of blue, on the red of the tile, to make a kind of cross shape (illustrations 3–4). Too simple! To get the ambiguity of this cross shape, which seemed relatively simple in the drawing, I had to make a very complex design indeed (illustration 5). This tile has forty centers in it, just to get the right amount of ambiguity. A sample of these colors — red tile, with shimmering turquoise blues, and purples, had the right feeling. It was just beginning to unify the space.

But the tile still seemed harsh in *design*. I lay with my eyes closed, and tried to get a vision of the shimmering surface of the tile. I realized that

(7) A continuous loop braid which forms centers in the
squares, centers at the middle, centers between the
squares, and a center in the whole.

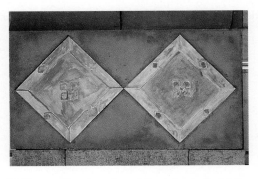

(8) First cardboard mockup of tiles using the braid idea.

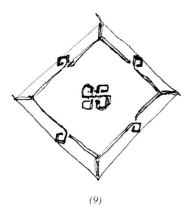

(9)

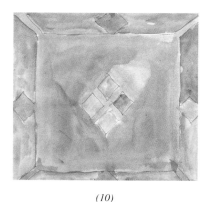

(10)

the main problem was in the fact that none of these tiles had yet managed to unify the concrete and the tile. So far, the two had always stayed separate. My first thought was that the red tile should perhaps be smaller, and the grey bigger. But this still left the two colors separate. And then — to tie the red and grey together and to unify the space — I began to see a design with knots drawn so that they would explicitly join the tile and the concrete (illustrations 6–8) I thought the concrete surface could be continued by a grey glaze around the edge of the tile — so there would be an ambiguity between concrete and tile. And, in the same zone, knots of turquoise blue, would create a further ambiguity and connection in the space.

This design went in the right direction. However, when I tried it the line of the knots was obtrusive: oddly, it seemed to create a division between the grey design and the red instead of unifying them. Also and the complexity of design seemed out of character and too fiddly for

the building: also incredibly hard to do — technically — on 4000 tiles.

Finally, looking at this painting, late in the afternoon, after a full day's work on the design, frustrated by the difficulty of the task, I suddenly realized that we could get the essence of this design, in two colors, not three, just with the grey and the red (illustrations 9–12).

At last this wall created the needed unity. It is the interlocking and ambiguity of strong centers, which creates the unity of space in the wall. This is supported by the choice of colors. Above all, the centers are used to unify the space. It is the desire to unify space by creating this endless ambiguity in space, which motivates and forms the centers through the fundamental operation.

The main job, of any task of creating centers is *always* to melt away the divisions between things. The interlocking diamonds of the red inside the grey, and the corresponding grey ones inside the red, the grey octagon which melts the difference between concrete and tile — all this finally achieves the one elusive thing, which has been the object of all this effort. *The wall no longer has divisions in it* (illustrations 12–13)

To do it, it was necessary to go through six different mockups, learning progressively more about how to do it. The final tiles *each* contain more than twenty strong centers: altogether the two-hundred foot wall contains some 60,000 to 100,000 living centers. And in order to make this wall, we had to paint four thousand of the tiles by hand. That is what it took to unify that wall.

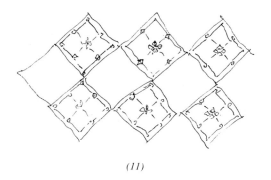

(11)

(12)

(13)

11 / EMERGENCE OF THE FIFTEEN PROPERTIES

In the Julian Street Inn, we see how creation of centers, and the focus on creating living centers one by one, stretches from the largest centers of the building, to its smallest ones. The volume of the building as a whole, its two-donut form, its courtyards, and the important dining hall, were all formed as centers early in the process. To the extent possible, these centers were made living centers. Each was given structure which embellishes the centers, and makes each of these centers dependent on the parallel life of other centers, and of smaller ones. The largest centers, gain their life from the fact that they help still larger centers — Montgomery Street, Julian Street — to have life.

Because of this interdependence of the centers, the building, and its centers are full of the fifteen properties. STRONG CENTERS, LOCAL SYMMETRIES, ALTERNATING REPETITION, BOUNDARIES, ECHOES, are all visible. They have come into existence naturally, as a result of the structure-preserving process.

In middle-sized elements — the courtyard, the columns of the colonnade, the trusses in the dining hall — once again have received their form from a process which creates centers one by one. The more detail elaboration of the floral truss, and the way structure-preserving processes helped even in the conception and calculation of engineering for the structure is described in Book 3, chapter 7. All these middle-sized elements, once again, are replete with the fifteen properties, depend on one another for their life. This came about, naturally, as a result of the impact of the structure-preserving process that was used from beginning to the end.

The smallest centers, too, spots of colored glazing on the tiles made specially for the building, also have these qualities, and once again we see the fifteen properties emerged throughout the structure of the tilework and its ornaments. There is DEEP INTERLOCK we see in the arrangement of the squares and diamonds; there is ALTERNATING REPETITION, very strongly, between the centers and the boundaries of the tiles; each tile has dozens if not hundreds of LOCAL SYSMMETRIES; each tile has, at its core, THE VOID.

So we get a picture of the process of creating a building in which these centers from large to small, emerge, are elaborated, and consolidated, as the building finds its form; and that it is this process which brings the form to life.

12 / SUCCESSFUL ADAPTATION

We have a beginning idea, now, of the way that adaptation in a complex system, requires the constant shaping and forming of individual centers, in relation to the whole. The success of the adaptation comes from the freedom which the center-forming process has to make each center strong, to make it centered in relation to other nearby centers. As we have seen, this process is *essentially* and necessarily dynamic. It can only be done, step by step, as the conception of the building, and its details, evolve, in planning, in design, and in construction.

The process able to carry out these thousands of adaptations, and the process by which centers may be formed as living structures, within living structure, depends on the detailed conditions of the actual laying out, and of the making process.

It is instructive to review a few of the examples. The shape of the building, the inward courtyards, came from adaptation to the noisy traffic on Julian Street; it created quiet areas for the members of the homeless community to recover, to find themselves. That placed demands on the construction (since the wall of the building had to be curved). It placed demands on the setbacks, since buildings had to be nearer to the boundaries than usual. The process required involvement of the homeless people in San Jose. Without their direct input it would not even have been possible to conceive the right shape. But this took effort. It was permitted by the city of Jose, and that made it possible.

I once spent some time talking to a homeless man who had been staying a few nights in the Julian Street Inn. I was just sitting in the building, and we struck up a conversation. He did not know I was the architect. After talking about many other things for fifteen or twenty minutes, I told him that I had built the building. He was very surprised, introduced himself, and said to me, out of the blue: "This is the only building I have ever been in, where absolutely everything is necessary."

I was pleased by his comment, but surprised because — by conventional later-20th-century standards — the building has many details which other people might consider *un*-necessary. In further discussion with him, I realized that he had somehow assessed the fact that all the ornamental details contributed to the wholeness of the place, and made the larger wholes — courtyards, dining hall, street front, arcade and so on — work better. The smaller details contributed to the life of the larger centers: and that is why he judged them to be "necessary."

It was not always easy to accomplish. As the exterior face of the building developed, it became clear that it would be necessary to build smaller centers — benches or seats — along the exterior face, both to enhance the centers formed by the big column bays, and to provide a source of life on the outside, a place where people could sit. The City of San Jose Planning Department refused permission for these benches to be built on the grounds that the city did not want homeless people sitting outside the building. When I built them anyway (secretly, during construction), the mayor of the city passed an edict stating that homeless people were not to be allowed to sit out in public, on these sunny benches, where they could be seen. He wanted to hide the homeless people so as to stop them from "dirtying" the street. The benches are still there, and people do sit on them when they can; but the official policy is that they are not allowed to, thus maintaining a nice clean street for the city of San Jose. Alas!

The refined tiles which I have described, were made by hand, in a process which allowed them — their design and color — to be adapted to the whole. That was possible, because we used the shimmering light they created, as a basis for fine tuning. But without the feedback we could get because the process was under our direct control, it would not have been possible to adapt the tiles to the whole with such finesse. Mass-produced tiles could not have done it. In design, color, glaze, and softness, these tiles were fabricated, precisely, in relation to the whole and their position in it.

13 / THE PERVASIVE GENERALITY OF THE CENTER-MAKING PROCESS

It seems possible to me that a person who has read up to this point in THE NATURE OF ORDER could start to be impressed by the idea of the field of centers, and might begin to believe that this struc-

ture holds the key to life in considerable degree. But such intellectual knowledge is far removed from the practical awakening to the idea that *there really is nothing else going on in the process which creates life* — that when we make something, every single moment, every single act of attention, every single act of design — no matter at what scale — is controlled by our ability to make strong centers of everything we have to touch.

It is not necessarily easy to do. In many cases it is hard to pack in so many centers as are needed; easier to be lazy, and make a few centers while leaving all kinds of space littered about between them. To succeed in re-arranging things so that everything is locked together with centers, so that every single part has life in itself because it is a living center — to prune a design, and look at it over and over again, searching for any little parts that are not centers — and then work at it, compressing, cutting, simplifying, re-arranging, until every single part, and every part of every part, and every part between the parts are all centers. This is tremendously hard work.

In Book 3, the pervasive generality of the center-making process is illustrated by an enormous range of cases (chapter numbers are all for Book 3, except as noted): GIVING LIFE TO A NEIGHBORHOOD (Book 3, chapter 10), MAKING A PARKING STREET WHICH WORKS (Book 3, chapter 3), MAKING A DRINKING GLASS (Book 3, preface), DRAWING AN ANIMAL FOR A TILED FRIEZE (Book 3, chapter 18), LIVING ROOM OF A HOUSE (Book 1, chapter 11), BALUSTRADE IN THE OPERA 14, PLANTING A ROSE BUSH IN THE GARDEN (this book, page 218), DRAWING A FLOWER (this book, page 598), MAKING A BEAUTIFUL WINDOW (Book 4, page 283), MAKING THE APPROACH TO A MAJOR FREEWAY BRIDGE (Book 4, page 294), MAKING THE STRUTS OF A STRUCTURALLY SUCCESSFUL TRUSS (Book 3, chapter 7), MAKING MEADOWS IN THE BRUSHLAND AT THE CITY'S EDGE (this book, page 220), GIVING LIFE TO A FISHPOND (Book 1, page 432), MAKING A BEAUTIFUL CEILING IN A ROOM (Book 3, chapter 15), LAYING OUT THE PLAN OF A MAJOR PUBLIC BUILDING (Book 3, chapter 4), BUILDING A PUBLIC BENCH WITH ORNAMENTS (Book 3, chapter 12), LAYING OUT THE SUBDIVISION OF PRIVATE LOTS IN A COLOMBIAN NEIGHBORHOOD (Book 3, chapter 13).

NOTES

1. For a precise definition and analysis of living structure in buildings, see Book 1, throughout, and especially chapters 1, 2, 4, 5, 8 and 11.

2. This may be understood with a physical example. Imagine a chair in a room. As an experiment, I get a big ball of scrap iron, on a rope, and hang it so that the scrap iron is hovering near the seat of the chair. In conventional thinking, the chair is unchanged. I have simply brought a bundle of scrap iron near the chair. But seen from the point of view of wholeness, the situation is quite different. When the chair stands by itself, there is one set of most salient centers in space. The chair in its wholeness is then defined by this system of salient centers. When I bring the scrap iron towards the chair, the wholeness changes. Suddenly, for instance, the bowl-shaped seat of the chair is less coherent as a center than it was before. New centers, formed by the scrap iron, have meanwhile become *more* salient. New configurations have become more vivid, old configurations are less vivid. As a result the chair itself has changed. Its wholeness has changed, because the system of centers is altered: if I view "the" chair as defined by its wholeness, the chair itself has changed.

This is a new point of view. It is no longer true to say that the same chair is there, and has merely been juxtaposed with some scrap iron. Instead since the new wholeness is altogether changed, and since the chair, properly seen, *is defined by its the wholeness*, the chair after the scrap iron is a different chair from what it was before, even though the scrap iron is not touching it. Its space, and the system of salient centers have been reconfigured. It has changed.

Although it could seem like a small revision of terminology to see the world like this, it is a profound change of consciousness of the world as a whole. It recognizes that wholeness is a very subtle structure, changing all the time, and vulnerable to very small encroachments in its surroundings. What we see as the physics of the chair, its mathematical structure, is not constant and fixed. It is changing, subtly, all the time, as influences from the world around enter the picture, and modify the relative salience of different centers in and around the chair, thus forming, reforming and altering the wholeness which was "the chair."

3. The experimental process of judging the extent to which a transformation preserves structure, has been described in this book, chapter 2, pages 59 ff.

4. An elegant example of such an experiment was published by my student Yodan Rofe in his Ph.D. dissertation. He examined neighborhoods in San Francisco, asked people what places were damaged and what was well, and what kinds of actions would be needed to fix the damaged places. Yodan discovered astonishing degrees of agreement, and tabulated them statistically.

CHAPTER ELEVEN

THE SEQUENCE OF UNFOLDING

GENERATIVE SEQUENCES ARE THE KEY TO
THE SUCCESS OF LIVING PROCESS
WHENEVER COMPLEX STRUCTURE
IS BEING FORMED

1 / INTRODUCTION

Unfolding, the essential feature of all living process — which we may also call differentiation — comes about, and succeeds, because it always occurs in a certain kind of *sequence*. It goes step by step, we already know that. But it goes step by step *in a certain order*.

The classic example of a generative sequence occurs, of course, in biological morphogenesis, where sequence is well known. When an embryo grows, it must grow in a certain order — a preordained order. If the events were to occur in another order (or if artificially altered to force events to occur in another order) the effects would be disastrous. Instead of orderly form, we would get chaos, monsters.

This is natural enough. In an evolving whole, one thing follows from another. One kind of pattern has to be laid down first, so that another kind of pattern can be introduced to it, can be laid down to complete it. But this is not merely true of biological morphogenesis where it happens necessarily, just because of the way things work. It is a fundamental rule in *all* unfolding. It is linked, inevitably, to the differentiating aspect of the fundamental process. And yet, among the features of living process described in these chapters, it may be both the most surprising rule, and also the most essential one, the one which goes deepest to provide the necessary underpinning of all living structure.

2 / SEQUENCES OF UNFOLDING IN ARCHITECTURE

Artists and architects are familiar with the idea of sequence — although the idea is not often talked about as being about "sequence" per se. Rather, a good artist knows that an emerging work will come out well to the extent that the artist does things in the right order. This order is not usually written down, nor is it pre-fixed. But many artists are aware, while making a new work, that what is first laid down, what is done next, what third, what fourth, that controls the quality of work that comes out. A good artist is keenly aware that the power, fluidity, depth of a new work, depend on the order in which its features are created. That much is common knowledge.

And in that sense the concept of a sequence of unfolding is consistent with well-known features of traditional art in many disciplines. As a more general rule, too, it is often doing things in the right order, which allows the emerging form to become natural and well formed. In the exam-

ple of the Julian Street Inn (chapter 10), it was usually the order in which different centers were created — the sequence in which they were established — which made them living, or not, in the design. Placing the dining hall as the center of the project, *after* the two courtyards had been formed, allowed the dining hall to complement the courtyards.[1] If the dining hall had been placed first it might have been placed anywhere, and the courtyards would then have had more difficulty finding their most useful size and proper shape. The reason is that in a morphological sense the courtyards were bigger than the dining hall — bigger in their impact on the wholeness. To make the process work smoothly, in such a way that each center could find its proper, well-adapted shape, they had, therefore, to be fixed earlier.

Altogether, in every process aimed at getting life, centers must be created in the right order. If we create centers in random sequence, when we are designing something or when we are building something, the evolving form will likely turn out confusing and chaotic. Although the tortured view of art, the struggle to go this way and that, gnashing one's teeth until a form emerges, has become part of our popular mythology of design, it is more true to say, I believe, that the greatest art of the past was most often created without this tortured effort, and came about by a process of differentiation in which the steps were done in such a sequence that profound results emerged.

When properly constructed, the sequences which arise from proper use of the fundamental process are *generative*. That means they can create living structure, easily, nicely, smoothly. That is indeed, just what we mean by *unfolding*. The form unfolds, as if without effort, very much as natural form such as a developing embryo unfolds in nature.

Living structure comes into being effortlessly, simply as a result of following the sequence.

3 / GENERATIVE SEQUENCES IN TRADITIONAL SOCIETY

In traditional society, these generative sequences, being precious, were known, rememberd, recorded, and re-used many times over. I referred earlier to the canoe building process in traditional Samoa.[2] Among the traditional boat builders of Samoa, there existed a chant. The chant was a line-by-line description of the way to build a traditional Samoan war canoe. The first lines were:

· *First find your tree.*
· *Cut down the tree.*
· *Hollow out the trunk.*
· *Next carve the prow.*
· *Shape the hull of the canoe.*
· *Start shaping the inside to form the seats . . .*
· and then, much later...
· *Shape and carve the prow to form a figure*

and it went on from there, line by line, describing the operations that were needed, step by step, to find the tree, fell it, hollow it out, carve it, and finally transform it into a full-fledged, carved and ornamented war canoe.

The chant created beautiful and *coherent* canoes, because it virtually guaranteed that the builder would be able to unfold a coherent whole by following the instructions of the chant, because the actions, done in this order, worked

smoothly. Each one further elaborated the result obtained from the previous actions.

The Samoan canoe chant is an example of a generative sequence. It *generates* canoes. The generative sequence is essentially the same each time that it is used, but each canoe that is generated is unique. The operations of the generative sequence guarantee success for a wide variety of conditions, making it possible for the designers and builders to create unique canoes each time they use the process, because of the way the successive operations act on one another and on the context (which is always unique). Because the generative sequence is based on the proper unfolding of centers for the canoe, the canoe comes out coherent.

It is perhaps helpful to draw attention to the differentiation which takes place at each step, just as the fundamental process prescribes. First the tree is trimmed (by SIMPLIFICATION). Then the tree trunk is hollowed out (by DEEP INTERLOCK, STRONG CENTERS, and POSITIVE SPACE). Then the front of the canoe is sharpened (GRADIENTS, BOUNDARY, and GOOD SHAPE). Then the shape of the hull as a whole is refined (GOOD SHAPE, LOCAL SYMMETRIES, and ROUGHNESS). Then further differentiation forms the seats (STRONG CENTERS, ALTERNATING REPETITION, and DEEP INTERLOCK) and so on. The differentiation goes forward following the scheme of the fundamental process very closely, and it is because of this progressive differentiation — because it unfolds so smoothly, from one step to the next, each step perfectly paving the way for the next — that the canoe as a whole can become beautiful.

4 / VITAL IMPORTANCE OF THE "RIGHT" SEQUENCE

In architecture, as in other things, the importance of sequence is both simple, and potentially shocking. Even when there are only two steps to be taken, the order in which they are done may be all-important. And it may be highly surprising.

Consider for example the process of laying out a house on a lot.

"Common sense" says that you should *first* place the house, and *then* place the garden. This is common sense; but it is wrong. To make the environment and the formation of house and garden together come out right, you have to reverse the order of these two operations, as follows:

1. First: *Locate the garden in the best and most beautiful place.*
2. Then: *Locate the house so that it helps and supports the garden.*

This example is fascinating because it illustrates the enormous significance of sequence. If you place the house first, you are stuck with the leftovers as places for the garden. In all likelihood the garden will not become a pleasant place. Positive space will amost certainly be violated. So will view, smell, noise. But if you locate the garden first and then place the house volume in a way which supports the wholeness of the garden, the garden will come out better *and so will the house.*

Of the two available sequences for these two operations, one sequence is wrong, and one is right (90% of the time). The sequence which is wrong, is correct according to conventional wisdom, and probably considered obvious by millions of people. The one which is right (and which gives you insight, makes things more understandable, and gets wholesome results), flies in the face of common sense, and would be rejected by nine out of ten people who first hear it. Yet it is the right answer.

Few examples explain the enormous power and significance of sequences more vividly. And as you can imagine, if the sequence — the order of steps — is significant when dealing with only two operations, how much more significant it will be when dealing with ten, or twenty, or fifty steps. There the chance of getting the sequence right by accident, is extremely small.

5 / EXAMPLE OF A LARGER GENERATIVE SEQUENCE: A JAPANESE TEA HOUSE

In the next example we shall see a much longer sequence of steps where we see and feel the progressive differentiations very clearly. Each differentiation acts on the product of the previous differentiations, and as it does so new centers are formed and unfolded, and in turn themselves — later — get differentiated further.

The following twenty-four steps give the generative sequence for a traditional Japanese tea house.[3] To understand the extraordinary power (and effectiveness) of this sequence you should, if possible, ask someone to read it to you while you sit with your eyes closed, and allow a vision of a tea house to form in your mind. Because it works by successive differentiations that are smoothly related, you will find the design forming, one step at a time, in your mind, as you go through the sequence. Do nothing in your mind except follow the statements you hear being read. After you have heard all 24 statements, with a bit of luck you will have a complete vision of a teahouse in your mind. The process is almost effortless.

Please, if possible, do ask someone to read this to you, now. And please do close your eyes while you are listening, so that the images can form freely in your mind (as they cannot if you merely sit here and read the words yourself). Start by imagining a real place where you might want to build a tea house.

1. SECLUDED TEA HOUSE. *The tea house is in a secluded garden.*

2. GARDEN WALL. *Some kind of wall or barrier surrounds the entire garden. From inside the garden the public world is not visible, and hardly audible. If there is a family dwelling associated with the tea house, the dwelling may be part of this wall.*

3. INNER AND OUTER GARDEN. *A low barrier divides the garden into two parts: an outer garden and an inner garden. The tea house is in the inner garden.*

4. GARDEN PATH. *There is a slightly meandering path running through the outer garden, past the low barrier, and through the inner garden to the tea house.*

5. STONE PATH. *The meandering garden path is composed of mossy stepping stones, and is loosely bordered by trees and bushes.*

6. OUTER GATE. *Where the garden path meets the edge of the outer garden there is a gate, connecting the outer garden to the public walk. The gate is opaque. There are no direct views from the public path into the outer garden.*

7. MIDDLE GATE. *Where the garden path crosses the low barrier, between the inner garden and the outer garden, there is a gate called the middle gate. The middle gate is small with a roof or low door on hinges.*

8. BRANCHING PATHS. *In the outer garden the garden path may branch in several places along its length. Any given branching path may or may not lead eventually to the tea house.*

9. GUIDE STONES. *Where the path branches there are guide stones set near the stepping stones. The host closes off some branches by placing a guide stone on the stepping stone at the branching point. Before the guest arrives on a given day there is only one path open through the garden to the tea house.*

10. WAITING BENCH. *In the outer garden, near the middle gate, there is a waiting bench. The bench is roughly 7 feet long, and may be covered.*

11. WAITING NEAR HOUSE. *If there is a family dwelling associated with the tea house, then the waiting bench is usually near the dwelling. If so, the waiting area may be connected with the physical structure of the dwelling.*

12. TEA HOUSE APPROACH. *The length of the path from the middle gate and waiting bench to the tea house, is rarely more than 20 feet.*

13. STONE WATER BASIN. *Somewhere along this 20-foot path through the inner garden, between the middle gate and tea house, there is a stone water basin and running water.*

14. RECESS SHELTER. *If the tea house is to accommodate long meal sessions, then there is a covered bench a few steps away from the tea house where people can sit and view the garden.*

15. KNEELING-IN ENTRANCE. *Where the stone path meets the tea house there is a window-like entrance in the face of the tea house. The entrance is roughly 2 feet high, 2 feet wide, and 2 feet above the path. A person entering must stoop down and kneel in.*

16. TEA HOUSE HAS THREE PARTS. *The tea house is made up of three parts in plan: the tea room proper, the tokonoma and an anteroom. The tea room is the largest part — it is where the guests gather and the tea ritual occurs. The anteroom is a tiny area off the tea room where equipment is kept and some preparation is made. The tokonoma is a shallow alcove off the tea room where objects, art, and flowers are displayed.*

17. SIZE OF THE TEA HOUSE. *The floor area of the tea room is limited to four sizes: 1.5 mat, 2 mat, 3 mat and 4.5 mat (a mat is roughly 6' x 3').*

18. 4.5 MAT CONFIGURATION. In the 4.5-mat tea room, the half mat is placed in the center, and the 4 mats are laid evenly around it in a spiral.

19. CENTRAL HEARTH. A small square hearth is fitted into the floor at approximately the center of the tea room. Guests sit on pillows around the hearth.

20. HOST'S ENTRANCE. The host enters the tea house through a sliding screen door. The host's entrance is always in a different wall than the kneeling-in entrance.

21. CEILING HEIGHT. The tea room has a roughly 6.5 foot ceiling in it.

22. DIM LIGHTING. There are very few windows in the tea house walls. Where there are windows they are high, near the ceiling — and placed to give a dim indirect light throughout the tea house.

23. TOKONOMA. The tokonoma is an alcove off the tea room, which is visible on entering the tea house. The size of the tokonoma varies with the size of the tea room. In the smallest tea house the tokonoma is simply a curve in the wall.

24. TOKONOMA PILLAR. The tokonoma contains a small pillar on which an object, a work of art, or a vase of flowers may be placed. The pillar is made of wood — a kind of wood not used in the rest of the tea house.

When you have heard all twenty-four statements you should have generated a complete and coherent picture of a tea house in your mind. You will probably find that the process of getting this picture has been almost effortless. It should virtually have formed itself.

The process is effortless because the differentiations have been read to you in the right order. Each new differentiation introduces a new center by making a further division in the configuration of previously existing centers. The new center you create in your mind's eye at each step is easy to create because the context for creating it has been built up coherently in the steps before. The next center emerges easily and naturally, because the evolving structure which gives birth to the new center is complete and coherent at each step and gives birth to the new center almost by itself. This is what we mean by a process of unfolding.

It is important to point out that the tea house is able to unfold effortlessly in your mind, because it unfolds *as a whole.* A coherent picture has built up in your mind because the steps are arranged in such a sequence that no step contradicts the structure which has been built up by the steps before it. At each moment you have a wholeness in your mind. As the wholeness develops it gets differentiated. It gets more and more structure. Each step is designed to operate on the previously existing wholeness that is in your mind. As a result, the wholeness unfolds a little further each time. The sequence is chosen so that each differentiation unfolds naturally from the one which preceded it.

Generative sequences which work by differentiation existed pervasively for traditional buildings and allowed people to create traditional design in nearly effortless fashion. The user was able to pull a new design almost directly from the interaction of the generative sequence with the specifics of their own needs and context.

6 / THE ROLE OF SEQUENCE IN PRESERVING STRUCTURE

A generative sequence not only guarantees feasibility and the emergence of coherent form. It also provides the conditions in which structure-preserving transformations can occur successfully.

For instance, in the tea house, if I try to locate the waiting bench too early, at a moment when I do not yet have the location of the middle barrier, the context for placing it does not yet exist. But more important, it is also not possible, in this case, for me to use the waiting bench and its location to preserve the structure of the rest. For the waiting bench to preserve the structure of the garden, I have to put it in at a time when the garden has developed. I can make the structure-preserving process work, only if things come *at the right time, in the right order.*

Consider the division of inner and outer garden. If I make this differentiation early, while the field is still fluid, I can place the inner and outer garden in a natural way, which preserves the structure of the overall garden, its boundary, the natural sites, views, sounds, which are nearby. I can, for instance, place the inner garden at a quiet spot, as it needs to be. I can place the outer garden in a way that continues elegantly from the location of the main gate. But suppose that, willfully, I place the tea house itself too

early, because I think I know just the right spot for it! Then I have (without explicitly intending it) made commitments about the location of the inner garden, which may not be consistent with the larger issues. It may, for instance, now be difficult to get a nice path from the gate, through the outer garden, to the inner garden, and have the inner garden in a quiet place. I can probably still twist things around to make it work *somehow*. But I no longer have the ability in a relaxed, smooth, and simple way, to do just what I have to do, what should be done, what is natural and necessary to do. In this case, my willfulness has disturbed the possibility of laying this garden out in a way that preserves the structure of the whole. As a result the chances of getting a living structure have been reduced. And all because I did things in the wrong order.

7 / THE MATHEMATICAL SCARCITY OF GOOD SEQUENCES

So, the chief ingredient of unfolding sequences, and the feature that makes them work, is this: *A sequence works, or does not work, according to the order of the steps.*

In principle, a good sequence (steps in the right order) can be defined mathematically by asking, for each center, which other centers need to be in position before that center can be formed. One sets up a flow chart among the steps, defining an arrow for every case where one center must precede another. This gives a partial order on the steps: And one can then define a linear sequence (a collapsed partial order) which minimizes the cases where arrows form cycles or are reversed.[4]

Since good sequence is mathematically defined in this way, we may infer that one should, in principle, be able to define an unfolding sequence for any problem, once one knows what the ingredients are. As soon as one knows what kinds of centers a given type of building will have in it, one should then be able to work out a

sequence which will allow these centers to unfold smoothly as they do in the traditional examples.

For a given task, the number of all sequences which work is tiny by comparison with the huge number of all possible sequences. For example, in the case of the Japanese teahouse there are 24 steps, and therefore 24! or approximately 6×10^{23} different possible sequences of these 24 steps: billions upon billions of possible sequences. However, among this huge number the number of sequences which "work" for the 24 steps is very limited indeed — a few million at the most. Even if there are a million workable sequences, that is still an infinitesimal proportion, something like one in 10^{14}. From observation of working sequences, I believe, further, that the sequences which work are all variants of the same broad flow, all essentially similar, in which one or two steps may be transposed, but which have broadly the same overall pattern of unfolding. Other than these, as sequences get more and more scrambled and out of order, the effect will be that, when being read, incoherence in the unfolding will occur, and important structure will be lost. In short, less than a trillionth of all the 6 x 10^{23} possible sequences actually work well enough to allow smooth unfolding. This underscores the difficulty of finding a *good* sequence for such an unfolding process.

It is not possible, at present, to give a precisely defined way of identifying the sequences which work, although some progress has been made in this direction. That is to say, we do not yet know a purely mathematical procedure which can identify the sequences which work.

However, the sequences which work can be identified experimentally by a well-defined procedure. If one applies a sequence of steps to a given context, and if one then observes the unfolding process, it is possible to identify, unambiguously, whether the process engendered by the sequence at any time contradicts itself — that means, whether one is forced to backtrack, because step B which comes at a certain point

in the sequences forces one to undo the results of the previously taken step A. By doing experiments on test cases, it is possible to winnow out, and ultimately to eliminate the bad sequences, thus gradually finding one's way to the few sequences which have the property that no such backtracking occurs as the project unfolds. One technique for finding good sequences is to identify bad *sub*sequences, and eliminating all sequences which contain these bad subsequences. There are a variety of ways of getting to the good sequences, and it is very hard work. But, with time, it can be done.

Since the identification of backtrack-free sequences can be made experimentally, it is clear that the concept of backtrack-free sequences is — in principle — well-defined even though in practice hard to discover.

The important thing is that such backtrack-free sequences are relatively stable. Once discovered, a backtrack-free sequence remains backtrack-free for nearly all contexts. Thus the backtrack-free sequences lie at the core of the theory of living process.

8 / A GENERATIVE SEQUENCE FOR APARTMENT BUILDINGS IN PASADENA

In the next seven pages I show a backtrack-free sequence of this kind, constructed for a limited class of apartment buildings. My colleagues and I were asked to write a zoning ordinance for the city of Pasadena, California, an old town with a nice history recently ruined by an influx of ugly multi-family apartment buildings. The zoning ordinance was to set guidelines for a new class of apartment buildings, which — it was hoped — would respect tradition by making courtyards and gardens, and building relatively low compact apartments around these gardens.

What surprised nearly everyone associated with the project was that it was possible to write a successful and fairly simple generative se-

quence for apartment buildings of this type.[5] The sequence was of such a nature that it allowed the creator, or designer, to produce a design for a particular site by an unfolding process that automatically met the necessary conditions for a good apartment building.

To get the sequence, a pattern language similar to the languages illustrated later (chapter 13), was first constructed for these multi-family apartment buildings, then re-formulated as a generative sequence.[6] In its sequence form it gives the user a process of unfolding in such a way as to allow a building with good plan, volumes, and organization to be made, very easily, to fit the particular conditions of any given site.

This generative sequence is given below. It is printed here in more or less the same language that we wrote for the ordinance, and asks the user (the applicant for a building permit on a new site) to follow the instructions while laying out his apartment building.

The sequence has eleven steps. The steps are designed to go smoothly, one by one, so that the applicant can fill out the application forms easily and with a minimum of interpretation.[7]

The process is also designed to facilitate the actual design and planning of new development projects, and to encourage new projects of high quality. A builder who wishes to check the possibility of a project on a new site can pencil out a feasible project within a short time, simply by following the steps in the order given. This will then enable him to create a project which meets all legal requirements, and to examine the possible results of a conforming project, both quickly and economically.

Since the sequence is based on what we consider as essential patterns, one can say that any successful apartment building, for this context, *must* meet these conditions. The sequence is therefore essential, functional, and does not merely satisfy legal requirements. It goes — my colleagues and I believe — to the root of a successful apartment building in Pasadena.

STEP 1

MAP THE CONTEXT AND SURROUNDINGS.

To begin the layout process, and to make sure that your project does something useful for the neighborhood, it is necessary to start by understanding the essential structure of what exists around the site, both on your lot and in the immediate vicinity.

Draw a map at a scale of 1 inch equals 50 feet. The map must show your lot, two lots on either side, the back 50 feet of the lots behind these five lots, and the front 100 feet of the five lots across the street. On this drawing, survey and identify:

(1) Lot boundaries.
(2) Footprints of all buildings on surrounding lots. Each building or part of building must be shown with its approximate height in feet.

Step 1: Mapping the site to show its good points

(3) All gardens on surrounding lots. Examine how big they are, where they are located, what their shapes are. In particular, you must identify adjacent gardens which are worthwhile sitting and looking in their direction and enjoying them.
(4) Beautiful open space in the street, which helps to create the atmosphere of the neighborhood.
(5) Parking structures on surrounding lots.
(6) Big trees on your site or on the street, and on adjacent lots.
(7) Existing driveways and back-alleys on nearby lots, with special reference to any possible pattern of access in which these existing driveways and alleys might serve the back of your lot.
(8) Setback dimensions on adjacent lots.
(9) Any windows on next-door buildings facing your lot, which serve living areas, and must have good light preserved.
(10) Groups of doors or other entrances on next-door lots, which create a pattern of movement and pleasantness that must be preserved, and which may form the basis of a new space or focus in your project.
(11) Walkways and entrance paths on surrounding lots.

STEP 2

DECIDE BASIC ARRANGEMENT OF PROJECT AND ITS OUTDOOR SPACE TO ENHANCE SURROUNDING PROJECTS AND THE NEIGHBORHOOD.

The character of the neighborhood which is described in this ordinance can only be obtained when each individual project is made to work together with its adjacent lots. The beauty and character which the city hopes for will only arise as a result of coherent relationship and connection between parcels with regard to gardens, courtyards, parking, buildings, and driveways.

In particular the following types of connection between adjacent lots are all critical:

(1) Connection between position of gardens or open spaces, either in the interior or front of the lot, to form larger gardens and open spaces.

(2) Spatial cooperation between adjacent building volumes, to maintain the coherence of open space and light access, and to permit growth of relatively long stretches of building volume parallel to the street.

(3) Sharing between driveways and back alleys, with the possibility of obtaining easement on adjacent driveways, to reduce the number of driveways.

(4) Connection between parking lot positions, to improve accessibility from driveways and alleys.

(5) To achieve these types of connections, examine the context of map with regard to the following matters:

(6) Identify next-door gardens with which the proposed garden on your lot can connect to create a larger garden; or any beautiful open space along the street on adjacent lots, which is worthwhile preserving and extending by your acts.

(7) Examine the position and configuration of building volumes on adjacent lots and consider the possibility of placing your volumes in a way that creates continuity of building volumes along the street.

(8) Consider the possibility of obtaining easement for the use of existing driveway on adjacent lot.

(9) Examine the configuration of existing parking on adjacent lots, to see if any possibility exists for combined use of parking, or combined access to parking.

(10) After considering these possibilities, and before beginning the detailed design and layout of your project, *it is necessary to get a single basic vision of the position, size, and nature of main garden.*

Step 3

DECIDE BASIC ARRANGEMENT AND POSITION OF MAIN GARDEN.

The garden must be large, no less than 28 feet by 45 feet. In addition, choose the position for this large main garden which does the most possible to connect with existing spaces on next-door lots, and which also does the most possible to provide a balanced variety of space in the neighborhood.

There are numerous ways according to which the main garden can do this:

(1) If there is an existing large interior garden on the adjacent lot, the proposed main garden should be placed adjacent to it so that the two spaces work together.

(2) If there is a beautiful front garden in the street, or a

Step 2: First idea of where the gardens go, to connect the project to the neighborhood around the site

broad lawn with the front of the buildings at least 30 to 35 feet back from the sidewalk, the proposed main garden should connect with existing front gardens on at least one side, so as to form a "long" garden along the street.

(3) If there is a need for a deep open space on the street, part of proposed building frontage should be located at least 75 feet back from the sidewalk, so as to form a "deep" garden on the street. In this case, the front garden must be enclosed by existing buildings of adjacent lots on at least one side.

(4) If there is a need for a spacious internal courtyard on the block, proposed main garden should be an internal courtyard entirely contained within the lot. This is mainly possible on a lot wider than 80 feet, and is difficult on narrower lot.

(5) If there is a beautiful tree or stand of trees, the proposed main garden should be placed so that the trees form a focal point of the main garden.

(6) If there is an apartment building on an adjacent lot, with entrances facing the proposed building, the main garden should be placed so that those entrances are on the edge of a large shared space which includes the main garden.

(7) If there is a single-family house next door, the main garden should be placed so that there is a large space next to the house, for light and view.

(8) Of course the way which the main garden can best improve the positive qualities of the existing place depends on the specific site itself.

Step 4

CALCULATE NUMERICAL PARAMETERS.

Once the position and size of the main garden are approximately clear, calculate areas which will be devoted to building volume, parking, and driveways.

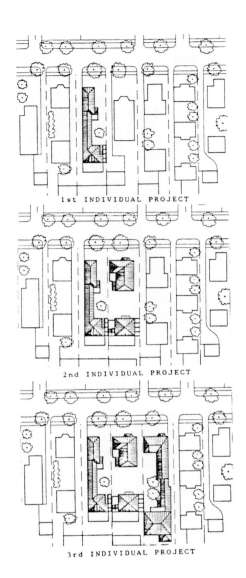

1st INDIVIDUAL PROJECT

2nd INDIVIDUAL PROJECT

3rd INDIVIDUAL PROJECT

A sequence of three developments, on adjacent lots, showing how each new apartment building is asked to "join hands" with existing ones to create useful and lively outdoor space, gardens, and shared parking and driveways.

(1) First obtain context restrictions on size of garden and building heights, as a result of adjacent projects. Then calculate the maximum possible volume of built space, by considering setbacks, garden size, and building height restrictions, in combination with number of parking spaces and parking type. At the end of this step, you should have a definition of the areas which will be devoted to the following:

(2) Main garden

(3) Other open space

(4) Surface and/or half-depressed parking

(5) Underground parking (if any)

(6) Driveways

(7) Footprint of building at grade

(8) Building footprint built over parking

(9) Total area of built space

(10) Number of units

(11) Number of parking spaces

(12) Assume, at this stage of the calculation, that the building has two stories overall. Later adjustments will be made to correct for volume and building height.

Step 5

LOCATE PARKING AND DRIVEWAY.

Locate required parking in a position where it cannot be seen from the street. After getting the numerical parameters, choose the parking type in relation to these numerical parameters. Once parking type is clear, it is possible to decide the position of parking, and on position and type of driveway.

(1) All at-grade parking, when aggregated, must be located at the rear 40% of the lot. There are limited exceptions.

(2) All naturally ventilated underground parking must be located at the rear 50% of the lot. There are no exceptions.

(3) Mechanically ventilated parking must be located under building volumes. It should not be built under the main garden, with some exceptions (30% of the main garden).

(4) If possible, acquire easement on any driveway on an adjacent lot. The City encourages the acquisition of easements for the use of adjacent driveway, and makes it permissible to meet parking access in this fashion. If either of the two adja-

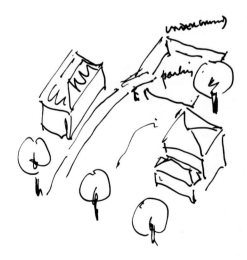

Step 5: Placing the parking, in a way that is not obtrusive for the street

cent lots has a driveway which is capable of providing access to the rear of your lot, then you may be able to share the use of this driveway, if the owner will agree to give an easement. It is recommended that there be a negotiation between yourself and the adjacent property owner, in which you try to plan your main garden and building volume so as to protect your neighbor's property values, in exchange for a driveway easement. If you succeed in obtaining an easement for the use of an adjacent lot driveway, then you are entitled to a density bonus as specified on the density charts.

(5) If no easement is available, you must provide a new driveway. If you have chosen not to use an existing driveway, then you must provide an eight to ten foot driveway. No more than one driveway is allowed per lot. Locate the new driveway along the property line.

(6) All other details of parking layout are to be worked out later.

STEP 6

DECIDE ON LOCATION OF BUILDING FOOTPRINT AND DEFINE ROUGH SHAPE OF BUILDING VOLUMES.

Now locate and shape the buildings according to the beauty of the garden and the character of the street. Locate the building volumes in a way that provide substantial enclosure to the garden. The maximum width of building volumes is 35 feet. You must therefore surround the open space defined in step 3 with long narrow volumes of building. At least 60% of the perimeter of the garden must be enclosed by buildings. At the same time, allow for connections and passages between gardens and open spaces. In addition, if appropriate to the configuration of the main garden, try to place one of your building volumes parallel to the direction of the street, to enclose the garden and contribute to the shaping of the street front. Bear in mind that in order to give good daylight to apartment units, and to enclose outdoor space effectively, the maximum width of building volumes is 35 feet. At this stage you may assume that this volume has an average height of two stories.

(1) While locating and shaping your building volumes make sure that your interior garden is visible from the street. Interior courtyards and gardens should be experienced from the street, and be visible from it, so that they contribute to the beauty and liveliness of the street. Some interior gardens will be wide open on the street and some will feel secluded, connected to the street through a passage. This type of variety is extremely desirable. At the time your project reaches this

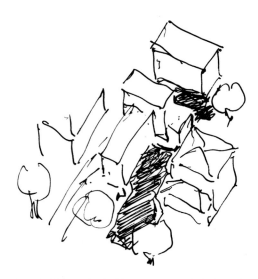

Step 6: Placing the building volumes to help form the gardens, and to contain the right number of apartments

step, the feeling of the whole street, from the point of view of visibility of gardens, has to be assessed. The new building should be open or enclose its garden towards the street to a degree that contributes mainly to the liveliness and character of the street as a whole.

(2) Pay attention to the front setback line. Limited amount of single-story building volumes are allowed to project forward of existing front setbacks of adjacent buildings. These volumes or portions of volumes must be built in such a way that the front is 10 feet from the property line.

(3) If there is no other building on your side of the street, within 200 feet in either direction, that projects forward beyond existing front setbacks, then you are strongly encouraged to place part of your building out to within 10 feet from the front property line.

(4) You may build closer than 5 feet to the rear and side lot line in order to create continuity of building volumes, and are encouraged to do so, provided that you meet requirements concerning light access to windows in adjacent buildings. There are two major reasons for allowing and encouraging zero setbacks. No open space is wasted on leftover strips of unusable space. And the fact that a building volume can be on a side lot line allows for connection between adjacent building volumes. So, it is possible to introduce building volumes parallel to the street together with building volumes perpendicular to the street, thus enabling the formation and enclosure of gardens and courtyards.

(5) Make sure that minimum separation requirements between proposed and adjacent buildings are satisfied. If you have placed the building volume closer than 5 feet from side or rear lot line, you must pay attention to existing major windows and entrances of adjacent buildings.

(6) Now, re-calculate your total building volume again, and adjust story height in different parts of the building volume. Throughout the building volume you have defined, the average building height will need to be two stories, to get the maximum allowable density.

(7) In order to bring the building volume into line with the allowed development, the following adjustments must now be made. Any building volume projecting beyond adjacent front setbacks must be one story. Any building volume within 50 feet of the street, for at least 50% of its length along the street, must be softened by one-story porches, alcoves, room extensions, or galleries. Any three-story construction needed to complete the full allowable density, must be placed on the back 30% of the lot (see standards). Three-story construction may be built over parking.

STEP 7

REFINE THE GARDEN SHAPE IN RELATION TO BUILDING AND ADJACENT GARDENS.

Now embellish, adjust and refine the size, extent and shape of the main garden, taking into account the following: The main garden is to be aggregated in the form of a single rectangular entity of space, as specified by the open space standards. Seventy percent of the main garden must be on natural ground, not over subterranean parking.

(1) There are limited exceptions, specified in the ordinance.

(2) It is also important that the main garden can be enlarged and extended by other developers on the neighboring lots on either side. To make this possible, the main garden must always touch at least one side lot line, except in cases where the lot is more than 80 feet wide.

(3) Place secondary gardens to encourage connection between gardens. There must always be some garden touching one of the two side lot lines. Where this requirement is fulfilled by the main garden, there need not be any secondary garden. All required open space can be used for the formation of the main garden.

(4) On a lot which is less than 80 feet wide, where the main garden must touch one side lot line, a secondary garden is not required. On a lot more than 80 feet wide, if the main garden does not touch at least one side lot line, a secondary garden must be created along one of the lot lines.

STEP 8

LAY OUT DETAILS OF PARKING.

Put in enough details of parking, even at this early stage, so that number of available parking spaces and adequacy of driveway widths and turning radii will be near enough right so that later development of the design will not upset the way that everything has been worked out.

(1) Locate parking spaces, following the design standards specified in the ordinance.

(2) Design driveway and curb-cuts following the design standards specified in the ordinance.

(3) If driveway is adjacent to the main garden, give it detailed position and treatment to protect the garden.

(4) Shape parking space as positive and usable space.

STEP 9

DIVISION INTO APARTMENTS

Within the overall building volume which has been established, the apartments permitted by the ordinance, may now be identified.

(1) First define the location of the apartments. Cut up the total volume into apartments in such a way as to define the best and most pleasant apartments. There should be no attempt to make apartments of standard shape. Rather, each apartment should take a shape which is appropriate to its unique position in the building volume and with respect to daylight, access to outdoors, and entrances. The living room or main room of the apartment should have a garden view if possible.

(2) Provide for access from the parking to the apartments through the garden. The pattern of circulation which is created, should encourage very simple access from the parking lot, through the main garden, to the apartments.

STEP 10

PLACE AND SHAPE APARTMENT ENTRANCES

Place entrances facing main garden. In as many cases as possible, the apartments should have access from the main garden.

(1) Provide apartment entrances from the street. At least one, and possibly two apartments should be entered directly from the street side, with entrances visible from the street.

(2) Make apartment entrances individually identifiable. Some entrances to apartments may be embellished with porches, stoops, steps, or stairs. This should be done only for those cases where this element helps the overall structure.

STEP 11

DESIGN DETAILS OF GARDEN

Embellish the garden with various details that will make it a pleasant, social, and useful place for individuals, and for the inhabitants as a group.

(1) Locate path from street to units.
(2) Locate path from parking to units.

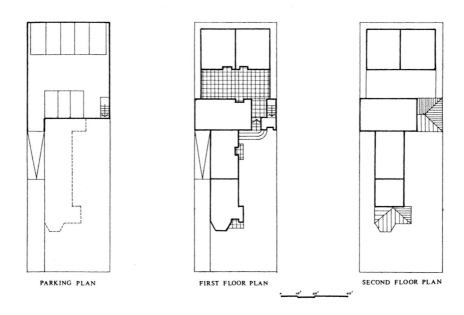

PARKING PLAN   FIRST FLOOR PLAN   SECOND FLOOR PLAN

Parking, and first and second floor plans, showing individual apartments and their entrances

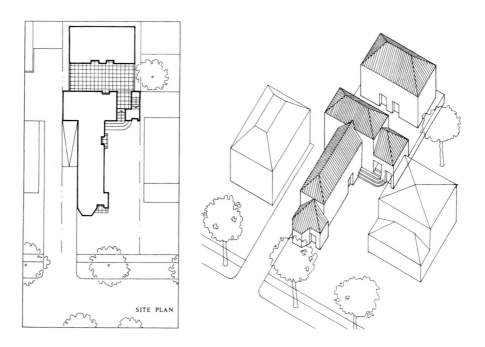

SITE PLAN

The finished building

(3) Place low walls, trellises, hedges, trees, etc. to provide additional enclosure for main garden.

(4) Place low walls, trellises, hedges, along building front.

(5) Define position of major trees in the main garden and secondary gardens.

(6) Locate lawn areas, paved areas, and benches in the garden.

(7) Define position of trees along the street.

(8) Define special embellishments for the front garden and areas along the street or connecting with the street.

9 / UNIQUENESS OF DIFFERENT APARTMENT BUILDINGS GENERATED BY THE SEQUENCE

Uniqueness of each apartment building generated by the sequence, is clearly visible.

On the pages 313–16, we see a few examples of the variety of apartment buildings that can be created by this generative sequence. These are different apartment buildings, designed for a wide variety of site conditions (lot width, orientation, and so on) that occurred in the city of Pasadena. Each of these designs was made for a specific lot in Pasadena, and is unique to that lot. The lots vary in width and depth. They vary in the density for which they have been zoned. They vary in orientation. And, of course, they vary in the character of street which lies beyond the lot, and which must somehow be helped, made more whole, by the insertion of the new apartment house.

The buildings show a surprising variety, all containing the same key invariant features specified by the generating sequence, but nevertheless each unique according to its context.

Dimensional factors are interesting. There is no hint of modular rearrangement in these designs. Rather, the building widths and configurations are pushed, pulled, squeezed, to form well-adapted structures for the conditions that exist on each lot. The variety which occurs, rather more like true organic variety, shows

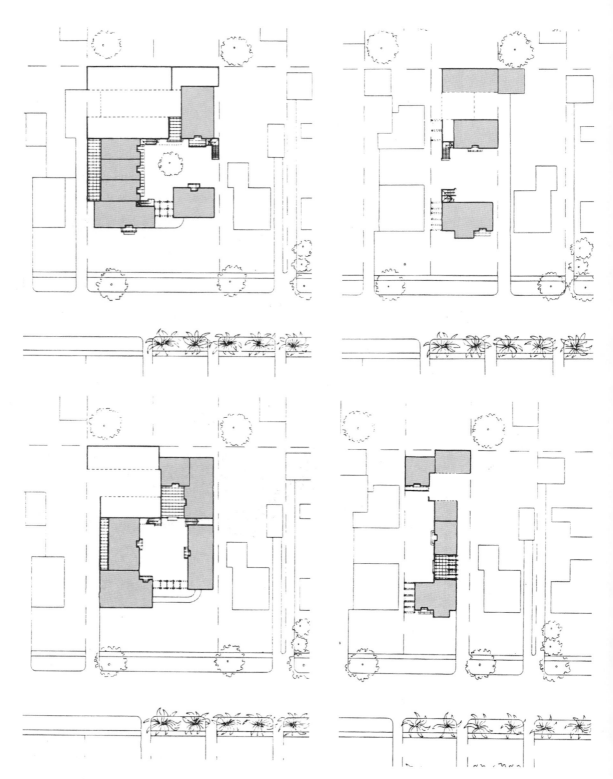

Low density: Four apartment building plans generated by the sequence, for different conditions

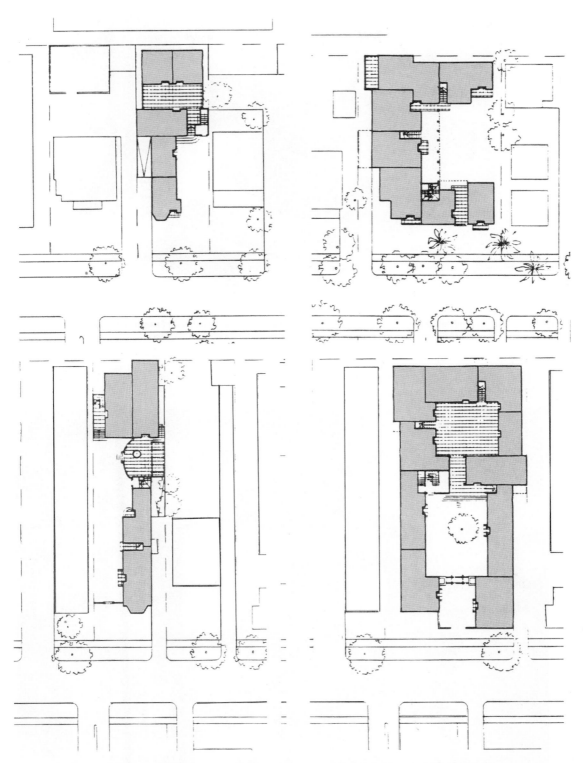

Higher density: Four more apartment building plans generated by the sequence, for different conditions

Another model of an apartment building showing the kind of detail and uniqueness that typically develops as a result of using the generative sequence.

A model of a block in Pasadena, in which a dozen different apartment buildings are visible, generated by the sequence described in this chapter. The simulation was carried out by my students at the University of California.

each one as unusual, with its own presence and its own life. In form, these buildings are less like typical apartment buildings of the late 20th-century era, and — at least in this one respect — slightly reminiscent of buildings in various traditional societies.

Although the generative sequence itself is fixed (and needs to be fixed in order to embody the dictates of the fundamental process), the variety this sequence generates, when interacting with a variety of contexts, is very great indeed — indeed, it is essentially infinite.[8]

10 / THE MENTAL CHANGE NEEDED TO ALLOW YOURSELF THE POSSIBILITY OF USING A GENERATIVE SEQUENCE WHILE MAKING A DESIGN

The crux of every design process lies in finding the generative sequence for that design, and making sure that sequence is the right one for the job. Because such a generative sequence is hard to find, people do not easily grasp the fact that such sequences exist, and therefore find design much more difficult than it needs to be.

Another way of saying the same thing is to observe that for many people, perhaps the most difficult thing of all in understanding living process, and in getting a proper sequence for the unfolding of the whole, is reconciling oneself to the idea of doing one thing at a time. Yet, according to prevailing norms, many architects and designers think it is impossible to get good results by working in this way.

That is because the prevailing wisdom about architecture suggests that since a building is a complex whole, a designer has to do everything all at once, in a kind of incredible artistic tour-de-force, where he sees everything all at once in a single coherent vision. This is nonsense of course. But it is based on a rhetorical question something like this: "How could one possibly succeed in design, doing one thing at a time, since a complex whole is a unitary undivided whole which cannot be separated into parts?"

It is precisely the trick of the unfolding process to solve this problem. The unfolding process allows you to go one step at a time, *precisely because* it is based on a sequence which permits this without disturbing or screwing up the unfolding of the whole.

The reason it works is that, like any system in nature, what is actually unfolding is indeed the *whole*. The key to any human unfolding process, is that the artist or builder visualizes the thing as an entirety, as a whole, from the first day. Even before you start, you already fix on it and see it as if it were a whole. You feel it as a whole, imagine it in its wholeness . . . and gradually tease out from it the features of this wholeness. At each step you do something which has a significant (and good) effect *upon* this whole, seen *as* a whole.

The effect of understanding this point can be dramatic. I remember a student, I will call him X. For months I tried to teach him. He was an outstanding student, but he was — at that moment in his life — still weak in design. He just did not seem to have the knack of putting things together to make something beautiful.

He struggled and struggled. And for months I tried to teach him. Then we came to a design class in which he had to design a house. He worked and worked at the design. Couldn't get it right. Never knew what to pay attention to. The mess on his drawing board was pretty bad.

Of course, when someone can't design, it is usually because they confuse themselves by taking things in the wrong order. The continuous back and forth between all possible issues causes confusion instead of clarity.

Finally, one day I sat with him, and I said "*Look, I am going to talk you through your design project today. Forget what you have. Erase the whole design. Start with nothing."*

Next I asked him, *"Now, tell me, what is the most important thing about the site and the most important thing your design must do in relation to the site. Dont worry about anything else. Just tell me the answer to that one question. Tell me."* He told me.

"All right, so make a mark. Put in just that one thing. Forget everything else." He did it.

"All right. Now tell me the next most important thing." He thought about it. I questioned him. Finally he told me what it was.

"All right, now put that in. Just that second thing. Nothing else."

He put it in.

We went on like that for an hour or so. If he told me something was important, when I doubted that he really felt that, I just looked at him, and said, no, tell me really *what is the next, truly the most important thing?* Then he told me that. I kept on like that, forcing him to say, genuinely, what was the next most important thing. And each time, when he had told me what it was,

defined it, and I believed it, then I told him, "Do it. Now put it in." Then after he had done that I asked him to choose the *next* most important thing he knew about the (not-yet-existing) building. Then I asked him to put *that* in. And so on.

At the end of an hour he had a beautiful building. It was straightforward, simple, fundamental. Above all it was beautiful. The thing he had never been able to do — to make a beautiful design — he had suddenly done. He was able to do it. At the end he came and said to me, "I had no idea it was so simple. I never understood it before," and, as if amazed by his own insight: "Finally I understand it, I understand what you have been saying. You just take one thing at a time, and do it in the right order. That's all there is to it. Just do the most important thing. Finish it. Then do the most important thing. Finish it. And so on."

He was astonished. It seemed like the most important lesson of his life in architecture school. In this exercise I taught him that it was just the *sequence* that underlies our ability. By doing things in the right order, he was able to make a beautiful thing.

11 / THE VITAL INTERPLAY OF FORM AND SEQUENCE

I do not believe that it is possible to understand the nature of sequence, or the idea of generated structure, if one has not actually constructed a sequence which works.

I have pointed out that good sequences are extremely rare, that for any given problem there are trillions of bad sequences, compared with only a few good sequences. But even this piece of information does not prepare one for the actual difficulty of making a sequence which works.

Consider, for instance, the task of making a sequence for construction of low-cost housing for urban India. A simple-minded view of this task would be that first we define the generic centers which are going to be in the housing: For the community, streets, houses and so on this

would be done according to the ideas expressed in chapter 13. Then, armed with the list of generic centers (patterns) which are good for people in these buildings, we could then try to arrange them in different sequences, so that they unfold nicely, and thus create a generating sequence for the urban housing (as it might be used by families for themselves, perhaps in cooperation with urban community officials).

But this is very far from the actual task, and from the nature of the difficulties we experience. What happens is that as we write the pattern-like entities down, in order, trying to put them in a nice order which will unfold smoothly, we find that we have to keep changing the patterns. Sometimes we have to combine two. Sometimes we have to divide one into two new ones. But, more surprising than that, sometimes we find that we are having to invent new patterns altogether.

And sometimes, as we work out a smooth sequence that really differentiates space well, step by step, we find that we may altogether change the content or relative weight of one pattern or another, thus, entirely changing the meaning of the form which will be generated, and ultimately even changing the whole form itself.

Thus the arduous task of building an effective sequence leads us into a thicket, not only because we are considering so many possible sequences, rejecting the bad ones, and trying to simulate, in our minds, the effect of going through the sequences we consider, to see how they unfold, and whether they unfold nicely.

It leads us into a deeper thicket of intellectual challenge, because we find out that even a minor change in the sequence changes — not only the effectiveness of the sequence — *but the whole meaning and content of the form itself.*

Thus, while we thought we were merely constructing the tool with which to create or generate the form of a house, we find that we are struggling, at every turn, with the form itself — with the actual form of the houses and buildings and community, even when we are simply working on the structure of the generative sequence.

12 / FURTHER INSIGHT INTO THE REAL NATURE OF LIVING FORM

It is worth pondering the meaning of this discovery. I have spoken about form, and I have written at length about the nature of generated structure, and the fact that form only has life when it is a generated structure.

In chapter 6, my discussion will have left the impression that the importance of generated structure lies mainly in two things: first, in the tinkering that we do, to adjust things which makes subtle and correct adaptations; and second, in the differentiating process which allows the generated structure to be born from successive differentiations. It is true that these are two fascinating and important points. But we find out now, that the nature of generated structure is much deeper still, and even more interesting than we may have suspected.

In the process of messing about with the possible sequence that we are trying to build, we play with its steps (the patterns), we play with their arrangement in time, *and we have to play, also, with the actual contents of the steps themselves.* What we are doing there is to try and find a sequence of differentiating steps that will, all in all, generate a nice structure. This idea that a sequence of differentiations can be nice, or not so nice (and believe me, this is a *real* distinction) means really that the differentiations are nice when as we go forward through the sequence, each step does something nice (graspable, simple, beautiful) to the product of the previous steps. When we finally get it so that this is happening all along, we then have a nice sequence of differentiations, and as a result, then, we get a nice form.

Now this is completely surprising. What it means is that the form itself, the form of the result, is nice or not nice, according as the sequence of differentiations which led to it is nice or not nice. And this means that when we see a form and consider it harmonious, *it is because it has unfolded from a nice set of differentiations,* and that we are subliminally aware of this, even if not conscious of it.

Thus the idea of a generated structure contains a third thing, over and above the step-by-step adaptations, and over and above the raw fact of the differentiations and the structure they have introduced. It contains the third thing, that a structure is truly generated, and perceived as such, and perceived as having life, *only when it has unfolded from a nice, beautiful, sequence of differentiations* — and this is perhaps the most important point of all.

Here we have, finally, come to a real insight about the nature of living form. We now know that the form itself and the way it has been generated are part and parcel of the same thing, and are an indissoluble entity. This casts new light on the depth and importance of the generative process, in the creation of living form in buildings. To make the point clear, consider the following example which comes from work Howard Davis and I did on the development of a system of sequences for high-density urban housing in India. This system of fourteen sequences deals with everything from community planning to ornament. The particular sequence illustrated here concerns construction of a house plinth for each house.

We started with the point of view from work done earlier by B. V. Doshi in India. Doshi had a model in which there was a prefabricated concrete box, containing plumbing for bath, toilet, and kitchen, within two prefabricated cubicles. This fitted contemporary thinking about sites and services as practiced about 1980.

SEQUENCE — DRAFT 1. We decided to start with the assumption that this entity, the plumbing core, should indeed be placed near the back of the lot, before everything else, as Doshi had done.

SEQUENCE — DRAFT 2. Then we introduced the very important idea of a plinth for every house, a traditional pattern in much Indian housing, which has the effect of raising the house above the monsoon rains, and providing each family a stable, well-built base on which they could continue with their own construction.

SEQUENCE — DRAFT 3. As we thought about the plinth, and its necessary expense, it seemed to us pointless to provide the prefabricated bathroom cubicle and that it was better to spend available funds on the plinth, itself an expensive entity, and to provide the plumbing core within the plinth, but without walls or roof. The families could, we felt, provide those elements for themselves, when they chose to do so.

SEQUENCE — DRAFT 4. We now added, to the idea of the plinth, the traditional entity called an *ottla*. Howard pointed out to me that the *ottla*, a raised terrace *in front* of the house at the same level as the plinth, provided a wonderful social spot where people could sit, work, talk, look at the street, interact with neighbors. We thus provided (in the sequence) a second plinth in front of the main plinth, forming the *ottla*. The traditional *ottla* has steps, contained within it, leading from the street, onto the *ottla*, and thence to the house front door.

SEQUENCE — DRAFT 5. We went back to the plumbing core. After further discussion, it seems that even provision of the sewer and water should be left to the family, not provided at the outset: And that World-Bank emphasis on the importance of the bathroom, was out of proportion, when water and toilets can be provided communally, until people have built their own. We therefore modified the notion of what was happening in the plumbing core, and decided that we would instead provide a chase (still at the back of the house), within the plinth, which could later accommodate any pipe work for water, sewer, drains, and so on, the family wished to provide.

SEQUENCE — DRAFT 6. Finally we made explicit provision for the cutting of steps in the *ottla*, at the appropriate place to go towards the front door as the family settled their house plan.

We see in this chain of revisions, a gradual change in the whole character of the sequence. The centers generated by the sequence changed dramatically in meaning, content, and form. And the ensuing house form evolved and changed enormously with the evolution of the sequence. Referring back to these examples, we may also get an example of what it means to say that one sequence can be "nicer" than another.

Consider three sequences out of the above six drafts. The first sequence (#1) places a prefabricated concrete box, containing plumbing, near the back of the lot. The third sequence (#3) first places a plinth, then a plumbing core on the plinth. The sixth draft sequence (#6) places a plinth, then a smaller plinth (the ottla) in front of it, then cuts a chase for future plumbing in the back of the main plinth, and finally cuts steps into the ottla giving access to the house.

Of these three sequences, the last sequence (#6) is evidently the nicest. It has a comfortable order of events which provides meaningful structure and unfolds smoothly. The first of the three (#1) is the least nice sequence in this sense. #6 is better than #3; #3 is better than #1. And the same may also be said of the *forms* which are generated by the three sequences. The form generated by #6 is better than the form generated by #3 and that is better than the form generated by #1. Sequence #1 merely places a nearly random thing at the back of the lot. It neither contributes to the whole, nor does it come from the whole. Sequence #6 is the one which in the most profound sense unfolds the whole, and develops and differentiates it to make a meaningful place that is both beautiful and works for people.

13 / CONCLUSION

The idea that sequences of instructions can create coherent building form with infinite variety, holds the promise of a new era in architecture.

When I described the Pasadena apartment-building sequence and other examples to a prominent computer scientist in Silicon valley he said to me, with an astonished look on his face: "You mean the generator problem, for architecture, is solvable?"

I told him that I did mean that, and that my colleagues and I were on the way to solving it for a large number of particular cases, and believed it to be solvable in general. But the idea that it was in principle solvable was so massive in its implications that he nearly jumped out of his chair. In other words, although from another discipline, he at once understood both the problem and the significance of solving it.

Many examples of generative sequences are given in Book 3: for office layout (chapter 11), for individual houses in a specific culture (the generative sequence published in Book 3, chapter 11 is for houses in Colombia); and for a construction system (Book 3, chapter 17) for low-cost housing construction in Mexico. Prototype generative sequences for a variety of architectural problems, have also been posted on the website at Pattern-Language.com. The topic is also discussed more extensively in chapters 18–21 of this book.

Once the problem of creating, using, and working out generative sequences for a wide variety of architectural and environmental problems has been solved and worked out practically, the mental landscape of architecture will change, since lay people will be able to lay out, for themselves, houses, gardens, neighborhoods, streets, shops, factories, office buildings, and public buildings. At that stage, the promise of a world in which living structure appears all over the face of the earth, governed by generative sequences, can become a reality.

But there is a further complication. At each stage in a living process, the needed sequence for the steps that are to follow comes from the wholeness which has unfolded up until that time. It is the wholeness *itself*, coupled with the fundamental differentiating process, coupled with the use of structure-preserving transformations, which tells us exactly what the proper sequence is for the next steps. This is the crucial point of contact between the idea of the wholeness, and the idea of the sequence. The single most important thing that happens during the process of making anything, is the ever watchful task of getting the next bit of sequence right and modifying it as we go along. Paying attention to what has to be done next, and getting this right, is as important as what one actually does. The more one understands the idea of unfolding, and the more one understands the key role which sequence plays in the unfolding process, the more it becomes clear that the process of design and the process of construction are inseparable.

Compare an old-style cabinetmaker with a new-style woodworker. The old timer always knows how to make things in just the right order. He can set up a vertical in a cabinet without worrying about the next step. Then he sets the rail. Then he trims the rail. Then sets his drawer. Each element follows from the previous element. Because the sequence is right, the thing unfolds without complications. The sequence gives the thing its perfect ease and simplicity.

By comparison the modern, arty woodworker tries to be much more clever. He gets his "conception" . . . it may be complex. Then he figures out how to put it together. Each part is fabricated so that it all goes together perfectly. The end result is not relaxed but contrived, highly precise according to some previously created image. This thing does not unfold. It is made to conform to a rigid conception.

In this comparison, we see the essential fact: The power and relaxedness that come from a proper sequence are *immense*.

NOTES

1. See chapter 10, pages 283–84.

2. See page 82

3. The 24 steps of the tea house sequence were studied in 1972 in a seminar with my Ph.D. students. We made efforts to find algorithms for obtaining consistent and backtrack-free sequences. Other mathematical and LISP methods of obtaining good sequences as a function of temporal priorities defined among centers, were worked out at that time.

4. This is mathematically identical to a well-known problem in flow chart analysis (PERT charts) common in industrial engineering.

5. This apartment house sequence was worked out in a collaboration with Artemis Anninou.

6. See chapter 13, throughout, for techniques necessary to obtain relevant and vital generic centers as the substrate for a pattern language.

7. See note 8.

8. The generative sequence described here, was, in the end not implemented as part of the Pasadena ordinance. The circumstances are of interest. My friend Dan Solomon, the San Francisco architect with whom I was joint-venturing the creation of the zoning ordinance, came to me and told me that he felt the generative sequence was an offense against architects, that it abrogated the individual freedom of expression of any self-respecting architect who might wish to apply for a building permit in Pasadena, and that he could not agree with the idea that the ordinance would contain the sequence as a major component. He also made this feeling clear to the Pasadena Planning Commission, and we were forced to drop the idea. It is significant, I think, that the fundamental rightness of generative sequences, as a source of life in buildings, was so deeply misperceived by a fellow-architect, who felt it to be a denial of freedom. It was, of course, only a denial of the freedom to do something willful and "creative" in the name of architecture: just the very aspect of architecture which caused so much damage in the 20th century. But the generative sequences are the *origin* of real freedom in the creative process — if that freedom is aimed at creating living structure.

CHAPTER TWELVE

EVERY PART UNIQUE

A PROCESS SO
FINELY TUNED TO CIRCUMSTANCE
THAT EVERY PART BECOMES UNIQUE

1 / GEOMETRY: UNIQUENESS, REGULARITY, DIFFERENTIATION

Almost the most distinctive mark of living process lies in one aspect of the geometry of the results. Simply put, *Every part of the world that has life, and every part of every part, becomes* UNIQUE. *It becomes unique because each part is adapted to its context and because, in the large, no two contexts are ever the same.*

During the onrush of the late 20th century, love of the unique — at least in places and things — sometimes appeared almost quaint, a desperate search for humanity among the inhumanity of dull repetition, stereotypes, and nearly identical McDonald's shops and Japanese cars. Uniqueness, a lost quality, still existing only in a few fishing villages, was regrettably now kept only for vacations. Daily life itself was marked by replicas, by sterile repetition, by the *loss* of uniqueness. Video-tapes of films, identical cars, bags, packages, refrigerators, houses, windows, streets, created a sense of a modular world in which parts were not unique. We were informed, solemnly, by the architectural theorists of that century, that modularity was an inevitable aspect of production, part of the march of progress, and that it would lead us to triumphs of technology.

But uniqueness — the uniqueness of every spot, every part of every place — is a *necessary* aspect of living structure. It is possibly the most fundamental aspect of living structure, and it follows necessarily and without break from the fundamental process itself. It is only in its uniqueness to unique conditions, made necessary by fine adaptation, that anything takes on living form. This is true to such an extent that if the structure of uniqueness at every part does *not* occur within a structure, we can be *sure* that it is not an unfolded whole, not living structure at all.

Indirectly, then, the love that we can feel for a place, for a building, is made possible by living process. When we visit traditional towns and villages, we love them, very often, because each part is recognizable. Each house, door, curtain, garden gate, seems a unique being, specific to its place and time, unique in all the world. That is why we love them. As the little prince says in Saint Exupery's fable: "I love you because you are unique."[1] It is the uniqueness of each mountain, building, person, spot, that makes it possible to love it, or him, or her. The uniqueness that creates our relation with the place is made possible by a living process. By creating uniqueness everywhere, the living process touches, directly, the issue of whether the world will be a world we love, or not.

2 / REGULARITY: FACT AND FICTION

Ultimately, all order and all form come from repetition. Even a meandering line is repetition: the line repeats the relation of the one side to the other, continuously, along the line; and it repeats the continuous quality of the line segment, and, locally, its degree of curvature. Galaxies, stars, atoms, cells, waves, leaves, people, are all repeated endlessly — they all appear millions upon millions of times. It is their repetition which forms the world. And in the sphere of buildings, too, walls, columns, windows, doors, roofs — they all repeat, millions upon millions of times.

Thus everything in the geometry of the world is essentially organized repetition. The final target of unfolding is to find and create just those repetitions which are required — and from

Dewdrops

them, to give birth to form. Hierarchy and repetition, of an organic not mechanical kind, ultimately create the architecture of the whole.

But when a process is a *living* process, the repetition is of a very special kind, quite different from the mechanical kind of repetition we learned to recognize in the 20th century.

During the 20th century, our ideas about repetition and uniqueness were distorted, I believe, by two important but erroneous strands of thought. First, by a conviction (often carried by architects) that it was inevitable that a modern industrial process could only make exact replicas, if it was to be efficient, via mass-production. Indeed, the 20th century was dominated by a too-simple idea of modularity. Throughout much of the 20th century, artists and architects were obsessed with the idea of modularity, of modular components as building blocks. On the surface, we were led to believe that this kind of modular repetition had to be introduced by architects for reasons of efficiency, speed, and so on. But more deeply, I believe, it was an aesthetic idea, a philosophical ideal, an intellectual extension of the ideas of mechanism.

Second, our concept of repetition was distorted by a conviction about atoms and fundamental particles, which seemed to provide a basis for thinking that the world is, in its essence, modular. This philosophical ideal originated in the deep-seated 19th- and 20th-century belief that the world is *ultimately* modular in its construction. At one time physicists believed that atoms — then thought to be the ultimate constituents of matter — were the modular units from which everything was made. Later, it was thought that electrons, neutrons, protons were the identical modular units from which everything was made. Later still, quarks and strings — even smaller and more fundamental — were to be the repeating units from which electrons and neutrons were made.

At the base of this philosophical ideal was the idea that each atom (of hydrogen, say) is *exactly* like every other hydrogen atom. Atoms of a given type were thought to be truly identical; the variety of the world coming simply from the geometrical combinations. As the 20th century came to its second half, the intellectual bias of the century was often mixed with the philosoph-

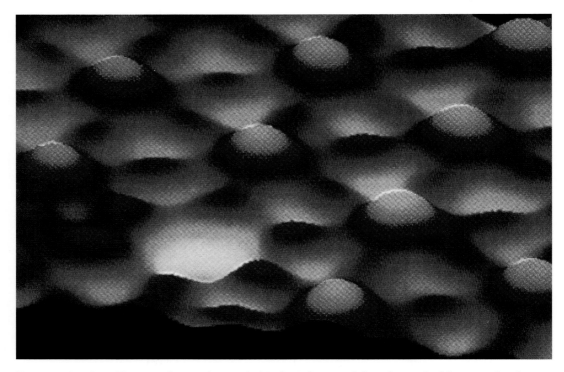

Every atom is unique. The array of atoms photographed in this iodine crystal shows how each of the atoms, though at one time, according to conventional 20th-century, thought to be identical, is in fact slightly different in its detailed shape from its neighbors. What we see here are indirect traces of the outer electron shells, but the geometrical and spatial differences from atom to atom are very clear. Photographs of individual atoms were taken for the first time in 1988 on a scanning tunneling microscope, at the IBM Research Center in San Jose, California.

ical (and practical) dream of a small number of components which could be combined in infinite richness of arrangement to create beautiful things.[2]

Such an ideal is not consistent with the nature of wholeness. If the idea of wholeness as it is expressed in Book 1 turns out to be correct, and if the unfolding of wholeness described in this book turns out to be fundamental, *then one must come to expect that each atom and each particle will be different according to its context*, and that there are no ultimate identical constituents of matter at any scale.[3]

For the case of atoms this has recently been confirmed. About ten years ago, people were able, for the first time, to take photographs of individual atoms.[4] When one examines these photographs (usually photos of many "identical" atoms in arrays as in the photograph of an iodine crystal, above) one sees that indeed each atom is

slightly different — each according to its context. This is directly visible in the photograph, where we see that although neighboring atoms are very similar, they are not identical. On the basis of theoretical and ontological reasoning, a similar view rejecting any "ultimate" constituents of matter was proposed by David Bohm. The view is gaining in acceptance among many theoretical physicists today.[5]

It is hardly surprising that atoms differ. If the nucleus of an atom were a sphere 1 cm across (the size of small marble), the electrons forming the outer part of the atom would be in a three-dimensional spherical zone about 1 kilometer away from the marble. Since the electrons move according to forces induced by other particles, it is intuitively obvious that the detailed movement of each electron in the orbit around the nucleus will go (slightly) differently, according to the local configuration of other particles, and

Clematis growing on a wall of my farm. Here, there is true uniqueness in the repetition.

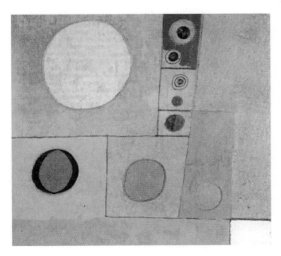

A painting by a famous painter, Ben Nicholson. Though it is graceful, interesting, beautiful — it does not have the same profound structure as the branch, even though it has its kind of variations. Ultimately, as a structure, it is far less subtle, less complex.

it will indeed therefore be slightly different for each atom. The uniqueness of each atom is clearly visible in the photograph of an iodine crystal shown. The electron shell is defined by a wave form; the electronic orbital, which establishes electron position in relation to nearby atoms and their orbits, is unique according to the nearby spatial and dynamic conditions.

Thus the mental, historical, and almost moralistic stereotype which holds that there *ought* to be modular units in a configuration is erroneous, and we should give up our adherence to it. In larger systems the same is true. When a living process is working, it creates a very special kind of geometrical order in which every part is whole, unified, and in which every part is unique, according to its conditions. *This is a particular type of geometry which, though highly regular, makes every part unique because it is consistent with its context, not only with its essential character.*

A type of repetition, in a postmodern building, which has none of the qualities of the repetition generated by a living process

Consider, for instance, the clouds in the sky. Each cloud has a geometrical order, which is just right for its position in the sky, its character, its uniqueness at that moment. Each cloud, and each part of each cloud, is different according to its place in the weather system and its history, making every cloud, and every part of every cloud unique. The uniqueness is highly subtle, just right, not exaggerated, never more than what is required.

This non-modularity of the living world is a necessity of the world's structure, that the world cannot have living structure *unless* it has this feature. In a living world every part must be different and unique according to its conditions.

Let us consider the same issue at another scale. On page 325, I show a photograph of branches growing, in winter, outside my kitchen window in Sussex. At first sight, the raindrops and twigs look similar, nearly the same. Each drop is round, and about the same size. Each twig looks "the same." But of course, the beauty of the dew and of the branches lies just in the fact that they are not in fact the same, not identical, but that rather, each part is unique in a subtle and extraordinary way. It is this rich *non*-modular structure, which gives the whole such life.

If the reader has any doubt, it may be useful to compare a painting by Ben Nicholson with a photograph of a clematis branch (page 327). The painting is charming, fun. But it is a work carried out in a simpler, more nearly modular geometry. It does not have the life of the clematis branch, it does not have the capacity to move us, touch us, make us feel the wonder of the world to the same degree.

There is something in the uniqueness-filled geometry of the living structure which is precious, subtle, goes to the core of things. The living structure is *based* on the fact that every part is unique: Not merely that the cells inside the flowers are unique, but that the atoms in the cells are also unique, all according to their orientation and location.

So, in a living structure, we have a configuration which is unique and highly defined in its details, in this all-encompassing utterly beautiful way. From the electrons to the atoms to the branch itself — it and all its elements are unique and precious. Yet it is all repeating.

The repetition is important, vital. It is very important to observe that repetition in the world is inevitable, since indeed similar conditions do keep recurring, and since similar conditions will keep spawning *similar* configurations. One must not interpret uniqueness in a naive hippielike way, to imply that each building (or wall, or window, or street) would be better off if it were utterly different and without relation to others. Calm repetition, the calm beauty of the rows of vines in a vineyard, is of the essence of living

*The real endless repetition in a traditional city—in this case Jerusalem—
where each repeating part is varied from the next, and has been made unique.*

Moshe Safdie's earliest experiments from the 1960s, where he tried to achieve variety by conceiving building as a combination of modules. What he was searching to achieve was the beauty of Jerusalem (previous page), but this method of repeating modules could not — in principle — achieve that goal.

structure. But the operative word is *similar*, not *same*. For the vineyard to be living, the rows must be very similar. But for it to be living, they must not be the same.

Nothing that is made by combining rigidly identical modules, can have this kind of living structure. It is for this reason, above all, that so many works of the 20th century failed. The identical houses, the identical boxes or units of mass fabrication, the identical lamps in the street, the identical doors, windows, roof tiles — all intended to make better things cheaper and faster — *all* have an essential problem: they are sterile. The postmodern developments made to include features of 18th-century buildings are still sterile in spite of the effort to make them less so — because they are manufactured from large-scale modular units (both in design and construction) which are not adapted to their local conditions. Because they are modular and repeti-

tive in this negative sense, they are not adapted to the local conditions each one experiences. As a result, they can only take their position in a dead structure.

Even new and sophisticated modular construction does not solve this problem. If I speak to a manufacturer of modular components — someone, say, who makes hotels from modular assemblies that become rooms — he may tell me that these modules (perhaps 30 feet long and 14 feet wide, and weighing 10 tons) are potentially context-sensitive, because each one can be given slightly different interior contents.

But that is not the real thing at all, only an horribly impoverished form of variation. Living structure is not merely context-sensitive at a single level. If a system is truly context-sensitive at every level, from the largest to the smallest, each part is unique, because all of it, throughout its fabric, has been generated in this marvelous way

Habitat, built in the 1970s by my friend Moshe Safdie. This structure was a breakthrough at the time. It was intended to provide uniqueness to individual apartments, while also being modern, efficient, and sophisticated. Unfortunately, it does not have the deep structure of true living structure. Instead its repetition, unlike that visible in the living structure of Jerusalem, and though a serious effort, was actually still banal and deadening in spite of the serious effort made.

that makes each part perfectly adapted to its position, just right, and perfectly unique at its place in the world.

That is what was missing from the 20th century. I believe that, at root, this is one of the most profound reasons why people of the

20th century began to feel alienated and despairing. Deep in our hearts, I suspect we know that every situation is unique, each person, each moment, and therefore each place, must be unique. To live in a world which denies this truth, by creating an appearance of sameness, and then perhaps forcing us unique creatures into that mold of sameness, is degrading and impossible to bear.

The mathematical concept of wholeness I have put forth in Book 1, has the consequence that wholeness changes dramatically, even from the slightest and most subtle variations which occur in the wholeness field. This is because a very slight change in the configuration, can cause a major change in the centers which are generated. A tiny point, added, can alter the the deep structure of the wholeness enormously at the scale of yards or even miles.

The necessity of uniqueness, at all levels, in the universe, follows from this mathematics. If then, there is to be a living world of the future, the present processes of fabrication must be replaced by other deeper and more sophisticated processes which, like nature, are context-sensitive from top to bottom, and create unique living structure at every level, so that each part of the world becomes unique.

3 / UNIQUENESS ARISES NATURALLY FROM SEQUENCE FROM DOING THINGS IN THE PROPER ORDER AND FROM THE APPROPIATENESS OF REPETITION

The uniqueness of the world is connected, deeply, to the sequence of unfolding discussed in chapter 11. When a developer makes a series of apartments which are "modular," identical units, that are to be arranged like building blocks inside a larger plan, it goes without saying that the units will not be unique. This is closely connected to the fact that the design of the units came "at the wrong moment" in sequence — indeed at an inappropriately early moment, which did not allow each apartment to take its own floor plan, according to position and conditions, as adaptation requires. Similarly, if we place modular windows in a building, the design of the window precedes the moment when the building reached the decision point for size and shape of windows according to their positions, the light, size of rooms, view, and so on. On the other hand, if the emerging building truly unfolds in the fashion I have explained for living process, then of course the apartments must be given their shape, plan, design, only *after they have been placed*, and in response to the unique conditions arising, each in its different position (For such a scheme see the process and plans illustrated on pages 306–16). And similarly, if we do things in the right order, when it comes to window design, then each window will be designed only at a moment *late enough in the unfolding* so that each room knows what its needs are, the view, the light, the room size, the most important place in the room.

The organic unfolding of a building tells us *when* these various decisions must be made. And the *consequence* of deciding things at the right moment, when correctly done, is that the building and all its parts become unique. The sterile modularity and inappropriate sameness of 20th-century parts came about directly as a result of taking things in the wrong order.

What kind of repetition, on the other hand, is generated by a living process? In the products of a living process, what is the relation between repetition and uniqueness?

The way that the fundamental process creates living structure is like biological and natural unfolding, but *unlike* much modern architectural design and construction, in the all-important respect which concerns the size, character, repetition, and non-modularity of component elements.

I can illustrate this through an example, by referring to an ultra-high-tech furniture system which my colleagues and I worked out for the

Repetition—but not modular *repetition—in the interior of the Sweet Potatoes clothing factory. Christopher Alexander with Gary Black, Artemis Anninou, Kleoniki Tsotropoulou, 1988.*

furniture companies, Haworth and Herman Miller.[6] We were trying to find a way of making a furniture system which would allow each worker in an office to create an environment that was well adapted to that person's needs; personal, particular, and well adapted to the room, or space, where this was happening.

The prevailing type of office furniture system which existed at that time was one built from modular units: Standard desk, filing cabinets, etc., each in two or three standard sizes, which could be freely placed and arranged to furnish an office. It was the prevailing assumption that by arranging and re-arranging these fixed elements, each person could create the environment they wanted in a "unique" configuration (I have put the word "unique" in quotes, for a reason that will be obvious in a minute).

I became convinced from many experiments with people laying out their own offices in different spaces, that in order for them to realize the configuration that suited them, and suited the room, what was required was a different kind of furniture in which both the configuration and the pieces of furniture themselves arose by differentiation *from* the general configuration of the space. This means that the pieces, in the positions they took, were sized and shaped by subdivision of the whole, according to the needs of the position they were in, just as kernels of corn are squashed up against each other in a growing ear of corn.

Years ago, I wrote a computer program which allowed people to create a room layout in this way, by differentiation.[7] My colleagues and I also created a layout procedure, and a system of dimen-

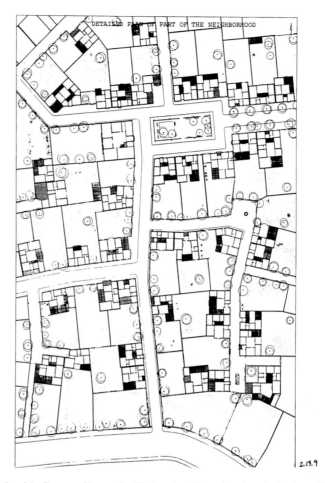

DETAILED PLAN OF PART OF THE NEIGHBORHOOD

My plan for a neighborhood in Guasare, Venezuela (Christopher Alexander, Artemis Anninou, Hajo Neis, Ingrid King, Jonathan Fefferman, 1982).

sionally changeable components which could be delivered cheaply and quickly to each client, and then re-sized with infinite variations to match the configurations developed in this fashion. The room arrangements that people generated in this way were genuinely personal, genuinely well-adapted to the rooms, or corners where it was being done. They were altogether different in character from the stiff and unworkable arrangements that can be created by arranging a few standard components in a few rigid arrays. They were richer, contained a potential for more variety, had the capacity to seem and be "whole," and had a geometric structure which was more reminiscent of biology than of modular-component art.

Above all, the richness was greater than the combinatory richness of a normal modular system. This occurred because the infinity of configurations that can be created in a differentiating system, is a richer and *larger* infinity than the infinity of geometrical arrangements that can be made by arranging and re-arranging standard components.[8] But, in addition, the *character* of a whole formed by splitting and differentiation, is more genuinely organic, and more unified, than anything that can be achieved by combined and rearranging fixed parts. The illustration of the mouse foot on page 33 (from a phase of biological growth), explains this point in a single image.

It may be said that any living process, built up from repeated applications of the fundamental process, works, by creating configurations

334

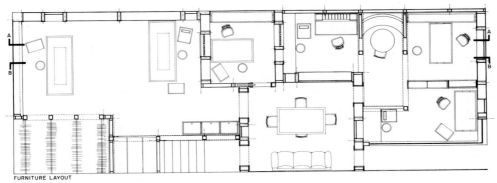

Subtle rectangles in the differentiated plan-form of the Sweet Potatoes factory:
This is the plan of the factory shown in the photograph on page 333.

from within this much larger infinity of possible configurations. It is — for this reason — able to create genuinely adapted results which, incidentally, also look more natural and more organic, because of their unfolded character.

What emerges from differentiation is not a loose, funky, rounded, kind of organicism. The buildings which the fundamental process creates, in the sphere of building, are still dominated by rectangles or near rectangles — because the rectangle is, after all, the main shape of easily built inhabited space that has positive space on both sides of every wall. But the differentiated

complex of rectangles is a richer and more subtle texture of configuration, a more profound morphological substance. This may be seen in the photograph of Jerusalem (page 329), where traditional forms are chiefly made from such complex rectangles. Like the furniture layouts, the building configurations which arise from a differentiating process are better-adapted. They come closer to doing what is wanted, fit the circumstances, and pay attention to the vastly larger system of constraints and needs and local centers, which is needed to create true living structure in the world.

4 / EVERY LIVING PROCESS IS — AT ITS CORE — A PROCESS WHICH IS DEVOTED, THROUGH ADAPTATION, TO MAKING EVERY PART UNIQUE

Why is uniqueness of all parts in a living structure so hard to understand? I am constantly astonished that students — even artists and architects who seem to understand wholeness — continue to have trouble understanding the balance of repetition and uniqueness.

I remember one group of students, advanced students, very good students, who had been doing beautiful work with me. Professor Hajo Neis and I asked them to make a model of a housing project we were working on: 300 apartments, a big site. We asked them to make a model at 1/4

inch scale — rather large. Each building was about seven inches high; the whole model was the size of a room: ten feet by fifteen feet.

For a week the students struggled. They made many cardboard models, but there was nothing very worthwhile there, still just a bunch of cardboard buildings. Nothing particularly good. The students were frustrated. They didn't know what to do. They couldn't grasp what it was they hadn't done. I kept asking them to do better. But they had no idea what was actually needed to make it better.

A portion of the Amazon project for student housing, University of Oregon, 1992, where one can see how every part, and every space, has become unique, because of its particulars.

I told them it was all in the geometry. My saying this, over and over again, did not help. They still didn't get it. It was, to them, just words. They kept on with their nice ideas, with the attempt to make it ecological, or socially good, or beautiful. But none of this did much good. What I really meant by saying "It is in the geometry" was not getting across to them. They became bored, then finally started getting angry with me. I let them stew for a few days, in the hope they would discover, for themselves, the core of the essential point.

Then after they had worked for a few days, I once again looked at their model with them. I remember looking at one particular place in the model, a zone no more than about three inches across in the model (standing for a twelve-foot diameter in real life). I said: "Imagine standing here, at this spot. Let us ask the question, *Is it wonderful to be here, just at this spot?* Please, really stand inside this place, ask yourself if it is wonderful here." And of course, after examining it honestly, they saw "No, it is not. Of course it isn't." So I said to them, Let's work at that one

spot, until it *becomes* wonderful there, in that one small spot, twelve feet across, for a person being there. Three or four of them worked at it, seats, view, good surface, enclosure, and so on. Finally they had made it nice. In the model you could feel how nice it was. So then I said, OK, now you are done with that. Let's now take another place, ten feet away (two-and-a-half inches away in the model). Is it wonderful to be in *that* spot? No? Then work at that one, too, until that second spot, too, becomes wonderful, wonderful to be there, standing there, walking there, sitting there. And then, later, "Are you done with that one? Now go to a third spot, and then a fourth, and so on, keep on going like this, until every single spot, every spot in the whole area you are designing that a person could be in, is wonderful."

After a while, the whole thing became at least *good* — and sometimes, here and there, even wonderful. And in this whole, it was, of course, the *geometry* that made or did not make it wonderful at every spot. It is because every single place had an appropriate and intelligent adapted

There is simplicity and repetition. There is widespread repetition. But when one looks carefully, you see that still, every part is made so that it is unique. Model of part of the Amazon housing, University of Oregon, 1992.

uniqueness, caused by its real adaptation to circumstances. When *that* is done, you feel each place as a real thing, and can see its reality enough to make it really good.

This point is so simple. There is nothing complicated about it. It seems rather astonishing that all this complexity boils down to something as simple as this. It is a little bit like the proverbial slap from a Zen teacher. The student thinks it is all complicated, deep, profound. He twists his head this way and that way, trying to "get" it. Then the teacher finally slaps him to wake him up, as if to say, "Stop thinking about such complicated matters: Just eat, just walk, just sleep." Or (in the case of architecture), *Just make it nice at every spot.*

Following this rule, the geometrical structure, which creates life, living space, is not too hard to make. All you have to do is pay attention, keep on paying attention, work at it, and work at it, and work at it, and gradually each center gets transformed, and life enters the structure.

So why is it so hard to explain? One reason that it is so hard to explain is that each time you do it, it comes out differently. Each case is unique. What does it need to make *this* space have life? It comes out differently in every part, and differently as a whole according to its context each time you do it? That is the whole point. Life is unique. We could even say: *Life is exactly*

that property of space in which each spot becomes unique according to its place in the larger scheme of things. So, if there were a spatial formula which would explain in detail how to make living space, it would fail, because, by virtue of being a formula, it could not succeed in treating each place as unique.

But there *is* a formula of living *process*. If you pay attention to the wholeness, intensify it, intensify it some more — gradually then it becomes unique.

In a further discussion of this living space with my students, after the same class of students finally succeeded in making some life happen, throughout a larger model, one student, Rueta, who had experienced the process, told me: "I got there, but I don't know how I got there. It is like reading a book, over and over, and then finally I have absorbed its meaning, but I do not know just how or when this happened." Another said: "I understand it now: but I do not know at what moment I understood it, or what happened. It is like an enlightenment. Suddenly it seems obvious, and the difficulties are gone."

The main thing is that you have to pay attention, work hard, look at each case as unique. That is the most important part. You just have to try and understand what would be living space, each time, whatever you are trying to do, and accept the fact that every time the result always comes out different. In our Amazon housing for the University of Oregon, a project for about 300 apartments, no two groups of buildings were the same, no two apartments were the same (see drawing and photograph on pages 336–37). Even in this infinitely repetitive problem — mass housing — the living process was of such a nature that each part became unique.

Everything hinges on the understanding that every part must become unique when living processes are working. This is the key. It is a particular type of geometry which, though highly regular, has every part unique because it is true to its context and therefore to its essence. What we began to appreciate is that every repeated entity is different: that we have to look, carefully at every single case as fresh.

Making it, designing it, laying it out, is immensely hard work, harder than what we are used to — but it *works*. Indeed, finally we understand that this is the *only* thing which works.

5 / THE *SURPRISING* CHARACTER OF WHAT UNFOLDS

The many features of the Fort Mason bench, San Francisco. By making the bench reflect and extend the structure which is there, it takes on a unique character that emerges from that one place in the world.

Because of the uniqueness which unfolds, the results of living process will often be unexpected, even turn out surprising. This unexpectedness is typical of all structure-preserving transformations. Although the concept of structure-preserving transformations sounds conservative — to some people it may even sound as if you don't invent or create anything — in reality the process is very different. By preserving structure one always gets surprising results.

Consider the case of the San Francisco bench (for details see Book 3, chapter 11). I began with a clear sketch of what I thought it ought to be — a rectangular U-shape. As we began working, the structure-preserving process then taught us something quite different. Using the

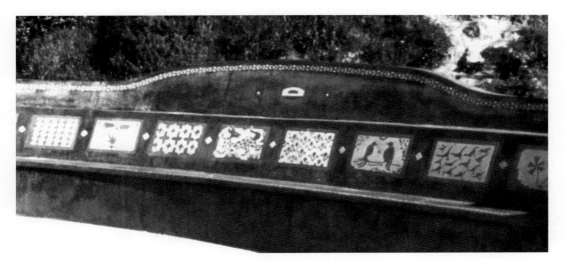

The bench from the front, showing details of the hand-made terrazzo panels designed and shaped and cast in place to fit the landscape and the place while we built the bench

structure-preserving process, first with concrete blocks, then with a group of people simulating their natural way of sitting in relation to the landscape and to one another, the initial rudimentary idea of the bench was slowly transformed into something entirely unexpected. The structure-preserving center-making process first generated a gentle curve (a GOOD SHAPE); then the ROUGHNESS of the ends of the curve to make POSITIVE SPACE with the surrounding pier; then BOUNDARIES in the structure; then a backbone shape for the back of the bench (GOOD SHAPE again, and STRONG CENTERS; then a stair on the back of the bench forming a special place; then an unanticipated octagonal table with lobes (LOCAL SYMMETRIES); then ornaments of richness and variety with ALTERNATING REPETITION of green and white, with a curved line of black and white diamonds with LOCAL SYMMETRIES once again preserving and intensifying the larger structure of the curve. The deep structure of wholeness, being made of centers, is such that the work of enhancing and preserving that structure — although it sounds passive — *is more active than anything, more inventive than a mythical "wild" artistic imagination.* In fact it is the work of enhancing structure which gives rise to the most imaginative, inventive, and wonderful new creations.

6 / RESPECT FOR WHAT EXISTS

The creative work is to illuminate, to reveal what is already there . . . but this takes depth of perception and love . . . certainly profound knowledge of the nature of space and its structure. To do it, successfully, we are called upon to make another crucial revision in our views about the nature of things: We have always assumed that the process of creation is a process which somehow inserts entirely new structure into the world . . . in the form of inventions, creations, and so on. Living process teaches us that wholeness is always formed by a special process in which new structure emerges directly out of existing structure, in a way which preserves the old structure, and therefore makes the new whole harmonious. Thus the process of making wholeness is not merely a process which forms centers or the field of centers in space . . . it is a process which gives special weight to the structure of things as they are.

The enigma is that something new, unique, previously unseen — even innovative and aston-ishing — arises from the extent to which we are able to attend to what is there, and able to derive what is required from what is already there. . . and that all this, then, will lead to astonishing surprises.

In this context, creativity looks entirely fresh. The act of creation is not a willful process like the art of Michelangelo, which we evaluate according to its novelty. It is, instead, a process in which we most deeply express our reverence for what exists.

If we concentrate on understanding by what process each part must become itself — in just the right way which emerges from its position in the whole — it will be tied to the whole, harmonious with the whole, integrated with the whole, yet unique and particular according to just the unique conditions which occur in that part of the whole. This will give us the living process, and our understanding of it, too, in its entirety.

It is this requirement for uniqueness which most profoundly shocks the system of architecture, construction, and thought, that we allowed to develop in the 20th century. It is in the ability to make each part, unique, adapted to the whole, that we have the most to learn from traditional society, from traditional landscape, and from traditional art. I make this building stand forward a little bit more. I close this space, a tiny bit more firmly. I am clear I want to be able to walk through here. I am sure that the shape of this garden should be like this, not like that. And each time I am sure of one of these small things, I put it in. Gradually then, the work grows under its own laws. Each of these tiny acts, makes something useful, something definite happen. Very gradually the whole shifts, emerges, comes into focus. In each place, a being slowly emerges from the mist.

NOTES

1. Antoine de Saint Exupery, THE LITTLE PRINCE (New York: Harcourt, Brace & Co., 1943).

2. Many eloquent treatises on this subject were written, in art by Max Bill, Victor Vasarely, in architecture by Ezra Ehrenkrantz, by Moshe Safdie, by the British proponents of modular coordination (1955-65), and by 20th-century construction companies trying to sell large-scale units of construction and fabrication.

3. This discussion was first taken up in early drafts of Book 1, about 1983.

4. Hans von Baeyer, TAMING THE ATOM: THE EMERGENCE OF THE PHYSICAL MICROWORLD (London: Viking, 1992 and New York: Dover, 1998).

5. The fashionable thing has been to say "Yes, atoms are not perfectly modular, but instead it the much smaller quarks which are perfectly modular, or yes, but it is the even smaller strings, which are perfectly modular." The theory of wholeness as characterized in Book 1, would lead to a different conclusion — namely, that it is in the very essence of things that wholeness is non-modular, and that subtle variations will always occur at every level, no matter how fine one looks. This point of view was also expressed eloquently by David Bohm, in the following passage from WHOLENESS AND THE IMPLICATE ORDER (London: Routledge & Kegan Paul, paperback edition, 1983),pp. 48-50. On page 49 Bohm writes: "Of course modern physics states that actual streams are composed of atoms, which are in turn composed of elementary particles, such as electrons, protons, neutrons, etc. For a long time it was thought that these latter are the ultimate substance of the whole of reality... however it has been found out that even the elementary particles can be created, annhilated and transformed, and this indicates that not even these can be viewed as ultimate substances. . . one may suppose that this deeper level of movement may be analyzable into yet finer particles which will perhaps turn out to be the ultimate substance of the whole of reality. However, the notion that all is flux into which we are inquiring here, denies such a supposition. . . At any stage, further properties of such collections may arise, whose ultimate ground is to be regarded as the unknown totality of the universal flux."

6. See Herman Miller, HMI, publications of CES, 1988 (further described in Book 3).

7. The computer program I wrote was different from the typical CAD-type programs which, like much contemporary system-furniture, work on the assumption of addition, by arranging and re-arranging modular components. My program worked by differentiating space, allowing objects of different size and shape to crystallize out from the space, in the shape and size they needed, for their particular role, in the whole.

8. The point can be expressed simply. If we consider a straight line one foot long, and have three component segments whose combined length is one foot, there are only eight possible arrangements of these three segments along the line. On the other hand, if we make two cuts, anywhere along the length, in such a way as to first divide it in two, and then divide one of the segments in two again, there are an infinite number of ways these two cuts can be made — and hence an infinite variety of possible resulting configurations, even for this simple case.

CHAPTER THIRTEEN

PATTERNS

GENERIC RULES FOR MAKING CENTERS
OR
''MAKING LIFE ENJOYABLE''

1 / INTRODUCTION

In previous chapters, I have discussed unfolding mainly from a formal point of view, discussing the way that centers grow, and how they grow in such a way as to allow coordination and adaptation among the parts of the emerging whole as it becomes a building.

But, of course, there is an enormous subject, not yet dealt with at all: the question of the functional origin of a building, and the definition of the functions that are to go into it. In any sane process which is able to make living structure in buildings, giving proper attention to the functional basis of the building — to what people need, and want, and desire, in order to make themselves comfortable — is paramount. For a building it is the essence of its worth.

I have not discussed this subject earlier, because the way that functional information enters the building process, cannot be well understood without a grasp of the geometrical aspects of the formative process. Even the question of what the building does, and how well it does it, can be understood properly only in the context of the geometry.

We have now had a sufficient preparation in geometry and structure, to begin a detailed discussion of the functional basis of a building.

2 / STRUCTURE-PRESERVING TRANSFORMATIONS AS THE ORIGIN OF FUNCTION

At the beginning of every building design process, it is necessary to get an idea of what is going to happen in the building, how it is going to work. But this activity of defining functions ahead of time is far more subtle than it might seem.

As I have said in Book 1 (chapter 11, pages 403–39) that all functions, when they are working well in a building, are associated with living centers. This means that all the "functions" which are to be defined for a building need to be expressed as rules for making *centers*. And, above all, the *choice* of these centers is vital: To a very great extent, the finished project will be defined, controlled, in its behavior and its feeling, by the *choice* of key centers which are to appear in it.[1]

Simple examples of traditional function and its centers. A rose trellis around a cottage door is simple enough: It forms a center, it creates enjoyment through color, smell, and it enhances the love of living things. Though it is small, and the center is not high among the more significant centers in the built environment — still, the choice of this one type of center has a huge effect on house and village. It is just one center, and a small one; but it has a *huge* effect on what life is like in that place. In another case, a repeating center and its functions may be very large, visible, and highly significant in the way that function and behavior are made to change. Dulles airport for Washington, D.C., was largely defined by the mobile lounges which Eames and Saarinen invented as a new way of getting from the airport to the plane. It was a new kind of center that transformed the way an airport works.

Such examples show us how the quality of human culture is embodied in the repeating centers which are current in a place. Indeed, as we know very well, the needs which people have in buildings are richly modified by culture. A house for an Arab family in Morocco, for a Japanese

The circle of houses typical in Trobriand society. The circle was one of the major patterns which defined their culture

Physical character of the Trobriand houses around the circle. Here is another major pattern which defined their culture.

family in Japan, for an English family, a Russian family — are all quite different things. In any particular society, the centers which are recognized are specific, and identify a particular (culture-borne) way of life.[2] The way of life of Americans in Fort Lauderdale, the way of life of Trobriand islanders in a Trobriand village; the way of life of Indians living in a high density part of Delhi — each has its own complex system of centers. In each of these cases, the way of life, the existence, is defined by centers that are peculiar to that culture.

So, for instance, the Trobriand islanders in a village typically arranged their houses in a circle around a common area.[3] The chief's house at one point of the circle, with storehouses on either side, created the axis of the village. Collective yam stores were placed at points around the inner circle, on either side of the axis, leading to the chief's house and main common house. This was the way the world made sense for Trobrianders, was comfortable, and was consistent with their culture, their values, their beliefs. It was all embodied, summarized, in the centers that appear in this typical layout of a village. The archetypal centers, which define the classic Trobriand village, are the physical and geometrical embodiment of a wholeness which will then support, reflect, sustain, the essence of their culture.

Thus, the task of defining centers, for a new building, or for a neighborhood, is one of the deepest and most significant kinds of work which can be undertaken, in trying to establish a new way of life, and a physical environment which supports that way of life.

The process of choosing or defining functional centers, if it is to be part of a living process, must itself derive, then, in some fashion, from the existing wholeness. Like the elaboration of geometry itself, the pre-operational phase when the centers-to-be are being defined must be drawn from the existing wholeness by structure-preserving transformations.

What exactly does this mean? It means, mainly, that the centers that are to be injected into a new building project — the generic entities or patterns which are to be the building blocks of the project, and which are to define it — must come in large part from the human *culture* where the project is happening — and therefore, of course, from the culture that *exists*.

When we begin a building project, our clues about what should be built, what should be done next, must come not only from the land but from society, too, and from the culture where this is being done. We are faced with the empty canvas, and we puzzle about what to do. It is the human family which makes us build a house, it is the concept of transportation and community which makes us seek roads and sidewalks; it is the way that people are in their custom and behavior, which provides the all-important physical subtleties. So, the response to the land, even if it is to be structure-preserving, a true unfolding process, must be rooted, always, in the whole, in the cultural and human whole *and* the land *and* the ecological and natural whole *and* the physical wholeness of that place which forms the context of our work.

3 / PATTERN LANGUAGES

About twenty-five years ago, my colleagues and I invented a class of theoretical systems modeled on the generative systems used in traditional society. We called them pattern languages.[4] A pattern language is essentially a way of defining generic centers, and then using them, sequentially, in design projects. The entities we called *patterns* were — albeit in an early formulation — somewhat similar to the entities I now call *centers*. One might say that every pattern which was defined under that theory was, in effect, a rule for making or partly making some important type of center, necessary to the life of a living human environment.

The theory of pattern languages was first put forward in A PATTERN LANGUAGE and in THE TIMELESS WAY OF BUILDING. Secondary statements of the theory were published in HOUSES GENERATED BY PATTERNS, A PATTERN LANGUAGE WHICH GENERATES MULTI-SERVICE CENTERS, and THE OREGON EXPERIMENT.[5] There are, in addition, a great number of recent publications by many other authors who have used these ideas and built on them during the last twenty years. Many are in the field of architecture.[6] In recent years a rich and varied addition to the literature has come in from computer scientists, writing in the field of software design.[7]

The essential ideas of pattern language theory are the following:

1. In traditional cultures, successful environments were always built by using pattern languages. They showed people how to make an almost infinite variety of buildings by combining and recombining the patterns, and contained within the process a modest guarantee that the buildings would be successful. Hence the great variety and beauty of buildings built by traditional societies.

2. Each culture had its own pattern language. The pattern languages reflected differences from culture to culture, and often nearly embodied the culture as a whole, in the form of rules which defined the spatial structure of the built environment.

3. The patterns were, for the most part, based on human needs, understanding, necessity. They reflected the deep practical daily concerns of people and were, as rules, expressed in a form which made it possible to put these things into the built environment in an immediate, practical, and effective form.

4. At the same time, although patterns vary from culture to culture, and while human needs vary and are highly specific in different human cultures, there is a core of material — a central invariant structure — which is common to all cultures. A portion of this invariant core — or at least a sketch of such a thing — is described in A PATTERN LANGUAGE.

This much of the theory is descriptive. But for the most part, the main purpose of the pattern language theory was not descriptive, but *prescriptive*. We discovered that it is possible to create pattern-language-like systems, artificially.

That is:

5. It is possible to create pattern languages for our own time, which, like traditional languages, embody knowledge, cultural subtlety, human need, and empirical information about the structure of living environments, in a form which may then be used to generate living centers by a combinatorial unfolding process.

6. It is possible to invent and create new pattern languages, artificially, by trying to see what new patterns will solve problems that exist in a given context. Although these may be new, in the sense that they are newly defined, many of them may, obviously, be versions of ancient patterns, familiar in different cultures, but so deep that in some form they are still relevant to our new era and new settings.

8. The objectivity of the patterns is context-sensitive, and always includes a built-in reference to the context for which that pattern works.

9. The patterns, because of their explicitness, allow discussion, debate, and gradual improvement of the material.

10. The artificial language will work well only to the extent that it embraces *a whole* — that is to say, to the extent that it comprises everything that needs to be said about a given building situation, and that the various patterns it contains work together as a whole system, which accounts for all morphology that is required to design, plan, design, or make, a complete building of that type and its immediate surroundings.

11. These artificial languages, like traditional languages, can then be used to steer processes of design and building, just as traditional languages played that role in traditional society.

12. For *any* new building project it is necessary to construct such a language, merely to provide a clear functional basis for the character and organization of the building. The language that is written down, at the beginning of a project may be invented from scratch, composed of known languages that have been re-combined, or may be a modification of a known language developed earlier. This will vary, according to the degree that the project is new, not yet fully understood, or old and familiar.

One might say that every new pattern defined under the theory of pattern languages is a rule for creating a certain type of (new) living center, needed and appropriate in a given range of contexts. More precisely, one may express the relationship of the two theories like this: Each pattern is a rule which describes a type of strong center that is likely to be needed, on a recurring basis, throughout a particular environment or class of environments. Further, a pattern not only describes a recurring center, but also describes a relation between *other* generic centers. The pattern both describes a generic *center*, and describes a generic *relation* among other generic centers. But it must be remembered that the pattern describes a *generic* center, not a particular center. In this sense the pattern is not so much like an element in an erector set, but more a rule for making a certain kind of center capable of making an infinite number of particular centers of the same type, whenever they are needed.

4 / PATTERNS AS GENERIC CENTERS AND THE EVOLUTION OF NEW CULTURE

Let us now ask how we may go about *creating* a system of patterns or generic centers to provide the elements for a given building process?

A living process only rarely creates living centers from scratch. In most cases, the living process makes use of solutions or partial solutions to previously encountered problems, in the form of pre-established coded schemes, or rules for making instances of generic centers.[8] The process then uses these generic centers again and again as it encounters different real-world situations. In organic nature, this is familiar. A gene is an organism's way of remembering how to form previously successful adaptations in ensuing generations of new organisms. The gene essentially remembers, and allows re-use of, a generic solution to a recurring problem. In architecture, traditional pattern languages played the same role. When we build a house, or a door, or a path, or a garden, these words describe worked-out culturally defined generic centers — pattern-like concepts which can be generated in a thousand forms to make actual centers in the world. The good environments in traditional society could be built because people had pictures of what worked; these pictures were agreed upon, and used and re-used, over and again.

Memorized nuggets of solution, like the patterns in traditional society, like genes in the growth of organisms, are necessary to any complex adaptive system and its process.[9] But in architecture the use of re-usable patterns does not only occur in *living* process. After all, damaged 20th-century building process, too, had its patterns — for example, many principles of traffic, building, and planning that were (and are) in use. The trouble is, of course, that many of these present-day patterns did not lead to creation of living structure, but rather the reverse — because they were based on criteria for success such as profit or insurance or limited managerial efficiency, which had little to do with the fitness of the living structure as a whole. For example, the common practice of placing motels and apartment buildings over at-grade parking, common in the United States during the 1970s and 1980s, was efficient because it was the cheapest way to do it. But it caused serious damage to the living structure of the pedestrian world and community fabric.[10]

The key difference between the patterns which arose in the 20th-century profit-oriented system and those which must accompany a living process, is that in a living process the patterns define types of centers which reinforce, support, bring out the life of the whole.

For a society to have living processes, attention to the whole must once again become the framework, so that the system of patterns which are used as support for the living process acts together to take care of the whole. Only this will make the living whole a possible outcome.

The crux of the whole thing is that we seek patterns which are *good*, patterns which will generate life when we create them in a building built in the context we are facing.

In our modern world, where societies are often in flux, the stability and coherence of such a traditional society is rarely found. Instead, people are usually struggling to create for themselves a system of coherent environmental objects and spaces, in which they can live well, be comfortable, and feel at ease.

But this means that people must *create* (artificially) what was taken for granted in traditional society: a system of patterns describing centers which can form the backbone of a new wholeness in a new society. Equally, the ecologists and biologists and forest management people try to create a system of patterns for centers which will provide the underpinning of a living ecological communities; educators create patterns for centers like classrooms, seminars, group discussion, individual education, which might provide the underpinning of a stable and healthy process of education; transportation experts try to create a system of new effective patterns for freeways, roads, parking. Throughout society people are working to create the basic underpinning of what may be a healthy world, capable of being coherent, realized within new building forms; capable of sustaining new kinds of community, family, society. And of course the patterns which are being created — and the centers which these patterns describe — vary from nation to nation, from village to village, from culture to culture, from subculture to subculture within the mosaic of a modern metropolis like London or Tokyo or San Francisco.

The process of finding these deep generalized culture-borne centers, discussing them, evaluating them, settling on them, and then applying them to the construction of the world, is a major part of the work of creating any physical part of the world, large or small, collective or private. It is, necessarily, the first and most essential part of the general unfolding process which takes place as we construct our world.

5 / HUMAN CULTURE AS A PART OF PHYSICS

In what follows, I shall argue that the process of defining a good pattern language, is not only related to culture but to wholeness, and that culture in relation to wholeness, is not merely social but a part of physics. This will seem an esoteric point. But I need to make this point for the following reason. Throughout this book, I have been arguing that living structure comes about only from the evolution of wholeness through structure-preserving transformations. For consistency, then, I need to be able to say that the definition of patterns, itself, as an activity, is also either structure-preserving or not, since this will be the basis of our ability to make *good* patterns — all this in the hope that we can then strive to make sure that our efforts to define new and better pattern languages are, indeed, structure-preserving.

But further, in order to make sense of the idea of structure-preserving transformations, in a realm as subtle and non-physical as culture, I need to argue that culture itself, and the wholeness which culture induces in the world, is as physical as the rest of wholeness. Only if we have a glimpse, at least, of that idea, will we be able, with all our energy, to focus on the problem of defining patterns which are indeed structure-preserving to present-day culture, yet searching, pointing towards, some new culture — and that the culture-wholeness system, too, can be considered as more alive, or less, so that the patterns we define contribute to the creation of a living world.

To understand all this with sufficient clarity, we must go back to the definition of wholeness and try to see how wholeness is influenced by culture.

Suppose I am sitting in my living room. The big chairs, the carpet, the tables, the windows, form centers in the room. These centers are more or less congruent with the way my family and I use the room. But suppose now that I have invited two friends from India to tea, and I am sitting with them. In their minds may be a cultural pattern, or predisposition, to sit on the floor. In India, the floor is more salient, more of a habitable space, than it is in California. My friends carry this in their minds.

While my friends are in the room, the wholeness has changed. The saliency of the tables, and the saliency of the table-chair system in the room has decreased slightly; the presence of half-formed centers nearer to the floor, perhaps a system of centers which includes cushions, carpet and the floor, has increased. So the wholeness, which is the system of *all* the centers with their relative strengths, is changed. I do not mean that while we are sitting there our *idea* of the world has changed, or that our image of the world has changed. In this example, I mean that, while those people are having tea in my living room, the living room *itself* has changed. Its *physics* has changed slightly.

To make sure that this point is clear, I shall give a more dramatic, purely physical example. Imagine a chair in a room. As an experiment, I get a big ball of scrap iron, on a rope, and hang it so that the scrap iron is hovering near the seat of the chair. In conventional thinking, the chair is unchanged. I have simply brought a bundle of scrap iron near the chair. But seen from the point of view of wholeness, the situation is quite different. When the chair stands by itself, there is one set of most salient centers in space. The chair in its wholeness is then defined by this system of salient centers. When I bring the scrap iron towards the chair, the wholeness changes. Suddenly, for instance, the bowl-shaped seat of the chair is less coherent as a center than it was before. New centers, formed by the scrap iron, have meanwhile become *more* salient. New configurations have become more vivid, old configurations are less vivid. As a result the chair itself has changed. Its wholeness has changed, because the entire system of centers is altered: if I view "the" chair as defined by its wholeness, the chair itself has changed.

This is a new point of view. It is no longer true to say that the same chair is there, and has merely been juxtaposed with some scrap iron. Instead since the new wholeness is altogether changed, and since the chair, properly seen, *is defined by the wholeness*, the chair after the scrap iron is a different chair from what it was before, even though the scrap iron is not touching it. Its space, and the system of salient centers have been reconfigured. It has changed.

Although it could seem like a small revision of terminology to see the world like this, it is a profound change of consciousness of the world as a whole. It recognizes that wholeness is a very subtle structure, changing all the time, and vulnerable to very small encroachments in its surroundings. What we see as the physics of the chair, its mathematical structure, then appears subtle and vulnerable: it is not constant and fixed. It is changing, subtly, all the time, as influences from the world around enter the picture, and modify the relative salience of different centers in and around the chair, thus forming, re-forming and altering the wholeness which was "the chair."

In the light of this example, let us consider a more drastic cultural example than before. Point Lobos is a beautiful small peninsula near the Big Sur, California. Consider the wholeness of this place at two different epochs, one as we know it today, the other as it was at the time of the Yurok Indians. The Yurok had a very strong affinity for rocks, trees. These things entered into their lives in a profound and practical sense, and their life was intertwined with them; each thing in the world was, for them, its functional character: a certain rock was "fishing rock," a certain tree was "meat-smoking-wood-tree" and so on. Let us now imagine such men going to Point Lobos, today a park with rocks, cypresses, seals swimming off the coast, chipmunks, waves, pebbles. We view this as a place of a natural beauty. The salient centers are the paths, seals, cypresses. Each of these things has its saliency, as a tourist attraction, as a precious nature preserve. But at the time of the Yurok, the relative saliences were different. The rocks and seals and fish formed centers of a different character and different saliency. Thus, at that time, the wholeness was a different wholeness. The wholeness, made as it is from the centers that exist in that place, each with its different saliences, was *actually* different. Like the chair, modified and changed when the scrap metal hangs in front of it, the world of Point Lobos as a physical system was something different then from what it is today.

When that place was inhabited by the Yurok, the relative saliencies of centers had one structure. When it is inhabited, as it is today, by us modern-day Californians in nylon shorts, with our ideas about the world, the saliencies are different. Above all, the place is now different because its wholeness is now different. It does not merely *seem* different, or have a different human picture of it. It *is* different. Mathematically, it is a different thing.

If, then, we seek to allow the world to unfold, thus creating life, it is this, the subtle, modified wholeness, affected as it is by culture, which must then unfold truthfully, to produce a living thing. The wholeness is, in large part, defined by the culture of that moment. *The proper unfolding of wholeness is both an unfolding of space from the culture which exists, and an unfolding of a new (future) culture from the culture of the present.* And all this is to be defined by the pattern language which reflects the inner needs and inner character, of the human and physical situation.

6 / DISCOVERING NEW PATTERN-LANGUAGES: HOW TO DRAW A VISION OF THE FUTURE FROM THE STUDY OF THE PRESENT

There was always one great difficulty with the theory of pattern languages, and with the languages my colleagues and I, and others, published. *Where did the patterns come from?*

Much of our early work implicitly made use of the idea that good patterns were to be derived, somehow, from existing culture, thus ensuring a relation to the subtleties of culture variation, and preserving things that were good and important, which had been swept aside in the onrush of techno-civilization. But there was always hanging over this process, a sword of Damocles. If — as a procedure — one takes the patterns from existing culture, then one merely reiterates what is being built. That is not *necessarily* good.

Who is to say which bits of culture are to be preserved, and which bits laid aside? In many cases the reason for studying patterns in the first place was to define better patterns, deeper and better generic centers, in the hope of making a more sustaining, more life-giving environment. But these patterns which we discovered were obtained partly by judgment.

I have said earlier (Book 1, Preface, pages 17–18), that the patterns in A PATTERN LANGUAGE were judged by many to be *true* in some sense. But this truth was of a new type, which recognized the life of a situation, or of a building, as a real thing. The truth of a pattern had to do with the question, "Does injection of this pattern into contexts of the stated type, in fact make these envi-ronments more alive?" This required making *judgments* about generic centers and the degree to which they sustain life, and judging which generic centers do the most to create, or contribute to, the life of the environment!

So how was one to find good patterns? Was this a process of observing existing culture — hence very conservative? Was it an arbitrary process — without a solid basis that one could determine? Or might it be a process where one could somehow make legitimate judgments about culture and society as they are, yet then use these observations to move forward to a new state, in a non-arbitrary way? In this latter case, which was perhaps our hope, one seemed to face the most profound and disturbing moral problems, since it was not clear how one could ever reach "the truth" about such matters.

Was there, indeed, any way in which one might, by observation of culture *as it is*, decide in what direction that culture *ought* to go, in the future? Could one, then, draw the future from the present, by any kind of objective process?

This is of course, exactly what the unfolding process seeks to do. But at that time, twenty years ago, the idea that there might be an unfolding process which would allow one to derive the patterns (which were to generate the structure of present and future environments) from the wholeness of *existing* culture, and so solve this problem, was never explicitly addressed.

7 / A NEW LANGUAGE FOR HOUSES IN PERU

For the sake of an example of how this process goes, let me describe what my colleagues and I did when we visited Peru in 1969. We were in an international competition, organized by the United Nations, to design low-cost houses for Peruvian families. There were 30 competitors,

Activity nodes

Car-pedestrian symbiosis

Car-pedestrian symbiosis

Shops on the corners

one from each of 15 countries outside Peru, and 15 Peruvian architects. We were the American team. To do the preliminary work, our team of four Americans went to live in Lima for a month. Each of us found a family to live with, and we met every night in a room we rented in Lima to compare notes, and write down what we knew.[11]

Before going to Lima, we read various anthropologists' reports about Peruvian society. It all seemed very exotic, but none of it seemed even remotely useful when we were living in our Peruvian families. For instance, ethnographic reports claimed that Peruvians kept the windows closed at night, even in hot weather, because they

didn't want ghosts to come through the windows with the night air. I never heard anyone say anything like this while I was living in the district of Victoria in Lima.

I found that I could imagine the Peruvians' feelings best just by being one of them. For instance it was a dangerous place, and it wasn't safe to leave windows open at night. That was really all the explanation one needed for why the windows had to be closed, even when it was sweltering hot. I found that if I looked at life from the point of view of being one of them, my *own* feelings, and my *own* knowledge of what had to be, was more reliable than anything else as an indicator of what was needed for a Peruvian family.

Family in the comedor, the heart of the house

Front door recesses

Watching the street: the activity which defines the mirador

The traditional Peruvian mirador

The *comedor* (dining room) in the middle of the house, where everyone came by, watched TV, or sat and talked on the way in or out, was a wonderful place. Being a member of that family, I knew that I needed and wanted such a room — and I could feel exactly where it needed to be in the house (in the middle of everything). I could feel that it needed to be positioned so that everyone came through it, on their way in, or their way out — I barely needed to ask any questions about this: *I could feel it*, all of it, but I could feel it only by being one of them. I, myself (as Chris Alexander) didn't have a house like that, and I don't want a house like that — because for me, in Berkeley, with my family, it would not have

made sense — it would not have been part of things, or part of the way my life works. But as a member of that Peruvian family, in the Peruvian culture, in the context of that family which I was a part of, it *did* make sense. It was natural, necessary, and I could feel its necessity, as part of *me*.

There were four of us making these observations. When we four team members, each making this kind of observation in the family where we were staying, compared notes, if anything didn't check out with all four of us, we rejected it. So, any mistake, caused by the idiosyncrasy of one family, or caused by our own idiosyncrasies as observers, got pushed out. What was left was only that stuff which corresponded to common feelings, felt by four different people, in four different families.

When we published the pattern language for the Peruvian houses, people in Peru said that our pattern language and our houses we designed from the pattern language were a more accurate reflection of Peruvian reality than even the Peruvian architects had managed.[12]

People wondered how we did it. But it was really very simple, and we did nothing more than I have just described. We identified the centers by getting so deeply into the situation that we could feel, *in our own bodies*, just which ones needed to be there.

The essential technique in the observation of centers, in any social situation, and in any culture, is to allow the feelings to generate themselves, inside *you*. You have to say, "What would I do if I were one of the people living here, what would it be like for me?" thus inserting yourself into the situation, and then using your own common sense and feelings as a measuring instrument.

Of course you must always check with people, explicitly. You cannot assume you are right. You have to check. On the other hand, checking doesn't mean just do what people say; their own sense of what is involved can also be in error. One must always go to the root, asking what is likely to create the most life, and maintaining a cautious skepticism, even while pursuing these difficult and soul-searching questions.

For concreteness, I reproduce the following list of patterns my colleagues and I identified in 1969 for Peruvian communities and houses:[13]

SUBCULTURE CELLS
DEGREES OF PUBLICNESS
LOOPED LOCAL ROADS
T-JUNCTIONS
DIRECT VISIBLE PARKING
TINY PARKING LOTS
PASEO
ACTIVITY NUCLEI
CAR-PEDESTRIAN SYMBIOSIS
PEDESTRIAN 50 CM ABOVE THE CAR

KNUCKLE AT ROAD CROSSING
CENTRAL MARKET
EVENING CENTERS
WALK-THROUGH SCHOOLS
VISIBLE KINDERGARTENS
WALLED SOCIAL GARDENS
CELL GATEWAY
MULTI-PURPOSE OUTDOOR ROOM
SHOPS ON CORNERS
CENTRIPETAL PEDESTRIAN PATHS
STREET FOOTBALL
FLOWERS ON THE STREET
LONG THIN HOUSE
PERIMETER WALL
CROSS-VENTILATED HOUSE
LIGHT ON TWO SIDES OF EVERY ROOM
PATIOS WHICH LIVE
TAPESTRY OF LIGHT AND DARK
THE SALA: INTIMACY GRADIENT
BATHROOM POSITION
PUERTA FALSA
FIESTA
STAIRCASE STAGE
THICK WALLS
FAMILY ROOM CIRCULATION
FAMILY ROOM ALCOVES
KITCHEN COMEDOR RELATIONSHIP
HOME WORKSHOP
TWO SERVICE PATIOS
ELBOW-ROOM KITCHEN
INDIVIDUAL BED ALCOVES
BED CLUSTERS
MASTER BED LOCATION
MASTER BEDROOM DRESSING SPACE
OLD PEOPLE DOWNSTAIRS
SERVANT SLEEPING SPACE
TWO-COMPARTMENT BATHROOM
CLOTHES-DRYING CLOSET
ENTRANCE TRANSITION
FRONT DOOR RECESSES
MIRADOR
FRONT DOOR BENCH
GALLERY SURROUND
TRANSLUCENT OPENING PATIO ROOF
LIGHT FROM TWO-STORY PATIO
SUNSHINE IN PATIOS

TWO-METER BALCONY
SHOP FRONT POSSIBILITY
RENTAL
CONTINUOUS FLOATING FLAB
MORTARLESS BLOCK WALL
COMPOSITE BAMBOO FOAM BEAM
COMPOSITE BAMBOO FOAM PLANK
SULPHUR REINFORCING
PLUMBING ACCUMULATOR
CONTINUOUS ELECTRIC OUTLET

What is the status of this list of centers? To some degree these centers are based on observation; they reflect Peruvian life as it was in 1969. Some are idealized, they contain our ideas of what might be a better way to arrange pedestrians and cars, or parking lots. Some are almost no more than ideas about how something might be done: the use of sulphur as structural reinforcement, for example. Still others are highly general — so much so that they were later generalized and included in A PATTERN LANGUAGE and remain, to this day, as observations of what makes people comfortable, almost all over the world. These, then, are rooted in psychology. Some are specific to climate and place, not exactly to culture.

So, this list of centers describes what we took, at that time, to be the core of the cultural background in Lima, into which houses had to fit, and from which houses might be generated. We tried — in our inexperienced fashion — to identify the centers which really existed in everyday life (SHOPS ON CORNERS), and those which

we believed existed in people's consciousness (THE SALA), and those which existed, latent, in dreams and traditions but were actually disappearing from modern Peruvian society. Others reflected modern aspects of Peruvian city life. FOOTBALL IN THE STREET described the peculiarly Peruvian form of street football, CAR-PEDESTRIAN SYMBIOSIS described the way that cars were, then, a focus of activity.

All in all, this list of centers is a partial picture of the wholeness which existed in Peru at the time. Yet, because these centers exist in culture, they have a carrying force, a generative power. They may be used to create copies of themselves, or many specific individual centers, in Peruvian communities and houses, which reflect and embody these generic culture-defined patterns. So a certain person may now build a sala in his house, and this sala then exists in his new house as a new center which has unfolded from the wholeness of the culture, and has, in its specific details, also unfolded from the particular geometry of the house and its setting in the street. Thus the fact that THE SALA is on the list of centers, gives birth to real centers in the world, *generates* them.

The culture-borne centers play a genetic role, not unlike the role played by genes in an organism. They describe what *is* — in a deep, inner sense. And they also describe how the world can be generated, to become congruent with people's inner feelings, aspirations, habits, and society.

8 / THE TYPE OF OBSERVATION WHICH LEADS TO DISCOVERY OF LIVING CENTERS: SEEKING TRADITION AND SEEKING THE NEW

What exactly is the relation between fact and fiction, cold observation and inspired vision, in these patterns? And to what extent is the traditional nature of some of these patterns necessary, or typical? To what extent is the appearance of a

hypermodern pattern like CAR-PEDESTRIAN SYMBIOSIS also typical of what must happen when true unfolding takes place? Let us concentrate on the extent to which the process of finding, discovering, these generic centers, is a true unfolding which can carry a culture from its past state, into the future.

Certainly the majority of these patterns from Lima were rooted in observation. We did not invent them. We *saw* them. We extracted them, as we thought, from the situations we saw around us, and in the people we were with.

Yet we were looking at people with charmed eyes. We asked ourselves, like psychiatrists, what was best in them, what were the things about the people we were with that were most deeply rooted, in which these people felt anchored. What conditions — we asked ourselves — did create for the people of Lima a condition in which they felt most whole, at peace with themselves? Of course, the answer to that question is bound to be both traditional and modern.

A person feels at peace in the special small living room near the front (the *sala*) because it reflects ancient Peruvian ways, the degree a stranger can come into the house, a comfortable, formal place, to "show." So of course people feel comfortable, deep in themselves, continuing something like this.

Yet at the same time, boys and girls and teenagers also feel comfortable leaning against the battered old cars, talking in the dust and mud of the unpaved street and glaring sun. And of course, they also feel at ease in a small narrow dark patios, where the glare of the incessant equatorial fog of Lima is cooled by the dark shade. And of course the family in the *comedor*, now gathered around the TV set, is something entirely new, yet also makes people deeply comfortable, because it is so real, so exciting, so everyday.

Which of these patterns, then, does the most to nourish the inner person? It is just those things, those generic centers, which fall out of the ground of their cultural existence, and yet maintain a thread with the past, stand on the past, because it is the most ancient and fundamental relationships and spaces, in which — in the end — people are most anchored — touched, brushed, transformed, by the hypermodern conditions of our age.

What we are looking for, in our attempt to find patterns NOW, for our lives, for our age, for new kinds of centers which will come about by unfolding from the wholeness of the present situation, are these deep patterns, half-existing, and yet carrying forward from the present, the truth about the present wholeness, preserving its structure, yet making themselves consistent with the new age.

9 / THE PROCESS OF FINDING A GOOD CENTER

To show in rather more detail the degree to which the list of centers that are unfolded from what lies deep in people's hearts — hence in their "culture" — is crucial in the life of a building, I will describe the evolution of a single center for a single project. This example happened in 1982, during the early stages of making a single private house in Berkeley, California, for André and Anna. At the moment when this event took place, we had already determined the size of the house (about 1150 square feet) and its overall volume. It was to be a three-story tower, 20 feet by 20 feet in plan on each floor. This was the only arrangement that would allow us to get the price down to within their budget, since it reduced both roof and foundation price.

We began to face the question of the spatial organization of the inside of the building. To do this, we had to find the most important major centers in the house. I asked Anna and André, What is the house made of? What are its principal rooms?

In the conventional wisdom of the mid-twentieth century (still active then, in 1982), it used to be normal to assume that every house had a kitchen, a living room, and a dining room, one for cooking, one for sitting, one for eating. But in the 1980's I began to notice that almost all our clients experienced some kind of extreme discomfort with the separation of these three functions.

The problems were manifold. The living room was often too formal. The dining room was too formal. The person cooking (in those days usually the wife) was too far from the action while cooking in the kitchen. And where were the children supposed to play?

One solution that had been common in mid-century America was to include a fourth room, "a family room" as an extension of the kitchen. However, this often left the formal living and dining rooms as deserted wastelands which no one ever used, which then became even more formal and even more dead.

I found that discussion of these problems often caused genuine anguish in almost every family, because as they discussed it family members began to see that the real forces in their lives were just not consistent with these conventional rooms like the conventional living room and dining room they may have grown up with. And yet emotionally, they were still attached to them. People felt more and more distress as they found out that the reality of their own day-to-day lives was not consistent with their emotional attachments to a given system of centers. The centers in people's *minds* were different from the ones in their *actions*.

In the case I am discussing, André quickly realized that this discussion was not merely a practical one. It was, as he put it, a discussion about his whole way of life. Anna felt the same. Both of them felt that their future as man and woman, as a couple and as a family, was on the line. The discussion of spaces, and centers, itself harmless, but profoundly disturbing in its implications for family life, for the relation of man to woman, and much more, created tremendous anxiety. We had to stop talking for a while.

After a three-day period of anguish, I took André and Anna to the site one day, and asked them to stand in the middle of the land, and asked them to visualize, to remember, the most wonderful house they had ever known, the place which made them most comfortable, and where — if they were there now — would make them feel most comfortable. I insisted that they keep their eyes closed while we were doing this, and try to abandon all their preconceptions. A smile came to André's face, and he turned to me, and said that he had begun to see, in his mind's eye, his grandfather's house in the south of France, a big room with a fire and a table, and with the south light streaming in from the outside.

There followed, in the discussion, an immense peacefulness and relaxation, when the idea arose of using a farmhouse kitchen like the one André had known in his grandfather's house in France.

At this moment, indeed, an entirely new way of life presented itself: A big table in front of an open fireplace, with the kitchen counter in the background, and food storage in a pantry,

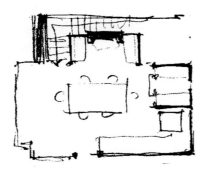

Diagram of the farmhouse kitchen, as first conceived after the pattern was created, 1982

The farmhouse kitchen for André and Anna and their children, as built, 1983

out of the way. Life was to revolve around this room. All the functions were redefined. Suddenly, the turmoil of confusion implicit in the various other versions of living room, dining room, kitchen and so on, fell into place in a comfortable and easy configuration, which was both practical and emotionally satisfying. This simple hard-won insight was completely responsive to the actual behavior and feeling of André's family.

At this moment we had the beginning of the house plan. And, indeed, in the finished house, it is this insight which provides the core of the life of the house.

We must see that what has happened here is something generic, not specific. The discussion was not about this particular house, and its geometry, as much as it was about the generic system of centers which made sense for this family, wherever they might live. Perhaps, by extension, it even touched questions of a general cultural nature, and how men and women in California were to live together. The new center which had

been formed, the farmhouse kitchen, changed the generic system of centers in the culture, and changed — by implication — the houses which would be generated by the culture. At least, anyway, as far as it touched Anna and André.

I must emphasize that this story describes the addition of only *one* new center to the list of centers for this house. The house was not defined by this one center. But the example suggests, by extension, how emergence of a list of items like this would gradually build up an understanding of how a given building is to get its life.

It is essential to realize that what happened in this case was not merely a redefinition of *function* (a phrase often used by architects). The process was powerful because it defined a new *center* — a *center* of function. Having arrived at an understanding of a particular *center* which must be in the house, our physical grasp of the essence of this house then became practical — and we were on the road to being able to make a house that would have a real life.

The example is typical, not just for houses, but for all kinds of building problems. It is the precise definition of building functions through new types of centers — and often the reconfiguration of the essential centers which have to carry the functions — which brings a project to fruition. It is not only a question of defining certain functions and then accommodating them in the geometry. *It is a question of rearranging the functions, redefining the nature and meaning of the way the thing works — which suddenly opens the door to a new comfortable life, which will actually work.*

In this example, we begin to see centers, not merely as nodes or central elements in a physical composition, but as nodes or centers of energy in the configuration of a life. As we see from the ex-ample, it is not enough to say that a building which comes to life solves its functional problems correctly. Instead the inner functions themselves, no less than the geometrical order, have to be re-arranged, created as centers, so that the truth of the real forces in the system can unfold.

I hope it is clear to the reader that the process which created this insight was, in a new guise, once again the fundamental process. It was because we asked ourselves, collectively, "What next thing can we do that will positively affect the life of this household?", and pursued this difficult question to its end, that we got the result, and were able to define this one new center — even though, at that stage, still abstractly.

10 / ESSENTIAL CENTERS NOT GIMMICKS

A living process works only to the extent that it is based on patterns which go to essentials: patterns which really create centers that support the deeper aspects of human life. A picture of wholeness will be a true picture only to the extent that it describes essentials. It is the *essential* content of the centers in a place which creates its life; their basic *content*, not their outward form. The life comes about when the centers have been chosen for their essential character. They go to the root of the life in a place. It is the essence which is contained in the centers that define the life.

To illustrate this point, on pages 358–59 I show six examples of generic centers from the small town of Ravello in Italy, pairing them with six examples of modern developer-construction in California. In each pair, the example from California is on the left, the example from Ravello is on the right. Italians, traditionally, have a way of doing things which often focusses on *essential* content. As a result, the centers they use are more concentrated, more spare, and go more to the heart of the matter, to the heart of the way a place or a building lives.

At first sight, the examples from Ravello seem crudely made. We may consider them rustic, or old-fashioned. However, most of them, though they look old, were made in the 20th century. No matter how crudely made they are, their essence is in their content.

For example, in the first picture, look at the flowerbed along the top of the wall. There is a walkway which goes from the upper street down past the cathedral, to the square. In this wall, there is a flowerbed, actually made as a channel in the top of the wall.

The effect of this flowerbed is incredible. It puts the flowers at eye level, just where you see them most intensely. Their smell is beautiful, just near your face. Walking alongside this wall, you have a center, the flowerbed, at the same height as your eyes, your nose. It is unforgettable. Compared with the powerful impact it makes on you, the exact design, or shape is totally unimportant. It is the choice of a strong center that might be called FLOWERBED AT EYE-LEVEL ALONG THE TOP OF THE WALL, which is the crucial thing.

Development: Redwood planter box, hexagonal for "design."

Ravello: Flowerbed growing in the top of a wall. The flowers are at eye-height for a passer-by.

Development: A bench made to impress

Ravello: A bench with a view

Development: Fancy railing with no purpose

Ravello: Ordinary gutter and drain—just right

Development: "Designed" light pole — made to impress

Ravello: Ordinary light and electric box — only for light

Development: Heavy-handed and authoritarian bollards and paving in developer-built place: they tell you what to do, and give no options.

Ravello: Flowerpots used as traffic markers in Ravello's square: they allow cars in, but suggest they should stay out. It works.

Development: Fancy balustrade from a pretentious house

Ravello: Painted steel rail in a Ravello palace: modest

In each of the examples, the "design" is less important than the *choice* of just *this* center. That is what governs the life and atmosphere of that place. If we look at the comparable details from a contemporary Californian suburb shown on the left of each pair, we may be astonished because in the Californian case the accent is so often on the non-essential image, not on the essential centers. On the left of each pair, one sees examples of developer architecture and postmodern "image" architecture, which put the accent on image, not on the essentials.

In the redwood planter box, the accent is on the box, not on the flowers. The box is supposed to create an impression of concern for plants. In the Italian case, the rough plastered trough for flowers is unobtrusive, what matters is the flowers. The flowers are intense, they are at just the right height to see them, smell them, experience them. The place stays in your memory.

In the fancy staircase balustrade, all the emphasis is on the *impression* which the balustrade will make — not on the problem of holding on. In the economical iron railing, which comes from an 11th-century palace, the essential thing is the beauty of the steps, and getting upstairs to the door.

In each pair of examples, the left hand one is image-conscious, and sterile; the right hand one is simple, often cheap, and goes to the guts of the situation in a way that matters, and in a way that has the capacity to enhance life. The right hand ones are real; the left hand ones are phony.

In addition, the Ravello centers illustrated on the right of each pair, are the ones whose presence is already latent in the culture. They go the heart of the structure that is already there, they summarize and encapsulate the essence of the real life that is going on in people's hearts.

11 / THE SYSTEM OF PATTERNS EMANATES AS A WHOLE

For a building project, it is not enough that individual patterns or generic centers solve essential problems and work well. In order for a system of patterns to provide the basis for a true unfolding from an existing situation, it is necessary that the system of centers works *as a whole*, emanates *as a whole* from the situation, and has the capacity to create a holistic and ordered system which is *coherent and complete*.

Whenever we define one center, it is always defined by other centers: a larger wholeness in which it is embedded, some centers which are parallel to it in scale, and some smaller centers that cooperate to bring it to life. Defining one center actually means seeing, at least in rough outline, all these relationships together, and sensing the way that they cooperate to create the whole. In some instances, we might not yet know what subsidiary centers are needed to make the center in question come to life, but we do know that something needs to be there. We may pose it as a question for further investigation. Therefore, even when making the first attempt at defining a list of centers we need to see the system as a whole. When it is written in such a form we can test it. Does it form a coherent whole in our mind? Can we envisage it? Does it seem to answer the needs and latent centers as we understand them from the project's requirements? Does the system as a whole create a life-filled entity which will make the purpose of the project meaningful? Finally when reading the list of centers, does it shed some light on the project itself? Do we understand better what are the problems felt by the people who initiated the project, the deep reasons for its existence? If those questions are answered in the affirmative, than we have a good beginning.

The following example, a project for the cultural center of the city of Samarkand, shows what it means to focus on this larger wholeness.

The project, sponsored by a competition for

Samarkand held by the Aga Khan foundation in 1991, called for the reconstruction of a central city area about 1000 meters by 500 meters, and which was to contain a great variety of activities that would form a new city core.

I wrote the following "poem" — a list of partially formed centers — at the very beginning of our work on the Samarkand project, almost the day we began, long before we had worked it through.

1. It is a sequence of public squares, gardens, and buildings, which will form the new center of the city of Samarkand, uniting historic and traditional buildings and quarters.

2. There is a new dimension here, a center of spiritual life. It is not a commercial center, not a cultural center, not a religious center in the old idea. It is not a convention center. Somehow, this new center of the city of Samarkand, unites old and new, weaves together the thread of the silk road, the tomb of Timur the Great, with the modern world, and a vision of the world in which comfortable human concern, and a spiritual awareness of the importance of life, is visible, felt, and active.

3. It is an inspiring place to go. A place of pilgrimage, which will receive visitors from the five continents, in increasing thousands.

4. A network of beautiful paths, formed by columns, colonnades, brick walls, buildings, gardens. This network of paths, which passes across the whole area, is formed by the building masses which arise out of it, and by formal gardens.

5. Do the paths open into courtyards, ponds, gardens, hidden places? Are they formed only by mysterious buildings, rising in color, tile, and marble? Are there figures, statues, animals, Gods, people, statues standing at the places where the paths cross?

6. Are the animals themselves covered with mysterious animals?

7. Is there any reference to voyages?

8. The main thing one is aware of is a network of green and beautiful jewel-like streets. Each has lush trees, seats, platforms, streams.

9. These green streets, made by their trees, benches, sitting platforms, and edges, form a lacework of places to walk. They are like parks, long and narrow, you can explore for many hours, walking around these streets.

10. Each one of the streets arrives on some new treasure. Each building is like a treasure, arrived at by the green streets.

11. Samarkand, historically, and in the time of Ulugh Beg, was a crossroads of the world. In the Tang dynasty period, every conceivable exotic substance, or idea, or artifact, or art on earth, came through Samarkand. No matter where it went, or where it came from, it went through Samarkand.

12. Somehow, then, one may imagine these green heavenly paths, as a network — almost a mythical bazaar in which reference to these many exotic substances exists.

13. The blue tilework of the Timurids, the hand-painted blue tiles, with small black, yellow, and white detail, on mud brick — these tiles, and the yellow bricks are in evidence on walls, domes, courtyards throughout the center. It is a thread which connects.

14. The whole network of paths is almost like a forbidden city. A place which is walled, punctured at very occasional places which allow one to enter, a special area that contains its own magic.

This was the very first list I wrote for the project. After trying to understand the system of patterns as a whole, and as we worked on it, the list was then transformed as a whole to modify the global feeling and content of what this place was going to be — as it matured in our understanding. We kept on thinking of the *whole* way of life which would be created by these patterns, and then changed the patterns, intensified them, improved them, made the centers more explicit, as our understanding of this whole increased. We kept on working at it until the living whole revealed itself, as fully as we could manage, in the list of centers. After much more work, the list — or pattern language — for the project ended up with the following centers: Note, the earlier statements are written in the active form, in italics, which sketches the content of each possible center. The second, longer list which

A model of the new city center for Samarkand built for the Aga Khan competition. This model embodied, in diagrammatic form, the geometric meaning of the pattern language we wrote for Samarkand, 1983.

follows is given in small capital letters, to indicate that by this stage the ideas had materialized and solidified as *centers* — as potentially solid objects which were reliable and recognizable as entities.

THE FORBIDDEN CITY
MASSIVE SURROUNDING WALL
THE FESTIVAL PROMENADE
VIEW TO REGISTAN
THE OBSERVATORY
THE ORCHARD OF PEACH TREES
MAIN TERRACE
OUTDOOR THEATER
CRAFT SCHOOL AND BAZAAR
THE INNER CITY
SMALL HOTELS
WALLED PATH
MUSIC SCHOOL
INNER CITY GATE
FIVE SMALL WALLED GARDENS
CHAIKHANAS
MAIN STREET FROM THE REGISTAN
FOUNTAINS AND STREAMS
EXHIBITION HALL
COVERED BAZAAR
THE LIBRARY
THE MANUSCRIPT MUSEUM
ARCHED BRIDGE

THE MAIN BRIDGE
SOCCER AND GAMES
WALL OF ARCHES
GATES IN THE OUTER WALL
THE HOSPICE OR KULLIYE
INNER PART OF THE FORBIDDEN CITY
BLUE-TILED WALKS
THE MOSQUE

The photograph above shows the model we made for the project, on the basis of this pattern language.

This example gives an idea of the vital role which generic centers can play in creating a whole. In this example these centers, *the list alone*, creates an almost magical atmosphere. As soon as we name them, *just from naming them*, we begin to feel the aura of the place. The patterns are evocative. It doesn't even matter in what order we take the centers. The mere list, itself, already conveys a profound atmosphere, and defines, in great degree the atmosphere of the place which will be made up of these centers. It creates the atmosphere right away. It is these centers which play the defining role. In Book 3, chapter 4, I show a drawing I made with my apprentices to show the physical character of this system of centers when they are realized.

Our entire approach during the pattern language stage of work on a living process, is to get a glimpse of the centers that will make the building which is to be designed, come to life *as a whole*. We keep on making lists, doing experiments, trying to find out what the list will generate, trying to find out the key centers, until we have a system of centers in mind, which, when it is let loose in a real situation, will make something that comes to life.

The essence of the point, is to find — or create — a set of centers which, together, will generate a complete and coherent object of the type we are looking for. We keep trying out our rudimentary list to see what sort of whole this list of centers will generate. We then use intuition and feeling to judge the deficiencies in the whole which is created, to make us aware of *more* centers that still need to be created.

12 / THE EISHIN SCHOOL PATTERN LANGUAGE

In the next (and last) example, I give excerpts from a much longer language, the list of centers for the Eishin school in Japan, constructed between 1983 and 1985. The full list contained about 200 patterns, and defines a way of life for a high school and university.[14] At our client's request it was different from any existing school in Japan at that time (1981). We can see and feel, merely by reading the names of the centers and their rough description, that what was going to happen in this new school would be very different from what we are familiar with.

Above all we can see this new way of life as a *complete* whole. The way it works is completely defined by the list of centers. Thus in all important aspects the *life* of the new school is *contained* in these centers, and the list of centers defines this way of life it its entirety. This gives us tremendous insight into the vast extent to which the life of any given building or building complex, is defined by the list of centers which it will contain.

I. GLOBAL CHARACTER

· *There is an outer boundary which surrounds the site.*
· *Inside the outer boundary, there is an inner boundary which surrounds a smaller area; about one-fifth of the whole site.*
· *The area inside the inner boundary is called the inner precinct. It is a dense area where the school and college have their major buildings.*
· *Between the inner and outer boundary is the outer precinct: an area filled with gardens, sports fields, and various freestanding outer buildings.*
· *The buildings and the site are given their character by stone foundation walls, wood columns, white walls, a few special places with red lacquered wood, wide overhanging roofs, dark roof surfaces, stones and grass on the ground.*

2. THE INNER PRECINCT

· *The entrance to the inner precinct begins at the outer boundary. At a key point in the outer boundary, there is a gate.*
· *This main gate is a building.*
· *From the main gate to the inner boundary, there is an entrance street. The entrance street is flanked with walls or trees, and is extremely quiet.*
· *Where the entrance street meets the inner boundary there is a second gate.*
· *Inside the second gate, there is a public yard. This public yard is formed by a great hall, which forms the main side of the yard.*
· *Beyond the public yard and through a third gate is the essential center of the school and uni-*

versity. This essential center is reached through several layers, which have been described. And it contains further layers and further levels of quietness, within itself.

· *This essential center is fairly large — itself a world, bounded, within the inner precinct and formed by paths and gates. This essential center contains a large part of the high school and a large part of the university.*

· *Opening from this essential center are those parts of the university and high school which are specialized and separate.*

· *Since the essential center is at one and the same time, the heart and crossroads of the school and university, it has the rough form of a cross — formed by crossing paths. Because it resembles the character* ta *(a cross in a square) we have therefore named it the Tanoji Center.*

· *At the crossing of the streets and paths which form the Tanoji Center, there is a smaller center: This place is the kernel of the busy part of the Tanoji Center.*

· *And, opening from the far side of the Tanoji Center is a higher and most peaceful place that we call the college cloister. This is the inner sanctum of the university, and the most peaceful place of all. It is chosen to be in a place which invites contemplation.*

· *Also opening directly from the Tanoji Center is the homebase street. The homebase street is a wide, lively, sunny street formed by the individual home room buildings where the high-school students have their classes.*

· *Opening through gates on another side of the Tanoji Center is a lawn. This lawn, especially for the use of college students, is surrounded by the college buildings, and leads directly to the lake.*

· *The lake is a peaceful place, to rest. . . .*

. . . . . .

A further excerpt from the pattern language gives some of the details:

. . . . . .

8. INTERIOR CHARACTER

· *The interior character is warm and subdued: wooden columns, floors and walls in places; pale yellow wall color, comparable to golden chrysanthemums, paper or silk; near-white sliding screens and ceilings.*

· *Floors of many buildings are raised, slightly more than usual, off the ground.*

· *Classrooms have polished wooden floors, or carpets, and shoes are not worn inside the classrooms.*

· *All homebase classrooms have big windows facing south.*

· *Many rooms have gallery spaces to one side, where light comes in beyond, and shines through screens.*

· *Many walls and other surfaces are wooden, with natural unfinished wood.*

· *The classrooms and other rooms are furnished with very solid wooden desks, which several students share.*

· *In the larger buildings, there are mirrors where students see themselves.*

· *Outside the buildings, there are often flower beds.*

· *And inside, here and there, throughout the school, there are surprising soft highlights of color, shining out among the subdued colors of the rest, a figure painted in pale kingfisher blue in one place; a golden yellow iris in another.*

The full original pattern language which we constructed in 1982 contained about 200 centers.[15] These centers, completely governed and defined the life of the school. Even before we had any idea about the physical configuration of the buildings, their shape, or design, or the way these centers were to be made real in space, it was already obvious that the school was going to be given its life to an enormous degree, merely by this list of centers. Regardless of the particular architecture which followed from this list of generic centers, or the *way* these centers would later be embodied in a real place with real form,

In the rain on the Eishin campus, students hurrying from class to class. Christopher Alexander, 1985

the list of centers *alone* already defined the essentials of the place and its way of life, and its *degree* of life, to an enormous degree.

Once again I go to a single detail in this list of centers. One of the patterns in this pattern language for the Eishin school, describes the fact that classrooms are separate buildings, and implies, therefore, that it is will be necessary to walk in the rain to go from class to class.

One could have made a different choice, to keep the classrooms together, and to protect students and teachers from all rain. The key centers in the two cases are these (here again I use small capitals to emphasize the entity-like character of the centers):

A standard Japanese high school contains these patterns:

CASE I

ONE BUILDING FOR ALL CLASSROOMS

CLASSROOMS ATTACHED

WALLS OR FLOORS BETWEEN
    CLASSROOMS

COVERED PASSAGES PROTECTED
    FROM RAIN

Instead, the new kind of high school formed by our pattern language contains these patterns:

CASE 2

SEPARATE CLASSROOM BUILDINGS

EACH BUILDING LIKE A HOUSE

GARDENS BETWEEN CLASSROOMS

PATHS CONNECTING CLASS-
    ROOMS EXPOSED TO RAIN

365

In what sense is the second list more essential than the first? *It is more essential, because it deals with feeling, and at a much deeper level.* The second system of centers is more deeply connected to human feelings *as they really are*. This large topic is taken up fully in chapter 14.

It is also useful to understand that the second system is rooted more in the wholeness of the Japanese culture itself. Before we began our work in Japan, the old Eishin school (on its previous site) was arranged like case 1. There was one huge block with many classrooms. But if one examined that wholeness carefully, one could see that within it (the world defined by the case 1 patterns), the truth of the second set of centers (the world defined by the case 2 patterns) lay there, latent, waiting to be derived. The desire for autonomy of different teachers, and different classes was already a real thing in their lives. The enlivening character of the rain on people's faces was even then a real thing, observable in life. The deadening effect of being in passages all day long was also a real thing, also observable. The centers of autonomous classrooms in the second list were latent in the actual existence of the people and the place *as it already was*. The centers of rain on your face and centers of unprotected paths were latent in the actual existence of the people and the place, *as it all was*. The centers of gardens between classrooms was latent in the actual existence of the people and the place *as it actually was then*.

What, then, defines essential centers and distinguishes them from trivial centers? The answer, briefly put, is this. The essential centers are those whose presence is already latent in the field — which go the heart of the living structure that is already there — which summarize, or encapsulate, the essence of the real life which is going on.

Of course, in a period of history where people like to stress the arbitrariness of all things, such an idea may seem doubtful or impossible to accept. But the crux of all life is, nevertheless, the difference between recognizing the essential thing and separating it from the trivial thing.

13 / THE DEEP NATURE OF PATTERNS AND PATTERN LANGUAGES

A pattern language is a created thing. It is a work of poetry, a work of art. It is potentially as profound in its way as a building can be.

The intensive character of questioning people, to find their deep wishes and deep needs, might, mistakenly, be thought to be some kind of market research, or opinion survey. But the power of the pattern languages, such as the one developed for the Eishin campus, hinges on something very different which they contain: A geometrically constructive aspect of their emotion and their content.

A well-constructed, deeply constructed pattern language has the power, within it, to help people visualize geometric configurations that are whole. This arises, because, deep inside the elements of the pattern language there are references to, and hints of, the fifteen transformations. Thus, the agenda of the pattern language not only aims to record and objectify the positive things and relationships which are needed by a given culture, or a given population, or a given group of people. If it is any good, it also has, within it, a driving force which will make geometrical wholeness easily visible and more easily attainable. This arises because the fifteen properties are embedded, sometimes loosely, sometimes precisely, in the patterns.

So a pattern language, if it has been well-constructed, sublimates the inner desires and necessities which have connection to our feelings and dreams, transforms them into geometry, expresses them in a deep enough way to make art of them, casts them in such a way that they have the power to become living flesh in buildings.

14 / LOOKING FOR GLIMPSES OF ETERNAL LIFE

The pattern language, then, is that aspect of the world which steers buildings towards the creation of a living state. For example, the decision implicit in the definition of high-school classrooms as far apart, makes it necessary to use umbrellas. And that, in turn, makes it inevitable that the students will feel the rain. Here we looked inside the culture, as it is, and tried to bring forward a deeper truth, a cultural reality beyond or inside the present cultural reality, yet legitimate and, I think, necessary, because it is more true to people's deepest feelings.

This rain on their faces is not harmful but beneficial. By experiencing the rain, they become more one with themselves: the existence of the rainy streets, the umbrellas. The umbrella-filled street is a being; it is a picture of the self, quite different in its poetic substance and in the life which is experienced there from the dry, air-conditioned perfect concrete-box schools and classrooms of the 1970's. Among the Italian examples from Ravello, the flowerbed in the top of the wall is a strange and unexpected thing. Yet it touches the heart immediately. If I ask myself which is closer to my self — these odd channels in the walls with flowers at head height where I can smell them, or the pristine flowerboxes of the developer's project — it is easy to answer that it is the Italian flowers on the wall top which are closer to my heart.

This is what it means to have centers which have life in them — that the entity defined by a pattern digs deep into the experience of life, and creates a feeling of life lived, life passed, the sadness and tranquility and happiness of actual life, raw as it is.

Before starting to make anything, or design anything, one has to choose and define the con-tent of the centers functionally and geometrically, and their relationships. This list of centers out of which the thing is to be made is sometimes expressed as a pattern language. But this is only one possible way of doing it. The main thing is that you must get clear what the essential centers are which will give the thing an actual profound *life*. Once you have that clear mentally, you can start the actual geometrical unfolding of the plan or the design.

Ultimately, the success of your list of centers, your pattern language, determines whether or not the thing which is created will have life. So, the effort to make a list of centers is a way of trying to predict the way the life is going to go, and what it is going to depend upon. It succeeds if, indeed, life comes about because of it. And the list of centers — even before it serves to make a building — must be judged according to the likelihood of its creating life. This can be done. You can often tell just from looking at a list of centers that it may not produce life, because you can tell that it has obvious gaps, or problems, or misses the main point in some essential way.

Above all, what we are looking for are just those centers which will intensify the life of the place. To do this, we have to work, with a constant intuition about the life, at what is going to intensify this life. This can only be done in a spiritual state of mind. We shall arrive at the stuff which produces life only by having a sense, in us, of what will actually make life in the real thing.

The extent to which I am able to do this depends on the extent of my own mental and emotional awakening. I have to ask myself, first, What is real life in a person? What kind of thing will produce real, deep life in an event? What will bring real life to the conditions of a building, or garden, or street, or town? What kinds of events make us feel close to our own wholeness? And in the end my ability to ask these questions requires that I ask which kinds of centers will do the most to produce real spiritual life in people: which things, events, moments, kinds of centers, will create a spiritual awakening in a person or a person's life.

Finally, then, I am in the state of trying to see, like Bashō, what will most concretely reveal the most translucent inner being in a person.[16] When I eat, eat. When I walk, walk. I am trying to find those aspects of sight, sound, smell, the sandwich eaten on the back of the truck, the sun's rays on the bedroom floor, which will illuminate existence and make a person come in touch with his eternal life.

NOTES

1. The case that it is the defining elements or entities which define most of the structure in any given environment, was originally made in Christopher Alexander, DETERMINATION OF COMPONENTS FOR AN INDIAN VILLAGE (London, Pergamon, 1963).

2. The fact that every environment is given its essential life by the key generic centers, is now receiving wider and wider recognition. See also Christopher Alexander, Sandy Hirshen, Shlomo Angel, and Sara Ishikawa HOUSES GENERATED BY PATTERNS (Berkeley: Center for Environmental Structure, 1969). Also published in Christopher Alexander Sara Ishikawa and Murray Silverstein, A PATTERN LANGUAGE WHICH GENERATES MULTI-SERVICE CENTERS (Berkeley: Center for Environmental Structure, 1967). Christopher Alexander and Daniel Solomon et al., A CITY OF GARDENS: ORDINANCE FOR MULTI-FAMILY HOUSING IN PASADENA (Pasadena: City Planning Department, 1987).

3. Ken Costigan, "Pattern Language for the Trobriand Islands," Department of Architecture, Masters thesis, first written 1975, formally approved 1996.

4. Christopher Alexander, THE TIMELESS WAY OF BUILDING (New York: Oxford University Press, 1979); Christopher Alexander, Sara Ishikawa, Murray Silverstein, Ingrid King, Shlomo Angel, and Max Jacobson, A PATTERN LANGUAGE (New York: Oxford University Press, 1977).

5. See references in note 2.

6. Andrés Duany, Sarah Susanka, Dan Solomon, and others have also begun to recognize the importance of patterns as defining entities, and have put forward versions of the same idea in pattern books, provided as tools for planning in a growing number of communities.

7. Among the pioneering books on pattern languages in computer science: Erich Gamma, Richard Helm, Ralph Johnson, John Vlissides, DESIGN PATTERNS: ELEMENTS OF REUSABLE OBJECT-ORIENTED SOFTWARE (Menlo Park, California: Addison Wesley, 1995); James Coplien and Douglas Schmidt, PATTERN LANGUAGES OF PROGRAM DESIGN (Menlo Park, California: Addison Wesley, 1995); Richard Gabriel, PATTERNS OF SOFTWARE (New York: Oxford University Press, 1996).

8. John Holland has given an extraordinary and up-to-date mathematical account of the way schemata *must* appear in any successful adaptive system: ADAPTATION IN NATURAL AND ARTIFICIAL SYSTEMS (Cambridge, Mass: M.I.T. Press, 1992), especially 66-74.

9. Ibid.

10. In an investment-oriented economy, the profit motive can easily gain the advantage. Patterns which are good for profit, are easy to define. And they spread easily.

11. Discussion of Peruvian patterns in Alexander, Hirshen, Ishikawa, Angel, Coffin, HOUSES GENERATED BY PATTERNS was reprinted, in part, in David Lewis, THE GROWTH OF CITIES (London, Elek Books, THE ARCHITECT'S YEAR BOOK 13, 1971).

12. Juror's Report and Minority Report on the International Competition for Low-Cost Housing, United Nations, Lima, Peru, 1969–70.

13. From HOUSES GENERATED BY PATTERNS.

14. Taken from Christopher Alexander and Hajo Neis, BATTLE: THE STORY OF A HISTORIC CLASH BETWEEN WORLD SYSTEM A AND WORLD SYSTEM B, (New York: Oxford University Press, to be published).

15. The complete list, with discussion of the process used to obtain the pattern language and the patterns, will be published in BATTLE: THE STORY OF A HISTORIC CONFLICT BETWEEN WORLD-SYSTEM A AND WORLD SYSTEM B.

16. The reference to the poet Bashō is to *all* his work, but I should like to refer perhaps especially to THE NARROW ROAD TO THE FAR NORTH, a book of prose and haiku on Bashō's journey, in which the ordinariness and concreteness of existence is illuminated.

CHAPTER FOURTEEN

DEEP FEELING

THE AIM OF EVERY LIVING PROCESS IS,
AT EACH STEP, TO INCREASE
THE DEEP FEELING OF THE WHOLE

INTRODUCTION

We come now, to the most important and most profound aspect of living process. I believe it is the deepest issue in this book. I believe it is the most enlightening and appealing. Yet it may also prove, intellectually, to be the most controversial and the most difficult to accept.

The issue has to do with feeling.

I assert, simply, that all living process hinges on the production of deep feeling. And I assert that this one idea encapsulates all the other ideas, and covers all the other aspects of living process. It may also be said that this vision of living pro-cess is, or if true may turn out to be, in the end, of the greatest importance for the future of mankind.

Yet perhaps there is no other place in this book where the intellectual paradigm I offer is more at odds — at least on the surface — with the Cartesian paradigm. At first sight it would almost seem absurd to claim that every living process may be recognized, or measured in its degree of efficacy, according to the depth of its capacity to produce deep feeling. Yet I believe this is so.

1 / WHOLENESS AND FEELING

How, in practice, can a person keep paying attention to the whole; how can one achieve successful differentiation and structure-enhancing transformations at every step of a living process?

I have mentioned elsewhere that wholeness and "deep structure" are enormously difficult to see.[1] Especially in a complex, real-world case, the task of finding the most structure-enhancing step available is therefore, in practice, extremely hard.[2] Our current modes of perception are not always tuned to seeing wholeness in the world around us; and the exact definition of the structure of whole-ness — the system of centers at all scales, with their attendant degrees of life and coherence — is cumbersome and hard to grasp when we try to grasp it by analytical means. Yet in order to move forward, and to find agreement in larger, commu-nal projects, it is imperative that we do have a workable and practical method of seeing whole-ness, and assessing the degree to which any pro-posed next step does increase the life and whole-ness of an evolving structure. Otherwise there is no effective way of choosing the next step forward in any given process. How is this to be done?

This difficulty is experienced even in a small task like the ongoing work of a painting, even in the placing of the next brushstroke. The difficulty is more clearly experienced during the work of making an emerging building plan of a new design: how to take the next decision about content, position, size. And it is experi-enced most vividly in a large project when many people together are taking decisions and where — together — people must decide what next step will do most to preserve, extend, and enhance the life of a larger place in a city neighborhood.

Yet people in traditional society seem to have managed these tasks with less difficulty than we do. How were builders and artisans in traditional society able to pay attention to the whole? How could they stay focused on the life of the whole? What did they do to accomplish this? What did they do to make their actions structure-enhancing?

In part, we already have a theoretical answer to this question, as explained in Book 1, chapters 8 and 9. Each observer is able to judge the whole, to see and experience the whole, by paying attention to the question: Is the emerging building increasing *my own* wholeness? Is it increasing the feeling I experience when I am in touch with that thing? Is it becoming like a mirror of my own self? Is it becoming like the soul?[3]

But, less obscurely expressed, the extent to which a building is coming to life can be steered by the extent to which it has deep feeling in it, deep feeling that we experience. This can be done for any emerging entity — room, painting, garden, pottery bowl, plaza, table, window, street.

The living process can therefore be steered, kept on course towards the authentic whole, when the builder consistently uses the emerging feeling of the whole as the origin of his insight, as the guiding light at the end of the tunnel by which he steers. I am suggesting that if the builder, at each step of a living process, takes that step which contributes most to the feeling coming from the work, always chooses that which has the more profound feeling, then this is tantamount — equivalent — to a natural process in which the step-wise forward-moving action is always governed by the whole.

Roughly this, I am almost certain, is what traditional builders did. They paid attention to the *feeling* of the emerging structure: and thus were able to stay within the guidelines of the existing and transforming whole. Guided by feeling, they were able to function almost like nature: They were able to make each small step count in the emergence of a new unfolding whole.

For us, in our era, it is not so easy. The word "feeling" has been contaminated. It is confused with emotions — with feelings (in the plural) such as wonder, sadness, anger — which confuse rather than help because they make us ask ourselves, *which* kind of feeling should I follow? The feeling I am talking about is unitary. It is feeling in the singular, which comes from the whole. It arises in us, but it originates in the wholeness which is actually there. The process of respecting and extending and creating the whole, and the process of using feeling, are one and the same. Real feeling, true feeling, is the *experience* of the whole.

Being guided by the whole, and being guided by feeling, are therefore nearly synonymous. What I call feeling is the mode of perception and awareness which arises when a person pays attention to the whole. When people pay attention to the whole, they *are* experiencing feeling. It may seem far-fetched to suggest that all questions of city planning, engineering, transportation — not to speak of building — should be decided by feeling, by the feeling of the whole. But that is, indeed, exactly what I am proposing. It is an intelligent and practical way forward.

This principle may be formulated as an essential rule: *In any living process, or any process of design or making, the way forward, the next step which is most structure-enhancing, is that step which most intensifies the feeling of the emerging whole.* Feeling thus gives us human beings our access to structure-preserving transformations. It is the process of intensifying deep feeling in the whole which gives us direct access to the core of living process. Although extraordinary, if judged by the standards of 20th-century positivism, this process is nevertheless sober and exact.

2 / DEEP FEELING MUST BE THE CORE OF LIVING PROCESS

My emphasis on feeling is not meant to say that you or I, the architect or the builder or the user, should *express* our feelings when we are working.

During the early part of the 20th century there was a school of thought where a great deal was said about artists *expressing* their feelings, as if

---

ART AS EXPRESSION

THIS IS NOT VERY INTERESTING

puts feeling

artist———————————>into work

Not this

FEELING IN THE WORK OF ART

THIS IS ESSENTIAL AND IMPORTANT

generates feeling

the work——————————>in me

This is what must be happening

---

this was supposed somehow to be the purpose and pathway of art. Artists sometimes tried to do this by placing paint to record their emotions, throwing paint at the wall, pouring their emotion *into* the work. In each case the artist tried to send his feeling *into* the work, in the name of: "I am expressing my feelings." In all these cases the idea was that the feeling goes from the artist *into* the work while the work is being made.

Producing a building which *has* feeling is something different. Creating a building which works as a whole by using structure-preserving transformations through deep feeling is quite another matter. In this case it is not important whether the architect's feeling goes *toward* the building. *What matters is that the building — the room, the canyon, the painting, the ornament, the garden — as they are created, send profound feeling back towards us.* It means that if I am the builder I set out to produce a neighborhood, or a landscape, or a building, or a window as if it was an instrument, as a specific geometrical substance which will work back on me or on any other person and create feeling in me or in that person. The feeling comes *from the object back to me after it is made*, does not go from me to the object while I am making it. Here the question all the time is: Within the step that I am taking now, can I take the next step in such that way that the evolving work has its deep feeling increased the most? What step, of all possible steps, will add the most to the feeling we experience when we are in or near that place?

In the course of using this method, we shall also find, from time to time, that as we move forward, *before we take an action*, we can grasp the latent structure as an emotional substance, we may feel it as a vision — a dimly held feeling

which describes where we are going, but is not yet concrete, in physical and geometrical terms. This means we can sense, ahead of time, the quality of the completed whole — even when we cannot yet visualize it. We then keep this quality alive in our minds and use it as the basic guiding light, which steers us towards our target. The final target, then, has the *feeling* which we anticipated much earlier, but often has an unexpected, unfamiliar *geometry*.

The feeling which steers us in this fashion is a vision — but it is *not* an arbitrarily *invented* vision. It is a vision of something we may call the *emotional substance* of the coming work, a feeling which arises in us, as a response to the wholeness which exists. It is therefore reasonably accurate, reliable, and stable. We can get it, and then keep on coming back to it. It evolves, as the project does, and as our concrete understanding evolves. Thus, as the geometry develops, the feeling is kept intact, but becomes more and more solid — provided we do not depart from the feeling that existed in us at the beginning. So, this feeling which guides us is our response to the wholeness — first to that wholeness which existed at the beginning. Subsequently it is our response to the wholeness as it evolves and emerges from our actions. It is our knowledge of what kind of thing is needed to complete that wholeness, and make it more alive.

I have previously described wholeness in mathematical detail so that we understand the wholeness as a *real* structure. It is something real and substantial in the world. But even though it can be described as a mathematical structure, it is too complex to take in by purely analytical means. In order to get the whole, to grasp it, one must feel it. Its wholeness *can* be felt. Using our own feeling as a way of grasping the whole, we can put ourselves in a receptive mode in which we grasp, and respond to, the existing wholeness — together with its latent structure. This is not an emotional move away from precision. It is, rather, a move *towards* precision.

The feeling we seek is a condition in which the artist, builder, or participant opens himself to the whole, allows the whole to appear within him, and allows it to act within him: It is, then, the feeling which arises from the work itself. Above all, that which is latent, the structure just below the surface that is "trying" to appear, can be felt. And this is the core of what must be observed, felt, and perceived in order to make structure-preserving transformations feasible. Thus, during a living process, feeling is being used as the surest and

most reliable way for the artist or builder to receive the wholeness, nourish it, and respond to it, preserve it, and enhance it.

From the feeling that exists in us as our reaction to the wholeness that was originally there, we progress, step by step, towards a geometry which induces in us, a more and more intense feeling. I judge my success as an architect, at each moment and at every step in the emerging process, by the degree to which the work, as far as it has gone, intensifies my feeling when I am there — and, by extension, intensifies the feeling of every other person, too.

That is the essence of living process. It is a movement towards a structure which is precious. And, above all, it is a movement toward a structure which makes us feel our own existence most deeply.

INTERWOVEN MEANINGS OF THE WORD "FEELING" IN A LIVING PROCESS

. Since the word "feeling" has several different interwoven meanings in relation to a living process, I shall recapitulate the different ways that feeling and living process are connected.

1. I am talking about feeling as a way of grasping the wholeness of a situation. We grasp wholeness by feeling it, we obtain a nearly visceral feeling of the whole which puts us in touch with the whole.

2. I am also talking about a feeling of what to do next — at any given instant in the unfolding of the whole. This feeling, too, is generated in us *as* a feeling. We confront the whole, look at it, in the state it has reached, and we can feel where it wants to go or where it should go as its unfolding continues.

3. I am also talking about the importance of the idea that a building or any made object, when it has life, creates — generates — deep feeling in the person who encounters it. This principle that a thing, given life, has the obligation and function in the world to induce deep feeling in people — that is a third ingredient of my discussion.

4. Fourth is the fact that while making something, and when it is begun, or not yet finished, sometimes before it is begun, we carry the feeling, in the form of a dimly held vision of emotional substance. We begin with a dim awareness, and we carry that dim awareness with us, as we move forward through concrete acts of struc-

ture-preserving unfolding to generate a new and vigorous whole.

5. Fifth is the fact that this feeling or vision of emotional substance comes into our minds *from* the whole which exists. It is the existing whole that inspires the feeling or vision of what it might become as it unfolds. This is why feeling helps us to perform structure-preserving transformations. By following feeling, we are able to come close to the process of structure-preserving unfolding that must characterize the living process.

6. We have the fact that as artists, or as citizens, we need to be aware that any made thing — building, room, street, or ornament — has the obligation to create experience of deep feeling in us. We may think of this by saying that the thing *itself* has feeling when it lives.

7. Finally, there is always a structure latent in any given wholeness. This latent structure is the weakly held system of centers that are not quite defined yet, only partly articulated as a structure — yet which carry the inspiration of what this thing might be, where it might go. Every wholeness carries within it this "vector" in time, pointing in some direction, and indicating where it might go. This is the most important aspect of wholeness, and the reason we must try to "feel" the structure when attempting structure-preserving transformations, hence every step of a living process. That, too, is experienced by us as feeling.

3 / A PANEL OF YELLOW BLOSSOMS

How can all this — a vision of a given wholeness experienced through feeling — affect our actions? Let us consider a panel painted for the interior of a building as a tiny part of the wall surface. In the panel which I show here, from the wholeness of the place where I was doing the work, I began with an inner feeling of a shining blue. It was an intense blue, sky-like, yet more intense, illuminated by the light of yellow stars.

During the work of painting, this inner feeling of blue which I could see clearly in my mind's eye, though it was not yet realized, acted as a kind of vision to guide the work of the painting.

I began by trying to find an actual physical color which matched the light I saw in my mind. I found a beautiful soft shining blue, manganese blue, white, and cerulean blue, with a touch of ultramarine and grey. I began by painting this blue over the whole panel. When I filled the panel, I painted small yellow stars all over it, in an effort to make the blue shine more. It was, at this stage, partially beautiful.

However, it seemed flat and incomplete, and did not yet match the energy of the heavenly blue I could still see in my mind's eye. I began trying to intensify it. I worked for eight hours, adding more and more color — big daubs of orange and

Yellow Blossoms, oil on wooden panel, 1987

yellow towards the top; blobs of dark red near the bottom. After eight hours of work, the painting was ruined, a mess. But there was a spark created by the yellow daubs. I noticed that the way they interacted with the blue, did begin to make it shine in just the way that I had seen; a glimmer of that feeling had begun to enter in.

In frustration at the build-up of thick paint, I wiped the whole panel clean with turpentine. But I had discovered the essential thing about the physical device needed to realize the deep feeling of heavenly blue that remained in my mind's eye. To make the blue shine, in the way that created the feeling I had experienced, the painting needed big yellow blossoms towards the top.

I began again. This second time, I *started*

with these yellow blossoms, put them in first. Even now, the painting was *about* the shining blue, but I only painted yellow blossoms. Then gradually, over the next few days, I painted the pale blue blossoms, dark grey panel, red panels, green stems, and in between the yellow blossoms, the small amount of blue. Even in this blue, most of it was pale, reddish, towards lilac. Only one spot, no more than one square inch, has the literal color of the original shining blue. Yet the painting is still mainly about this blue, and what it takes to make it shine — to realize the feeling of that original blue in my mind's eye.

From the beginning to the end, even when the panel reached its final "yellow" state, I held the vision of the inner shining blue, that had first prompted me to make the panel in that place.

4 / GRASPING THE FEELING OF A FISHPOND AS A WHOLE

Here is another example of the way feeling must be the clue to wholeness, when we seek to make something alive. I once had an interesting discussion with Sim Van der Ryn. He was arguing that feeling is not enough. In his view it was too vague, too emotional. For instance, he said: "In making a sustainable fishpond which works, you just have to concentrate on the facts about fish life, water, plants, and so on, ecological facts about a healthy pond." I told him: "It is true that these ecological facts are a necessary part of our knowledge, our understanding of how to make a pond. And it is true that many of us know too little about what it requires to make the world sustainable, harmonious in its biological and chemical detail, and so on. But suppose, indeed, that we are trying to build a fishpond. The facts about the ecology of the pond — no matter how detailed by themselves — will not tell us how to make that pond good. Even if we have theories and facts about sustainability, edge plants, fish breeding, water temperature, types of weed,

types of insect, and so on — even with all of this we will not succeed in making the pond have life unless we also have a clear inner feeling — a subliminal perception, and awareness, and anticipation — of what life in that pond will be like." That means we must have a dim awareness within us, of what a pond with life is like, as a whole and in its feeling. If we do have that feeling of life clear (for the fishpond), we can then use it to guide us. It will help us move towards a pond which does have life. But if we do not have such a feeling clear in us, no amount of knowledge about ecology and sustainability will get us to a pond that has life in the sense I am discussing. We shall just be left scrambling mentally, churning about, marshaling our facts, making experiments perhaps — but still not clarified by an inner vision which tells us what to do. Building the pond, stocking it, putting weeds in it, placing bushes around it, we need to be guided by an inner vision of good life in this pond. We must have a feeling, in us, which will

Ecological fishpond

reliably tell us when we are going in the right direction, and when we are going in the wrong direction. It is ultimately this inner feeling, this inner vision of feeling, which is our only reliable (and necessary) guide. In short, we must be able to imagine the pond — not as a copy of another pond, or with detailed factual vision about dimension, depth, plants. We must be able to summon up, inside us, an inner sensation of the feeling of a healthy pond, which makes us remember

or create the kind of feeling which a good fishpond has: the slow movement of the fish, the edge, the light on the water, the kinds of things that may be present at the edge — all this, not in biological or architectural detail — but as a morphological feeling which allows me, in my inner eye, with my eyes closed, to remember, breathe, the kind of soft and subtle feeling of life which such a fishpond requires. It is that vision of feeling which, above all, must guide me.

5 / CHOOSING AMONG DOORS
ACCORDING TO DEGREE OF FEELING

For further illustration, I should like to show a small example of what it means to examine different alternatives for a given situation, trying to decide which ones have deeper feeling.

I ask you to imagine a wall, with an opening in the wall that has yet to receive a door. Let us consider some quickly sketched possible doors to fill this opening. Some have more feeling, some

A. Virtually no feeling at all

*B. Does have feeling, perhaps the most
feeling of all the doors illustrated*

*C. The barn door: not much real feeling in it,
even though it corresponds to a 'feely' stereotype*

*D. Does have feeling: the potential
for a great deal*

*E. Quirky and unusual. But in the right context, painted
the right colors, this door might have profound feeling*

*F. Might have feeling if made well: in this
embodiment doesn't have much feeling at present.*

G. Lots of detail, but not much feeling as it stands.

*H. A little bit of something here, as far as feeling goes;
but feeling is not developed*

have less. For each door, I ask you to pay attention to the feeling which the door *creates* in you.

The judgments one can make about the feeling created by these doors in the wall are necessarily incomplete, since the degree of feeling of each one — if it were a real door — would depend on more information about the context and character of the building in which the door is to be placed. Nevertheless, we can see different degrees of feeling in each door, even in these rudimentary sketches.

The door A will have relatively little feeling, no matter where it is placed. C, too, though it looks like a door that is supposed to have feeling, actually has very little. B has a lot, perhaps the most of the eight doors on the page, though of course it would only make sense in a certain kind of context. D, though similar, has rather less. E is strange looking; but in the right context (a brightly colored earth building for instance), it could have the potential for a great deal of feeling. H is a little strange: It does not have much feeling in this context, and it does not preserve or extend the latent structure that is there. F might only work in very special circumstances, a warehouse or industrial building perhaps, to account for the width of the doorway. G has some feeling: In a simple block building, with flowers round the door, it might have a great deal of simple substance.

I hope it is visible that the ones which have most feeling are also the ones which (probably) best preserve and extend the deepest latent structure in our imaginary wall, and are the ones which will do the best job of creating and increasing life in this wall. Of course, in a real case, it would depend enormously on the character of the wall itself. But, still, you get the idea.[4]

6 / THE BLACK COLUMNS

Now for a larger-scale example. Let us explore the idea of emotional substance further, through an example from a large auditorium. In 1984 I went to Japan to work out the colors of the inside of the Great Hall in the Eishin school. Getting these colors right was one of the most exhausting things I have ever done.

While I was designing the hall I always had two impressions. First, that it should be very dark inside, a feeling of darkness. That quality is already present in the early cardboard model shown on page 239; and, as a feeling, was present in me from the very beginning of my thought about this building. Second, that in the darkness, colors were somehow glowing. I imagined bright colors, even reds, yellows, blues — on the columns and capitals — but darkly glowing in the darkness — never bright. This was my starting point.

When I went to Japan in February 1985 the building shell was finished. All the columns, capitals, beams, walls, windows were there. And the darkness was there. So I stood for days, in the dark hall, trying to imagine concretely what colors would create the proper feeling.

It was hard work. Nothing obvious came. Most of the first colors seemed wrong. Then, after several days, I spent almost half a day sitting in the bath — my eyes closed — simply trying to see the inside of the hall. I sat for hours and hours. Finally, after many hours, I began to see the inside of the hall and its columns as black. This was startling and unexpected — not something that had ever occurred to me. But it had the marks of an authentic vision. And on the surface of the black, something faintly glowing.

I made a first sketch, very hastily.

The vision maintained itself. The chevrons on the column, which had been in my mind ever since some earlier sketches — now seemed darkly red. By chance, since I made the sketch

My original sketch of the columns

A slightly later sketch

hastily, in the train, on the way to the site, the drawing was done in ball point which left faint bluish lines, even after I had painted the red and the black. The faint bluish aura was important, and essential to the way the color glowed.

Back at the site, I now began full-scale mockups in the building, painting huge pieces of paper, and covering the real columns. It was very hard to get the right colors. The black, as I found necessary to make it work, was actually a dark, dark, reddish gray — not dead black, which was too harsh.[5] The red, too, was hard to get. At first simple reds had a terrible bright decorator-like quality, completely different from the feeling I saw in my mind. Finally, I began mixing a series of reds which had an unusual amount of black in them; so much, that I myself could not believe that they would seem red. And yet, on the column, it was these blackish reds which glowed in the right way, when the chevrons were made of them. There was so much black that I couldn't even persuade my assistants

to mix them correctly — they kept making them too red, not black enough.

The size of the blossom on the capital was also crucial to the color.

Then the faint bluish haze. First I tried very fine blue lines, between the red and black. It was hopeless, and only trivialized the red, made it seem pink. Then, I tried putting blue — actually white with a faint bluish cast — on the ceiling of the gallery, behind the columns. But the right color was not blue. It was green. The green, a very, very pale sea green — looks blue. The blue looks too bright. So I got the bluish cast for the black and red by painting a sea-green white.

Now the whole thing was still only half done. The columns and ceiling were clear; but the beams, upper columns, and main ceiling, were still totally unclear. We tried many, many colors — red, grey, greyish red, reddish grey, white, black — on these other places. None of them amounted to anything. They didn't continue the feeling of the black and red columns.

First vision of color based on the feeling developed earlier: Black, red and faint traces of a bluish haze are all visible

They were just colors. I realized that once again, the thing was lacking on the level of the inner vision. So once again, I simply sat in the water of my bath, looking, looking, with my eyes closed. For hours, nothing came. Finally, after many hours, I began to see a faint shimmering of black and white — something entirely different in quality, in feeling — from what I had been trying to paint.

I went to the office, and tried painting something like this, on the model I had on my desk. It seemed strange and unfamiliar. But it had some hope. But time had run out. The pressure of time, caused by the construction work, and my own schedule, put me in a corner. I had no more than a few hours left. I was in a terrible panic. I went over to the hall, certain that I had failed. And then, in my moment of failure, I grabbed a brush, and angrily, hurriedly, splashed

some colors on a mockup of the main beam — a huge sheet of paper, three meters long and seventy centimeters high, which represented a short section of the beam. I asked one of my assistants to put it up. And up there, amazingly, it fit just perfectly. It was a new animal, something different, amazingly different from the darkly glowing intensity of the black columns — but with just the right life to hold its own against them and yet support them at the same time.

It was solved. But once again, the key thing in the solution was not the work, the actual painting, the trying different things. It was the shimmering sense of black and white, which was quite different from anything I had tried before, which I saw only after immense effort.

It was the initial vision, the initial sense of color-feeling, which was the essential element. The hours of sitting intensely in the bath, eyes

Paper-covered mockup in the Great Hall, during construction, 1985

tightly shut, waiting until an authentic living vision entered my mind, was fifty times more work, emotionally, than the actual work of painting, trying, mockup, etc. That is where the value of the whole thing came from. At every step one takes, in an unfolding work, it is always the process of knowing the emotional substance — and then getting it clear enough, so that it exists alive, in one's mind, and can be followed and materialized — which is so hard. This is the hard work, this is where the thing begins, and this is where its success or failure is determined.

The Great Hall interior, as it was being completed. Here the formless feeling of the whole was kept alive for months, years, and then embodied, more or less successfully, within the whole that one sees here.
Eishin campus, Iruma-Shi, Tokyo, 1985.

7 / THE FORMLESS BUT SPECIFIC FEELING OF THE WHOLE

In each of the examples I have given, the essence was that at each step of a living process one must be able to feel, ahead of time, the *feeling* which will later exist in the finished object (building, painting, canyon as on pages 260–61, or pond), without yet knowing its form in detail.

We are able, somehow, to identify and carry in ourselves, this feeling which must be in the finished thing — and we can carry it in us eloquently enough, and specifically enough, so that as we move forward in the creative task, we can constantly check to see if the next action, the emerging form, this detail or that, does have *that* feeling and not some other.

The very specific nature of this feeling — when accurately experienced — can be remarkable. But it is very difficult to explain just what this feeling is like in character. It is not verbal, it is not visual, it is not auditory. Yet it is articulate and highly specific, very particular, unique each time that it occurs.

It is so articulate, and so specific, that it allows us to use it with great accuracy. When it is understood and felt clearly enough, it is so specific that it will allow me to consider 100 possible ways to make a roof, and reject them all, because they do not have this feeling, then to accept the 101st because it *does* have it.

In my view, our ability as artists depends very largely on our ability to experience, formulate, and carry such a feeling — first to feel it and witness it, then to carry it forward, remember it, keep it alive within us, and insist on it. Few buildings have anything profoundly significant in them, if they do not start with this. Few paintings or drawings, or details in a building, or rooms, have much

The Great Hall interior finally finished, black and red plasterwork complete.
Christopher Alexander, Hajo Neis, Ingrid King, Miyoko Tsutsui, and Ishiguro-san, 1986.

deep quality in them, if they do not come, first, from such an experience of feeling, which is first kept alive, and manifested then in actual geometrical form.

You know the *feeling* which the thing will have. But you do *not* yet know the *form*. In fact, you keep having to change the form, because as the work unfolds, you find out many, many details which have the wrong feeling, which do not function, in response to the whole, as you thought they would. Because you keep the *feeling* constant, you *have* to change the form.

If the form were kept constant to your original idea, then the feeling would be insubstantial, and would change. That would not protect or extend the wholeness. Instead of that you hold the feeling constant (that which *does* extend and protect the whole), you keep it alive in you, this formless feeling which is so vivid, so particular, that you can judge all your form-making as you make the thing, by matching it against that feeling. Thus we have, as a natural part of living process, the idea that a kind of emotional substance — something more solid than a feeling, but less formed than a thing — is guiding the process of designing and making at every step. It is solid enough to be clearly felt, and clear as an appropriate, fitting response to the nature of an object or a place. But it is as yet without geometry, without outline or solid form.

What I am saying then, is that before making anything, large or small, and before each step in the process of making it — *before each step* — we must be able to feel its emotional substance. We must get this emotional substance clear in our minds, and be clear that this emotional substance, and no other, is the one which is called forth by the conditions which that place or object creates.

That is what creates the whole, successfully, and allows life to emerge.

8 / DESIGNING A MUSIC CABINET

I will now describe the process of using feeling, repeatedly, as the origin of a step-wise process to make a music cabinet. In this example, feeling guides and dominates the process, from beginning to end. The cabinet is not wonderful — though it perhaps has a living quality to a modest degree — but I am using it as an example because it just happened that I made extremely detailed notes while I was building it. These notes give helpful insight into the painstaking and minute process which is usually required to find the feeling in a thing.

It began with a request from my wife, Pamela, who is a professional singer, a soprano. She wanted the cabinet for her sheet music. Each song is only a few sheets, so the music is too floppy to stand up and must be stored flat. What she needed was something with many, many thin flat shelves, one on top of the other. That was the basic idea of the cabinet. Because this functional idea is unusual, it has its own character which arises from the music sheets themselves.

Sketch 1. Pamela told me roughly how big a cabinet she wanted — fairly high so that one could place a vase on top, and wide, too, but not so wide that it couldn't be moved around. At first we had an idea of something about four feet high, and three to four feet wide. I began making small sketches. In one of these, I had the idea that the bottom of the cabinet was deeper than the top, and formed a base. I drew two versions, and she picked the simpler of the two.

Sketch 2. Then I began to develop the proportions of the cabinet. First, I simply took the proportions which common sense seemed to suggest: A width of about 40 inches; a height of about 54 inches; and a depth of about 11 inches at the top, a little deeper at the base. It was clear that the cabinet shown in this sketch did not have the right proportions. It was rather ugly, too squat, not graceful, certainly not a picture of the self.[6]

Sketch 1

Sketch 2. More detailed, but it lacks feeling, and is much too squat.

Sketch 3: Versions of the top board

Sketches 3–7. In the next steps, I made a sequence of free sketches of the cabinet looking for the right proportions. I started sketching a three-dimensional isometric view from a perspective that I knew would give me the overall

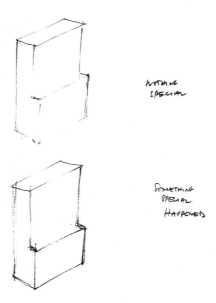

Sketch 4. Sketches of the upper part of the cabinet. In the lower drawing, the more elongated body begins to have a real feeling. When the pencil had got as far as the first drawing, nothing much had happened. By the time the pencil made the lower drawing, some real feeling entered in, and it was worth stopping there.

Sketch 5. Getting the relation between the top and the bottom just right. The upper of these drawings shows something OK, conventional, but without any special feeling in it. The lower, perhaps too extreme, has a trace of some real feeling, so that when I stand and look at it, I become aware that it has some real feeling which it sends out to me, and that it makes me feel my existence and my life in some poignant way.

feeling of the thing. I began sketching just the top surface by itself. Here already there was a sense of proportion involved, since I knew the top was important in its effect on the whole. While I was drawing, my pencil was searching out different possible widths and lengths for this top board. I did not allow myself to be guided by any abstract knowledge (such as "it has to be 36 inches long and 11 inches deep"), but searched only for a board that had the feeling I could already feel as part of this project.

Sketch 4. Next I tried to decide the character of the top portion of the cabinet. Again I made sketches to explore the possibilities, not stopping until I discovered one which continued the feeling in a significant way. The one I chose, the one which seemed to me to have the most feeling, is the lower one. It is the one which also has most *presence*. Is it more a picture of my self? Yes. Using the language of Book 1 (chapter 9) I could also say it is the one which most strongly makes me feel my own humanity.[7]

Sketch 5. In the next set of drawings, you can see what happens when I first start paying attention to the height of the "waist-high" shelf. I first

draw it conventionally, then try dropping the line. In the first drawing nothing special happens. In the second, where I drop the line, all of a sudden a self-like quality jumps out. I am watching for it, waiting like a hunter, for it to show up. The moment it shows up, I stop the pencil. The shape of this volume is critical. For the first time a glimmer of real feeling appears in the cabinet as a whole. So now I know, with some certainty, what shape the upper part of the cabinet is going to be.

Sketch 6. And just to show you the same phenomenon of feeling acting as a guide, yet *again*, look at the upper shelves in these two drawings. These are very narrow shelves, each one no more than about three to four inches high, in which sheet music is to be kept lying flat. In these two drawings, the only difference is that the lower drawing has one extra shelf. Once again, the lower drawing has something more; it pulls you in. Using the picture of the self criterion, the second of these drawings is more like my own self.

	inches	×25	×30	×28	×31	
Height	2.2	55	66	62	68	
Width	1.3	32.5	39	36	40.3	
Height of base	1.0	25	30	28	31	
Depth of top	0.4	10	12	11	12.4	
Depth of base	0.57	14.25	17.	16		
Height of small shelves	0.125	3.125	3.75	3.5	3.875	3
	inches on sketch		↑ Best.			

Sketch 7. Handwritten notes showing different interpretations of the dimensions obtained from my two-inch high sketch. The first column shows dimension in the sketch, the next four columns show different scalings, according to the height chosen for the cabinet as a whole.

Now I have the proportions of the whole cabinet. But even now I still don't know exactly how big it is. Of course I know *roughly* how big it is, and it is my sense of the approximate size that has enabled me to keep making decisions correctly. For instance, I told myself that the small shelves are about three to four inches high — and it was this sense of scale that made it possible to decide roughly how many shelves to have. But, in detail, I still don't know how big the cabinet is. So I used the second drawing in *Sketch 6* in order to find out how all the parts are to be proportioned in relation to one another.

Sketch 7. Now I need to do some arithmetic, to find a system of dimensions which *will preserve the feeling (and sense of proportion) which exists in the rough design I have made*, yet also keeps the actual dimensions within the range of real practical usefulness and common sense. I do know, for instance, that I don't want the real thing to be more than about six feet high; I don't want the narrow shelves to be more than about four inches high, nor less than about three inches; and I know that the waist-high shelf should be not less than about 25 inches high, and not more than about 32 inches high. I know this from making measurements against existing pieces of furniture. I also know that shelves need to be at least ten inches deep, but should not be

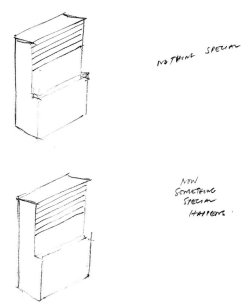

Sketch 6. Once again I look at the way the shelves sit in the cabinet, to try and decide which arrangement has the deepest feeling. The upper, with five shelves, is OK. In the lower, with six shelves, some special feeling appears. It is more significant. I feel myself, and experience my own humanity, more profoundly in the presence of the second.

too deep — and that large music books need about 13 or 14 inches of height when standing. I do this by trial and error, using a scale and a small pocket calculator, until I find a way to interpret the drawing, at a single scale, which makes all the heights, shelf widths, and so on, come out to numbers that are within the reasonable limits I have just set.

To get the right dimensions, I first measured off the lower drawing (*Sketch 6*), exactly, in millimeters. The key dimensions, as measured off my original perspective sketch, are shown in the first column of the chart I made (*Sketch 8*). Then in the next four columns I try a variety of different multipliers, and write down what actual dimensions (in inches) each part would have, for each different multiplier. I then tested the dimensions given in these different columns with a tape measure, to imagine the base, the width, the shelf height, and so on. Although all four sets of dimensions were possible as real cabinets, the second column which has a multiplier of 30, and makes the cabinet 66 inches high, is the one which most closely corresponded to the feeling and dimension that each part ought to have. The

base, at 17 inches, was a little deeper than I would like (I should have preferred a base depth of 14 or 16 inches); but it was a small price to pay for everything else being just right.

At this stage I had a design for a workable piece of furniture, with practical measurements. Because of the process I have followed, it retained the feeling nature of the thing I originally found through my early sketches.

The photograph shows the finished cabinet. It has some of the feeling described, perhaps not as much as I would like, but twenty years later we are still using it. In the picture on the next page, I show a second cabinet, built later, in the course of working out office furniture for Herman Miller. The second piece is more developed and has deeper feeling; its form is more carefully thought out in construction, is really beautiful. It is a pleasure to be near.

The finished music cabinet

A later, green version of the cabinet made as a piece of office furniture for Herman Miller

9 / FEELING AS THE ORIGIN OF THE ARTISTIC WHOLE

I assert again the very close connection between feeling and wholeness. When I say that we should aim towards the feeling created by a building, I might equally say, we should always try to shape each part so that it works to create the whole. These two rules are essentially one and the same. If I work towards making a thing which has true feeling, I am necessarily aiming at, conceiving, imagining, and thinking, about the quality of the whole. And it is true, then, that I will, because of my mental concentration, work in such a way that each part supports the whole, and is shaped by its presence in the whole and by its contribution to the whole. Easily said. But not trivial. It does mean that what is made, to create a whole, must originate from the effort to create feeling in the whole, not from intellect. Intellect is too crude a net to catch the whole.

In the following examples, I try to go a little further to show how these two concepts — created feeling in the whole, and the whole itself — are linked in practice.

CATCHING THE FEELING OF THE WHOLE THROUGH COLOR AND MATERIALS

It is important to understand what it means to pay attention to the *whole*, and how the feeling induced by that whole can then come into play in different ways. For example, in the choice of materials, what is "the whole"? When I begin a project, I often make a palette in which different materials are looked at in their proportion, so that one can discover, and then establish, the balance of materials that will make the project good. That statistic is one of the most global

First test

Second test

things about a project. Here in an early stage of the Eishin project in Japan, we see four different mockups, each containing different relative proportions of concrete, concrete block, white plaster, black plaster, green plaster, wood, stone. After studying these, a particular one (the fourth) was chosen, and provided the project with its wholeness of feeling.

Such a statistical distribution for overall material percentages is no less important than the expression of the overall type of plan, or the broad brush configuration of the plan. In each case one makes that choice which has the most profound feeling, and which fits — emanates most successfully from — that particular site.

When I visited the site in Japan, and spent a few days there in 1983 at the beginning of the project, I began to experience the wholeness of the site as a kind of light. I can still see it, and feel it, in my mind's eye, as I sit writing these words today, seventeen years later. It was both bright, and soft, yet brilliant and harsh in its

softness. I was able to carry in me the feeling of the buildings — even their forms and colors — that would be congruent with that light, sustaining it and sustained by it. The wall mockups I made, a few weeks later, shortly after returning from Japan, and illustrated here, were made as an answer to the feeling of the light which I experienced in Japan, in Iruma-shi, on that site, in 1983. The fourth mockup came closest to realizing the light in its harmony.

A TINY LIBRARY MOLDING AND ITS IMPACT ON THE WHOLE

Let us use a microscope to look at such a process more carefully.

A few years ago, I built a library in my house. It has floor-to-ceiling bookshelves all around. The bookshelves have a small step at waist height and may be seen as they are in the room in the photograph on the next page. Because of the step at the waist-high shelf, there

Third test

Fourth test

The finished library. "… I look around after an hour of labor, and realize that this may be the best reading space I've ever been in… The room doesn't shout… it has light that is good, and from two directions, that is constantly changing. The relationship of the chair to the table is just right for a long read. The details all come together in a way that makes me feel peaceful and watchful and attentive and comfortable reading a complicated book for a long period of time." Joel Garreau.

was a slight problem in the corner. There is a gap between the two verticals at the shelf (see diagram). How should the gap be closed? While I was building it I began a discussion with the cabinetmaker, how to close this gap.

There were three main possibilities. The thing could be made with two boards that form a right angle going into the corner. The thing could be made with two boards that form a right angle coming out into the room. Or the gap could be closed with a 45-degree board chamfered to fill the gap.

To decide the issue, I made a very simple experiment. When the gap was there, between the boards, I made a mockup with my hands — putting my two hands to go into the corner, putting my two hands to come out into the room, and putting one hand to make a 45-degree "board." Looking at my hands, in these three arrangements, it was possible to see which one had the

best effect on the room as a whole. I chose the third of them, with the chamfered corner. My carpenter was surprised, and resisted this one slightly. I did it, though, because from the experiments, I knew that it would make a better corner for the room as a whole. And, in the finished room, these corners do indeed make a beautiful whole. They have an effect which makes the entire room feel more finished, and more complete.

Here we have a case where a decision that is at the scale of three or four inches affects the life of a large center that exists at a scale of about 15 feet.

Consider another similar example from the same room. I had to place a small crown molding to close the gap between shelves and ceiling. I chose a crown molding, and had the idea of painting it. I thought if we use the same redwood, it will make a harsh connection with the white of the ceiling.

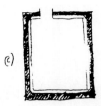

Plan view of the whole

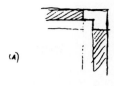

Configuration corner empty

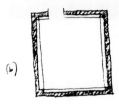

Plan view of the whole

Configuration projecting into room

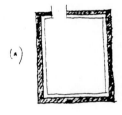

Plan view of the whole

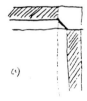

Configuration chamfered corner

First I thought about colors — and mentally went through the possible colors. It seemed likely that red would be the most harmonious. Then I got a small piece of the molding, and tried a few reds on it. I had expected that the red would need to be pale, halfway between the color of the redwood and the white of the ceiling, to tie the two together more effectively.

However, as it turned out, the thing which was most quiet, and which tied the room together most effectively, was a dark red, a scarlet with black mixed into it. Here again is a case where a very small center, at the scale of two inches, when carefully colored and intensified in just the right way, has the effect of calming and

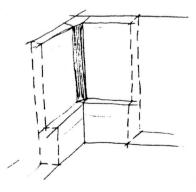

Perspective view of the chamfered corner

The part of the campus where the library was to be built.

binding together the whole room — again a center at the scale of 15 feet.

In both cases (chamfer and color), a small center, only a few inches across, helps the life of a center which is many times larger. The large center of the library as a whole, gets its life and depth of feeling from the careful way these small centers are chosen to help it.

Now, when people visit that room, they often comment on an enormous silence which appears to emanate from the room. A stillness one can hear in the room, even before entering.[8]

It is easy enough to understand the idea that an existing wholeness is helped by a small center, if it is done right. However, what I have found, is that people have difficulty *seeing* the wholeness accurately, so that they know what to do there.

THE SHAPE AND POSITION OF THE LIBRARY ON THE EISHIN CAMPUS

In the diagram, you see the plan of the university portion of the Eishin campus near Tokyo, as it was at an early stage while my colleagues and I were working out the plan. It is a long ridge, a natural feature of the land, which later was lined by long narrow buildings along either side. At the left hand end (east) is the Judo Hall. That forms, as one can see, a kind of stopping point, a focus, towards which the whole is ori-

Diagram of the ridge, judo hall at the left-hand end, library at the right-hand end

Sketch of the library, as it was to be built

ented. And at the west end, is the Library building. That library building is shown in my sketch. The whole building is conceived, shaped, given its cup-shaped plan, its height, its organization — by the task of becoming a focus which energizes the whole top of that ridge *as a whole*. The cup shape enhances the larger whole of the ridge. This is geometrically true. When we paid attention to the feeling that emanated from the land, and did our best to create the deepest feeling, it was natural (and appeared inevitable) to place the library in that position on the ridge, and to give it the half-cup form, which completed the natural form of the ridge itself.

That is a simple example of what it means, on a larger scale, to get feeling in a building by making it contribute to the life of a larger whole.

10 / WILL DEEP FEELING REALLY BE POSSIBLE? IN 21ST-CENTURY SOCIETY

It must be admitted that our society, modern industrial society, does not usually work in such a way that the whole *can* be given profound feeling. The fragmentation of process has made it difficult, if not impossible, to pay attention to the whole in almost all building processes.

One might say, then, that feeling is an unattainable ideal for us. We might reflect sadly on the passing of traditional society, where feeling was present in almost every building, and say, with a shake of the head, that for us in post-industrial society it is no longer possible. I shall return to this massive theme in Book 3. But I do not believe that a negative judgment about the matter would be helpful or accurate. I am certain that a society of human processes, based in the fashion I have been describing on the emergence of feeling, is an attainable ideal. Early modern buildings — the works created in the first half of the 20th century — were (oddly) more often engaged by feeling than postmodern buildings — those from the second half of the 20th century. Social and industrial processes can, with the right intent, be refashioned to allow feeling to guide and dominate the whole, no matter how impossible that may sound to our cynical contemporary ears.

It is worth reflecting on this as a realistic possibility.

11 / CLASSROOMS IN THE RAIN

If I repeat the process of relying on feeling again and again, gradually I do get something which has life. The proof of the pudding is that the life generates deep feeling within *me* — a profound kind of ease.

What is responsible for this kind of ease?

The subtle details of human experience must be accommodated. Yet though they are subtle, they are extremely specific. We feel them strongly. And they do actually exist in the reality of the events which will happen there, practical physical events, and emotional events.

A small story about a discussion I had with one of my apprentices, Friso Broeksma. He had been working on the Berryessa house for Mr. and Mrs. Lighty for three or four months, and I asked him what he thought of the feeling in the building. I asked him, if he felt that he now understood the principle that every step taken in the Lighty house was based, always, on trying to deepen the feeling. He said: "Yes, in *theory* I do. But in practice it seems different. I am worried, for instance, about the fact that the house has so many stairs — this will make it very hard for the Lightys when they get old. And the fact that the bedroom is separate from the main house — it means you have to go through the rain when you go to bed."

I told him that these were just the kinds of problem I was concerned about: That he was exaggerating certain practical matters, and therefore losing his own connection with the deeper feeling. To begin with, the Lightys and I together had laid the buildings out, among the oak trees, in this rambling way, with the necessity of moving from building to building, just to get from room to room. It came from them, because they loved the slope and the oak trees so much. Why should someone *else* come along and say that it is not functional? I told Friso that thou-

Rain on the Eishin campus. students hurrying from class to class

sands of traditional buildings he himself admired, in Holland, Africa, Russia, China, have all kinds of anomalies. These so-called anomalies come about for practical reasons that allow them to be true to the unity of their situation. They are a little strange, occasionally. But the strangeness bothers almost no one, because, what is more important, we sense and feel and experience their commitment to *life*.

So I told Friso that the issue of stairs for old people, or the issue of not getting wet, are not as all-important as he was claiming. The main lesson is to gain a greater sense of perspective, in which feeling has its place, and practical issues about getting wet and keeping dry also have their place. It is *feeling*, above all, which has the greatest chance of dealing with the whole in a balanced way, because it is precisely the nature of feeling that it does embrace the whole — while intellectual ideas more often concentrate on parts and end up getting them out of proportion.

What is most important is the feeling, the life one experiences there. You consider them

charming and never dwell on or exaggerate possible functional problems. But, for people educated in the functional architecture of the 20th century, it is the tyranny of functional problems, created by a rigid frame of mind, which exaggerates some things, and then makes it impossible to get the feeling or the wholeness right.

In the Eishin project, we had many fights with the teachers about the idea that the classrooms were separated from one another. They said: "How can you make a school where you can't go from one classroom to another without getting wet?" I told them, "Rain is part of life. It is not only necessary to avoid the tyranny of simple-minded functional thinking so as to relax the plan and allow the wholeness to develop. Also, getting wet is good for you — it increases your own sense of life. Think about Zen, and recognize the importance of the rain. It will be impossible to build a beautiful campus, if you insist on rain-proof connections between all buildings."

We argued and argued. Finally I reminded them that it had been their own choice to make classrooms separate (because the home-like atmosphere was better for the students and for the teachers), but that this separation and homelike atmosphere brought with it a second reality — namely, that the classroom buildings really *would* be separate, *would* have their own gardens — and that one would then have to go out into the rain when walking from one classroom to another.

So finally we did decide to allow the buildings to be separate. A year after the buildings were finished, I asked them if they minded getting wet between classes. They laughed. "We like it," they said. "We have umbrellas. Or we run. We feel more alive." The deep feeling which I am talking about concerns the whole. It includes feelings of life, the sense of living. Within the terms that I am talking, the feeling of the Berryessa house is profound because it allows parts of the house to sit on the slope — looking at the purple mountains which the Lightys loved — without disturbing any oak trees. The tyranny of "old people mustn't have stairs" or "you must have a covered indoor path to the bedroom" would disturb the whole, and disturb the feeling far too much.

12 / A NEW WHOLE EMERGES: LIFE V. MECHANISM THE ESSENCE OF UNFOLDING WHOLENESS

The obligation of the building is to help the street; the obligation of the fireplace is to help the room; the obligation of the wall is to help the roof: the obligation of the building is to help the garden; and of the garden to help the street.

It is this endless, upward-streaming hierarchy which produces life.

Everything in living process is meant only to underline this idea, and to show what it means to make this practical in buildings. I am proposing that in the course of planning, conceiving, designing, and making something, throughout that process we have a *single* step-wise process which may have 10 steps or 500 steps or 100,000 steps — but the essential nature of each step is exactly the same. It has only one purpose: to allow the wholeness to unfold correctly, *through feeling and by creating feeling.*

The process of putting feeling into the thing can be understood soberly. Consider an imaginary building task. It starts on the day you first hear about the job. It continues when you visit the place, meet the people; goes on while you get an idea about the building; get a rough idea about the plan of the building, the treatment of the site; continues while you work out the building volumes; goes on when you see the first visions of color and materials; when you have to pay attention to the codes; keeps going as you start working out movement, structure, and the placing of individual rooms. It goes on while you prepare drawings, and submit them to the building department; it goes on while you make mockups of the various kinds of construction which will be used in the building; working out what kind of building details you will use.

In every case, we do everything we can to intensify the feeling. It goes on when we start forming foundations; continues as we pour foundations; continues in the cutting and planing of every piece of wood; goes on while we decide details during construction: move walls, place windows, decide details of a seat here, an ornament there. It continues while we paint, place colors, on the building — and it continues in all the years after that while you, or others, add to the building, change it, improve it, and take care of it.

During this process, we make hundreds of thousands of individual decisions. Some of them take no more than a second: It may be an instinctive placing of a line — here instead of here.

Others may take months of discussion among us and our fellow builders, or between us and the client. Others are brief. I include the way your pencil travels along a line while you are drawing. I include even the time it takes to move the plane in a single stroke on a piece of wood you are planing — or the time it takes to take a loaded paint brush, and place one brushful of paint on the wall.

I even include the way you look at something, when you are trying to decide a question. Suppose, for instance, that we are considering two ways of making a concrete casting for a column base. We try two mockups in the builder's yard. As we look at the two samples, and think about them, we use a certain mental process — this mental process is affecting my eye, and helping me to make the choice between the two. We include even the choice of blade, when we are preparing to make a certain cut on a piece of wood. Again, the choice of this blade is one of the steps I have taken in making the building.

In a house, if we make one decision a minute over a two-year period, there may be as many as a quarter of a million decisions. For a big project there are many more. In a painting, where you sometimes make one decision a second for several hours, there may be several thousand decisions made even in a day. Even if there are a million steps, and a million wholenesses which I

pass through on my way to making something, I still use the same fundamental process, the same operation, for every one of these million steps. *In every step, I try to increase the feeling in the thing.*

Each step in the process is governed by this consideration. It applies equally to the moment when you first start thinking where to put the building on the site, and to the moment when you first try to grasp the main form of the building, and to its main structure and arrangement of columns, and when you first try to decide what shape to make the windows in a bedroom. It applies equally to the conceiving of the idea of what is happening in the downstairs inside the entrance (a functional problem), and to the idea of what color to paint on the wall of the kitchen, and to what plants to plant around the lawn, and to what animals to carve into the posts and how to carve them.

For some, this living process, based on the feeling which the whole creates, might merely be thought of as a general criterion that moves us forward through the art of building. But it is more than a criterion. It is an active principle, a particular and definite kind of action, which starts at the particular stage you have got to, and propels you forward to the next stage.[9] It doesn't matter whether this propelling forward takes one second, or six weeks, or sixty years: What guides it and propels it is the same.

NOTES

1. In appendix 3 of Book 1, I have described experiments illustrating the nature of the difficulty.

2. The experiments described on pages 54–7 help. And the techniques described in Book 1, chapters 8–9, also help. Nevertheless, it must be admitted that as a practical matter the task is sometimes difficult. Yet it is central to the living process.

3. These various versions of what is essentially a single criterion are more fully discussed in Book 1.

4. Of course I am simplifying the situation drastically, since in a real case, my decision will be affected by the extent to which this door *in its context*, has the most feeling. That would make an enormous difference. The most profound center would be affected and modified by the context — would, indeed, grow out of it — just as the door with most feeling, would also be modified by the context. But I want to be clear that even without this re-

finement, the question makes sense, and can be answered, as in this elementary example.

5. Sadly, the delay between my work of finding this color (1985) and the time when Mr Ishiguro did the plastering work (1987) caused my mockups to be lost. The beautiful reddish black which I had created was lost. Misunderstanding his memory, our manager had the plaster executed in pure black because he remembered it that way, and did not check with me. As built, it is impressive, but rather cold, and has never had the depth of feeling which it would have had, if it had been made, as I have described here, with a deep almost blackish-gray-red instead of black. The difference is clearly visible in the photographs on pages 381 and 382. The mockup has the reddish black. The actual building has the pure black.

6. See Book 1, chapters 8 and 9 throughout. This statement is merely another way of stating what I have

otherwise described in chapter 9 as the mirror of the self. A center is a good center, or a profound center, when it seems to be a picture of my own self. However, in order to probe this idea, to establish this idea concretely, and to put this idea into the objects, buildings we make — indeed, into the world we make — I must have the utmost clarity about what it means. What it really means is this: A center is a valuable one when it makes me feel the ultimate existence of the world, most deeply. Everything hinges, in the end, on my ability to make this happen. It therefore depends on my ability to experience it, to feel it, and to act upon it. And it also depends on my ability to understand what it means, in the most concrete fashion. Dozens of examples are given in Book 1, chapter 9.

7. Yet another way of talking about the basic criterion of Book 1, chapter 9.

8. This description of the feeling in the library comes from an unpublished manuscript by Joel Garreau, "Christopher Alexander," written for RESTORATION MAGAZINE, 1997.

9. Even so, there is a deeper question here. Just *why* a building which is profoundly based on feeling, should solve, simultaneously, these seemingly unrelated functional aspects is a profound mystery. This mystery touches the most unexpected aspects of the nature of space and the nature of matter, and will be examined again in Book 4, chapter 2. For the time being, I simply want the reader to be conscious that an approach rooted in feeling will go to the most vital practical nature of environmental structure. It engages *the* underlying nature of the whole environment, *the* most fundamental aspect of the physical world.

APPENDIX / THE HARD WORK OF CREATING AN ENGINE THAT PRODUCES GENUINE FEELING

I cannot emphasize strongly enough, that the production of a work which has feeling, may be imagined as the creation of an engine which makes this certain kind of feeling. It is careful, empirical, cool-headed. It succeeds, or not, in the degree to which this created engine is able to work, function successfully — that means that when the engine is finished the feeling appropriate to the context pours out from the engine, just as is appropriate to the place and time where the engine is placed. The hard work involved, the coolness of this work, is perhaps the most surprising thing, which must be understand by any architect.

As before, I shall give an example from painting, because in painting, somehow, the engine-like character is visible more exactly, and with less confusion. It is a painting of anemones. I hope the example will show how the search for profound geometry, even in a small thing like a painting, is the core of the hard work, and, when successful, ultimately then becomes the core of its success.

When I first saw the flowers, what struck me most about them, as a whole, was an intensity, a glowing darkness in the reds and blues, under-lined by the black centers. It was a feeling almost as if black-eyed peas had been unloosed to give life to the glowing reds and blues.

I began the picture by making a few small sketches of a handful of anemones in a jar. In each of these small sketches I was really just drawing the flowers as I first saw them, but looking for some glimpse in the work, of the kind of geometrical engine, which would be capable of creating the feeling which I have just described in the onlooker. These sketches are rough, hasty, and were made only in an effort to explore the possible geometric order which might create feeling: thus, as diagrams of the possible "engine," to find out what kind of engine will work successfully.

The sketches (page 398) were tiny, each one no more than 2 inches by 3 inches; one is even smaller, done with colored crayon on a tiny rectangle marked out on a board. All I was looking for was the way a geometrical structure in a picture might create the feeling which these flowers actually created in me. In the early sketches there are just hints of what might work. For instance, in the first there is a way in which the hints of dark masses,

First sketch

Second sketch

Third sketch

Fourth sketch

Fifth sketch

Sixth sketch

Anenomes, the finished painting

separated by light thin boundaries, has the capacity to touch a certain feeling. In the drawing with the spoon, we see the individual flower heads and petals, showing a capacity for some kind of feeling to be generated. Finally, playing with the arrangement, searching for an arrangement which makes the color speak, I found a sketch in which the pattern of black and white, like a beat in the background, allowed the color of the anemones to come to life. There, the feeling of the intense color and the "beat of the black-eyed peas" comes to life for the first time: This is an engine capable of creating that atmosphere. When I had done it, I realized that I had found, for the first time in this series, a thing which "had something." The geometry of this particular sketch, for the first time, created the feeling, substance actually felt at first. It is the rhythm of the dark and white on the wall in the background, small on the right, large on the left; and the fact that the eye of each anenome, also dark, but against a lighter group of petals, is then connected, almost becomes an extension of that wall. This is the geometric engine which does the work of creating feeling. Once I had understood that, by drawing it, the real work was done. I was then able to make a complete oil painting from this tiny sketch in no more than 10 or 15 minutes; an amazingly short time for an oil painting. It was because the real work was all done by then. In the small sketch, it had become quite clear how the geometry works to create feeling, and in the painting all I had to do was to re-create this geometric structure, in the same colors, without any going over. The finished painting, 10 inches by 14 inches, in oil, is an almost exact replica of the last sketch. By then I had found the finished engine which does the work. At this moment I no longer needed inspiration, I understood the geometry which made this work, and it only remained to put in into oils. The final painting is perhaps a tiny bit less subtle than the last sketch. But it works the same way.

It is the geometrical engine which does the work, and which creates the feeling of the color. That is what has to be created in any work of building. To find the geometric engine, the profound geometry, which will create the feeling actually needed in the building as a whole.

CHAPTER FIFTEEN

EMERGENCE OF
FORMAL GEOMETRY

APPEARANCE, FINALLY, OF COHERENT FORM

1 / GEOMETRIC ORDER

In order to achieve living structure, at a certain stage, it is necessary to seize hold of the building design and force it into an almost brutal, simple, massive geometric mold.

This happens when one is far enough along, so that can then almost view the building as pure art. The elements of space are to be made positive. The sub-elements of space, they, too, are all to be made positive. The massive elements of which the space is to be composed, they, too, are to be made positive. By pushing these very positive and massive elements around, the building takes on its force. It becomes a pure act of art, where the masses — these rectangular and positive elements — are unfolded, and moved, and shaped, until they have a definite, strong syncopated harmony. They will be repeated. Often what starts needs to be a tough and brutal repetition, which gets a rhythm going. Then these elements, their ratios, their proportions, their rela-

tions to one another, are varied to fit them to the context of the details, to give the whole thing life. At the same time, it is their spacing, the size and distance of the masses, and of the spaces between the masses — all looked at together — which then speak, which give out a subtle harmony — and a profound feeling from the strength of their definiteness.

These massive "stones," then, create the elegance, coherence, and strength of the whole. This is the moment when the building becomes architecture.[1]

Let me put this in context with other living processes. *All* living processes use unfolding to create geometric order. Throughout my discussion of the features of living process, I have suggested again and again, how the unfolding of coherent order — especially through the use of the fifteen transformations — occurs continuously. It is no exaggeration to say that when we contem-

The castle of Eilean Donan, on the west coast of Scotland. What appears superficially as the informal, relaxing, rambling roughness of the pictures shown in this chapter is actually a deeper order than the norm.

plate any living process at all, we always see that the length and breadth of the process will be suffused by steps through which a coherent geometry unfolds. But the origin of its particular geometry varies with the type of system. In the formation of water, it is the wave motion of the water which most clearly gives rise to the geometry. In the formation of solids it is the coalescence and crystallization of periodic arrangements of molecules that provides this tendency. In the formation of plants it is the successive unfolding of symmetrical leaf structures round the growing stem that provides the source of the order. In the case of buildings (if the process is a living one) the fountain of geometrical order comes, above all, from building *structure* (columns, walls, beams, vaults, and so forth), specifically from the aperiodic, tartan-like grids which form the abstract underpinning of the building structure. I will show in this chapter how it is ultimately the powerful formation of this structural core that provides a living building with its geometrical substratum.

2 / FORMATION OF BRUTAL AND MASSIVE CHUNKS IN THE VISITOR'S CENTER AT WEST DEAN

The transformation of the structure during construction. Starting from a plain rectangle with long walls pierced by windows, I introduced four massive cross-walls to make the final structure of the West Dean building.

I can show a very simple instance, from my building at West Dean: the Visitor's Centre of West Dean Gardens in Sussex. I had begun the building with a carcass, a simple one-story rectangle, with massively thick walls eighteen inches to two feet thick. It was crowned by a single very high roof. Windows were set into the walls in the right places, and at the right size with a bay system that corresponded to the beam-spacing of the roof and ceiling members. It was a powerful, though rather simple conception.

However, at the drawing stage, and during the early engineering and building stages, this conception remained incomplete. I was aware of something vital still missing, some element that would transform it: All I knew was that I was not yet quite there.

Once the walls were partly built, and one could feel the exterior volume and interior space, and also feel the weight of the massive walls, I began to see that what was missing was sufficient transverse structure, which had weight compa-

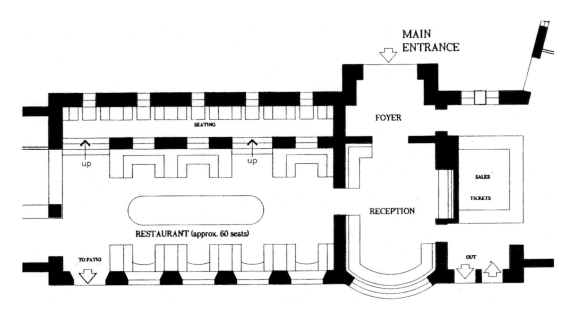

The plan of the Visitor's Centre at West Dean, showing the massive walls

The emerging order of the West Dean structure and its massive walls

The order of the details confirms the order of the whole.
Visitor's Centre, West Dean College, West Sussex, England. Christopher Alexander and John Hewitt, 1996.

The emerging order of the West Dean structure seen in one of its arched cross-walls

rable to the already-built longitudinal structure. I saw the arched openings of the windows in the long walls, by then already existing. But the cross walls were not yet comparable. I recognized that the *ends* of the main rectangle, especially, were not yet coherent or experienced because they were still weak and too poorly defined. So, in a space of a few days, I determined that the hull of the building must be supplemented with a series of massive transverse walls, pierced by arches. These walls can be seen in the drawings on pages 403 and 404.

You can see that the force of the building, as it was finally built (photographs on this page and the three preceding pages) lies in this nearly brutal effort to seize hold of the rectangular bays, bring them to order, make each rectangle continuous with the others, yet distinct. They are simple, and all in a row. Yet the spacing of the walls is unequal. The syncopated spacing and the

thickness of the transverse walls are not arbitrary, but caused by necessary positions which relate to the structure. And, all in all, what has happened is that now we have a system of positive entities — the main rectangular volume, the smaller rectangular volumes, the space, the walls themselves — forming a series of levels of scale. All very simple, yet as a whole, complex, and having a certain majesty.

It gets its weight as a building because the conception of the arrangement has been intensified, and made into something emotionally real, by the injection of the structure, and its beauty, its main massive elements. The transformation that took place was that the carcass, the building structure in itself, was made into a beautiful thing, not merely a structure, but a beautiful structure, guided by the process of its making as a beautiful thing in itself. That is a huge statement, and is the essence of the transformation.

3 / REASONS FOR BRUTAL GEOMETRIC ORDER TO EVOLVE

I want to explain exactly why the appearance of distinct levels of mass and scale must happen inevitably in a living process as one develops the building structure, and explain at the same time why the appearance of the geometry as it ensues in the building, may be described as almost brutal.

In many respects when we try to make structure-preserving buildings through living process, we are at first likely to find an order which is "informal," not too rigid, rather soft and harmonious as it fits itself to a landscape, or to a valley, or to a street, or to the seeming disarray of neighboring buildings. This *softness* is what characterizes the "old" way, and is what generates the beautifully harmonious order of Marakesh, or Rothenburg, or the back streets of old Kyoto and Nara, or the sweet subtle order of Jaisalmir in Rajasthan, or the subtle site-placing of a farm in the mountains of Wales. But even so, as we try to create this kind of soft order, there comes a time, inevitably, when we (as architects or builders) have to *impose*. We have to create a geometry that comes almost from the space itself, from the discipline of rectangles (because spaces are mainly rectangular), and from the discipline of equal or nearly equal structural bays (because structural bays are, by and large, roughly equal and regular). So we need to introduce this almost alien, slightly rigid, formal order of the built nature of a building, into the soft landscape of surrounding forms. And no matter how subtle we may try to be, this "something" which needs to be introduced is something inevitably alien. It has its own laws, it is deeply regular or massively crystalline, and its regularity may seem — and sometimes *must* actually *be* — brutal in a certain sense, because it comes from *itself*.

By that I mean that it comes from the need for the internal geometrical coherence of the building, not from the surroundings. Of course, as we introduce this formal geometry, work it, care for it, we do our best to make it harmonious, we tame it, we introduce necessary irregularities to make it fit the surroundings as well as possible. We fit it to the terrain, the idiosyncracies of street and site and neighboring volume.

This makes it more harmonious, not purely rigid or crystalline. The regularities flow with the land, the structure adjusts to subtleties of interior plan, and all thereby becomes softer. And, of course, we have made the decision about the geometric form — *which* rectangles, *how* big, just *how* brutal? — on the basis of a volumetric conception and a conception of positive space which all have their origin in the land. So it is reasonable to hope that from that origin, too, the geometry will not be brutal; will, if we are successful, have a balance of geometrical hardness and terrain-induced or interior-induced softness.

But in spite of these reasons for hoping that what we do may after all end up soft, well-adapted, comfortably fitted to the harmony of what exists, and thus be structure-preserving to the world, there is at the kernel of the whole process, an inevitable moment of truth which really is rather brutal, the moment when geometry, coming about for its own sake, imposes a discipline of its own that *must* be introduced. No matter how hard we work to make the building in harmony as far as possible with what exists around it and with the subtleties of its interior plan, still, taking this step is undeniably a brutal act, frightening for an artist who has sensibility for the beauty and softness of the land and of what others have built before him. *Yet it is from this moment of brutality, that real order must come.* The moment cannot be avoided. The nature of artistic creation — even, we may say, the biological character of order itself — demands it.

It is this injection of definite, strong, geometrical order that allows the profound depth of the made thing — the building in the land — and it is from this that the order must and will arise.

4 / THE APERIODIC GRID

Another way to express what I have been calling "brutal," is to say that there comes a time in the evolution of a building form when we must forget the context, the plan , even turn our back on these things, *and focus only on the pure beauty of the structural order*, the building as a thing of beauty in itself.

That means that for a time we become almost irresponsible, we forget practical matters temporarily, and we focus on the structural order — walls, columns, beams, vaults — as a three-dimensional object which evokes feeling through its geometric order alone, almost as if it were pure sculpture. It is the arrangement and shapes, of the structural order alone, which comes to the fore — and we focus on the question, whether this structural order, in itself, is beautiful enough to move us, as a whole, purely by virtue of its geometric force.

This is focused on beauty. It is brutal, only because, to do it, we must forget our responsibilities and the subtleties of site and function, and enter the play of pure forms with as much emphasis on feeling, art, and structure alone as we can.

This geometric substance that I call the brutal order comes, in fact, from the need to allow a certain regular rhythm of members to arise within an irregular envelope, because it is fitted to irregular circumstances. In the sequence of development, once we have a rough idea of plan, shape, size, and volume, we must then "grow" from this rough idea a regular packing of columns, walls, beams and structural bays which is regular enough to be a sound engineering structure, to have good horizontal behavior, good disposition of loads. And, inevitably, from this need, we will arrive at a system of rectangular

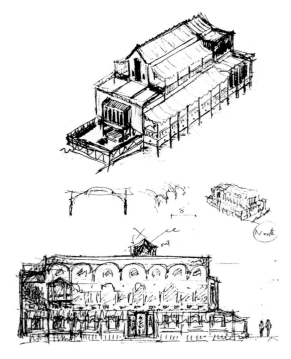

First sketches

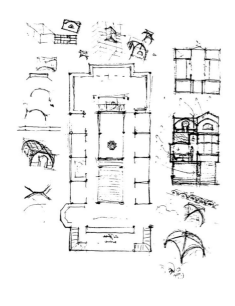

More sketches

My early sketches of the Linz Café, 1980.

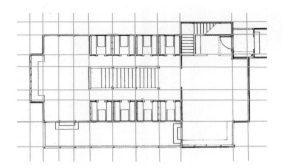

Tartan-like or ''aperiodic'' grid. This is a rough sketch of the aperiodic grid from which I generated the Linz Café

bays, more or less regular, yet imperfectly so — more or less repeated — yet fitted to the irregularities of site, variation of room size, and quirks of individual position. This cannot be done by an additive process. It can only be done — as a practical matter — by trying to cover the whole plan as accurately as possiblewith a *nearly* regular grid, squeezed, distorted just enough to cover the

peculiarities and necessities of plan. It usually looks like a tartan (left).

The work starts with the attempt to find grid lines (not spaced with perfect regularity, but spaced to fit the usual imperfections of plan) pushed into slight variations that fit the irregularities, so that the grid as a whole has an overall simple coherence. The resulting regular-irregular, tartan-like grid is what I call the "aperiodic" grid.

The gist of the process, what I call the formal or *brutal* process, lies in the use of very simple geometry, first introduced with force, after one makes sure that the inspiration has arisen from the place, and from the introduction, then, of just enough syncopation into the order, so that it truly fits the necessities of site and place and time, without doing violence to them.

We may see this phenomenon easily in a small example. On these pages, I show the plan of a small café I built in Linz, Austria, years ago.

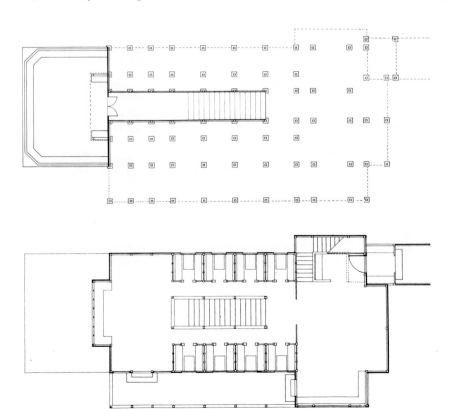

The Linz Café, floor plan

Interior, showing the effect of coherent structure on the feeling

The Linz Café, Austria, exterior view, 1981.

The building was inexpensive, and had, within its volume, various complexities of space. As one sees in the drawings on page 408, the rough sketch of the building had various conceptions of rooms. Then it came time to make a structure of this semi-regular arrangement. To do it, I drew a free-hand grid, similar to the drawing at the top of page 409. In order to fit the structure to the spaces I had conceived, this grid had differentiated spacing of the grid lines. Some were wide, others narrow. And this happened in both directions, in the long direction and in the cross direction.

The main building interior, where the regularity of the array is visible, and dominates

The result, once smoothed out, and made more carefully, is a perfect grid, but one whose spacing is fitted organically to the nature of the spaces in the building. Because of its regular and semi-regular character, it arises *from* the arrangement of spaces as conceived in the land.

We see, then, in the plan of the Linz Café, just how the use of the aperiodic grid works as the basis of a generating process. First we see a very rough plan laying out the kinds of spaces, and sizes, and their positions. One then tries to construct the simplest grid which could encompass these spaces, unchanged, making allowance for all the variations of scale. The largest space in the middle, the small spaces on either side, the syncopated alternation of large and small — all of these happening in both directions, of course, making a design almost like a Scottish tartan.

At that moment the order is essentially fixed. We have only to place columns at all the grid positions, recognizing that to some extent beams and columns will vary from floor to floor: The structural order of the three-story building is all but complete. The formal beauty of the interior is now almost assured, and comes in very large part from this array.

5 / THE SAPPORO BUILDING

Look here, at the example of Sapporo, a ten-story building which was to have been built in downtown Sapporo, on the northern island of Japan. This building, of concrete-encased steel, was to be built over an existing clinic. Because the existing clinic was hard to remove, and needed to stay in operation, I conceived the idea that the back part of the whole building would stand on massive legs, straddling the old clinic. These massive legs gave rise in my mind to a structural conception in which twenty truly enormous column clusters (see pages 415–16) ran all the way through the building from top to bottom. At the bottom they are indeed solid and massive, and visible as legs. Higher up, they are pierced — indeed they are so large that they con-

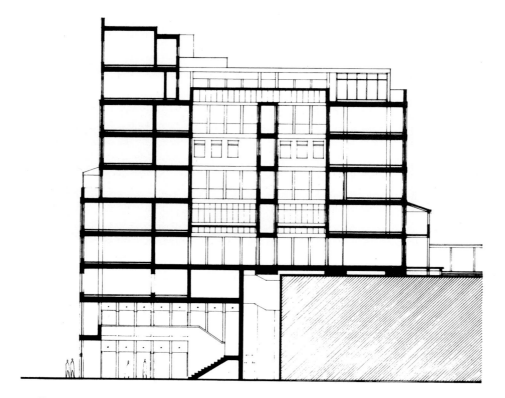

Sapporo ten-story apartment building, Longitudinal section, Christopher Alexander and Ingrid King, 1984

Model of the Sapporo building

Model of the Sapporo building, looking down into the light wells from above

tain arches, and each one splits into four smaller columns, and these four columns then become the crossings where the circulation and passages of the upper floors all meet.

In order to achieve this discipline, a very strict geometrical order had to be created. The overall structural idea is that of several frames, each made of columns, at different plan posi-

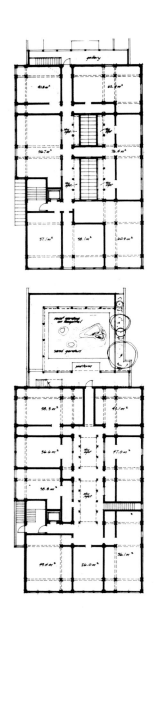

Sixth, seventh, and eighth stories of the Sapporo building   Fourth and fifth stories of the Sapporo building

north elevation

*Cross section of load-bearing structure
in the Sapporo building*

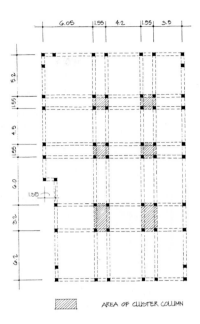

AREA OF CLUSTER COLUMN

*Plan of column layout. The column clusters where four
small columns make one massive column, are shaded.*

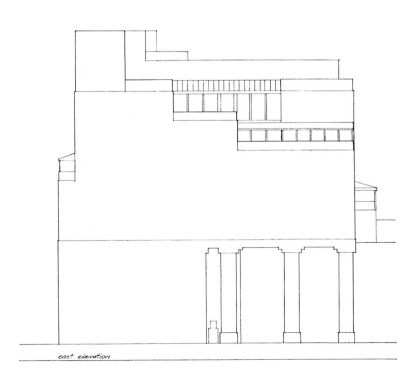

east elevation

Side view of the Sapporo building showing massive legs

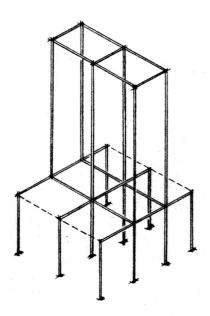

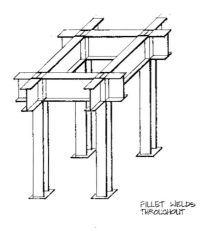

FILLET WELDS
THROUGHOUT

Overall axonometric sketch showing the whole building arrangement in diagrammatic form to illustrate how the vertical loads, from the central rectangular zone of steelwork, send their loads through massive beams, to the outer legs.

Detail of steel fabrication in one of the four-column clusters which appear repeatedly within the frame: structural engineering by James Axley and Gary Black.

tions, allowing and forming a core of two light-wells in the building, with the apartments grouped around the outside, and the passages and movement going around these inner lightwells. At each frame position, there are four sets of columns, each of these columns itself formed by four small columns with an archway passing through the opening, while maintaining structural rigidity. And the load from these inner columns is transferred to the outer legs, by massive beams passing across the building, above the arches at each floor. In the diagrams illustrated we see how highly determined the order has to be in order to work this way; and we see that even the column-connections, making possible a division of the "big" column into four smaller columns, requires rigid organization of steelwork to make it possible, itself again demanding a rigid and almost tyrannical geometry.

The four-column grid is caused partly by the passages and galleries typical of Japanese traditional space: They surround apartments to create an intimate scale in the interiors. Thus the geo-

metric order is highly organized, independent of site and people's preferences. This is what I mean by "brutal." Yet it is also conceived to be flexible, to have variety from floor to floor, to allow each apartment at each level to be unique, and to cope with the changing circumstances, as light, floor layout, terraces, and symmetry all change systematically as one goes higher in the building. Perhaps even more important, more exciting, is the fact that the same structural scheme goes through every floor, while the floors themselves are all different: Ten different floors one on top of the other, each specific to its circumstance as far as light, and view, and arrangements of apartments or shops is concerned — yet all held together by the repeating structural order that runs through the lot of them.

Thus the building is rigid in the definiteness of its geometrical conception, yet loose and subtle in the way the different floors are able to adapt to different conditions at the different levels. And it is also flexible with regard to grid spacing, which varies from bay to bay in each direction.[2]

6 / WHAT IS REALLY HAPPENING IN SUCH A CASE

It is my experience that this "successful" structure can be *generated*, with fair certainty, by people who know what they are doing, if they follow an orderly differentiating process to do this "brutal" thing.

It is after all also true that nearly all great traditional buildings contain such successful structure, making us believe that this differentiating process must have been a predictable and reliable process. It is also true, of course, that such middle-range order appears, without fail, in biological structures of all sorts, again making it virtually certain that there must be a predictable process which can create such order, and which does create it reliably in biological cases.

What is the essence of this process for buildings? How is it related to the "brutal" aspects of process I have been describing? How is it related to the repetition of the fundamental process that is required by all living processes?

I see the following key points.

First, the volume is already fixed. Let us hope that it is a good volume, a majestic exterior volume, which is simple. That is a major statement. Even a gigantic building must still be made of a relatively simple series of exterior volumes which form a single largest center (for further explanation of this process see chapter 4 of Book 3).

Second, we have a rough idea of the way space is to be disposed inside this volume. In broad terms, we have divided the thing up into areas and positions, possibly including exterior areas or spaces (for further explanation of this process see chapters 6, 7, 13 and 14 of Book 3).

Then comes the crucial step when orderly geometry of structure is introduced. We apply, to this configuration of roughly conceived spaces, a special kind of sharpening process: we use it to construct the simplest aperiodic grid consistent with the harmony and variety of the building plan. The aperiodic grid is a grid of parallel lines, not necessarily equally spaced, but parallel as far as possible, chosen so that all the main spaces or groups of spaces fit inside the grid. It is natural that this aperiodic grid contains both thick grid bands and thin grid bands, distributed in a harmonious way so as to form boundaries and levels of scale in a natural fashion.

If the grid has to be adjusted to make up for non-rectilinear aspects of the building volume (curves, or non-90-degree angles) imposed by exterior conditions, the grid is tweaked to adjust to these configurations by juxtaposition of slipped grid lines.

Consider, then, the following process.

· *It starts with the creation of a building volume in the land (application of* ROUGHNESS, POSITIVE-SPACE, GOOD-SHAPE *transformations).*[3]
· *That is followed by another process in which rough "cells" or internal volumes are made to fill this exterior volume — so far only roughly, but so that proportions, relative areas, and position are about right (application of* LEVELS-OF-SCALE, LOCAL-SYMMETRIES *transformations).*[4]
· *And that then is followed by a process of making a syncopated grid, which makes the disposition of volumes regular (but irregular), and which, at the same time creates boundaries, levels of scale, and alternating repetition, through creation of massive elements which are themselves felt and seen as living centers (application of* ROUGHNESS, POSITIVE-SPACE, LEVELS-OF-SCALE, BOUNDARIES, ALTERNATING-REPETITION *transformations).*

Virtually the same process can be applied to the largest buildings. On the next pages I show our unbuilt design for the huge Tokyo Forum, whose largest hall is the size of a football field. Here the structural elements are mainly massive walls, not columns. And there, just because the project is so massive, the overall order is made of two or three

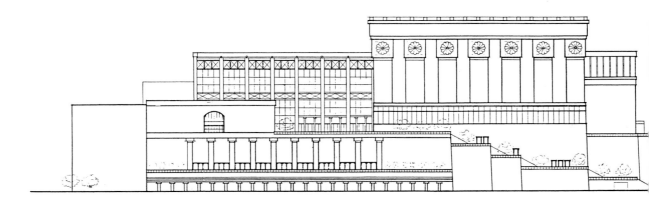

The massive Tokyo Forum, west elevation

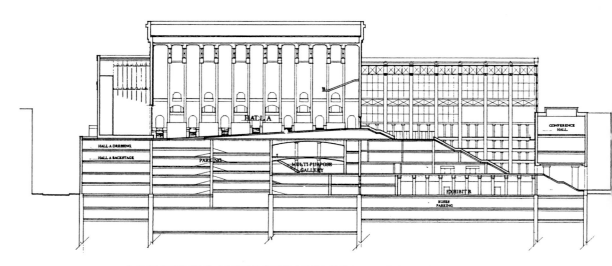

LONGITUDINAL SECTION THROUGH HALL A AND GRAND LOBBY,
FACING WEST

The massive Tokyo Forum, longitudinal section, from the east

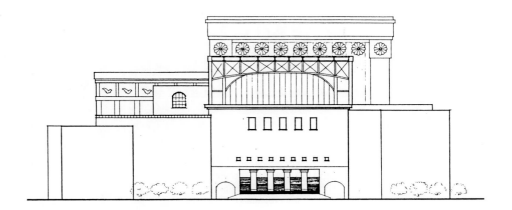

The massive Tokyo Forum, north elevation showing main entrance

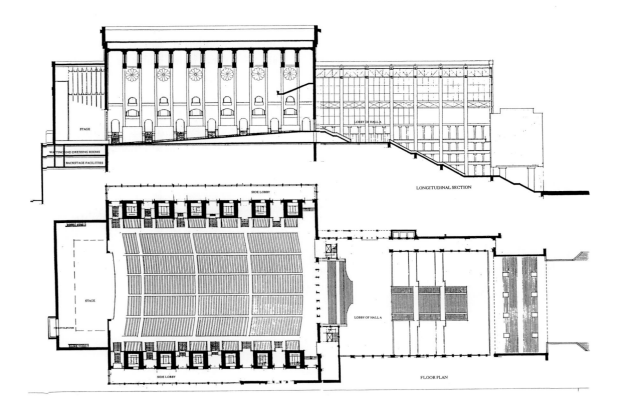

The massive Tokyo Forum, $750,000,000, designed for the heart of downtown Tokyo, Christopher Alexander with Artemis Anninou, Annie der Bedrossian, and others, 1993. Plan and principal section.

The massive, geometric order of the Tokyo Forum auditorium: 100 meters long and 50 meters wide, and 20 meters high

major rectangles falling together, the outside form is not quite so simple. But in essence the main idea is the same, and the use of the syncopated grid as a generating process for the geometric order, nearly identical.

It is very striking to see how, because the building is so enormous, there is an opportunity for a huge range of scales, which become visible in their hierarchy on the side view of the building especially. It is hard to grasp that this building is fourteen stories high, and the arcades and stairs at human scale are almost tiny as they appear on the side of the building. But the brutal order which comes from the geometry, comes from the wonderful and dramatic range of scales — several more jumps in scale than are typical on other buildings.

Once the geometric order is established, walls are made to follow the syncopated grid; and the most subtle order, in which large, smaller and very small alternate, follows nicely. In this case the main columns of the biggest hall are so huge that they contain whole rooms within their own dimension.

But the toughness, the possibility of real feeling in these spaces and their access and cooperation — the ground plan for all that has been established.

7 / OUTWARD SIMPLICITY OF FORM AND PACKING OF FORM

In some cases the "brutal" effect of geometry takes rather simple character. It is not always a matter of load-bearing structure as it is in the previous case. In the case shown here, the Sala house in Berkeley, it is more a matter of pure geometry, once again relying on the framework of an aperiodic grid as the basis for differentiation — but applied to the *space* and rooms, not only to the building structure.

In the Sala house, whose section is shown below, I determined on an extraordinarily simple outside volume: a three-story tower, more or less square in plan (20 feet by 20 feet). However, what may be seen in this section is the way the house is then crammed with smaller, ordered spaces, each unique in position and configuration. Yet the whole is managed so that these various small volumes pack tightly and neatly, without leftovers. This creates a strong and definite form, geometric in its essence, yet adapted and flexible and able to contain what it needs to contain, without any raggedness.

We see a similar thing in the ground plan of the Fuggerei in Augsburg. This plan (built in the

SECTION

Aperiodic grid visible in the cross-section of the Sala house

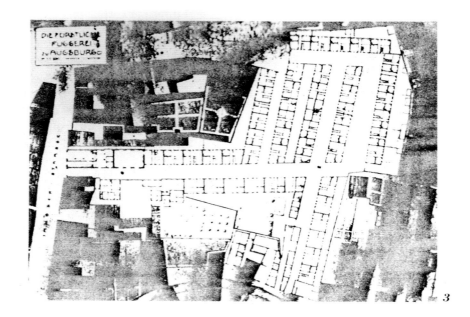

Aperiodic grid visible in the ground plan of the Fuggerei, Augsburg

16th century) contains a series of small rows of workers' houses, arranged in very strict rows. Yet because of the site, its boundaries, and an orientation created by originally existing orchards, the rigidly drawn lines and repetition fit the land, fit the boundaries, and create a unique and unforgettable internal configuration — one of the most beautiful small in-town villages in Europe.

In both cases (the Fuggerei and the Sala house), the principle is the same. A rigid and definite geometry is introduced in a nearly brutal manner, but is then treated, bent, filled, and modified, so that its coherent existence, while being adapted to rooms, circumstances, needs, and land, is nevertheless able to happen beautifully within a visible and satisfying order.

8 / A FURTHER STRUCTURAL EXAMPLE

Let us examine one more case in considerable detail. Here I show one of the college buildings from the Eishin campus. Although the presence of these buildings on the site is necessarily loose to fit the land (see site plan in Book 3, chapter 6), the buildings themselves are the simplest possible rectangles, *but laid into the ground in such a way as to make the land harmonious.*

What is the sequence of events that shaped this building? First, the building got its long shape simply from the way it was needed to sur-

round and form space. The simplest response to this shape was that it should be a firm, precise rectangle. There was no reason to make the building bend or wiggle. There was no reason to make it go in and out. The idea that a building becomes more "organic" if it has a more complex form, even when based on notions of the interior organization, is almost always wrong. In this case, the best and simplest solution was for it to be a rectangle of the right length to do justice to the land. Density prescribed that it be two sto-

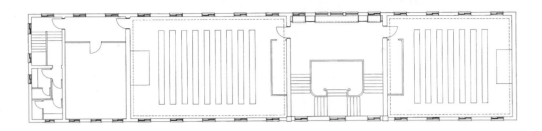

Upstairs plan of the Northwest college building, Eishin campus, 1987.

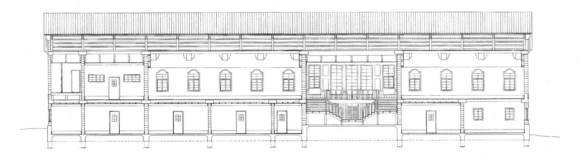

Interior longitudinal cross-section, looking north

ries high; examination of this on a site model confirmed its accuracy. Next the building had to be subdivided to form classrooms. In this particular building, two large lecture halls were required with flexible seating (loose chairs); the two rooms were of different size. These spaces cut across the building at asymmetric points. The entrance, a space in itself, obviously had to be between them. The downstairs plan required a wide arcade. The full dimension of the building, above the arcade, was needed for these two large lecture rooms. Thus an extraordinarily simple division of the rectangle made just the right sizes and shapes for the necessary rooms. Downstairs, below the two big lecture rooms, classrooms are smaller, and simply needed a regular array of small rooms.

Now the arcade required regular spacing of columns. The ceiling, with its massive beams, is an array that creates a horizontal mat of beams, acting as a horizontal moment-resisting diaphragm, to provide resistance to horizontal forces caused by earthquake.

Further subdivision of the main room ceilings by these beams was done in such a way that the space between the beams, and the beams themselves, were also of satisfying shape and dimension. That, as it turned out, worked just right from a structural point of view.

To understand just what I mean by subdivision and the potential which this process has for creating profound order, the following elementary example may be useful. We may grasp what is going on by looking at a very simple problem. Consider two ways of subdividing a rectangle, as illustrated here. First, I might simply cut it into four equal parts (as shown in the upper sketch, page 425). Or, more profoundly, I might divide it

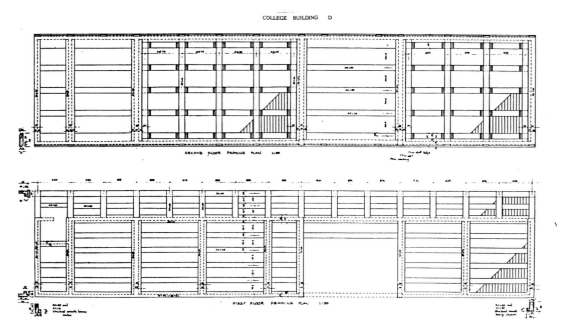

The pattern of beams at first and second ceiling levels which emerged from the orderly process of subdivision.
Differentiation, as defined in chapters 6 and 7, here gives rise directly to the needed aperiodic grid.

Interior of Northwest college building, showing the simplicity of form, and the mat of horizontal beams acting to transfer
horizontal forces through a moment-resisting diaphragm formed by the beams

Northwest college building from the arcade side, Eishin campus

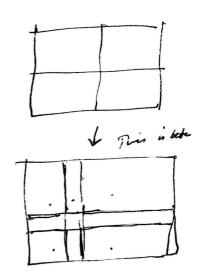

Simple grid and aperiodic grid. The aperiodic one is better because it is more differentiated, contains more centers, more boundaries, and more opportunities for useful and coherent structure.

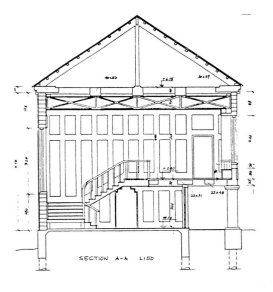

Cross-section of the building

as shown in the lower sketch. This is a more profound cut because, by making an asymmetrical division, I already introduce different LEVELS OF SCALE among the room sizes of the four created rooms. But, further, by introducing a thin band of space between the four divided rooms, a second smaller level of scale is introduced, and the diagram suddenly gets LEVELS OF SCALE, and BOUNDARIES as well. To be sure, this is a very simple example. But it shows how consideration

Northwest college building, Eishin campus

of geometry alone, taken on its own merits, and acted on with ruthless strength, will generate a more profound, more living form. It is subdivision, and subdivision again, and further subdivision of the parts, which creates the form. A purely geometric process creates the order.

9 / A GLIMPSE OF THE IDEA OF A GENERATING SEQUENCE FOR BUILDING STRUCTURE

In these last two examples we have seen how the order, the difficult, "inspired," geometrical order of a building, comes about from step-by-step application of a relatively simple sequence: the sequence that uses the fifteen transformations to build a highly regular aperiodic grid that fits decisions about volume and interior spaces which have been established earlier.

Since this aspect of buildings — the structural grid — is often treated too lightly, and since the sequence of steps I have described catches the important core of architecture in an almost simple way, we have a glimpse here of

what I have stated more generally in chapters 6 snd 7. Namely, as we pay attention to living process, we shall find various fragments of sequence in which living structure of a building is created by nearly routine application of repeatable steps to an emerging form. These will sometimes provide us with a general method of the utmost importance.

We may say that in this case, we have identified a general sequence, which will give us the form of a building, in a powerful and simple fashion, which is repeateable in a wide variety of circumstances.

426

10 / A GENERATIVE PROCESS FOR
MIDDLE-RANGE ORDER IN THE BUILDING STRUCTURE

There is a further aspect of the process I have described, which is of great interest. In all the examples, we have seen, alongside the use of the aperiodic grid, we have also seen, again and again, how *middle-range order* appears in the buildings which are formed by this sequence.

What I mean by "middle-range order" is the existence of entities — centers — at the scale of rooms, bays, portions of a building. Examples are especially visible in the plans and sections on pages 418–19, 423–24, and 428 of this chapter. These middle-sized entities, of a size so that there are perhaps four or five of them across in any one direction, provide the bridge — in terms of scale — between the large entity of the building volume and the smallest entities such as columns, beams, windows, doors, and other individual structural elements. There cannot be profound order in the building unless these middle-range entities exist. And, what is more important, there cannot be order in the building unless these middle range elements have a beautiful pattern, a beautiful pattern of arrangement among themselves. That in itself is remarkable, important, and was first noted by Ingrid King.[5] It is, indeed, this pattern of the middle-sized entities, which most strongly gives overall geometric order to the building. Without it, a building is very unlikely to be beautiful.

It is the generating process and the use of the aperiodic grid which produces these middle-sized centers. I should like to try and characterize what has been going on in these examples, so that we understand how this comes about — how it is related to the fundamental process and to the idea of living process, and to the use of the aperiodic grid. When we construct an aperiodic grid, the critical issue is the alternation of narrow grid bands with larger grid bands: This is what allows for the creation of boundaries and levels of scale inside the building, and paves the way for a variety of bay sizes at the intersection of the larger grid bands. It is also this which then stimulates the formation of strong, middle-sized centers.

Within this grid, it is certainly obvious that STRONG CENTERS, LOCAL SYMMETRIES, GOOD SHAPE, AND LEVELS OF SCALE play a huge part in the kind of process I have been describing. The outer shapes, the envelope, the plan, the sections, the walls, the structural bays, are all creating strong form at a level of scale which is intermediate to the building volume.

Thus, these centers are marked, first of all, by their intermediate scale. They are not as big as the building, but they are not small either. They exist at a scale roughly halfway between the two.

The existence of these halfway, middle-range centers in a living structure sheds a great deal of light on the unfolding process. The living process *must* give rise to coherent entities at a middle range of scale. In buildings, especially, the success of the process will be judged by the extent to which these middle-range entities appear with their own distinct symmetries, with their own definite and distinct force as strong centers, no matter where they are, and how they fit together in the building.

I have described this geometrical process almost viscerally as "brutal," because that is how it does present itself. But even so, although it is the most naked and forceful artistic act, this too must be seen as an *unfolding* which uses nothing but the fundamental process.

The effort is, at each moment, to make each "thing" positive. Space is made positive. Mass is made positive. Each element is given a positive and definite form. Each element contained within it is given a positive and definite form. And the masses of which the elements are made, they, too, are given positive and definite form.

Niche in the Central building, Eishin campus

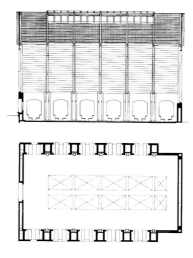

Plan and section of the Central building

Thus, the elaboration of form which occurs, is a raw harmony made of the simplest elements, in a telling and geometrical order, which is balanced and gauged to convey raw feeling. It repeats. It is often brutally simple in its regularities. But each mass is calculated to oppose, or complement, or complete, the harmony of the other elements.

This process, which circles around a bit, is the process of trial and error in which the solid geometry receives calculable, massive weight. When you are done, if you have reached what you aim for, you feel the impact of its "presence." *This* is how architecture comes about.

Interior of the Central building

11 / WHAT SEEMS LIKE AN IMPOSITION OF GEOMETRY IS NECESSARY AS A PART OF EVERY LIVING PROCESS

What I have said applies to buildings. It is the process through which the great volumes and spaces, in their proper hierarchy, are fitted together with small elements, even with the masses of which the walls and stones are made, to arrive at one solid packing that endows its surroundings and its occupants with the presence of a living center.

I believe — but am not in a position to affirm with certainty — that a similar "brutal" and purely geometric process always occurs somewhere in other kinds of unfolding that generate living order. I have had conversations with colleagues who are trying to extend what I have presented in this book. They tell me that at least something similar is going on in poetry, in dance, in the formation of social structure, in planning, even in the creation of healthy family relationships.[6]

Does this formal creation of geometry really apply to other living processes? Does it apply to the formation of a community? Does it apply to the creation of a human group; does it apply to the brushwork of a delicate painting? Or to the construction of a song played by a flute? To all these questions, it is probable, I think, that the answer is "yes." I believe the language of this chapter, pretty much as I have written it, applies not only to the construction of small buildings, and great buildings, but also to the emergence of any coherent whole, in almost any medium.

Thinking about creation in this way, brutal and too-decisive though it may seem, is the process by which the guts of a thing, its valuable force, is made.

NOTES

1. The whole chapter owes a great debt to Ingrid King. The difficulty of writing it and this difficult topic had been plaguing me for years, but I felt unable to write it down successfully. The way of treating it which I have chosen finally became clear in the course of several intensive discussions with Ingrid, in which we reviewed, together, many buildings which we have built, and which other people have built. During these discussions the logic of this chapter became clear.

2. See discussion of the Sapporo building in Ingrid Fiksdahl King, CHRISTOPHER ALEXANDER AND CONTEMPORARY ARCHITECTURE (Tokyo: A+U, ARCHITECTURE AND URBANISM, Special one-volume issue, August 1993, 151 pages).

3. For more detail of this process see Book 3, chapter 6.

4. For more detail of this process see Book 3, chapters 7 and 12.

5. Ingrid King, "Notes for a lecture on 'middle range order'," lecture given in the Department of Architecture lecture series, Kroeber Hall, University of California, 1981.

6. The expansion of the nature of order theory into these various subjects has been proposed to me and written about by various authors, including Richard Gabriel (poetry), Jenny Quillien (anthropology, human behavior, and organization theory), Peter Block (society and institutions) and many others. Of special interest is Richard Gabriel's extremely detailed application of the theory to the writing of poetry and to the criticism of poems. In his short book he constructs a parallel theory to the effort undertaken in this book, with extraordinary success. See THE NATURE OF POETIC ORDER: AND ITS APPLICATION TO THE PROBLEM OF LOCATING FAILURE IN POEMS, Department of English, Stanford University, 1999.

CHAPTER SIXTEEN

FORM LANGUAGE AND STYLE

HOW CAN HUMAN BEINGS IMPLEMENT A GEOMETRICAL DIFFERENTIATING PROCESS SUCCESSFULLY?

1 / INTRODUCTION

In the end, the lasting product of architecture is the shape and reality of the finished building. Everything in architecture comes from layout, organization, form, shape. And how elusive this is! Even now, after discussing so many aspects of living process, I have still not said enough about the actual shapes, the style, the 'typical' geometry of buildings which have living structure. What do they look like? What *should* they look like? From where should they get their "look"?

Operationally, too, this question poses daily problems for the architect, the artist. Each one of us architects struggles to make a beautiful thing. We work at it. We want to achieve this beauty. Is there anything, besides the advice already given in the last dozen chapters, which can guide us in this hardest task of all, the artistic task of formation, geometry-making, which will show us how to make buildings which have surviving shapes, resilient, for ever, shapes that will endure.[1]

Where, after all, when all else is said and done, should we look for shape and style and substance. As we begin to make a building, where should we get the building from, its shape, its style, so that the building ends up beautiful?

2 / THE FORMAT OF OUR ART

This comment is far more serious than it might seem. It is not merely a lament for the difficulty of the task, or a plea that this problem, too, should be addressed. Rather, it turns out, quite surprisingly, that this problem and its solution *must* lie at the very center of the idea of living process in the sphere of building; that indeed a living process MUST address this problem, since a process cannot work successfully if this problem is not addressed. It is not merely an individual problem, a natural personal concern of each individual artist. Rather, *it is a fundamental issue that belongs square in the middle of the analysis of living structure as a product of society.*[2]

We may start from the fact, obvious enough, that we do not start each new design from scratch. Somehow, we learn, over years, the ingredients that make a building good. Somehow, this knowledge is kept by us, occasionally transmitted to others, but mainly kept by us, in our minds, as a store of knowledge, which we may draw upon.

All this is a roundabout way of saying that more important than anything, in our work, is the combinatory system we grow in our own minds, the form language we use to speak the words that come out as buildings

And what format must this form language have? It is the box of tricks, the elements, rules, ways of making roofs, edges, windows, steps, the ceiling of a room. The way to make a wall, the way to make a column. The shape of the edge where the building meets the sky. The ways which will not only make a coherent and beautiful work, but one which can be built, in our time, by means we understand, control, and can execute for not impossible amounts of money.

More accurately put, at any given period of history, in any particular society, there are a certain number of schemata which provide rules of thumb for designing and constructing buildings.[3] The form-language is the (usually unspoken) combinatory system of these schemata (social, technological, geometric, stylistic, etc) which architects and builders have in their minds about how buildings ought to be organized, how built, how they must look. We may even call form-language the repository of style.

The most basic fact of all concerning these schemata is the following: At any given time in our history, we are able to create only what can be "made" from the schemata which we already have in our form-language. This is true even if we have been thinking in a very good way, with intelligence, concerning living structure. It is inevitable, therefore, that since we cannot help working within an existing form-language — itself, of course, based on the available processes of our time — then even with the best will in the world, *we shall only be able to reproduce versions and combinations of what can be "reached" by that form language.*

I want to be quite sure that the logic of this argument is clear to the reader. For reasons given above, the nature of human cognition is such that people will, in any case, use schemata as the basis of their building operations. It is, in essence, the shared form language of society. Good, bad, or indifferent, *some* kind of form language *will* be used. This is true whether it was a good period of architecture or a bad period. The schemata can be good or bad; the stylistic components available for recombination may be good or bad; but no matter which, it is the traces of the then-current form language of combinable schemata, which, dictate and shape the form of the world in any given period.

However, for reasons already hinted at in the last few chapters, the kind of geometry which is needed for living structure, and which must emanate from proper use of any living process, is not necessarily attainable within the combinations of today's form-language. There are reasons to believe that the form languages of traditional societies helped people to work in living process, allowed them to form buildings well adapted, and truthfully differentiated from the whole, in harmony with the whole. These reasons have been given in chapters 3 and 5 and 6; and it is plain that the conditions of living process were more often met in traditional societies than in our own period. But the form languages of recent periods, for various reasons, do not serve this purpose well, and in fact often even prevent the process of living process, and the natural process of differentiation.

It is reasonable to ask, therefore, what a modern form language would need to be like, *if it were to help us reach the goal of living process in our highly modern and technically sophisticated society?*

It might be said that, compared with this question of form-language, no other question will play such a decisive role in the formation of the environment. If we want a living world, and we want one which is created and generated by living process, *it is imperative that the form languages we use, and the form languages available to us, help us and support us in this task.*

Briefly put, then: Unless we have a form language which supports the necessities of living structure, then living structure is simply out of our reach. Even if all the conditions of chapters 6–15 are satisfied, it will still not be enough. Without a form language that supports the living structure, the nearly-living process will fall down, and not be effective. If a society has inadequate style, inadequate shapes and forms, then no matter how hard the builders and architects try, the environment they create will not be, *and cannot be* a living structure.

We come therefore, to one of the most vital targets of my search in Book 2. In order to make living process possible, we must take at least first steps towards a new form language — in effect, steps towards a new architectural style, which is general and which follows from the nature of living process. How, in practice, is such a language to be discovered? What are the strokes, the brush strokes, the gestures, the lines, the shapes, with which we are to paint our pictures, conceive our buildings? What are the materials, techniques, in which we execute these buildings? In what style should they, must they, might they, be executed? What is the language of shape and form in which we may create the stones of a living architecture in our time?

I must admit, frankly, that in this chapter I do not solve this problem. In most of the chapters so far, I have given what I consider at least a tentative and satisfactory answer to the problems raised by that chapter. But this problem is more difficult. I shall indicate the general lines of a solution, but I cannot claim to solve it fully. I hope that it will be taken up by many architects, together, in the decades ahead of us.

3 / HISTORICALLY, WHAT KIND OF THING DID A FORM LANGUAGE DO?

As a point of departure, we may start by making clear what a form language is and what it can do.

In earlier chapters, I have presented a conception of living process, in which sequences of steps — each step creating centers — allow a person or a group of people to create a building, or a part of a building, with reasonable expectation that it will be well adapted to its context, and will have living structure. The patterns in the sequence provide the geometric content which is specific to purpose, culture, climate, and so on. The sequence is organized so that the form unfolds coherently, and allows all the necessary patterns to appear in the finished structure.

Traditional sequences, however, went further. In traditional society, the sequences which people used to make their buildings also created the form, the geometry, the style, so that the entire building production of a society had a deep coherence of style and substance, with the result that buildings and outdoor spaces and their details, cohered together to form a living, geometric unity. For example, the 18th- and 19th-century houses in Virginia, described by the historian Henry Glassie, look alike, have the same shape, have the same kinds of plans, have the same roofs, the same chimneys. They are widely different in size and position, but are all versions of a single type of form.[4]

Like this language of rural Virginia, the pattern languages and sequences in use in tradi-tional societies, nearly always specified form, shape, volume, material, style, ornament. They embodied a coherent geometric, visual, physical style, so that now, long afterwards, the architecture of each given place and time, is still recognizable as part of the geometric living unity which was created by that culture.

It is to emphasize this point, that in the text of this chapter I shall keep on calling such geometric languages, which create building form and style as well, not merely pattern languages, but *form languages*.[5]

I shall argue that the creation of living structure in a society, cannot rest on the living process alone, as I have described it thus far. The emergence of living process requires, for its success, tools which directly give people the language of form, the shapes with which to work. It requires that the people shaping things, planning, making the buildings, can, through the sequences of form language, share some coherence of style and geometric substance. That is what is needed, for people to have the competence that they need in order to make complete buildings, geometrically. If there is to be a living structure in our society, the people of our society need such a form language. And I shall argue that it is our own responsibility (as architects) to create such a form language, both for our own use, and for the millions of people who are involved in making buildings.[6]

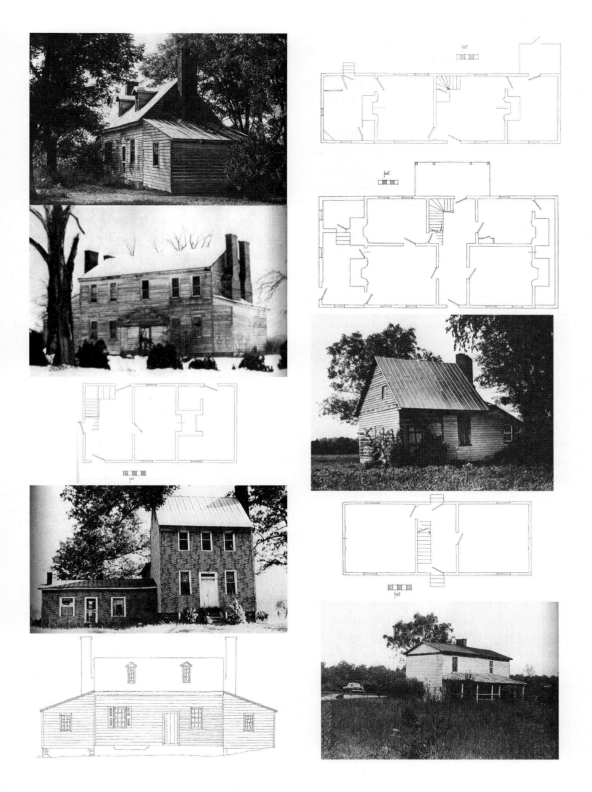

Some of the Virginia houses described by Henry Glassie, and generated by the form-language he described.

4 / TWENTIETH-CENTURY STRUGGLES TO INVENT A FORM-LANGUAGE FOR MODERN ARCHITECTURE

This thought is hardly new! Throughout the 20th century, architects began a great struggle to invent or discover an appropriate form language for the modern era. This was the undercurrent and expressed intent of much building and design that ranked as high architecture. Adolf Loos, Walter Gropius, Richard Neutra, Le Corbusier, Mies van der Rohe, and Frank Lloyd Wright all tried to reach this goal. But these 20th-century attempts to find a form language were not generally linked to a capacity to create buildings by living process. Indeed, the need for living process, and the results of living process, have not, up until now, been an explicit part of the architectural agenda of modern times.

Twentieth-century efforts made by architects started with the early and middle periods of modernism, in which there was a focus on asymmetry, massive repetition, simplicity of formwork and elements, large elements, prefabrication (of panels, beams, sheets of glass, assembled components (windows, doors, roofs even, wall panels, and trusses), often with a mixture of arbitrary shapes thrown in. These ideas created the style of the middle years of the 20th century.

Later, in the last decades of the 20th century, a new language was created by architects, one which one may describe as playful interpenetration of large fabricated elements (as, for instance, in the work of Frank Gehry). One saw sheets of glass, corrugated steel, slender steel rods, guy wires, gaskets, prefabricated machine-made furnishings. These — sometimes mixed with ironic references to historic elements like pediments and arches — created the core of the postmodern and deconstructivist imagery.

In the background, there was also a brave attempt — not always inspiring — to build sensible buildings which resembled ordinary buildings of traditional value, houses which appealed to traditional sensibilities with brick, clapboard siding, traditional looking windows, all occasionally mixed with nostalgic and historical forms.

None of these — neither the first, nor the second, nor the last — have played much of a useful role in helping the evolution of a modern form-language which can help us create living architecture. All in all, the schemata created by modern and modernistic architectural efforts in the 20th century are too crude to carry this load. They are too forced, too gross, not capable of the subtleties of form which create a living geometry.

Of course, occasional helpful steps were taken in the 20th century. Among architects who contributed to the invention of material which does have a role to play in living process, we may include Auguste Perret and the use of reinforced concrete; Wright with his cast Mayan blocks and intentionally small scale cross sections; the natural building movement placing emphasis on the use of earth and other ecologically friendly materials; other contemporary efforts to make transformations of frame construction towards something humane. The works of Geoffrey Bawa in SriLanka, and Ragnar Östberg in Sweden, helped pave a way for true physical beauty, unsullied by artifice. John Habraken's worldwide effort to achieve "open building" helped to modify the languages in use, with the intent of allowing individual acts of construction a greater role in the urban fabric.[7]

But even what came from these various positive directions has not yet laid the foundation for a recognisable worldwide living process for our time. We have still not achieved a useful and coherent geometry — a form language — which lays geometrical stepping stones toward the creation of a living world *that can, now and in the future, be attained by us for the production of coherent, vivid, geometric form.*

Although various modernistic schemata have by now occupied us for almost a hundred years, they have still not given us a form language capable of letting us make a living architecture. The *geometry* they have created is inadequate. They have not shed enough light on the actual *shape* the built

world must have if it is to have true life. Nor have they yet increased our consciousness of the fact that the geometry of the world is the absolutely indispensable underpinning for all living process.

5 / THE STYLE NEEDED FOR UNFOLDED, LIVING FORM

Why did the experimental form-languages of the 20th century not work? The reason is not hard to see. It is rather as if someone gave you a ruler and T-square, and said "Use these drawing tools to draw a human face." You would say, "But that is almost impossible: the ruler and the T-square create the wrong kind of geometry. A human face is made of different shapes and different relationships than can be drawn with these tools."

Just so with buildings that have living form. Of course, most buildings have a more or less squarish character, not so often rounded; and of course the situation in the buildings of a city is a little more complex than drawing a face. Nevertheless my example is appropriate. It is an apt comparison. The kinds of shapes which appear as a result of unfolding when it is done right, and which occur as a result of the processes we have been studying from chapter 6 to chapter 15, are highly specific in geometic type and character. The shapes are mainly rectilinear, but they include roughness, they include shapes in which angles are nearly square but not quite square; they necessarily include imperfect repetition, where one column and the next and the next are almost the same, but not quite the same, and each one is placed to make space positive, requiring that things were bent, adjusted, made carefully to fit the nature of an emerging whole. Twentieth-century form language did — and could do — none of this.

The kind of thing that is required may be seen in the stair shown on page 436. Here, the gradual forging of the geometry came about through acts of construction, not only design. The example, once again, is small, but real. It is

an unfolded form, *visible* as unfolded form yet with a definite physical character. It is coherent and geometrically whole, yet it is almost without a conscious, artificial style.

There isn't anything exceptional to this stair; it is fairly humble. But there is unfolding visible in its geometry. When we look at it, we can see the trace of a smoothness of process. We see the result of continuous stepwise adaptations. We can see that, one by one, its features have unfolded. I should like the reader to try and grasp what I mean by this. If we look at the stair, and try to imagine the decisions being made in time, we can see that the placement of the stair was established first, followed by a true unfolding. The stair is brisk, spare in outline, but has the character of accurate formation that follows from the proper adaptive unfolding of architectural form.

First, the landing was established; then the walls and their banisters were established in relation to the stair; then the ornament, which forms the top, was established in relation to the walls.[8]

All this may sound obvious, but it is not. If you concentrate on it, I believe you will *feel* the unfolded character of what is there. We can feel that one thing was established, then another was established in relation to the first, and so on like that. Each smaller thing has been given its shape after, and in relation to, the larger thing that was established first. It is *that* which creates the harmonious feeling, since it is that which makes each part adapted and comfortable. The stair is gently ornamented, but simple. Each part is, more or less just right.

As a result, the building form has a very definite character. Yet it is a character without conscious or deliberate imagery. It is nearly what

Unfolded geometry: A stair on the George house, 1998, Christopher Alexander and Randy Schmidt

one might call a formless form. It arises from un-folding of differentiations and symmetries, and little else. This kind of form is *necessary* in order for unfolding of a building design to occur smoothly. A prefabricated stair, for instance, cast in one piece in a factory, and lifted in by crane, could not have this quality. It cannot look as if it has unfolded. And it cannot have the deep adaptation typical of an unfolded structure.

Perhaps one is led to wonder if unfolding is even possible in our era of modern construction. Yet the stair in the photograph is an entirely modern construction, built in 1998 at a modest budget, using conventional concrete blocks, sup-

plemented by poured concrete ornaments poured into styrofoam molds, and a wooden portion cut out with modern saws and tools.

The form language which can support the creation and emergence of such an unfolded thing, must be made from elements and transfor-mations which support, one by one, the various steps in the emergence of a whole. That requires something simple, and direct, but above all some-thing which corresponds at every step to the kinds of thing which happen when a living structure is unfolded by differentiation from its context.

What kinds of new form language might help us achieve this: might let us create simple

Twentieth-century form language: The schemata here are not useful for creating living structure.
Daniel Libeskind, Felix Nussbaum Museum, Osnabrück

and unconscious, unfolded form for all the thousands of types of buildings we deal with in the world today?

If one were trying to make a staircase like the one shown on page 438, by combining schemata mentally, what kinds of schemata would they have to be? What language is needed, even to be able to *draw* such a building, or —

equally — to be able to build such a stair? The answer is: It would have to be a language of shapes, forms, differentiations and symmetries, which go just exactly to what is needed at each subsequent step. They would need to be simple, modest, small. And, certainly, the rules of the game needed for such a purpose are not the schemata which are being introduced today.

6 / WHY TWENTIETH-CENTURY FORM LANGUAGES WERE NOT HELPFUL

In chapter 4, I described the way in which modern forms that are not structure-preserving to their environment, are so obsessed with images that they cannot be achieved by structure-preserving steps.[9] They are conceptual, but are not

attainable in easy, natural steps which arise from the context.

To see that clearly, we need only look at examples of buildings which were considered avant-garde in 1998. The two shown here are by

Twentieth-century form language: The schemata here cannot create living structure.
Renzo Piano, New Metropolis, Center for Science and Technology, Amsterdam.

Renzo Piano and by Daniel Libeskind. The forms of these buildings do not allow such an unfolding to occur. They patently do *not*. Rather, the Piano and Libeskind examples show idiosyncratic modernistic forms, certainly able to draw attention to themselves, but which are not suitable as a source of schemata for living structure (pages 439 and 440).

Even when the architect working in a modernist or postmodern idiom tries to make buildings "organic" or more natural, they are likely to fail. Look at another more recent example of postmodern design done by one of the same architects (Renzo Piano) who is, in this case, con-sciously trying to be "organic." On pages 441–2 I show his design for a cultural center for the Pacific island nation of New Caledonia. In this design, we see modernistic building forms that intentionally follow the image of traditional New Caledonian huts. It is intended to create harmony between the two.

The aim is laudable. But what is hoped for is not achieved. The achieved image is an illusion, perhaps even a mockery, and the implied similarity between the two systems with the suggested harmony between the two, is none of it real. The two systems of forms are utterly different in their deep nature.

Renzo Piano, Community center, New Caledonia

Yet the architect himself has stated that his work somehow mirrors or reflects — and fits into — the traditional forms from the South Pacific. What features of the forms might create this impression in Piano's mind, and encourage him to make this claim? The forms are rounded (in plan). They are asymmetrical. They are incomplete. They are semi-transparent. They very roughly resemble (in outward shape only) the huts of New Caledonia. But these characteristics, which admittedly create an illusion of something different from other more typical modern forms, still do not correct the essential problem: their lack of unfolded, adapted, geometry. If we look at the real traditional huts of New Caledonia (shown in the foreground of a picture of the newer building, lower picture), they resemble, of course, *all* huts of primitive society *in that they have an unfolded structure*. This unfolded form does not lie in the superficial qualities such as those I have just mentioned. Rather it lies in the following: The shape is imperfect. Its symmetries are imperfect. They are not gross asymmetries, but *imperfect symmetries*. Its unevenness is not a gross asymetry, but a small twist in the shape, caused by some unpredictable reality.

The traditional huts of New Caledonia, visible in the foreground, have quite another kind of form, and the apparent similarity of form language is almost a "trick," hardly more than an illusion.

Thus the form-languages of the two cases are entirely different. In the cultural center, the forms are brittle, asymmetrical, open, where the older forms are soft, symmetrical, and closed. The new forms create the language of deconstructivist imagery, and inject this into the the older idea, achieving a superficial connection, but more deeply a travesty of intent and feeling in the actual substance of the buildings. The form language which Renzo Piano has used, is a language of dead form — it is this which creates the slightly grotesque quality and lack of resemblance. The form language of the traditional hut, on the other hand, is alive because it is unassuming and sequentially generated by unfolding. It is made with the language of unfolded form.

One sees from this example, that the possible use of schemata based on such features as curvature and form and shape, if it is maintained within modernist or post-modernist or deconstructivist imagery, will not accomplish a path toward unfolded living form, *because it does not take seriously the* CONTENT *of living structure*, and only strives to create an apparent similarity, while leaving the deep gulf between the two languages of form unchanged. It is evidently not deep enough. The main problem is that these works — though filled with effort, and regarded by some as important steps toward the evolution of a modern form-language — in fact contribute little to the practical capacity we have for making living structure.

This is the crux of the matter. An effective living process for our time must not only, in principle, be able to generate living structure. Somehow, the process must also contain the right elements, the words and syllables which do actually make it possible to create living structure in buildings. That means, a living process in architecture must contain schemata specific to architecture, which may be combined and recombined to build living structure.

As for the schemata which are capable of that — for the moment, in the contemporary idom, they simply don't exist.

7 / THE MODERN THEORY OF LANGUAGE

It is unlikely, in my view, that we can make much progress in finding a new form language, adequate to the world-wide purpose of forming living structure, without drawing upon the most modern discoveries in the field of language. During the 20th century, the concept of "language" was given a precise formal meaning by several mathematicians, for example, by the mathematician Emil Post[10] — and for the case of natural language by Noam Chomsky who coined the phrase *transformational grammar*.[11] In both domains, the basic idea was this: a string-creating system was defined; the starting point was usually a null sentence consisting of a single character, or word, or the null string. The language provided a series of rules which allowed certain kinds of transformations which would elaborate a given string, and turn it into another string which was allowed (hence the term transformational grammar). Typical allowed transformations might include substitution, inversion, concatenation, etc.

The rules of the language *were then these transformations*. A legitimate sentence in English was any sentence that could be derived by successive transformations. A legitimate proposition in arithmetic was any sentence (string of characters) which could be obtained by successive transformations of the base string.

You see how similar this is to the idea of differentiation as defined in chapter 7. In a transformational grammar, we start with a simple or empty string, and gradually elaborate it by successive transformations, until we get a completely differentiated structure, by substitution, inversion, concatenation, etc. In a form language for architecture, by analogy, we would then need a system of transformations which is able, gradually, to differentiate a previously less differentiated context, giving it more and more structure, until finally it becomes a completed building for that context.

Possibly the first person to try and write down such a formal language for architecture was Henry Glassie.[12] Almost thirty years ago, in his study of 18th-century houses in Virginia and their language, he did capture, as nearly as one might imagine possible, the actual production of a given class of existing buildings, through a well-defined transformational grammar.[13] The grammar he defined gives a system of transformations needed to define the house designs typical of those Virginia houses. It is valid for a wide range of sizes and conditions, and provides volume, plan shape, plan organization, length and width — and then proceeds to give positions of partitions, walls, entrances, windows, and ends with window sizes and important construction details.

Professor Glassie's grammar is of course, for a traditional system of architecture, one existing in the 18th century, and for a very narrowly defined culture and locality.

More recently, members of another school of thought, have been trying to make progress with the idea of form language. George Stiny and his colleagues have made an attempt to develop what they call "shape-grammars" in a comparable way. So far, these latter studies have not borne as much fruit as one might hope, in terms which an architect would understand as useful. This has happened, I believe, because they have been undertaken, so far, within the context of the value-free, postmodern attitude, which almost by definition is not able to deal with problems of life and tries instead to study its subject within a purely neutral conception.[14]

If we ask ourselves how we may construct a form language which can deliver (and help us create) living structure in buildings and communities as I have described it in this book, we are led to search, once again, for transformations: and of course the obvious place to start is with those transformations which appear naturally in the differentiating process. These are just those fifteen transformations associated with the fifteen properties, already depicted in chapters 2 and 7.

I list the fifteen transformations once more, to remind the reader of what they are: 1. LEVELS OF SCALE, 2. STRONG CENTERS, 3. BOUNDARIES, 4. ALTERNATING REPETITION, 5. POSITIVE SPACE, 6. GOOD SHAPE, 7. LOCAL SYMMETRIES, 8. DEEP INTERLOCK AND AMBIGUITY, 9. CONTRAST, 10. GRADIENTS, 11. ROUGHNESS, 12. ECHOES, 13. THE VOID, 14. SIMPLICITY AND INNER CALM, 15. NOT-SEPARATENESS.

Each of the fifteen transformations designates one way in which a structure may be transformed into another structure, while increasing its life. Any sequence of these fifteen transformations will therefore provide us with a basic, non-arbitrary scheme of differentiations that can be performed during the unfolding of a living structure. Thus, the fifteen transformations, potentially provide us with the underpinning of a form language, in the exact sense understood by the modern science of mathematical linguistics.

There is, of course, the enormous challenge of making such a language concrete, and culture-specific, while not hampering it with traditional or historical reference. I shall not attempt this here, since it is too vast a topic, necessarily to be taken up by others. But it is possible to see the first outline of an adequate form language in the fifteen transformations themselves, and in their immediate impact on geometry. From this, we may see glimpses of a new style, that could emerge, in hundreds of culturally different versions, but one which is nevertheless quite recognizable geometrically, and utterly different from the geometry and style we became used to in the 20th century.

8 / BUILDING A FORM-LANGUAGE FROM THEORY

Let us ask how the creation of such a form-language might begin.

Briefly stated, we may say that a successful building, one which has life, will always be entirely made of living centers, so that every part, and every part of every part, and every part between two parts, has been shaped and made as a tangible being — that is to say, a living center.[15]

In order to describe the creation of a building in these terms, we may then, reformulate the

A view of the town of Mardin, Eastern Turkey

idea of the iterated application of the fundamental process, creating centers one by one (as already described in chapter 7) as a system of transformations in which each transformation introduces further living centers into the unfolding structure. In Book 1, I have shown hundreds of examples of living structure; and as we have seen, in every case this living structure is made of a dense profusion of well-adapted, coherent, living centers, tying the whole into the larger world-whole which surrounds it. Very succinctly indeed, then, we may say that a form language able to produce life must be a system of transformations which allows such living centers to be created, one by one, or a few at a time, gradually creating a profusion of coordinated and interdependent living centers, each well-related and supportive to the larger wholes around it.

A building which comes as output from such a language — if the language is properly applied — can have life. A building made in some other framework — as for example in the conceptual frameworks popular in the late 20th-century — will not easily ever have life. To see such a form language at work, let us look at an ancient tower built in Mardin, Eastern Turkey, and reconstruct the action of the fifteen transformations on the geometric emergence of this tower and its form.

We may see how this tower was conceived. if we imagine a series of transformations, starting *only* with the general idea of a tower (a tall, thin, stick-like building). Let us consider what happens if this undifferentiated stick idea is transformed by a succession of transformations based on the fifteen properties.

(1) First, we give the "stick" a top — this is the BOUNDARY transformation.

(2) Next we give it a base — another boundary transformation.

(3) The shaft is now given a good shape (by

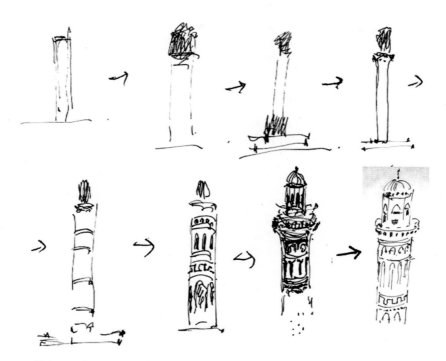

Eight transformations in the evolution of this tower, from nothing. See pages 443–44.

the STRONG-CENTER and GOOD-SHAPE transformations).

(4) The ensuing shaft is now transformed by a series of horizontal bans or belts — the ALTERNATING REPETITION transformation.

(5) We now introduce elements — into these belts. They differ from belt to belt — that is the most important aspect — and is created by the CONTRAST transformation.

(6) We now introduce living centers into one of the belts — a series of arches. This is the LEVELS-OF-SCALE transformation, acting together with STRONG-CENTERS .

(7) We also pay attention to the graded series of elements, from top to bottom, in the different width of the belts. This is produced by the GRADIENTS transformation.

(8) We make sure that each element introduced within the belts is locally symmetrical — this is produced by the action of the LOCAL-SYMMETRIES transformation.

(9) We also place the elements — arches — in such a way that the space between the arches is as strong as the arches themselves — the action of the POSITIVE-SPACE transformation.

(10) As we introduce elements in further bands, we maintain a general similarity of form — applying the ECHOES transformation.

(11) We elaborate the top of the tower, with ribs, (the ALTERNATING-REPETITION) transformation, and with a beautiful pregnant shape (the GOOD-SHAPE transformation).

(12) To elaborate it further, we give the top a balcony that projects out into the air around the tower (The DEEP-INTERLOCK transformation).

(13) Again and again and again, we apply the LOCAL-SYMMETRIES transformation, the POSITIVE-SPACE transformation, and the ALTERNATING-REPETITION transformations.

Repeated use of these transformations, snd little else, has created the tower.

It must be noted that the production of the tower as a living center, is caused, not by the historical period, or by any particular style, but primarily by the repeated application of these very general transformations.

9 / THE FORM OF FUTURE BUILDINGS
SKETCHES TO ILLUSTRATE THE OUTPUT FROM
A NEW FORM-LANGUAGE

Let us now consider a non-historical example. Consider the following sketch of a tiny building front (page 447). I show six steps, taken one at a time, which led to its form.

- *First, the ground and the roof plane are established (Step 1).*
- *The roof gets ears to mark the ends (Step 2).*
- *The corners of the volume are drawn in (Step 3).*
- *A mark is made, to indicate the door — actually it is the window above the door.*
- *The door is filled in below (Step 4).*
- *A first window is roughed in (Step 5).*
- *It is then embellished with a round arch above.*
- *Another window completes the composition (Step 6).*

Though informal, the building form which results from these steps, performed one at a time, in the order given, has a very definite character. It is visible, strong, a definite being in its own right. Yet it is a character without conscious or deliberate imagery. It arises, only, from unfolding of differentiations and local symmetries.

I give this *very* simple example, in order to emphasize, again, the vital role of *unfolding* — the process by which form is created through differentiation — and to see clearly how this comes about, what kinds of elements and local symmetries will typically be generated by unfolding. It must be noted that this statement is highly abstract, highly general, and not oriented to history. It certainly should not invite an architect to some form of romantic historicism. There is *nothing* about this statement which suggests that buildings, to be living, should have historical antecedents or allusions. Indeed, buildings made with an eye to the past will most often fail to have living structure, because the process of historical reproduction somehow turns vivid,

living structure sour. It congeals, without having real force or real vivacity.

It should also be understood, once and for all, that the buildings which do have living centers in them, though they have often been despised by modernistic theorists and dismissed on the grounds that they are about history, are in fact not about history at all. Modern architecture turned the entire architectural process on its head, because it managed to confuse people into thinking that all buildings that have beings in them — living centers — must inevitably be historical, or imitations of history. Nothing could be further from the truth. This one lie, caused, in a sense, the whole sorry upset we now look back on as modernism and post-modernism.

Indeed, the step-by-step evolution of living centers, in a progressive differentiating process, is *necessary* to the adaptation process. It is not a cultural decision, not an emotional decision, but a biological necessity — an essential part of the adaptation of a complex system. I have tried to demonstrate this conclusively in chapters 6–15. And we may say, therefore, that this geometric process of differentiation is the necessary underpinning of any building which is functionally well-adapted to its terrain.

To continue, I want to illustrate, more substantially, the difference between the geometry of a *natural* form language (as it arises from the patient use of the fifteen transformations) and the geometry which was chiefly accepted in late 20th-century architecture.

Please consider the small sketches on the next eight pages. These sketches might seem hardly more than doodles in the margin of a paper napkin. However, as a group they share a definite morphological character, similar to the example just given, though more complex. It is a character largely different from our current as-

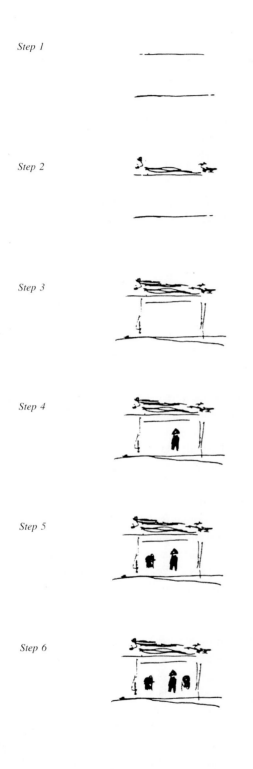

Step 1

Step 2

Step 3

Step 4

Step 5

Step 6

Six steps in the unfolding of a small building or building wing. Simple as it is, there is a syncopated complexity which enters in, that is impossible to achieve within the framework of modern ideas of design.

sumptions about architecture, yet necessary, I think, for any living structure. It is precisely in this difference that the modern problem of architectural form resides. That is why I wish to illustrate it, draw attention to it, and make the reader understand why something at least *like* this morphological character I show here, must come about as a result of any living process.

What is it that appears in these sketches? On first seeing them, a person who is used to modern idiom may say that they have an archaic character. But my view is different. It seems to me that these sketches show three things:

(1) They have an informal character, a rough and ready character, which is typical of highly adapted structures, not typical of technically produced or image-produced structures. It is, very much more, the result of an unfolding process.

(2) The sketches also have a humane character. One feels that they have a kindly relation to human existence, and to the vulnerable side of human nature.

(3) The buildings illustrated in the sketches contain the fifteen properties profusely. This must be there, of course, from the repeated use of the fifteen transformations to obtain structure-preserving unfolding.

I believe one may go further, to say that the sketches shown, for all their apparent naivete, show precisely the kinds of forms which MUST *in all likelihood follow from any program in which these fifteen transformations are progressively unfolded from a neutral beginning.*

In short, I am claiming that the forms shown in these sketches, far from being archaic, are, if anything, ultra-modern and represent in summary form a geometric character which will, in some version or other, have to be present in *any* future world of unfolded, living, functionally well-adapted buildings.

To help make my argument clear, let us look at the sketches in detail. They are sketches of imaginary but possible building projects meant to show what living form is actually like in its geometry. These sketches are not drawings of actual projects. Rather, they are drawings which

A drawing moving towards a generic house type

convey, in an imaginative fashion, what living structure looks like when it appears in an environment when it is harmonious with human existence and might, above all, have life.

Consider the sketch on page 447, NEAR OPEN LAND, below. Here, in a situation where a reasonably high density part of a city, abuts open land, we see many features of living structure have been generated in the drawing. The interaction between buildings and contours, creates subtle changes in the footings of the building, causing a cascade-like GRADIENT-like quality in the building masses. The stairs sit in the ground, each one unique, thus causing the uniqueness characterized by ROUGHNESS. The near buildings are made stronger as CENTERS, by the falling away of the smaller buildings in the distance. Buildings and stairs repeat in an ALTERNATING REPETITION. The stairs are marked as STRONG CENTERS, and as LOCAL SYMMETRIES; the buildings themselves, each within itself, has local symmetry. The building forms, the stairs, the windows, and the land contours are all related, in their form, thus showing ECHOES: they are generated by the pen which drew upon these echoes. The land forms in front have INTERLOCK

with the stairs and paths, leading toward the buildings. the roof structure, modest almost hidden, nevertheless gives each building GOOD SHAPE. Above all, the casual, formal, yet informal character dominates the scene.

Unfolded, modern, one step at a time, moving toward unfolded structure, the process of drawing the sketch *itself* followed the process of creating one center at a time, in respect to the existing whole. The same is true in all the sketches on the next pages. We may see, if we look carefully, that these building forms are thick with the fifteen properties. Their character, the character of each of them in its entirety, comes from the interplay of these fifteen properties.

But we see not only that the fifteen properties *appear* in these sketches. It is the fifteen properties consciously used as transformations during the process of drawing, which also *generated* the form of these buildings. The fifteen transformations are the ground rules of the language in which these forms are written. In chapter 2 I said that the fifteen are inevitable results (and ingredients) of structure-preserving unfolding. But here the fifteen properties are not merely *generated* by structure-preserving trans-

Bridge with buildings and usable offices within the structure.

formations going on while the drawings were made — they also *provided* a combinatory language of transformations which has the capacity, in human hands, to generate unfolded geometry — the kind of geometry which must follow from a living process.

Another example. In the two houses shown on this page, we have — for example — a natural way of making GRADIENTS. We have a natural way, an expectation, of making emptiness near complex highly differentiated structure — thus making THE VOID near portions of busy repeating structure. We have a kind of repetition with variety, so that inherently, we expect to repeat elements, which vary as we repeat them, because each instance unfolds differently from the matrix in which they occur. There must be an element of the language which allows the building mass to follow the earth, be part of the soil, NOT-SEPARATENESS, in its movement, in its roughness, in its ordinariness. These characters,

needed to allow creation of the adequate, unfolded form, are the same, in essence, as the fifteen properties.

I am asserting that, as human builders who wish to generate living structure, we must carry these fifteen transformations with us, as elements of a form-language which gives us — in part — the building blocks, the tools of the trade, the raw material, from which unfolded structure can be made. That is the ultimate material, from which living buildings must be made. It is this fact, and this process, which transcends the sterile simplification that has been typical of buildings in our machine age: and it is a forward-looking to an era in which living buildings, are our targets, our aims, the dream of achievement which we carry with us, as part of our art.[16]

In addition, let me say that the accompanying sketches should be taken rather literally. I do not mean them as rough drawings of a more

In a city

Near open land

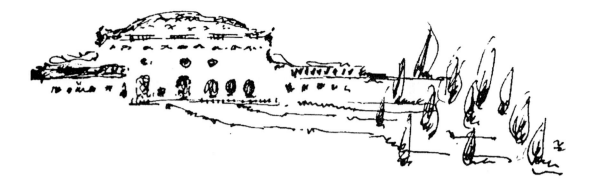

A museum or public building among cypresses

A house.

Another house.

pristine reality. Instead, I mean that their actual ROUGHNESS, and the visible soft morphological character they have because of this roughness, *are of the essence* of the fact that they are living. What I am trying to show in the sketches is that if it is to be truly living structure, it must actually be built with this character as I have shown it.

A MUSEUM OR PUBLIC BUILDING AMONG CYPRESSES

The trees grow where they will; the contours are almost physically visible as rills in the ground. the building takes a position of prominence, natural to the site, yet it is formal. Its formality is accomodated by a stepping of terraces, which allows it to sit, in its massive solidity, without imparing the ground. The shallow dome dominates the structure, but the structure is somewhat informal, even among its formal shapes, windows, doors, arise in syncopated fashion, within the overall movement of the building volumes.

There are smaller parts and larger parts. Openings vary. Ornaments form a BOUNDARY along the top. The left hand end fades into the hill, NOT SEPARATENESS between the building and the land.

INTERIOR OF A GREAT SPACE

Looking through the arch, the central space beyond at first seems regular. However, if we look at the ring below the dome, we see a dark patch, further away a light patch, as if the surface, and the openings, change in magnitude. Below the beam line, arched openings appear. They do not follow the rhythm of the dome's symmetry, but are placed according to the way rooms beyond need to look into the larger space.

Interior of a great space.

A wall in the landscape

In size, shape, arch shape, they vary. A variety of LEVELS OF SCALE are visible. The columns visible in the wall between these openings, are placed where needed, and do not follow a simplified repetition, rather a more syncopated ALTERNATING REPETITION. Near the beam, small openings or brackets, appear in repeating rhythm, but with irregularities dependent on the surroundings. The whole is magnificent in its simplicity, but subtle in shape and line.

A WALL IN THE LANDSCAPE

One of the most important sketches. Here there is just a wall. But we can see in the sketch that the wall and the gate and the steps which lead to the wall, are all integrated with the land in its nature, so deeply, that the land and the wall and the trees are all one: there is virtually no seam, no separation between them. They are all

of one character. The wall follows the ground. It dips, the top of the wall is thicker in one place where creepers are growing on it; the posts of the gate rise out the earth, each from its clump; the wall follows the contours, up, down, slopes. A seat on the left, leans into the wall. The top of the wall on the left hand side is accentuated near the gate, trails off further away.

In all this the physical fabric of the wall is like, and part of, the physical fabric of the earth and plants and trees. It follows them, it behaves like them, it has the same roughness, and the same discipline. We look at that wall, and we are looking at a part of nature.

AN ORNAMENTED SURFACE

An approximate packing of triangles, rhombs and parallelograms, with POSITIVE SPACE between them. However, the individual

Sketch of a tiled wall panel with coloring, to be built full wall height in a house in California.

An ornamented surface, showing both formality and roughness.

triangles are adjusted to fit the space between the adjacent parallelograms. Each four-sided shape is slightly different according to context; what is most uniform, are not the dark shapes of the tiles, but the width or thickness of the white space (mortar?) in which the tiles are bedded. the whole takes an overall form of a cartouche. What is achieved with the simple shapes is adherence to a growing whole, not packing of preformed shapes. Among shapes, and spaces, no two are quite the same. What governs their individual shapes is the pattern of the whole which remains recognizable, repetitive, and coherent.

A CORNER OF A CITY

Thus, for example, in this drawing of a corner in a city, the tops of the buildings have no windows, or less windows. There is a differentiation in the regularity. The three floors of windows which are shown have GRADIENTS whereby the windows change character systematically from floors 2 to 3 to 4. The roof structure is graded from one building to the next, roofs are smaller, somehow rambling. The bottom of the buildings on the right suddenly step out for a few feet. The floors of buildings on the left, as indicated, slope more gently away. Perhaps that should not be taken quite literally, but there is an

unexpected irregularity in the ground plane of these lines ... the buildings on the right cup, surround, and form a place where someone has put some tables and umbrellas — a STRONG CENTER is formed there by the buildings, and enhances the buildings.

These features all occur as a result of adaptation, thus as a result of unfolding. They are a direct result of living process.

AN AIRPORT GATE AREA

We have come to think of an airport as dehumanized, fast-moving, governed by technical or space-travel images. But in this drawing one sees an airport departure gate: the planes are outside; the relation to the planes is there, open, and friendly. The place itself seems — for some reason — made for people. Is it archaic. I dont think so. But the windows are made to look through. Each is a STRONG CENTER in its own right. So is each bit of wall between two windows. The airplanes are regarded as things worthwhile in their own right, worth enjoying. There is acceptance of the fact that arrival at the departure gate is often too harried, unfriendly, packages. Here the living structure of the place appears simply in response to my effort to draw a place where one might actually like to *be.*

A corner of a city: a group of buildings forming a public place with a cafe, not as a result of a developer's dream, but naturally, because the place is generated by the circumstance.

A MANY-LAYERED MEETING PLACE AND CONFERENCE ROOMS

This last very rudimentary sketch, once again using more or less the same form language, shows an additional feature that is valuable. It shows a conception of a building with entirely new content, a human need for gathering, meeting, and communal discussion, widely felt, but rarely if ever provided in a working form. Yet it is vital to many projects and to most communities.

Throughout a living process, and in all the sketch examples given on the last pages, the brunt of the work of formation is being done by the ROUGHNESS transformation and the LOCAL-SYMMETRIES transformation balancing each other. The other transformations work within this framework.

An airport departure lounge.

A many layered meeting place and conference rooms.

10 / ENSOR'S MASKS:
THE FORM LANGUAGE OF AN ULTRAMODERN PAINTING

The same form language in a painting by James Ensor, Masks and faces, 1927.

There is a considerable danger that readers might insist, all my counterarguments not-with-standing, that the form language I propose is somehow too archaic, is still invested with too much of a sense of history, and can never be suitable for the far distant future, or for our truly modern age of cellphones, airplanes and computers.

I have therefore chosen a painting, which embodies our modern age in an extreme form, and which is yet composed, without any doubt, in the approximate version of the form language I described. This painting was painted in 1927, sixty-five years ago.

What is it that makes this painting truly modern? Its inner horror gives us one reason.

There is no saccharine here, no allusion to the sweetness of bygone traditional times. It is raw, it deals with suffering. Indeed, it is possibly no accident that it was painted at the very time the murder of millions was being dreamed, for the first time, on the continent of Europe. Its colors are bold and unrealistic, again quite unlike the painterly saccharine sense of the nineteenth century. It places emphasis on deep feeling and awareness, not on appearance. It stabs at the reader, confronts the tragedy of human suffering and of our era. And yet it is profoundly human, too.

No one can deny its place in our recent modern history.

I feel therefore, that if the reader can accept that this painting, too, was composed within the same fifteen transformations, much as I have illustrated them, that reader (man, woman, architect, artist) will feel more free to recognize the power of the language I have drawn, and be more likely to use it in his and her own built constructions.

Why do I say that this painting has been made within the form language of the fifteen transformations?

The heads float free — as in a dream, each one a grotesque CENTER in its horror. The emphasis on the heads is indeed as CENTERS, more than heads. Each mouth is drawn as a CENTER, blood red in its CONTRAST and defined in its GOOD SHAPE; the hair sits, shape like, on the head and around the head forming a BOUNDARY to the skull; the ring around the eyes is drawn as a BOUNDARY; the teeth, savage, are drawn more from ALTERNATING REPETITION than from realism or a dentist's chart; the skull floats on a stick, not on a neck, shaped by GOOD SHAPE, affected by deep interlock, given its wedge shape by a GRADIENT; the shirts are colored by ALTERNATING REPETITION; the central shirt is given

its order by screaming CONTRAST, from the surrounding shirts, and the mask from the lower face; the dimensions of eyes, teeth, lips, hairs, are not governed by realism, but by LEVELS OF SCALE. Even the hairline of one man is given its shape by waving ALTERNATING REPETITION, not by the nature of hair.

I believe Ensor, in his visions, used this language, the language not only of a true architecture, but also the language of our archetypal fantasy, to make a thing which is profound in its horror, profound in its magnetic drawing power, and that he composed this picture (as other similar ones), drawing from this language, to substantiate his dreams.

If the language can do this, I believe we have no reason to be afraid that it is too sweet, too traditional, too saccharine, or that it will paste an untruthful sentimentality onto our buildings. The language can, I am confident, serve any purpose, I believe, that is deeply related to human (not mechanical) experience.

A pedestrian street on the Eishin campus, the comfortable space, gritty concrete, laundry lines, but elegant details — all, somehow, speaking in a way reminiscent of the Ensor painting.

Not an ancient style: but essentially a building without style, that follows directly from the structure-preserving transformations, according to the simplest moves. The Great Hall of the Eishin campus.

11 / POSSIBILITY OF A FORM LANGUAGE FOR ALL FUTURE TIME

I show three photographs of completed buildings (pages 455–57). They embody, in actual built cases, the kind of results this form language of fifteen transformations, when used in building projects, is likely to create. First (page 455), a street in which buildings, and space achieve a comfortable, formal, but comfortable harmony. Second (above), the Great Hall of the Eishin campus, seen across the campus lake. Third (opposite), the high, enclosed living porch of the Heisey house in Austin, Texas. All three were built during the last twenty years. I suggest that in any building process governed by construction, it will be the fifteen structure-preserving transformations which may most easily become the formal tools with which people can create well-adapted forms, allow coherent geometry to emerge, and manage, effectively, to assist in the creation of living form by adaptation and unfolding.

It is examples like these that encourage my belief that these fifteen transformations can provide us with a natural "alphabet" of living process. They are the most natural elementary transformations for a form-language that is able to generate living structure in the world.[17] It seems possible to me, that the conception of a universal form language, made from the fifteen transformations, applied, repeated, cycling and recycling in different concrete forms, recursively, so that every part and

456

Once again, not ancient style: but again a building without style, that follows directly from the structure-preserving transformations. This is the unfolded geometry of an elaborate porch.
Heisey house in Austin, Texas, Christopher Alexander with Randy Schmidt and Saul Pichardo.

every part of every part, will ultimately be formed *in its geometry* — could take root in our time, and in the future. It would be simple and elegant. And it would preserve and generate the elements of style which are necessary to a living world.

The form language which appeared in the works of several modern painters, most notably Matisse, Vlaminck, Bonnard, Derain, Nolde, Ensor, also provide schemata with which one can think, or decipher, or elaborate, a building in a natural way, something that goes the same way as the small sketches or the unfolded, built stair. These painters described and generated — above all — a new geometry of form and color which can be part of nature. It may also, with study, turn out to be a significant part of our growing effort to determine a generic form language for our time and for all future time.

12 / A SKETCH

A rough sketch I drew to express the sense and direction of the new form language: Direct output from the fifteen transformations. True, it looks like a child's drawing. But if taken literally, color and all, as something from which to build the world, we see the beginning of an entirely new geometry.

NOTES

1. For example: Can we get what we need from A PATTERN LANGUAGE? Is the published pattern language itself a form-language? When I first wrote the pattern language (and before I understood the importance of form-language), I assumed that people would soon start using it to make more beautiful buildings. It seemed to me that what my colleagues and I wrote together was common sense, and would follow from the directness and strength of the patterns.

But I was wrong. Oddly, many buildings were designed by people using the pattern language, which were *not* coherent. Rather, they incorporated patterns, *but within overall building forms which were typical of the architectural fashions of that time (1970s)*. This gave the buildings, often, a funky, ungainly, look. When A PATTERN LANGUAGE was first published, many architects who used it created buildings typical of the then current style of the 1970s and 1980s — unusual roof shapes, plywood sides, etc. Even though the plan, shape, volume, created by the patterns did not require (or even invite) this treatment, it was as if people only knew how to create an output by

pouring it into the then popular, known, receptacle of available geometric forms. The result that came out was not what was *required*, because that form-language (the then-current developer's architectural vernacular of the 1970s) was not capable of holding the content actually created by a living process. The resulting buildings often had a rather tired quality, looked like second-rate, not very good architecture. This was true whether the designer succeeded, or did not succeed, in incorporating the patterns.

All this happened because people simply *cannot* create buildings without a form-language. Buildings are, in essence, and at root, geometrical. Even with the powerful tool of pattern-language helping them to conceive living structure (in plan, volume, and content) the lack of form language meant that this output could not be consolidated as coherent form.

Evidently, the real stuff, the core geometry of the created form lies — and must lie, at least much of it — at a level deeper than the level of the pattern language. The 1970s architecture which appeared in such examples (even when the positive content of the patterns was included) was based on a different and unsuitable language of form which was more basic, and which carried most of the style, and meaning, and geometry.

The same will be true of any contemporary process, living or not. The building forms generated by a living process as I have described it so far will still have to be pieced together in whatever language of forms, shapes, combinations is now current. Unless we can develop a new form-language with the capacity to generate the kinds of forms I have described, the inner content of living process cannot be consolidated by these older forms. To make the unfolding work successfully, a new form-language must be created which is capable of holding this content . . . and that means, it must be one which supports the formation of living centers. This requires innovations, technical solutions that are surprising, practical and simple. Without such work as a foundation, the results of unfolding — as they truly are — cannot be upheld or widely built, at all.

2. Adequate formulation of this chapter has not been easy, especially because the work needed is so extensive that it cannot be not complete. In the final preparation of the chapter I owe a great debt of gratitude to Jenny Quillien and Nikos Salingaros who both helped me in discussion and clarification, not least by expressing their enthusiasm for the importance of the content.

3. Sir Frederick Bartlett, Jerome Bruner, Ernst Gombrich, and others, established half a century ago that human beings cannot undertake complex cognitive tasks without what they called "schemata." Whenever human beings create buildings — indeed when we solve any kind of recurrent problems — we always rely on pre-existing forms and patterns in our minds. Whenever we try to solve a problem, or create new design, we do it, necessarily, by relying on some language of forms which we already have available to us, and then combining and arranging and rearranging these forms to get new results. It is in the process of combining and recombining schemata, that we actually make progress. That is how creation actually occurs. This is true whether it was a good period of architecture or a bad period. The schemata can be good or bad; the stylistic components available for recombination may be good or bad; but no matter which, it is the traces of the then-current form language of combinable schemata, which must dictate and shape the form of the world in any given period. F. C. Bartlett, REMEMBERING (Cambridge: Cambridge University Press, 1932); Jerome Bruner, Jacqueline Goodnow, George Austin, A STUDY OF THINKING (London: Wiley, 1956); Ernst Gombrich, ART AND ILLUSION (London: Phaidon, 1960).

4. Henry Glassie, FOLK HOUSING IN MIDDLE VIRGINIA (Knoxville: University of Tennessee Press, 1975. For further discussion of Henry Glassie's work, see note 14, and page 441 of this chapter. I am much indebted to Howard Davis for making me aware, far too late in my life, of Glassie's beautiful work.

5. In view of my work on pattern languages, I must stress the distinction between *pattern* languages (also described in chapters 12 and 13) and *form* languages.

The idea of pattern languages was inspired by traditional languages, and drew much of their structure and content from traditional languages. However, the emphasis I gave, in the published pattern languages, was to the functional content of the patterns which the language dealt with, and created. In the late 1960s and early 1970s, the content of architecture was so seriously damaged, that it was not only marked by a breakdown of form, but more horribly, by an almost total breakdown of sensible human content. It was vital, at that time, to focus on the objective nature of the patterns required for comfort (and life) in human surroundings: and to find ways of making this content visible and usable. The task of doing this was so urgent, and so massive, that my collaborators and I spent six or seven years, merely accumulating material to undertake this task — and in so doing we neglected the equally important task of finding publicly accessible ways in which the actual geometric form of buildings could be unfolded, successfully, from the patterns.

6. But of course, unlike any one particular historic culture, which was able to embody its necessities in a particular language of forms that could be repeated, what we need for our time, and for all future time, is an understanding deep enough and general enough to include the coherence and the geometric unity of these past examples, while yet being free, open, flexible — able to take many individual forms, according to place, culture, and climate, and able, too, to change and evolve with changing history and changing technology.

7. See, for example, John Habraken, THE STRUCTURE OF THE ORDINARY: FORM AND CONTROL IN THE BUILT ENVIRONMENT (Cambridge, Mass: M. I. T. Press, 1998).

8. See earlier discussion in chapter 8, pages 228–33.

9. See chapter 4, pages 126–31.

10. Emil Post, "Absolutely Unsolvable Problems and Relatively Undecidable Propositions — Account of an Anticipation", first written 1921, and first published forty years later, in Martin Davis, THE UNDECIDABLE (New York: Raven Press, 1965) pp. 338-433; and ...1897-1954 SOLVABILITY, PROVABILITY, DEFINABILITY : THE COLLECTED WORKS OF EMIL L. POST , ed by Martin Davis (Boston, Birkhauser 1994).

11. Noam Chomsky, SYNTACTIC STRUCTURES, (The Hague: Mouton, 1965); Charles F. Hockett, LANGUAGE, MATHEMATICS, AND LINGUISTICS, (The Hague: Mouton, 1967).

12. Henry Glassie, FOLK HOUSING IN MIDDLE VIRGINIA.

13. Ibid.

14. To be fair, I must say that these writers have, in all likelihood, not set out to do the job I have defined here. So far, their studies have been mainly academic, and they may truly not be interested in this question which I raise here. Nevertheless, they are dealing with the same subject. See, for example: Stiny, G. and Gips, J., 1972, "Shape Grammars and the Generative Specification of Painting and Sculpture" in C. V. Freiman (ed) INFORMATION PROCESSING 71 (Amsterdam: North-Holland, 1972) 1460-1465. Republished in Petrocelli, O. R. (ed) THE BEST

COMPUTER PAPERS OF 1971 (Philadelphia: Auerbach, 1972), 125-135; Stiny, G., "Introduction to shape and shape grammars" ENVIRONMENT AND PLANNING B: PLANNING AND DESIGN, 1980, 7, 343-351; Stiny, G., "Shape rules: closure, continuity and emergence" ENVIRONMENT AND PLANNING B: PLANNING AND DESIGN, 1994, 21, s49-s78; Stiny, G., SHAPE: A PRIMER IN ALGEBRA, GRAMMAR AND DESCRIPTION (Cambridge: Cambridge University Press, in preparation).

15. In order to describe, fully, the fundamental language scheme that I believe to be necessary, I am using, here, the concept of beings, an apparently fanciful, but nevertheless succinct, more accurate, and more expressive way of talking about living centers. It is described in fully in Book 4, chapter 5.

16. In Book 3, I shall try to show by concrete, built examples what will happen when we use such a form language to make buildings. But I want to emphasize that as elements of form language, these fifteen properties are not arbitrary. They are the very simplest things which can possibly be used as a basis for assembly of a living thing, and it is from simplicity that they ultimately derive. Thus, we may come to see that they are useful, valid, and profound, because they eschew all complexity that is not needed.

17. An example of a very crude form language, which nevertheless showed considerable power, is to be found in the documents from the last formal class I gave at the University of California, before I became Emeritus. The class was explicitly based on the idea of searching for an appropriate form-language for modern times.

I wanted to find a way of teaching students how to approach the art of building, in a way that made sense, and which gave insight into a new style, and a new way of thinking about the form and substance and appearance of buildings, in the context of a modern city.

Here are the eleven principles I sketched out for the students as the working form-language for study and experiment:

Principle 1: The Fundamental Principle: Every building must help to heal the world.

Principle 2: Materials Materials reflect nearby buildings and materials.

Principle 3: Positive space. The building form comes after creation of positive space on all sides, thus connecting the building to all nearby buildings by positively formed outdoor space in each direction.

Principle 4: Normal walls Walls are normal walls, heavy and thick, with openings in them, that are distinct from the walls, so that each piece of wall is felt as a whole, and the windows are felt as whole.

Principle 5: Good windows: Windows are solid and have nice shapes within the wall. That means (a) window sits in a substantial wall, (b) bottom of window is good (c) top of window is good shape (d) window has real depth in the wall.

Principle 6: Structure is real. The structure works, and is taken seriously, as the essence of the building. We have not yet had enough discussion to know what this means.

Principle 7: Ornament. There is some sense in which

the whole buildings and exterior space made is beautiful as an ornament. And actual ornament plays at least some visible role in the exterior and interior construction of the building.

Principle 8: Form is of the place. Geometrically, it is "of the place" and gathers together, morphologically, the buildings forms, and land character of the surrounding few blocks.

Principle 9: Simplicity   The building, inside and out, is made as simple as possible: this does not mean that it is mimimal. It means that what is done (shape, and substance of each part) always helps the unity of the whole to be cemented. Things are chosen, like the smile of the buddha, to help connect one thing to another, until the whole it is so perfect that it is indivisible.

Principle 10. Beings Each project is a being.

Principle 11. Every project must be conceived, and worked out on a large-scale cardboard model of the city block where it is to be built, and where one was able to see the overall space created by existing buildings, and was then able to relate the new project to this space while it was designed, and test it until it became harmonious.

The students found these principles difficult to wrestle with. This is a comment more on the stranglehold of modernistic thought, than on the ability of the students. Even something as obvious as the second principle (determing the materials on the basis of materials in nearby buildings), was at first anathema to them. They wanted to make their mark as designers, and they fought tooth and nail for several weeks, against a principle which would reduce their license to be arbitrary, hence, as they thought, would prevent them from "making their mark." Only after a few weeks of seeing models, discussion and so on, did the obvious and straightforward simplicity of this principle, and its obvious importance for healing urban form, make itself felt. Afterwards, in review, most of the students agreed that it was this step and the third step, positive space, which had the most powerful effect on what they did, on the beauty of the results, and on changing the framework of their thinking. All eleven principles are, of course, embodiments of the fifteen transformations.

In the class, each student did a number of sketch design problems, in which they were to show their ideas about how to knit the city of Berkeley into a coherent modern fabric. All the projects were for individual buildings, both small and large, all undertaken in the downtown area of Berkeley. They included a museum extension, an apartment house, a new student office building for the university campus, and a subway station for the main station in downtown Berkeley.

The projects were free, inventive, yet harmonious in a way that was remarkable. They were unpretentious, many of them delightful, well-worked out, and the urban space created always had a useful, pleasant, and inspiring coherent and coordinated character. Yet the projects were entirely inventive, each one very different from the next, and there was no sense of stylistic imposition rules or doctrinaire order that was not inherent in the projects.

That such a simple form-language could produce such powerful results, was remarkable.

CHAPTER SEVENTEEN

SIMPLICITY

1 / THE DRIVE TO SIMPLICITY

Simplicity has always been a strong motivating force in architecture. Many great works of architecture are marked by the architect's goal of the simple. The works of Mies van der Rohe, Le Corbusier, Alvar Aalto, were only the latest in a long tradition of purifying buildings, making that which is most simple. Seven hundred years ago, St Bernard of Clairvaux strove for simplicity in another way which led to the pure monastic buildings of the Cistercian order. And the great Japanese tradition, going back even further, formed by Buddhist monks about the 5th century A.D., also aimed at simplicity and purity, as a way of making the essential in life come forward, and allowing the inessential to be laid aside.

Our modern conception of simplicity has gone wrong. Simplicity as *depth* has been replaced by a mechanical idea of simplicity as the geometrically banal. And most recently, in reaction to the banal simplicity of cubes and spheres, postmodernism has reintroduced complexity and ornament in a way that is too often merely dross, icing, fruitcake, and trinkets, overlaid on the fabric, shape and substance of our buildings.

In this chapter, I shall try to introduce a new definition that is consistent with the nature of living structure. We shall arrive at a conception of simplicity which shows it as the most pure thing which can arise, truthfully, from a set of given circumstances, in a way that preserves structure, and as *the defining quality of a living process.*

2 / WHAT IS SIMPLE?

I shall argue, now, that living process, in its very nature, may, in a certain special sense, be called deeply simple — that it may be *characterized* by the idea that it is the simplest process which exists in any given set of circumstances. What has appeared all along, the idea that complexity is a manifestation of deeper, more intricate structure created by structure-preserving unfolding, may be understood better yet when we appreciate that it is always the *simplest* step which governs: And that the drive provided by the SIMPLICITY AND INNER CALM transformation is, necessarily, at the very root of living process.

The things we call simple in design — cubes, spheres — appear simple conceptually because they can be represented by simple mathematical schemes. But they are not, in any *real* sense, the simplest things which can be created at a given place and time. The simplest thing which can be created, in real terms, is that thing which goes furthest to resolve, complete, hence to elaborate and underpin the structure of the world, its wholeness, which exists at that place. In this sense a volcano, a cobweb, an oak tree are truly more simple. . . because as nearly as we can judge, they perfectly resolve the forces, processes and conditions at that place, with the greatest economy of means and the greatest economy of form.

It is for this reason that the simplest forms ("simplest" in this organic and complex sense) must be our targets in any conscious, human-inspired, human-engineered process which aspires to the production of living structure. A process which purports to be a living one, but fails to create beautiful and living simplicity in the physical form it generates, must have something wrong with it. Stated again: the thing which matters most about a living process is — quite simply — that it produces beautiful and coherent

Stone garden at Ryo-anji

geometrical order. That is not only the necessary *result* of a living process. It is also the talisman by which we may know whether a given process is truly living or not. If it is a living process, it will create beautiful geometric structure. If it does *not* create beautiful structure, it can *not* truly be a living process. Thus the creation of coherent, beautiful, simple geometry and form is not merely an incidental offshoot from the living process. It is the *essence* of any living process.

This gives geometry and beauty — and simplicity above all — a special and central role.

3 / HOW IS THE SIMPLE TO BE ACHIEVED? A SPIRITUAL SIMPLICITY OF HEART

To approach the idea of simplicity as the target of all living process, I propose to begin with a new analysis of what simplicity *is*.

In my description of the fundamental process, I have stated that what happens next (at any moment in the unfolding of a living process) is the *simplest* thing that can be done to intensify existing centers. It is necessary that it must be simple because if there is too much extraneous clutter, the clutter gets in the way, makes less room for new necessary structure that the unfolding process is trying to achieve. Thus, "doing the simplest thing," only the thing which is *required* and nothing *beyond* what is required, is a practical and efficient necessity.

What is going on here is more than a *procedural* simplicity. It is also a *visible* simplicity. When an unfolding process has succeeded —

when a living process has succeeded — we may always recognize its results by a visible simplicity in the geometry and character of what is produced. The buildings which are most intensely living, most profound, are marked by an intense simplicity. This occurs because it is necessary to what they are and to what they have become during the process that gave them life. Further, simplicity is also not merely a geometrical ideal, but an attained internal purity — something we grasp and experience as associated with a spiritual state.

Simplicity is a spiritually achieved state of art. Among great works of art in history, those of greatest depth have nearly always been simple. Their simplicity comes from the Ground; their spirituality lies in their simpleness of attitude (see pages 492–94 at the end of this chapter). From a human point of view, this simplicity is easy enough to understand. Since a humble attitude requires that what is created is a perfect and indivisible unity, it implies that complexity of structure must gradually melt away to pure simplicity. Things cannot become deep until they reach a state of extreme purity that we might call purity of heart. This purity of heart cannot be attained unless a thing is pure — and therefore simple. All the extraneous stuff, whatever is not essential, must be removed. In this fashion, it is intuitively clear that only a very simple thing can be spiritual.

Door of Hauglid stave church, Norway, 13th century.

Marble utensil from the Greek Island of Naxos, prehistoric.

Using the language of Book 4, I may say: Those objects whose order makes them capable of reaching to the Ground, giving us a glimpse of it, always seem to have simplicity. They seem to need simplicity to touch the Ground.

I can rephrase this spiritual dictum in other words. Any good example of living structure always has a very high density of sustaining relations among its parts. These sustaining relations, which are always made, in some form, from the fifteen transformations, occupy a great deal of "space" — so much that there is usually not room for all of them in the relatively small extent of a physical object. However, there is room for all of them when they are extremely compressed, when their density is very great. This kind of compression, in which the density of sustaining relations is very high, can only be attained in a thing when that thing is extremely simple (For further detail, please look back to the discussion on pages 198–200).

In Book 1, I concentrated on the idea that the field of centers is complex. This was a necessary emphasis in the earlier chapters. In the 20th century we were living in an era when crude oversimplification of design existed widely, and the subtle complexity that is characteristic of wholeness was often lost. However the idea of living structure will be misunderstood if we do not now pass beyond complexity to reach simplicity.

Spiritual art is always simple. Shaker furniture, Romanesque architecture, Japanese tea bowls, Nigerian sculpture — these are things where human spirit seems to lie captured, where it seems directly present. Complicated forms — baroque architecture, Victorian furniture, the paintings of Raphael, trinkets of Faberge — these are more decorative — we could almost think of these as bedroom art — something where spirit is less present. Even those spiritual forms which are physically complex — carved

Plan of St. Gall, drawing of an ideal, imaginary monastery, drawn about 800 A.D.

1. church
   a. library&scriptorium
   b. sacristy&vestry
   c. monks' lodging
   d. school master's lodging
   e. Porter's lodging
   f. porch
   g. porch
   h. porch
   i. master of hospice lodging
   j. monks' parlor
   k. tower of St. Michael
   l. tower of St. Gabriel
2. annex for communion
3. monks' dormitory
4. monks' privy
5. monks' bathhouse
6. monks' refectory&vestiary
7. monks' cellar&larder
8. monks' kitchen
9. monks' bake&brew house
10. kitchen for disting. guests
11. house for disting. Guests
12. outer school
13. abbot's house
14. abbot's kitchen, cellar&bathhouse
15. house for bloodletting
16. physicians' house
17. novitiate&infirmary
    a. novices' chapel
    b. chapel for the sick
    c. novices' cloister
    d. cloister of the sick
18. kitchen&bath for sick
19. kitchen&bath for novices
20. gardener's house
21. goosehouse
22. fowlkeepers' house
23. henhouse
24. granary
25. collective workshop
26. annex of coll. workshop
27. mill
28. mortar
29. drying kiln
30. house of coopers&wheelwrights
31. pilgrims'&paupers' kitchen
32. pilgrims'&paupers' kitchen
33. house for horses&keepers
34. house for knights
35. house for sheep&sheperds
36. house for goats&keepers
37. house for cows&keepers
38. servants' house
39. house for swine&keepers
40. house for brood mares&keepers
W. monks' cloister yard
X. monks' vegetable garden
Y. monks' cemetery
Z. medicinal herb garden

geometric panels from Nigeria or the carvings of interlaced snakes and dragons on the entrance panels of Norwegian stave churches (page 464) — are always somehow simplified, distilled. No matter how much material is actually there, no matter what wealth of invention — even so, it is absolutely still in its spirit.

The famous plan of St. Gall embodies the archetype of simplicity in complex organization. Drawn by an unknown monk, about 800 A.D. at St. Gall in Switzerland, it was never built. But this drawing, on a single sheet of parchment,

later became the model for most of the monasteries in medieval Europe. I love the St. Gall plan because of its simplicity. Each element is drawn as simply as possible. The vegetable garden, the cloister, the shoe-making shop, the carpentry shop, smithy, forge, bedrooms, refectory — they are all there. Almost all of them are shown as simple rectangles. The plan is thus composed of the very simplest symmetries. And yet, each one is exactly where it should be; and, amazingly, each part is unique according to its place. The overall arrangement is extensive and intricate, but still perfectly simple-hearted. Each essential thing is given not one element of structure more than it requires. Complex shapes appear only when they come about naturally, from the interaction of the elements. The author of the plan was too childish to add any extra structure; it would have seemed like showing off.

The process which produced this plan was certainly practical, but leavened by great simplicity *of heart*. It consisted — I believe — of taking every step in the sequence of structure-preserving transformations in the simplest way possible. When new centers could be made symmetrical, they were. When they had to be asymmetrical, they were made so. As the monk of the St. Gall plan followed this process in his drawing, he gradually got something which became more and more complex (in a comfortable, organic way) but was still gentle and simple in heart.

4 / DOING THE SIMPLEST THING: THE BASIS OF ALL STRUCTURE-PRESERVING TRANSFORMATIONS

Let us get a more concrete vision of these ideas. To do so, we go back to the fundamental process, and to the concept of structure-preserving transformations. Suppose at some stage in a building process there is a certain field of centers. Now you want to transform this field in such a way as to deepen certain latent centers, while leaving the overall structure of the field intact. To succeed you must introduce new structure in the "least" way — that means, in a way which causes the least disturbance to the existing field. To do this, you must choose the simplest thing to do, at every step, because anything more than exactly what is required will tend to complicate and destroy the structure which exists.

Imagine a beautiful hillside, overlooking the ocean. A wild hill, grassy, a few scattered trees, plunging down to the ocean far below. Suppose that we are going to place a small gazebo on this hillside. What shape will be best for the gazebo? Of course the hill itself, as far as its structure is concerned, is complex and loose. The terrain rambles; trees are placed irregularly. The rocks plunge down at different angles. The grass is green here, yellow there. There are bushes in this hollow; over there on the slope there are orange poppies. In short, the whole thing is complex and asymmetrical.

Now, what shape of gazebo preserves this structure best? An irregular, asymmetrical, "organic" building will *not* fit well into the landscape. It will merely be tedious, and forces attention on itself (below, left). Surprisingly, the best one is the simplest: perfectly symmetrical, possi-

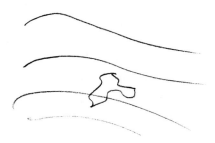

Effect of an asymmetric structure on the land: Not harmonious

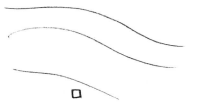

Effect of a symmetric structure on the land: Harmonious

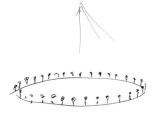

First sketch of a simple light   *Simple light as it now hangs in the Great Hall*   *Ugly light proposed by contractor; too much irrelevant structure*

bly square, possibly octagonal or round (page 467, right). In any case, not itself complex and irregular. The simple little square leaves things around it more alone. It concentrates its structure inward towards itself, and does not spread out its feeling or its structure into the surrounding landscape. Thus it does not contaminate the wild beauty of the hill.

The appearance of local symmetry in this example is very interesting. That is because the symmetrical structure induces one new center just where it is needed and nowhere else. Asymmetrical structures tend to induce many centers in many places, and so create unnecessary extra structures of centers that interfere with the existing order. In most cases, a symmetrical increment is the one which more leaves the field of centers alone; it is the most relaxed. Often it is the one which preserves structure most profoundly.

On this page I show another example of such a process at work: The lights of the Great Hall on the Eishin campus in Japan. At a certain stage, when the building was already under construction, we had to decide what form of lights to use. I knew that the light for this big dark hall would have to be made of many small lights, high up. A single big light would make too much glare. So I just drew absolutely the simplest ar-

rangement for a large number of small lights that I could imagine: A circle of lights, hanging from a point (above, left). In the end this was also, the form of the actual lights we built, almost exactly (see middle photograph).

The act of making this drawing contains a fairly pure example of the rule "always do the simplest thing." In early discussions we had already decided that the lights were to be candelabras — hanging lights with many small lights attached to them. And we had, also, decided on the positions of the lights. There was to be a single row, down the middle of the nave. So, now it was a question of just drawing the simplest center which had these qualities. It was something hanging, something with several bulbs. The thing I drew is the simplest structure which has these qualities.

That is all. There was nothing else we needed to do. When it was built, after careful mockups to decide its exact size, its material, and details, it came out very much like the drawing (above, middle). But we had to build these lights ourselves, since the contractor declared himself unable to do it.

In the third picture (above, right) I show a catalog photograph of the light fixture proposed for installation by the general contractor while the discussion was going on. It is ugly, irrelevant, harsh to the circumstances. It is harsh and irrelevant because it has too much structure that is not required by the situation. For example, the octagonal shape. What calls for an octagon? The small plastic triangles. Why do they have to be there? The strong edge around the top. Why is it there? The octagon made of triangles at the bottom. Why is it composite? None of these questions has a good answer. By comparison, the lights we built (and installed) have a more simple-hearted peacefulness because they contain nothing other than what is needed. In this sense they are more completely childish.

Again I want to emphasize: The appeal of the light is that there is nothing there except what is required. When I first drew it, Hajo (our executive architect in Japan) thought it was *too* childish. There was a shocked look on his face. I, too, thought that it was perhaps too childish. Yet childishness is what we see in the St. Gall plan, too. The result of a process in which, at each moment, the artist introduces the simplest possible thing to extend the existing field, and copes as sparingly as possible with the existing necessities through structure-preserving transformations.

5 / NATURAL SYMMETRIES

The geometry of living structure — what comes from the fifteen transformations — is the result of a process in which a complex system becomes at one and the same time *both* richer *and* simpler. Each new bit of structure, each new center, adds new differentiations. But each time, as soon as we get the new differentiations, we at once try to boil the garbage away so that the structure is simplified and concentrated. We try to keep it continuously simple, even while we fill it with more and more structure. The ultimate aim of this process is to find a perfectly simple structure which contains an immense wealth of structure.

We are constantly trying to simplify, to produce a system of centers and symmetries which is the simplest possible. The more we keep to simple symmetries when there is no reason for anything else, the more the whole thing gets purified. When we can, we remove smaller local symmetries, and simplify them even further, by enlarging the symmetries. We aim, by the end, to remove all extraneous structure. What we want is to cut and cut and cut until there is almost nothing left.

To clarify the connection between symmetries and simplicity: Complexity (in the bad sense) consists of distinctions which unnecessar-

ily complicate a structure. To get simplicity, on the other hand, we need a process which questions every distinction. Any distinction which is not necessary is removed. To remove a distinction we replace it by a symmetry. During this process the building gets simpler. Gradually we get just that syncopated system of local symmetries, rough but regular, symmetrical in details but syncopated in the large, that is typical of all real life.

Since each step will be most structure-preserving when it adds only the simplest symmetries, we may then expect that the end-result of a long sequence of such steps will be almost entirely made up of *local* symmetries. This means that the geometry of a wholesome living structure will be almost entirely made up of *local* symmetries, while yet being mainly asymmetrical in the large.

In Book 1, pages 188–92, I described an experiment which showed that the number of local symmetries in a thing has a big effect on its coherence. Now I want to go further and develop the idea that the structure of local symmetries may be nearly all there is, and that this is the most fundamental way of understanding living structure. Look at this sketch of a niche from a

Turkish prayer carpet. Every part is a symmetrical thing. Consider any part that appears asymmetrical, like the hooks. These are still, themselves, made of symmetrical things. Of course the hooks are asymmetrical in the large. But the stem of each hook is symmetrical. And each hook itself, is formed by a symmetrical isosceles triangle. So even though the hook as a whole is asymmetrical, it is still made of symmetrical components.

I am talking about *rough* symmetry. Even the triangles are only *roughly* symmetrical. If we measured them exactly, we would find them asymmetrical. But I leave aside for the moment the difficult task of defining the exact distinction between things which are roughly symmetrical, and those which are asymmetrical. Let us keep going with the main point. I claim that everything is made up of parts which are *roughly* symmetrical.

But, you may argue, if we divide the world up fine enough, any design at all can be composed of symmetrical elements. For example, if we go down to the level of pixels or photographic grain, we know that we can represent any object simply as a pattern of black and white dots of various size. And each dot, within this array, is symmetrical, no matter what the large-scale design is like.

But I am talking about higher level symmetries than that. I am talking about the fact that all the discernible pieces, the natural "wholes" of which the thing is made, are *themselves* either symmetrical or made up of symmetrical parts.

If I draw a hand, the symmetry is in the fingers. Each finger is symmetrical. Again, you may argue that the body of the hand is not symmetrical. The wrist is not symmetrical. But, in the sense that I mean, the wrist is composed of symmetrical parts. We can see it as a roughly symmetrical wrist, then, with a bone sticking out and forming a local symmetry in another direction.

Or take this railway engine, made in Brighton about 1880. This shows the property I am talking about very strongly indeed. Of course the engine as a whole is asymmetrical (viewed from the side), but it is made of parts most of which are symmetrical in themselves: the smokestack, the boiler, the cab, the cab door, the handrail, the handrail knobs, the number plate, the buffers. Certainly there are some items which are not symmetrical. For instance, the coupling hook is not symmetrical, the whistle levers, the side of the tender at the

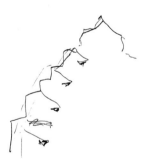

Carpet niche: the design made of many local symmetries

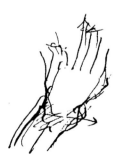

Hand's structure is also made up of simple symmetries.

Locomotive made in Brighton about 1880.

back of the cab. I don't know how to look at these cases. My feeling is that they don't matter. There are two ways we might try. We can try to explain that each one is itself composed of symmetrical components that are smaller. Thus, for instance, the splash guard over the front wheel is made of a symmetrical square box, which houses the oil mechanism, and a segment of a circle, which goes around the wheel. Of course, the multiple composition of the two has distorted the square box so that it isn't perfectly symmetrical. But anyway, a few asymmetries here and there are quite all right. What matters is that the maker *tried* to make each part symmetrical wherever he could, and a few times he missed. This is a more accurate statement of the process that was happening here. These symmetries are quite different from the pixels of a photograph. The pixels in the photo are symmetrical, but trivially small. The components I am showing you in this locomotive are quite large. What is remarkable is that most of the relatively larger pieces of the locomotive are almost symmetrical, or at least

distortions from symmetry made under a continual attempt to be symmetrical.

In the locomotive we see a continual striving for symmetry, which is abandoned only in those cases where there really is no other way. We see exactly the same in an industrial warehouse. And in a piece of machinery where the asymmetry is really essential, we feel an equal grace: For instance, a modern jet fighter has wings, tail, which are symmetrical in the large, but not symmetrical in themselves.

In many beautiful ancient buildings we see such a conglomeration of symmetries, too: It is this which creates their peacefulness. Many ordinary 20th-century things also had the same: For instance, a cement yard, or an oil refinery. In such 20th-century industrial structures, we often find the same loose agglomeration of symmetries (page 477). But many more recent *designed* modern structures (buildings and other things) possess an immense number of asymmetries — and *there* the overwhelming feeling is that the asymmetries are arbitrary, not forced by *necessity*.

6 / SYMMETRY, SIMPLICITY, AND JUST WHAT IS REQUIRED

The crux of the central connection between symmetries, simplicity and necessity lies in the following. Very often, when we look at something, we have an immediate, intuitive sense of its rightness or wrongness. This sense of rightness or wrongness most often comes directly from the symmetries we see and our sense about these symmetries.

The essence of this rightness or wrongness hinges on the issue of necessity. There is an intimate and fundamental connection between arbitrariness, necessity, and symmetry, which says, in a nutshell, this. *Everything in nature is symmetrical unless there is a reason for it not to be.* When this law is violated, we feel that something is unnatural, and that is the way in which symmetry plays such a fundamental role.

Let me give an example. Imagine you are looking at the sky one day. Suppose suddenly you were to see a cloud which is perfectly square. Without even thinking, you would know that it was not a natural cloud. You would know it must have been made by an airplane, or by some other non-natural process. You know this instantly, within the first tenth of a second. Why is this so? It is because you have an immediate familiarity with clouds as symmetry structures. Although clouds are loose and asymmetrical, still their characteristic form, the quality which makes them clouds, is a definite symmetry structure *of a certain type.* If we were to see a square cloud, we would be seeing a different kind of symmetry structure, and we would know, at once, that it was artificial. We would know it cannot have come about as a result of the normal cloud-making process because the cloud process does not produce that *kind* of symmetry structure.

This example shows that the symmetry structures in the world are very close to us. We perceive them instantly and subconsciously, without even knowing it. This mode of perception gives us an intuitive sense of which symmetry structures are appropriate or not appropriate in various situations. When we see the square cloud, we instantly register that something is "wrong". Our sense of what is right and what is wrong thus depends on subtle and detailed awareness of the kinds of symmetry structures which are appropriate and natural in various different situations.

Here is another example. A few years ago, a student showed me a drawing of a proposed

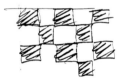

Student's checkerboard plan. It has too many symmetries (between buildings and gardens) to be the plan of an apartment building

apartment house design which he had drawn. It had the form of a checkerboard. He told me that the black squares were apartments, and the white squares gardens. Immediately, without hesitating or even thinking, I said, "It must be wrong". He was quite taken aback. "How can you say that so fast? You haven't even looked at the drawings yet".

"No," I said, "but I already know it must be wrong. In a checkerboard there is a symmetry between the black squares and the white ones, they are the same size and the same shape. But gardens and apartments are *unlike.* There could not be a natural structure, in which two things which are so different in their nature, could have exactly the same form. So I know this design must be wrong, before I even examine it."

Each thing in the world is subject to various influences. It has various degrees of similarity

and difference compared with other things, according to its situation. And in itself also, it has various degrees of similarity and difference. This is what we call its symmetry structure. Symmetry is a precise way of talking about similarities.

We observe that in any thing, there must be just the right amount of similarity and difference. Its internal degrees of similarity and difference must match, exactly, the degrees of similarity and difference which it experiences in the world.

When we make something which is just right, we have hit the degree of similarities and differences — its internal symmetries — just right. On the other hand, when we are wrong we can also always analyze the wrongness of what we have made in terms of symmetries. Either the symmetries are less than the situation requires. Or the symmetries are more than the situation requires. To understand the idea that the symmetries in a structure are "just right," consider, for example, the flow of electricity in two parallel wires. Other things being equal, the current will flow equally in the two wires. Why is this? If we want to, we can invoke some rule like Ohm's law or the principle of least action, to show why the wires carry the same current. But the deepest explanation, the most profound one, is simply this: There is no reason for the two wires to carry different currents, because the situation is symmetrical. Therefore, they carry the same current. In the absence of any reason, things distribute themselves symmetrically. Asymmetries occur only where there are reasons powerful enough to generate them.

In general, a harmonious structure — and the simplest structure — is one whose internal similarities and differences correspond exactly to the degrees of similarity and difference that exist in its conditions. That is the best definition of simplicity. Consider the shape of a bubble. When we have a soap bubble floating in the air, it roughly has the shape of a sphere. Although we can give various sophisticated mathematical explanations for this fact, there is one very simple explanation, more fundamental than all the oth-

Vermeer, Woman pouring milk,

College buildings, Christopher Alexander and Hajo Neis, 1987

Early 20th century: not enough symmetries. Everything had to be asymmetrical, in order to be modern. Le Corbusier, Ronchamp.

Late 20th century: too many symmetries. Postmodernism, like neoclassicism, tended to put in toomany symmetries, more than were appropriate for a given situation.

An unusual building, odd, yet strangely natural. Not influenced by either modernism or postmodernism, although quirky, this building has the number of symmetries about right.

ers. It is simply this. The air pressure on the inside of the bubble presses out with equal force in all directions. The same is true of the air pressure outside the bubble, pressing in. It presses with equal strength all over the bubble. Under these circumstances the bubble must take on the form of a sphere, because a sphere is the only volume-enclosing shape whose surface is the same at every point.

Suppose you saw a bubble in the shape of a

Even simpler. A system of local symmetries, relaxed and well-adapted to its circumstances. Here the number of symmetries is just right.

cube. You would know, right away, that something was wrong because a cube has too many differences in it. Mainly, the corners of the cube are different from any other points and the edges are different from the middle of the sides. Such a structure could only come about under circumstances where the forces or processes also had a comparable level of complexity, where the pattern of forces somehow gave rise to eight points which were "special." Since you know the forces in a bubble aren't like that, you know the bubble can't take on the form of a cube.

We can express this idea, in the most general way, by saying that things which are similar must be similar, and things which are different must be different. Or I can put it more precisely: The degree of similarities which exist in a structure must correspond exactly to the degree of similarity of the conditions there, and the degrees of differences which exist in a structure must also correspond to the degrees of difference in the conditions there.

This is a profound idea, which — I believe — no one has so far managed to express in a fully mathematical way. If it could be expressed precisely, it would be the rule from which everything, all form, derives.

Let us come back to architecture. A building which is perfectly made, and perfectly simple, is one in which the symmetries correspond exactly to what is required — neither more, nor less — just as we see in nature. Please look at the four pictures on pages 472–73. In the first period of the modern movement, when Ronchamp was made, architects and designers were very much afraid of symmetry. Everything had to be asymmetrical in order to be modern. So, generally, things had *too few* internal symmetries to be perfectly natural. We wince when we see these structures because the symmetries feel wrong.

Now, in the present period of so-called postmodernism, the pendulum has swung the other way. Postmodernists, as neoclassicists used to do, put in *too many* symmetries, more than are appropriate for a given situation. So we wince when we see them because in this case, too, we can feel the wrongness of the symmetry structure at once.

Making a thing whose symmetries are ex

actly right is extraordinarily hard. It means, that we have to be so simple that all the necessities are in perfect balance. Simplicity is the state in which all structure is removed, except exactly that structure which is required.

7 / THE IDEA OF A NATURAL SYSTEM OF SYMMETRIES

To understand the idea of "only what is required" further, let us consider what we might call a natural system of symmetries.

Here, for instance, is a Chinese brush painting of bamboo. The twigs and branches hanging down form symmetries. But the symmetry we

see in the tree is very gentle. The leaves are not perfectly symmetrical. They are approximately symmetrical. The clusters of twigs and leaves hanging down form local bundles which are almost, but not perfectly, symmetrical. The tree itself is not perfectly symmetrical. Yet it has a

Branches of a bamboo tree: depicted in a Chinese brush painting: natural symmetries.

Two buildings, the utmost simplicity. Eishin campus, Christopher Alexander, Hajo Neis and others, 1985.

rough overall symmetry, which produces order. Thus we see systems of symmetries, which are roughly symmetrical locally and are all nested, forming a hierarchy of approximate symmetries.

This natural system of symmetries is one of the defining marks of all living structure. I cannot for the moment define what I mean by call-ing this natural structure a "balanced" and comfortable system of symmetries. I only draw attention to it. Look at the character of the symmetries, and pay attention to the way they work.

Look at the courtyard of the house in Copenhagen (page 478). In this courtyard we also see the phenomenon I call a natural system of

Courtyard house, Copenhagen. Here uneven, syncopated, local symmetries form a perfectly harmonious whole.

Office building, Dallas. Here there is an uncomfortable feeling about the symmetries: too gross, too dominant, they destroy the ease.

symmetries. There are various local symmetries in the arch, the windows, the individual pieces of wood which form the windows, the local portions of the structure. There are also approximate larger-scale symmetries in the courtyard, in the building mass. None of the symmetries are perfect. They are syncopated, uneven, comfortable, relaxed. That is because the symmetries only occur where they are *generated*, where they *have* to be.

On the other hand, look at the lobby of an office building shown on the right. Here, too, we see symmetries. Some are small, some large. But overall, there is an *uncomfortable* feeling about these symmetries. The building looks too perfect to be true. It is *over*-simplified. The symmetries we see are perfect, very rigid, one might say almost obsessive in their perfection. The loose comfortable balance of symmetries which was visible in the drawing of the bamboo tree, bopping here and there within the structure, is not visible here. This is a building which lacks a natural system of symmetries.

To contrast with the over-technical perfection of the symmetries in this last building, please look at two typical industrial sites (opposite). In these industrial sites we tend to see more loose systems of symmetries. That is because the lack of need for "image," again makes it possible for people to do just what is required, and nothing else. There are local symmetries where they are needed and nowhere else. Some of the elements are symmetrical. Large scale symmetries are visible. On the other hand, wherever the symmetries need to be interrupted, they are interrupted. They do not suffer from an image of a controlled overall plan, which tries to tie the symmetries down. They exist where they please — that means, only where they *need* to exist. Again, this is comfortable.

Making a building which has life is essentially a problem of creating such a balanced system of symmetries. Whenever we manage to create a great work of art, we manage it only because we manage to discover a natural and comfortable system of balanced, nested, symmetries.

Power station
Here there is a more natural balance of symmetries.

Thousands of local symmetries in every bolt, crane,
stanchion, handrail, funnel, bucket.

It is not an overpowering, overall symmetry. The system of symmetries have the same balance and easiness which we observe in nature. We may typically see a natural system of symmetries in an ancient farmhouse. We may see it in an ancient palace. We even see it to some degree in the early skyscrapers built in Chicago (Burnham and Root, for instance) — though we rarely see it in the more recently built skyscrapers.

The point which I am making is that this particular balance of symmetries, which seems like an almost accidental pleasantness or easiness, is in fact *a highly specific structure*. This highly specific structure must be present in order for something to have life, and it takes very precise form because this is the structure something has when it is true.

We may summarize the relation between life and symmetry by saying simply this: Life requires a natural system of symmetries. Or, in dynamic terms we may say this: A living process must generate a natural system of symmetries in order to make something whole. This rule is di-

rectly related to the theory of structure-preserving transformations in which we produce living structure by unfolding the wholeness (field of centers) step by step. *The unfolding of the field of centers may be considered as a process in which we introduce one symmetry at a time.* The wholeness is the end-result of this dynamic process; it is the trace left by a process which produces one symmetry at a time.

Successful life which creates unity in a building and holds it together is generated by the balanced, syncopated, off-beat quality that the natural system of symmetries creates. "Balanced" and "offbeat" seem to be opposites. But the idea that a structure exists which has both these attributes at the same time is precisely one of the most important attributes of living structure. At first sight, being tight in terms of symmetry, and being loose seem opposite. One is orderly, one is disordered. But the real unity is precisely that quality which is generated by the balance in which both exactness and looseness exist together.

8 / AT EACH STEP GET RID OF EVERYTHING
THAT IS NOT REQUIRED
"MAKING LIFE" AND "BEING SIMPLE" ARE THE SAME

Let us try to understand the creation of simplicity still more deeply.

What happens dynamically in a living process is that the wholeness is being constantly differentiated, step by step, by the insertion of new centers into the system of existing centers.

However, there is a further, and powerful effect of the basic rule of the fundamental process. The basic rule says that, at each step, what happens next must be that thing which does the *most* to preserve and intensify the existing wholeness. It is a wholeness-enhancing process which never introduces extraneous structure, but always keeps as close to the previously existing wholeness as it can. When the process is working properly, the new local symmetry which is created will always be the simplest possible. It is the *simplest* elaboration of the existing system that can occur and yet be consistent with the patterns of differentiation present in the wholeness.

The chain of symmetries that is generated, each one the simplest possible at the moment it was created, generates that unusual mixture of complexity and simplicity which is familiar in the works of nature. It is helpful to dwell on this pattern of symmetries explicitly, since its character tells us a great deal about the nature of a successful unfolding process. It also works as a kind

Grassland: simplicity and symmetry among the blades of grass

480

Atmosphere of the Central building, Eishin campus, caused by simplest symmetries, with no fuss, and with a relaxed mind.

of diagnostic tool, telling us whether a particular process is honest and free, or whether it is distorted and contrived. This is extremely important since the naturalness and simplicity of the finished product (and its spiritual purity) will depend, in the end, on this graceful quality. It is a mark of a living process that it does lead to this result. If there is any deviation from the pure system of symmetries, we may use it as a signal that something image-ridden, hostile, or impure has entered the unfolding process. So we may use the emergence of simplicity as a test to be sure that any given process is working well.

Consider the blades of grass shown on page 480. What we have is a system of local symmetries. We have overall complexity, made of local symmetries, piled upon symmetries piled upon asymmetries. The structure arises because of the process which creates symmetries, asymmetrically, on the back of other symmetries.

What I want to emphasize is that unbalanced, awkward systems of symmetries which depart from the natural are created by deviations of process. They are not only unhealthy in some

way, but their ego-deviation is visible in a surfeit of symmetry or in a loss of symmetry.

On the other hand, when a process is pure, and exactly right — and it may be made from any combination of the processes I have described in the last twelve chapters — then we do, gradually, get from the process itself, just the right distribution of symmetries: pure simplicity. This means that as we make something we must continuously purify it, get rid of all the structure which is not absolutely necessary.

The idea of differentiation is strongly interwoven with the existence of symmetries. Within a structure subject to no influences creating differentiations, everything would be symmetrical. Thus, there would be a single homogenous undifferentiated continuum in which no point is distinguished. Structure arises from distinctions. As soon as distinctions arise in the structure, they give rise to other distinctions. As a result, asymmetries arise. The system of asymmetries which occurs in space is, effectively, the history of the differentiations which have been called forth. A structure which has life is one

Interior gallery at the West Dean Visitor's Center, 1996, Christopher Alexander and John Hewitt

in which there were only those differentiations that were called for, and no others. This is a perfectly simple system.

The conception is deeper than it seems. For if we consider the world as a homogeneous space in which all distinctions come about for reasons, then the system of differentiations and the system of living centers are one and the same system.

To restate: To get life we *have* to make things simple. In fact, trying to be simple in the complex organic sense I have described *is the main thing needed to get living structure*. We may even say that living structure *is* simplicity. But what we mean here by simplicity is subtle, far from the naive, contemporary idea of what is simple.

The SIMPLICITY AND INNER CALM transformation keeps everything straight, simple, and direct. It is the practical equivalent of Occam's razor — the medieval philosophical principle which requires that we use only the simplest

theory which is required, nothing more elaborate.

If we want to, we can understand every step of the 10,000 steps, as a step adding structure — of adding a center. The center that is added will most often be a local symmetry, since there is rarely any reason to add something which is not a local symmetry. But the local symmetry that is placed, usually creates an asymmetry, too, at a larger level.

Thus, the unfolding process will always create a huge system of local symmetries, syncopated, irregular and asymmetrical in the large, with a hierarchy of axes and main points and minor points.

This particular characteristic balance of symmetry and asymmetry is fundamental to the nature of order. It always occurs in life. It will always occur in any project which has life, because it is a natural, and practical result of the unfolding process.

In the illustration of bamboos from the Mustard Seed Garden manual of painting, we see this characteristic appearance. The same characteristic appearance comes about in the site plan for Samarkand (this book, page 362 and Book 3, page 126). In both, there is a certain syncopated balance of highly symmetrical things, distributed unevenly according to the terrain, with subtle asymmetries appearing here and there, always themselves made again of smaller, locally symmetric things. It is far deeper in the bamboos, than in the drawings of Samarkand.

If we follow the unfolding process faithfully, we shall nearly always get this characteristic appearance. It sounds frivolous. But it is not. It is fundamental, and helps us to understand something fundamental about the nature of the unfolding process. In a thing which has life, there will always be a characteristic balance of symmetries and asymmetries. It will include a lot of local symmetries, an amount which is "just right." But there will always be a lot of asymmetries, too, again an amount which is "just right."

If the balance of symmetries and asymmetries is off, this is the surest and fastest intuitive way of telling that something is wrong — either with the wholeness, or with the process that produced it. The symmetries and asymmetries, and the balance between the two, are therefore invaluable as diagnostic tools to help us see if we are getting to the right stuff while we are making something. They are especially invaluable because we can tell so very fast, intuitively, if they are just right or not. It is therefore one of the fastest ways we have of telling if things are going right in an unfolding building, and of correcting our work as we go along.

9 / JAPANESE ASYMMETRIES

The proper balance of symmetries which occur in a real or natural thing may be made very clear by paying attention to the Japanese love of asymmetry. We can agree, probably, that the art and architecture of traditional Japan is certainly one where the qualities of life that I have spoken about have reached a high point. Yet the Japanese, traditionally and explicitly, reject the idea of symmetry. Their art is full of consciously asymmetrical compositions. I have even heard that according to tradition in Japan, the number 4 is the number of death, because it is so perfect in its symmetry, while 5, which cannot be symmetrically represented, is the number of life.

Thus one of the great cultures of human history, famous for the depth which it has reached in the attainment of life in buildings, seems, explicitly, to reject the importance of symmetry. Yet in the argument put forward in these books, the idea of symmetry has a major role. How may this apparent contradiction be reconciled?

To start with, we can hardly deny the fact just mentioned — that the great Japanese masters did explicitly reject symmetry, and derived the greatness of their works from conscious attention to the importance of asymmetry?

But when we study their attitude, and study these works which rely on the presence of asymmetry for their beauty, we shall learn something essential about their preference for LOCAL SYMMETRIES which will reinforce our understanding of its importance in a living process.

Does this seem strange? Let us consider some examples of asymmetry. On page 483 is a plan of a Japanese temple precinct. As you can see, it is entirely different from a European Renaissance villa, or from a medieval compound. The buildings are placed with much greater irregularity, the whole thing feels more like nature in its roughness and complexity. We can hardly argue that, after all, it is symmetry which is important here?

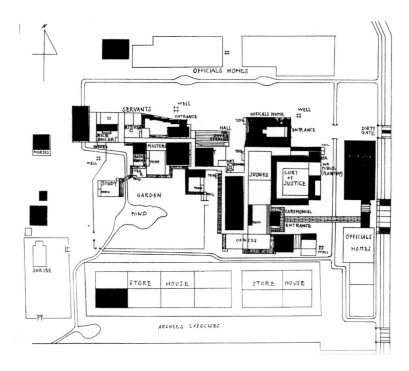

A Japanese temple precinct in Takayama; the whole is highly asymmetrical: the individual elements are purely symmetrical.

But we must also note, to start with, that *locally* the layout of each building is almost rigidly symmetrical. Look at the plan. Although the overall layout is very loose and organic, the *elements* which appear in the plan are rectangular buildings with the strongest internal symmetries. This is undoubtedly true.

So there is an overwhelming presence here of local symmetries, even at the level of the plan. But what about the asymmetrical character of the overall complex? Well, these buildings are placed exactly where the previously existing centers of the site asked that they should be placed. The apparent asymmetry comes from the most painstaking adherence to the exact positions of important natural centers, axes, wholes in nature and the buildings, which existed there before each next building was built. Within the framework of these asymmetrically occurring natural centers, the builders created as much symmetry as possible.

If you want to see how important the symmetry is to the calm and restful feeling of the

whole, you have only to replace the buildings with structures that are asymmetrical within themselves. Then you would get something like the drawing on page 485. As you see, it is a horrible chaos, reminiscent of some of the excesses of 20th-century high architecture.

So we cannot avoid a recognition that the asymmetry of the Japanese temple precinct is derived from a forceful use of *highly* symmetrical structures. And this balance of symmetry and asymmetry is more complex than it seems. Nature creates asymmetry only when necessity forces it. But unlike nature, the Japanese are doing something more: In many famous cases, they created asymmetry *deliberately*, with full intention, in order to create tension, balance, life, where the thing would otherwise be dead.

Look, for instance, at the use of a natural tree trunk as a column in a famous tea house (page 488). The tree trunk is bent and twisted, while a properly made column would have been symmetrical and perfect. This is *deliberate* introduction of asymmetry for its own sake, not be-

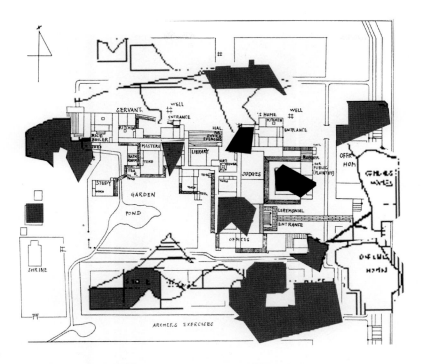

Humorous transformation of the temple precinct in which each building is made into an asymmetrical "design."

cause it was made necessary by contextual circumstance. The same is true in the stone garden at Ryo-an-ji (page 463). The rocks are placed in the raked sand with intentional, and deliberate, departure from symmetry.

And the same is clearly true in their famous drawings and paintings, kimono designs and ornaments which often introduce a deliberate asymmetry, in order to give harmony or life to the whole. For instance, the kimono (page 486) with the asymmetrical arrangement of the great blossoms, is completely inundated, formed, by its asymmetry.

But before we think we have mastered the situation, let us think yet again. Look at this kimono carefully. Once again we notice that the main elements of the asymmetry consist of parts that are themselves locally symmetrical. For instance, the kimono itself is symmetrical, as a whole. And the blossoms in this example are also symmetrical, within themselves. The effect of the asymmetry which interests us so much would be less powerful by far, if the ele-

ments of which it is made were not themselves symmetrical? For instance, if they were random, rambling shapes the effect of the asymmetry would be less startling, and less interesting.

But what about the big asymmetry itself? How do we explain *this*? For it is this *asymmetry*, not the symmetries, which make a counter-example to the thesis of the previous argument. Obviously we must admit that it is intentional, not merely an accident. Yet is not forced by necessity, as the asymmetries of nature are.

To understand this properly, we may go back to the discussion of symmetries in physics. You remember that a thing is typically symmetrical when there is no reason for it to be otherwise. A falling drop is axially symmetrical because there are few horizontal forces on it to cause asymmetries: It becomes symmetrical by default. Now, consider the man (or woman) who is placing these blossoms on this kimono. Of course, the blossom design is an endlessly repeating one — of which we see a fragment here. Well, suppose, now, that the weaver, or the maker of

Symmetrical blossoms, asymmetrically placed on the kimono

the kimono, had ONLY placed one blossom, symmetrically, in the middle of the body — in the middle of the chest, say.

What explains why this was *not* the right thing to do? Well, if the blossom were in the middle, one would ask oneself, "Why is that symmetry present there?" The blossom has a reason to be symmetrical. And the body has a reason to be symmetrical. But there is no reason at all why these two symmetries should coincide. That would be an accident. So, the weaver thinks to herself, we shall therefore, instead, portray the more "general" case: We introduce no structure which is not inherent in the situation, so we place one blossom markedly off symmetry, in order to make sure that an arbitrary, false coincidence of symmetries is not introduced.

The beauty of the placing in this great red kimono lies in the clarity of this distinction, and the fact that it has done just exactly the right thing.

But, now here comes a problem. If I showed you another robe which was symmetrical — a roman catholic priest's robe, for instance, from the Middle Ages, with a great cross on the robe, exactly symmetrical, what would you then say. This, too, may be profound and beautiful. But this one is beautiful because it does *not* have asymmetries as part of it. So what is the right explanation, and the right way of thinking about the symmetries? If you can use the same argument to prove anything at all, whether the thing comes out symmetrical or asymmetrical, then what is there but words here? Can we identify any general, operational rule which we can follow, which would tell us whether to make a particular robe symmetrical or asymmetrical, or a particular design symmetrical or asymmetrical?

We must admit this is the crux of the problem — but, also, that for the present there is no obvious answer.

Another complex asymmetry, in which elements are placed to show the general case, of asymmetries
made from symmetrical bamboos and symmetrical leaf clusters,
beating against the symmetry of the human body on which the robe is placed

Can we, in any case, agree that what the Japanese achieve with these kimonos, or with their other beautiful deliberate asymmetrical placing of things, is somehow close to nature, in spirit? It reminds us of nature and it seems to have the structure of nature in it somehow. We don't know how to make this precise yet. But we may agree, intuitively, that it seems roughly true? And at least we can say, certainly, that it is this which makes it beautiful. Are we able to go on from here?

Let us take an example of a tree, growing in nature, which also has this quality — a tree twisted by the wind, perhaps, trunk and branches growing at a wild angle to the vertical. Well, the tree, of course, also has within itself many local symmetries — the symmetry of the trunk, of the branches along their own axes (rough of course, but nevertheless still cylindrical

symmetries), also the local symmetries of individual leaves, each one roughly symmetrical about its own axis. And yet in its largest aspect, where the tree *could* also be symmetrical, it is not symmetrical: It leans over. The tree leans over, because of wind, or because the soil moved, or the sun shone more brightly from one direction than another. There are asymmetrical influences forcing it away from what would otherwise be the potential symmetry of the whole. But the priest's robe has nothing like this in it. Even in our explanation of the asymmetrical pattern on the red kimono, we did not claim that there is a reason for the asymmetry — only that the asymmetry is a more general case than the symmetry of the way the two things interact.

In theory, then, the most general representation of a tree would show the archetypal tree, which is not perfectly symmetrical. It would be

Asymmetry of a natural branch introduced into the veranda of a Japanese house

hard to recognize if we made it perfectly symmetrical, which is a more unusual case; so the asymmetrical case shows us the more typical, more fundamental tree.

Once again, this is true. And if we are making a picture of a tree we are right. But the tree *itself* does not become asymmetrical for similar reasons. The drawing is asymmetrical because it is supposed to illustrate a general case. The tree is asymmetrical because there is some particular force making it so.

So nature hasn't helped us all that much. What happens in the natural case is not the same as what happens in the Japanese case. And yet, we must admit that the Japanese are trying, and

succeed, in imitating nature. That is why they do it. But the Catholic priest, who places the cross on his vestment, is he imitating nature or not? And is the profound symmetry which he creates more valid, or less valid, than the case of the asymmetrical kimono?

These questions are still too difficult. Within the the living cases, we know there is always a balance of symmetry and assymetry. But we do not know a way to formulate this balance.

For the time being this question is too hard. It alerts us to the subtlety of the balance. It tells us that simplicity is a deeper matter than we thought. But as to the details: For the moment, we must just declare them an enigma?

10 / FINAL SECTION ON SIMPLICITY

The creation of simplicity is a constant struggle. Not only is one removing, cutting, pruning, so as to lay bare the structure of what exists, uncluttered. That is hard enough. But one has to maintain a continuous awareness that our present use of the word "simple" is contaminated and erroneous.

In the 20th century we assumed that to be simple is to use drastic geometric shapes

Eishin campus in springtime. Among all the buildings I have built, and all the pictures taken of my buildings, this picture stands out as my favorite of all. It is a snapshot, not a great photograph, taken with an instant camera. But it shows, more closely than any other of my pictures, the simplicity reached for in this chapter. I took the picture at a moment just after one of my clients told me that in these buildings we had reached what they all thought had been the unattainable.

lacking in structure. Yet nature teaches us that what is truly simple — a waterfall say — is vastly complex — as a structure — and yet vastly simple in its essence. Thus we must strive for something which is utterly simple, in the sense that there is nothing unwanted there, nothing extra. At the same time we know that if we succeed in being truly simple, we reach a fine filigree of levels upon levels in which every part is unique, each adapted to the one unique spot in the world where it lies.

Perhaps no one worked so hard at the creation of geometric space as Gauguin (next page). His canvases, too, are geometrical creations. There we see the fabrication of ordered space. He places, touches, arranges, stretches, twists, until the feeling comes into play.

It is easy to look at such a picture, once finished, and say, "How easy. How beautiful. How breathtaking the color."

But what lies invisible below the surface are the unbelievable hours, days, weeks, months of work to twist one canvas into shape, to arrange just this patch of blue here, and just this lilac, just this green wrapped around, so that the geometry itself creates the feeling.

And that, too, in building. It is the geometry, this pattern of pure organization, which has the ability to connect us to the universe, to mobilize our feeling, to induce deep feeling in us — and to connect us to ourselves. It does not really matter what the "content" is. When we listen to a Mozart piano concerto, or Beethoven's quartet #14 in C-sharp minor — the music has tremendous meaning. Obviously, this does not happen in a *practical* realm. The thing which has this effect on me is a pure organization of sound.

In architecture the same is true. Although the real content is there all the time, in the background — and although it is real human life, ecological life, and social and spiritual life which is at

Paul Gauguin, Horseman on the Beach, 1880

stake — still, too careful or too penny-pinching a regard for these practical problems will always produce trivial results. What matters is the organization itself, the geometric organization — and the ability of this geometric organization to penetrate to the core of being human.

So, what matters in the building is the pure physical pattern of the centers, how deep it reaches, how far it manages to go in activating my feeling. My effort, in making the building, must constantly be to create, and activate, a pure pattern of physical geometry — ultimately material and light — and the depth of the impact which this pure pattern of organization has on me, on my self, on my soul — to what extent it mobilizes my feeling.

Even knowing this, as I do, it is such a struggle to keep on with the geometry. In painting, I try to make a realistic scene. I look at the life there. I try to make the picture come to life, and half of me is asking, What makes it real? What makes it real? I try to paint what I see. But I have to shout at myself, all the time, play, play, play, stop worrying about realism. Just make sure the actual shapes are beautiful, and that the geometry works, that the arrangement of the shapes is beautiful. This means all the shapes, the space between things, and the things, and the shadows, the creases, the fold in the tree trunk. Each shape must be beautiful, supporting the other shapes. This is an incessant work. I have to keep forcing myself, reminding myself. That is why the idea that the spirit and the life, in the end, lie only in the geometry, has to be repeated every day, every morning, every afternoon.

In building, the same thing. More difficult, even, because it is more obvious. I work hard, hour after hour, month after month, I try to make the building right. I pay attention to the passage, the width, the length, the feeling, the light, the comfort, the size of the window, and so on. Always I am trying to make it comfortable. But again, what I have to do, to make it live, every shape must be beautiful. The window sill. The top of the column. The door. The window over the door. The wall between the windows. The edge of the roof. Is it the most beautiful I can make it? Just don't forget. Just don't forget. Keep doing it. It is only when I do *that*, have joyful fun, do nothing else, just keep on doing that, to make each shape beautiful, that the thing begins to gain its life. It ought to be easy. But it is *so* hard.

O Gauguin.

11 / ALL THERE IS

I believe that the drive toward simplicity, is possibly the deepest feature of living process, and its most essential feature.

Anything that does not have this drive toward simplicity cannot, really, be taken seriously as a living process. And this is a very tough criterion, a hard task-master. Consider, for example, the buildings and furnishings that are rich with "patterns." What I mean, here, are the growing number of objects, rooms, houses, buildings, where architects have tried to overcome the stark and deathly character that was common in the middle of the 20th century. Now, too often, they replace that starkness with something too lush, too fruity, too rich, too much like a wedding cake, or sickly cream-filled dessert. Although many architects who seek living structure most genuinely do their best to reach it, the multilayered pattern-filled environments which people make in their desire to do better, often do not have enough cold stark simplicity to have been generated by a living process — and end up merely sentimental, not something which can ennoble, or deepen, a quiet and examined life.

Economy, simplicity, drive the formation of ice on a pond. They drive the formation of flames in the fire. And they drive the formation and simplicity of what is most valuable in the sparseness of a simple room that contains hundreds of complex relationships boiled away almost to nothing, leaving only a quiet which approximates the void.

We have, then, a guiding force: The search for simplicity, newly defined as the search for the living. Every living process searches for the simple. The structure that is created by successive application of the fifteen transformations, with the incoherent continually boiled away — that is living structure.

Living structure may be understood, remembered, as that which remains behind from a continuous striving for the simple, and from the removal of dross. But this "simple" will be both simple and complex. It will be a deep structure capable of holding the most intricate content, yet boiled away, until nothing is left in it, except the few lines which awaken the heart.

METAPHYSICAL NOTE
THOUGHTS ABOUT SIMPLICITY WHICH ARE TOO DIFFICULT TO EXPRESS IN SCIENTIFIC LANGUAGE

The following passage was written long ago. It is, I believe, true. But its truth is difficult to pin down accurately. It deals with mathematical issues that I have dim awareness of, and about which I have even proved preliminary theorems: But the contents are still too rarefied, and too incomplete, to be expressed in precise and common sense terms. Yet the passage may have some value since it allows a poetic perception of an even deeper nature that exists inside simplicity. This may, for a willing reader, throw light on the ultimate nature of the simple — something not yet fully reached in the preceding scientific text.

NOTHINGNESS

I have tried to show that the conditions of the fundamental process are necessary and sufficient for the creation of life. They allow the unfolding of the wholeness of the world. Living structure will come about, as a result of the repeated application of these conditions.

In effect, that is the end of this part of the story. We now have a grip on the process, and it is precisely defined. The main difficulty which remains, is in applying it to real cases. In many instances, it takes years of experience to learn how to apply this step repeatedly, to any given situation.

However, one additional bit of information casts light on the process of unfolding taken as whole, and gives us a holistic overview of what it really does. This is the overview we get if we examine the *inner* meaning of simplicity.

The enigmas of section 9 (pages 486–88) are mirrored in physics. I have mentioned before that even in physics, the idea of simplicity — whether embodied in Occam's razor, the principle of least action, minimum principles, Hamiltonian, geodesic light rays, least energy paths, calculus of variations, or rate of entropy production — is surprisingly obscure. Although there is a general rule that nature follows the simplest path, it turns out to be *amazingly* difficult to give any one completely general formulation of what this means.

In this chapter we have found the same. Although we have good general intuitions about simplicity, it is difficult to give a tough-minded general definition which tells us how to identify the "simplest" thing in any given case.

I believe the reason is this: The idea of simplicity is rooted in the extent to which a given thing comes in contact with the Ground (something I shall not discuss thoroughly until Book 4). For the time being, you may think of the Ground as the substrate of everything, an undivided plenum. I believe, to put it briefly, that there never can be any purely mechanical formulation of the idea of simplicity. Instead, we shall end by accepting that what is simple is just that which is in contact with the Ground, and the more it is in contact the more simple it is.

However, the simplicity itself, so wonderful and so clear in feeling, still hovers uncertainly over the issue. In order to understand, with as much clarity as possible, the meeting point between the field of centers, structure-preserving transformations, simplicity and symmetry, I shall now explain a crucial idea about structure-preserving transformations, which I have not described before. It goes to the root.

If we consider so called empty space, it has its own structure, and its own wholeness. I have sketched a version of this particular wholeness on pages 61–63, showing sequences of transformations that start with a row of evenly spaced dots: an approximation to the structure of nothingness. Within the structure of nothingness there is an endless system of repeating centers, all rather weak, but all *equally* weak, overlapping continuously. In mathematics this structure is called *the continuum*. We may also call it simply emptiness. In any case, emptiness or nothingness is not without structure. It has its own wholeness like any other thing.

Now, as I showed on page 61, we can introduce structure-preserving transformations of this nothingness which lead to various new designs and forms. Each of them, too, has its own wholeness. And these in turn can be transformed into other designs and forms, more complex, with *their* own wholeness. I show this family of forms, all descendants of nothingness, by means of the first line in the accompanying diagram. Each arrow stands for a structure-preserving transformation. Each dot stands for a form which can be reached from nothingness by structure-preserving steps. All of nature is included among the dots which are descendants of nothingness.

There are other designs and forms which can *never* be obtained from nothingness by structure-preserving transformations. These also form a family. In the second line, each arrow stands for a structure-preserving transformation. Each jagged figure in the second line stands for a form which cannot be reached from nothingness by structure-preserving steps.

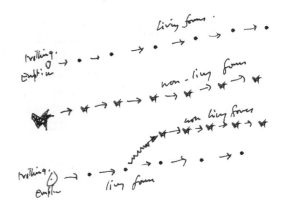

Line 1 shows forms descended from the structure of nothingness or living structure, through structure-preserving transformations.

Line 2 shows forms descended from NON-living structure. No matter how intently sp-transformations are applied, the forms almost cannot get back to the line of living forms.

Line 3 shows a line that starts with nothingness, goes along with structure-preserving transformations. Half way along a SINGLE transformation BREAKS structure. The forms which arise from this transformation are forever damaged. Only a huge further effort to clean them and apply new structure-preserving transformations can bring them back to the first line.

The two families are forever separate. You cannot get from one family to the other by structure-preserving steps. To get to the descendants of nothingness from a descendant of jaggedness, you have to destroy structure. To get to a descendant of jaggedness from a descendant of nothingness, you also have to destroy structure. For instance, the third line of my diagram shows how, once damage has been done and nothingness disturbed in an emerging thing, the ripples and after-effects of that damage will continue for a very long time, and can only be repaired at great cost, and with enormous effort. What goes forward smoothly from nothingness is delicate and precious. But the after-effects of jaggedness, once introduced, are nearly lethal, and very hard, *very* hard to repair.

All the things with profound life, are in the first family. The works of nature are in the first family. The works of great architecture and great art are in the first family. Everything which is simple, and whole, can be reached from nothing-ness, and is a transform of nothingness.

On the other hand, the things in the second family, which can only be obtained from nothing-ness by structure-DESTROYING transformations, or from one another, can only be obtained by tear-ing structure: and they cannot be alive. This is an extension of the experiments described on pages 61–63. It is as if only those things, forms, condi-tions, which can be obtained as structure-pre-serving transformations of nothingness are those which are alive. All others are less alive.

It is highly significant that structure-pre-serving transformations are connected with the idea of nothingness. A natural thing is a trans-form of nothingness. A beautiful thing is a trans-form of nothingness. Anything which has life, which has deep wholeness, *also* is a transform of nothingness. What this means is that a thing which has life, no matter how subtle, how com-plex, how apparently intricate and highly orga-nized is, in effect, a multiplication of elabora-tions, always preserving inside it, the structure of nothingness. Like water, like the Void, this shows us ultimate simplicity as an inner attribute of everything that has true life.

A remarkable conclusion: Namely, that a thing which is well-made, and beautiful — and a thing which touches the living quality which I am reaching for in these four books, will always be iso-morphic to nothingness — it will have the same structure as emptiness. On the other hand, a thing which is wrongly made — something which has ego-filled, perverse structure in it — will always be partly isomorphic to jaggedness, to SOMETHING.

This strange conclusion, odd as it sounds, corresponds to certain intuitions. The feeling of things which are very beautiful, which are lim-pid, clear, smooth — so gracefully simple that, like water, they touch us almost without touch-ing us — is expressed exactly by the strange phrase that they share the structure of nothing-ness. Each approaches nothing, it *is* nothing. Its depth comes from its kinship with the great Void. It rests tranquil in its simplicity, because it has, ultimately, no structure and it disappears.

This strange conclusion corresponds, also, to the thoughts which have been expressed by mystics throughout history. In another form, this is the teaching of the Tao, which tells us to be like water. It is the teaching of Hua Yen Buddhism, one of the antecedents of Zen, which tells us to realize that everything is empty. It is the teaching of the Sufis who dance to become one with nothing.

There is no greater vision of what it is that we are doing when we make a thing. We try to reach a structure which, in all its possible complexity, is ultimately so simple that it shares the structure of emptiness and is derived from it.

In the chapters of Book 4, we shall see that beneath the field of centers there is a Ground which is personal, potentially full of feeling, per-haps animate or being-like. The Ground appears not like a material substance, but more like self-stuff or self-substance.

Here, in anticipation, we see something al-most equally mysterious. That Ground, in some fashion, is nothing-like. It is the original empti-ness. A thing which is truly whole, respects that nothingness. The nothingness is still visible in it. Only a wrongly made thing which is too compli-cated, too filled with ego, disturbs this nothing-ness, and lets itself be seen and felt.

True simplicity — the thing which is truly whole — leaves the nothing undisturbed, quiet, like a lake.

If we imagine a mountain stream crashing and tumbling and then reaching a still pool, we may see the water in that pool as dark, and slightly tur-bulent. As the surface of the pool becomes quieter and quieter, we see further and further into the darkness of the water. In the same way, as the steps which make a building let it become simpler and simpler, we see further and further into the Void. Our connection with the Ground becomes more tangible. Our glimpse of the Self which is the Ground becomes more definite. These matters are taken up further in Book 4.

PART THREE

A NEW PARADIGM
FOR PROCESS IN SOCIETY

EVOLUTION TOWARDS A SOCIETY WHERE
LIVING PROCESS IS THE NORM

I have done my best, in Part Two, to present a concrete picture of the character of living processes as they must occur in the successful construction of the environment. Processes which are living ones, are step-by-step structure-preserving adaptive processes whose main characteristic is their ability to focus on the whole, and to improve and deepen the whole. Each step — when it is going right — heals and improves the whole. All of the steps — as I believe — focus on the creation of living centers. All of them rely on intensifying feeling as they occur.

And the sequence in which the steps occur is always vital to their ability to be effective. The steps generate living geometry in a way that is appropriate to circumstance, only when the sequences are right. These are some of their most salient features.

In order to work, these living processes — especially when applied to the large urban areas and modern agglomerations of urban regions — require freedom of action, freedom within the process. That means that each process must allow every step of each adaptive sequence sufficient latitude to go wherever it needs to go, IN THE CONTEXT OF THE WHOLE, to make the whole more alive. This requires freedom of action at each step.

For the most part, the necessary freedom of action cannot be provided within the context we came to know in the 20th century as totalitarian democracy. By totalitarian democracy I mean the system of thought and action which is prescribed by the rules, procedures, lock-step processes of the modern democratic state, which attempts to create buildings by social routines that are military and regimented, not free or organic. In virtually every walk of life, as we have come to know the processes of planning and construction from the 20th-century heritage, freedom of the kind necessary to create profound wholeness is hampered by our institutional norms and by the normal processes of our society.

This is strange, and not easy to get used to. In modern democracy we have come to believe in the freedom of our own society, and we look with intellectual detachment (touched with a smug feeling of superiority) at the great literature of George Orwell's 1984, *Aldous Huxley's* BRAVE NEW WORLD, *Eugene Zamiatin's* WE, *as if these works describe caricatures of something which may have occurred in other societies — in Communism, in Totalitarianism, in Fascism — but never in our own. Rarely have we understood that our own society, too, our own democracy, though originating in the ideal of freedom, has nevertheless created a system of thought and action, in the sphere of architecture, which makes living structure all but unattainable — at best* BARELY *attainable.*

The problem creates a new kind of challenge for democracy. To create living structure, we need a kind of freedom which the founding fathers of the American constitution (for example) did not dream of, because the issues involved in the creation of life in the environment simply were not visible to them. To create living structure in the environment of our age, and in the future age which stretches before us, we must now find ways of turning society beyond its too-regimented path, and towards paths of design and planning and construction which allow the life of every whole and the life of every part to emerge freely from the processes by which we make the world.

CHAPTER EIGHTEEN

ENCOURAGING FREEDOM

STARTING TO MAKE CHANGES
IN THE CHARACTER OF PROCESS

1 / INTRODUCTION:
WHAT DO PROCESSES ACTUALLY LOOK LIKE IN EVERYDAY SOCIETY?

What would make it feasible to introduce living processes all over the Earth?

In modern society there are hundreds of thousands of different generic processes in everyday use. But what are they like? Looking at the instructions in a software manual; using a mouse to control a computer; flipping hamburgers; filling out tax forms; applying for a building permit; following a rule of accounting; repairing a street with an asphalt laying machine; using a backhoe to dig a trench; painting the back fence; repairing a roof with new flashings; running to catch a plane; loading baggage on a plane; selling plants in plastic tubs, with instructions about shade, sun, and soil type for best results. Sending a package by FedEx, drawing up a table of square feet needed for a new building.

These are the outward forms of our present-day social processes. There are great numbers of such processes all over the world. Many vary greatly from culture to culture; some are shared across groups of cultures; and some are nearly universal. They include all aspects of family life, school life, hospital life, parking enforcement, automobile manufacture.

Let me go on with my examples. The use of rules of order for conduct of a meeting; the competitive bidding of a construction project from drawings; transfer of funds from one bank to another; discussion of an architect's drawings around a table of a board room to decide whether or not to accept the design of a new building; allocation of budget for an improvement project; spending of funds at the end of a fiscal year in a frenzy to use up the funds; election of public officials; awarding of public design projects by invited competition; use of bulldozers to maintain weed abatement in the fire-prone hills of northern California; use of bulldozers to cut fire roads into wilderness; selection of pre-painted colored galvanized iron sheet for a roofing job; assignment of a milling charge when special cuts are made in a lumberyard; legislation allowing police to roust homeless people who sleep in bus-shelters; use of full sheets of plywood to design wall panels, and resulting standard ceiling height of eight feet; application of fire safety laws to make all staircases at least three feet wide; purchase and installation of sprinklers in lawn grass; dredging harbors; hanging out on street corners; panhandling for money; purchase and sale of guns; manufacture of shoes in Southeast Asia and importation for sale to the United States; use of electrical equipment in the garden; use of weed-killers on driveways; common decision-making among committees charged with building design; the architect's use of tracing paper as a sketching medium; architects use of CAD drawings as a way of specifying buildings and working drawings.

These current processes — and the hundreds of thousands of others like them, as formulated at present — are not primarily intended to generate, or modify, or heal, or create a living environment. They are processes which have grown up for many reasons, some concerned with planning and construction, some concerned with other aspects of day-to-day life in society. Most of them, nearly all, have an impact — usually indirect — on the shape of the world. Some of them are living, that is "healing" in their effect. But even these, for the most part, *do not look like the idealized processes which I have drawn in chapters 6–17.* They are more banal, perhaps more ordinary, more down to earth. They are not directly concerned with the life of the result, are not concerned whether they have impact on living structure or not. They are simply rule-defined procedures (some defined through informal or unspoken rules, others through formalized written rules) which thousands, often millions, of men and women use in daily life. These processes, with their effects, form the backbone of what we know as our society.

They are not chiefly *living* processes. They are not all *non-living* processes. But they do all have effects. Most of them have some kind of effect on the geometry and structure of the world — hence on the architecture and cities we create. The world is shaped by these processes, is given its style, order, character, and functional form by these hundreds of thousands of processes acting in concert over the surface of the Earth.

2 / IMPROVING PROCESSES

If we seek to improve the living structure of our world, we must increase the presence of *living* process all over the world. This in turn requires (or at least common sense strongly *suggessts*) that our effort must start from these everyday processes as they actually are, and modify them. It would be far too hard to replace all the everyday processes with new ones. That could only be done in a utopia, in some kind of science-fiction.

We must therefore find a way — a practical way — of slowly, gently, transforming today's processes from what they actually are today, to making them better, making them more workable, without creating too much disturbance, without upsetting society too drastically, as the changes occur.

That slow, incremental change towards more living process is the subject of the next four chapters.

An example to show what I mean. Consider freeways and highways, and the process of locating them, through land acquisition. What are the rules and policies which govern the location of new freeways and highways? Such policies vary from country to country, often from region to region. They are, of course, dependent on the cost of land, the degree of urbanization in the area being considered, and on the prevailing political attitudes (business *v.* environment, for instance) of the government. Let us compare two possible policies. The first states that *the freeway should always be located to minimize acquisition cost of land together with freeway construction cost.* This is a rough approximation to the process actually used in making roads today. A second policy, while giving some weight to these cost matters, also contains an explicit policy along the following lines, thus: *Up to a certain limit, and regardless of extra length, the position of a new freeway should be chosen to leave beautiful and harmonious land untouched, and should be built as far as possible (where available) on land which is itself damaged (though it may create views to beautiful land from a distance).* Following this second policy, a new stretch of freeway will thread its way through a landscape, using as far as possible only the most damaged available bits of land, both for the road itself and for the landscape on either side of it. The long-range effect of this second policy, on the Earth, is somewhat more positive.

The first, purely cost-based process causes acquisition of beautiful bits of land for roads (and the destruction of their beauty), without regard for the damage done to ecology or health of the land. The pure cost-based process is therefore implicitly a life-destroying process. Even though it must be argued that cost reduction achieves important social goals and thus indirectly helps to create life in other areas of society, this process does, unmistakably, damage and destroy life as a direct consequence of its narrow formulation.

The second process, on the other hand, with its emphasis on maintaining places of natural beauty and on juggling funds and costs to make this feasible, is implicitly a more living process, since it preserves and extends living centers where they exist, and builds the new center of the freeway roadbed and its right of way in such a way as to *increase*, not reduce, the harmony of the land taken as a whole, while also trying to conserve funds. The second process is a more living process because it helps create gradual improvement in living centers in the world. The emphasis on centers is hidden, once again not easily visible in the way the rule is formulated. Yet the distinction between this process which does emphasize life, and the purely economic version of the process which does not, is considerable.

In particular, it interferes with our freedom to do what is right. It neither encourages us to create life, nor does it even *allow* us to create life. We know what is right, often, and could act on it, if we were free. But the processes that govern do not give us the freedom to do the life-creating thing. The second kind of process creates a policy framework in which we are free to create wholeness when we can see it — whereas the first process, being purely cost-based, does not give us the freedom to create wholeness in the world.

3 / IMPROVING ZONING RULES

Consider the process of zoning. In 20th-century society, many communities use a zoning ordinance in city planning. This zoning ordinance often includes a "setback" process. In a typical American case for house lots, this process might create a 5-foot setback along each side yard, and a 20-foot setback at the front and at the back.

Such a process will not — in general — create living structure. How do we know this? On a small urban lot, it fails to create positive space in the garden of the house, indeed leaves the space lying in useless narrow strips on all four sides of the building. The presence of living centers is thereby reduced. That, in turn, damages the connective fabric of the neighborhood. It is highly wasteful since it does not allow the family to benefit from the space which they own and have paid for. Especially for small houses on small lots in higher-density neighborhoods, it does not create circumstances in which smaller centers — flower beds, lawn, workshop, whatever is appropriate — can flourish easily, since the outdoor space, being cut up, has little room (or sunshine) for anything useful in any one area.

We can predict that the loss of the centers in the space of the garden inherently reduces life, since the building, unsupported by next-door centers, will have life to a lesser extent than it might

if the space around were used to good advantage. Under these circumstances it is harder for an individual house to make a contribution to the larger neighborhood. That is because, given the extreme rigidity of the zoning rule on a small lot, the house volume has little play left in it — it is virtually fixed in its position (and ultimately in volume) by the four imaginary lines parallel to the lot lines which define the zoning envelope. The effect of this imposed rigidity is to give the builder less freedom to make the house contribute in an imaginative way to the structure of its surroundings.

The picture of sterile neighborhoods as they have in fact been created by present-day mechanization is already visible in this sketch. But it is not merely a mechanical character which has been created: The centers which the house and garden need at many levels in order to form living structure are harder to create because of this process. The imposition of the setback rule makes it harder — often nearly impossible — for a family, or a builder, or an architect — to create living structure. Once again, we are not *free* to do what is right, what is most natural, what is best for the neighborhood.

Knowing all this, of course, does not yet answer the challenging question: What kind of better process might both protect buildings against fire and guarantee them light and air (the present function of the setback rules), and also protect the living character of house, and garden, and street? Nevertheless, it is plain that one could, at once, start looking for an alternative social process, which does these things better while also stimulating the growth and formation of larger and smaller living centers, in the vicinity of the structure.

All this thought about one small topic arises from the definition of living structure already familiar from Book 1. We evaluate the relative life of a process by making predictions based on thought-experiments or simulations. We gauge the likelihood that living structure will appear under the impact of this particular process. We try to imagine a better process which solves noise and daylight problems between neighbors, while generating more positive space.

Whatever form this new process takes, even if only partially successful, it will make us more free to do what is right, and what is best for the neighborhood, and best for our individual homes.

4 / IMPROVING STREETS TO ENHANCE NEIGHBORHOODS

Consider neighborhood streets. Around 1975, the City of Berkeley—under the impulse of radical thinking of that era—decided to close certain neighborhood streets. The object was to slow down traffic in neighborhoods, to make streets safer for pedestrians, possibly to encourage bike traffic, and to make neighborhoods more pleasant and more quiet.

The Public Works Department then initiated a program to close streets with barriers made of huge concrete tubs, sometimes connected with steel guard rails (the photograph below shows what these barriers look like). All in all, perhaps as many as a couple of hundred barriers of this kind were built. The process which the Public Works department set in motion to build the barriers, went roughly like this:

· *1. Define a place in the street network, where a closure (often at an intersection), will reduce through traffic flow.*
· *2. Define the type of closure needed.*
· *3. Place prefabricated concrete tubs and steel guard rails to implement this decision.*

One of the traffic barriers as installed by the Berkeley Public Works department

A tree planted in a Berkeley street fulfils a similar function but creates living structure instead of destroying it

In the thirty years since these barriers were built, many Berkeley residents have come to realize that these barriers are not as pleasant as the idea of them at first seemed. Let us ask, therefore, to what extent the process of locating and installing barriers was a life-creating process?

There are three main difficulties in the process, existing at three distinct levels of scale:

At the largest level of scale, the decision to close streets, rather than slowing streets down, was often not very carefully done: Instead of feeling like a loop, the road feels frustrating to outsiders, and the actual path that works is no longer intuitive, nor intuitively visible.

Second, the actual "permeability" at the barrier is often badly chosen. You need to go through, and it would be quite all right to slow a car down, since if the slow-down was effective, it would do the neighborhood just as much good. But again, because of obstacles in the road surface even where the barrier has an opening in it, there is an ugly feeling of frustration that accompanies the experience, and it does not help the neighborhood, nor the area around the barrier.

Third, the barriers themselves are physically ugly; they have a mechanical and unpleasant structure. They also cost far too much, $8,000 for each tub in 1975. They were made of inappropriate pieces of steel and concrete that were entirely insensitive to local context. On the whole, then, one could not call this process a life-creating process. This process may (I emphasize *may*) have been better than what preceded it; but it was still not creating profound life. Merely having the intent to create life, or to make something good, does not guarantee that an ensuing process actually will create life.

A process that would have been better:

· *1. Identify a street where the neighborhood would benefit from slower traffic.*
· *2. With respect to through-traffic, make it slower: Hence, reduce street width and road surface, but without closing the street.*
· *3. Locate a spot where a constriction (a narrowing) in the street might be helpful.*
· *4. Make each of these narrowings something useful like a small park, even just a flower bed which takes its shape, form, and substance from its immediate context of sun, wind, light, and size and position.*
· *5. In one famous Berkeley street (illustrated in the photograph) a tree in the middle of the road makes the street extremely safe, and beautiful.*

This modified process is not enormously different from the one that was implemented. But it places more emphasis on the context. It allows people in the process to create things which are more alive in themselves. It encourages creation of living centers at a large scale, at a middle scale, and at a small scale, all simultaneously. It is more likely to be structure-preserving. It is more likely to be respectful of the real feelings and needs people have. It is more context-sensitive, and encourages each place to become locally unique.

This is a more living process. The result is likely to be more humane, better for the neighborhood. We judge its greater excellence because of our intuitive grasp of probable consequences, as much as by its conformity to the abstract scheme of chapter 7. It will create a more humane, more livable, more refreshing, and emotionally supportive environment.

5 / IMPROVING COMPUTER-AIDED DESIGN (CAD) PROCESSES

Consider computer design processes. There are, by now, thousands of applications in which people use CAD (computer-aided design) to design, plan, draw, buildings. There are, on the market, many systems which enable a person to lay out their own kitchen, or bathroom, or house, for themselves. Typically, for example, consider the following kind of kitchen layout process that is available commercially on a CD.[1]

· *1. Take the kitchen floorplan.*
· *2. Decide where you want the outer wall.*
· *3. Decide how long to make the counter.*
· *4. Decide where to put the refrigerator.*
· *5. Decide what color to put on the walls.*
· *6. Decide what tiles to put on the floor.*

A process of this type is, within certain limits, under the control of the user. We might assume, therefore, that in principle it must be a living process. But it is not. It will enable people to create virtually any arrangement they wish. In principle that is better, let us say, than having an impersonal housing authority or tract-builder make the decision in a bad way. But it is a very small advance. The process is still not a living one.

Why do I say that it is not a living process? I say this because the process does not encourage the use of structure-preserving transformations. It does not encourage the creation of living centers. It does not even draw the user's attention to the idea of living centers, nor to the possibility of making centers, stronger and more living in the kitchen, so that the user can direct himself to this aim.

The CAD-based system can therefore just as easily create a monstrosity as something good. Why do I blame the CAD drawing tool for this? The CAD drawing tool allows one to draw a bad project as easily as a good one. One may therefore say that the process is entirely neutral. But, of course, my whole point throughout Book 2 is this: *There is no such thing as neutrality in such matters.* A process is either life-creating, or it is not. To be

life-creating, even in some degree, it must have the effect that it encourages the formation of living structure — increases the freedom of the user to find his way to what is useful and appropriate — hence to find living centers, which preserve and extend the structure of the world.

It is perfectly possible (in principle) that computer-based processes could be life-creating — because such processes could, of course, be made in such a way that they systematically encourage the formation of living structure. I am merely saying that the kinds of CAD-based programs which existed in the era of 1990–2000, because they were intentionally neutral, most often did not have this character.

Instead, we have posted, at PATTERNLAN-GUAGE.COM, a kitchen design sequence which does focus on centers and their emergence, and on the adaptive process which allows a person to use these centers for themselves. This sequence has the following steps:

· *1. Think about the activities in your kitchen, and formulate them as generic centers.*
· *2. Decide the size and shape of the kitchen.*
· *3. Place windows in the kitchen, to bring beautiful light into the room.*
· *4. Place a big kitchen table as the main focus of the kitchen.*
· *5. Place a fireplace to form a secondary center in the room.*
· *6. Place an outdoor kitchen garden, according to sun and wind and view.*
· *7. Place a door leading to the outdoors.*
· *8. Place the kitchen counter and your workspace in a good relationship to the main centers.*
· *9. Put in thick walls around the room, to supplement the table, fire, and counter.*[2]

6 / THE BREADTH OF PROCESSES THAT CAN BE IMPROVED

I want to emphasize that almost any social process can have a relatively *more* living character, or have a relatively *less* living character. The pro-

cesses of architectural design, of engineering, of banking, of planning and zoning, of construction and the application of construction codes, even the typical processes which take place in an architect's mind — these are all originally socially defined processes, and these are *all* capable of being relatively more living, or less living.

Relatively minor groups of processes, too, may be living or not. The way a truck driver drives his rig on the interstate freeway. The way a zoning officer conducts the process of filling out a zoning application. The use of organic material in building systems. The fabrication and shaping of components in a concrete casting plant.

Any one of these processes can, in principle, *help* to create living structure in the whole, or it may work *against* the formation of living structure in the whole. That means, broadly speaking, that any process may help, or hinder, the formation of living centers, and may help or hinder the emergence of life in the whole.

Suppose, for instance, that a group of architecture students are asked to make designs in a studio class, and are then asked to bring their drawings for presentation to a jury of several faculty who will make comments about all the designs. This process was widely used in 20th-century architecture schools. It, too, is a *process*, a process traditional in contemporary architectural circles and part of the process of design which these students are being taught. Unfortunately, this process is harmful, and has a strong tendency to work against creation of living structure in building design. It is harmful because it encourages students to focus on image more than on reality. In the first place they learn to equate design with drawing, and are not taught that it is the quality of the *building* more than the quality of the *drawing* which matters most. Second, the jury system encourages presentation: Those who draw the most beautiful and slick images tend to gain sympathy from jurors who only have a few moments to study each design. Further, the process is far too quick, and too casual. Jury members sit in judgment, often without understanding the schemes they are judging; the whole procedure encourages a trivial attitude to buildings.

This process, though commonly found in schools of architecture, cannot be considered a life-encouraging process, since it does not encourage students to create life in designs, nor even to know what it means to create life in buildings.

If we wish to, we can try to correct it. For example, one might have a modified jury process in which rough working models, not drawings, are presented and discussed and judged. The models will tend to focus attention better on the real content. Or one can ask students to stake out imaginary buildings on real pieces of land, and then visit these staked out buildings, walk through them, and around them. That will bring judgment and discussion closer to the real life of the student designs.

In principle, every social process which plays *any role at all* in the formation of the environment is potentially a living process. One process may be defined by a paragraph in a handbook. Another may be defined implicitly by a kind of paving typically available in a local do-it-yourself store. It may be enforced as a matter of practice, within an institution, without being written down. It may be expressed as a formula, if it is a checking process in an engineering code, or the application of an investment rule in a bank. It may, more rarely, be context-sensitive and based on observation, such as the rules now governing forestry in a wilderness area, where the cutting and pruning and culling of trees will be done on according to rules that are governed by the spacing, age, growth, size, slope, wind, and exposure of a given site, in a forestry handbook.

All extant processes may be scrutinized, tested, examined for the degree to which they are life-creating or not. And it is reasonably clear that *all* types of processes, since they *all* have some impact on the formation of the environment, should be made more living in order for our towns and buildings and our outdoor landscape to come to life. In short, not one of the processes in any of these categories should escape our scrutiny.

7 / SLOW IMPROVEMENT OF *ALL* SOCIAL PROCESSES

I hope my point is becoming clear. The processes at work in society take a great variety of ordinary outward forms. All these processes can be modestly improved. We are beginning to see that making changes in the social process is possible, even when conceived in a vast array of different spheres, all having effect on the shape of the world.

During the last forty years I have experimented, repeatedly, with more global changes of process. A partial list of innovations in process that I have tested during these years (given below) gives some idea of the scope and range of the process changes one might contemplate. Most of them deal with the *global* character of a given process, and were not only making small changes in one sequence or another. I proposed these serious modifications for many of the processes that create buildings, because for forty years I have been trying to identify the kinds of process that are *capable* of intensifying wholeness. These processes included more subtle analysis of a design task in terms of its functional roots.[3] They included involvement of users and lay people in the design process of their houses and workplaces.[4] They included management of construction.[5] They included new forms of construction contract.[6] They included innovations in the flow of money.[7] They included inventions in construction technique designed to create physical processes that could allow formation of well-adapted, cheap, buildings.[8] They included proposals for the nature of the human process that is used to lay out a building.[9] They included various experimental human processes needed to improve layout of building interiors.[10] They included changes in process for consecutive layout and siting of buildings in urban design and construction of city downtown.[11] They included mechanical innovations in setting out the foundations of a building.[12] They included innovations in engineering process and analysis to get better results in engineering design.[13] They included innovations in public diagnosis of a community environment leading to changes of process.[14] They include processes where users play a major role in construction, even in ordinary projects. They include innovations in the relative sequence of items in a construction procedure.[15] They have included innovation in the manufacturing process for office furniture designed to make the furniture better adapted to individual needs.[16] They include proposals for changes in the maintenance of buildings, and the maintenance budget and its distribution over the lifetime of the building.[17]

These proposed innovations have all been innovations of *process*. I made the innovations long ago, and in most cases, long before I wrote this book, *simply because I knew the living architecture I was aiming at would be dependent on changes in the character of process.* Furthermore, these processes all embodied (in one form or another) the fifteen transformations at every stage of their action. They were, therefore, morphogenetic processes (as defined below). At the time when I first made them, these process innovations were often dismissed as dreaming, as too radical for an architect to propose.[18] Nevertheless, fundamental practical innovations of process are inevitable consequences of thinking correctly about the nature of living structure in buildings, and of facing honestly the task of creating living structure in the world.[19]

The reader knows as well as I do, that the social and institutional processes we are familiar with today (and that includes most of the large processes of society as we know them) have a very different character from the ones I have been calling for, and are not always life-creating. More important, and in particular, *it is precisely those innovations which attempt to change the system of processes most deeply, that are hardest for society to accept,* and therefore hardest to implement.

This is because the really deep changes are ones which change jobs, and which therefore actually alter the capacity of the social system to let people create wholeness in the world, or to allow it to be created. These kinds of changes — the fundamental ones which are actually needed in society — are at odds with many institutions, not only with individual processes, but in some cases with the whole structure of our institutions as they have developed during the last sixty years.

The processes of construction, planning, banking, cash flow, social organization, business practice, planning law, and above all development — as well as a host of minor everyday processes, too, such as those involving community decision-making, maintenance, building codes, traffic enforcement, labor laws, and distribution of city budgets — as they exist today, are too often inconsistent with the demands of a life-giving or life-creating process. That means, then, that modern society, as it has been organized during the past sixty years or so, was inherently unable to create life in the environment.

Some might say that our contemporary political reality, therefore, rules out the possibility of living structure in the modern era. I do not believe that such a conclusion is justified. My deeper claim is that, up until now, we have simply misunderstood the nature of architectural process. We have not understood how profoundly living process in design and building is related to life, altogether, and how life then emanates directly out of living process in society. The practical impediments to the creation of living structure in the world will gradually be removed, I believe, once we begin to recognize that social process must necessarily be *architectural* process, and that architectural process must *necessarily* be life-creating, a process *which can support the continuous creation of an emerging living structure in the world.*

That requires not merely that we improve the sequences and processes of our society. It requires, specifically, that we make these processes architectural. That means they must be morphogenetic.

8 / MORPHOGENETIC PROCESSES

"Morphogenetic" means "creating or generating shape, morphe, form, gestalt." A sequence is morphogenetic if it does actually unfold to generate a coherent form.

The elements of a sequence being morphogenetic are twofold. First, a sequence is only morphogenetic if it embodies the fifteen transformations, and if it is structure-preserving. Second, a sequence which is morphogenetic will embody, to a greater or less degree, or at least support and encourage, as many as possible of the features of living process, which permit adaptation, structure-preserving transformations, uniqueness, feeling, and simplicity (chapters 7–17).

This is a pretty complicated idea, which encompasses, in one word, all of Book 1 and all of

Book 2, wrapped up in a single package. What I call morphogenetic is not different from "living" — but it places the emphasis on the *form-creating* aspect of the sequences. It is, therefore, "architectural." It creates the form of the world.

To create life on Earth, the sequences which generate the built world, and which help people do it, must be morphogenetic. That is simple to say and hard to do.

From the last few pages, we may begin to have a new view of the generated character of the built environment and of the physical world.

Implicit in the description of living process that I have given are whole-seeking processes which can occur in design and in construction — in short, processes which might typically be used by architects and builders and planners.

But the built world on Earth is formed by a more diffuse and more extensive system of processes, which comes from all walks of life, and all facets of society. Our built environment, as I have stated, is formed by the interaction of thousands of day-to-day rules, procedures, habits of thought and action. It is these processes, embedded in society, which create the form of the world: streets, parks, buildings, rooms, windows, gardens.

Although the myriad rules and processes that exist today can be made slightly more living, by incremental improvement, *the larger task of making these processes genuinely morphogenetic — so that they generate deeper and more coherent living structure — still lies on the horizon.*

9 / THE PRIMARY FUNCTION OF SOCIETY

Why is freedom associated with the morphogenetic character of social processes? Because it is the shape-creating, organization-generating, aspect of process which ultimately allows people to do what they want, what they desire, what they need, and what is deeply adapted to life as it is lived and to experience as it is felt. The *humanity* of the environment comes about only when the processes are morphogenetic, are whole-seeking, are placed in a context that gradually allows people to work towards a living whole in which each person plays a part. If this point is not clear from what you have read in this book, please read Book 1, chapter 10, to understand more fully what I mean.

I believe we may take on this task, collectively, and can gain effective, instrumental knowledge of our generative system, and thus some measure of awareness and control over the system of processes that generates the world. I choose to define society as that system which creates the human world, and say that its *primary* ongoing function, and the criterion we should use to judge it by, *is its capacity to create and re-create a living world for us.*

In this vein, I wish to propose the concept that society — the huge system of process-rules and principles we know as society — should be viewed as having as one of its major functions the continuous creation and perpetuation of a living physical world. The processes which are created and maintained by society, by our culture, provide the world with its genetic material. If we want to understand how the formation of the world works, we need to study this system of processes and their action of the form of the built world. If we want to judge the extent to which society is able to form living structure, we need to compare its system of processes with the action of living processes. If we want to influence and modify the world, to make it more living as a structure or more adequate to human need, we need to influence the action of this system of processes.

It may even be said that we could approach a new point of view in which THE *primary function of society would be understood as the function of generating a healed structure in the world through morphogenetic processes — and that this primary function is to allow us, the members of society, to adjust progressively all the small processes in such a way that individually, and together, they will more and more effectively create a living world.*

But there is one very large-scale obstacle. As things stand in society today, there are forces at work making the transition to a morphogenetic regime very, very, difficult. Although it is possible to imagine minor improvements in some of our processes (as in the small examples given in the last ten pages), and we may be able to imagine small-scale improvement in the degree of life our processes create, changes on the larger order that is required are — for the moment — prevented.

In the next chapter, we shall look at present-day social process, with an eye to understanding how deep we have to go to modify the system as a whole, profoundly, and what may be needed to inject and establish morphogenetic processes in place of the processes we have today.

NOTES

1. A typical example of such a program was Doug Carlston's HOME ARCHITECT, manufactured and distributed by Broderbund in the mid 1990s.

2. This is one of many new sequences which may be found at PATTERNLANGUAGE.COM.

3. Christopher Alexander, NOTES ON THE SYNTHESIS OF FORM (Cambridge: Harvard University Press, 1964).

4. Christopher Alexander with Sara Ishikawa, Murray Silverstein, Max Jacobson, Ingrid Fiksdahl-King, and Shlomo Angel, A PATTERN LANGUAGE (New York: Oxford University Press, 1977).

5. Christopher Alexander, Howard Davis, Julio Martinez, and Don Corner, THE PRODUCTION OF HOUSES (New York: Oxford University Press, 1985).

6. Christopher Alexander, Gary Black, and Miyoko Tsutsui, THE MARY ROSE MUSEUM (New York: Oxford University Press, 1995).

7. Christopher Alexander, Halim Abdelhalim, Marty Shukert, Ed Hazzard, and Howard Davis, THE GRASS ROOTS HOUSING PROCESS (Berkeley: Center for Environmental Structure, 1973).

8. Alexander et al., THE PRODUCTION OF HOUSES

9. Christopher Alexander and Hajo Neis, BATTLE: THE STORY OF A HISTORIC CLASH BETWEEN WORLD SYSTEM A AND WORLD SYSTEM B, (New York: Oxford University Press, in manuscript).

10. Christopher Alexander, THE LINZ CAFE (New York: Oxford University Press, 1983).

11. Christopher Alexander with Ingrid King, Hajo Neis, and Artemis Anninou, A NEW THEORY OF URBAN DESIGN (New York: Oxford University Press, 1987).

12. Alexander et al., THE PRODUCTION OF HOUSES, pp. 209–43.

13. Ibid., and Alexander et al., THE MARY ROSE MUSEUM, P. xxx.

14. Christopher Alexander with Murray Silverstein, Sara Ishikawa, Shlomo Angel, and Denny Abrams, THE OREGON EXPERIMENT (New York: Oxford University Press, 1975).

15. Alexander et al., THE PRODUCTION OF HOUSES, pp. 234–62.

16. Christopher Alexander and others, THE PERSONAL WORKPLACE: A SYSTEM OF OFFICE FURNITURE DESIGNED FOR COMFORT, Volumes 1–8, (Berkeley: Center for Environmental Structure, 1989), prepared for Herman Miller, Inc., Zeeland, Michigan.

17. Alexander et. al., THE OREGON EXPERIMENT.

18. See for example, the review of THE PRODUCTION OF HOUSES by Michael J. Crosbie, AIA JOURNAL (74, No. 12, December 1985), 88–89, where the fundamentally altered process of housing production which is presented in that book was dismissed as something for hippies, and the reviewer appeared to turn his back on the need for this altered system in mainstream society.

19. A client named Ellie Moller once asked me to plan a small town for about a thousand people, on the banks of the Sacramento River. As part of this work, I began working out a money-flow process for the first twenty-five years of the project, but one day she telephoned to say that she was worried about mis-using my genius as an architect. She didn't want me to spend so much time thinking about the money flow, since other people could do that, but she *wanted me to think more about the "design."* By that she meant the static pattern of buildings, streets, shapes, and so on. It took me quite some time to convince Ellie that the flow of money, year after year, and the way this works to create a flow of construction in the town, are essential features of its life — every bit as essential to its design as the layout of buildings — and that if this task were put in someone else's hands (an accountant's, for example, working according to today's accounting practices), it would become separated from the building forms, and therefore almost certainly wrong and inimical to the life of the place. The notion that beauty is the result merely of "design" deeply pervades our contemporary consciousness. Ellie had looked at beautiful buildings built over centuries, had loved them, but was unaware that they *could* only have been created by a certain *process*. Although she had recognized the beauty of the buildings my colleagues and I had sometimes managed to build, and wanted that beauty for her own project — that inner thing which catches life — she was simply unaware that what made our buildings live was the process we used to create them.

CHAPTER NINETEEN

MASSIVE PROCESS DIFFICULTIES

1 / THE GENERATION OF MONSTERS

In theory, every process can be modified and made more living. One can therefore, in theory, imagine a slow evolution in which all the millions of disparate processes in modern society are gradually modified, one by one, until we reach a system which more and more will generate a living world. Using the information presented in chapters 6–17, and working on everyday processes in the fashion depicted in chapter 18 — we may imagine a future society containing thousands of processes, each one capable, in principle, of more and more improvement, moving it slowly towards a living process.

Though optimistic, this picture is helpful because it does show, in principle, how we might gradually transform our world, merely by paying attention to the individual strands of process that occur in everyday life, and making them better, more living, one at a time, according to the definitions of living process.

Unfortunately, though, the deep process difficulties of today's society cannot be solved so easily. There are *massive* large-scale aspects of our modern society which stand in the way.

Above all there is, in today's society, an overall atmosphere, a quality of attitude and fact which again and again and again, seems to conspire to make living process difficult, even impossible. This problem is so severe that — if it were not absurd — one might almost imagine that modern society has been created, intentionally, to make living process hard to implement, to drive it from the door.

And then, too, there is a second problem, related to the first. Living processes, as described in chapters 6–17 and in the last section of chapter 18, are *morphogenetic*. They create form intentionally and explicitly. They are *directly* aimed at the unfolding of life, they have the unfolding of living structure as their *goal*. Modern processes, for the most part, are not morphogenetic. The thousands of processes I have referred to in chap-

ter 18, exist very much *as a fragmented multitude*. They are not ordered, not coordinated, not coherent as a system.

For example, 20th-century zoning-ordinances have impact on the forms of apartment buildings. The buildings are dense, compact, they fit the maximum space into the envelope, the rooms typically have light on one side; the apartments typically open off elevator halls, or long dark passages without natural light; there are no gardens to speak of. These are unappealing buildings. But their unappealing morphological character is not a deliberate, considered effect, which generates coherent well-formed apartment buildings of a horrible type. It is more a kind of idiot consequence, coming from the confluence of effects that no one understood or thought out. The resulting apartments have too little light and air, have cramped access, have access which is not private enough, have walls and floors not always thick enough to insulate sound, do not allow the formation of private dwellings which make people able to enjoy the space where they are living, nor to feel well.

It is as if — and indeed this is true — the society which spawned the 20th-century processes, did so without realizing that these processes would have morphological effects. The effects are chiefly negative. Even when positive, they are clumsy, awkward. Thus 20th-century society, in respect of apartment buildings, entered a kind of monster phase, a Frankenstein phase, where government decisions indirectly generated horrible living conditions without intending to.

If this bad effect were confined only to apartment buildings, that would already be bad enough. But comparable effects exist in almost every part of urban and rural society. Bad conditions and bad building form are generated indirectly by regulations, processes, and influences, in almost every part of a modern urban region; and their bad effects come from the deepest layers of ethos, practice, and assumption, often spread pervasively and forming the substratum of society.

In the case of public downtown we have a similar example. In the case of individual houses and offices, we have another example. In the case of the global warming and destruction of the ozone layer we have a similar example. In the case of destruction of rain forest we have another example. In the pollution of rivers we have another example.

The effects of bad-structure-generating social process are hideously widespread. The rules and processes that have been introduced do generate a world. But they generate a world that is destroyed, that strongly lacks living structure. And, they do so with a ferocity and speed which could make someone from outer space believe — if it were not patently absurd — that it is being done on purpose. How could rules, laws, and processes which generate such obviously harmful structures, have been introduced and replicated throughout modern society, unless it were on purpose? Yet of course, it is not on purpose. It is all *by mistake*. And it is by means of a very particular kind of

mistake. We, the first children of the modern age, have not yet understood the huge extent to which *the physical structure of the world is generated by its processes.*

The processes do have huge impact on the way the world is shaped. But these impacts are most often unintended, tangential. So the structure-*destroying* transformations which run rampant in creating our modern environment are on the loose, uncontrolled, created by idiot processes for which no one takes morphogenetic responsibility. We have let loose a system that generates monsters. And we do not even realize that it is we who created this system of processes and we who continue to let it loose![1]

Of all these examples, possibly the most vicious, and most devastating to life, is the process now known as "development" (see pages 520–21). Yet in the western world, we accept this monster as normal, and are blissfully unaware of the vicious dangers surrounding it. That is discussed in full on .

But, in any case, it does embody a norm of social process which essentially rules out the possibility of generating living structure.

2 / LONG-IN-TOOTH DIFFICULTIES OF INSUFFICIENT FREEDOM AND APPROPRIATENESS

The most fundamental difficulty today — and the one we are perhaps most fully conscious of in day-to-day events in our bureaucratic society — is the fact that events, actions, processes, are not sensitive to context. They are tailored to a standard situation, and fail to pay attention to the wholeness which exists.

Ask yourself, for example: During creation of a new street in our modern era, is it possible that the shape, length, width, of the street, its arrangement, its trees, its parking spots, the entrances to the buildings — may be calculated, shaped, divined, in a way that arises naturally out of the unique circumstances, landforms, and

personalities of the people on that street? No, it is highly unlikely. Streets are governed by rules which do not encourage — sometimes do not permit at all — attention to the unique qualities. Could a few parking spaces be smaller than usual? Could they be at unusual angles? Could one lane be narrower than another, at one point to protect a glorious flowering bush? If not in a pedestrian zone, could the street be largely pedestrian, with possibilities of vehicles moving only slowly through the walking people? Could the surface of the street be a mosaic, depicting a scene of spiritual meaning, and be laid, pebble by pebble, by the people in the street? Again, no, and no, and no! These possibilities are remote. We know that they are all nearly impossible in modern totalitarian democracy. Yet common sense tells us that all these particularities might arise in response to a careful adaptation in which topography, feeling, culture, personality could play a role and be recognized in the resulting shape of the city.

3 / EXCESSIVE RIGIDITY OF RULES

The same kind of dynamical argument can be applied to almost every contemporary structure, whether it be a new city hall, creation of a plaza or an airport, whether it is the waterfront, a forest, a new bridge, a house, a garden, or a neighborhood. Rules are wrongly formulated. Processes are too rigid to allow adaptation. They cannot allow life to occur.

Here, another example: I describe an event that happened during construction of the Lighty house in Berryessa, California, which I built many years ago. This was a house, small, but consisting of six buildings on a slope, looking towards distant mountains in the Napa valley. The road above was on a plateau. The site itself, then, was on a slope falling away from the plateau and it was there on the slope that the very small house was constructed, almost palace-like, among the oak trees.

The plateau above, at the edge of the road, was more or less flat, and had to include a garage, and space for two cars. At the same time, there was a magnificent old white oak standing in a key position; and the entrance of the house itself, the front door and stair that led down the slope to the house, were located near this old oak tree.

The question was, How to place the garage? Because of the site conditions, and the Lighty's infrequent use of cars, I had determined that the garage needed to be long and narrow (one car behind the other). More important, this building had the capacity to create a positive space with the oak tree at its center, then taking the arriving person in a most natural way, through this courtyard, towards the front door.

Only one problem existed. A very small change of distance, had a huge impact on the life

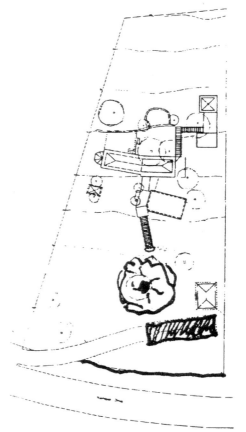

The plan of the Berryessa house, emphasizing the garage, the white oak tree, the stair and the front proprty line. If the garage had been moved one foot to the north, and closer to the tree, the space around the oak tree would have been damaged.

of the structure which could be created. The position of the garage was governed by a setback regulation of 10 feet. But, to make the garage work, while leaving the space around the great oak tree in good condition, the roadside edge of the garage would have to be no more than 9 feet from the road; 9 feet 3 inches would have been possible, at a pinch. But 10 feet would have crowded the tree, and destroyed the living space around the tree. To solve the problem, the set-back requirement *had* to be violated.

What to do? In theory, a variance could have been sought, and possibly granted, to allow the needed minor deviation from the setback rule. However, this procedure would have taken at least several months — time that neither the clients nor the project could afford. Further, it was unlikely that it would have been granted. A legal desire for consistency would probably have held sway. The intent of the setback rule was to create a uniform street facade ten feet from the edge of the road — a rather simple-minded, rule-bound attempt at protecting the larger whole. This rule was insensitive to the more subtle wholeness, which existed on different sites and in this case included the great tree, *and* the garage, *and* the house.

To solve it, briefly and easily, what we did was to confuse the building inspector on the day he came to measure the building: "Could you hold this end of the tape, please, I will measure over here," that sort of thing — and make him believe that the nine feet, were actually ten. Of course, it had already been marked as ten feet on the drawing.

But this stratagem, though effective in our particular instance, did not alter the fact that the process — viewed as a whole — *did not contain the capacity to create a living structure*. It contained the capacity, only, to create a poor approximation to living structure, by following a rule-bound scheme that could not even see the wholeness, much less appreciate it or protect it.

If a process were to be defined, which might replace the too-rigid setback rule, it would have to be one that both protects the larger whole, and is sensitive to the variations and needs of smaller local wholes.

4 / INTENTIONAL RIGIDITY OF RULES
THE INFLUENCE OF FREDERICK TAYLOR

Where did the 20th-century passion for rigidity come from? It came, in part, from Frederick Taylor.

Taylor was one of the individuals who had the greatest influences on the 20th century. An American machinist working at the very end of the 19th century, Taylor conceived the idea of time-and-motion studies, studies in which we would make the repetitive production of objects more efficient.

Taylor first inspired Henry Ford's factory at Dearborn, the first highly efficient modern factory. Ford employed Taylor as a consultant while he planned and built this factory. Later, as a direct result of Taylor's work, almost all natural and organic processes throughout the world which relied on judgment, participation, and common sense were replaced by a way of thinking about process, which relied on rules, rigidly

applied, codification of category, task, function. What we know as the modern organization with machinelike repetition of processes, came from Frederick Taylor.[2] What we know as modern bureaucracy — American, British, Russian, Swedish, or Chinese — with its system of rules, questions and answers, which make little provision for human actuality or human difference, came from the application of Frederick Taylor's ideas to large human institutions.[3] What we know as modern construction, is the application of Taylorism to the assembly of physical components. What we know as modern agriculture, lies in the application of Taylor's ideas to farms, animals, crops, water resources, fertilizers, and machines on the land.

It is amazing to realize that Taylor himself very well understood the positive social and human conditions of the living process he was trying to replace. Here is a quote from Taylor himself: "Now, in the best of the ordinary types of management, the managers recognize frankly that the workmen who are under them possess a mass of traditional knowledge, most of which is not within the possession of the management. The most experienced managers frankly place before their workmen the problem of doing the work in the best and most economical way. They recognize the task before them as that of inducing each workman to use his best endeavors, his hardest work, all his traditional knowledge, his skill, his ingenuity, and his good will, in a word, his initiative, so as to yield the largest possible return to his employer."[4]

Taylor understood all this extremely well. And then, for reasons of money and efficiency, *he deliberately set out to destroy it.* Three principles of Taylorism are: (1) Disassociate the labor process from the skills. Labor must be independent of craft, tradition, and knowledge (Taylor spent years putting his own trade of machinist onto index cards). (2) Separate conception from execution. (3) Gain monopoly over knowledge to control labor process. The increased productivity of identical widgets created by application of these principles, decreased labor costs and increased management control. As Taylor himself wrote:

"*The full possibilities of my system will not have been realized until almost all of the machines in the shop are run by men who are of smaller caliber and attainment, and who are therefore cheaper than those required under the old system.*"[5]

Here we stand face to face with the magnitude of the task which faces us in trying to create a living society once again. To replace structure-destroying transformations with structure-*preserving* transformations — in short, to re-introduce living processes throughout society — we must succeed, slowly, over a period of years, in transforming the effect of Frederick Taylor's thinking.

5 / INAPPROPRIATE SEQUENCE CAUSED BY ADMINISTRATIVE CATEGORIES

The application of rigid procedures and formats, has created an extraordinary loss of contact with natural sequences — sequences that are able to allow a whole to unfold organically, in a fashion that is naturally required — and this frequently has unfortunate, negative results. Consider, the design of the Mary Rose Museum, a $15 million museum in Portsmouth, England. The Mary Rose ship lay, at that time, in dry-dock #3. I was commissioned to design a new museum that was to be built over the existing dry dock. The loads were great; the muck and debris in the foundation clay, was unstable, and unreliable.

I asked our client for permission to hire a soils engineering firm, to make the necessary preliminary borings so that we might have at least a rough working sense of what lay beneath the dock. I did this, knowing, of course, that the character of the soils would have enormous impact on the possible design; thus we asked for a soils test, at an unusual time, not part of the accepted conventional wisdom, which more typically calls for soils test only at the time of working drawings.[6]

My client, the shipping company, Sea Containers, agreed to the cost of the preliminary soils test. However, according to conventional protocol, they wanted to keep the soils-testing process separate from my design process, or from my company. This made sense, according to the conventional separation of tasks. In Taylorian fashion, they felt it would muddy the waters to have too close a relation between architect and soils engineer and wanted to give me only a completed packet.

I, on the other hand, insisted that the soils work had to be under my control. I argued that the questions I wanted the soils engineer to ask, would depend on the preliminary design I had in mind, which in turn depended on his first rough findings, and that I needed to keep the question and answer process going, dynamically, between myself and the engineer, while the work went forward. I insisted, therefore, that it was necessary for me to control the soils work, and to pay for it. They would not allow it.

In another project, the Frankfurt housing, I asked that we have the structural engineers involved from the beginning, since to meet the cost we had to perform actual engineering calculations. For two years, the client refused to start the engineer (even though contract demanded that engineering be paid by them), because, as in the other case, they wanted the engineer to be brought in later, when the first architectural scheme was already complete. This made genuine and effective cost-squeezing impossible during the early design process — the very phase of work when it had to be done in order to be effective. Yet the essence of the project was the requirement that

high-quality buildings were to be built at low cost, and this needed the most sophisticated design from the beginning in regard to structural members, floor design, and wall design.[7]

Most amazing of all, throughout this two-year long discussion, the client insisted that I provide a guarantee of building cost — something I most warmly wanted to provide — yet he could not understand or accept that we could not provide the necessary cost assurances without benefit of engineering.

This man was not silly, as this story makes him sound. He was simply caught in the rigidity of contractual separation between different professions, thus making workable and responsible attention to the whole impossible.

In both instances — Mary Rose Museum and Frankfurt apartments — this kind of damaging compartmentalisation and refusal to allow processes to unfold in the right order, had negative impact on the shape, form, cost, and life of major buildings.

6 / FURTHER DIFFICULTIES OF INAPPROPRIATE SEQUENCE: THE NEW JERSEY WETLANDS

An experience I had once in New Jersey, may serve as a more subtle and more extensive example of this complex yet massive point.

A client asked us to build about a dozen houses on a site of 15 acres in Mendham Township, New Jersey. I went to look at the site, with the idea of getting a first rough idea where the houses would best be placed.

When I got there I was astonished. I had forgotten how lush and overgrown New Jersey is. The site was completely overgrown. A pond at one end, bushes, thickets, a maze of thick undergrowth, and trees everywhere. There were several thousand trees, saplings, and bushes, large and small.

As I stood there, struggling even to walk through it, one thought was constantly in my mind. How are we going to get started?

I tried to explain the problem to Karl, my client, and found the greatest difficulty in communicating it to him at all. I was trying to imagine the actual machinery we would use, what kind of task it was to clear this site, without damaging it. He said, "What's the problem?" I suppose he was imagining that I would make a plan on paper, and he would then get a group of bulldozers to clear it. That was the normal process in 1989. But I was trying to imagine it, *actually*. I stood there, and realized that this one task was a task of two or three months at least, just to do selection of trees, culling of trees, and designing. The longer I looked at it, the more difficult I realized it was, and the more complex the problem, because I realized that as things stood it wasn't even possible to decide where to place the houses. You couldn't see enough of the land, to see where to put the houses. Just to decide where to put the houses, one had to clear some trees, some underbrush, grade some land. And in doing those elementary first steps, to see where to put things, one was already making decisions, merely in the act of finding out how and where to make the decisions.

I explained it to Karl another way. He had brought me into this project because he wanted to learn how to preserve the natural wetlands of New Jersey, and show how houses could be built without destroying the natural wildlife. This meant, a process of selective cultivation . . . a process in which one thinned out and tamed the wild land. But not a process which is *too* respectful of nature. Rather, a kind of process of establishing a form of nature, half-tamed, half-wild, where human settlement, houses, gardens could interact harmoniously with nature, not by leaving it alone, but by creating a mixed, balanced continuum in which gardens are wild and nature is tamed . . . something rough and natural, but also cultured and tamed and formal.

To make this thing, it was necessary to have an intelligent process, in which each act of cutting a bush, pruning a sapling, removing trees, grading a small stretch of land, was being done in a dynamic way so that the complex and beautiful finished reality would arise from the process itself.

It would have been impossible to create a sensible drawing of this complexity, showing the future of each one of 5000 trees. Imagine drawing 5000 trees, and marking on the drawing which ones to leave, and which to take! But it would also have been inherently impossible because, when done correctly in a living process, it would be the *sequence* of cutting the trees, one by one, alternating with the sequence and process of choosing lots, deciding house positions, seeing what is left, cutting one or two more trees, finding the position of the next house, then cutting again, at the right distance . . . *all this, which would make the beauty of a successful building project in which a dozen houses could be harmoniously related to the land.*

Today, no such process exists as part of the kit of tools in the architect's tool-bag. Within the mainstream profession of architecture, no one knows the rules for such a process — especially not if time and cost are taken into consideration as a relevant part of the issue. It was this that made me marvel, and stop in astonishment as I stood at the edge of the wood that day, wondering how we were going to do it. The complex intelligent process (not too costly) in which people, bulldozers, equipment, and care and love for the forest would all interact to produce a new half-forest half-garden, in which the right balance could be struck. And the fact that this process had to be dynamic, and could not be predetermined by drawn plans.

To imagine what this process might be like, one has to imagine a process of gardening — especially in an old and rather wild garden, where the pruning, gardening, weeding, are all selective, and where the wild plants and cultivated plants grow together, and emerge from the act of gardening itself. It is then the dynamics of the process in time, and the intelligent and motivated process of reacting to successes and failures, which creates the final whole . . . not some static image, which can be drawn on a plan at the beginning.

It is a coordinated process of decision-making, coupled with the use of heavy equipment, in a delicate and selective fashion, together with basic decision-making that has the authority to place lot lines, and house-footprints, while the pruning, and cutting is going on. The process is then able to create positive space among the trees, sites that get sunshine, sites that are visually protected from each other, and sites, gardens, and views, which benefit from the natural lie of the existing trees, and the existing lay of the land.

This is a new kind of process, not consistent with existing processes. And because of the way such a process works, it is not practical to create this life by first making a drawing, and then asking someone else to build it. That division of activities is not consistent with the inner logic of the process.

7 / DIFFICULTIES OF SEQUENCE CAUSED BY SEPARATING DESIGN FROM CONSTRUCTION

The way that sensible adherence to a sequence of unfolding, is likely to impact real social processes, is nowhere more clear than in the relation between design and construction. In conventional 20th-century process, most people made the assumption that design and construction *can* be separated successfully, and *should* be separated, that design comes first, ending with preparation of detailed construction drawings, and is then followed by a construction process which executes the design specified by the drawings.

If we pay attention to the sequence of unfolding as it actually needs to happen, and to the formation of living centers from the whole in a way which enhances the whole, we find ourselves repeatedly in the circumstances where we MUST jump back and forth between the two. This is easily visible in the sixty pages of the appendix. At the time we place a foundation, we must make allowances for design, since rocks, or trees, may influence the overall line of the building. If we go back to the design process,

we may find that at an early stage in a design, a tree has to be cut down, or a piece of land excavated, in order to further the evolution of living centers which then permit the continued evolution of the design. We find that a step in the design cannot be taken responsibly, without first taking a step in construction; or a step in construction cannot responsibly be taken, without taking a step in design.

Thus, in as living process, design steps and construction steps *must* be interleaved and entangled. The idea that they can be sharply separated as they were in much of the 20th century, does enormous violence to the needs of living structure. On the other hand, careful attention to the natural sequence of events in a living process that is truly capable of creating a good building leads inevitably to a form of process (and social organization) in which these two are entwined.

This topic is discussed at length in the appendix of this book, and is also a major theme throughout Book 3. See especially chapter 16, *"All Building as Making."*

8 / DIFFICULTIES OF SEQUENCE WHICH ORIGINATE IN ARCHITECTURAL EDUCATION

The difficulty of our situation during the last decade of the 20th-century, was never made more clear to me than during a short visit to the Architecture school of the Queen's University, Belfast, in 1996. At the invitation of Dean Tom Woolley, I went to talk to the fifth-year students and graduate students. I gave a talk, lasting about an hour, explaining to them how and why one could not make a good building without standing in it, shaping it during construction. I gave innumerable examples of the way that de-

tailed floor layout can only be worked out after one is standing on the slab, of how window positions and detailed window shapes can only be worked out once standing in the room; how entrance positions need to be fine tuned by walking towards the door; how the height of a wall, or of a ceiling, can only be judged accurately, in full three-dimensional reality, while standing in the place where the wall or ceiling are to be.

The examples were convincing. During that hour, I managed to paint a picture of the way the beauty of a building, its suitability for life, comes just from these accurate decisions, made while the building is under construction. After hearing dozens of detailed examples of adaptation, and fitting of form to detailed functions, I believe the students accepted, thoroughly, that if one was to build good buildings, it had to be done this way.

I explained, then, that one could only have the ability to make these changes in the emerging building, if one had actual responsibility for the construction itself, and within the framework of a new kind of construction contract — since change-orders made under standard bid contracts were too expensive, and far too clumsy.

This, too, the students accepted. They asked me, then, how they themselves could gradually move towards this kind of life. What training could they get? What employment might they seek, to move them in this direction?

I started out by telling them that at the very least they needed to work in construction, full-time, during their last year at school, so that they might have a thoroughly mobilized ability to understand and feel material construction process and the joy of the site. They asked me how, and in what framework, they should do this. I said, "Well, your Dean is favorable to these ideas. Just arrange your curriculum so that your classes, in this last year, are of that kind, and in that spirit." But Tom Woolley, ruefully, told me that although he personally favored this approach — and had run his own class this way — none of the other instructors would agree to it. They would insist on the students continuing their drawing exercises. Even he, as Dean, in his own words, "did not have the right, or the power, to tell his fellow teachers what to do in this regard."

"But then, the students cannot learn this at all, and will be unable to learn it later either," I told them, and him, together. "And why is that?" "Because, once you leave school, you will need to find employment. As junior draftsmen you may be employable. But as construction workers you are not employable. Many of you do not even know how to hold a broom, let alone a wheelbarrow or a trowel or a saw. So, you cannot get work on a construction site, at a wage that will keep you alive. It is necessary that you learn these things, *now*, during your precious student years, when your family have made a budget for you to help you study, and when the need for a paid job is not controlling you."

"But," they told me again, "within the school, as it was set up, that would be impossible." And that was true.

So, what it boils down to is this. Most present-day architects like *talking* about construction, but are afraid of construction tools, and have little feeling for them. In many cases, getting their hands dirty scares them. In order to protect their trade, they refuse to allow the students to work on construction sites, because they want to force the students to be like them. But, later on, once the students have left the school, it is too late for the students to do anything about it.

This is a drastic problem — almost of the "you can't get there from here" variety. Here the processes of our existing society are so entrenched, that it is not even easy to visualize how a person can make the jump, or find a bridge, to a newer and more living process.

9 / FURTHER DIFFICULTIES OF SEQUENCE CAUSED BY THE SEPARATION OF CONSTRUCTION FROM DESIGN

The problem caused by these separations of process goes further. Almost everything deadening we see in the present-day results of constrction may be atttibuted to this difficulty. For example, no one really likes the repetitive soul-destroying apartments and offices in modern cities. The sense that we exist as packaged wheels in a machine is all too obvious. Nearly everybody feels it.

But all this is, of course, another result of the sequence used to create buildings. Drawings cost money. To make a drawing of an apartment building in which every apartment is different is hugely expensive. It is therefore difficult to get enough information, to provide a reasonable and sensible basis for making the apartments different. Why should they be different? It takes time and effort to understand, for each one, why and just how it ought to be different.

Further, much of the information is not available until construction is under way. You cannot get the information from a map of the site, from drawings, site plans, and so on. Only when standing on the floor of the real place, can we begin to appreciate the uniqueness of each spot, to be able to do anything about it. But in today's sequence of construction, it is far too late by then. The building permit has been issued, and the building contracts have been let.

And further still, the present process allows too little interplay between users, workers, families, and the places they inhabit. It allows a worker to put a family photo on a desk, but not the profound adaptation of a place to idiosyncrasies of feeling and need experienced by different women and men.

So, the semi-automated, wrong-headed sequence of the present process, commits us to having thousands of identical apartments and offices.

The mystification of professional expertise causes further difficulties. In order to achieve local adaptation of the millions of centers in a living structure, it is necessary that decision-making control over these centers is decentralized as far as possible, placed in the hands of the people who are closest to it. Yet in modern society an extraordinary number of men, women, and children are convinced that they do not know enough to lay out a house or an office or a road — that it is an arcane matter for professionals which only professionals can do. This deep-seated and wrong-headed belief

has been inculcated by the heavy-handed tone and legal character of design and engineering professions, leaving people as impotent recipients of the designs handed to them by their more competent "betters."

The architect's claim to be the only person in society who can manage design capably, is not only manifestly false (because architects have done such a bad job). It is also, from a deep theoretical point of view, inimical to the growth of a living environment, because it concentrates too much design authority in a handful of people, making successful adaptation impossible.

We see here, a principle of local autonomous adaptation, needed for successful adaptation of the larger system. It requires a level of knowledge and expertise in the hands of people of society at large. That means, simply stated, that the layout process for different pieces of the environment must be widely available to millions of players. The possibility of such widespread knowledge and empowerment lies in the generative capacity of different pattern languages — generative sequences.

But the critical issue lies in the matter of competence and permission. It is necessary for people to have access to the minimal competence to lay out small parts of the environment, in a way which is living, and which is good for the whole, supportive of the larger wholes in the world. This competence must lie *within individual hands of people who do not have special training*. And it requires, also, that some similar competence for local design of streets, public space, shared space, is in the hands of groups of individuals, again unskilled, again using rather simple generative sequences to create well-adapted plans. And, most important of all, it requires a system of social arrangements which ALLOW people to have control over these parts of their environment, which touch them so deeply.

In the computer age it has become possible, in principle, to create such generative schemes, and to make them widely available, in our mass society. But, so far, this fact has only just started to influence the process of development.

10 / THE BIGGEST SOURCE OF MONSTERS
PROFIT-BASED DEVELOPMENT: LENDING, BORROWING, AND SPECULATION

The various ways in which society has made living process all but impossible, culminated, in the 20th century, in the system of processes that became known as "development," and in the activities of the generic individual who became known as the "developer."

Even now, we have inherited from the 20th century, a quiet acceptance of the idea that "development," stimulated by the actions of a "developer," is the natural way for the buildings of our Earth to be created. We take it for granted that office buildings, hotels, housing, private houses, roads, movie houses — even parks and public buildings — are built by borrowed money and — very often — it is money borrowed from people who are *speculating* with money.

The effect on the world has been devastating. In the later half of the 20th century, this borrowed money has been taken too far away from the site where adaptation must be happening, thus removing the control from the process of adaptation itself. This has happened because nowadays the money is often money that is leveraged — that means, it is money, borrowed from someone who has no interest at all in the actual thing being built and is only looking for a general, monetary return on investment.

One may say that the developer is harmless, and that developers — people who build for profit — have existed for centuries without doing harm. But the scale and scope and character of modern development, are entirely new. If a 19th-century businessman or developer built a factory for his own profit, at least he was still involved, it was local to him, he was able to make personal adaptations, there was, often, even vision in the undertaking. Above all, money and profit aside, the vision of the factory was still most often based on feeling . . . on some kind of feeling for the whole.

The modern development process is based *solely* on money, not on tangible physical results. A group of investors are based in Florida, say, and Singapore and London. This group of investors place a certain capital sum in the hands of an agent, or broker, who seeks to "place it." He finds a project going on in Aspen, Colorado — a group of apartments to be built for weekend skiers, say. This looks like an attractive investment. He recommends it. The money goes down. It is handled, locally, by a third agent, a real estate broker in Snowmass, Colorado. The actual builder of the project is a fourth individual, and the craftsmen are fifth — now five steps removed from the investors in Singapore, London, and Florida. All of them, at all levels in this process, have one driving rule, only, and that is the profit — the return on investment — which they are able to pass up the line, while each agent takes his cut. Finally, at the end of the line, the investors in Singapore and Florida need 10%, 20%, 30% on their money.

The project as a whole is driven by this motive. The long-distance investors in the investment group control the execution of the project., by demanding monetary certainties (a plan that will easily "re-sell," for example, thus making it less well-adapted to the land, and more well-adapted to the realtor's little red book. Any motive seeking to make the project well-adapted to the land, beautiful, touching to the people who live in it — is entirely secondary. Sometimes, a glimmering of this motive enters the picture because — in expensive projects — it is thought that such "amenities" will add to the monetary value, and hence to the return. But the motive is still money. Thus, even these beautiful and important aspects of living structure are introduced, in this case, only because they may increase profit, and they are done, cynically, then, with an eye to the bottom line, as it is experienced, in cash, by the investors in Florida and Singapore — people who have never walked that land, who have, to a near certainty, never even seen pictures of the land — and who do not care about the outcome, except insofar as it brings them monetary rewards.

That, in a nutshell, is the modern process of development. And versions of this process are used — were used — even by the governments in Communist countries. There, once again, the government builds what they build in a way that all the primary decision-makers are absent from the project, uncaring about the individuals or the land, and caring only that the project works financially as an investment for the People's government.

Socialist or Capitalist, it is all the same. The modern process of development, has all but destroyed our capacity to create living structure in the world.

The result of all this, of course, is against life. It is against life because the motives controlling decisions are different *from* life. The control of the project comes from the source of money; but the immediate adaptation, the connection to human beings, the connection to the land, become secondary. We are not looking, in such a project, at the prudent garnering of cash, to do the best possible for the land. We are, rather, looking at an object which is created in order to become an instrument for making money into more money — quite another thing.

The abstract and alien face of housing, motels, warehouses, as they exist in the modern landscape of Dallas, Johannesburg, Vancouver, and Singapore, is caused, first and foremost by this characteristic of development. Architects have, for the most part, been unable to resist this process, and now, in very many cases, consider themselves to be working for developers. Often they regard developers as their primary source of clientele. Many architects of the late 20th century considered this the badge of their modernity, of their professionalism.[8] Yet, by so doing, they were often directly working against life, and toward the death of the land.

It is particularly hard to grasp the real nature of this insidious problem. People will ask, innocently, isn't it true that the builders of the great railroad stations borrowed money? Is it not true that farmers borrowed money to create their farms, even in the 18th century, when living structure was so easily produced? Yes, it is true. But that borrowed money was entirely in the control of the borrower. So it could be used to make the best and most living structure possible. Today's leveraged investment capital is something very different. The use to which the money is put, is not judged by its success as a living structure, as a living part of the community — it is judged by its ability to create cash, perhaps 10% of its value per year, perhaps even 15% or 20% of its value per year. When that becomes the motive, the impulse towards living structure usually gives way to an impulse towards something else, something that is ugly and distorted.

Development is defined, in its essence, by a five-step sequence:

· *Find land with potential for profit.*
· *Architect makes plans.*
· *Bank approves plans.*
· *Permit is given for the plans.*
· *Contractor builds plan.*

Throughout the second half of the 20th century, this model was used more and more for the creation of environment. It was used for houses, roads, public works, bridges, public buildings, parks, agriculture, beaches, and so on. By the end of the 20th century almost all the world (with the exception of third-world squatter housing) was being built this way.

The development process was largely independent of the issue of public or private property. The same model, originally developed in so-called Capitalist countries for private development, was later used equally as the basis for publicly owned housing in so-called Communist countries. The expansion of private development in the private sector increased towards the end of the century, and then became the model, also, for public projects all over the world. The model is profoundly intertwined with our present understanding of society.

And this model remains consolidated and reinforced, by a wide variety of institutions. Banking regulations, banking practice, property law, the laws which govern the control of streets, the nature of private property, zoning ordinances, building codes, fire laws, the expectations of local governments, the structure of income tax, the character of traffic laws, the nature of ecological protection, the laws governing handicapped access, the nature of cash draws made by contractors — all these institutions, and many more, cooperate to reinforce and consolidate this model which we call "development."

The construction which has followed this model has created a vast volume of buildings. Three-quarters of all the urban environments *that have ever been built in the history of mankind* were built in the 20th century. And most of this new construction — with the one massive notable exception of squatter settlements in many countries of the world — has followed the model of "development." Essentially, then, this is *the* most pervasive model of order production which humankind has invented in modern times.

But, at the same time, as I have argued, it is virtually impossible for a living environment to be created in this fashion.

Here we see a huge system effect, in which processes do not merely generate dead structure individually but as a whole, throughout the whole of society. There is an intransigent, ineluctable whole, and the system of society acts as a monolithic whole so deeply connected, so intertwined in its resistance to living structure, that its effects are far more pernicious, and present us, overall, with a very, very serious problem.

11 / THE DEATH OF BEAUTY: A HUGE SYSTEM EFFECT WHICH DESTROYS ALL FEELING

I showed in chapter 18, that the positive way in which individual processes can be made more life-creating has a severe limitation. Living process is by nature morphogenetic. That means a living process acts, in every facet, as a whole, and in all its aspects, is aimed at creating POSITIVE SPACE, is aimed at making form coherent. A living process — and this, too, is how I have described it in chapters 6–17 — is oriented in its entirety, towards the creation of wholes.

The present-day piecemeal and fragmented processes of our society, are *not* oriented towards creating wholes. They are highly organized, yes. But they are *not* oriented, in their substance, towards the creation of living wholes. They are oriented coherently, but towards making money, or creating power . . . other matters entirely.

How then can this too-rigidly coherent machine gradually be changed? Is it possible for a merely piecemeal process, grafted onto the existing fragmented system, to change it gradually towards a morphogenetic process, much more like the idealized living processes I have defined earlier. If that is so, then we may face even more difficult hurdles, before we can succeed.

Once again, we are led to the realization that a piecemeal modification of society, along the simple lines envisaged in chapter 18, will not be powerful enough to work. It will not work because the force and integration of the present life-destroying process is so massive, and so thoroughly organized. What we became used to in the 20th century as the process of development, prevented people from acting according to their feelings, still to this day prevents people from shaping the environment in a way that is appropriate according to the global nature of the whole — and prevents the successful evolution, as unfolding would suggest, of buildings and landscape.

Thus the 20th-century process interrupts the process of paying attention to wholeness, the unfolding of wholeness, and the process of shaping the surface of the Earth correctly. At the same time it also robs people of the simple joy of acting appropriately, in a way that is fulfilling.

The connection between the two — the rise of developers and the loss of feeling — is not accidental. It may seem ridiculous to say that the world will be improved — in its organization — if people are able to act, at every scale, according to their feeling. *But it is the* WHOLE *that is being damaged by the loss of feeling.* By not allowing people to act according to the global feeling of the situation, that means that each of the prevailing processes — whether they have to do with

development, or land purchase, or transportation planning, or banking, or speculation, or construction-contract administration — they all, in their present form, have the capacity to damage feeling and therefore to fly in the face of the interests of the global whole.

Worst of all, perhaps, is the fact that the processes which exist — which we now take for granted — in many cases virtually outlaw living process, make living process fundamentally and practically impossible, impossible even to *imagine*, since the ground rules of the processes we know today have driven them out so far.

12 / THE FOOTSTEPS OF THOMAS KUHN
A VITAL NEED TO RECONSIDER
THE RULES WHICH
GOVERN SOCIAL PROCESS

What changes are needed? What changes are possible?

Thomas Kuhn became famous for describing the seasick feeling one has, when in the midst of a shift of paradigm.[9] It will help focus attention on the fundamental nature of changes that are required, in implementing living process, for me to describe certain practical experiences in these terms.

During the period 1963 to 1998, I created a special program at the University of California, Berkeley. In 1987 it became known as the Building Process program. This program showed students, in early outline, what is contained in the four books of THE NATURE OF ORDER. Teaching in this program my colleagues and I tried to show students what it would be like to work in a world where living processes exist.

The program became the focus of remarkable hostilities from the faculty. The hostility, I believe, arose out of the intellectual incompatibility of the program with then prevailing forms of architectural education. These difficulties arose because the ways of thought that exist in

present-day prevailing processes, are literally incommensurable with the ways of thought put forward in THE NATURE OF ORDER. Some of the incommensurables seem superficially unimportant. For example, I was unwilling to subject my students to juries because I did not believe in them; I often declined, too, invitations to take part in other people's juries. That is because, in the mentality of unfolding, it does not make sense to look at a drawing that purports to be a finished design. Yet my objection could not be translated into the thinking of architects teaching at that time, and they assumed that I was rude or uncooperative. No explanation that I ever found could bridge the gap between the two world-views.

I insisted on the possibility of teaching students in the context of real projects and in real construction. I did this, of course, because the student projects which were then popular — drawings of imaginary projects — are literally nonsense according to the theory I have put forward, and can have little sensible role in education. But since real projects have their own time scale, which does not fit with university semesters, my grades were sometimes late: And, worse, the demands I placed on my students, quite understandable to the students, were incommensurable with the requirements placed on them by teachers who saw no problems in a normal academic curriculum.

There was, too, a far deeper problem. Students who had been trained in our program understood, as a matter of course, that value was a matter of substance, something to be worked through and discussed. Yet visiting architect-professors from the rest of our Department still assumed (according to the older paradigm) that there was no such thing as value (as an objective thing), and rather that each person should be free to go in whatever direction he liked and thought interesting. Thus faculty visitors to my classes, who almost inevitably came with that theme in mind, often forced us to go through an agonizing (and for us time-wasting) explanation and debate often lasting several hours since they did not agree with the philosophy of value they heard put to them by students trying to explain their projects — all simply because of the difference in initial assumptions about whether value actually exists or not.

The examples of incommensurable ideas ranged from minor to enormous. You may see what a devastating lack of communication existed even in a university setting, one supposedly conducive to reasoned discussion. How much worse, and how much more serious, this problem is, when it arises in a real-world setting, where one tries to make these changes and innovations in process against the backdrop of present-day procedural assumptions in planning, architecture, and construction. It is relevant to consider these difficulties, because they are surface manifestations of the very deep inconsistency between thinking about living process and the present organization of society as reflected in current training of architects.

The lengths that I have gone to in my own life, and have needed to go to, during the last thirty years, in order to make living process work, have sometimes been extreme.

I have often made construction teams from ordinary men and women and craftsmen, but outside the world of commercial construction. The reason is that the commercial construction people knew what to do (knew the rules of the game) so well, that, without meaning to, they often created an impossible atmosphere on site, and did not, or could not, make the physical moves needed; nor did they have the right attitude to their work.

I have not always done what my clients wanted, and have occasionally jeopardized relationships with them when the client's desires seemed to be at odds with the needs of the whole: Once, for example I had three clients who suddenly wanted to divert money from the common land between their houses, to the fixtures in their bathrooms and kitchens. Because I had the contractual right to the last word on allocation of construction money, I refused to do so. They wanted to focus on their bathrooms. I wanted to focus on the whole. Even though the whole was theirs, not mine, their private greed interfered with their grasp of their own whole as a group.[10]

I have already described the special unit I set up at the University of California, with the purpose of training students who would understand the nature of living process. As the years went by, gradually hundreds of our students were beginning to show a tendency to see the importance of these new ways of understanding architecture, compared with what was offered in conventional classes. Many of our students began to doubt the value of the existing methods being taught in the school, and to express these doubts. Fearful of an intellectual avalanche, conservative faculty members took surreptitious steps to close the program, so that students would no longer be able learn this material. Although I had been a full professor for more than 35 years, out of fear and antagonism, the new approach to architecture was now deliberately withheld, and students were threatened when they sought access to these ideas — all because they contain a new paradigm, incompatible with existing concepts and methodologies.

Similar difficulties can arise in the construction industry. For years I have run a construction and architecture business, sometimes without insurance, because, combining the two trades as I have always done, we could not always get insured. I had to endure a lawsuit. We made a beautiful terrazzo floor, for $12,000, very low budget, red, green, yellow, hundreds of small panels of intricate color. It was to be built over an old slab which was cracked. I told the clients that to prevent the terrazzo from cracking, a new reinforced slab needed to be built underneath, at a cost of $10,000. They said they didn't have the extra $10,000, and asked us to build the terrazzo over the old, cracked slab. The floor came out beautifully, but developed minor cosmetic cracks, as predicted. Even though they loved the floor, our clients then took the cracked floor to arbitration. The arbitrator heard testimony that a standard professional bid for the floor (that we built for $12,000) would have been $80,000 for the terrazzo alone, that the client had an extremely low price, a very economical way to spend money, and advance notice of the likelihood of minor cosmetic cracking. But he awarded a judgment of $4,000 to our clients, and told us that if the clients couldn't afford the slab, we should not have built the floor at all. In the context of the old paradigm, the beauty of the floor they received almost as a gift, and the good faith relationship we trusted, were less important than the pittance they received from arbitration.

Yet I believe their original choice had been a wise choice — the arbitrator notwithstanding — since to spend an extra $10,000 to avoid cosmetic cracking would have been a less useful way to spend the available budget, and would have taken money away from something else in the project and produced less overall value. But, as you can see from this story, you risk a great deal when working within a new paradigm which includes a) human relationships of trust, b) on-going decisions about trade-offs, c) the overall wisdom of how to spend a given modest amount of money to get the best from your money. It is risky within the current

system based on a) legalisms b) blueprints and contracts that preclude sensible adaptation, c) profit and gain, and d) too little human trust.

People who attempt to do these things will be in jeopardy when they attempt to do them within the present system.

The very same can happen even in the ethical problems of user control. I have often worked with users and sometimes had to give them the ultimate right over design, in defiance of an institutional client: For example, went ahead and built benches on the outside of the homeless shelter I built in San Jose, in spite of the fact that the mayor of the city issued an edict to say homeless people could not sit on the benches I had built outside the building because he wanted the city street to be "clean" of homeless people. When asked to make hundreds of bus shelters for the city of San Francisco, with the condition that the bench in the bus shelters must be made too short to lie down on ("we can't allow tramps to defile the city by sleeping in our bus shelters, so we will make it impossible for them to do it"), I refused. I have worked with Habitat for Humanity, and stood against the insistent will of their construction managers to standardize self-built houses, when a few tiny moves allowed the families to make each house individual to their own wishes, without increasing cost.

All in all, for more than forty years I have had the experience that — on any given issue — three times out of four, what I instinctively wanted to do because I thought it was right, was at odds with *somebody's* picture of how things ought to be. For years, this seemed like a coincidence. Sometimes it seemed to my friends that I was just plain stubborn, ornery, "against everything" — that I had a built-in desire to be in conflict with people. But then, gradually — and only fully in the last ten or fifteen years — it began to sink in that this apparent source of conflict had a straightforward origin. It came about, because my instincts were governed, as often as I found possible, by respect for life, respect for wholeness in the world (at least up to the limitation of my own ability to see it). What I did came from my desire to see the whole, and my desire to build according to the whole, and my refusal to give up on the whole.

In this framework, my encounters and battles with others, with institutions, with corporations, sometimes with society itself — came about because *whatever I did* (at least in the 20th century: in the 21st it has at last begun to change) *in order to get wholeness* — *that* was getting in their hair, *that* was the pain-in-the-neck, the loose bolt in the machine.

The pursuit of wholeness, pure and simple, was at odds with virtually every institutional and social reality of the 20th century.[11]

It was when I finally understood *that*, that I began to see, fully, what a vast task we face, and what a vast task it would be for us to regenerate our society so that it can allow people to pursue life and wholeness: life in the world, and wholeness in themselves.

Of course the adventures which I have been living for more than forty years, now, and the observations I have made, might still be attributed to the monomania of a solitary individual, over-zealous, who had a blindness to the format and procedures that are proper in the worlds of architecture and society.

But it is more appropriate, I think, to see that the vast 20th-century net of interacting processes that we inherited, and now accept as normal, was indeed deeply abnormal and against life. It is our obligation to do what we can to reject these defunct processes, to transform them, to fight with every breath against them, and to search in our daily actions, for all the means we need to preserve the sacred quality of our life and the life of our cities and our planet, and to seek a new form of processes in which we can be whole.

13 / ELEMENTS OF SOCIETY IN WHICH CHANGES MUST BE MADE

Consider the following list of elements, all describing major parts of the 20th-century development process, and of 20th-century society. All the following elements of the modern building process — *in their past and present forms* — create their own sequences and processes, and do so in a way that have deep, negative impact on our ability to create a living, unfolding process for the built world.

· *The process of banking*
· *The control and regulation of money*
· *The way money flows through a project*
· *The conditions in which risk is deployed*
· *The process of development.*
· *Speculation in land*
· *Construction contracts*
· *The role of architects and engineers*
· *Organization of construction companies*
· *The nature of planning*

· *The nature of master plans*
· *The nature of construction contracts*
· *The process of ecological evaluation*
· *Evaluation by lending institutions*
· *Architectural competitions*
· *The size and scope of architect's work*
· *The teaching of architecture*
· *The priorities of manufacturers*
· *Building codes and regulations*
· *The role of town planners*
· *The mortgage process*
· *The process of housing ownership*
· *Control over housing*
· *Ownership of public land and streets*
· *Protection of the wilderness*

Every one of these elements, in its late-20th-century form, contains features which actively inhibit the possibility of implementing living process. Each of these categories of process, in its late 20th-century form, contains issues at least as serious as the examples I have given in this chapter. Some are still deeper in their implications, and more rigid in their effect.

One might easily be led to a kind of despair by this analysis. It would seem that changing the institutions I have listed, requires a wholesale making over of much of society. Yet it has to be recognized that the system of mechanized social relationships, rules, and bureaucracy, which was invented at the beginning of the 20th century, does work, almost inevitably, against the creation and unfolding of living order.

The very methods that render bureaucracy efficient — whether in banking, or planning, or manufacturing, or accounting, or construction — namely, the application of fixed rules in the wrong kind of way, and the early 20th-century version of systematization of rules and procedures so that people can be replaced — work against the processes which are necessary to allow accurate unfolding to occur and which allows a living structure to appear.

The advent of computers has changed some of that. For the first time, mechanized procedures are available which are inherently flexible, context-sensitive, capable of responding uniquely to differences, and thus approximating, in human-created fashion, the organic living processes of nature and of traditional society. It is now for the first time sometimes possible — to seek context-sensitive modification of procedures — to replace mechanized bureaucracy with a new, more organic form of human organization that is more capable of creating living structure — because it allows individual processes and sub-processes to be free — that means, to respond appropriately to what is happening in the whole.[12]

But this noble purpose, is extraordinarily difficult to implement, difficult even to conceive. That is because the form of social organization, and the structure of social processes we created during the 20th century, again and again create a mental catch-22 situation where the means needed to escape from the anti-living process, are prohibited by the very process we are trying to replace.

14 / THE NEED FOR A TRUE SHIFT OF PARADIGM

Given the extraordinary strength of the present system of society, and the consequent range of social difficulties inherent in encouraging new living processes to grow in modern society, I shall — in the next chapter — focus on the possibility of a global transformation of society, which is undertaken piecemeal. I shall sketch the outline of an overall view, showing us some of the practical conditions most needed to allow a living structure to evolve throughout society.

It must be borne in mind, throughout this discussion, that we are concerned here — and in the most radical fashion — with that thing that Thomas Kuhn wrote about: A fundamental shift of paradigm. We have, for more than a hundred years, been used to a fully mechanized process where the human organization of con-

struction is itself mechanized (not by equipment, but by the character of the *human* process). What people say and do, what their responsibilities are, how their work is defined, how institutions cut up the process into bits — by the end of the 20th century, the mechanical nature of all these human processes was accepted as normal, and is today taken for granted. But, in spite of the advantages this has provided to the modern age, the processes are also damaging to life.

In order to institute a widespread, *overall* living process in our 21st century, this must be (slowly) swept away. We must find ways to transform, *throughout society,* our mental ways, our processes, our ways of thinking and doing, in every field that touches the environment.

NOTES

1. Our lack of awareness in this regard, is encapsulated in a surprising story, already told in chapter 10, but directly pertinent to this text. In chapter 10 I described a process for generating apartment buildings which was, in part, commissioned as part of our work on the zoning ordinance for the City of Pasadena. But, my partner in this work, a prominent San Francisco architect, refused to allow this version to be put forward to the city. He argued that a generative system of this kind, could not be allowed because it would take away the liberty of architects, abrogate every architect's right to make his own design. In pursuit of this argument he forced, by political means, a tepid compromise in which what finally was adopted as an ordinance, was a set of criteria for apartment layout, but not the sequence which has the power to generate good buildings.

Dan Solomon is very sophisticated about rules and regulations and their impact on building form, and has great knowledge of the issues attending such problems. However, under the circumstances of our contract, he only felt comfortable making changes in the rules and system of rules, more or less consistent with the form these rules and regulations have today. A new kind of system of rules, with greater generative power, was beyond what he could tolerate: thus suggesting that, in spite of his vast and sophisticated knowledge, he had too little awareness of the damage which present-day *form* of such systems of rules can impose on buildings.

Yet he is a person sophisticated in such matters and in the important role of rules in architecture.

The fact that he, of all people, did this simply underlines the extent to which the generated structure of the built environment is — for the moment — hidden from our society.

2. Frederick Taylor, PRINCIPLES OF SCIENTIFIC MANAGEMENT: THE ONE BEST WAY (New York: Harper, 1911), reprinted Dover 1998.

3. Lenin, too, was a great admirer of Taylor's ideas.

4. Frederick Taylor, PRINCIPLES OF SCIENTIFIC MANAGEMENT.

5. Ibid. I have given a short summary of Taylor's ideas because even those of us who are thoroughly sick of the bureaucratic and machinelike character of modern society, will, in general, not be aware of the extent to which it all started with the work of one man, nor the extraordinary extent to which these changes were deliberate, conscious, willful. Obviously, if all this was created by the deliberate thought of an individual — as indeed it was — it becomes easier for us to conceive the possibility of changing it. It becomes conceivable that within a short space of time — perhaps, no more than another fifty years — another, entirely different system of processes can be made to grow in society.

A living process takes the condition of a place, and asks, "What must be done, what is most appropriate to that place, to heal it?" That question is answered by the *process*. And when that has been done, the living process asks, again, what must be done now, to heal the half-formed form which has emerged so far. And when *that* has been answered, then the living process will ask, again, what must be done now, to heal *that* state of the half-formed form, what detailed development must be supplied.

The social revolution in part originating from the work of Frederick Taylor, must be held responsible for the loss of this most important feature of any life-creating process. It caused this loss at almost every level of modern society.

6. Christopher Alexander, Gary Black and Miyoko Tsutsui, THE MARY ROSE MUSEUM (New York: Oxford University Press, 1993), pp. 48–78.

7. This was a large housing project for workers of Hoechst Pharmaceutical AG, in Frankfurt, Germany. The design is described in Book 3, chapter 3, pp. 84–90.

8. The theme that the architect must go along with the social processes of the modern era, was a professional battle cry from very early days in the 20th century. It could have been no more than a cynical decision to go where the money is, and certainly is little more than that in some contemporary alliances that have been forged between architects and developers. For a most serious discussion of a move towards a new way of seeing the architect's activities, see Howard Davis, THE CULTURE OF BUILDINGS (New York: Oxford University Press, 1998).

9. Thomas Kuhn, THE STRUCTURE OF SCIENTIFIC REVOLUTIONS (Chicago: University of Chicago Press, 1970).

10. The common land, which was almost destroyed by these actions, and finally saved, may be seen in the discussion of the Texas project, Book 3, chapter 3, pages 80–83.

11. Explicitly discussed in Christopher Alexander and Hajo Neis with Hisae Hosoi, BATTLE: THE STORY OF A HISTORIC CLASH BETWEEN WORLD SYSTEM A AND WORLD SYSTEM B (New York: Oxford University Press, in manuscript).

12. Many authors have begun to write about this problem, in a variety of fields. See for example, James C. Scott, SEEING LIKE A STATE (Newhaven: Yale University Press, 1998); Henry Mintzberg, THE STRUCTURING OF ORGANIZATIONS (Englewood Cliffs, N.J., Prentice Hall 1979).

CHAPTER TWENTY

THE SPREAD OF LIVING PROCESSES THROUGHOUT SOCIETY

MAKING THE SHIFT TO A NEW PARADIGM

1 / MORPHOGENETIC PROCESSES
A PIECEMEAL APPROACH TO THE PROBLEM

A true living world will arise only if its processes are morphogenetic: That means, if the processes are — roughly — given the qualities which I have described in chapters 6–17. Of these, the most important are those which emphasize the whole, calling out the fifteen transformations repeatedly, creating living structure as they do so. If processes are in use, which have these attributes, then we may have the real possibility of a living world.

However, as we have seen in chapters 18 and 19, the sequences in general use in our present era are *not* usually morphogenetic. And, in addition, there are massive systems at work in contemporary society, which actively work against the use and spread of morphogenetic processes.

We shall now turn our thoughts, therefore, to the practical problem of effecting a gradual transition to a world governed by morphogenetic processes. It is perfectly plain that an effective solution to this problem can only work by piecemeal means. The present system is massive, powerful, and extremely widespread and entrenched. There is no 'revolutionary' approach

that has much hope. The present system cannot be destroyed and replaced: it is too widely present, and too deeply embedded, in too many institutions. And it is, besides, for all its faults, serving us too well, in too many areas of life, for us to *want* to destroy it or replace it.

I take it for granted, therefore, that the practical means we seek must be gradual, incremental modes of change, which somehow manage to inject living sequences — and morphogenetic ones — into the present system of processes, in such a way that as deeper and more morphogenetic character gradually gets a foothold, is established, and slowly becomes the norm.

The vital point about morphogenetic sequences, is that they are based on the fifteen structure-preserving transformations. They really have to do with the unfolding of wholeness. So we have sequences which do some good, piecemeal. . . in tiny amounts. Then we have a class of small morphogenetic sequences, which are truly based on the fifteen properties, and which therefore truly have the capacity to inject living structure into the damaged system.

2 / SNIPPABLE GENES
THE OPTIMUM SIZE OF SEQUENCES FOR EVOLUTION

The key to the idea that will allow a system of workable morphogenetic sequences to evolve in a not-too great length of time, is highlighted in the genetic ideas of John Holland.[1]

Holland has shown how an information system which guides a real world system may evolve and "learn" by gradually building effective models of functioning, in the form of "genes." In Holland's analysis, he describes the genes which

we know in organisms as a special case of a much more general phenomenon which allows learning to take place through the exchange and evolution of individual processes that contain encoded solutions to small, limited problems, and are then replicated and spread.

Perhaps the most important element of Holland's analysis is his discovery of mathematical reasons why the learning, and spreading, and successful evolution of the genes, will occur most successfully to the extent that the genes are *small* and independent. One example of his argument, is simply the fact (in biological genetics) that at the time of meiosis, when male and female chromosomes cross over and intermingle, the shorter the genes are, the less likely they are to be damaged at the crossover point, and the more likely, therefore, to survive and be passed on to later generations.[2] This particular argument is merely one example of a more general argument which shows that *small* independent "lumps" of coherent problem-solving information, the *smaller* they are, and the more independent, the more likely they are to survive and spread into the gene pool. Sequences, too, are most likely to spread when they are small.

All this is mirrored in biological genetic evolution. Biological evolution also works because the evolution of processes is taking place in very small increments. The evolving system is not asked to take unfeasibly large jumps, but rather, very small, and advantageous steps, which leave everything working, while making one improvement at a time.

What is essentially remarkable about the genetic system is that, individually, genes are small — each one only a few bases long, along the chromosome — and are largely interchangeable. Amazing, but true, that a gene which causes a certain desirable kind of enzyme activity can be transplanted from a fish to a person, sometimes even to a mushroom. Most genes are highly general in what they do. What they do is limited, but "snippable" — each one can be cut out and used, individually, by itself. The "snippets" — the individual genes and gene complexes — are effectively almost context-free. A gene is small, interchangeable, and can be transplanted effectively from one system to another — in many cases with success.

This is the secret of biological evolution. I believe it will also turn out to be the secret of the evolution of the genes controlling the living structure of the Earth and of the built worlds on Earth.

3 / THE GRAMEEN BANK SEQUENCE:
A SINGLE SNIPPABLE GENE
WHICH HAS BEEN HAVING A PROFOUND EFFECT

Let us consider a dramatic change in society, which occurred through introduction of a single snippable gene. Consider, for example, the laws and policies which govern lending. A few years ago, Professor Muhammad Yunus, then Professor of economics in Pennsylvania, was interested in lending money to very low income families, without collateral, in a village in Bangladesh.[3] He approached several major banks with this idea, but they refused him. Finally, he decided to try it himself. He lent a total of $42 to twenty-seven borrowers, without security, but based only on trust, and based on his feeling for their situation. They all used the money effectively, and paid back the loan (at normal interest rates). He knew the people, he was interested in their projects, and he had to be concerned because his being paid back depended on their wisdom, so he was of course *genuinely* interested in what they were doing. After his success, he went to a major bank and said, Look, it worked in this one village. Please undertake a scheme of this kind. Yes, they said, It worked in one village, but it wouldn't work in another! He could not get the money. So, in a second village, he tried the same process, again with his own money. It worked again. The money was paid back. People did useful things with their money. Again he went back to the major bank, to get them to try it . . . Yes, it is all very well, it worked in two isolated cases, they told him, but it would not work in five. In frustration, he began to lend money himself, first in the next five villages, then more and more and more. The failure rate for the tiny loans he issued was less than 2%, an unheard of low for normal banks. Ninety percent of the borrowers turned out, over the years, to be women. Gradually these very small loans became larger, and now operate sometimes as high as $100, sometimes even as high as $5,000 at a time. People did intelligent things with their tiny loans. One woman bought a cellular phone, in a village with no wiring for phones. People all over the village used her cell-phone to make their calls, and paid her accordingly. Gradually the village entered a more robust state of economic life, as a result of what the phone calls accomplished. Making the batteries needed for the cell phones, became a small side business for another family.

In essence, the Grameen Bank idea may be described by a short sequence:

· *Lend small amounts, without collateral.*
· *Lend within a small face-to-face community.*

·

Lend to people you know, and only when you truly understand what they are going to do.
· *Charge normal interest.*
· *Lend to those whom you trust instinctively.*

Today, seventeen years later, the Grameen Bank has assets of $400 million, its methods operate in 52 countries, and it has lent money to 10 million people, helping to bring them out of poverty. The Grameen Bank sequence has been copied all over the world. It is highly successful. It operates on the basis of feeling, on what is appropriate. Decisions to lend, or not to lend, are based on intuitive assessment, on trust, and on the decision as to the positiveness of the feeling the lender had, about the project which was to be underwritten by a loan — no matter how tiny.

The example shows that fundamental change, even in high-profile rigid processes like banking, is possible and has been demonstrated in our time. In the case of this example, the time taken to go from pilot projects to widespread copying of the new process was less than a generation.

4 / OTHER RECENT STEPS IN THE EVOLUTION OF SOCIETY WHICH HAVE BEEN TAKING PLACE THROUGH THE SHARED USE OF PATTERNS

A similar, though far less dramatic phenomenon occurred in architecture with the appearance of A PATTERN LANGUAGE. The buildings of 1970 were stark, often box-like, cold, unadorned; windows and doors were plain; ceilings were of uniform height; gardens were often stark, without benches often with harsh kinds of plants and bushes; ceiling lighting was cold and dreadful; furniture was often so strangely shaped as to be unusable.

Buildings are so different now, it is even hard to remember or visualize the sterile way most newly constructed buildings looked about 1970. Since the advent of A PATTERN LANGUAGE, hundreds of patterns began to spread — partly

through the appearance of that book. Patterns that come to mind especially are LIGHT ON TWO SIDE OF EVERY ROOM, WINDOWS WITH SMALL PANES, CASCADE OF ROOFS, INDEPENDENT REGIONS, FARMHOUSE KITCHEN, CIRCULATION REALMS, CEILING HEIGHT VARIETY, A ROOM OF ONES OWN, . . . and so on.

Of course the published pattern language was not the only origin of these changes. During the last decades of the 20th century, many of them were in the wind, and felt by many. However, the book played a significant role in the evolution of these changes in the built world. Although the static non-process format of the patterns was less powerful than the sequences under discussion in this book, still the patterns had a very large effect. The building forms that were introduced in this "genetic" way have now, twenty-five years later, become part of the vernacular of our time. It is reasonable to expect that sequences, with their inherently far greater power, will have a greater effect.

5 / MORE SNIPPABLE SHORT SEQUENCES
CONSTRUCTION SEQUENCES AS PROCESS GENES

Let us apply the insight of the Grameen Bank process to the evolution of social processes. Suppose, for instance, that a new contractual process is invented for construction.

Let us assume that the sequence is long and complex with many interlocking features.[4] A move to adopt this new construction system will put stress on the human beings, the skills, the economics of the process, the city building department, the architects involved, the available contractors, the licensing laws, the insurance policies, and so forth — all this making it less likely that the innovative process will take and enter the system at large.

It is difficult to find social conditions in which *all* the features of the construction process can change *at the same time*, hence extremely difficult to introduce such a new process as a whole.

But suppose that the same improved process of contracting is broken up into, say, twenty separable sequences. Together the twenty smaller processes define the new system in its entirety. But let us also assume that these twenty sequences (or genes) are carefully defined, and chosen, so that each one, individually — *any one of them by itself* — is separable from the nineteen others, and can therefore be successfully injected *by itself* into an otherwise normal or mainstream system of construction. If the snippet works well, it may be adopted, and may spread to new construction methods, even in the context of different attitudes. (Of course, this is the way technological evolution takes place, *anyway*. But we are talking, now, about the possibility of injecting *morphogenetic* sequences into the mainstream).

Now expand to a situation where each of the twenty snippets is in circulation. We then have available a mixed system of approaches to construction: But the essential, new, morphogenetic ingredients can flourish one at a time. They can be tested, improved — and can spread deep into society and existing social processes — simply by virtue of the improved performance they create "without rocking the boat too much."

What was difficult or impossible as a larger act of social transformation, becomes possible when one uses a genetic approach to achieve the same aims. What is needed is simply a way of "cutting up" the original innovative process, into a small set of process genes or *small* sequences that work individually, and that are robust enough to work in a wide variety of contexts, even when not supported by other parts of the new system.

6 / MORE ON THE LENGTH OF SEQUENCES

I said earlier that during the last thirty years, my colleagues and I have experimented with many new forms of process, under full-scale project-conditions.[5] The experiments have been extensive, and have included planning, architecture, design, construction, engineering, financing, participation, neighborhoods, towns, emergence of new culture in institutions, construction of large buildings, construction of small buildings, and so on.

Many of these experiments succeeded. Over a thirty-year period my colleagues and I demonstrated, in field after field, that we were able to construct models of process which do allow living sequences to occur, to dominate a particular construction project, for a limited space of time; and we have often been able to show the positive results which come from the living process in these special contexts.

The shortcoming of our experiments was that they demanded too much. In our early experiments, we often went to almost unbelievable lengths to get some new process to be implemented, and to get it to work. But the amount of effort we had to make to get it to work — the very source of our success — was also the weakness of what we achieved. In too many cases, the magnitude of special effort that had to be made to shore up a new process was massive — too great, to be easily or reasonably copied.[6]

We succeeded because we replaced an existing system with a large system in which every aspects of procedure, process, attitude, rules, were changed: *it worked*. But such an inhuman effort was not easily repeatable. It was, indeed, almost impossible to repeat, and unreasonable to expect that others would repeat the nearly superhuman effort needed to make the process work. Toward the end of our first generation of experiments, even we ourselves could scarcely muster the special energy needed — emotionally, politically, financially — to sustain our effort.

Stated in abstract terms one might say that our new or revised living processes were too "large" to be widely copied. Some path-breaking process models take a very great deal of time to think out, simulate, test in real circumstances. Ours often had too many new components. They required too much change. It was therefore hard to adopt them in their entirety, and there-

fore also unlikely that they would be spread widely, or be copied widely.

For example, after a series of experiments in construction contracts, which began in 1976, in 1986 we developed a wholly new kind of contract and began using it and testing it in construction projects during the years 1987–97. By the end of the 90s, we had a model which was worked out, tested, and effective. This needed a nearly 20-year development period. But to succeed in copying this process, an architect needs to become a contractor. He needs to meet, head-on, the special insurance problems caused by the fact that liability insurance will most often not cover a firm that is both designing and building. He needs to meet the client problems which arise from the fact that expectations are, often, based on client-experience with old types of building contractors. The architect needs to have trainees who have manual and craft skills, where an architect is more often used, typically, to hiring drafts-people or those with clerical skills. During the course of the contract, it is occasionally necessary to make engineering changes while the building is being built. If these engineering changes are made by outside engineers, they can be prohibitively expensive so it is necessary to have in-house engineers (as, indeed, we have had during the whole working life of my own firm).

The sum total of these special conditions is complex and arduous — so much so that it is unlikely, at present, that many people can copy them. Unlikely, therefore, that anyone can repeat the complex living process which has been invented, and which has been proved to work.

Again, in 1970 I began testing living processes that would allow a group of families to lay out and design their own houses and common land for themselves. In 1976 I was able to test this process for the first time in a real case. I was able to test it for the second time only recently in 1993, seventeen years later. With something so experimental, it is hard to find the circumstances and hard to put it to the test.[7]

What *has* been copied in that instance — the process sometimes called co-housing — is superficially somewhat similar in appearance.[8] In co-housing, families meet. They design houses with the architect. They lay out the commons with the architect. But because the co-housing process has been led chiefly by architects forced to work within today's paradigm, the results come out much too much like the half-dead environments typical of upscale 20th-century housing tracts. The co-housing process contains a few good features that make it slightly better than existing tract housing. But it is far from a living process.

Nevertheless, in spite of its limitations, the co-housing process has been copied all over the United States because it is compatible with 20th-century professional definitions of architect, contractor, and so forth, and *precisely because* the deep roots of sequence change that would be needed to achieve a fully living process are *not* required by it.

The housing process which my colleagues and I developed is closer to a living process. It allows families to design and control the houses, and allows flexible construction management, so that each house, and its garden are more truly living places. The process does allow — for fundamental reasons — each house to become something heartfelt and unique. It allows the common land to develop from real experience. It is, overall, a living process. But, unlike the cohousing model, this process is

hard to copy. It requires more fundamental changes, to succeed. I am not sure that what we achieved has ever yet been copied by others, because, once again, copying it is arduous, and few individuals or groups have either the training or the will to copy it.

The root of our failure, in the past, to make new processes which spread widely, lay in the fact that the living processes that we specified and carried out existed as indivisible wholes. They could not be copied successfully, part by part. They were copiable only in their totality — and that was just too much to achieve. Unlike the patterns in A PATTERN LANGUAGE, which are copied widely because they *are* small and snippable, our process innovations — though far more profound — remain largely unknown.

All in all, we may summarize like this. When models of a new process are too intricate, too complete, too indivisible, they require specially trained people to carry them out, they put unworkable demands on the practical social system in which the innovation occurs. Also, people who can act according to the new process which has been worked out, are very highly skilled, hard to train, and above all rare. There are not many of these people around. So, for that reason, too, it is extremely hard for the new process, even when it has been shown to work, to spread — because it is too hard to do.

7 / THE SPREAD OF ONE, SMALL, "SNIPPABLE" GENE WHICH CAN BE WIDELY SHARED

In order to illustrate the positive consequences of keeping sequences small and independent, and to illustrate the idea of a small "snippable" sequence, let us once again consider the construction contract as a sequence.

A fully flexible management construction contract (for design and construction) which provides for continuous change within a fixed

budget, under the architect's direct management, is a fairly complex (and, for some, forbidding) proposition.[9] Many architects do not have enough experience to make it work. The responsibility is great. It is hard to get the necessary experience or training to make it feasible. So — when taken as a single whole — many architects may say — reluctantly — "I cannot do that."

But let us consider a single very small sequence from that group of sequences: One of the short sequences through which the architect directly controls just *one* craftsman or subcontract without the intervention of the general contractor.

For concreteness's sake, let us consider the process of tile-setting inside a building. Or, alternatively, we may consider the process of building and installing specially sized windows to make the house more beautiful. Direct management of interior tile-setting is quite feasible, even for an architect with little experience in construction. It is not difficult for the architect to insert — into a conventional general contract — the idea that a certain phase of operations — window-making, say, or tile-setting — should be directly in his hands, and under his control. Finding a custom window-maker to work with, within a limited budget, needs more experience. But it, too, is feasible.

That means that for this limited phase of construction the tile-layer or the window maker will be working directly under the architect. This is an attractive proposition for the architect, and not so frightening. The architect cannot get too badly burned having only the windows made directly under his supervision. There is not enough money involved to get too worried about it. Since the window-maker will take responsibility for the quality of the windows, and their non-leak character — there is not a great deal, either, that the architect can get sued for, or reprimanded for, if something goes wrong.

In addition, there are readily available models of procedure. In Mexico, and in Spain, for instance, it is commonplace for architects to run craftspeople and subcontractors directly. This has been a tradition for a long time. So, in countries where architects do not usually control construction (as in the United States or England), this small process gene can easily be supported, in part, with an argument that says, "Look, they have been doing this for generations in Mex-ico — it is no big problem. In fact, we can try it, too."

Further, introducing this process gene into architecture creates very positive advantages for the architect. Architects are hurting. They get fewer jobs, they get paid less, they are hurting for work — and the drafting work is not so much fun. Taking direct responsibility for supervising and managing the construction of tilework or windows is fun. It can make a strong visible difference to the beauty of a building. It is exciting. And, of course, it enlarges the architect's scope of work and brings in extra money. If the management gets paid 20% of direct costs, and the windows for a typical house cost — say — $17,000, the architect gets some $3,500 for taking care of the windows. In the case of tiles, if there is perhaps $3,000 available for some special interior tiling, the architect gets $600 — still a welcome income — for choosing tiles, working with the tile-setter to lay them in, possibly even getting involved in the joy of actually doing it himself.[10] So she/he gets money, has more fun, and her building gets better. The whole thing is do-able, and fairly painless.

Once having done it, the likelihood that the architect will do it again, in another craft or specialty, is increased. After doing it two or three times, it is very possible that the architect will choose to take on responsibility for additional subcontracts on the next job. After gaining experience of this kind, gradually, the idea may coalesce spontaneously that the architect might — for a small project — take *several* major subcontracts. Ultimately, perhaps even all of them. But there is no need to think about this at the outset. What matters is that the small increment of process is in itself feasible, attractive, fun, and financially rewarding.

As a result of injecting it into the normal process, daily life for architects, clients, and tile-setters, becomes more meaningful. And the buildings get better.

The chance that this process gene will spread is quite considerable.

8 / WHAT IS IT THAT WILL ALLOW THIS SEQUENCE TO BE IMPROVED MORPHOGENETICALLY?

How will the evolution of such a snippet sequence make it become a *morphogenetic*? The answer to this question is that to become morphogenetic, the sequence *must* be reconstituted as a series of steps which emphasize the action of the fifteen structure-preserving transformations.

Thus, in the case of the tile work, the sequence must not only redefine the way the work is contracted, organized, and paid for. To become morphogenetic, the sequence must also contain specific aspects of the fifteen transformations which are relevant to tilework, relevant to position, color, design of tiles, and to the design as a whole, applicable to the installation of tilework in a building.

The designing of the tiles and tilework must be active when they are being laid. Designer and layer, whether two people or one and the same, are to work in response to the tilework that they lay, have the ability to introduce a more subtle color as they feel it is needed, are free to introduce a small jarring shape to relieve a monotonous homogeneity if it occurs, can actively choose background color and space in the tiles, so that the POSITIVE-SPACE transformation and the ALTERNATING-REPETITION transformation can become effective in making the work better.

One example of such a sequence can be found on our website under ornament.[11] The ornament sequence is a series of steps which begins with the structure of a building while it is as yet un-ornamented, and then, step by step, introduces elements of a design: first large centers, then smaller ones, which are all generated to be consistent with the whole and structure-preserving to the whole.

What might this be like, in detail, for tiles? For example:

· *Find an overall gesture relevant to the whole.*
· *Find a color harmonious and structure-preserving to the colors in the room.*

· *Find a way of making* STRONG CENTERS *come out from the gesture, within individual tiles and groups of tiles.*
· *Introduce* ALTERNATING REPETITION, *thus a second system of* CENTERS.
· *Then strengthen the* CENTEREDNESS *and* LOCAL SYMMETRY *and* GOOD SHAPE *of individual elements of the design.*
· *Place the tiles, roughly at first, to make* POSITIVE SPACE *between the tiles.*
· *Put in finishing touches, edges, monochrome* BOUNDARIES *of stark color, to complete the overall feeling of the work.*

This group of steps all have to do with the design. Further steps may be introduced into the technique and practice of the tile-setting work, to provide ways that make it possible to do these structure-preserving actions from a practical point of view, without increasing cost. These might include, for example:

.

Hand making of tiles on a short firing cycle.
· *Cutting technique to make onsite cutting easier*
· *Types of tile-setting compound to allow special setting of fragments*
· *Using types of grout with substantial body and color to take up the slack in hand-set designs*
· *Less emphasis on the perfection of the surface flatness.*
· *Recipes for glazes and firing temperatures for special tiles.*
· *Use of sealants and hardeners to protect low-fired glazes (often needed for beauty of color, because low-temperature glazes have a wider range of color which can be tuned more finely).*

As may be seen in these loosely sketched examples, a morphogenetic sequence will tend to increase both the architect's and the tile-setter's capacity to produce living structure. This is built into the instructions themselves: and will then achieve more life through the action of the transformations that appear in the sequence.

Consider the future path of this innovation, in which some architects (a few hundred, say) decide to take on the work of managing, directly, the subcontractors or craftsmen doing tilework in a building. For those architects who find this very small process feasible and likeable, there is a likelihood that the sequence will then evolve, and as it is copied, be thought about more and more carefully *as a sequence*. The sequence is likely, then, to be improved with time, and made more life-creating.

Among the improvements the process qualities defined in chapters 8–17 will slowly get introduced into the tile-making and tile-setting sequence. For example (numbers refer to chapter numbers):

- *The sequence will emphasize the step-by-step process of designing and making good tilework, and encourages both architect and tilesetter to abandon rigid drawing as a specification for the design, encourages them rather to place tiles and designs in a more fluid way inspired by the surroundings (Ch. 8).*
- *The sequence will teach designers and tile-setters how each bit of tilework laid should be chosen, and designed, to help the design of larger whole get better (Ch. 9).*
- *For both architect and tile-setter, the sequence underscores the need to create stronger, more subtle, and more living centers at each stage of the laying process (Ch. 10).*
- *Ways are found to allow the sequence aspect of the work itself, to get better. Within the sub-contract the architect has the freedom to design, make, and lay tile, in a sequence that more fully allows living structure to appear (Ch. 11).*
- *Fabrication techniques make it possible for the tilework to be done in a way that allows variation and uniqueness of individual tiles to appear in the design together with repetition — in balance — to occur (Ch. 12).*

- *Ways are introduced to allow the tilework to be based, in part, on generic patterns that are worked out ahead of time (Ch. 13).*
- *Depth of feeling is encouraged — and therefore present, and created — at every stage (Ch. 14).*
- *The tilework is done in such a way that large-scale geometry appears (Ch. 15).*
- *The patterns of the tilework may follow known geometric prescriptions that provide a basis for deeply affecting forms to be made (Ch. 16).*
- *Simplicity must govern, and the sequence reflects ways of moving towards a greater spiritual simplicity in the design (Ch. 17).*

Accompanying these kinds of changes, other innovations will also appear in the sequence; technical innovations that make tiles better, cheaper, more colorful, easier to cut, easier to lay. In all likelihood, future manufacturing techniques will allow greater individual control of the tiles before fabrication, by the architect himself, so that the architect or artist, using the most modern technology, is more and more fully in control of the design of individual tiles and of their arrangement.

It is not hard to see that even this relatively simple subject is rich, and that attention to the sequences which control both tile design and tile laying, will gradually allow architects and craftspeople, together, to lay more and more beautiful tiled surfaces in the buildings they make together. Their judgment will improve as they gain more knowledge of the sequences and more control. And their technical ability and craftsmanship will then improve as they find themselves moved by doing better and more beautiful work.

Gradually, this one small, snippable tile-laying sequence will get better, will become morphologically more profound, better at carrying the essential content of living structure. Very gradually then, but in a finite and realistic way, we see how one sequence in the "pool" of sequences available on Earth can be improving. There is a chance that it can, within a reasonably short space of time, come closer and closer to being able to contribute limited areas of living structure in the built world.

9 / CRITERIA FOR EVOLUTION
SEQUENCES AS A MEDIUM OF DISCUSSION, EXCHANGE, MODIFICATION, AND IMPROVEMENT

The crux of successful evolution, even for a simple short sequence, or of a modification in a sequence, is the criterion for *quality* — that is, the selection criterion for sequences we regard as "morphogenetic." Up until the end of the 20th century, such a selection process might have been difficult, since choice and quality were considered matters of opinion. New theory changes that. What is contained in these four books is based on the assertion that, for the first time in modern history, ways of thinking are available, which can make the criteria for deciding what is "living" both *potentially* sharable and *actually* shared. This means that the criterion of life, as it is defined in Book 1, may be extended to cover the life of sequences and processes. *That* creates the opportunity for people to make sequences better: It allows sequences to evolve purposefully towards a more living condition. It also provides the possibility that by careful attention, public sharing and public use, by discussion and piecemeal improvement, the sequences will evolve in a positive way, and to the benefit of us all.

I have been told that by 1998, there were some 10,000 computer scientists and software engineers using software patterns as the medium of their discussion and exchange about software design.[12] This occurred, to start with, as a result of a conscious effort by Coplien, Gabriel, and others, to promote this idea in the computer science field, and it coincided with the appearance of several books by several different groups of authors, all writing their ideas about what made software "good," in a common medium of exchange.[13] Once this had happened, it moved out of the hands of individuals and became an autonomous phenomenon among computer scientists. They found it advantageous to express their ideas as "patterns," and they — the members of a very large, world-wide community of scientists — then began a process of evolution of ideas about software design, which all of them were able to share.

The same thing did not at first happen in architecture, perhaps because at the time the pattern language was first published, architects were less conscious of their common need to focus on the profound substantial question, What makes a building have life? But in the intervening years, since 1977, the atmosphere has changed. Architects are more aware, now, that they do need to share ideas. Lay-people, in all walks of life, and builders, developers, banks, planners, craftspeople are all becoming aware that commonsense ways of talking about design and construction are needed. They, too, now recognize a need for a common medium of discussion and exchange.

10 / THE GENE POOL:
FURTHER PROCESS OF IMPROVEMENT AND SELECTION OF THE SNIPPABLE GENES

Where are the sequences and gene-snippets to be located? If snippable sequences are process genes, where do they mix, mutate, and get improved. How are they to be established, and where are they to be held? Where is the gene pool located? Where is the repository of the evolving material? The natural answer to this question for the 21st century is, of course: The Internet. For the first time in human history, there is a public, world-wide, communal memory that is — in principle — accessible by everyone, and instantly accessible.

Under conditions of the Internet, good sequences can be exchanged and spread rapidly. The Internet, a medium where effective sequences can — in principle — be quickly described, shared, modified, and used and reused by millions of people, makes it possible, and vastly accelerates the speed at which information can be exchanged and transformed.

It is natural to conceive that a vast system of sequences could be available, and forged, on the Internet. People will then be able to use it as they choose, and the possibility of new and better sequences spreading will almost be assured.

Starting in the year 2000, my colleagues and I began to post on the Internet, at WWW.PATTERNLANGUAGE.COM sketches and first drafts of a variety of life-creating sequences. These sequences range enormously in scale and scope. One of the smaller ones, only about seven steps, allows a person to create an entrance transition. Another defines a process for laying out a comfortable kitchen. Larger sequences define adaptive sequences for creating and placing house volumes in a piece of land. Others generate street patterns, others transform streets from a car-dominated state to a healthy combination of pedestrian life and car life. One of the larger-scale sequences defines a process for creating and culling healthy meadow land from fire-prone brush land; others generate waterfront areas that allow a living relation between animals and people and the ocean and the beach. The largest of all define sequences for generating beach ecology, forests in relationship to water, urban land in relation to agricultural and natural land, and for maintaining city downtown areas and the structural organization and form of large, downtown high buildings.

The sequences are relatively simple in character. *And they are operational.* That means they give practical instructions which allow people to create or generate versions of things unique to a given circumstance, in a natural and unfolding way. And they are simple enough, so that judging their effectiveness, and seeing how to make improvements is relatively easy.

The key thing about all sequences that are LIV-ING *sequences is that they generate centers in an order which lets each center unfold naturally from the centers which have been laid down before.*

It is very hard work to get this character in a sequence (see pages 317–19). Even the short 5- or 7-step sequences mentioned above take many trial-and-error efforts before the sequence is just right, and can generate a structure which unfolds successfully. But in the end it can be achieved.

Exactly what that means — although it is theoretically clear — is likely to promote intense debate, healthy debate, and vigorous disagreement, too. I have little doubt of that. But what matters is that the goal of a living world has become fairly well-defined. This means that the evolution of sequences can be kept orderly, and does have a useful value-quality which all human beings, from all their different cultures, can — in principle — agree on.

If my predictions are fulfilled, the PATTERN-LANGUAGE.COM site will in the end be only one of many similar sites: all carrying evolving sequences. And we must hope that the movement and evolution of the sequences goes, by common public agreement, towards those which do sustain life.

11 / THE NETWORK OF SEQUENCES

When functioning properly, morphogenetic sequences have, in their nature, a further vital aspect beyond their individual character as sequences. They are linked to each other.

I have, during the course of Book 2, essentially created a correspondence between *centers* and *processes*—a correspondence in which each living center is associated with some sequence of repeated actions by which that center is typically created and made living.[14]

Now, each living center has life to the extent that it is linked to other living centers (see Book 1, chapter 4). And in just the same way, each sequence that has the capacity to form a certain type of living center, is linked to those other sequences which have the capacity to form the linked centers which provide this center with support. As each center is created, other centers need to be created, too, strengthened, made more alive. So, the sequences that generate living centers are interdependent, just as the centers themselves are interdependent.

Let us say, then, that we have a sequence which generates good houses. This process is a process which enables people to lay out, on a given site, an organic and beautiful house. The process is of such a nature that the house which results will then turn out unique to the site where it is to be built, unique to the people for whom it is built or designed, and by whom it is laid out. Examples of such houses are given in Book 3; construction of one such house is shown in detail in the appendix of this book.

It is possible to create a highly *general* generative sequence—that means, a sequence which can be used successfully in a wide variety of different contexts—which enables a person to go through the house-layout process successfully. The process is definable and predictable in the steps that must be followed. The steps, and their sequence, are more or less the same (with big variations, of course) each time the sequence occurs.

This process will generate thousands of instances of one kind of living center, in this case instances of houses. Of course, the process will vary from culture to culture, and from region to region, since different specific aspects of climate, density, family size, family type, will all cause necessary changes in the generative process. However, even processes from widely different regions and cultures will have similar (not identical) components, steps, and sub-processes.

A single successful sequence may allow a thousand, or ten thousand, or a million families, to lay out successful houses for themselves. The houses will, by virtue of the process, come out with a reasonable degree of living structure, and will be unique, each to its site, budget, and family, just as genetics of oak trees cause every oak tree to be well-formed and yet unique. It is the interaction between the generic process, and the uniqueness of the conditions, which works to generate a unique individual oak tree. Just so, a single generative sequence for houses can generate a million unique houses, each one highly successful in meeting the special needs of special individuals and families: and each one well adapted to the particular site where it occurs, thus—at least in part—healing the land.

Now comes a critical point which addresses the linkage among sequences and the network as a whole. The generative process which allows a person to lay out a beautiful house, must—in order to succeed—call other living processes, which play other roles, and have valuable effects on the other aspects of the living structure of the world around the house. For example, when it comes time to *build* the house, the layout process may call on a flexible management process for construction—by that I mean specifically the contract which allows money and management to be used wisely to create a living house in practical and material terms for a given sum of money.

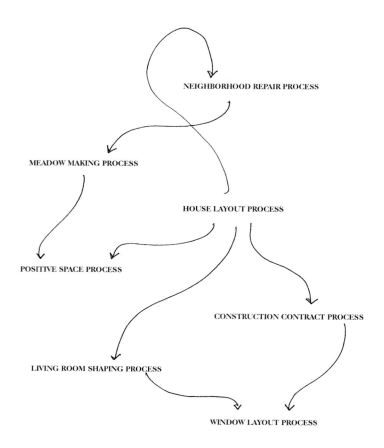

NEIGHBORHOOD REPAIR PROCESS

MEADOW MAKING PROCESS

HOUSE LAYOUT PROCESS

POSITIVE SPACE PROCESS

CONSTRUCTION CONTRACT PROCESS

LIVING ROOM SHAPING PROCESS

WINDOW LAYOUT PROCESS

The triggers among processes: The way that one process triggers another, indicating the resulting ripples throughout the system of all social processes.

Or, considering a parallel process, the house layout sequence may call on a sequence that has the unique function of generating centers of positive space on the land around the house. This is a kind of outdoor space that is shaped, coherent, and useful, with its own living structure.

And, again, in order to help the house to make a contribution to the neighborhood, the house sequence may, at some stage, call a sequence for street repair which shows how the volume of the house can help play a role shaping the public space of the neighborhood.

So this one sequence will not merely allow the house to flourish as an individual, separate entity, but will help it to contribute to the larger whole, encouraging, gradually, construction of a coherent neighborhood.

We may picture the situation in a diagram like the one above. This shows dependencies and connections among sequences which call upon each other. From a relatively small number of component processes, then, a system can be built in which each process triggers the action of other processes. This triggering will ultimately play a decisive role in making the environment whole. As a person decides to design a house for themselves, this will then trigger another process which will make the space around the house and near the house have positive attributes (via the POSITIVE OUTDOOR-SPACE PROCESS). At another moment, the house design process will trigger some facet of a NEIGHBORHOOD-REPAIR PROCESS which will make the street outside better and more favorable for communal life. At another

544

time, the house process will trigger a new kind of CONSTRUCTION-CONTRACT PROCESS which will allow the house itself to be built organically, without increasing cost, but while paying better and more detailed attention to interior items, distribution of items, shape of individual rooms, window placement and so on.

The placement of windows while the house is being built will then come from the WINDOW-LAYOUT PROCESS.

A main problem in the environment today is that the fragmentary processes which exist only rarely direct attention to organic, reparative, attention to the whole and there is no way—presently—in which each process triggers the other processes that are needed, together, to take care of the whole.

In the system I am describing each process—as it is initiated—triggers other processes, and the widening circle of processes continues to trigger other processes, and to repair the whole. In the illustration opposite, merely from the HOUSE-LAYOUT PROCESS, other processes are triggered which repair the open space around the house, which repair the street and make it better for the neighborhood, which initiate construction management which gets the best

value for money, and which permits gradual improvement of the house and continuing adaptation while the house is being built. In the course of that management process, other minor processes are triggered, making rooms the best shape possible within the house; another locates windows to make them as beautiful as possible.

Even if nothing else but this handful of processes were implemented regularly, throughout the urban area, wherever houses are being built, or added to, or improved, the positive impact on the environment would already be enormous. Yet this system of processes can be described in very little space. The processes themselves take no more than a few pages to describe; each is tiny, so modest that it can be described in a few paragraphs. It is easy to see that a wide system of processes can be economically described, and triggered, and that with almost minimal effort, this outward rippling system of processes can gradually be introduced into society.

From such a system of processes, if it is evolving gradually according to people's experience of what makes the world around them living, then the environment can gradually be healed.

12 / INTERDEPENDENCE OF SEQUENCES

The triggering system I have described will work as a whole only if the various processes actually do trigger each other. But, if we achieve a widespread use of the processes by ordinary people taking care of their own environments, the processes are used by unconnected people. And the use of processes is of course voluntary. Can we encourage people to see and use linked processes, according to the natural interdependence of the sequences?[15]

In order to make the system of living processes work best, what is necessary, above all, is that the linked processes actually are

initiated when needed. How, then, can the linkages be activated? In order to see it clearly, it may be helpful to compare the system of environment-creating processes, with the system of sequences we have come to think of as "arithmetic." Naively, we think of arithmetic as consisting of a few separate processes, addition, subtraction, multiplication, division. A couple of more sophisticated processes include taking powers and taking factorials. These might all be thought of as independent processes, which we bring into play when we need them, essentially when we feel like using them.

In this view, arithmetic would be a system of isolated, unlinked sequences whose use is voluntary. But the real nature of arithmetic is not like that. The sequences are linked. Each process calls on other processes. Division, for example, as a process, calls on multiplication at certain times, and on subtraction at times. Raising a number to a power draws on multiplication: or if we work with several powers that are multiplied, it calls on the process of addition. The fact that one process calls on other processes is not voluntary. It is essential to the nature of arithmetic. Arithmetic does not work unless we recognize that each process is, in part, defined by the way and pattern in which it calls on other processes. That is simply the way that arithmetic works. If we want arithmetic, we must learn the way the different processes are linked to call on one another, and use them accordingly. If we do not do it, the system does not work, and we cannot get good results.

There are similar linkages among environment-generating processes. I believe the MEADOW-MAKING PROCESS (for maintaining grasslands) *must* call on the PARKING-LOT MAKING PROCESS. That is because the creation of meadows in the areas on the urban fringe, requires that the meadows be useful, hence that people drive to them sometimes, hence that a few cars can be placed modestly and quietly, without huge parking lots. So, in the act of making meadows, we *must* call on a sequence which teaches us how to make modest, hidden, cheap, yet workable parking lots. This is neither voluntary nor compulsory. It is simply a part of what it means to understand the MEADOW-MAKING PROCESS.

If I say that the house-layout process must call on the FLEXIBLE-CONSTRUCTION-MANAGEMENT SEQUENCE, that is because we know that a good house cannot be achieved without some version of that FLEXIBLE-CONSTRUCTION-MANAGEMENT PROCESS. No matter how good the design, the design will not lead to a good result if it is not followed by, and does not call upon, this FLEXIBLE-CONSTRUCTION-MANAGEMENT SEQUENCE. And that second sequence does not work unless, during the course of the construction, it does not call on the WINDOW-LAYOUT SEQUENCE. That again follows from knowledge of the real situation while making a building. If one ignores the connection, and if one wishes to ignore the linkage, of course it is possible to do so. But it simply means that a less good house is being made. It is simply in the nature of things, as much as it is in the nature of things that the unfolding creation of a human being in the embryo state must call on the LEG-MAKING SEQUENCE; and just as, in arithmetic, the LONG DIVISION PROCESS must call on the MULTIPLICATION-PROCESS or on the SUBTRACTION PROCESS.

13 / THE LINKAGES STIMULATE EVOLUTION OF FURTHER SNIPPET SEQUENCES

It is surprising how quickly even a small network, gains power from the cumulative effect of the sequences. Individual short sequences, like the ones mentioned on pages 539–40, can seem almost trivial. Each one has a certain interesting, perhaps even important content. But it hardly shakes the Earth, or makes one feel that an enormous tide is coming.

Yet, when we look at a system of half a dozen short sequences, even as modest as the tiny network illustrated on page 544, the situation changes dramatically. These half a dozen sequences, taken together, can have a very big effect on the environment, we are suddenly face to face with a wholly new way of conceiving space and shaping space — and the potential force that exists in these few short sequences, interacting with one another, and calling one another, suddenly appears in a dramatic and powerful light.

We see how a whole world, in its essentials, can be defined by a surprisingly small number of sequences, acting together. This is really remarkable. Perhaps even more important, I know from experience that this situation then strongly inspires the creation of further sequences, thus causing an expansion of effort, and an expansion of effect which is almost geometric in its increase: As we add a single new sequence, we multiply the spread, reach, and power of the network as a whole. The effect of the few sequences, and the increase of effect inspires the creation of more and more sequences of similar type, so as to cover, cope with, and extend the living character of more and more environments.

14 / THE NETWORK EVOLVES

Let us try imagine such a passionate new process in which all we members of society together generate a vessel for our lives. Let us try to imagine a widely available, worldwide process for the repair, construction, reconstruction (even including the necessary destruction) of the world, in all its breadth, put together in such a way that it allows each of the buildings of society to become a living structure, at every place, and all the time.

What might this new world be like? What, in practice, would the system of society be like as the paradigm shifts, and living processes give us the right to experience and consolidate our feelings and our passions? I believe four general features of the overall system of society will turn out to be fundamental:

1. All processes having impact on the environment (any impact) will slowly need to be re-thought and reconstituted as morphogenetic sequences. We thus move away from the inchoate conglomeration of individual rules and processes described in chapters 17–18, and start replacing them with processes that are explicitly *morphogenetic*. We begin to envisage a world in which every process — every rule, every human interaction, every purpose-filled act which touches the environment — has among its tasks the major task of creating coherent living form. And, slowly, this needs to be understood by everyone: By administrators, inventors, actors, users, builders, children. We begin living in a world in which the ongoing, continuous creation of living structure through processes aimed at *shape* becomes our conscious aim, in every part of daily life.[16]

This means, concretely, that all the processes in common use will contain the fifteen structure-preserving transformations, will resemble, more nearly, the fundamental process defined in chapter 7, and will be composed of chains of application and iteration of the fundamental process with the attributes described in chapters 6–17. Over time, that will have the effect that among the billions of living wholes, worldwide, more and more are being created daily, are everywhere being shaped, nourished, and healed.

2. The morphogenetic sequences at large in society slowly coalesce to form a more coherent system. Thousands of morphogenetic sequences will exist in people's minds: Although these sequences may exist freely, and independently of one another, they will slowly become linked to one another, forming a continuous net of sequences, mutually calling on each other. In the future, the members of society — all of us together — will begin more and more to see, feel, think, and conceive these "shaping"-sequences as linked. This will have the result that a fluid over-arching process, created piecemeal by the actions of thousands and millions of people, slowly begins taking care of the whole, and we understand how it does so. Within that whole, smaller processes will take care of some of the smaller centers, and we understand how they do so. And then, once again, still smaller processes will take care of the still smaller centers, which are needed to fill out and complete the positive space and the space between things. The system as a whole, although widely distributed and based on actions performed by millions of independent individuals will slowly take care of the whole Earth. Every part is touched. Every part is nourished by some person. Every person has some part to nourish.

3. Our shared focus shifts towards the task of improving these world-wide sequences through evolution. Continuous and deliberate creation, improvement, and evolution of the generative sequences, becomes a widespread feature of discussion in many segments of society. At present, since sequences are largely hidden from view, or unconscious, there is little opportunity—little point, too—in discussion or debate about the relative merits of different sequences. But as morphogenetic sequences come more and more into view, and are used by more people, it becomes natural for people to consider making or modifying their own sequences, sharing and exchanging ideas, trying consciously to improve the sequences they know—and then, finally, people begin to see that it is part of their obligation to share the material they have, to deposit improved sequences in the common gene pool, so that others may gain the benefit, also. Even the large-scale process embodied, for instance, in the concept of "development" can be summarized, in its essence, as a sequence of operations (a sequence that is, in this case, *not* a living one), and efforts made to improve it.[17] Profound morphogenetic processes are also based in one way or another on sequences. Such sequences *all* have the important character that deeper aspects of structure are laid down first, and that subsequent steps always follow smoothly.[18] This, too, merits discussion, and will slowly become a matter of common awareness.

4. More generally, I believe, we shall all gradually come to feel a concrete and realistic obligation to make sure that every action taken, by anyone, in any place, always, heals the land. A widespread ethical change begins to appear. Healing the land is understood by more and more people: Throughout society, slowly each person comes to recognize his or her fundamental obligation to make sure that in every act of *every* kind, each person does what he or she can do to heal the land and to regenerate, shape, form, decorate, and improve the living Earth of which we are a part.

15 / THE EMERGENCE OF SEQUENCES THAT CONSECRATE OUR SACRED HUMAN LIFE

The physical world and its places and its buildings reveal more poignantly, more accurately than almost anything else, what is really happening in human life. The form of the world—the form of the buildings—tells more poignantly than anything does, what will be happening there, what life will be like. And the *making* of a living world—that process is not only more revealing, it is more potent, closer to the bone, closer than anything else to our frailty and our reality, the nature of our society.

When we build a world for ourselves, we are not only building a world which is convenient, where we can be comfortable, where we can—as far as possible—be alive ourselves. We are also actively building a picture of our own sacred life, ordinary, dumb as it sometimes is, even—but a picture of the life which truly lies within us.

In a healthy world, each one of us must, in some degree, participate in this work, and allow our individual thoughts and desires to shape, at least a part of our small world. The world, what we call the world, is our work of sacrifice, our adoration, that we make this thing, this container, this world, which then makes us, and allows us to live.

But to create this thing, obviously *we* have to be — during the process — in touch with what we *are*. In touch with what it means to be a person, man or woman or child. In touch with what it means to be a father, a friend. In touch with the desire for a cup of coffee, for the smell of the freesias loosely gathered in the bowl on the table, for the special taste of the strawberries when they are sliced thin in the bowl with cream, in touch with the dung of animals, with dead leaves on the ground, in touch with the noisy blowing of the storm.

If we are to imagine a process which can allow all of us in society to create our communal life together, then this process must — to an extraordinary extent — allow these ordinary feelings, our ordinary thoughts and passions, to enter the world and therefore to enter the processes

by which the world is made. No bureaucrat can handle this for us. No well-meaning master-architect, alone, will do it for us, not if what matters in the end is the tone of the jukebox, the smile of the waitress, the slightly raucous atmosphere in which the locals lean on the bar and eye each other, swapping tales, stifling their loneliness.

For all that to be contained, captured, brought to life, it must be *us*, mustn't it — *we ourselves* — who do the deciding and at least some of the building, so that it is ours when it is finished, and we can still feel what it means to be alive in that thing, built, unfinished, but nevertheless open to our ordinary stories and our ordinary human life.

Well, now we can see why a refined and politely worked-out process will not do, why something conceived in the planning department, or in the professional pages of legislation, or in a professional code of ethics, will not sufficiently catch the glint of that *something* that engages us, here, in our life on Earth.

16 / FORTY THOUSAND MORPHOGENETIC SEQUENCES

There are — a rough guess only — perhaps two thousand *long* sequences which may be needed to make the environment well. And let us say that each of these long sequences, when cut apart, contains some twenty smaller sequences. That suggests that the total number of short sequences or process genes which could com-

pletely transform the built environment may be no more than about forty thousand. Although one or two decades might be needed to achieve this — it is reasonable to think that after one generation, great steps forward may have been made — and that a transformed society may be in sight.

NOTES

1. John Holland, ADAPTATION IN NATURAL AND ARTIFICIAL SYSTEMS (Cambridge, Mass: M.I.T., 1992).

2. Ibid., especially pages 89–120.

3. Muhammad Yunus and Alan Jolis, BANKER TO THE POOR: MICRO-LENDING AND THE BATTLE AGAINST WORLD POVERTY (New York: Perseus Books, 1999).

4. Such a long sequence is provided, for example, in the innovative construction contracts already referred to, Alexander et al., MARY ROSE MUSEUM, pages 92–98.

5. See chapter 18, pages 505–06, for a listing of some of the process innovations my colleagues and I have introduced in real projects.

6. See note 5. If you examine these references, you will find it to be true of many of them, that they are so long, the processes defined so complex internally, that they are hard to transplant separable parts, and one has the strong impression that to work, they need to be taken lock, stock and barrel, as a whole.

7. One example of this process, built in Mexico, was described in THE PRODUCTION OF HOUSES (New York: Oxford University Press, 1983); another, built in Texas, is described in Book 3, chapter 3, pages 114–17 and Book 3, chapter 13, pages 370–77.

8. Co-housing was first invented in Denmark, and has since then spread widely in the United States. Publications are widely available, and may be found through CO-HOUSING: THE JOURNAL OF THE CO-HOUSING NETWORK

9. Management contracts.

10. See Book 3, chapters 18 and 19 on ORNAMENT and COLOR.

11. See http:/www.patternlanguage.com/ornament/ornament.htm.

12. Personal communication from Jim Coplien.

13. For example: James Coplien and Douglas Schmidt, PATTERN LANGUAGES OF PROGRAM DESIGN (Menlo Park, California: Addison Wesley, 1995); Erich Gamma, Richard Helm, Ralph Johnson, John Vlissides, DESIGN PATTERNS: ELEMENTS OF REUSABLE OBJECT-ORIENTED SOFTWARE (Menlo Park, California: Addison Wesley, 1995); Richard Gabriel, PATTERNS OF SOFTWARE (New York: Oxford University Press, 1996).

14. I spoke, in the preface, of the idea that the relatively static vision of Book 1 is here replaced by a more dynamic vision in which each living center is understood as the continuing output from a living process.

15. In the future, the processes themselves might easily be made available on the internet, in computer form, on CD-ROM, or in written manuals. The step-by-step descriptions of process, programs which describe each process, are not difficult to write. Some examples have been given; other examples are given throughout Book 3. A computer technique in which these many different processes are linked, with the linkage available and growing, is also not hard to implement. The idea that as each process is carried out, the attention of the users is then guided toward other processes, is consistent with the nature of wholeness as it is described in these four books, and consistent with the nature of living process.

The growth of organisms, too, during development, works like this, by means of a network of triggers setting off processes in chains occasioned by the causal network that binds and forms the organization. Because the system of processes (many controlled by enzymes) trigger each other and are triggered in response to evolving events within the developing organism, at particular times, and in response to the appearance and completion of other processes, the organization can find ways to become whole. See Stuart Kaufmann's discussion of auto-catalytic networks in AT HOME IN THE UNIVERSE (New York: Oxford University Press, 1995).

16. Max Jacobson demonstrated, by experiment, that lay people could do this successfully. Max Jacobson, LAY PEOPLE DESIGNING HOUSES WITH THE PATTERN LANGUAGE (doctoral dissertation, Department of Architecture, University of California, Berkeley, 1975).

17. See chapter 17, pages 520–22.

18. Chapter 11.

CHAPTER TWENTY-ONE

THE ROLE OF THE ARCHITECT
IN THE THIRD MILLENNIUM

1 / THE ARCHITECT

In essence, the present view of architect as the only "designer" of the building — is far too remote from real building process altogether. What governs the shape of the environment, what can create living structure, is the *whole* system of sequences and processes by which buildings are *made*. This system includes money, contracts, financing, loans, construction details, engineering, timing, user involvement. It is the process which, in England, is called procurement. The process of procurement, the process of getting the environment, and its structure, is a huge process extending over many thousands of people.

The obsolete 20th-century architect, making drawings, but otherwise standing outside the procurement process, might be compared to an (imaginary) designer of the moon-landing project in 1969 who might have said: "I am a designer. My job is to decide where on the Moon we are going to land. How we get there is someone else's problem, not very important." The architect's too-exclusive focus on the drawing as the architectural process is hardly less myopic. Such a definition confines the architect so narrowly, as to make the architectural effort almost marginal. It all but ignores the architect's love for buildings, and the necessity of involvement with craft, making, manufacturing, engineering, people, money, and public discussion.

Yet architects did, in the late 20th century, steadfastly refuse to consider the procurement process at all, let alone to consider it as a single whole. They were rarely willing to consider procurement as an important theoretical and practical problem. And only very few were willing to get their hands dirty enough to get themselves involved in it.[1]

As a result, the profession became more and more marginal.[2] Where architects could once command a fee equal to 7-15% of construction budget, towards the end of the 20th century this fee percentage began dropping steadily, as part of a society-wide perception that architects had little to contribute. I recently heard of a case where in a series of six-million dollar jobs for the Ministry of Defence in the United Kingdom, the architect's fee was routinely set at 0.3% — a thirtieth or a fiftieth part of what it once used to be. The engineer in charge of the procurement told me "frankly" (as he put it) that this was the extent of the value which architects in his experience contributed to the projects. The profession was collapsing towards the end of the 20th century, because architects too often failed to do good work, would not pay attention to the creation of living structure, and did not know how to take responsibility for or direct themselves towards the really hard work, the *content*, the significant points which matter, the human heart.

2 / A NEW DEFINITION OF ARCHITECTURE

Throughout this book, I have said that it is *living processes* which govern the creation of living structure, always *processes*. The process of unfolding, and the fundamental process, and good sequences, are the essential pre-requisites for the generation of living structure in the world.

The question arises, then, what we can do, the architects of the world, to help implement such living processes? How can we — through the use of living sequences — create and help others to create living structure in the world? The 20th-century definition of the architect, framed by the drawing process, was unable to provide a living process in so many ways. There was no natural way (intrinsic to the way the profession is defined) to bring people (users, clients, owners) into the process, there was no natural way of controlling money, there was no organic way to permit unfolding to occur, no natural way to incorporate feedback by building in what works and eliminating that which does not work.

It was hardly even possible — for a 20th-century architect working within the conventional framework of professional practice — to combine structural engineering with the design process, since the structural engineer today (as defined by architects) is a person who will take the architect's sketch design (not based on structural thinking), and then make it buildable by inserting structural elements to make it "stand up." So it was inevitable that architects, working in the 20th-century framework, were not able to contribute to an unfolding process even in the realization of structural design. Yet engineering structure is truly the core of architecture.

In short, the sequences of action which defined the architect and his activities in the 20th century had little to do with the needs of living structure, and they only rarely followed lines that could embellish or sustain the use of living process. Within the 20th-century definition of the architect, architects were largely impotent to make living structure, or to help it to occur.

What is still worse, in very many cases, the definition of the architect, and the definition of the processes which define the concept and activity of the architect in today's society, actively work against the formation of living structure, make it, indeed, more difficult, sometimes impossible, for it to occur (See note 3 for detailed discussion).[3]

The difficulty is gradually being recognized. I was interested, not long ago, by a remark made to me by Tony Abbate, former president of the Fort Lauderdale chapter of the American Institute of Architects. He and I were discussing the prospect of making the Progresso district in Fort Lauderdale come to life, what it would take, how it could be done.[4] We were discussing, too, the rather strange effect his discussion with potential collaborators drawn from the architectural profession had recently had on him, and on the delineation of the project. He had, at that time, just found it necessary to "un-invite" some potential collaborators, because though they were far-thinking and innovative, the impact they brought, with the inevitable techniques and baggage of the architectural profession, their own needs for recognition, and the standards and methods of the typical large project done by professional-architecture as-it-was-in-1997, had depressed him, and forced him to turn away in search of a new process. As he said to me, on the phone:

"I shall spend the next months searching . . . to find out how we might be able to do this . . . We need something entirely new. I don't think architecture, as it is defined at present, has anything to contribute. We must essentially start from scratch."[5]

This from someone who had been president of the AIA in an important town in Florida.

3 / A VISION OF THE FUTURE

Yet in spite of so many problems with the profession, in the modern era, the possibility of beauty in the built world remains largely in the hands of architects. It is we who hold a candle in the dark, it is we who are the keepers of the flame. And, in spite of the horrible mistakes we have made all over the world, during recent decades, it is still mainly we who, in society's eyes, hold the possibility of a beautiful and living world.

How are we to do it? How is it to be done? Good or bad, it is we architects who need to work it out. And the good thing is, that for us architects, it is the physical vision, the vision of loveliness, the beauty and life of buildings which draws us on. Purely generative methods, the methods of social scientists, indirect methods of computer networks, will not by themselves actually *create* loveliness. Only the work of builders will do that. If the world is to be made lovely all around us and — to a growing extent — in every part and every place, *how, in practice, is this to be done by architects, builders, and the rest of the people in society?*

I should like to think that in THE NATURE OF ORDER I have set out true statements on how life emerges from structure, and that these statements, taken together, can provide the underpinning for a renewed sense of hope, and for a new architecture that is worth something, for an architecture that is capable of being profound and universal.

I hope, in short, that a person armed with a better understanding of the phenomenon of life will have a chance of a new view of the nature of architecture — one which deals fully with the most ordinary practical questions, and one which deals with the most profound questions of art as they arise in the art of building. I called Book I THE PHENOMENON OF LIFE because the life I have described, and the structural nature of this life, is indeed a *phenomenon*. Like other phenomena, it cannot be denied. It is simply there. And because it is there, it is there for all of us. All of us, who live together in the world, have access to this life, and to the knowledge of it. That means — if we choose to — we may draw upon it. We are free, if we wish to, to create an architecture that is based on life. Or we are free to ignore it. How could we choose ignorance?

Most of the architecture in human history was based — in intuitive, implicit form — on knowledge of the life which I have written about. Certainly the greatness of traditional architec-ture had its origin in this kind of knowledge. And the shallowness of our efforts in the past hundred years only came into being because we lost touch with the phenomenon of life — and were unwilling or unable to be guided by it, because conditions in society made it unwelcome, sometimes impossible.

Nevertheless, I believe it is possible to make conscious knowledge of living structure and of the nature of order, a part of our normal awareness as architects; and I believe that we may then build and help to build, for ourselves and for our companions on the Earth, a living world which reflects this knowledge.

I see the architecture that will arise in such a future time as marvelous beyond imagining. In my mind, I see buildings, golden vaults, simple massive dark walls of permanent materials, windows that are filled with light, and which fill rooms with flickering light; gardens, small, and subtle, yet allowing a peaceful spirit to enter into the quiet stroller, who walks by the water, and by the bush.

I can imagine soaring structural designs, a lacework of fibers forming roofs, ceilings, vaults, and domes, of unimaginable simplicity and beauty — besides which even the marvels of Ravenna and Chartres, and of the great temples of Kyoto, may one day seem almost lesser.

But to reach these marvels, I see this architecture of a future time as something that generation after generation of young architects and builders must work their way towards, must fasten onto, listen to, study, and prepare for. I see generations of young men and women finding this new architecture in which the phenomenon of life is caught, by which it is inspired, and in which we human beings may once again have our existence affirmed by the beauty of our surroundings.

This beauty is our task, in the small and in the large. That is what we have dedicated ourselves to do. But we must prepare, consciously, to find our way towards such a future.

4 / MY ASSUMPTION ABOUT OUR PROFESSION

To start with, I do take it as my assumption, that we architects are responsible for the life and well-being of *all the buildings on the Earth.*

I imagine a new role for the architect, in which we take more seriously our responsibility for *all* form and space in the world, in which we try, first by theory, then by practice, then by craft and art, to help the many societies in the world gain control of the processes which govern the shape of the built world, so that each place may become a living structure, and so that the world as a whole may become beautiful.

No one has told me this. It is not widely accepted. But, to me, it is the only conception of architecture that truly makes sense. Just as doctors, as members of their profession, take the responsibility for the care of illness and disease — and take this responsibility, in principle, *for all the people on the Earth* — so it seems to me only natural that the life of buildings and the built world, that precious quality which makes or breaks the pleasure and significance of human life on Earth, must be taken most seriously of all by those of us in the profession devoted to the love of buildings, who see buildings as our task and our passion, and who — in principle — know more than other people about the nature of these buildings. It is we to whom the people of society most naturally turn, when buildings, and the quality of the built world, are being discussed. And it is we to whom they will ultimately look, for the overall quality of the built environment.

Could architects, in principle, take care of all the buildings in the world? There are, at present, about six billion people in the world. There are, by some estimates, as many as two billion buildings in the world.[6] And there are about half a million architects in the world.[7] Let us say that, on the average, our two billion buildings have an average lifetime of some 50–100 years. That would mean, then, that at present world population, each year about 30 million buildings need to be renewed or built from scratch. If there are 500,000 architects, and if all these buildings were to be taken care of by architects, each of us architects would need to *build* some 60 buildings per year.

Please take a moment to reflect on this number and what it would mean. It would mean, on average, that you start work on a new building every four working days. If you have an office with four architects in it, the members of this office would need, together, to finish some 240 buildings per year, an average of one per day. How might this be possible? Few of us have, I think, tried to imagine such a scale of action, or thought seriously what these figures would mean if we took on such a huge responsibility. Yet, in principle, if we — architects — were to believe ourselves responsible for the geometry, the form of the built world, that is the responsibility we would need to accept. And if we believe that the form of buildings truly makes a difference to human life, there can be little point in following a way of thinking and acting which could, at best, deal only with a tenth or a hundredth of what needs to be built. We should aspire to deal with all of it (if we consider it truly important), or give it up as a luxury and deal with none of it (if we believe that it does not really matter). The seriousness of our intent must force us, in effect, to take on this responsibility, and address the question of how it might be done.

Up until our era, architects have never, so far, considered the possibility of taking such responsibility. Nikolaus Pevsner's famous statement "A bicycle shed is a building, Lincoln cathedral is a work of architecture,"[8] did, in its supercilious 20th-century elitism, take away from us the very task which architecture, by definition, sets out: *The making of the whole created world in its geometry.* Instead, during the 20th century, and, indeed, during the whole history of professional architecture so far, the work covered by architects has focused on a limited special class of buildings, a too-narrow segment of the class of all buildings.

Yet since the built world is all one structure, all of it either dead or living in varying degrees, then we architects — if we hold ourselves re-sponsible for the order of the built world — must have some idea how *all* this built world, vast in extent, is to receive its form. And we should, too, have a clear idea how we can go about helping to take care of it, *all of it*, bringing it form, nourish-ing it, making sure that it is OK, that it has its life. This is a massive responsibility.

5 / FIRST MAJOR PROBLEM: THE VERY LARGE
HOW TO ENLARGE THE ARCHITECT'S RESPONSIBILITY
BROADER SCOPE WITH LARGER IMPACT

Let us continue our calculation. Altogether, the Earth has on it about 51 million square miles of land.[9] Of that land, about 2 percent, something like about 1 million square miles, are urban and semi-urban land. About 4 million square miles are in use for cultivation and habitation together. That is roughly the extent of human habitation on the Earth.[10]

Also, as stated above, there are at present about 500,000 architects in the world. From the numbers given above, we may infer that if the work that has to be done were to be distributed evenly, then each architect in the world would be responsible, during his lifetime, for 8 square miles of built environment, an area nearly 3 miles by 3 miles, including all its buildings, and all its exterior space: its roads, gardens, parks, and public works.[11]

If we have a serious wish to make the physi-cal built world better, and if — in any sense — we architects see ourselves as the guardians of the world's physical world of buildings and streets and gardens — it means then, that on the average, in an architect's lifetime, this architect must take care of (design and complete and maintain) the buildings and exterior space over a total area of something between 2 and 8 square miles, or about 1300–5000 acres (500–2000 hect-ares). This calculation is very rough, of course, but the orders of magnitude are near enough.

Let us assume, further, that an architect has a professional working life of some 40 years. This means then, that our average architect must, on the average, design and complete buildings which cover a total of about 70 acres per year. Or, if we imagine a small architectural firm of four architects, these four working for a year must then together design and complete all the buildings, roads, gardens, on about 300 acres, and they must achieve this once a year, *every single year of their working lives*. This is a huge number, compared with the size of work we ar-chitects normally do today. Certainly, it is a much, much higher average than can be reached by conventional contemporary forms of practice.

How is it to be done? How could the archi-tect's ability, and scope, and capacity, be magni-fied suddenly, to such a degree? If there is such a thing as living order of the kind I have defined in this book, an order which comes from the particularities of individual people and particu-larities of place — then we must ask: How is this order to be generated on a worldwide scale? That is the first problem we confront when we face our real professional responsibility.[12]

In principle, one architect could take respon-sibility for such a large part of the Earth. But it is certainly far beyond what one architect can design directly using today's conceptions and to-day's techniques and today's processes. It could only be done if it were done *indirectly*, by indirect generative means, so that this one architect sets in motion processes which allow hundreds of others (users, builders and so on) to do the necessary volume of work, *but to do it in the right way.* That means, to do it using processes which allow ordinary people — the people who live and work there — with only help or guidance, to generate order by generative means like those described in this book. From the architect's point of view, this would mean he, or she, would be working with these people by guiding, helping, and steering their work — while allowing them a great deal of power and decision-making influence — essentially thus magnifying the impact of his/her effort, and allowing much of the detailed adaptational order to come from the place it has always come in past societies — from people themselves and their local craftsmen. But the architect might well become, in a future society, a person who is responsible for *creating* such generative systems, making them work smoothly, making languages and ways of building which hundreds or thousands of people can use to make their own beautiful surroundings by themselves — and, when needed, with her/his help. That is what I mean by the architect's new role in creating order.[13]

In my vision of this activity, I propose that the architects view themselves in this activity as creators, that they take responsibility for the beauty, order, wholeness of the result, so that they have a very great deal invested in their success in defining languages which people can use successfully, because it is then, through these people, that the architects are able to make beauty in the world, a hundredfold or a thousandfold as large in its extent, as anyone can manage today.

Of course architects might say that they have no wish for such indirect responsibility, and that they prefer to draw a few buildings. But, how else is the task to be done? And there is a moral argument as well: The education of an architect is expensive. Society has given each of us architects a gift, by allowing us to be architects. It seems to me that to take on a responsibility, commensurate with the gift that we have been given by our training, we ought to think out ways we can shoulder the responsibility that actually falls on us.

Because of the numbers (population, area, and number of architects), the methods an architect must use in the 21st century, to have the right kind of relationship to the environment — *can* only be *indirect* methods. We can only accomplish our aim, by finding some way of creating living structure, without personally having to design every bit of it, without personally having to shape it all. This must — can only — lead to an indirect, generative method.

6 / SECOND MAJOR PROBLEM: THE VERY SMALL
HOW TO DEEPEN THE ARCHITECT'S RESPONSIBILITY
FINER SCOPE WITH MORE SUBTLE DETAIL

Let us now go to the other end of the spectrum, the very small and the very beautiful. Everything that I have said throughout this book, makes it clear that successful design and creation of living structure needs *more* care, not less; *more* input, *more* information, *more* slowness. To make the details of a building right, we need to be closer to the craft, closer to materials, closer to every step and every window sill, closer to construction, fabrication, ornament, color. In Book 3, especially towards the end (chapters 15–19), we shall see this in considerable detail.

This means, simply put, that architects must — if they wish to have any kind of serious relationship to the making of beautiful buildings, and wish to generate life in buildings — they must then move back towards the profession they once came from, the profession of builders.

It is really not possible to carry out the living process, as I have described it, unless the architect is making things, taking responsibility for money, craft, sequence of construction, modification of construction — all in all, the building, to become beautiful, must be an emerging work of art *under his hands*.[14]

The example shown in the appendix of this book, describes such a process. It is rewarding and effective. But it is plain that somehow, such an approach increases, does not decrease, the amount of work which must be done by architects. The examples of Book 3 confirm this judgment.

Furthermore, the problem of adaptation itself plainly suggests that in a world of living structure people at large need to be involved, massively, in the construction of their buildings and their neighborhoods. Who knows the most about a place? *The people who live there and work there.* Who is capable of providing all the detailed twists and turns, the detailed nuances, the detailed lovely subtleties, required to created a well-adapted structure? *The people who live there, and the people who work there.*

This means, then, that a well-adapted environment must include participation, effort, and ownership in some form, by millions — no, billions — of people. If this were to be done in anything like the present framework, it, too, like the need for craft, would take more man-hours, more effort, from the tiny band of half-a-million architects, who are already grossly overloaded!

Yet the calculation just made also suggests that the total amount of construction we have to take care of is greater than what is accepted in today's current practice by a factor of ten or a hundred. Thus we have what seems to be an almost insuperable problem confronting our profession. To meet the ideals of quality we need to go more into depth, work more closely, work more in construction, making, fabricating, craft — and also give more time to working more with families, owners, occupiers. All this makes the work slower. Yet to take care of our responsibility as guardians of the Earth's built environment, we need to do fifty or a hundred times as much work as we do today, because we have responsibility for all the buildings, not merely a few of them.

Unless we go into detail, and take care of fine adaptation, we shall not be able to do a good job — it will be more of the same bad stuff which was built all over the Earth in the 20th century. But unless we also increase our scope and the breadth of our responsibility a hundred-fold, we shall not even begin to take care of the Earth's surface, and shall not therefore be able to cope with the real problem of a living environment in a realistic or useful way.

How can these two apparently irreconcilable requirements be reconciled? Ethically, artistically, and biologically, how can we architects act in a responsible way towards the Earth and towards the people of the Earth?

In the way I have described living structure, the building becomes a living thing, only when it is conceived, throughout its fabric, as an ornament. The geometry of the work, the fine geometry, as in a work of sculpture or a work of painting, is the thing which makes the building beautiful. Where roofs, walls, windows, rooms, passages, floors, ceilings, steps, sills, moldings, tiles, material surfaces work together — all of it — as an ornament which touches the soul.[15]

By my arguments, this is not only beautiful in conception but *necessary*. The proper adaptation and shape of detail and ornament, plays a role in the unity of living structure not very different from the role played by molecules in a leaf. You cannot keep the leaf yet not have the properly adapted molecules within it. Just so, you cannot have a large-scale environment 8 square miles in extent, with buildings, bridges, roads, all working properly, all alive in the large, if the details of which it is made, the bricks and mortar, windows, plants, and ornaments — do not make sense, and do not have life themselves. And that means that all this material, too, must be controlled by people who understand living structure very deeply, and who are close enough to actual material, to be able to shape it with love and grace.[16]

To achieve this highly complex adaptation successfully, in every cubic inch, it is impossible merely to draw drawings for others to build. The connection to the material, its working through, the dynamic development of shape, color, form and substance in the evolving building, must be controlled by the architect or builder or craftsman, if a living structure is to be made.[17]

All this suggests — *requires* — that, even in the largest buildings, the architect must become more of a builder, must come closer to the direct control of money and material, and time, and process, than a conventional architect can do. It means that we must find a way for the emergence of a new kind of architect-builder, consistent with the conditions of modern contracting, yet placing the architect, or his and her evolved future counterparts, more directly in control of the real art of building, and of the physical results which only such direct control can bring.

7 / LARGER *AND* DEEPER

So, according to my analysis, our scope must be larger; yet at the same time the physical and geometrical refinement must be far more detailed. We must learn to increase our scope by looking through a telescope *and* to increase our scope by looking through a microscope, at the same time — as we change our profession.

If living structure is to be created in the world, it is a virtual certainty, I believe, that the presently obsolete 20th-century architect (which we ourselves embody) has to be replaced by a new and different kind of professional, undertaking different tasks, playing a larger role, increasing the scope of what is covered — yet at the same time also playing, at least half the time, a smaller and more modest role, a more engaged role, more embracing in her/his artistic responsibility as a maker.

If I am right, and these two changes come together, as I believe they must, we shall be able, in the 21st century, to embark on a new era where architects become both more able to generate living structure in the world in large amounts, yet also able to do it with a finer and more detailed, more caring attention to detail.

We shall see both these new kinds of activities in most of the examples given in Book 3. On the one hand a more generative role, which allows architects with other people — sometimes hundreds of people — to play their creative part in forming the environment, creating a more comprehensive wholeness on the largest scale. On the other hand a more detailed and more modest, but more concrete, artistic role which guides the making of buildings, gardens, roofs, walls, seats, windows, rooms, ceilings, and floors and ornaments, all as works of art, in a way which pays more attention to the wholeness — thence the life — of the environment.

8 / WHAT PLACE, THEN, FOR US ARCHITECTS?

In the last twenty chapters I have painted a vision of an immensely complex world, which, to be made living, is to be generated autonomously, by millions of people acting for themselves, within the framework of living process as I have defined it, with the benefit of the fifteen structure-preserving transformations, supported by pattern languages. I have imagined a situation where the practical version of these living processes are emerging, developing, evolving, and being applied by agencies, social institutions, families, individuals, and businesses.

In this vision, the craft of the architect — the forming of the environment in its beauty, in its majesty, in its humanity — is to be assisted by semiautonomous generative sequences that help millions of people to become creative.

The traditional province of the architect, then, what is it? What is an architect to *do*? How best may an architect play a role in this new, wider-ranging landscape?

Four words encompass an answer, and define a balanced system of life, in which each architect takes on, in some measure, each of these four things, as part of daily work.

> *Making*
> *Designing*
> *Building*
> *Helping*

Making. Practicing, oneself, the art of making, laying bricks, pouring concrete, molding, firing tiles, undertaking wooden joints, shaping plastic steel, and glass in their elements of fabrication, so that the architect's own hands have the pleasure of the art in them. Using, in all these cases, well-defined new sequences which introduce the possibility of living structure into the physical construction techniques themselves.

Designing. Arriving at drawings, schemes, sketches, for the more important buildings, for those special buildings which stand for something that the people or community would like to have. Using new generative sequences to make designs, sequences which are integrated as necessary with the process of making, allow life to be created on the land and in the city — and which show, above all, the structure-preserving aspects of each project, so that it heals the world.

Building. Acting as a contractor who manages money, manages construction, who has responsibility for balancing budgets and who has the dynamic power to modify the building while

it is being built, so that its functionality and beauty can gradually shine out more and more, while it is being made.

Helping hundreds of people to design and layout and build their own structures, adding a touch here and a touch there to make the largest processes go well. Helping to invent, create, provide the generative sequences and languages which make this very large-scale activity possible, and helping people and communities to use them well, in a framework which also has our guidance. Once again, the emphasis of these generative processes must be on the beauty and coherence and positive space within the *large*, as it results from the cooperative work of hundreds.

The Summary. In my view we need to change in two especially important ways. First, the architect needs to be closer to the work of building, more detailed, closer to the material construction details, as a craftsman, contractor, builder. Second, paradoxically, the architect also needs to be more remote from the work, less egocentric, more in a position of creating *generative* schemes which apply to really large segments of the environment: thus creating rules and generative processes for whole neighborhoods, communities and even regions.

Is there a place for such an architect? How does the architect fit in most effectively, in the context of a system of myriad living sequences? How is the artistic and creative urge to build, something that has been with human beings for as long as society itself — how is this to be nourished, how expressed, how is this creative urge to play a role in the creation and generation of the environment of the future? How should we come to understand our own future, in these terms?

In all this, we must remember that the architect's job — ultimately — is to create beauty, harmony, living structure both in the large and in the small. *It is the dazzling beauty of darkness and light, color and silence, warmth and material and vegetation, which makes us gasp. That is what an architect's life is for. That is what we stand for. No matter how sophisticated the work of procurement, no matter how powerful the generative sequences may be, it must be organized in such a way that it helps and inspires the architect to make beautiful and miraculous buildings which make all of us experience the soul.* And, along with this, living structure must be created worldwide. That, too, is something that must have attention. And we, the architects of the world, are uniquely placed by inclination and tradition to take on the job of safeguarding and creating the living structure on the Earth's surface.

If that is to happen in this new century, it will require a very large change. We architects need to form, as a major part of our profession, of our curricula in schools of architecture, as a major part of our vision of the future, a concerted effort on the question of procurement: To invent ways of getting living structure in the world, to ask how we can guide and cooperate in large-scale processes that will genuinely create and generate living structure in cities and outside cities. If we do not do it, someone else will do it, and our profession will collapse.

In Book 3, I shall try to show how, armed with living sequences that embody the fundamental process, we may apply them thousands of times throughout the landscape of a modern city — and so gain the capacity to generate living structure at every level of scale. I shall try to show what such a future world which we create might look like. By looking at examples of the kind of city which the unfolding process generates we may begin to grasp the real meaning of the fundamental process, and the kind of world which different realizations of this process will create.

9 / THE ARCHITECT'S DREAM

Thousands of young architects want — somehow — to create a living world.

They want, and see hope for a vision of glorious buildings, neighborhoods that are sparkling, vibrant with human life, some quiet and beautiful, some pulsating with idiosyncrasy which celebrate the individual human beings in all their differences, beautiful places to dream of, and to lift the spirit.

In the mind such things create a glorious world, a miraculous vision, something worth striving for, something worth living for.

But how is this vision to be attained. What practical steps can make it last a lifetime, make it repeat, what steps create some hope, some possibility of success? Many architects, many of us, young and old, are too often frustrated, because there are few models available of the ways in which they might be able to work at a suitable scale large enough to make the world beautiful in its entirety, small enough to allow love of craft, and making, and detail, to find expression in every project. The present definition of what architects do (and hence of what an architect "is") interferes again and again with our ability to play a useful role in the worldwide unfolding process.

For this reason I have tried, within the examples of Book 3, to show living sequences being used in a hundred ways to define some of the new roles an architect might have (and perhaps *must* have) in a new and future state of society which is truly concerned with creating living structure in the world. To a large degree, then, the examples which follow in Book 3 not only show fragments of a form language, a new way of seeing and making the world. They also illustrate many of the most important ways a new architect may live and work.

NOTES

1. The issue is profound. Because of course the very terms "architect" and "architecture" are themselves defined by sequences. The legal definition of the architect in California, for instance, is the administrator of a contract between owner and builder. This view, of course, imposes a very specific legal sequence — and hence procedural ideas of professional practice — on the architect.

What we call the architect, is a person with certain rights, certain skills, certain aims — of course — but it is, above all, defined by the *procedures* which the architect follows, by the sequence of what she *does*, by what he *does*.

During the entire period from 1950 to 2000 — what the architect did — hence what the profession of architecture *was* — was very narrowly defined. Our present profession of architecture has a definition (largely based on development) which implies first, that nearly everything in architecture is to be done by drawing — that is, by *drawing* buildings — and then having others build them. This process is consistent with the methods of developers — who seek to borrow money, and make money on the borrowed money by building. For a developer it is natural to need a drawing, then to get it built, whether it has living structure or not.

2. For an overview of the historical process which led us to this point, see Mark Crinson and Jules Lubbock, AR-CHITECTURE, ART OR PROFESSION? THREE HUNDRED YEARS OF ARCHITECTURAL EDUCATION IN BRITAIN (Manchester: Manchester University Press, 1994).

3. Tragically, indeed, the situation is even far worse than that. The narrow definition of the architect, as it was accepted throughout the second half of the 20th century, is by now so well established, that the contribution of the architect, and perhaps without anyone's intending it, often works actively to *prevent* unfolding from happening. For example, my colleagues and I once designed a system of furniture for Herman Miller. During the process of working on the project, I became curious why the living quality of natural workplaces, which was something we were aiming to support — had been replaced by a sterile landscape of hard furniture and furniture systems. During our preliminary investigation, it turned out that it was the *designers* — interior designers and facilities managers — who themselves wanted this un-living environment, because it was easy to manage, and because it flattered images which the designers (architects) sought consciously to achieve. The harmonious living environment of a real workplace, was something that these property managers and interior architects actively sought to change and destroy, and to replace with the dead environment that played on the pages of illustrated magazines.

In one place I visited, Computerland in Hayward, California, I drew attention to the accounting department as a lively place where people enjoyed working, compared with the floors of offices with new furniture systems which were so unfriendly that they were almost empty, since (for their own comfort) workers all made arrangements to work elsewhere. The facilities manager to whom I described this problem, apologized profusely to me for not yet having transformed the accounting department (which I was praising) with a new system, and told me emphatically that they would be installing the new furniture system in the accounting department within a few weeks. He behaved almost as if he had been caught in some dreadful sin. He assumed, I suppose, that because I was an architect, I must be looking down my nose at him for not yet having transformed the accounting department to the sterile office landscape that had been created everywhere else.

As in this example — but multiplied hundreds of thousands of times, all over the world — many of the activities of the architect in the 20th century had serious and too-often negative influence on the world.

4. The planning of the Progresso district, Fort Lauderdale, is further discussed in Book 3, chapter 10.

5. Private communication from Tony Abbate, June 1997.

6. Howard Davis, THE CULTURE OF BUILDINGS, (New York: Oxford University Press, 1999), page 3.

7. Estimating this number proved difficult. No organization that I contacted was able to give me the figure for the world, and could only give the count of their own membership, a very poor basis. Department of Labor figures indicate that there are some 100,000 working architects in the United States, in a population of 260 million. On the assumption that the number of architects is a function of GNP, not population (because there are proportionally more architects per capita in first-world countries), this would extrapolate to about 500,000 architects, worldwide. The number could be higher, but is very unlikely to be more than one million.

8. Nikolaus Pevsner, EUROPEAN ARCHITECTURE (Harmondsworth, Pelican, 1942).

9. This figure comes from the Population Reference Bureau, Washington D.C., 2001.

10. Also culled from statistics provided by the Population Reference Bureau.

11. 4,000,000 (square miles) divided by 500,000 (architects).

12. The concept that an architect has the skill to take responsibility for very large parts of the environment, has been put forward, brilliantly, by Andrés Duany in his work on town planning. The codes which he and his colleagues have created do attempt to control architecture at a very much larger scale than architects normally attempt, and I believe, in future, his efforts will be seen as major pioneering steps in the effort to change the profession. I do not agree with all the details of his method, still less perhaps, with the attempt to press the codes into a legal framework thus using coercion instead of persuasion and occasionally resulting in a certain deadness. But the brilliance of Duany's attempts to deal with the large scale, and the boldness of his methods, cannot be denied. They have historic importance.

13. Discussions of the generative role of the architect have been put forward in many ways by many people.

See, for example, the lengthy and careful study of the subject by Howard Davis, THE CULTURE OF BUILDINGS (New York: Oxford University Press, 1999). For another example, see the section on Generative Methods in Christopher Alexander, "The Origins of Pattern Theory, The Future of the Theory, and The Generation of a Living World," Keynote speech to OOPSLA conference, San Jose, California, October 1996, reprinted in PROCEEDINGS OF THE IEEE, August 2000.

14. The possibility of treating construction and building as art, requires new concepts in the realm of building contracts. One version of the powerful contracts my colleagues and I developed over the last twenty years to make this possible, is printed in full in Christopher Alexander, Gary Black and Miyoko Tsutsui, THE MARY ROSE MUSEUM (New York: Oxford University Press, 1993), chapter 3. Related concepts, such as more flexible drawings with more room for interpretation, were well known in history. See, for instance, Lothar Haselberger, "The construction plans for the Temple of Apollo at Didyma," SCIENTIFIC AMERICAN, December 1985, Vol 253, No 6. pp. 126–32, and J.J. Coulton, GREEK ARCHITECTS AT WORK: PROBLEMS OF STRUCTURE AND DESIGN (Ithaca, New York: Cornell University Press, 1977).

15. This topic of the creation of building detail, and the necessity for small structure to play a main role in the adaptation of the environment, is discussed at length in Book 3, chapters 15–19.

16. See commentaries in, for instance, Christopher Alexander, "The Architect Builder: Toward Changing the Conception of What an Architect Is," SAN FRANCISCO BAY ARCHITECT'S REVIEW, September 1977, No. 4, p. 4., and Soetsu Yanagi, THE UNKNOWN CRAFTSMAN: A JAPANESE INSIGHT INTO BEAUTY, Kodansha International Ltd., Tokyo, 1972.

17. A summary of these results is given in "The Real Meaning of Architecture," by Thomas Fisher and Ziva Freiman, in PROGRESSIVE ARCHITECTURE, July 1991, pp. 100–107, and in Christopher Alexander, "Manifesto 1991," PROGRESSIVE ARCHITECTURE, July 1991, pp. 108–112.

Making, designing, building, and helping.
Colored sketch for a medallion in a marble floor
Made for the lobby of the Athens Music Megaron, Christopher Alexander, 2001

CONCLUSION

LIFE-BASED SOCIETY
A VISION AND A LONG-RANGE OVERVIEW

1 / DEEP FEELING AS THE GUIDING PRINCIPLE

The revolutionary consequences of chapter 14 can hardly be exaggerated. If living processes, guided by feeling for the whole, and guided by *feeling*, were to shape all acts of construction in society, then everything, nearly, that we know about modern society would be changed. Above all — and what I wish to say now is not a small thing — it means that people would have a self-awareness, a knowledge of reality and wholeness as it is, quite different from the ignorance of inner feeling we came to accept as normal in the 20th-century.

The idea that feeling — above all *feeling* — should become the main anchor of the huge, hundred-million-variable process which creates life on Earth, seems hard to take seriously. Above all, it seems hard to implement. We live in a world of computer process, banking, strictly controlled procedures. How is it possible to contemplate a world in which the freedom exists, that could allow natural unfolding — the unfolding governed by deep feeling — to control processes of such magnitude?

Yet I do mean this seriously. Let me make three small points.

(1) By feeling, the reader must remember that I mean adherence to the whole. It is not an idiosyncratic touchy-feely kind of thing, but serious, holistic connection with the whole, which provides a wholesome feeling in the actor.

Market in Guadeloupe. Although ancient, it is of the far distant future, too.

(2) Next — a feeling-guided process was typical in most human societies, during much of the Earth's history. That alone should give one pause in dismissing it too quickly. Why should it not also be possible for us?

(3) What I have called a feeling-based process — the fundamental process as I have described it — is demonstrably necessary for the production of living structure.

Some writers — Lynn Margulis[1] or James Lovelock[2] among others — might say that a texture of living structure on the Earth is required for Earth's survival. They argue for biological reasons, and I argue for architectural reasons, that living structure is a necessary feature of a reasonable, surviving, nourishing world. If we want an Earth which is covered with living structure then, according to what I have argued in this book, this wholeness-based form of action must, indeed, become the norm. And that means that construction processes guided by feeling for the whole must, too, become the norm.

But perhaps most interesting, most inspiring, underlying the material of this book there is the *vision* of a world which is guided by feeling.

Instead of technology, *feeling*: At the beginning of the 21st century, even the biologically oriented views of complexity theory, are chiefly guided by interaction of complex variables, mathematical attractors in phase space, and so on. The power of the techniques that have been elaborated is startling. But it remains true that human beings, and human nature, are intuitively more in tune with feeling than with mathematics. Our humanity — humanity itself, our sympathy for one another, and for ourselves — all has its origin in issues concerned with archetypal feeling. From this point of view, the importance — in my view — of the techniques I have described, is their capacity to create a living world which is rooted in human feeling, because that will create a world in touch with *us*, with our true nature, with our humanity. The idea that feeling itself can become both criterion and instrument — that what is done, no matter how large or how small, can become personal, connected to the personal self of all human beings — and that this process then opens the door to a new form of society. That is truly revolutionary. That can shake the world.

2 / REPAIRING THE WHOLE

I hope I have succeeded at least this far: That the reader of this book has begun to appreciate the possibility that in the future, a new form of building and planning process must come to exist worldwide, in the sphere of human creation, and in the disciplines by which we shape the Earth and our built world upon the Earth.

Nature is able to create living structure by smooth sequences of recursively applied structure-preserving transformations, applied again and again and again to the wholeness which exists on the surface of the Earth. The laws of physics, and chemistry, and hydrodynamics, and the laws of complex evolution — now called non-linear dynamics or complexity theory — all

of them at their core suggest the same process: The wholeness which exists gives way, incessantly, to a next wholeness, which preserves the structure of the previous one. This happens even in the process of destruction, in the process of simplification, death, pruning. It happens, too, in the more complex two-level process we call genetic evolution.

The key is biology. In this book I have proposed a process, able to propagate life in our built and natural environment, which is very similar to the way that biological processes propagate plant and animal life on Earth. A key and vitally important point is this: The pressure towards life in the local system is congruent with a pressure towards life *in the whole*. There is no conflict between the life of the parts and the life of the whole. Every living process seeks, at every single moment, to increase the life of the parts and the life of the whole, together.

Autonomous and purely physical processes of this class created organic life on Earth in the pre-human era. Similar, but human-inspired processes created the beauty of traditional towns and villages in the first human era. Similar, but more conscious processes can now be used to make buildings, rooms, streets, gardens, public squares, neighborhoods, landscape, and wilderness, even objects of daily use in our world. That, I believe, is what will come to pass in the second human era which is now just beginning.

In principle, living processes of this class might then also be used to create everything else. They might, for instance, one day even be used as the processes for building human institutions, family discussions, for choices, for decisions of value, even politics. But that is, perhaps, looking a very long way into the future.

Of course, there are hundreds of thousands of specific social processes which may have the ability to increase the life of the whole. Certainly,

I am not insisting that there is any one super-process, or only one kind of viable process. Rather, I am specifically insisting that there is only one *class* of living processes — albeit a very large class indeed — and that any particular process must, if it is to be a good one, belong to that class.

When we engage in building design, or building construction, town-planning, or agriculture, or engineering, or placing highways, when we build buildings, when we give permission to the construction of buildings, when we consider plans for land-use — in all these cases too, the same unfolding process which has created living structure in nature, could — if allowed to — also create living structure in our environment.

By inventing and re-inventing versions of the fundamental process in appropriate social forms, and applying these forms of process to all acts of making and building and repairing, this worldwide operation then contains within itself, the seeds or core of the biological unfolding process that occurs in nature, now applied to human society. Throughout human society, human beings who use it will be capable of healing and remaking the ravaged Earth.

3 / THE BIOLOGY OF OUR FUTURE WORLD

People used to say that just as the 20th century had been the century of physics, the 21st century would be the century of biology. The origin of this thought was that while the processes of physics that dominated our 20th-century technology were fascinating and unusual, they were often one-dimensional, linear, monochromatic, involving fairly small numbers of variables. The creation of life, on the other hand, is a highly complex process, involving thousands or millions of variables, working in subtle cooperation. It was felt that, as understanding of biology increased, so our mental world, and our ability to understand and

control biological process by subtle means, would increase, so that we would gradually move into a world whose prevailing paradigm was one of complexity, and whose techniques sought the co-adapted harmony of hundreds, or thousands of variables. This would, inevitably, involve new technique, new vision, new models of thought, and new models of action.

I believe that such a transformation is starting to occur. I also believe the repeated application of the fundamental process to the built world will inevitably have to be part of such a transformative society. In saying this, I must underline my belief that living processes belong to the *future*, not to the past. Although 20th-century social processes were so different from what I contemplate, and did not yet contain the wherewithal to create living structure (except for the small islands of exception I have cited)—there is now a natural swell in people's minds, a sea-change, and a change of intention, so that the turn towards generation of living process is, perhaps, one of the signal marks of the turn of the millennium, of people's changed awareness, of their hope.

Our future, as we begin to see it now, contains a vision of an entirely new kind of human process: A process, like the process of biology, which is attuned to human nature, makes more sense of human feeling and human common sense. In this process — and it applies to every step that is taken in society, whatever people are doing — you move forward in small, tiny steps. Each step accomplishes something concrete and good — one center at a time. Each step is taken forward, judged, by the impact it has on the whole. We are continuously evaluating the whole for its deep feeling, for its usefulness, for the support it gives to human experience.

This process, then, is potentially remarkable. As versions of such process are worked out for different situations in society, they may, ultimately, replace bureaucracy and the machinelike organization of large corporations and government. It is a process in which individuals do what is necessary, and what they can do, moving everything forward one satisfying step at a time.

You may wish to say that this is dreaming, even impossible. But that, I think, would only be the echo of the dying 20th century that talks, still, in our heads. It *is* possible. A few examples I have given in this book begin to make that clear. Other more extensive examples in Book 3 make it far more clear, and show how this process can, indeed, generate an entire living world.

Above all, we know that it must be possible on theoretical grounds. We know it because this is the process by which the biological world of plants and animals has already been created. Late 20th-century research on complex systems by Holland, Kaufmann, and others, showed how very complex systems with enormously rich and complex state-space have been built up, repeatedly, throughout biological history, by the process of unfolding, and by small structure-preserving processes, which go step by step, yet reach astounding results in the whole.

I believe that structure-preserving processes of the general type I have defined will be extended far beyond the bounds of architecture. Other preliminary demonstrations in the sphere of complex systems lead to the same conclusion. What I am pointing to makes sense as a way forward in the complex world of computer programming and software development, where the intricacy and internal architecture of systems has been shown to develop best under these kinds of impetus. It works in the world of biology. It works in the world of technology. And it will work in the world of architecture itself.

A world made in this way is truly a new kind of world. I do not know, for sure, that traditional society reached its goals by these means. What I do know, and am certain of, is that the society of the future, the long future of men and women on our planet, will — *must* — inevitably be carried forward by this kind of process which allows the nourishment of the individual to happen at the same time that vast, and highly technical developments occur.

The small, step-by-step process is not only the best way to build the architecture of a complex system, from the point of view of adaptation. It is also the most satisfying, the most nourishing — because it creates, at each step, something that makes us — the makers — feel more wholesome, something that makes us feel alive while we are doing it. It is nourishing, it is fun, it is productive, it is efficient. And, of course — best of all — a similar healing effect also takes place in the whole. Since it is the whole we are always looking to at each step, the whole which is transformed and made to have a deeper feeling, a lovely feeling consistent with everyday longings —

then the whole, the great architecture of the whole, will in the end serve us, give us a kind of world (born of just such a process) which is the world in which we want to live.

In Book 3, we shall see how the fundamental process, applied iteratively, thousands and thousands of times throughout the landscape of a modern city has the capacity to generate living structure at every level. By looking at examples of the kind of city which living process generates, the reader will, I hope, begin to grasp the real meaning of living structure.

4 / THE FAR-DISTANT FUTURE

In certain respects, some of the processes I have described in this book have something in common with ancient process. My respect for the language, and buildings, and processes of ancient society, is a respect for ancient wisdom. But far more essentially, these things — the processes and building forms that I describe — belong to the *future*. Indeed, in most respects, they belong more to the far-distant future than to the past or to the present.

The fundamental process and the structure-preserving unfolding process — these are things that belong to a visionary future for humankind — a future in which complex structure of the built world, its daily re-creation, its daily nurture, will be considered normal. It is this far-distant future — hardly yet contemplated — which I have been looking to for the last thirty years. To be well, we must set our sights on such a future, and recognize that complex processes of the kind that are needed to generate and sustain life in our surroundings will, *structurally*, be processes of the kind that I have been describing. That is so for reasons that are akin to the reasoning of biology, to the reasoning of complex system theory, and to the reasoning of ultramodern physics and computer science.

It is the vision of a future living Earth, which draws me on. Inspired by a thoroughly new view of structure, fueled by a view which sees living process as the origin of all life, this allows us to contemplate, for the first time, the idea that one day such living process will cover and completely generate, in biological fashion, the natural and human-made and built environment that we may ultimately learn to call our living Earth.

NOTES

1. Lynn Margulis, THE SYMBIOTIC PLANET: A NEW LOOK AT EVOLUTION (London: Phoenix, 1998) and WHAT IS LIFE (Berkeley: University of California Press, 2000).

2. James Lovelock, THE AGES OF GAIA: BIOGRAPHY OF OUR LIVING EARTH (New York: W. W. Norton and Co., 1988).

APPENDIX

A SMALL EXAMPLE
OF A LIVING PROCESS

1 / A RADICAL NEW PROCESS

Throughout Book 2, it has been my contention that when we design and build in such a way that what we build gets life, it is necessary to do things in a new way which respects the step-by-step unfolding of the field of centers. During the unfolding, each new center made at a certain time t is introduced and shaped in response to the wholeness that existed just before, at time t-1, and is then shaped according to its contribution to that wholeness. All this is accomplished by repeated application of structure-preserving transformations.

Although this may leave certain features of the professional architectural process intact, it also creates many revolutionary changes. To illustrate, this appendix contains one fully detailed practical example of the process, describing, in some detail, the making of a single house that I built in Berkeley for Christopher and Stephanie Upham during 1991 and 1992.[1] As we shall see, throughout this project the fundamental process and the fifteen transformations are used again and again and again, to get each new detail, as the whole unfolds.

This process is very different from the normally accepted process of architectural design and construction as it was in the 1990s.[2] To make the unfolding process possible, I was both architect and contractor for this house. The bank accepted the process, in spite of its innovative character. The submission of plans to the Berkeley building department was normal (however, see discussion on pages 604–05). The role of drawings was also very different from that in the normal professional process of today. Since the construction was indeed an unfolding process, we could not know how the house would turn out in detail, until it was finished. Although some drawings were made during the process — for permits, structural checking, and so on — all the participants knew that the drawings were merely a rough approximation of what was to become the finished building.

The house was carefully built to a fixed budget — according to contract — and came in *on* budget. The money was administered under a new kind of construction contract which I have developed with my colleagues over many years. This contract allows construction price to be guaranteed while unfolding is taking place, even though the design is not rigidly fixed ahead of time.[3] Thus the client does not have the financial uncertainty that such an open-ended project would create in a typical late 20th-century construction contract where many steps of the unfolding would be viewed as changes. Rather, in our contract the unfolding was a feasible process *within a fixed budget*, backed by the careful cost control necessary to make this possible. This was part of the agreement from the beginning.[4]

Our work was done by a small group of people including craftspeople, an architect, an engineer, apprentices and construction workers experienced in construction, an architect trained as an engineer, and people inexperienced in construction. The total calendar time spent was somewhat longer than usual. The fees were standard (though spent in smaller amounts over a longer period). The cost of construction management, fixed in advance as a percentage of the fixed construction budget, was also approximately standard (18%).[5] The Center for Environmental Structure (CES), the contracting body, is a non-profit organization, and it was part of the character of our agreement that every penny, except for the fixed fee, was to be spent on the building. CES had responsibility for allocating and reallocating the money dynamically, while design and construction were moving forward.

I am not proposing this example as a general model of all living process. Other processes will certainly need other new concepts to become living. Road building, land management, assignment of loans, zoning and planning, larger construction projects — all need different kinds of revision in order to include the features of living process. Each sphere of process needs different aspects of process to be changed.

However, the degree of difference this pro cess has, compared with standard design and construction, illustrates the general proposition that *all* process is likely to need drastic change in order to achieve living process.

The garden before the Uphams bought the land

2 / FINDING A SITE

THE HOUSE WAS TO BE ABOUT 2500 SQUARE FEET, A GARAGE FOR TWO CARS, TERRACES, SMALL GARDENS, A MAIN BEDROOM FOR CHRIS AND STEPHANIE, ONE FOR SASHA (STEPHANIE'S DAUGHTER), AND A THIRD SPARE ROOM.

We searched for two years for the site. I encouraged Chris and Stephanie to find a site where they had, from the outset, a strong feeling of belonging to that place.

To find the right site, with my help, occasionally we drove to a possible site and discussed it. Several that we looked at were either unsuitable or unavailable. I want to emphasize that, in keeping with the fundamental process, we rejected several sites that others might have accepted (buildable, financially sound, etc.), because they did not generate a sufficiently deep feeling of "this is ours" in Chris and Stephanie. At last, one day I got a call: "Come and look at this one." I went to a small beautiful garden, covered in flowers. It was part of another lot and was to be cut off and sold. A beautiful place, but very small, almost too small.

However, because it had the right feeling, we began the effort to build a beautiful house there, in spite of the site difficulties.

3 / FIRST ANALYSIS OF THE SITE WITH ROUGH TWISTED PAPER AND BALSA MODELS

FROM THE SITE, I FIRST DERIVED THE VOLUME AND POSITION OF THE HOUSE.

What was needed to preserve the structure of that place, that bend in the road? My first reaction was that it was a shame to destroy the beautiful garden. I talked to the seller, expressing my concern. He said that it didn't matter because he was getting old and couldn't garden anymore. But I felt that to destroy this garden might endanger or destroy the neighborhood.

The garden sat in the concave curve of a quiet street. It had a key position in the neighborhood. I noticed that to place a house there in a structure-preserving way, one would have to find a way of shaping the house, placing it, so that the beauty of the garden and the way it nourished the street could be left intact.

The idea of this was clear. What was not clear was whether the necessary volume could be put on the site without harming the street. I told the Uphams: "It is a beautiful site. But I am not sure I can do a good job there. It is so tiny; by the time we have a workable volume there, it may not be possible to preserve the quality of the street or of the garden. Before you buy the land, let's check it, to see whether a beautiful house with the qualities you want is possible there."

To check the site, I made a small clay model at 1:200 scale (1/16th inch = 1 foot) — and began playing with bits of balsa wood on this model, to find out what harmonious volume would unfold from the site itself. In essence, the problem was to find out how 2000 square feet of building

Roughest sketch model in modeling clay and balsa wood

could be put on the site, while leaving the beauty of the garden and street intact.

It turned out that it *was* possible. I was able to put the house rather snugly into the slope, not standing out, to preserve the structure of the land. The curve of the garden stayed as it was; the house and its curve preserved the system of centers formed by the garden and the curve of the street.

However, it quickly became clear that it would not be possible to build a two-car garage, without destroying the site. I had a talk with the Uphams about this. They said it was OK and that they would be satisfied with a one-car garage. With that difficulty out of the way, the overall volume of the house came, finally, as a rather awkward shape but the only relaxed and comfortable volume I could find, with its own proper centers, which made the site come to life

and left POSITIVE SPACE throughout the bowl of the site and towards the street.

To make this modeling process effective, the model was crude: bits of scrunched-up tissue paper, scraps of balsa. The roughness of the model was intentional, because it allowed me to play, move stuff around, see whether a harmonious arrangement of volume was possible. To find something good, I had to be able to play quickly, move fast, push things around. A carefully made model would have been disastrous because it would have slowed me down, constrained me by its cleanness. What was needed was a dynamic model in which I could tear things up, put them in, in which I could find out in a matter of minutes — even seconds when moving fast — whether something that preserved and extended the wholeness of that land and the surrounding buildings was truly possible.

4 / FULL-SIZE TESTS OF VOLUME AND POSITION ON THE SITE

FROM THE POSITION AND CHARACTER OF THE HOUSE VOLUME GIVEN BY THE SMALL MODEL, NEXT, ON THE SITE ITSELF AND FROM THE FEELINGS WE GOT BY WALKING THERE, WE GOT THE DETAILED DIMENSIONS OF THE VOLUME.

The next step of unfolding. With a general feeling for the overall idea of the volume from the model, we went back to the site to check it out in more detail. I stood with one of my apprentices placing stakes. The only thing we were trying to do at this stage was to get clear about any facts or fixed points that I felt we could rely on, as fixed aspects of the emerging design.

At the site, the existing terraces of flowers were more impressive than on the model. There was a clear sense of the main terrace as the focus, but it wasn't very wide. We placed stakes in such a way that this terrace seemed to become believable as a real and comfortable place.

Here we see the unfolding at work again. The terrace existed in our minds as a rough shape — a sized and positioned "thing" — but as we asked ourselves what detailed shape unfolded from this loose and general terrace idea, the shape developed and became more clear, thus creating POSITIVE SPACE in the terrace. As a result of this, a kind of gentle bow appeared in the plan, where the terrace became slightly bigger and where the house bent toward the sun.

Another thing that became very clear as a further unfolding was the strong sense one had that it was best to enter the site at the west end, up stairs close to the neighbor's existing garden stairs. This was at the opposite end from the garage, and therefore seemed surprising — even illogical — but careful walks up and down the road in front of the house, looking at the flowers, seemed to confirm a strong feeling that it was indeed best to enter the site at the western end, up

Another rough, but more detailed, clay and balsa study model

a similar small stair. It appeared that the structure of the site was preserved and extended by a stair at the left, far more than by a stair at the right. So I made the decision — which some might call irrational — of not placing the stair by the garage, but a rather long way away from it.

One further thing. Since the main terrace was *very* narrow, we felt the building wall that we began to visualize above it couldn't be too much of a cliff, since it would overshadow the terrace and make it uncomfortable. Here the structure of the site, as it existed in my mind at that time, had to be extended by subtle detail to preserve the structure of the house and not to destroy it. So I began to see a balcony or porch upstairs, essentially reducing the impact of the house volume overshadowing the terrace. Here, as a result of the unfolding process, a STRONG CENTER began developing, with GRADIENTS, and ALTERNATING REPETITION.

The small room down the hill, at the eastern (right) end of the house, already seemed like a real place — a very nice additional center of the house which formed the tail end of the house in

its cascade — and again forming graded variation, and thus strengthening the main strong center of the house.

I had very little idea about the interior plan of the house at this stage: only a rough idea of the living room in the middle, the entrance at the western end, the main bedroom upstairs — and a vague notion of the kitchen at the eastern end in the narrow wing of the house. As I told the Uphams, the crucial thing at this stage was to get the volume of the house to the stage where it had a beautiful harmony with the site. We had that now, and were lucky to have it.

Our work on the site was then summarized in a further rough model. I want to stress the ordinariness, the *apparent* awkwardness and roughness, of this model, too. As finished, the house is beautifully situated and keeps the street alive. It genuinely responds to the wholeness of the site, makes what is there more alive. In order for the house to help the street and preserve the structure of the neighborhood, the positive space which has been formed on the main terrace, in front of the house, is the crucial ingredient. It is this positiveness which maintains the neighborhood, the street, the garden.

All this became possible because of the informality of the model, which allowed the unfolding process and the center-creating process to take place unimpeded: indeed, encouraged them. I should emphasize my strong belief that an attempt to define this house volume on drawings, or by drawing, would have failed. The complex three-dimensional reality of site, house volume, space, slope, just could not have been visualized from a drawing. It was the little blocks of balsa wood themselves, and the arrangements they made on the sloping clay, that led to the volume.

A house designed in drawings, or merely staked out on the site, would probably not have come as close to preserving the wholeness of the slope as we managed, because there would have been too little information there. It was the feedback from the many errors that became visible in the tiny model while I was making it — and which could then be corrected — that made the center-creating aspect of the fundamental process work.

5 / A FIRST SKETCH

FROM THE POSITION OF THE HOUSE ON THE SITE, AS WE HAD STAKED IT OUT, I WAS ABLE TO GET A FIRST VISION OF ITS PHYSICAL CHARACTER, LIGHT, AND WINDOWS.

At this stage, I summarized the feeling of the house in a little rough pencil sketch (shown here). This was the first drawing I had made of the building.

The process of making this sketch was another step in the unfolding. The volume as I had understood it so far from the balsa wood model was, as a whole, too rough, too higgledy-piggledy, not harmonious enough. In this sketch, I gathered together what was visible in the model and on the site into a single graceful sweep which simplified the structure and made a single building form consistent with the feeling of the street.

This step of the structure-preserving process resulted in a house that was kinder to the street, and more consistent with its structure than the many-volume building suggested by the balsa wood model. The cleaning-out process — vital to all structure-preserving — introduced SIMPLICITY and INNER CALM into the emerging whole. I was getting rid of dross.

*First sketch of the house as seen from the street: this sketch adds a new overall simplicity
to the lumpy awkwardness inevitable in the rough study models*

The sketch now had the essence of the coming building. It had the volume, the feeling of masonry, the balcony upstairs with columns, the curve looking out toward the sun. It showed the bow, generated as a response to the view, swelling towards the south — and the wall of the small terrace. The balcony upstairs, stepping back the front wall of the building, was necessary because the terrace was so narrow. It came into view in the unfolding before there was even a suggestion of an upstairs plan.

Although the final building (see pages 630–31) is in *detail* quite different from this sketch, in the broad morphological sweep of the whole, it is the same. This is typical of the fundamental process, which first creates broad structure that remains intact later, even when subsequent unfolding greatly changes details.

Within this step, preservation of the existing centers of the garden, and of the centers of the street and surrounding land, had been very important; and preservation of the site's wholeness took precedence over the program. GOOD SHAPE has appeared in the building; ROUGHNESS has appeared in the entrance path; and the terrace has been formed as a BOUNDARY.

6 / CHECKING THE NEIGHBORS' VIEWS

WE NOW MODIFIED THE VOLUME TO PRESERVE FURTHER THE STRUCTURE OF THE NEIGHBORS' VIEWS.

To make sure of the volumes, we went back to the site and had someone stand with long vertical two-by-fours to show the top, roof edge, and so on as real positions. We then climbed up to the houses above us and went into their living rooms, onto their terraces, to check the views that would be left if the building stood where the two-by-fours were. We looked out from everybody's windows, decks, and gardens, all around.

We saw, from this experiment, that it would be best — for the neighbors' views and for ourselves — to tuck the house as far back *into* the hill as possible, and keep the height less than 11 feet off the ground slope at the back, and 19 feet off the ground at the front edge. These heights were recorded on a contour drawing. This insight was different from prevailing wisdom in the Berkeley hills, which would have told us to place the house on stilts, far forward on the site and up high, often as much as 25 or 30 feet off the ground for a two-story building. This "in-the-air" approach generates the cheapest foundations and is therefore common. Instead, we chose a more expensive foundation, digging deep into the hill, to preserve the hill, the garden, and the neighborhood's views.

To stay on budget, the expensive foundation had to be paid for later in the process with savings from other construction categories.

The impact of this step in the unfolding is to make the house long and narrow along the contour, thus introducing GOOD SHAPE and DEEP INTERLOCK into the volume of the building.

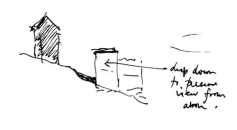

Tucking the building down into the land,
to maintain the neighbors' views

7 / FIRST EMERGENCE OF AN INTERIOR PLAN

THE FIRST ROUGH IDEAS OF ROOMS AND ROOM
PLACEMENT EMERGED BY GOING INWARD FROM
THE HOUSE VOLUME, WITH THE FUNDAMENTAL
PROCESS.

In my first version of the house, the great
curve, from the sketch, was a wonderful living
room, full of light, in the middle of the house.
The entrance was to one end (left on the accompanying plan sketch); other rooms were grouped
around the right end, stepping downhill. The
house would be entered from the northwest, and
a stair would run up the back side of the house,
to the second floor.

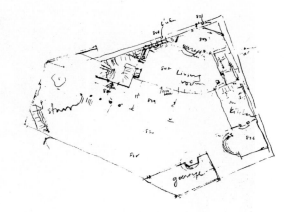

First sketch of interior layout.

8 / EXTENSION OF THE LOT: THE LITTLE PLUM TREE

WE NOW UNDERTOOK TO PRESERVE THE
STRUCTURE OF THE LAND EVEN MORE DEEPLY BY
ARRANGING FOR OUR CLIENTS TO BUY A BIT OF
LAND WHICH HAD A SMALL PLUM TREE WHOSE
PRESENCE HAD A PROFOUND EMOTIONAL EFFECT
ON THE HOUSE.

In the conception of the house which had
unfolded so far, the entrance, with a porch, was
to be at the western end. With the plan in mind,
I stood roughly on the site of the proposed porch
at the western end of the house and noticed that
as things stood, it was really too close to the lot
boundary to be a nice entrance. In addition, the
city had an ordinance which restricted the total
area of the house to 40 percent of the site area.
Given the very tiny site, and the configuration
which was developing, this would have forced
the house to be slightly too small.

Where I stood, just next to me was a little
plum tree standing at the western end of the
site — a beautiful spot, with a flat terrace, flowers, a couple of chairs. It had a magic and a pleas-

antness which would not really be present on the
site without it. To make the house have life, the
house *needed* that tree. I suggested to Chris and
Stephanie that the small area with the plum tree
to the west was needed to make this porch work,
by giving it a spark of life and a bit more space.

The same point may be understood, too, in
terms of unfolding. The site with the house as we
had roughly located it and this tree together
formed a complex. In this complex, the plum tree
itself and the space which connected it to the
house formed an essential center that was at that
stage only *latent*. This latent center might simply
be described as a potentially beautiful place to
the west of the house, where house and plum tree
together had the capacity to form a wonderful
"thing," a center. But this center was nearly
there; it almost existed already. In the unfolding
of wholeness, this center had, therefore, to be
preserved, cherished, extended. Without it, the
site as we were experiencing it would have been
lessened, damaged.

The beautiful little plum tree

I suggested to Chris and Stephanie that we broach the difficult topic of adding this piece of land to the property in our next discussion with the sellers. At first they refused. I wrote them a letter explaining that without this piece of land, the size restrictions imposed by the lot area would make the necessary house almost un-buildable. We held discussions for several weeks. Finally, they agreed to sell. Even then, an ex-traordinary number of special legal measures were needed to make the lot adjustment possible.

It took three months of work to get this one little thing. Its only purpose, really, was to inten-sify the one existing center — the terrace — with another — the kitchen porch — and to use the center created by the existing plum tree to make this possible. In the course of doing it, various subtle steps had to be taken to make the bound-aries just right within the restriction of the zon-ing ordinance — for example, a few feet too many and the sellers' original property would be-come illegal. We also positioned the boundary in

such a way as to intensify the beauty of the sell-ers' garden, too, in that area, its terrace walls and bushes.

The parcel which was formed when we added the plum tree was odd in shape and caused some legal nuisance. But this nuisance was re-quired if we were to follow the rule that the wholeness had to be obeyed and extended. This

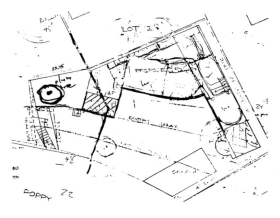

Extension of the lot, to include the plum tree

devotion to the wholeness, and the protection and weaving in of the plum tree, let the process of the house design and layout take an unusual path: It made everyone conscious of the wholeness, and breathed a special life into the process. The house itself also benefited enormously.

The odd shape of the new lot is a perfect example of ROUGHNESS coming into existence as a result of unfolding. The site, as originally drawn, was a regular five-sided figure. To intensify its wholeness, it had now become an irregular polygon, with a small piece stitched onto the larger shape. The roughness arose directly from the unfolding process.

9 / DEEPER QUESTIONS ABOUT THE FEELING OF THE PLAN

I BEGAN TO QUESTION THE DISPOSITION OF THE MAJOR ROOMS WITHIN THE HOUSE.

In the evolution of the plan so far, a certain pleasant feeling was emerging, more or less from careful attention to practical points, one by one: the preservation of the garden and the street, the volume of the house stepping back, the size of the terrace to make it comfortable, the beauty of the little plum tree.

But in the course of paying daily attention to feeling, one also sometimes has the experience of *wrong* feeling developing: The work does not always go right. Then one has to seize this intuition that the emerging form is wrong, stay with it, and change things at the right moment, to act upon the deep character of the form without drastic repercussion on cost.

That is what now happened in the evolution of the house interior. So far, what had followed from the volume and site, and from the location of the entrance at the left end, was a rough idea of the ground floor — the main entrance at the left, then the kitchen, then a big irregular living room in the middle, then a spare room or study at the far right end (visible in sketch on page 580).

As we got used to the site, I became uneasy about this arrangement since I knew the light in the living room might be murky, not beautiful, and the distance to walk from entrance to kitchen to living room seemed too cumbersome. I also had an uneasy sense that this layout did not arise naturally from the true nature of the Uphams' life, the character of their relationship, their feelings. In short, I had a dim sense that this house, as presently conceived, did not yet have enough that they would experience as profound feeling: It did not go to the heart of family life as they knew it.

I therefore suggested that they come and speak with me, privately, in my own house, over a few drinks, so we could discuss the uneasiness that I was feeling.

10 / A DEEPER CONCEPTION OF THE LIVING ROOM

THE UNFOLDING PROCESS NOW TOOK A DECISIVE TURN. BY REEXAMINING THE EMOTIONAL CONFIGURATION OF THE FAMILY'S DAILY LIFE, THE FUNDAMENTAL PROCESS LED US ALL TO A NEW SENSE OF THE NATURE OF THE LIVING ROOM.

When Chris and Stephanie got to my house, I asked them to describe, in more detail, the main centers in the house, as they now imagined them. I pressed hard, and asked that they describe the key centers in the house again, as vividly as possible. During this discussion, Stephanie finally broke down in tears, because she described her family as not real enough. It seemed to me that her tears were a lament for what she had lost by being the owner of a very successful children's clothing factory. A vision of a small rosy room, with its fire and comfortable chairs tightly grouped around, slowly came into being. Perhaps it arose directly from her lament, a place of comfort where her wounds could be healed: simple, small, warm, and strongly formed by GOOD SHAPE and LOCAL SYMMETRY.- Embedded in the plan, at its core somewhere, we had begun to imagine an intense smaller center at the very heart — quite different in feeling from the large living room we had originally shown in the earlier plan. This new room was small, deeply embedded, intense, compact. It was the center of the center.

This deep-lying center also arose from structure-preserving transformations — in this instance, from the character of Stephanie Upham's feeling.

I have often found that the fifteen properties — in this case, the small nugget-like rosy center — often come in almost archetypal fashion, from close adherence to the deep feelings people really have. It was I, not she, who started the process that brought this to light. But it was *her* feeling, the reality of *her* family life, which made it true, made it a productive and essential part of the unfolding process.

11 / LAYING THE HOUSE OUT ON THE LAND

NOW WE ESTABLISHED THE PHYSICAL GEOMETRY OF THE HOUSE FOOTPRINT IN DETAIL.

To get the layout of the ground floor more clear — getting the other ground-floor rooms in relation to this core — Gary Black (vice president of CES), Stephen Duff (one of my apprentices), the Uphams and I now staked out the whole ground floor of the house, room by room, on the land, as accurately as we could from what we then knew.

Afterward, working from these stakes, we constructed an exact plot of the house shape (shown in the drawing on this page). It was the first time we had seen an accurate picture of the house plan, based on detailed understanding of its relation to the land.

I want to stress the fact that the *stakes* came first, not the drawing. The drawing was made *from* the stakes. This is the opposite of the procedure architects more typically follow, by which they first draw a building on paper, and then use stakes on the land to indicate what they have drawn.

In the course of placing stakes, many points of the design became more clear: for instance, the profile of the front wall with the terrace as a thick BOUNDARY, and the position of the back retaining wall with the slope above it as another thick boundary made of STRONG CENTERS.

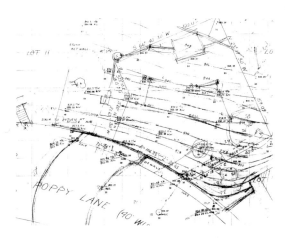

First stakes marking the terrace, and the south face of the building volume

12 / STARTING TO GET A GENERAL IDEA
OF CONSTRUCTION

DURING THIS TIME, I BEGAN TO ASK MYSELF WHAT OVERALL FEELING OF MATERIAL AND BUILDING CONSTRUCTION WE SHOULD AIM FOR: I TRIED TO DERIVE THE PROPER FEELING FROM THE FEELING OF THE LAND.

In a conventional process, one might now have gone on to develop the plan in more detail. But the unfolding process has peculiar demands. Having the core idea of the ground floor clear — emotionally — I noticed that what was missing now, most strikingly from the whole, was a sense of how this house was to be *made*.

It followed, therefore, that the next most significant aspect of the whole which had to be made clear was its actual material and substance. This arose, at this moment, because the vision of the core room, so deeply felt by the Uphams, was very physical, very material, in nature. It felt solid, more like plaster or masonry than like wood. We could not therefore really go forward without having a more developed understanding of this material aspect of the whole.

So I put to our group the following question, as we worked: What is the house made of? Can we feel its essence, its substance? What are its materials? What is it, as one sees it from the outside, enters it, walks about in it? In more detail, what is its general construction method, what are its materials, even what is its overall color?

In these discussions, I concentrated, at this early stage, and sought to lead the discussion, only on the most global aspects of construction: the weight, the relative curviness or straightness. What is the density? What is the overall feeling of the real material thing going to be? What feeling was consistent with the site, and with the emerging whole?

First cardboard model to explore the possible forms of material, construction, and color which might be consistent with the emerging whole

*Trying to imagine a texture of
concrete block and plaster*

Testing wall texture using blocks

Chris Upham on the site

*First mockup of poured concrete shapes
with cement plaster and styrofoam insets*

Another experiment trying a combination of red pavers, white plaster strips, brick, concrete, and concrete block

At this very early stage, we got the idea that the house would be made of concrete block. As a group, we began to see a balance of pale yellow washed over concrete block, with gray bands of ornament. The ornament on the blocks and poured concrete wall introduced LEVELS OF SCALE; the bands of ornament created ALTERNATING REPETITION. I was not sure yet whether these bands of ornament were poured or specially made block. To answer the question, I asked my apprentices to test some possible ornaments, likely colors, and different arrangements and mixes of these colors on what we now knew the rough volume of the house to be. And even at this early stage, I already started looking at the character of ornament in some detail. My apprentices and I started building possible blocks, poured-concrete blocks, and block and concrete walls in our construction yard. We made up some blocks which gave indications of a possible ornamented, but heavy structure. Some of these, with in-cut stars and crosses, were closer in feeling than others to the gestalt which was emerging from the unfolding process. The one that came closest was based on a Japanese ornamental concrete block. These details, even going to the actual ornamental shapes themselves and the sense of concrete, helped to fix the feeling of the house. The thickness of the concrete masonry introduced the possibility of BOUNDARIES at a smaller scale. We could judge, even now, that some of these ornaments had more business on the site than others, and this helped to establish the character of coming centers in the larger structure.

It should be borne in mind that at this stage we still did not yet know the room plan of the house in detail. But we were beginning to get a feeling for the building as a material structure.

13 / ESTABLISHING ROOMS

THE NEXT CENTERS TO BE ESTABLISHED WERE THE MAIN DOWNSTAIRS ROOMS.

Having the substance of the house clear, the unfolding process naturally turned back to the plan because the plan relationships and centers forming the plan were now the *next* most important features which must emerge from the emerging wholeness: a wholeness which now consisted of an uncertain plan with a small compact living room at its core — within a structure made of concrete or masonry.

I had by now completely abandoned the overall plan which I had while I was first deciding the house volume. That first plan had its stair too far from the main center; its big living room had nothing to do with the vision of the small intense rose-painted room I had seen. Instead, given the core importance of the small compact living room, I now placed the stair towards the back of the footprint triangle — with an entrance room in front of it, thus making this entrance room the very center of the house and intensifying it as a STRONG CENTER properly, making a GRADIENT to the stair at the back. That left the main room to the right of the entrance room, also as a strong center, but small, as it had to be to catch the Uphams' feelings.

The next center which became clear was a rather large kitchen, with a big table to one side, where the Uphams were to eat. This living kitchen had not been clear at first, but now we got from our discussion with Stephanie a picture of a big hollow room, spare, quiet, not too decorated, where the family was to cook and eat. At this moment, this kitchen became clear in character — but not, at first, yet clear in its position. However, it was time now to fix positions.

Where to put the kitchen? East or west of the living room? After thinking about the sunshine in the kitchen, the little plum tree, and

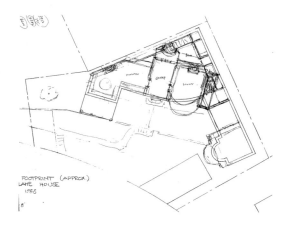

First-floor plan sketch with its major centers worked out.

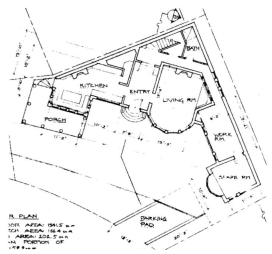

As drawn for submission to the city of Berkeley for the building permit

the approach to the house, we all together (the Uphams and my staff and I) decided to place the kitchen at the northwestern end where the porch had been on earlier sketches. Remaining rooms went to the southeastern end.

The combination of kitchen, stair, and living room now effectively defined the new layout of the house within the given volume. We drew the plan and prepared a set of preliminary drawings ready for submission to the city of Berkeley.

14 / UPSTAIRS ROOMS

WE ALSO TRIED — UNSUCCESSFULLY — TO GET THE UPSTAIRS ROOMS AS LIVING CENTERS.

I knew that it was too early to understand the upstairs rooms, since we were not yet standing on the second floor to judge them. However, we tried to get an upstairs layout, mainly to apply for a building permit and satisfy building requirements; it is shown here. Perhaps the most notable thing about this layout is the fact that by the time the construction process reached the upstairs, the drawn layout turned out to be entirely wrong and was then redone completely. Of all the upstairs rooms on this early plan, only one — the small bedroom at the southern end of the house — remained as it was.

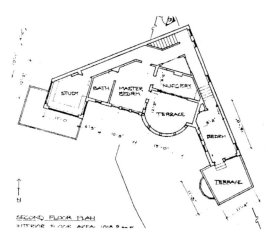

Upstairs plan as drawn for building permit

The wholeness which one needed to see in order to determine the rooms upstairs just was not yet visible, so it is not surprising that these judgments could not yet be made.

It is remarkable that the architect's belief in his own powers dies hard. No matter how many time I tell myself that perhaps, just this once, I can work out what has to be done in a building without being there, in the event I am always proved wrong, and it always turns out that the influences from nearby parts of the building and its environment which will determine and generate the plan, make a decisive impact not predictable at the time the building existed as a drawing (see page 610, below, where the second floor as it actually unfolded later, is shown in a plan view).

15 / ANALYSIS OF COST

IN PREPARATION FOR SETTLING THE WAY THAT WE WERE GOING TO BUILD THE HOUSE — REAL DETAILS OF CONSTRUCTION — WE HAD, SOME TIME EARLIER, BEGUN A CAREFUL ANALYSIS OF COST.

In the program-budgeting method I have used for years, we sit down, *before the building has been designed*, and make a plan of how to spend the money. That is — for a given amount of money, which is usually set at the beginning — we decide how much should be spent on walls, roof, foundations, terraces, exterior works, interior furnishing, and so on.

It is interesting to see how much of the picture of the finished building can be built up, merely by assigning numbers to the different operations and elements. For example, in the buildings I build we typically spend much more on construction of adjacent outdoor areas and spaces than is spent in other projects; we also spend more on the *structure* of the building than is spent in typical California buildings. From the very beginning, this has an effect on the architecture and on the whole way one sees the site.

In fact, one is able to visualize, judge, and modify the design, just from the numbers, even at this earliest stage when there is only a list of numbers on a piece of paper. *The list of numbers IS the earliest design.* It can already be visualized, experienced, from the point of view of the feeling it is likely to create.

In the case of the Upham house, our first cost picture of the building allocated rough numbers to foundations, walls, roof, windows, interior. This was an analysis made during early conceptual design. The problem with the first cost picture was that the overall cost was too high, and far more important, in proportion certain items seemed intuitively too low or too high, relative to one another, for the building that was imagined.

We then made a second educated guess about how costs ought to be apportioned, in the design, in order to make the overall feeling of the building sensible, and coherent. Here, for instance, we put high costs for windows (knowing that many large and beautiful windows were essential to the design). We put in expensive interior plaster work, also essential; and we put in masonry walls.

When we found out that these costs ran too high, we then had to decide how to keep things in proportion, keep the important things important (in terms of what was to be spent on them) and yet bring the whole cost picture to the level that the clients requested.

Some of the items we cut or raised in price, or lowered in price, may seem surprising by contemporary standards. We used more expensive flat roof membrane (since roof quality was essential in a flat roof building); we kept masonry construction on the first floor wall. We increased expenditure on outdoor items, but we removed a porch as inessential to the overall feeling. We kept terrazzo in the kitchen, but determined that it could be done by students, while the grinding of terrazzo could be done by Chris Upham, thus taking an expensive item, allowing it to keep its quality, but cutting its cost drastically.

On the other hand, we had cheap knotty-pine planks in the upstairs floor; kept wide cherry floorboards in the living room. Other things were reduced, too. Bathroom fixtures and toilets were kept low. The client agreed to paint the building interior and the exterior windows.

This judgment about the assignment of costs, what was reasonable, what created a good atmosphere, was based on the feeling which the whole had when one visualized the whole created by the budget amounts to be spent on different items.

16 / CONCRETE WALL DETAILS

WITHIN THE FRAMEWORK OF A TIGHTENED COST PICTURE, WITH PERCENTAGE OF 15 PERCENT ALLOCATED TO THE MAIN STRUCTURAL WALL OF THE HOUSE, DETAILS OF TECHNIQUE, SHAPE, AND FIGURE BEGAN TO EMERGE FROM THE MOCKUPS OF THE WALL CONSTRUCTION ELEMENTS.

Two things had been going ahead. As our cost picture was getting more detailed, we were starting to get bids from subcontractors on key items. We were also making progress on a number of items where the bid was not yet in or we didn't know how to perform the subcontract. Two examples were (1) the concrete front wall of the house and (2) the interior plasterwork. We were now sure that at least the lower floor of this building was to have concrete walls; but it had become clear, from the analysis of available money, that we could not afford to do the same upstairs — so we decided to use beautifully formed and poured concrete downstairs, and a cheaper, thick heavy concrete-like stucco over wood frame upstairs. I wanted the building to be something of permanent value — not like so much lightweight two-by-four frame construction, a temporary building which would be derelict after fifty years.

I began trying to imagine the concrete structure of the downstairs wall: columns, beams, openings, capitals. It was hard to visualize in detail. I tried sketching it, but couldn't get enough of a sense from the sketches; the problems were all three-dimensional, too hard to visualize in drawings. My apprentices made small models; but there wasn't enough detail in those models either, not enough to grasp.

Besides, the problem of cost of the formwork was looming as a huge problem. How could we build the complex shapes and articulation of columns, beams, capitals, frames — and not lose our shirts. How could we succeed in doing it within the budget.

I decided that the only way to get an idea of this thing was to build some full-size mockups in cardboard. Randy Schmidt (one of the main CES craftsmen on the job) and James Maguire (one of the CES construction managers) built a complete bay of the structure in cardboard, at full size. Interestingly, it was terrible at first, very crude. This is interesting because that first cardboard mockup exactly followed the drawings. It just showed us how far from a workable and desirable three-dimensional configuration the structure imagined in the first sketches had actually been.

It is worth noting that many of today's buildings which do not use such an unfolding process are doomed to just these kinds of mistakes, since in contemporary practice it is the drawn details which actually get *built*.

We made a second mockup, including a series of changes, looking at them while we did them. In heavy corrugated cardboard, this was very easy. The size of the columns, the offset of

*Looking at the cardboard mockup on the site,
to test its feeling in relation to the site*

the columns in front of the panel, the degree to which the beam came out over the columns — these aspects all changed during our efforts to make the configuration more harmonious, more real, and to give it deeper feeling.

And how could a capital be made, to make sense within this system? This was very hard to imagine because it was so complex with regard to water exclusion and flashings. But in the full-size cardboard reality, we began to be able to imagine the physical arrangement the flashings would need to have.

In the end, after a few days' work, we got shapes which meant something. They had solidity and feeling in proportion and mass. As a result of the development of the full-size cardboard models, GOOD SHAPE had made its appearance in the column capitals; CONTRAST, in the degree of offset between capital and shaft; ALTERNATING REPETITION, in the rhythm of columns and bay spacing; LEVELS OF SCALE, in the small details of reveal and depth in the modeling of the concrete surface.

*Cardboard mockup of wall construction. This mockup was very detailed, full size, and allowed us
to check the offset between one plane and another to the nearest half inch and quarter inch*

The columns, the bays, the thin column capitals, the panels above and below the windows — and, of course, the windows themselves and the reveals — all existed as substantial centers in their own right. It was this process, the instilling of the centers with life, in these construction details, which gave the whole process its energy — and its success.

17 / PLASTERWORK EXPERIMENTS

COMPARABLE DETAILS BEGAN TO EMERGE FOR THE INTERIOR PLASTERWORK (DETAILS WHOSE CHARACTER WAS STARTING TO BE WORKED OUT NOW) EVEN THOUGH THE ACTUAL PLASTER WAS STILL NOT GOING TO BE BUILT FOR SEVERAL MONTHS.

Before I knew how to make the plasterwork surface inside the building, I knew we would need to cast the panels ourselves, but didn't yet know how to do it. We began experiments. Randy Schmidt started a number of plaster models, exploring the possibility of making flowers and other simple reliefs in plaster and trying the kind of casting techniques we might be able to use. What we were looking for was a treatment of detail in the plaster which would have a shimmering surface in the large, and be simple and touching in feeling: NOT-SEPARATENESS and INNER CALM. We did the experiments by gluing cardboard and balsa wood surfaces, then casting from them, until surfaces began to appear which had a feeling of light in them.

By the end of these experiments with real casting plaster, the plaster panels emerged as flower-covered surfaces, embellished with leaves and latticework.

Closeup of one type of floral ornament which we tried

Early experiments in trying to make beautiful, but inexpensive, plaster panels for the interior

18 / START OF CONSTRUCTION

WE STARTED CONSTRUCTION IN OCTOBER 1990.

The idea of the house, as far as we knew it at this stage, was encompassed by the model shown on this page. In these days of working drawings, it seems peculiar to say that what we knew, at that moment, was what is visible in this rough model and little more. But that is the truth. We understood the broad configuration, and we understood, at this early stage, approximately how we were going to make it. Not much more. That is the honest truth.

Uncomfortable as it may be to admit it, in this age of hundreds of detailed working drawings for a comparatively simple building, that just is so. But I want to insist that the existence of this limited and partial knowledge, not full knowledge, at any given stage of the unfolding, *is of the essence of the unfolding process*. In a true unfolding process, you know certain things at different stages, but what you know about what is going to happen more than a few steps ahead, is always rather limited. That is the essence of unfolding.

And that is necessary in order to allow the unfolding process to occur. Rough as it is, this model showed us what we truly *knew* at this stage, together with a few construction details. Everything else was still unknown, and had yet to be unfolded.

Rough model of final conception, as we imagined it before we started to build

19 / THE RETAINING WALL

THE MOST IMMEDIATE PROBLEM WE HAD TO SOLVE WAS THE CONSTRUCTION OF THE RETAINING WALL TO HOLD UP THE MAJOR HILL BEHIND THE HOUSE.

In this building, the cost plan for the retaining wall and foundation was enormous: a subcontract of $90,000. We had already spent a lot of time getting ready for this subcontract to start, once again from the point of view of cost. Most bids for the work had been very high, on the order of $140,000. In our cost plan, we had allocated some $90,000, and not a penny more. To conform with the cost plan, we now began a search for a flexible method of doing the huge retaining and foundation job within the $90,000 budget.

While this work was getting prepared, we were making final changes in the way the piers would be drilled, to keep within the budget. There was a huge technical problem: the back of the retaining wall. How were we going to build it without massive formwork, and in such a way as to build a $140,000 retaining-wall system for about $90,000. The problem was that if we excavated the hill, it would need massive shoring to hold it up while the retaining wall was being formed and poured. This was aggravated by the prospects of rain, a wet hillside, and the weight of the existing house directly above, which might cause a cave-in.

With Stanley, our foundation subcontractor, we worked out an ingenious method which involved drilling long deep piers, reinforcing them, pouring them, excavating around them, and then filling in between with a poured retaining wall. The piers were big enough and close enough together to hold the hillside temporarily while the final wall was formed and placed between them. The photograph shows this technique, when the piers were half built and being excavated.

The piers exposed after drilling and pouring, and ready for forming the foundation and retaining wall between the piers

20 / MANAGEMENT AGREEMENT THAT FEELING MUST GUIDE EVEN THE MOST TECHNICAL ASPECTS OF CONSTRUCTION

THE NEED FOR FLEXIBLE DECISION-MAKING IN THE SEQUENCE OF CRITICAL CONSTRUCTION OPERATIONS FORCED A HIGHLY FLEXIBLE APPROACH TO CONSTRUCTION MANAGEMENT.

I had a talk with James Maguire who was then running the construction for CES. He told me about some problems he saw coming, including the position of underslab plumbing, the framing contract, setting the foundation boards, and a few others. In the course of discussion, I reminded him that he must be as relaxed as possible about the small details, which could always be solved one way or another — but that the big questions about the building, especially the most important open questions about coming major centers, must be kept open and flexible, with our minds constantly on them.

For example, the plan of the kitchen wasn't right yet. We didn't know if the room was OK or not. It had a strange shape on the drawing. If kitchen and living room weren't good, the house would be a failure. We therefore had to make sure that Stanley, the foundation subcontractor, was coordinated with our schedule. I wanted to have at least ten days of decision time set aside after he made his cut into the slope, so that we could stand on the real land, before he started drilling. Why? Because when he began to drill his front line of piers, that would essentially fix the front structural wall of the house.

If it was going to be necessary to make any changes in the shape or size of the two main rooms, that was the last time we would be able to do it, since it might turn out that we would have to modify the front line of drilling, or the front foundation form, to give the two main rooms a more beautiful shape.

This is a perfect example of how, within the fundamental process, feeling must enter even into major technical decisions.

21 / SETTING THE MAIN-FLOOR LEVEL

THE FINAL POSITION OF THE MAIN-FLOOR LEVEL CAME FROM A PROCESS DONE STANDING ON THE SITE.

On October 30, 1990, we set levels for the benching process. Walking on the site, standing on buckets, planks, judging the right height for different parts of the floor. After trying different dimensions the main-floor height was judged to be best at 24 inches above terrace height, instead of the 30 inches shown on the drawings.

This judgment was based, in part, on a straightforward combination of comfort and psychology. It simply *felt* most satisfactory. But this explanation does not fully explain the coher-ence which it created. To grasp it more fully, this "right floor height" that was finally chosen may also be understood as creation of a living center. It was the dimension which made the space between the terrace and the main-floor positive and comfortable. If you imagine the terrace as several steps below the floor there was, floating above the terrace, a slab of space, the same size and plan as the terrace and — depending on the decision that was to be made — either 30 inches or 24 inches thick. This slab of space hovering above the terrace, and connecting it to the main floor, had the potential to become a center, and was judged to be best, most life-supporting within the project as a whole, when the offset was 24 inches. At that dimension, the whole configuration created the most POSITIVE SPACE and GOOD SHAPE. This could be assessed by the methods described in Book 1, chapters 8 and 9, according to the feeling of wholesomeness which it created in us, the observers.

You see how even this very simple decision — like nearly every other in the process — was based on experiment. It was the choice of that dimension which created the most profound sense of life, well-being, wholeness in us, the observers — and was experienced by all of us, jointly, in that way.

22 / EXCAVATION

A MINOR CRISIS. WE HAD TO KEEP THE FOUNDATION SUBCONTRACTOR'S METHODS CONSISTENT WITH THE PROCESS OF UNFOLDING, NOT WITH HIS USUAL MODE.

I went up to the site and found that Stanley, our foundation subcontractor, had dug far too much away from the back of rooms, in order to prepare for pouring the retaining wall foundation. He had — before he started — been specifically told not to do this, but did it anyway because he had a convenient piece of equipment up there, and wanted to use it as much as possible.

I insisted that he hadn't had the right, and that according to our contract it had been agreed that we would look at the ground-floor plan of the house (and perhaps modify it) while excavation was going on, so that we could check details of wall positions. Now he had made this impossible because the site was so deeply cut up that no one could walk about: there were 3- and 4-foot drops, and we couldn't even stand on any one level bit of ground to imagine floor levels and so feel the reality of kitchen, front entrance room, and living room.

It was a difficult situation. Several days of phone calls; some upset. Finally, I was able to persuade the contractor that his crew had violated our agreement. They built plywood platforms for us, very cheap temporary ones, over the areas they had cut in error. This accomplished, we were in a position to start the fine-tuning of the ground-floor plan.

23 / FINE-TUNING THE PLAN AS WE FIXED FORMS FOR THE FOUNDATION WALLS

NOVEMBER 9. A NUMBER OF MAJOR DECISIONS WERE NOW MADE JUST BEFORE FOUNDATION FORMS WERE SET AND BUILT.

Kitchen fireplace position. The kitchen fireplace position (as drawn) was terrible. It could not be built where it was shown on the drawing since, as now became clear, it would ruin both halves of the room and split them. It had to be moved back. We moved it back 18 inches. From this, an entirely different feeling. Now the fireplace didn't jut into the room; it was comfortable for the sitting area, and nice to look at from the doorway. We also moved it six inches to the north so it fit nicely between two of the massive piers in the retaining wall.

Kitchen porch. As it turned out, the porch on the south face of the kitchen (on the real site) was narrower than we thought by about nine inches. I felt it was too narrow now to be pleasant. We had the option of extending the retaining wall out to make the porch, or to abandon the porch altogether and make it a pathway. It wasn't a natural place to sit anyway, as it turned out. I decided to give up this porch altogether.

Workroom floor level. The offset from the workroom level to the main floor was 15 inches as cut. We made the workroom nine inches lower, and dealt with drainage problem and waterproofing problem at the French window.

Spare room at the end. The spare room was a beautiful place. I was sure Stephanie would end up using it for herself. Very nice, nestled down low in the site. To keep this nestled feeling, we left its level as it was cut.

Stair coming down to the workroom. This interior stair needed to be further back, away from the workroom, to create psychological space. We started down by the bathroom door, and put winders in the stair to make that possible.

Living room bow. Quite a surprise. The bow of the window was bigger than on the drawing. Don't know why. It was very splendid. Was going to get lots of light. Moved the center of gravity of the room toward the south where this splendid bow was. Left as is, though surprising. Serendipity.

Living room door. We moved the door of the living room back from the house front door, to make a more generous and sensible center in the living room, on the right as you go in. Now the main fireplace to the left as you walked in (as shown on the drawing, on the back wall) seemed silly. Too squashed. It was impossible, by the look of it, to get significant light in above the retaining wall. We proposed moving fireplace to the long wall of the living room.

Main fireplace position. I asked Randy if it would cause chaos if we moved the chimney

We started to understand the position of the fireplace in the kitchen, and began making adjustments in its position. It was a situation where a foot in one direction or the other radically changed the feeling of connection between the kitchen and the big bay window eating area; and this fireplace was itself hampered in position by the back wall of the house, which was a major retaining wall that had to be built at the very start. Because the fireplace needed its own foundation, this position was critical very early on and had to be decided.

away from its position on the back wall, as far as the upstairs was concerned. No, he said, it was just taking up valuable space now. So we did it.

Line of doors. Tried moving the door from entrance room to living room even further back in the entrance room. It didn't help, somehow made the room seem funny inside. By moving doors, the line-up between living room door and kitchen door was no longer quite as nice. So we didn't change it.

24 / THE LILY TILES

THERE WAS A BREATHING SPACE DURING THE NEXT FEW WEEKS. DURING THIS TIME, THE BUILDING AS IT HAD DEVELOPED SO FAR NOW BEGAN ALLOWING ME TO GENERATE THE CHARACTER OF CERTAIN ORNAMENTS.

While the work on the floorplan changes was going on, I started to think about other details that would affect the house. I had been enjoying the idea of making small tiles to put in the front foundation wall. The first sketches I made of these tiles were of a small black octagon, with a yellow, red, and lilac star on it. I sized it against a bit of real concrete, and then made a tile sample. It seemed rather crude. Then I started wondering if the form of the insert should be tall and delicate, not squat and hard like an octagon. When I had first seen the site, there had been several tall pink lilies growing there. They suggested lilies as ornaments which might decorate the lower part of the foundation: I started to

Early experiments with an octagonal tile and a lily tile, to see which one fit better
into the landscape and into the wholeness of the site

*Holding up a full-sized drawing of a lily, in the rough position on the site where
it would occur, to see if it feels harmonious and fitting.*

imagine that the inserts might be lilies, also made of tile, but more realistic. The technical difficulty of making big clay lilies would have been formidable, but I pressed on anyway. I tried more mockups. Meanwhile, another version of the black octagon tile worked out better, with a delicate color, and began to feel right. I took it to the site to check its feeling.

The tiny question, octagon with star or naturalistic lilies, as the ornaments for the front foundation wall was growing in importance. I was very much aware that the main rooms were not yet fixed: The spaces of living room and kitchen were crucial but not yet perfect at all. I had the odd, intuitive sense that getting clear about this small decorative tile — whether to go for the geometry of the octagon, or the organic character of the lily — would help establish the nature of the house and would then guide the evolution of larger questions about living room space and kitchen space.

After a few weeks of reflection, the lily tiles were beginning to seem like the right thing to do, especially since the lilies themselves originated on that land. Randy and Lizabeth (my assistants) and I met on site to look at my first sketches of the lily tiles.[6] On site, the sketches were horrifying, too big, too gross. The big lily I

First painting of the final lily tile

597

had drawn on paper, about 18 inches high, did not in any sense feel harmonious with the land or with the house as we saw it or visualized its foundation. This feeling was clear, palpable. Also—a practical detail—we found out that the tiles couldn't be seen from the road—so whatever we put there would be seen only from close-to, from 10 or 15 feet from the house. Given that fact, the size of lily that felt natural was about seven inches high, not 18 inches as I had thought at first. We could feel, as we did experiments at four, five, seven, and nine inches, that the seven-inch lily was a natural continuation of what was there. All three of us saw this clearly and agreed.

On the other hand, the octagon I had already made did look beautiful. Color was vital to the place. One lily I drew on paper—a small watercolor—also looked very good. It was a red lily, green stem, sky-blue background. But after looking for a while, it seemed too sweet. Then we tried (one person held it up, while the others looked at it) a painting I had done of a red lily, with yellow spots, green leaves, blackish gray ground. This looked better.

We went back to my workshop and started making a three-dimensional lily in clay. The idea of a clay lily directly set in concrete which I had started with was not practical—I couldn't

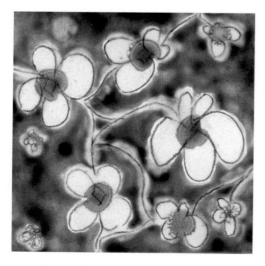

Blossom tile: another early tile experiment

figure out how to attach so many pieces to the formwork. So I tried a small clay plaque, the size of the painting—only seven inches high, with the lily in relief within the plaque—and the idea that we could cast recesses in the concrete wall of the foundation to hold these plaques.

After looking at the first rough lily plaques tried by Randy and Lizabeth, I asked for the clay they were using and began a much more basic thing, in which negative and positive really worked (POSITIVE SPACE). This meant rebuilding the whole lily design from scratch, as a low relief. It changed the design quite strongly. I played with the clay until its centers were more powerful (the leaves as centers, the space between leaves as centers, and the borders of the tile as centers). Then we made a plaster mold from the modeling clay, tried pulling a few clay tiles from the mold, and fired them. Meanwhile, a glazing sample began looking quite good, though a bit harsh compared with the subtle color of the octagon. I made many different color studies, on paper and with glazes, until the color of the tile began to feel right on the site. The one which had the deepest feeling was a striking color, with a red ground, purple surround, and yellow and orange glazes for the lily itself.

After a few days, we had eight of these lily tiles in a row and could see them on the site. We compared them with the octagon which I had still not given up completely. After thinking about it for six or seven days, I began to feel clearly that the lily was more true to the house than the octagon. The octagon was more elegant. But the lily had more of the real "original" feeling of the site.

From this, my knowledge of the emerging house took a huge jump. I saw the house changed. The unfolding had progressed not only in the emergence of this one detail, but in some subtle way that also changed feelings and qualities in the larger whole.

In effect, the size and color of the ornamental tiles unfolded from the size and character and spacing of the tile positions along the foundation wall.

Various hand-glazed lily tiles

25 / PLACING AND FINE-TUNING FIRST-FLOOR ROOMS

A MONTH OR TWO LATER, MOST OF THE FOUN-
DATIONS AND SLAB WERE IN. WE COULD BEGIN
TO VISUALIZE THE HOUSE IN EARNEST.

The essence of what we did now was to re-
form the rooms while standing on the newly
poured slab, and give them their final shape according to what we experienced there.

Standing on the slab, we could see the
wholeness, as it then was, of the ground floor of
the house. We could sense, feel, the right way to
divide this up into rooms. Even when they were

roughly the same as the division we already had
in mind on the drawings, we could now see *exactly* where to place each partition wall, because
the space was real and each room could be felt —
and then established — as a real center in its
own right.

We laid the rooms out in chalk, on the slab.
Several partitions moved a few inches. The main
thing is that we did it in such a way as to make
each room a beautiful and solid center in its own
right, where we *felt* comfortable.

Settling positions of columns, to form the bays and window openings of the living room bay window

26 / MAKING AND PLACING THE FIRST-FLOOR WALL

FROM THE NEW FIRST-FLOOR PLAN, WITH ITS ROOMS CHALKED OUT, WE NOW WENT ON TO FIX THE COLUMNS AND WINDOWS WHICH WOULD DEFINE THE FRONT WALL OF THE HOUSE.

This front wall was the poured concrete wall which was going to determine the load-bearing structure and appearance of the house. We had already decided earlier (see pages 588–89) that the wall of the house was to consist of articulated columns, beams, panels, and windows within the panels.

The method we used to make the decisions was ingenious. We had worked it out so that we would use the actual plywood forms into which the column concrete would later be poured, as mock-up columns to play with during the decision-making stage.

I had asked Carl Lindberg, the man who did the major concrete work, to make the column forms in a way that each column form would be a loose, movable, plywood box roughly nine feet long, and about 12 by 12 inches. We had about fifteen of these boxes, ready-made. They were made so each contained offsets and flashings to form a waterproof joint where wall panels would later come into the column.

These column-form boxes were stacked on the slab. Each was stable enough, by itself, to be moved, carried, placed, and braced, wherever we wanted it.

The whole ground floor of the building thus had an amazingly simple and elegant way of being formed. To get the wall right, now that we had the final room divisions, we used the column

Walking into the room, testing the position of the door, and trying to find out if the positive space of the bay window is large enough, when the door is in a certain position. We moved this door several times, and finally tuned it to within about two inches to get its best position.

forms themselves, moved the columns until we liked their positions (from both inside and outside) and then set and braced them accordingly.

————

PLACING THE COLUMNS, THE MOST IMPORTANT THING WAS TO RECOGNIZE THAT THE DECISIONS ABOUT COLUMNS WAS, IN EFFECT, A DECISION ABOUT POSITIONS AND SIZES OF WINDOWS.

Experience has taught me and all my crews that there is no foolproof way to decide window openings until one is standing in a room. In this house (given the column/beam construction) the rooms *could* not be there until the columns existed. But using the column forms as mockups gave us a way to break the vicious circle.

Each column form was a box. We had made these boxes, one for each column, and had them standing upright, but loose, on the slab. We had made them so they could be placed, moved, and adjusted, until the window openings were where we wanted them. Once we had them right, we connected them with horizontal 2 x 10's, which stabilized them, and could then be used as beam forms.

This was tremendously useful. It meant that we could stand in the main rooms of the house, adjust the column forms by eye, see how the windows had to be to make the room just right. Once we got it right, these forms were nailed in position, fixed, set with the horizontal members.

The steel was set, and within two or three days, the whole thing was ready to pour.

The design is such that the panels, corner panels, and the whole structure was prepared — and then poured — at the same time. When we were finished, and had the rooms just right, to our satisfaction, the position of panels and windows was quite different from the permission drawings we ourselves had made earlier. Not one room was the same.

We did one room at a time, placing the column-forms until the column positions and the shape and size of wall panels between the columns felt just right. We checked them from inside and outside until we were satisfied. Then we braced them, and tied them together with pairs of horizontal boards that would work as formwork for pouring concrete beams.

Thus we were able to move the columns around, by eye, using the column forms as if they were the columns themselves. When we were satisfied we stabilized them, and tied them together with beam forms. Then we placed the steel. Then poured the concrete. This technique allowed us to perform the unfolding just as it should be done. The larger configuration of the rooms created the context in which the exact position of the columns and column-bays as centers could be judged. The physical technique allowed it to be done, judged, and then set, without extra cost or time.

It was a nearly perfect embodiment of a natural unfolding process.

27 / FIXING THE LIVING ROOM: ITS DOOR AND FIREPLACE AND WINDOWS

DURING THE PROCESS OF PLACING COLUMN FORMS, THE DETAILED CENTERS WHICH FORMED EACH OF THE FIRST FLOOR ROOMS CAME FROM WHAT WAS THERE, NOT FROM THE PLAN DRAWN ON PAPER.

In order to get the first-floor centers right, we had to make very important decisions about

the layout. We had a rough layout, obviously, in the floorplans chalked on the slab. But we had to make the centers real; that means we had to make them into real rooms, in three dimensions, with beautiful light.

We started with the living room, the most important room. In this room, the position of the fireplace, the detailed character of the big bay window, and the position of the door from the entry hall to the living room were most vital. The door from entry hall to kitchen also played a role. We needed to place the two doors so that they didn't exactly line up, but gave a nice partial view through. One wanted to be able to sense the kitchen from the living room, but not see into it directly. One also wanted to sense the fireplace of the living room as one entered the house: but still that fireplace and the big bay window had to be protected, so that once inside the living room it was a comfortable and cozy spot. That meant the living-room door had to be far enough back in the house so that the living room and its bay window area were protected, not uncomfortably exposed.

To get all this right, we made many experiments, using cardboard for mockups, and sitting

Looking through the living-room door, towards the entrance room, to see what view of the front door is most comfortable

Sitting in a circle to get the "feel" of the living room, and to find out exactly how to place the fireplace so that fireplace, bay window, and door are all comfortable

around in a circle as if we were in the finished room. The fireplace (shown in the picture on page 603) is made of cardboard. We located that first, and gave it size and mass and dimension. Then we used cardboard walls to check and recheck the impact of the two door positions and the fireplace position, until we had them all just right.

One of the rather surprising things which materialized from these experiments was the need for a row of small interior windows in the back wall of the living room, between the living room and the passage behind the living room.

Finally — and as it turned out, very significant in the finished room — we changed the five

windows of the beautiful bay window. When we first tried placing the columns to make this window, using the assumption that all five parts were equal in size, we found that the window did not work so well. It did not have enough sense of focus. It was not, as much as I felt it could be, a living center. So, instead, I made the middle opening bigger than the others, then the openings next to the middle slightly smaller, and the openings on the outside smallest of all. We played with the proportions of the variation. Everyone checked it. It was much better. That is how we finally set the columns, and how the room is built.

28 / REMAKING OTHER FIRST-FLOOR ROOMS

ONCE WE HAD THE LIGHT IN THE LIVING ROOM RIGHT, WE WENT ON TO CHECK THE LIGHT IN ALL THE OTHER FIRST-FLOOR ROOMS: ENTRANCE ROOM, KITCHEN, AND THE TWO ROOMS AT THE EASTERN END OF THE HOUSE. THE LIGHT COMING INTO THESE ROOMS TOLD US WHERE, AND HOW, AND HOW BIG TO MAKE THE WINDOWS IN THE FRONT WALL, AND EVEN MADE US MODIFY PLAN, INTERIOR PARTITIONS, AND BOUNDARIES OF THE MAJOR ROOMS.

Recall that we could not see the actual light as it would ultimately be in any of these cases. The ceilings of these rooms were not yet built, nor was the front wall complete. But, using the column forms to represent the columns, we could for the first time guess at the light that would come in, because we had enough information from real walls, floors, trees, sunlight, reflections, orientation, to sense roughly what the quality of light at each point would be like when the house was finished. It was this partial, but real information, which provided enough feedback to help us make good decisions.

The entrance room provides an example. We could now see that the light in the entrance

room, if built as shown on the drawing, would have been catastrophic.

As usual, we started with a mockup that showed us what was on the drawings. In this case, using cardboard to close in walls, we could see that what was on the drawings was dank and awful. The room was unpleasant and far too dark. What was needed was obvious: a big window in the front wall, all around the door, so that the entrance room would be bathed in light.

But there was a difficult structural problem. On the design as submitted to the building department, we had placed a massive concrete moment-resisting frame in just that part of the exterior wall which formed the front of the entrance room. To make the entrance room light, we would have to take this away. But the shear resistance was essential to the building. It was just this one element which we originally intended to use for resistance to horizontal motion along the whole front of the house, especially critical there because this face of the house was mainly made of windows and openings. Something solid had to be there, somewhere. And to work, it had to be massive.

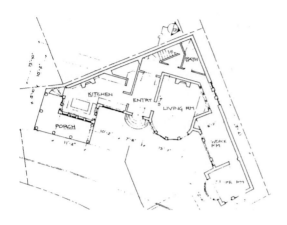

*First floor as drawn for submission
to the city of Berkeley*

First-floor plan as finally built

The anticipated forces were huge and could not easily be taken up elsewhere, since the whole front of the house had openings, doors and windows, all along its length. What to do?

Before trying to solve the problem we went on to the kitchen to see if there was any possible interaction which might help. In the drawings, we had the window above the kitchen counter huge and open. Standing in the room, this seemed far too big—almost grotesque. The kitchen needed containment, even a little darkness, to make the light spot in the big eating area at the western end of the room more attractive as the main center. So we set about sizing a much smaller window above the kitchen counter that would make the kitchen warmer, darker, and cozier and more contained.

So, suddenly, the solution of the shear problem fell into our hands. Since the kitchen window had to be smaller, we had room in the exterior wall for the extra columns and the very deep massive beam which the moment-resisting frame required, thus moving the shear-resisting element from entrance hall to kitchen. This needed some extra effort on computer runs, and a new drawing submitted to the building department, but we were able to solve it just nicely.

Things like this do not always happen. The shear-resistance problem caused by opening the entrance might not have been solved so easily.

But then we would simply have done something else — some other drastic change — to make the entrance room come out right.

The big windows at the western end of the kitchen got modified too. We found out just what sill height was needed to create a sense of privacy. That was quite subtle. Also, we put in an extra window looking towards the front door, looking east. And we put a door leading out to the little plum tree.

The strange L-shape of the kitchen was complicated and needed a lot of work. We more or less got it right at this stage. It would finally be resolved, later, by the construction of the big cylindrical fireplace (see pages 612–13, below).

In the two rooms to the east, the plan changed completely.

The long thin room — Stephanie's workroom — had originally had a French window opening to the garden. This was absurd in practice. The room was too narrow. It needed to be contained. We replaced the French window with a bank of four windows that made the room feel usable, pleasant, and not too exposed.

And the last room, the square room which drops down, was also quite wrong. On the drawings, we had shown it with a bay window looking out over the garage. This bay window seemed to be overdoing it entirely. And besides, one really didn't want to orient quite like that. We replaced it with a simple wall with windows, making the room square. It is now one of the nicest rooms in the house. And from the side, in an insignificant corner, we put a narrow French window out to the terrace, to make up for the one we had removed from the long thin room.

Finally, the back of the entrance room also had to be adjusted. To make the room have a beautiful shape, the way it narrowed to a neck, and then a landing, before reaching the bottom of the main stairs, was — in reality — entirely different from what we had shown on the plans. We had simply not been able to grasp the impact of the three-dimensional intersection of stair, entrance, passage, and walls, coupled with the change in floor levels. Being three-dimensional, it *could* be grasped only in the actual situation.

Every one of the five main rooms on the first floor changed fundamentally during this process. The position of walls changed. The spacing of windows changed. The positions of doors to the outside, the position of doors to the inside, the relative integrity of different centers in different rooms, *all changed*. If we had built the rooms that were on the plans, the house would have been all right, but barely acceptable — perhaps acceptable within the terms of reference of contemporary modern architecture, because this has become the acceptable level of what people get — but not acceptable in the true sense of something working well and being comfortable and beautiful.

The life which is now visible in the finished house as we built it simply would not have been achievable if we had followed the drawings. It came about only because we could see what we were doing in the actual situation, respond to it, change it, and make it live.

29 / COMPLETING THE FIRST-FLOOR STRUCTURE

WHEN THESE DECISIONS HAD BEEN MADE, WORK WENT AHEAD TO FIX AND BRACE ALL THE COLUMNS, FORM THE BEAMS, POUR THE CONCRETE STRUCTURE. THE STRUCTURE WAS THEN READY TO RECEIVE THE SECOND-FLOOR FRAMING.

As we began the second floor framing, one could begin to see the entire exterior volume of the building. This made it possible for the first time to take in the building as a whole, and to pay attention to qualities which were needed to complete this whole.

30 / POURING AND FORMING THE GARAGE

SUDDENLY ONE DAY I GOT A CALL FROM CARL LINDBERG, ASKING ME TO COME TO THE SITE. I WENT UP; HE WAS JUST FORMING THE GARAGE WALLS IN THE LOWER RIGHT-HAND CORNER OF THE SITE.

He wanted to get it in fast, so the upper part wouldn't collapse: As he started forming, he realized there were several open questions, unresolved by whatever sketches existed at that moment.

In order to form the garage roof concrete work, Carl had to know the final level of the terrace which will be above the garage. We had never decided it. The big issue was that it felt uncomfortable if low — because if it was too far below the house, it would not be used or usable. On the other hand, if it was high, several feet of earth would be required above the roof, resulting in a huge weight on the garage roof slab.

Or the garage could have a high ceiling, which would be very uncomfortable in feeling.

In addition, we had to check the appearance of the house from the southeastern end of the street. I had never done this before. It was vital that the structure of the garage plus terrace as seen from that end not be too high; otherwise, it would intrude on the house and look too huge and formidable.

We settled for a low ceiling in the garage, a thick slab to take a big weight, and several feet of earth on top, thus bringing the terrace to a nice position for the house.

Finally, we shaped columns and brackets, and flared entry walls, to make the entrance to the garage a STRONG CENTER. Mockups to de-

cide the shape of the concrete work. Cardboard cut-outs. The thing was heavy, very nice. Massive. Built after making the cardboard shapes.

Formwork on the massive concrete brackets which frame the garage

31 / GETTING THE ENTRANCE PATH JUST RIGHT

THE NAGGING PROBLEM WITH THE ENTRANCE STAIRWAY STILL EXISTED.

From the very beginning of the project, I had been wondering how to climb up the hill, from the left of the garage, to get to the front door. At an early stage of the project, I had assumed I knew how it went (from the left of the garage more or less straight to the front door), and had Randy place rough working mockup stairs in those positions, so that we could try walking up and down that path. It was never very comfortable. More recently, with the trench open for the gas and electric lines, Carl had built a rough stair going absolutely straight up to the left of the garage (photo page 608). This also was very unsatisfactory. It was far too steep, abrupt, and rather unpleasant.

Just before pouring the top retaining walls to form the terrace over the garage, we had to make a decision. None of the paths we had looked at seemed pleasant or graceful.

The one path which had always been pleasant — for everyone — was the forbidden one, which went on the neighbor's land at the left

end of the lot. Recently, she had locked her gate because our crews going in and out disturbed her — quite reasonable. But still, if we wanted to sneak in by the most comfortable route, that was the way to go.

I had tried to prevent myself, and our men, from going that way, so that we could experience

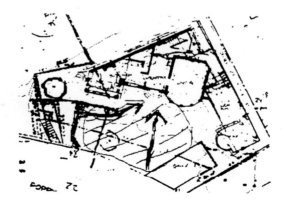

Two paths from the garage to the front door: The right-hand one crosses and destroys the positive space; the left-hand one goes around it and leaves the positive space intact. The garage is visible lower right. Hatching shows positive space.

*As planned, and tested: entry at the right of the site,
direct from the garage.*

*As finally built: entry at the left-hand end of the site,
then entering past the kitchen.*

the real options and get a feeling from the actual process of walking which ones were most pleasant.

But now, faced with the need to make a decision, it was this path, over to the extreme left, which seemed the only one that had a really comfortable quality. We were able to try a second path, not on the neighbor's land, but along the property line. We tried it, made a few tests. When we were sure, I called Chris and talked it over with him and Stephanie. They were quite comfortable about it, too — to my surprise. As it turned out, the conventional idea that the entrance must be near the garage meant very little to them. So the problem was solved. Randy be-

gan to build the stair (see photo). The only thing that we had to overcome was our own assumption that there would be something wrong if the path did not go directly from the garage.

One might say that it was POSITIVE SPACE which helped us to get this right. The space formed by the stairs going across the chasm near the garage was never positive. What we finally understood was equivalent to understanding that the only way to make this space positive was to treat it as a single inviolate lump of space, not to be cut by a stairway. The stairs then, instead, encircled the bushes and the main front part of the site, instead of crossing them, and so made the space and the system positive.

32 / REMAKING THE UPSTAIRS ROOMS

We were now able to stand in the upstairs, with an open floor and exterior walls given by the rough framing operation.

Framing the upstairs was, in our contract, divided into two operations: rough framing, which was to go very fast and cheap, and finish

framing, which was to be slow to allow for subtle adjustments to partitions, windows, and doors. We gave the finish-framing contract to James Maguire, one of our own most trusted people.

I had James construct rough mockups of the partitions, as shown on the plan, so that we could see them. Many aspects of the space which they created were surprising, even shocking. Because of the way the walls were placed, the whole upstairs seemed tiny — not right at all for such a large house — almost as if the Uphams weren't getting their money's worth — but in any case, definitely wrong in feeling.

Also, there was nothing really beautiful up there. Just a bunch of rooms. I decided to spend a few days letting the problem sink in.

The most crucial thing to get right was the beauty and shape of the main bedroom. I tried to imagine what would make this room beautiful, especially in relation to the terrace outside. I got a clear sense of its shape, with a big bed alcove and windows to the south and east. Then other things fell into place. The terrace had to be a little smaller, and the light on the terrace was amazingly harsh. We decided to extend the roof overhang, to give more shelter there and make the light softer. The space at the top of the stairs

was given a more beautiful shape. I reshaped the end of the bedroom so that it formed an octagonal shape that made sense with the door from the stairs. The bathroom was placed in the leftover triangular space, at the top of the stairway.

Now that the main room was beautiful, with its own shape, and coming nicely off the passage from the top of the stairs — that was the thing which brought the upstairs into a good state (STRONG CENTERS, GOOD SHAPE). I could now put a bed alcove opening off the main room. Chris's study was also in a totally different relation to the master bedroom, and to this alcove. And the bathroom was now in a totally different position.

It should be emphasized that, just like the downstairs, the arrangement of rooms on the second-floor level changed completely once we began looking at the real space in three dimensions. The main bedroom was entirely different. The bathroom was in a different place. The toilet

The upstairs after rough framing, and before new decisions were made. The cardboard walls and mocked-up partitions showed us clearly just how bad it was.

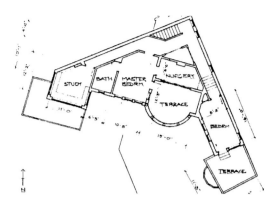

Upstairs plan as drawn for building permit

Upstairs plan as finally built

was in a different place. The main terrace off the master bed alcove was different in character, and even the wall bounding it was moved. The bed alcove was entirely new. Chris's study was to be approached in a different fashion. The stairs and the stairwell and landing were all new. As a result of our work on the second floor, the plan had become totally different, in almost every single room layout, from the way it appears on the permit drawings — all except Sasha's room, which, being in a wing by itself, stayed more or less the same.

Again, as with the first floor, if we had built what was on the plans it would have been acceptable, within the very low level of standards we have come to accept in contemporary architecture. But it would have had no significant life,

because it would have contained no significant centers. They were not visible, or, I believe, even imaginable at the time we laid out the plans on paper.

On the left is the plan as drawn and as submitted to the building department. On the right is the plan as actually built. Almost nothing is similar.

The significant life which the house now has, as built, comes about entirely because we were free to feel the centers that were needed and that were latent in the emerging structure, and we were then free to conceive them, refine them, and build them, all within the real three-dimensional space of the building envelope while we were constructing it.

33 / THE MASTER BED ALCOVE

Perhaps one of the most charming things that happened during the project was the decision about the master bed alcove.

Chris and Stephanie were standing with us upstairs, one day, studying their bedroom. We had a way of getting from the bedroom to Chris's study, but it made a passage where we didn't really want one. Then Chris mentioned Jefferson's bed at Monticello — a bed which was the only path to get to his study — and wondered if this

approach might work for him. At first I dismissed it as a charming but nutty idea. Later, however, we made a mockup of the bed alcove in the bedroom. The alcove was beautiful as far as its position was concerned; but it left the room dark and it was dark itself. I had to clear the darkness away. To do it, I just kicked out the back of the mockup. Suddenly the light changed, the room was filled with light, the light came streaming in from Chris's study beyond, and the

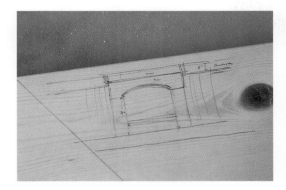

Bed alcove as I first drew it on a plank of wood that was lying there

annoying passage that had been ruining things was gone.

This was really a stroke — coming entirely from Chris's original idea. I called him to tell him about it. Now *he* got nervous. Couldn't we make a passage. Would it really work, to get into his study, only by crawling across the bed. I asked him, joking, if he had any women clients. He joked back that that was probably the reason why

Setting the position of the bed-alcove opening in the room

Checking the feeling of the master bed alcove, from inside and out

Jefferson built his bed at Monticello that way originally. Finally, after a lot of hemming and hawing, Chris agreed to do it: a wonderful stroke, which makes the upstairs of the house beautiful, just right, and very sensible; filled with light, it is an inspiration to be there.

When we got ready to build the bed alcove, we made a variety of cardboard mockups to determine the size of the opening, the arch of the opening, the exact width of the bed, the soft edge between the mattress and the wooden platform, and the position of lights inside. The most criti-cal thing was the exact position of the alcove in the wall. The view through the bed alcove into Chris's study depended on very slight movement up and down the room. And the strengthening of the part-octagon shape of the master bedroom also depended on the position of the bed alcove. Finally, it turned out that the opening needed a very broad set of boards — this showed up first in a small sketch, as when we were standing there a too narrow set of boards around the opening looked funny. The wide boards gave the bed its proper weight.

34 / THE KITCHEN FIREPLACE SHAPE

IN THE KITCHEN, A MAJOR NEW CENTER HELPED TO RESOLVE AWKWARDNESS AMONG EXISTING CENTERS.

We came to the kitchen fireplace. The Uphams had told us they wanted to bake pizza in it, every night. That made sense. It became a kind of oven. All along, the kitchen had had a strange and awkward L-shape, already discussed earlier. I looked and looked, what to do, but couldn't make it just right. To resolve the two

The kitchen mocked up in its entirety in cardboard, so we could see just how to make the kitchen fireplace. The idea of a cylinder had already occurred to me from seeing the room shape and recognizing its two lines of sight. Now we had to make the cylinder work, and to do that we had to have the full three-dimensional configuration, as it was going to be. We had to make many many versions before it all sat right.

parts of the room — to keep them separate, and yet unite them — it occurred to me, after looking and looking and looking, that a single great cylinder would have a relation to both and yet would give each one a better shape by itself. This sounded crazy, but when we made a small plasticine model of a cylindrical fireplace it looked rather good.

To check it, we built the fireplace in cardboard, in the room itself, with all the kitchen cabinets (coming later) in cardboard too, so we could judge how calm and simple it would be possible to make it.

It worked.

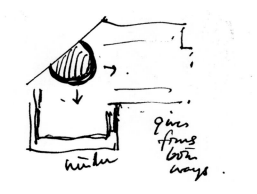

Position of kitchen fireplace as a cylinder: It gives a focus to both parts of the room, separates them, and joins them.

35 / THE KITCHEN FLOOR

THE NEXT CENTERS, TO SUPPORT THE KITCHEN, WERE CENTERS MADE IN THE FLOOR.

We always had intended to build one of our terrazzo floors in the kitchen. To make the cost of it feasible, we were going to do the styrofoam work (where the pattern gets set) with help from apprentices. We would place the marble dust professionally. Chris Upham himself was then going to grind the floor.

Stephanie mentioned her hope for green and red and yellow. That night, I made a small sketch of red, yellow, and green triangles. Shawn Bradbury, then one of my apprentices, made full size paintings to check the color in position. It worked very well. We settled the scale. Finding the exact colors for the green, red, and yellow wasn't so easy.

The rest was just hard work.

But after all the color effort, when it came to the actual placing of the material, we had the wrong mix for the green. The green came out too dark. It ruined the design. Randy did dozens of experiments to get a sealer which made the green lighter. He then painstakingly applied that special lightening sealer to all the green triangles (several hundred of them); this brought the balance back, and it works fairly well.

My first colored sketch of the floor design: red, green, and yellow

*Three colored mockups on butcher's paper, to try on the floor of the actual room
in order to determine the best scale for the floor pattern*

*Styrofoam forms from the making of the kitchen floor, in prepration for the first colored terrazzo
to be poured into the voids between the pieces of styrofoam (white)*

36 / PLASTERWORK

Now we prepared to make centers, thousands of them, in the plasterwork of the living room.

My first idea for the plasterwork panel design had been a pattern of tiny leaves. It had a comfortable organic quality. Randy made a beautiful mockup by casting plaster over a form made of relief built up from thin paper, and we then installed two or three panels in the room to look at them. Physically, they were lovely. Everyone liked the leaf design.

However, there was an uneasiness in me, a feeling that the leaf designs were pretty, but not substantial enough, too formless. Truthfully, because the space between the leaves wasn't very good, there were not many living centers in the design. I felt afraid that they did not have enough lasting power to make the room really good.

I asked Randy to make another, very geometric, pattern which was something like a basket pattern, tiny strips crisscrossing in low relief.

It was colder, and more formal. It had more strong centers. But it was also less pleasant.

When I first showed the two to our clients, they chose the pretty one, the one with the leaves. But this did not make my uneasiness go away.

I asked them to spend an hour, first sitting for half an hour with the leaf design, then sitting for half an hour with the geometric design, in both cases paying attention to the life and wholesomeness they felt in themselves while sitting in the room.

Faced with that question, and the staying power of the pattern, all of us came to the same conclusion. The leaf design was the more trivial. It did not sustain a feeling of wholesomeness in any of us as strongly as the geometric basket design. We chose the basket design.

Then we had to decide the arrangement of the panels in the room. We kept going back and forth between real full-size castings, fixing them and making paper mockups, in the room, until the whole room became still and comfortable.

Randy checking widths and details of the edge band on the plaster panels. On these panels, it turned out that a difference among one-eighth, one-quarter, and three-eighths of an inch was of tremendous significance.

Mockup in paper to test the overall pattern of the plaster panels on the ceiling. This part concentrates on the edge, where the width of the panels had to be chosen very carefully, to get a proper harmony.

During this process I found out, to my surprise, that the *overall* pattern of cast panel strips in the room was the most crucial thing of all. We therefore made several cardboard models of the room interior at 1 inch to 1 foot, trying different overall arrangements of one-inch wide white paper strips (not patterned), just to find the overall arrangement of the strips in the room that made the room most beautiful.

We ended up with wood panelling below waist height on the walls, a regular array of vertical patterned plaster strips above waist height, about 4 or 5 feet apart, with areas of smooth plaster between them, and a basketweave of

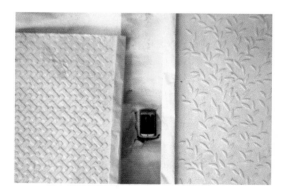

Plaster panels with the basket pattern and the leaf pattern placed in the living room, so we could compare the feeling each one created in that room

Trying the size and weight of one of the versions of the rosettes to go in the middle of the ceiling panels

Another view, looking at the middle of the ceiling

raised patterned strips in the ceiling, with flower medallions at the intersections of the strips. All the patterned strips had the same geometric miniature basketweave design in low relief, cast from a mold that we ourselves made in balsa wood.

All this had to be done now, before the house was closed in or windows installed, to allow us the lead-time necessary to make the plaster panels in advance.

We made them in our own workshops.

37 / WINDOW OPENINGS AND WINDOWS

ABOUT THIS TIME, IT CAME TIME TO DECIDE THE DETAILED WINDOW DESIGNS.

At the time of framing, window openings had been made specifically for each room. Now we had to look at the actual window design itself: the arrangement of lights, mullions, and glazing bars for each window and door.

In my experience, this is always torture. It seems easy, but is actually hellishly hard. We usually do it with surveyor's tape, pinned or stapled to the window frames, so we can look at the

effect of different patterns on the building, from inside and out. It takes days, sometimes even weeks.

The Upham house was no exception. We worked at it for several days, always looking at each room from the inside (that is usually the easier part), and then looking at the building as a whole from the outside. That is the hard part. Each room has its own demands, and tells you what the windows should be like, from the inside. In a complex building, it is very hard to get

Before ordering windows, we made cardboard mockups of the glazing bar and pane layout in every window in the house, and examined them from inside for their effect on the room, and from outside for their effect on the street

this pattern of window panes which make each room just right from the inside, yet let all the windows work together comfortably to make the building harmonious as a whole.

In this house, the big living room windows formed a kind of anchor point. With many, many lights in those windows, everything else had to go into the background, to fit in harmoniously.

The trick, finally, was to get things to a point where LEVELS OF SCALE was working as the dominant feature of the different windows, all working together as a whole.

The combination of windows in the finished house, as some of them looked from the outside. The frieze and balustrade completed

Cardboard mockup to test the size and distribution of glazing bars in the windows of the living room.
This was about the fifth version: it took that long to get it just right.

Close-up of living room windows after installation

38 / BALUSTRADES OF THE UPSTAIRS BALCONIES AND THE CONCRETE FRIEZE

Comparing the star-octagon frieze design with the lily frieze design

THE HOUSE ITSELF, IN RATHER UNEXPECTED WAYS, DEFINED THE GEOMETRIC ORNAMENT OF THE CONCRETE FRIEZE.

It came time to form and pour the frieze. Originally, I had assumed it would be a star-octagon design. That idea came from the very first mockups in our yard. So we started with a new mockup of the original frieze, on site, made in styrofoam. It didn't look quite right. I asked Randy to make it deeper, to change the size of the octagons. None of it seemed quite right.

Then we tried an entirely different frieze design, reflecting the lily tiles in the base of the house. We made long pieces of this new frieze. It looked silly, too decorative, not calm enough — pretentious, not simple.

In the end, we went back to the simple star-octagon design, but smaller, a scale which left the

building alone and a deeper cut for the relief, so that the design was more definite, more blockish, more calm. In this case, GOOD SHAPE emerged from the unfolding process.

A test of the lily frieze design with the balustrade design: This design didn't work at all.

39 / FRONT DOOR STEPS

*Using a simple board to judge the height, width, and length of a concrete parapet
which was to be built on both sides of the concrete front door steps*

THE FRONT DOOR STEP EDGES EMERGED NATU-
RALLY FROM WHAT HAD GONE BEFORE.

We had gradually built up an assumption in
our minds that there would be a beautiful concrete stair leading up to the front door, but had
never thought about the form it would take, what
it needed to be like in detail.

Instead of drawing, it was easiest and most
effective to hold up a board, showing the position of a wall that would contain the steps on ei-

ther side. In twenty minutes I suggested a few
key details. We looked at the steps in a mockup
of concrete blocks and cardboard. The width of
the top was an issue. The way the bottom tread
worked, whether it was straight or splayed out.
The information from these experiments was
given to Randy, who then formed and built the
steps.

They were built very quickly, with not too
much thought, beyond that one day's work.

40 / PAINTING WINDOWS AND EXTERIOR WOODWORK

ORIGINALLY THE HOUSE WAS GOING TO BE YEL-
LOW ABOVE AND GRAY BELOW. INDEED, I FIRST
MADE THE LILY TILES WITH THIS COLOR SCHEME
IN MIND, WITH AN AWARENESS OF THE YELLOW
QUALITY THAT WAS GOING TO EXIST ON THE
SITE.

However, once we had the house up, the
concrete formed, the upper plaster in place, and
the windows primed, the gray and white was so
beautiful that painting the upper wall yellow
seemed altogether wrong. Separately, Chris and
Stephanie, different craftsmen on the project,

A lily-tile in the stem wall of the foundation

One of the small balconies

and I all came to the conclusion that it was best as it was, and should be left alone.

But we had forgotten the lily tiles. When the tiles went in, it became clear that the house was no longer harmonious with them in that gray state. I had made a mistake and should have installed them months before, so that the house could grow around them, harmoniously. In fact, when it finally came time to put them in, I was afraid and didn't want to look at them; I felt sure that the house had grown away from them. In fact, it had. Luckily, not to a to drastic extent.

To make a correction, after the tiles had been installed, I realized that the colors of the windows had to change from the cream-white we had begun to be attached to, towards a color that reflected the tones of the lily tiles: red and yellow. Stephanie herself — a textile designer — made a big contribution here. I went to look at some window samples Stephanie had painted. There was a deep red and some very bright yel-

lows, even two greens. I was rather shocked at this boldness and asked if I could take a little more time, to find colors that were more subdued. I began experimenting with pale yellow, bright enough to sparkle in the gray — just as the white was doing, but less cold.

Once the lily tiles were all in, however, the situation changed dramatically. Suddenly the deep red and the bright yellows seemed right, not too bright, even sensible.

I asked Bob Walsh, one of my apprentices, who was an expert professional painter, to mix some samples which were in the range of the red and yellow in the tiles — a slightly reddish yellow, and a subdued red of some kind. He quickly found just the right red, bright, but soft. I could see that it was right. I began trying to find a way of painting the windows, which might have a red *and* a yellow together, without being too bright and silly. One on the sash, and one on the frame, or a hairline of one, with the other.

41 / FLOWERS IN THE GARDEN

FLOWERS AND FLOWER BEDS WERE SOON PLANTED.

Even before the house was finished, we began building flower beds. Chris and Stephanie filled them with flowers. These flowers were so lovely and so successful that when we came to build the main balustrade along the front edge of the terrace, I thought that the balustrade itself should be a long flower box, which could be filled with earth and planted. That is, indeed, how we made the base of the balustrade: a long flower box, gently curving, poured in concrete. When the carpenters first made the forms, the straight lines were distracting, too severe. I asked them to curve them gently, so that the line of the base followed the lay of the land more easily.

Flowers in the garden

42 / USE OF THE FUNDAMENTAL PROCESS

In all the processes I have described in this chapter — whether in discussion with the client, during early design or later design, or during construction — the very same process was taking place. The building and its wholeness were unfolding, step by step. In one fashion or another, we were using something like the fundamental process, again and again, to try and get good results.

At each step, we asked ourselves what could be done next to have the *biggest* and most positive impact on the wholeness of the emerging site considered *as a whole*. We asked this question, did our best to arrive at the answer, and did the necessary and appropriate

thing to have this effect. And at each step, our answer to that question was, in some form, "the creation of other living centers." Hundreds of times, we created new centers and tried to give them as much life as possible. The centers we created were large, small, tiny. They occurred at different scales, all over the building. But this much is common every time: We were always creating some living center which was, as far as we could manage, intense in its life. At each step, we were trying to create just those next centers which did the most, in our judgment, to make the house — indoors as well as out — together with the site and neighborhood, come to life as a whole.[7]

On the living room table: a vase of flowers from the garden

The finished entrance hall

The kitchen in use

43 / COMMON SENSE: AN OVERVIEW OF THE PROCESS

You might say that this is all just common sense. I believe you would be right. But this common sense flies in the face of many processes which 20th-century architecture and construction practice set in place.

When we try to make a building in such a way that it gets its life, what we have done here is the most natural way to do it: We get one thing right at a time. We do what we know. We get things right as we come to understand them. That gets good results.

Expressed in the formal language of this book, what has been described is not merely common sense. It is a process of unfolding, in which centers are established, modified, improved, one at a time. It respects the step-by-step unfolding of the field of centers. Each new center is born, then, as a result of the previously existing wholeness.

All this is common sense. Yet, oddly, this common-sense process, which is also a correct unfolding process according to the analysis of this book, flies in the face of current practice. Although it does leave a few features of the mainstream contemporary architectural process intact, it also requires revolutionary changes in procedure.

In practical terms, the processes for this house included a great variety of different operations, from the beginning to the end, that are different from present-day forms of architectural and construction practice. This included steps that were unusual in sequence:

The living room

for example, the idea of making the building volume before knowing what is in the building, and the idea of placing the outdoor space before the building. Throughout, the project included a very different approach to the use of drawings, and to the relation of drawings to the permit process, and to the construction contract.[8] Differences in on-site operations, during construction, for example, cardboard mockups, full size, of various building details. Others changes of process involved combinations of jurisdiction that were entirely unfamiliar: jurisdiction over money as a basis for making decisions about the porch. Unusual for an architect, jurisdiction over tiny details of construction-procedure, as in the basis for building the formwork of the columns to make them movable. Others involved apparent idiosyncracies of scale. For example, working out the building color so

early in the process, and placing such emphasis on the lily tile at an apparently early stage in the unfolding. Others involved drastic departures from conventional practice: non-adherence to the drawings, and changes of structure, even foundation structure, while construction was going on.

However, what is clear is that this process is feasible. The house you see here — and many, many other similar houses built in similar fashion by my company, CES — was delivered on budget. The manipulations of money needed to get this result, in spite of enormous changes — which would in existing methods of contracting be treated as unworkably expensive change-orders with increases of price — were treated within the contract we used as normal events and were covered without increase of cost.

This house is controlled by common sense. It comes out the way it is, according to the unfolding process, not controlled by image, but by reality.

"I've just been to see the Upham house for the first time. Its astonishingly beautiful. I ambled through there with a ridiculous grin on my face gaping about like some rube."

"Approaching on foot reminded me of nothing so much as my first glimpses, down the valley, of one of those stacked-up medieval villages along the Dordogne River. And it feels just as much a part of the place you built it as the troglodyte cliff dwellings that we climbed around in up above those villages. Here's hoping though, that the Uphams don't start selling souvenir pins and color slides out the kitchen window!"

Letter from Steve Sullivan, Berkeley, 1993

44 / END OF THE APPENDIX ON THE UPHAM HOUSE

The design and making of the Upham house, like the design of the Mary Rose Museum and the construction of the West Dean Visitor's Centre, is an ultra-modern example of the fundamental process at work. It uses techniques of engineering, construction, process, financing, and contract management which are nearly unknown today, and which belong to a more biologically oriented future society, where a syncopated process of this kind may become common.

In Book 3 we shall study these aspects of the fundamental process, in modern form, in more detail. I shall argue that an unfolding process in human society must meet certain necessary conditions. These conditions are surprising. They do not conform to the narrow scientific-technical conditions we have come to expect from 20th-century thought. Yet I believe that the conditions, as I state them, are necessary, and inevitable, and will be present in any successful future applications of the fundamental process. In this sense, then, I shall argue that the process of imagining, designing, planning, building, and repairing the human environment, is always — and necessarily — characterized by certain necessary features of the fundamental process, which may be seen as an invariant core of any living process in society.

Although the processes which human beings can use to create the environment are vast in number and will continue, I am sure, to be astonishing in their variety, nevertheless, I believe it is true to say that all these processes which are successful — past, present, and future — will share some of the features that I have described.

The finished house

NOTES

1. This house was described and analyzed by Kenneth Baker and Mark Darley, "New American Craftsman House," AMERICAN HOME STYLE AND GARDENING (New York and Atlanta: 1996) April-May, pp. 42–47.

2. As it has been for most of the houses I build.

3. For 1991, a fairly modest budget of $342,000 for 2400 square feet of construction, plus $96,000 for a massive 15 foot high retaining wall and sewer reconstruction caused by an unusual hill condition.

4. Contracts of this kind are described in somewhat more detail in Book 3, and provided in full in Christopher Alexander et al., THE MARY ROSE MUSEUM (New York: Oxford University Press, 1995).

5. In a normal bid contract, typical costs for the general contractor's operations vary greatly according to project size, but average about 20%, ranging from some 14% to 28%. Typical breakdown includes general conditions (4–8%), overheads (6–10%), and profit (4–10%) though the last is often supplemented by unseen profits that are not disclosed.

6. Randy Schmidt and Lizabeth Chester were two of my apprentices, both originally students at the University of California at Berkeley. Lizabeth helped to make the lily tiles. Randy undertook a great variety of specialized construction jobs on the Upham house, and it may be said that the beauty of the house is due to his craftsmanship, more than that of any other single person.

7. To remind yourself of the fundamental process and its full definition, see chapter 7, THE FUNDAMENTAL DIFFERENTIATING PROCESS.

8. When starting a building project, it is natural to make drawings at a certain stage — just to confirm to ourselves that the building we conceive is whole, and does work geometrically and structurally. But this drawing process has a limited role, not nearly as extensive as the one which was taken for granted in 1990.

For instance, we start the design with the site — not with a drawing, but with an experience of volume and position on the site. This is best done without drawing — because the closed eyes, or intuitive awareness of the site's wholeness works better in three-dimensional real space, than it does on a piece of tracing paper.

Once we have the general outline of the building given by the site, it does make sense to try and draw it. At this moment the correct process coincides with current practice.

But then, once the drawing reveals the overall outline of the building — its general arrangement of walls, columns, roofs — then the usefulness of drawing stops again. The detailed creation of the building is better done, under conditions where the building comes, by craft, from the general overall understanding of the thing — not from some fanatically precise set of working drawings that are only constructed for legal reasons.

In this respect the process of unfolding resembles certain ancient building practice, more than it does the legalistic system of architecture we are presently used to. For example, the San Francisco City Hall, a rather large building, was built around 1900 from five sheets of drawings — something almost unimaginable today. The drawings give the outline of the building: The builders and craftsmen filled it in according to their best judgment, as they went along. The Parthenon was also built from sketches — but as far as we know these sketches, made for the purpose of setting out the broad structure of the plan, were scratched on stone only to give the principal plan organization. Again the details of column, entasis, carving, etc., were worked out by the individual craftsmen as the building evolved in its actual substance.

The medieval cathedrals, too, were based on drawings. But once again, the drawing was often a single sheet — a broad layout, which set out the general terms of the geometry. The detailed filling in of column profile, vault shape, windows, floor, was made by the master craftsmen as they enjoyed their art.

These processes are not just historical accidents, now superceded by a wiser 20th-century America. These ancient processes were closer to the needs of an unfolding living, building — because they set just the right amount of detail in the wholeness which is established at the time of drawing — and they leave the right amount of room, for the evolution of details, as the building takes physical shape.

PICTURE CREDITS

My gratitude for all the help I have received with the content, ideas, discussion, and production of these four books from many, many people during the last twenty-seven years has been expressed on pages 345–54 of Book 4. In addition, I gratefully acknowledge the use of pictures, photographs, and illustrations owned by the following persons and institutions. All illustrations not mentioned belong to or are the work of the author, and are reproduced by permission of the Center for Environmental Structure.

Frontispiece
    p. i source unknown.

Author's note
    p. xv top left Bernard Rudofsky; p. xv top right © Ralph Richter, architekturphoto, Dusseldorf; p. xv bottom left Mark Darley, Esto; p. xv bottom right courtesy of Bitter & Bredt; p. xvii Bernard Herman, Michael Folco.

Preface
    p. 1 Ilya Prigogine, *From Being to Becoming: Time and Complexity In The Physical World*, Freeman, 1980, p. 200; p. 5 Bill McClung; p. 7 both, Temple Museum, Kyoto; p. 10 by courtesy of the office of Terry Farrell; p. 11 from popular song book, source unknown.

Chapter 1
    p. 21 top © Loren McIntyre; p. 21 bottom left: Mt. Wilson and Palomar Observatories; p. 21 bottom right James E. Gelson; p. 23 both: Ian Stewart and Martin Golubitsky, *Fearful Symmetry; Is God a Geometer?*, Blackwell, 1922, fig 7.3; p. 24 both Rene Thom, *Structural Stability and Morphogenesis*, © 1989, Addison-Wesley, plate 7, fig 5.18; p. 25 left: Ian Stewart and Martin Golubitsky, *Fearful Symmetry: Is God a Geometer?*, Blackwell, 1992, fig 7.3; p. 25 right: internet, source unknown; p. 26 top and bottom: Ilya Prigogine, *From Being to Becoming: Time and Complexity in the Physical World*, Freeman, 1980, p.17 (from James Riley and Ralph Metcalfe: p.16, NASA); p. 27 top left: H.W. Douglass Pratt, Bishop Museum, Hawaii; p. 27 center right: Ilya Prigogine, *From Being to Becoming: Time and Complexity in the Physical World*, Freeman, 1980, p.200; p. 27 bottom right: Ian Stewart and Martin Golubitsky, *Fearful Symmetry: Is God a Geometer?*, Blackwell, 1992, fig. 8.19; p. 28 top left: Peter Kain; p. 28 right John Tyler Bonner, *Morphogenesis: An Essay on Development*, Atheneum, 1963, fig. 4, plate 1 (after Egli, 1949); p. 29 both John Tyler Bonner, *Morphogenesis: An Essay on Development*, Atheneum, 1963, fig 34 (from Brown, The Plant Kingdom, 1935) and fig. 38 (from Sachs, Botany, Oxford, 1882); p. 30 top left John Tyler Bonner, *Morphogenesis: An Essay on Development*, Atheneum, 1963, fig.60 (from Thaxter, 1892); p. 30 top right and bottom Ian Stewart and Martin Golubitsky, *Fearful Symmetry: Is God a Geometer?*, Blackwell, 1992, figs 1.5 and 6.3; p. 31 lower left John Tyler Bonner; p. 31 right Harold E. Edgerton; p. 33 and 34: Lewis Wolpert, *Principles of Development*, Oxford, 1998, fig. 10.5 and Box 7A; p. 35: Gyorgy Kepes, *L'Objet Cree par l'Homme*, © George Braziller, 1965 (from Cornish, Ocean Waves, Cambridge, 1934); p. 36 top Peter Stevens, *Patterns in Nature*, Little Brown, 1974, fig. 69; p. 36 bottom John Tyler Bonner; pp. 37 and 39 Peter Stevens, *Patterns in Nature*, Little Brown, 1974, fig. 162, 116 bottom, and fig. 121; p. 40 all Brian Goodwin, *How the Leopard Changed its Spots, The Evolution of Complexity*, Simon & Schuster, 1996, figs. 4.1, 4.2, 4.9, 4.12, 4.13; p. 41 painting John Gurche; p. 43 left: D'Arcy Wentworth Thompson, On Growth And Form, V.II, Cambridge, 1959, fig. 462 (photo A. Robinson) and fig. 463 (drawing after Culmann and J. Wolff; p. 43 right Barnaby's Picture library; p. 44 left E. Eugene Stanley; p. 44 right internet, source unknown.

Chapter 2
    p. 54 Harold E. Edgerton; p. 63 Ian Stewart and Martin Golubitsky, *Fearful Symmetry: Is God a Geometer?*, Blackwell, 1992, fig. 1.5; p. 64 spider's web, Derek Locke; p. 66 left Harold E. Edgerton; p. 66 right © 1990 Amon Carter Museum, Forth Worth, Texas, Bequest of Eliot Porter; p. 67 Mt. Wilson and Palomar Laboratories; p. 68 Georg Gerster; p. 69 left I.W. Bailey; p. 69 right Rene Thom, *Structural Stability And Morphogenesis*, © 1989, Addi-

son Wesley, plate 7; p. 70 top Tet Borsig, *Designs In Nature*, Viking, 1962, plate 62; p. 71 left Peter Stevens, *Patterns In Nature*, Little Brown, 1974, fig. 162; p. 71 right D'Arcy Wentworth Thompson, *On Growth and Form*, V.II, Cambridge, 1959, fig. 554; p. 72 top: Yukio Ohama; p. 72 bottom Adolph Suehsdorf, ed., Picture, ASMP, pp. 42-43; p. 73 Carl Struwe; p. 74 © Ken Heyman, Woodfin Camp & Associates; p. 75 top © 1998, George Steinmetz; p. 75 bottom Gyorgy Kepes, *The New Landscape*, Theobald, 1956, fig. 190; p. 76 top Evelyn Hofer; p. 76 bottom © 1990 Amon Carter Museum, Fort Worth, Texas, bequest of Eliot Porter; p. 80 Ben More Coigach, Wester Ross, Sutherland, by permission of Vincent Lowe, ARPS, Scotland in Focus Picture Library, Ladhope Vale House; p. 81 Bob Gibbons, printed in Richard Mabey & Sinclair Stevenson, Reed International Books, Michelin House, London, 1996, p.352; p. 82 left and right Bryan Mumford, Mumford Micro Systems.

Chapter 3
    p. 87 Montana Historical Society, Helena; p. 88 source unknown; p. 89 top and bottom source unknown; p. 90 left E. H. Gombrich, *The Sense Of Order, A Study In The Psychology of Decorative Arts*, Oxford, 1979, fig. 85 (from A. H. Christie, Pattern Design, 1929); p. 90 right Z. Yesilay; p. 91 by permission of Vojtech Blau; p. 92 top left and right Herman Phelps, *The Craft of Log Building*, Lee Valley Tools, Ontario, 1982, figs. 54 and 15; p. 92 bottom Gunnar Bugge and Christian Norberg-Schulz, *Early Wooden Architecture in Norway*, Oslo, 1969, p. 6; p. 93 top: Herman Phelps, *The Craft of Log Building*, Lee Valley Tools, Ontario, 1982, figs. 6-9; p. 93 bottom Gunnar Bugge and Christian Norberg-Schulz, *Early Wooden Architecture In Norway*, Oslo, 1969, p. 119, top; p. 94 top Gunnar Bugge and Christian Norberg-Schulz, *Early Wooden Architecture in Norway*, Oslo, 1969; p. 94 bottom Dr. Eva Frodl-Kraft; p. 95 Bildarchiv/ONB, Vienna; p. 96 both Norman F. Carver, Jr., *Italian Hilltowns*, Documan Press, 1979, photos N. F. Carver; p. 97 Edmund S. Bacon, *Design Of Cities*, Viking, p. 108, 1962; p. 98 Scala/ Photo Fanelli; p. 99 top Steen Eiler Rasmussen, *Towns And Buildings*, Harvard, 1951, pp. 88-89; p. 99 bottom Sandy Lesberg, *The Canals Of Amsterdam*, Peebles Press, 1976, pp. 72-73, photo by Ab Pruis; p. 100 both Oktay Aslanapa, *Turkish Art And Architecture*, Praeger, 1971, figs. 27 and 128; p. 101 Hans Jurgen Hansen, ed., *Architecture in Wood*, Viking, 1971; p. 102 Georg Gerster, *The Nubians*; p. 103 Graham Stuart Thomas, *Great Gardens of Britain*, Mayflower,1979, p. 237, photo by author; p. 104 Roderick Cameron, *Shadows from India*, William Heinemann, p.45; p. 105 © Ken Heyman, Woodfin Camp & Associates; p. 106 Orhan Ozguner, *Village Architecture in the Eastern Black Sea Region*, Middle East Technical Univ., Ankara, 1970, fig. 79.

Chapter 4
    p. 109 Leonardo Benevolo, *The History of the City*, MIT, 1980, fig. 1223; p. 111 both *Labyrinth Stadt: Planung und Chaos im Staedtebau*, M. Dumont, 1975; p. 112 Leonardo Benevolo, *The History of the City*, MIT, 1980, fig. 414; p. 113 top and bottom right Ken Simmons; p. 114 bottom left and right Ken Simmons; p. 115 both Ken Simmons; p. 117 source unknown; p. 118 source unknown; p. 120 top Quinton Davis; p. 120 bottom photographer unknown; p. 121 © Stephen J. Krasemann/DRK Photo; p. 123 both: © Loren McIntyre; p. 124 Lee Nichols; p. 125 Oktay Aslanapa; p. 126 photographer unknown; p. 127 top Peter Leach; p. 127 bottom *The Japan Architect*, 1985-86, p. 276; p. 131 Architecture slide library, UC Berkeley; p. 132 Emilio Ambasz, *The Architecture of Luis Barragan*, Museum of Modern Art, NY, 1976, photo Armando Salas; p. 133 both Boesiger/Girsberger, *Le Corbusier, 1910-60*, Wittenborn, 1960, pp. 159 and 253; p. 134 all courtesy William Storrer, *The Frank Lloyd Wright Companion*, pp. 430, 431, & 461.

Chapter 5

p. 140 © 1946 Henri Cartier Bresson, Magnum Photos, Inc.; p. 141 and 142 Brian Brace Taylor, *Geoffrey Bawa*, Singapore and New York: Concept Media Pte. Ltd, 1986, p. 56; p. 143 Fairchild Aerial Surveys; p. 144 Steve Glischinski & Greg McDonnell, *Uboats: General Electric Diesel Locomotives*, Stoddart Publishing Co., Toronto, 1994 p.99; p. 146 Eurostar Magazine #22, Bernard Chevry, 1998, p. 33; p. 147 Carl Gossett, Jr., NYT Pictures; p. 148 The Cameron Collection, Brisbane, Calif.; p. 149 all Golden Gate Bridge and Transportation District; p. 151 top © The Estate of Andre Kertesz; p. 151 bottom © Bruce Dale, National Geographic Image Collection; p. 152 Scientific American, Oct. 1997, p. 73, Simulation Gec Alstholm; p. 153 Chester Higgins/NYT Pictures; pp. 154 & 155, *Frank Lloyd Wright: The Early Work*, Horizon 1968, p. 116, 33, 11, and 117; p. 156 top: *In/Sight: African Photographers, 1940-Present*, Guggenheim, 1996, photo Santu Mofokeng; p. 156 bottom: © Alex Webb, 1995, Magnum Photos, Inc.; p. 158 Mark Darley/Esto; p. 159 top right Mark Darley/Esto; p. 159 bottom Gregorius Antar/ Aga Khan Trust for Culture, *Architectural Review*, Oct 1992, vol. CXCI, no. 1148;p. 160 Andras Balla; p. 161 © 1993, Alex Webb, Magnum Photos, Inc.; p. 165 Sally Woodbridge, Bay Area Houses; p. 166 by courtesy Jean-Marc Bustamante; p. 167 top: Gina Corrigan, *Images Of China*, Occidor, 1966, fig. 129; p. 167 bottom: © 1987, James Nachtwey, Magnum Photos, Inc.; p. 168-69 Gina Corrigan: *Images Of China*, 1996, figs. 123 and 128; p. 171 *by courtesy Bob Gosani, In/Sight : African Photographers, 1940 To The Present*, p. 227; p. 173 © 1993, Alex Webb, Magnum Photos, Inc.

Chapter 6

p. 181 Howard Davis; p. 182 Witold Rybczinski, *How the Other Half Builds: Volume 1-Space*; p. 183 left and right Witold Rybczinski, *How the Other Half Builds: Volume 1-Space*; p. 184 top left and bottom right Witold Rybczinski, *How the Other Half Builds: Volume 1-Space*; p. 184 top right B.V. Doshi; p. 185 all Witold Rybczinski, *How the Other Half Builds: Volume 1-Space*; p. 190 bottom left Slesin, Cliff, Rozensztroch, *Mittel Europa*, Clarkson Potter Publishers, New York, 1994, p. 227; p. 192 B. V. Doshi; p. 193 Mark Darley/Esto; p. 194 left *Limousine City Guide*, Tokyo, Winter, 1983, cover photograph; p. 194 right: Royal Dutch glassworks catalog; p. 197 Lewis Wolpert; p. 199 Arthur Upham Pope, *Masterpieces of Persian Art*, The Dryden Press, 1945, plate 27.

Chapter 7

p. 205 © James Nachtwey, Magnum Photos, Inc.; p. 206 Giraudon/ Art Resource, New York; pp. 208–9 Laurence Deonna; p. 213 top right Demetrius Gonzalez; p. 214 Joanna Pinneo; pp. 221, 222, 223, 224 all Bill McClung.

Chapter 8

p. 231 Jackson and Perkins catalog, photographer Bjurstrom; p. 232 Rene Thom; p. 233 Nolli plan of Rome; pp. 242-244 from videotape *Matisse: His Life*; p. 246 Miyoko Tsutsui.

Chapter 9

p. 250 from video Matisse: His Life; p. 260, 261 Bill McClung.

Chapter 10

p. 272–275 © Richard Bryant/1988/Arcaid; pp. 286, 287, 289, 290, 291 and 295 bottom Mark Darley/Esto.

Chapter 12

p. 326 courtesy of Fran Heyl; p. 327 bottom by courtesy private collection; p. 328 source unknown; p. 329 Moshe Safdie; p. 330 Moshe Safdie; p. 331 Moshe Safdie; p. 333 Mark Darley.

Chapter 13

p. 343 both Ken Costigan; p. 356 Mark Darley/Esto; p. 358 top left from Kathryn H. Anthony, "Public Perceptions of Recent Projects," in *Architecture*, 3/85, p. 96; p. 358 center left © Steve Rosenthal; p. 358 bottom left source unknown; p. 359 top left, center left source unknown; p. 359 bottom left © Country Life Picture Library.

Chapter 14

p. 376 Cedric Crocker, *Creating Japanese Gardens*, Chevron Chemical Co., p. 70; p. 382 Ruth Landy; p. 383 Hiroshi Kobayashi; pp. 387 right and 390 Mark Darley/Esto.

Chapter 15

p. 402 source unknown, postcard vendor; p. 405 Nicholas Kane, *Perspectives Magazine*, August/September 1996; p. 422 UC Berkeley Architecture slide library; p. 429 *The Japan Architect* 1985.

Chapter 16

p. 435 all courtesy of Henry Glassie, *Folk Housing in Middle Virginia*, The University of Tennessee Press, Knoxville, 1975, p.50, 69, 76-77, 86-87, 99, 104-105, 186; p. 439 Bitter & Bredt; p. 440 © Ralph Richter, Architecturphoto, Dusseldorf; p. 441 both © Tim Griffith, Esto; p. 444 by courtesy Ana Sanat Dali; p. 454 James Ensor painting, by permission Christies, London; p. 457 Randy Schmidt.

Chapter 17

p. 461 Roderick Cameron, *Shadows from India*, William Heinemann; p. 463 Ken Domon Memorial Museum; p. 464 Teigens Fotoatelier, Olso; p. 465 Museum of Cycladic Art, Athens; p. 466 courtesy of Walter Horn & Ernest Born, *The Plan of St. Gall*, v.II, University of California Press, 1979; p. 473 Rijksmuseum Foundation, Amsterdam; p. 473 bottom Hajo Neis; p. 474 top left Steen Eiler Rasmussen: p. 474 top right Steven Brooke; p. 474 bottom Robert A. M. Stern, "Modernismus und Postmodernismus,"in *Design ist Unsichtbhar*, Austria, 1980, p. 270; p. 475 source unknown; p. 476 Mai-Mai Sze, *The Tao Of Painting: A Ritual Disposition Of Chinese Painting*, Princeton 1967; p. 478 left Hans Jurgen Hansen; p. 478 right Nick Merrick, © Hedrich Blessing; p. 479 left, Quinton F. Davis; p. 479 right, Ken Longbottom, *Liverpool and the Mersey, v.I*, Silver Link Publishing Ltd., p.31; p. 480 Ludwig Goldsheider, ed., *Leonardo da Vinci*, Phaidon Publishers (Phaidon Press Ltd.), 1951, plate 121; p. 484 Bruno Taut, *Houses and People of Japan*, Sanseido, 1958; p. 486 Seiroku Noma, *Japanese Costume And Textile Arts*, John Weatherhill, 1974, v. 16, fig. 37; p. 487 source unknown; p. 488 Bruno Taut, *Houses and People of Japan*, Sanseido, Tokyo, 1938, fig. 432; p. 490 © Christie's Images, London.

Conclusion

p. 566 courtesy CES Editions, Guadeloupe, Singapore, 1985

Appendix

p. 590 all Randy Schmidt; p. 622–27 all Mark Darley/Esto; pp. 630–31 Mark Darley/Esto.

Although every effort has been made to trace and contact copyright holders before publication, this has not been possible in a few cases. If notified, we will be pleased to rectify any errors or omissions at the earliest opportunity.